The Persisting Question

Current Research on Antisemitism

Edited by
Herbert A. Strauss and Werner Bergmann

Volume 1

Walter de Gruyter · Berlin · New York
1987

The Persisting Question

Sociological Perspectives and Social Contexts of Modern Antisemitism

Edited by
Helen Fein

Walter de Gruyter · Berlin · New York
1987

Published with the support of the
Technische Universität Berlin,
Zentrum für Antisemitismusforschung.

Printed on acid-free paper (ageing-resistant – pH 7, neutral)

Library of Congress Cataloging in Publication Data

The Persisting question.
    (Current research on antisemitism; v. 1)
    1. Antisemitism. 2. Holocaust, Jewish (1939–1945) – Causes.
I. Fein, Helen, 1934–   . II. Series.
DS145.P418   1987   940.53'15'03924   87-9030
ISBN 0-89925-320-2 (U.S.: alk. paper)

CIP-Kurztitelaufnahme der Deutschen Bibliothek

Current research on antisemitism / ed. by Herbert A. Strauss u.
Werner Bergmann. – Berlin; New York: de Gruyter

NE: Strauss, Herbert A. [Hrsg.]

Vol. 1. The persisting question. – 1987

The persisting question: sociolog. perspectives and social contexts
of modern antisemitism / ed. by Helen Fein. –
Berlin; New York: de Gruyter, 1987.
    (Current research on antisemitism; Vol. 1)
    ISBN 3-11-010170-X

NE: Fein, Helen [Hrsg.]

© 1987 by Walter de Gruyter & Co., Berlin 30.
Printed in Germany
Alle Rechte des Nachdrucks, der photomechanischen Wiedergabe,
der Herstellung von Photokopien – auch auszugsweise –
und der Übersetzung in fremde Sprachen vorbehalten.
Satz: Dörlemann-Satz, Lemförde
Druck: Hildebrand, Berlin
Bindearbeiten: Lüderitz & Bauer, Berlin

Foreword

This series, "Current Research on Antisemitism," organized and edited by the Zentrum für Antisemitismusforschung at the Technical University of Berlin, is aimed at improving our understanding of a scourge of mankind that has grown vicious in our century. "Modern antisemitism," most historians agree, began sometime during the 1880's. The main characteristics that set it apart from older forms of "anti-Judaism" were the rise of ultra-nationalist and racist thought; the development of antisemitic social movements and political parties; and the turn against the constitutional equality of Jews. The modern forms were seen to rest on centuries, if not millenia, of religion – based discrimination, defamation, and persecution suffered by the Jewish minority in the Christian world. Ever since Christianity and Judaism – its parent religion – separated and began to compete, ever since Christian thought and faith had affirmed their separate identities from Jewish thought and practice, ever since permissive Roman Imperial usages had collided with the often crude "adversos Judaeos" tradition articulated by the church fathers – the teachings of the Christian churches had given a special and ambivalent place to Jews and Judaism. Jews were assigned a unique place in the *Heilsgeschichte* of Christendom: their ultimate conversion to the true faith would provide the ultimate test of the validity and superiority of Christianity. Yet the alleged involvement of Jews in the death of the Christ and the collective guilt incurred thereby demanded that, until the last judgement would introduce new realities, Jews were to exist in a demeaned and lowly state as punishment for their deed. Christian anti-Judaism was carried on as a religious and cultural norm; it became a self-fulfilling social and political prophecy, the basic paradigm within which secular motives for prejudice and hatred at times acquired increased irrationality and viciousness. Ironically, even thinkers of the Enlightenment in France and England used traditional Christian defamations of Jews and their religion to attack Christianity. There is good reason to agree with those historians who see strong continuities between what was now called Christian "anti-Judaism" and modern "antisemitism." Still, the most destructive effects wrought by antisemitism, although occurring in a nominally Christian country and carried out by baptized Christians, were planned in an anti-Christian and racist context.

With the rise of the nation-state in Central Europe, and the crisis of liberal nationalism turning imperialist, Jews began to be blamed for the alleged ills of liberalism. Antisemitism fused with a broad range of political ideas and interests. Emancipated Jewries were identified with "modernizing" trends in Western and Central continental Europe by old conservative and new extremist nationalist forces. In Eastern and South-Eastern Europe, similar economic and socio-political influences united with rising national independence movements within the traditional empires (Austro-Hungarian and Ottoman empires and Czarist Russia) to exaggerate sharply traditional religious and "middle-man minority" tensions. Thus, when World War I broke out, the basic racist and ultra-nationalist ideas and alignments had been rehearsed, as "modern antisemitism" gave way to the "new antisemitism" of the interwar period, most pointedly in Central Europe in the wake of the dislocations attendant upon the lost war. Antisemitism served to project responsibility on local Jews, or a phantom "world Jewry," for the political and economic crises of the late 1920s and early 1930s. The Nazi seizure of power in Germany and their subsequent invasions and conquests of "space" for "racial superiority" brought ultimate horror and destruction to European Jewries. The government of one of the most civilized nation-states of Europe executed the most pernicious policy of persecution and extermination the world has seen so far. And although antisemitism has been recognized as one motive in the policies and opinions of other nations of the period as well, it did not match the final brutalities inflicted on the Jews by the Hitler regime.

Since the end of World War II, hatreds and prejudice have survived even as the horror of the Holocaust entered the consciousness of Western civilization. However, articulated attitudes of hatred and prejudice against Jews declined, expecially among the young. Except among unreformed Nazis surviving as marginal men in Germany and Austria, antisemitism has turned latent due to its total unacceptability in politics, public life, or cultural institutions. In recent history, it has surfaced when politicians in Germany and Austria were caught with heretofore unrevealed involvements in the Nazi past, or when intended or unintended slurs were mobilized for political ends. In place of prejudice against Jews taking center stage, the arrival of new ethnic, religious, or "racial" minorities in Western Europe led to new patterns of stereotypes and prejudice against foreign workers, seekers of asylum, or immigrants from the now independent former possessions of Western European countries. They have created new challenges for social action as well as for research and theory in European social science. In the USA, changes in the status of Blacks and other minorities, and immigrants from Third World countries, have woven new patterns into the rise and decline of discrimination and prejudice. And in the Third World itself, numerous tensions akin to those discussed in Western research have emerged, since decolonization has effected an entirely new pattern of national state formations based on tribal ethnicities. These ethnic conflicts have often led to tragically violent confrontations and to genocidal exterminations involving millions of human beings. At about the same period, a new world-wide phenomenon developed among communist and Third World countries. There a foreign-policy form of stereotyped hostility to Jews – anti-Zionism – emerged and revived, in turn, older antisemitic stereotypes, especially in communist-controlled Eastern European propaganda systems.

Thus the Zentrum für Antisemitismusforschung, the first of its kind in Europe, faced a complex variety of phenomena subsumed under the imprecise terms "antisemitism" and "anti-Judaism." It also confronted a research situation characterized by the co-existence of multiple strands of theory and empirical research concerning antisemitism and its scholarly *Unterbau*, the historical and social science disciplines dealing with prejudice, conflict, group tensions, minorities, and ethnicity. As a result, the Zentrum opted for approaches to the study of antisemitism that would prepare the way for basic theory and empirical research and for historic studies of more than local significance. This opting for basic and interdisciplinary research implies several assumptions. Antisemitism cannot be studied historically without being placed in the larger contexts of the economic, social, political, religious, and cultural histories of the discriminated-against group as well as its discriminators. Negative stereotypes cannot be studied without reference to the many positive forms of interaction and economic, cultural, religious, etc. relations that have formed positive mutual images at least since the beginning of Jewish emancipation in the middle of the eighteenth century. Antisemitism cannot be understood unless the *genera proxima* of its several forms are clearly conceptualized in the languages of several social sciences, above all in sociology and psychology. Thus, research on antisemitism requires not only historical and structural analyses of majority and minority, but the consideration of the full range of theories and empirical studies dealing with group relations in all their complexity.

This series, then, "Current Research on Antisemitism," has been planned to account for the state of international scholarly knowledge of antisemitism in the relevant disciplines. It assembles in five volumes what each volume editor considers the most valid or recent contribution to the *particular* problems of antisemitism, as well as to basic research in theory and empirical studies on general mechanisms and processes in such fields as group relations, prejudice, conflict, attitudes and behavior, to name just a few. Each volume consists of articles grouped in systematic chapters of the editor's choosing, and of introductions to each chapter by the editor, drawing the frequently divergent approaches and results of the several researchers into as coherent and concise a synthesis as possible.

Volume I (the present volume) deals with sociological research in its historical as well as systematic dimensions. It is edited by Helen Fein of the Institute for the Study of Genocide in New York. Volume II offers a path through the multidimensional contributions made by the several subdisciplines of psychology to antisemitism and prejudice. It is edited by Werner Bergmann of the Zentrum für Antisemitismusforschung, Technische Universität Berlin. Volume III assembles studies of modern antisemitism along systematic (typological), geographic, and chronological lines, and aims at setting guideposts for a comparative history of antisemitism in Europe and the USA. It is edited by Herbert A. Strauss of the Zentrum für Antisemitismusforschung, Technische Universität Berlin. Volume IV reviews the intellectual and religious history of modern antisemitism as revealed by the history of religion and philosophy, political theory, the critique of ideologies, the sociology of knowledge, and related disciplines. Volume V is based on the fact that the mass murder of Jews in World War II is being recognized by scholars as an event so unique that it has transformed the context within which antisemitism and prejudice can be studied. This last volume will review what the various disciplines have contributed to the complex processes that led to the genocide of the Jews and to the immediate and long-range implications of the multi-level traumata that resulted from it.

The editors of this series owe gratitude above all to the volume editors (excepting, of course, themselves) for whom working on their volumes was, to a large extent, a matter of dedication and responsibility. They thank the Technische Universität Berlin for adding an allocation for the publication of this series to the Publication Fund of the Zentrum für Antisemitismusforschung and thus making its appearance possible.

And they thank Walter de Gruyter Verlag, Berlin, for the courtesy and efficiency with which they have chaperoned this series, part of the program of the Zentrum für Antisemitismusforschung, to its realization.

Berlin, January 1987   Herbert A. Strauss
                                                   Werner Bergmann

Preface

To read or to write a new book on antisemitism demands a distinct *raison d'être*. My justification for expanding this library is not only that the question persists and is recurrent but that it has seldom been viewed from a sociological perspective apart from contemporary surveys, which ignore its historical origin, duration, dimensions, and its diffusion among states and civilizations. Most contemporary surveys have focused on the phenomenon in one point in time only, on individuals rather than on institutions, movements, and ideology, on attitudes rather than on behavior, and on the U.S. to the virtual exclusion of other western states and non-western states. Ironically, modern social-psychological studies, despite their explicit bias against ethnocentrism, have produced a literature on antisemitism that is not only ethnocentric but tempocentric, based largely on the experiences of and responses to American Jews during the forty years of the hundred years or less most members of this immigrant group have been in the U.S. This arbitrarily limits the questions we can pose and what we may learn.

The sociological perspective requires complementary historical and comparative analyses to answer the questions it poses: How is antisemitism similar to and dissimilar from other cases of inter-group hostility? Can it be simply regarded as an outcome of prejudice or social conflict? How has antisemitism developed to be regarded as an *ism*? How is it related to Judaism and the evolving role of Jews in different states and civilizations? How can it be understood as a modern social movement? We lack good comparative studies to answer such questions.

We begin in the usual way without defining antisemitism, considering its origins and the major types of explanation in Part 1, and sketching its historical development in sociological terms. Studying *antisemitism* rather than *anti-semitism* implies more than the deletion of a hyphen; it means taking antisemitism seriously as a thesis without an antithesis, for there is no *semitism*. Part 2 addresses the question how we can define antisemitism generically (considering the radical differences among authors presented), and considers contrary propositions about how its dimensions are related. What impact does antisemitism (as it is indexed now) have on political or other behavior?

Part 3 surveys the ecology of antisemitism, its specific relation to Christianity, and considers the status of Jews and Christians under Islam, both of whom were tolerated, subordinated, and excluded from the sanctified Islamic universe of obligation. This may also be related to the discussion of Arab antisemitism in Part 5. More generally, Part 3 considers how discrimination and hostility against Jews and other minorities are related to the roles such groups often play as *middleman-minorities:* groups who serve as traders, financiers, managers and entrepreneurs, and are strangers, members of diaspora or "overseas" nationalities, detached from but still identified with other nations. This affords us an opportunity to formulate and probe more general theories explaining the extent and intensity of prejudice, hostility, and violence, the charges and myths against the minority and to appreciate the circular or interactive nature of group relations. We explicate the contradictory implications of theses, explaining when antisemitism and other anti-minority ideologies erupt and grow, which reflect contradictions in the main body of sociological theory.

Part 4 focuses on the past impact of antisemitism on Nazism and the Holocaust. How well does antisemitism explain who supported the Nazi Party and the tolerance of the German people for the discrimination, segregation, and annihilation of the Jews between 1933 and 1945? How do these findings reflect on theories about the origin and mobilization of antisemitism and the differentiation of types of antisemitism?

Part 5 inquires about changes in the contemporary question and how Jewish status, claims, and nationhood (and the conflicts the Jewish state has engendered or inherited) impact on antisemitism, focussing especially on Soviet and Arab antisemitism. This also tests the pre-theoretical assumption often made that because we are studying a continuing question it is the same question, there are the same grounds instigating it, and that these grounds are mere justifications for underlying hostility.[1] By all historical accounts, the goals of antagonists of the Jews were not the same in 100 C. E., 1200 C. E., 1795, 1875 and 1935, and there is good reason to believe it is not today – it may not even be the same question in all states and contexts at the present time. Just as "the Jewish question" focussed attention and attributed responsibility to the Jews by labeling, labeling diverse phenomena as antisemitism may mislead, overgeneralize, and divert attention from the more menacing threats to Jews.

---

[1] The relationship between conflict and hostility is considered more theoretically in Part 2 and Part 3.

One significant question has been omitted: the impact of antisemitism on the Jews themselves, on their aspirations, their self-identifications and consciousness, their cohesion and cultural participation, and on the ideologies and movements to which they have been drawn in the contemporary world. Thus, the unwary reader should be warned. This book offers a constricted view, focussing on Jews as objects and victims rather than subjects and actors in history. Because of the focus of this book and the space the latter would entail, this is beyond our purview; however, the revolution in Jewish consciousness in the diaspora after the Holocaust and the establishment of the state of Israel have been discussed in the introduction to Part 5.

One can not but conclude reflectively. Understanding antisemitism may be a contribution to social-scientific inquiry and to Jewish self-understanding. Post-Holocaust generations of Jews are heir to an easily aroused latent dread of antisemitism which can appear as mindless pessimism or be masked as mindless denial, denial cloaking anxiety. Both are loaded with unexamined assumptions which may increase anxiety but decrease perception and discrimination. This book is an attempt to probe taken-for-granted assumptions, to substitute intelligence and analysis for defense mechanisms and mechanical defenses, to begin asking new questions. The delegitimation of antisemitism after the Holocaust seemed to many a great historical leap forward. But that optimism has faded over the last decade. Camus' *The Plague* yields the metaphor which corresponds to our fears of the chronic persistence of antisemitism:

. . . Dr. Rieux resolved to compile this chronicle, so that he should not be one of those who hold their peace but should bear witness in favor of those plague-stricken people; so that some memorial of the injustice and outrage done them might endure. . . . None the less, he knew that the tale he had to tell could not be one of a final victory. . . . And, indeed, as he listened to the cries of joy rising from the town, Rieux remembered that such joy is always imperiled. He knew what those jubilant crowds did not know but could have learned from books: that the plague bacillus never dies or disappears for good; that it can lie dormant for years and years in furniture and linen-chests; that it bides its time in bedrooms, cellars, trunks, and bookshelves; and that perhaps the day would come when . . . it would rouse up its rats again and send them forth to die in a happy city.[2]

---

[2] Albert Camus, *The Plague*, New York, 1948, p. 178.

The bacillus survives, but eruptions of the plague on a massive scale seem to have ceased as conditions for its growth are no longer common.

July, 1985   Helen Fein

Contents

Part 1: Explanations

Part 2: Dimensions / Effects

Part 3: Comparative Contexts

Part 4: Impacts On The Holocaust

Part 5: The Question Today

Part 1: Explanations

HELEN FEIN

Explanations of the Origin and Evolution of Antisemitism

We begin by examining antisemitism from the perspectives of distinguished scholars from different disciplines who have explained the origins or persistence of this phenomenon in different periods. It is arresting to observe how much they agree with each other despite different methods, concepts and stresses. They represent three major schools of explanation of antisemitism, differing in emphasis. The first school relates its historic origin to the dominant Christian definition of the Jews, focusing on hegemonic organizations, institutions and ideologies of western civilization.[1] The second focuses on the interactions of Jews and others. Such interpretations often assume without warrant that xenophobia or "the dislike of the unlike"[2] is universal among societies.[3] "I regard the very presence of the unique Jewish community among the other nations as the stimulus of the animosity directed at them" says Katz herein.

The third explanation is a neo-Marxist functionalist one, interpreting the functions of antisemitism as a device for the dominant class in modern capitalist societies to channel aggression against outsiders and, extrapolating from psychoanalytic thought, its function for the antisemite whose fears and hostility are externalized, displaced, and projected onto vulnerable minorities. Thus, both the psychic economy and the political economy of capitalism dictate the need for scapegoats. This approach does not consider the origin and functions of antisemitism in precapitalist (or non-

---

[1] Jules Isaac, *The Teaching of Contempt: Christian Roots of Anti-Semitism,* New York, 1964; James W. Parkes, *The Conflict of the Church and the Synagogue: A Study in the Origins of Antisemitism,* New York, 1969; Leon Poliakov, *The History of Anti-Semitism: From the Time of Christ to the Court Jews,* New York, 1965; and Ruether herein.
[2] Salo W. Baron, "Changing Patterns of Antisemitism," *Jewish Social Studies* 38, 1, 1976, pp. 5–38.
[3] Also shared by Eva G. Reichmann, *Hostages of Civilization: the Social Sources of National Socialist Anti-Semitism,* Westport, Conn., 1949.

capitalist) societies which are considered in Parts 3 and 5 herein. It was best developed and diffused by Adorno[4] and is represented herein by Sartre.

Both Ruether and Katz relate the development of antisemitism historically and may be read in conjunction with Langmuir (Part 2): they depict a sequence of interactions in which the agents of the dominant group define, limit, and, at times, evoke minority responses which reinforce the hostility of the dominant group. Yet, the self-definition, roles, and aspirations of the Jews have not simply been reactive, but are interactive and have changed in the modern era, Katz shows.

The trenchant analysis of Ruether of the theological roots of antisemitism shows how and why the church fathers devised the anti-Judaic myth of the rejection of the Jews, and how it was elaborated and transmuted into medieval Jew-hatred and antisemitism, pre-modern and modern, through cumulative and interacting causes over almost two millenia. More recently, Gager[5] has shown the divisions in the early Christian church regarding its response to the Jewish heritage of Christ and his first followers.[6]

Both Ruether and Gager agree that pagan attitudes toward the Jews were not consistently hostile and can not explain the later Christian doctrinal justification of hostility against the Jews. Both also agree that the anti-Jewish party won in the early church. Gager postulates other potential endings or hypothetical outcomes, concluding

> The results of our study require us, however, to confront again those who have sought to deny or minimize the contributions of early Christianity. Neither in paganism nor in Christianity is there evidence for a consistently negative understanding of Judaism . . . Judaism provoked among Christians and pagans alike profound *internal* divisions. Certainly for Christianity in its early stages, the real debate was never between Christians and Jews but among Christians. Eventually the anti-Jewish side won.[7]

---

[4] Theodor Adorno et al., *The Authoritarian Personality,* New York, 1950.

[5] John G. Gager, *The Origins of Anti-Semitism: Attitudes Toward Judaism in Pagan and Christian Antiquity,* New York, 1983.

[6] There were 1) the Judaizing Christians of Jewish and pagan origins who insisted that converts must fully follow the Hebrew law, 2) the Gnostics who disdained the Hebrew Bible and law and 3) lastly, Paul and his associates who (according to Gager) sought a middle path, admitting Gentiles to the new Covenant without any doctrinal necessity to observe Jewish law and ritual since it was abrogated for the Gentile Christians but not for the Jewish Christians. Gager agrees with the scholars who maintain that Paul recognized the authenticity of the worship of both Jews and Christians – both were chosen peoples – and solely fought against the assimilation of the new Christians as Jews. The more conventional interpretation of Paul (which Reuther credits) holds Paul responsible for the beginnings of the anti-Judaic myth.

[7] Gager, *op. cit.,* pp. 267–269.

In the beginning, Gager points out, Christians were a persecuted sect, competing for followers in predominantly Jewish and Jewish-influenced communities: they sought to rebut Jewish claims and prescriptions in order to preserve their cohesion and independence as a separate group, to assert their own legitimacy by ignoring, denying, or discrediting the legitimation of their religion of origin. But when they could not win the debate with contemporary Jews, Christians devised the "simple assertion that the Jews, as God's rejected people, were blind to the meaning of their own scriptures. At this point debate ended and diatribe began."[8] Thus, the church propagated the anti-Judaic myth first to justify its own separation; the myth served to legitimate segregation from and stigmatization of the Jews after Christianity became the state religion of the Roman Empire, and political solidarity began to be based on religious monism or likeness in contrast to the earlier imperial pluralism and toleration.

Katz's work assumes this background but puts greater emphasis on Jewish-Gentile interaction processes, and thus may be related to inter-group relations theory. This presupposes that majorities' and minorities' aims may agree or differ: the majority may seek to integrate or assimilate a group, incorporate group rights, or may expel or seek to destroy the minority. Minorities may seek to assimilate, integrate, or separate themselves and may accomodate to, resist, or defy the goal of the majority. When both the dominant authorities of the Christian majority and Jewish minority sought to preserve their mutual exclusiveness, intolerance was reciprocal.[9] The differential power of the majority allowed the church to define and stigmatize the Jews as a pariah caste. Pariah castes – closed, endogamous, segregated groups who are believed to be polluting, the lowest of the low – are usually tolerated as long as they accept their place. Jews' role as pariahs, later specializing in the medieval period in the despised (but demanded) function of moneylending, was accepted by rabbinical authorities, but seen only as instrumental to allow Jews to preserve their special honor – which, as Weber observed, was not confirmed by worldly honors as is the honor of dominant castes.[10] Before the

---

[8] *Ibid.,* p. 159.

[9] Jacob Katz, *Exclusiveness and Tolerance: Jewish-Gentile Relations in Medieval and Modern Times,* New York, 1961.

[10] There is disagreement about whether the concept of caste can be applied outside of a caste society. Caste and class are different principles of social organization, the former based on group descent or ascription, while the latter is based on individual achievement; in caste societies, ranking is on the basis of group status, while in class societies (the basis of capitalism), ranking is on the basis of individual achievement. Yet, caste has proved a

seventeenth century, the rabbis viewed Christians as the other, theologically and morally inferior, but still insisted that Jews must adhere to ethical
standards in business dealings with them that apply to any trade, for to do
otherwise would not only violate the law but endanger the whole Jewish
community.[11] There was no potentiality for assimilation in pre-modern
Europe without conversion which led to rejection by the Jewish community.

Katz relates (herein) the continuity and the development of modern
antisemitism to the underlying pre-modern Christian definition of Judaism,
denigration of the Jews and the Christian restriction of them to pariah
status. The disparity between their status after emancipation and their
pariah status evoked the resentment of Christians who then perceived
them as aggressive and illegitimate competitors.

---

persistent phenomenon in some modern class societies. *Pariah* castes – groups ranked
below the lowest caste or strata which were originally discriminated because they did dirty
work – still survive as in Japan despite legislation outlawing such discrimination. The
archetypal caste society, India, has preserved and transformed caste as units of class
society, group-identity mediating individual life-chances, despite legislation outlawing
untouchability and compensating for past disabilities.

Jews differ radically from Indian untouchables in not accepting their inferiority, traditionally viewing themselves as a chosen rather than an abased people. Weber's observations on
pariahs clearly pertain to the Jews:

> The sense of dignity of the negatively privileged strata naturally refers to a future lying
> beyond the present, whether it is of this life or of another. In other words, it must be
> nurtured by the belief in a providential "mission" and by the belief in a specific honor
> before God. The "chosen people's" dignity is nurtured by a belief either that in the
> beyond "the last will be the first," or that in this life a Messiah will appear to bring forth
> into the light of the world which has cast them out the hidden honor of the pariah people
> (Max Weber, "Class, Status, Party," in *From Max Weber: Essays in Sociology*, New York,
> 1946, p. 190).

Because of the many differences between the status and self-conceptions of Jews and traditional Indian pariahs, Werner Cahnman ("Pariahs, Strangers and Court-Jews: A Concep-
tional Classification," *Sociological Analysis* 35, 1974, pp. 154–166) challenged Weber's use
of caste to comprehend their situation. However, some other sociologists have followed
Weber in this use of caste to understand the situation of Jews (Celia Heller, *On the Edge of
Destruction: Jews of Poland Between the Two World Wars*, New York, 1977, pp. 58–61) and
Blacks, focussing on the dominant group's definition of the pariah as fundamentally
inferior and its ability to restrict their status over generations. Using it in this looser sense,
one may label the Jews in western societies a caste before emancipation (and in Islamic
societies which are discussed in Part 3). Since caste was perpetuated ultimately in caste
societies not by the belief of the untouchables but by the differential power of the dominant
caste(s), there is justification for this approach.

[11] Katz, *op. cit.*, pp. 158–167.

The introduction to Part 3 and Zenner (Part 3) consider the functions of a pariah caste for the dominant class in pre-capitalist societies and theorize how hostility to the Jews and other minorities results from the roles they play and why those roles are often deliberately allocated to pariah castes.

In retrospect, it is easy to overlook the interval before Jews were consigned to pariah status: Jews were not segregated, typed occupationally, or isolated from Christian and pagan neighbors in the west in the first millenium,[12] not fully distinguished by visible characteristics as outgroups, strangers to be exploited and deemed "fundamentally inferior", as Langmuir avers (Part 2). Had they been uniformly despised and scorned, the church fathers would not have needed to produce the *adversus Judaeos* texts which Reuther discusses, nor would they have needed to decree their stigmatization and segregation.

Widespread popular violence against the Jews did not occur in western Europe until the 11th century C.E. during the Crusades. It spread in the 12th century C.E. when the myth or chimera[13] that Jews committed ritual murder was invented, apparently by an English priest, eager to transform Monmouth into a cathedral center drawing pilgrims to view the bones of a martyr; this necessitated the discovery of a martyr and a dead boy was transformed into one by construction of this tale.[14] Waves of accusation, collective violence, and demonization of the Jews followed until they began to be regularly depicted as agents of the devil, committing more fantastic or chimerical crimes.[15]

The development of antisemitism may be used to illustrate and probe more general theories of conflict and intergroup relations, based on the following overlapping dimensions:

Power

Groups and nations may interact within a polity and across polities. Insofar as ethnic/national groups are organized as states, their behavior is governed by the rules and interests governing interstate relations. Insofar as national or minority groups reside in one state but are identified with other states, they may arouse hostility (or sympathy) depending on the

---

[12] Poliakov, *op. cit.*, pp. 26–37.

[13] Gavin, I. Langmuir, herein, Part 2.

[14] Gavin, I. Langmuir, "Thomas of Monmouth: Detector of Ritual Murder," *Speculum* 59, 4, 1984, pp. 820–846.

[15] Joshua Trachtenberg, *The Devil and the Jews*, Philadelphia, 1984.

relationships between the dominant state-people and state with the state with which they are identified.

Within the state, dominant groups usually define or limit the roles and status of subordinate or minority groups which constricts both their options and potential alliances. Minority groups' expectations of their place may accomodate to or differ from the design of the dominant group, depending on their cohesion, goals, visibility, aspirations and assessments of their future. Segregation and stigmatization are dominant-group mechanisms to keep the minority or subordinate group distant, demeaned, and disprivileged. Changes in social structure, political economy, and the state may cause the dominant group to redefine the role of the minority, creating competition and other unexpected behavior by minority-group members which are viewed as illegitimate by the dominant group. The dominant group can create conditions which instigate minority responses and behaviors which reinforce their perception that the minority merits discriminatory treatment, creating a self-fulfilling prophecy, and selectively evaluate minority behavior to conform to majority stereotypes of the minority; thus, the division of power and status leads to attitudes which reinforce discriminatory behavior. Individual members of minorities may seek to evade their status by assimilation while concentrated minorities may seek to negate their powerlessness by group separation. Insofar as their basis of ascription is visible, the majority can repel their assimilation. Insofar as minority-group members are stigmatized, but their stigmata are not always visible, their attempts at assimilation may be viewed as covert aggression by members of the majority and provoke increased majority-group cohesion, antagonism, and political mobilization to combat the threat of the minority, defined as illegitimate.

Group Cohesion, Cognitions and Conflict

Groups attempt to maintain boundaries to retain their identity. Within the boundary or circle, members are expected and socialized to reciprocate obligations. Group boundaries demarcate spheres of solidarity, defining the borders of the "universe of obligation" of the common conscience.[16]

Groups based on unity of belief, such as religious communities and cults whose universe of obligation stems from belief in a sacred and sanctifying authority, have a particular problem when such belief is challenged. Dis-

---

[16] Helen Fein, *Accounting for Genocide: National Responses and Jewish Victimization During the Holocaust*, New York, 1979, p. 4.

crediting the basis of unity is seen as renegadism, delegitimating sacred authority and splitting their essential basis of solidarity. As Coser put it in reformulating Simmel, "The closer the (original) relationship, the more intense the conflict."[17] There are several responses to such a conflict which include the physical and cognitive insulation of the more vulnerable group, discrediting the other group, and using secular power to prohibit the spread or practice of the other. Berger and Luckmann[18] discuss the uses of "ideological nihilation" of the opponent, negating or liquidating the legitimacy of the earlier system of belief.[19]

Yet the continued existence of a stigmatized out-group may also serve to preserve the structure of the dominant group. Conversion of the out-group may be a goal of the dominant group and/or it may become a "negative reference group," as Newcomb put it, defining the unity of the in-group.[20] A pariah caste, being below the lowest caste or class, raises the ranking of all strata of the dominant group and emphasizes their common status.

Insofar as conflict generates greater cohesion among the dominant group, groups threatened with internal schism may need and search for enemies:

> Such groups may actually perceive an outside threat although no threat is present. Under conditions yet to be discovered, imaginary threats have the same group-integrating functions as real threats . . . Such scapegoating mechanisms will occur particularly in those groups whose structure inhibits realistic conflict within.[21]

Myths, stereotypes, and collective defamations or accusations are most apt to frame social perceptions in crises when there is lack of objective and authoritative methods to determine the source of crises: what is seen and inferred, and who is blamed. Insofar as groups are depersonalized and defined outside the universe of obligation – as are pariahs –, they are more vulnerable to accusation and victimization. The more conflict is conceived of as collective combat, and the fewer over-arching bonds there are between antagonists, the more intense it will be, and the more likely is violence to be employed.

---

[17] Lewis A. Coser, *The Functions of Social Conflict*, New York, 1956, p. 67.
[18] Peter Berger and Thomas Luckmann, *The Social Construction of Reality*, Garden City, N.Y., 1966.
[19] Gager, *op. cit.*, p. 22.
[20] Coser, *op. cit.*, p. 90.
[21] *Ibid.*, p. 110.

This does not imply that all intergroup hostility is caused by contrived or projected conflicts. Part 3 and Part 5 consider to what extent conflict may be related to the roles Jews and other minorities play. Structural conditions which alter the potentiality for conflict include economic expansion and depression, the opening up of opportunities in new spheres or areas, population changes and the number, size, and relative status of groups in an ethnic hierarchy.

Political Mobilization

Ethnicity is a variable attribute in modern societies, depending both on how people construct their own identity, view their past, and how others define them. Both class and ethnicity are alternate bases for mobilization of parties and social movements. Whether class or ethnicity (race/religion) is the basis of appeal depends not only on the structure of belief and conflict but on the costs of each strategy and potential audience.

Ideologies defining which class or group is blamed for threatening conditions are instruments of mobilization. In pre-modern societies, religious belief and myth served a similar function, mobilizing popular rebellion against ruling elites or appealing to these elites by crowd action, bargaining by riot.

Ruling elites and classes may deflect popular mobilization against them by ideologies exploiting pre-existent myths blaming stigmatized minorities, increasing loyalty and cohesion on the basis of the likeness of the dominant group. Popular leaders or competing elites may mobilize against such groups both because they are seen as agents of the ruling elite, popularly viewed as the source of social problems, and because it is more economic to mobilize against powerless groups; there is less to fear in response than there would be were dominant groups attacked. Ethnic group mobilization allows organizers to appeal to cross-class constituencies and is thus usually a substitute and counter to class mobilization (the exception being where class identity corresponds uniformly to ethnic identity).

The following summary sketch of the development of antisemitism may be used to illustrate these dimensions.

I. Pre-Christian Era

1. The Jews began as a migratory nomadic tribe, becoming sojourners, agents, and clients of the Pharaoh, and foreign workers later reduced to slavery in Egypt; their flight – and the supernatural or natural collective

violence against their enslavers – is recorded in *Exodus*. In their flight and periods of sojourning before they became a nation, they made alliances in some instances and waged (or justified) wars of annihilation in other cases (*Joshua*) as was common in the ancient world.[22] Their behavior and the responses of the rulers of surrounding city-states toward them appear not to be based either on their religious beliefs or any underlying hostility but on whether their interests and goals were in conflict with those of the other tribe/state.

2. During the period of Jewish nationhood, the Jews were a dominant state-people but freely interacted and often worshipped with other indigenous tribes (pagans) dwelling among them. Frequent denunciations of the worship of Baal and of child-sacrifice in the *Torah* testify that, though the Jews were united on the basis of monotheism, they were not segregated or monistic in its observance; exogamy and participation in pagan worship was common among Jews.

3. The Jewish nation-state split and was reduced to colonial status in the Mediterranean world after the expulsions to Babylon due to the growth of warring, expansive empires and internal disunity. Partly in response to the dispersion and uprooting of the Jews, Jewish scribes and authorities codified Jewish law and prescribed endogamy, leading to fewer bonds with other tribes. Although group boundaries were reinforced, Judaism was still inclusive, open to converts.

4. Reinforced Jewish boundaries and their self-definition compelled Jews to reject common celebration with neighboring tribes and justified Jewish hostility or xenophobia towards pagans. Similarly, the hostility of the latter to Jewish self-separation (and specifically of Egyptians to the Exodus myth) led some to credit xenophobic and hostile myths explaining and deriding the practices of the Jews and alleging their unclean origin.[23] Thus, antagonistic Jewish and pagan attitudes or prejudices were reciprocal.

5. During the Greco-Roman period, there was a wide dispersion of Jews throughout the Mediterranean world in which they occupied a variety of roles as individuals and enjoyed state-recognized group rights – e.g., not

---

[22] Frank Chalk and Kurt Jonassohn, *The History and Sociology of Genocide,* Vol. 2, Montreal, 1984.

[23] David Winston, "Pagan and Early Christian Anti-Semitism," in Henry Friedlander and Sybil Milton (eds.), *The Holocaust: Ideology, Bureaucracy, and Genocide,* Millwood, N.Y., 1980.

working on the Sabbath. Jews were integrated in the Mediterranean world, both adapting to and adding to Mediterranean cultures.

6. Real and symbolic alliances between Jews and Rome and factionalism within the ruling elite of Rome led to conflicts between Jews and Egyptians in Alexandria resulting in collective violence and defamation (1st century C.E.). "Throughout this period anti-Semitism was firmly embedded in the structure of anti-Romanism; both were hallmarks of Alexandrian patriotism."[24]

7. As the Jewish community was open to converts, Jewish customs and thought gained adherents and influence in Rome. The growing influence of Judaism caused conservative Roman elites to defend Roman traditions by disparaging Judaism and mocking Jews whom they "saw . . . as essentially un-Roman."[25] At the same time, the Jewish revolts against Rome (66–73 and 115–117 C.E.) led to Roman revision of the earlier policy of toleration. Thus, hostility among some Roman factions to Jews was based on both symbolic and real conflicts involving them.

II. Early Christian Period

8. A new religious community emerged from the followers of Jesus, enlarging on the original Jewish core but including pagan "Judaizers", Gnostics and Christian Jews who were confronted with two problems demanding resolution: 1) the definition of borders and 2) a cognitive crisis. They had to differentiate church from synagogue because a) both the synagogue and most Jews had rejected the messianic claims of the Jewish Christians and b) the potential for outreach to pagans depended on accepting them as they were – not circumcized – and resisting their conversion to Judaism which might lead to their assimilation as Jews. Cognitively, they had to make sense of the dead Messiah, interpret the link between their Jewish heritage and their new faith, and (later) defend the abrogation of Jewish law and their separation from the Jewish community.

9. The definitions of both Christian and Jewish leaders became increasingly exclusive but the circle of potential followers to which Jews and Christians might appeal was the same. Competition led to increasing self-defense and aggressive rebuttal of the other. To lessen the threat of meaninglessness posed by the Crucifixion, to retain the biblical mandate

---

[24] Gager, *op. cit.*, p. 53.
[25] *Ibid.*, p. 59.

and to delegitimate Jewish claims, the dominant Christian leadership faction constructed the tenets of the anti-Judaic myth.[26] As Ruether points out, both the Jewish and Christian positions were mutually exclusive and intolerant but had different implications, for

> the Jewish view of "the nations" allowed Jews to coexist with Christians and with peoples of other faith, provided they let the Jews be themselves, whereas Christian universalism could allow for no such place for the non-Christian . . . For Christianity, anti-Judaism was not merely a defense against attack, but an intrinsic need of Christian self-affirmation.

Two reinforcing processes were at work: rivalry increased mutual antipathy and group separation increased in-group solidarity. The greater the competition was between Christians and Jews, the more the anti-Judaic myth was reinforced by hostility. The more social distance there was between Christians and Jews, the more credible was the defamation of the Jews.

III. Late Roman and Medieval Periods

10. The anti-Judaic myth which justified the above was reinforced as Jews, whose existence was tolerated by the reigning church for theological reasons, were defined outside the "sanctified universe of obligation – that circle of people with reciprocal obligations to protect each other, whose bonds arose from their relation to a deity or sacred source of authority"[27] after Constantine adopted Christianity as the state religion in the 4th century C.E. Being outside the universe of obligation implies that the dominant class has no obligation to protect the out-group or minority or to expiate violations against it, thus making it vulnerable to become a victim of collective violence or genocide.[28] Although the right of Jews to exist as Jews was theologically recognized by the church, their right to exist in any specific time and place depended on the tolerance of the princes and the state. Neither state nor church could usually protect Jews from mobilization against them which was stirred by the anti-Judaic myth.

Jews were incrementally denied equal rights and their status diminished by fiats of rulers of state and church in order to make Jews inferior to Christians: these included the decrees of Theodosius II (439 C.E.), Justinian (531 C.E.), Lateran Councils (1179 and 1215 C.E.) the Council of

---

[26] See Ruether, herein.

[27] Fein, *op. cit.*, p. 4.

[28] Helen Fein, *Imperial Crime and Punishment: British Judgement on the Massacre at Jallianwala Bagh, 1919–1920*, Honolulu, 1977.

Montpellier (1195 C.E.) and other medieval councils which stripped Jews of rights to hold office, bear arms, testify in litigation against Christians, employ Christians in a lower status, marry Christians, and finally segregated, labelled, and stigmatized them, compelling them to wear special badges and clothing. After being visibly stigmatized, Jews were ghettoized from the 13th to the 16th century C.E. in western and central Europe.

Thus the status of Jews in Christian Europe became inferiorized and regulated as is a pariah caste dependent on the dominant caste or class.[29]

11. The dominant nobility exploited the dependence of Jews on their protection by casting them in the stigmatized role of usurers[30] in order to fill a status gap in medieval society in a manner consistent with both Christian and Jewish law.

12. Jewish segregation and stigmatization reinforced Jewish cohesion which, in turn, was functional for their economic specialization.

13. The degradation of the Jews led to their physical powerlessness, making them more vulnerable to collective violence, because their inability to resist attack proved that there was neither a deterrent nor any cost in attacking them. The hostility to moneylenders among borrowers, the Jews' role as protected wards of the princes, and their powerlessness led to incentives to strip and despoil them.

Aggressive attempts to spread Christianity also led to violence against Jews as roaming bands of Crusaders mobilized against the infidels, who demanded that Jews convert and massacred the noncompliant, and were impervious to any social control which might check their violations against Jews.

14. Because there were no consensual limits to conflict as the anti-Judaic myth marked the Jew as an enemy, a people outside the Christian universe of obligation, conflicts in which Jews figured or in which hostility was displaced onto them were more likely to become deadly than other class or group conflicts. Conflicts in which Jews were symbolic or substitute targets (as clients or representatives of prince, bishop, or nobility) could also become deadly, leading to pogroms and massacres. According to Poliakov,[31] the higher clergy and nobility unsuccessfully tried to protect

---

[29] See note 10; Part 3 discusses their status in Islamic and Asian civilizations.
[30] See discussion of pariah capitalism im Part 3.
[31] Poliakov, *op. cit.*, pp. 45–50.

the Jews, and the lower clergy were more likely to lead attacks against Jews, but more research is needed to confirm this.[32]

Beginning in the 12th century, the anti-Judaic myth was reinforced by chimeric accusations (ritual murder), providing new sanctions for collective violence against the Jews. Popular mobilization – of crusades against the infidels or the anti-Christ, or of oppressed classes against their overlords – was likely to lead to attacks on Jews, both because of the anti-Judaic myth and the embeddedness of the Jews in real and symbolic conflicts.[33] Collective accusations – libels against Jews frequently based on chimerical crimes – might instigate or be used to justify collective violence.[34]

15. As a native middle class emerged to compete with the Jews, the utility of toleration of the Jews changed, and elites tolerated or encouraged their expulsion from western Europe, flights sometimes precipitated by violence. Their re-entry and migration depended on their changing utilities for elites and prospects advanced by elites in other, less developed states who offered toleration and protection in exchange for Jewish skills.[35]

16. When threats and crises arose whose source could not be understood or agreed upon, the anti-Judaic myth framed social cognition, leading to further victimization of the Jews; the attribution to the Jews of responsibility for the black plague is a case in point: thus the myth expanded. Jews viewed through this prism were likely perpetrators to be charged with horrendous and new chimeric crimes, the legends of which reinforced their stereotype; they began to be seen as non-human, diabolic.[36]

Given this perception, the myth could also be exploited by groups with antagonistic class interests to frame the Jews, as was observed by 14th century contemporaries who attributed Jew-burnings to the money their debtors owed them and doubted the accusation that they had poisoned the wells, used as a pretext to instigate these massacres.[37]

---

[32] The general prejudice against rioters, assuming they are "riff-raff" – an assumption not confirmed by much contemporary social-scientific research – informs Poliakov's assessment that "only the dregs of the population everywhere joined the slaughterers" (op. cit., p. 45). It is not clear, however, how this can be known without careful analysis and delineation of their class status.

[33] Heiko A. Oberman, The Roots of Anti-Semitism in the Age of Renaissance and Reformation, Philadelphia, 1984, pp. 41–43; Poliakov, op. cit., 1965.

[34] See also 16 following, Langmuir (Part 2) and Introduction Part 2 and 3.

[35] See Introduction Part 3 for further discussion.

[36] Oberman, op. cit., pp. 84–85; Trachtenberg, op. cit.

[37] Marvin Lowenthal, The Jews of Germany: A Story of Sixteen Centuries, New York, 1970, pp. 28–29.

Figure 1:
Interaction of Causes of the Degradation and Violations of the Jews in the Christian Era

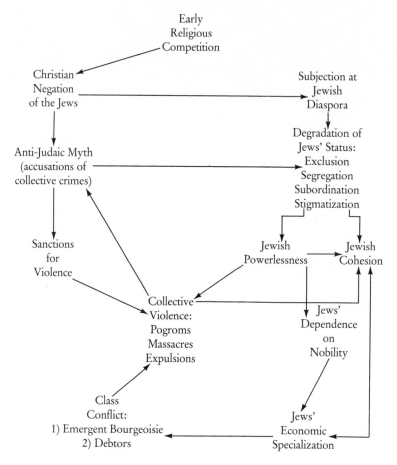

IV. Modern Period

Note this sketch focusses on the core states of western Europe; a focus on eastern Europe or the Iberian states would require taking into account their different course of political and economic development.

17. The demands of the leading classes in the developing nation-states for greater participation and freedom led to a movement within states to grant all male inhabitants equal status as citizens, leading to the emancipation of

the Jews in the core states of Europe in the 18th and 19th centuries and in the Americas.

18. As belief systems changed, ideologists and social movements seeking to comprehend and alter the modern world responded to these changes by amending and revitalizing the basic paradigm of antisemitism first incorporated in the anti-Judaic myth: the antisocial character and/or negative acts attributed to the Jews are said to be caused by their intrinsic nature or belief. These drew on pre-existent hostility to the Jews and similar psychic mechanisms for recognizing, generalizing and displacing blame which are embedded in the anti-Judaic myth.[38]

19. Emancipation of the Jews led to their individual acculturation and the integration and assimilation of some, and (in many cases) the division and reconstitution of the Jewish religious community on new sectarian and organizational bases. Integration, however, increased Jewish visibility for several reasons:

20. Competition between Jews and non-Jews in the middle classes increased, both because the roles Jews could play in the 19th century were no longer so restricted, and Jewish aspirations for social mobility were rising at a time opportunities were expanding.[39]

21. Increased competition and the greater urbanization of Jews than of non-Jews (which also increased the likelihood Jews would be competitors) led to heightened Jewish visibility, especially in the metropolises in which political events were made.[40]

22. Jewish acculturation, visibility, and the drive by some Jews to assimilate into the main-stream of European society led toward greater "consciousness of kind" among European Christians, increasing their need to reinforce group boundaries excluding Jews, resulting in increasing individual discrimination and social antisemitism.

23. Status threats associated with Jewish competition and the fear of downward mobility of non-Jews led to increased prejudice against Jews and defensive reactions including:

---

[38] See Katz herein and Goldhagen, Part 5.

[39] See part 3 Introduction for a discussion of how competition may relate to intergroup hostility and Hobsbawm, Part 5.

[40] Encyclopaedia Judaica 5, p. 1511; Salo Baron, *Modern Nationalism and Religion*, Freeport, N.Y., 1947, p. 220; Norbert Kampe, "Jews and Antisemites at Universities in Imperial Germany (1)," *Leo Baeck Institute Yearbook* 30, 1985, pp. 357–394.

a) symbolic attacks against individual Jews as representative of Jews as a
  collectivity;
b) the exclusion of Jews from fraternal and professional associations;
c) institutionalized quotas restricting the number of Jews entering
  schools, the professions, and the civil service, and discriminatory
  licensing requirements for the trades and professions; and
d) ideological antisemitism.

24. The rise of a mass electorate divided on class lines and the cross-class
appeals of the antisemitic movement made antisemitism a resource for
political contenders, especially useful in periods in which the status threats,
increased mobility (downward and upward), and dislocation associated
with early capitalism were increased by depression and national crises.
This was the case in the last quarter of the 19th and the second quarter
of the 20th century. Therefore, one would expect the success of political
antisemitism to be related to the extent of status threats as it was (in both
periods); the latter can be explained both by the extent of intergroup
competition and/or declining or static opportunities.

25. The antisemitic movement, like other social movements, both drew
on pre-existent beliefs and attitudes which might attract followers, and on
adapted contemporary modes of justification. Religious and secular or
racial antisemitism drew on traditional and modern modes of justifying
ideology respectively. Nineteenth century "scientific racism" – the doctrine of racial or group inheritances of unequal worth and the polygenetic
origins of mankind producing species ranked for all time – rationalized the
hierarchy of groups and contemporary European imperialism. Racial
antisemitism was reconciled with religiously-based antisemitism by the
invention of an Aryan Christianity, denying the Jewish origins of Christ.
The diversity of rationalizations for antisemitism enabled the movement to
appeal to the most diverse audiences.

26. Structural conditions in the interwar years in Europe (especially after
1929) led to the remobilization of the antisemitic movement in fascist and
radical right parties and paramilitary bands. The antisemitic parties in the
newer nation-states of central and eastern Europe were more successful
than those in the older states for several reasons:

> . . . ethnic competition was intensified in the interwar years, reinforced by the new states'
> opportunity structure that increased self-conscious group comparison, inducing envy of
> dominant collectivities or other minorities that had traditionally played critical roles
> within the nation-state. The new nations' prospective elites perceived visibly dissimilar

internal minorities sharing ethnicity of neighboring states and/or playing the role of the middleman minority. Poles, Germans, and Jews were suspect. The state was seen by such groups as the vehicle to transform the political economy, which could oust the strangers who had illegitimately infiltrated or usurped positions they now wanted for themselves ... Anti-semitism was an ideal tactic for radical challengers because it was simple, popular, and could be used to mobilize movement cadres to foment aggression. Where a tradition of collective violence against Jews did not exist, there was a tradition of collective accusation ... Anti-Semitism was also an economic means of arousing a constituency because of the empiric powerlessness of the Jews in political competition between ethnic groups, and the visible role that Jews often played as a middleman minority. Rather than serving as a catharsis for class conflict within a collectivity ... anti-Semitism was a functional tactic to raise tension within a collectivity against a substitute target for combat with another collectivity ... Similarly, anti-Semitism was a functional ideology for radical right challengers throughout Europe because the Jews were the only pan-European people who were culturally and politically visible, except for Germans.[41]

The myth of Jewish world conspiracy was embedded in the ideology of the Nazi Party along with a chimeric accusation that the Jews polluted the blood of Germans and a utopian fantasy of an Aryan master-race which was used to legitimate the state's right to exist, expand, and kill. The "Final Solution of the Jewish Question," Germany's extermination of the European Jews, was the acting out of this fantasy; it had earlier instigated Hitler (1939) to authorize the categorical murder of institutionalized German children and adults deemed defective. It later led to the annihilation of the Gypsies.[42] Part 4 considers what role antisemitism played in the growth and mobilization of the Nazi Party and in the toleration by the German people of the discrimination, expropriation, segregation, violation, and ultimate annihilation of the Jews between 1933 and 1945.

Part 5 considers how the re-establishment of a Jewish state and the role of Jews in other nation-states since 1945 has affected antisemitism and the perceptions of Jewry.[43]

Critical Sociology and an Existentialist Approach to Antisemitism

Perhaps the most popular post-World-War II explanation of modern antisemitism has been based on its social-psychological functions. Both the critical theorists and Sartre solely look at antisemitism as a modern phenomenon and begin with Marxian assumptions, relating it ultimately to class structure and conflict.

---

[41] Fein, 1979, *op. cit.*, pp. 85–86.
[42] *Ibid.*, Ch. 1.
[43] Katz also remarks upon this herein.

Figure 2:
Development and Impact of Modern Antisemitism Since 1789 in Western Europe

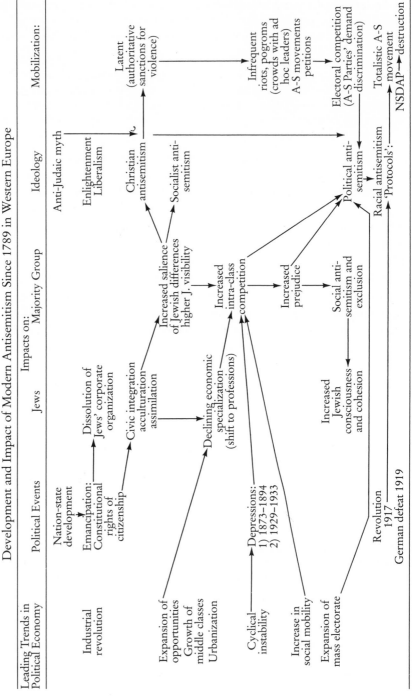

Sartre[44] explores the consciousness of the antisemite, rejecting as rationalizations explanations which account for antisemitism as a response to attributes of the Jews; Sartre, instead, relates it to the attributes of the antisemite: his sadism, his longing for certainty, rigidity, and "impenetrability." This is not to say that antisemitism is just a sign of individual maladjustment or deviance; antisemitism, to Sartre, is a fallacious attempt to create a classless society, a union based on exclusion in order "to give value to mediocrity as such, to create an elite of the ordinary."

Martin Jay, reviewing "The Jews and the Frankfurt School,"[45] showed that the members of this group did not conceive of antisemitism as a problem in itself before 1943.[46] Horkheimer and Adorno first viewed bourgeois antisemitism as a symptom of class conflict with Jews serving as scapegoats to displace hatred against capitalism. After the war, Adorno incorporated a psychoanalytic model which later became the basis for *The Authoritarian Personality*,[47] whose presuppositions are summarized by Pettigrew:

> Externalization theories of prejudice derive directly from psychoanalytic thought, . . . The most prominent are the authoritarian personality theory and the frustration-aggression hypothesis . . . central to the syndrome is anti-intraception, the refusal to look inside oneself and the lack of insight into one's own behavior and feelings. As children, authoritarians may have been punished frequently by stern parents, and in turn felt intense hatred for them. Unable to express these aggressive feelings for fear of further punishment, authoritarians find them threatening and unacceptable, deny them, and begin to project them onto others. If they feel hatred for their parents, they see hatred not in themselves but in the dangerous outside world.[48]

Such hatred could be manipulated by fascist demagogues in times of systemic crisis, projecting aggression and displacing blame onto minorities in their midst.[49]

Adorno did not seek to explain the choice of minorities as victims or the social cognition of the Jews, apparently viewing minorities as interchangeable scapegoats despite evidence to the contrary. Finally, Adorno interpreted fascist (e. g. Nazi) antisemitism as "false projection . . . equivalent to

---

[44] Herein.
[45] "The Jews and the Frankfurt School: Critical Theory's Analysis of Anti-Semitism," *New German Critique* 19, 1980, pp. 137–149.
[46] See also Ehrhard Bahr, "The Anti-Semitism Studies of the Frankfurt School: The Failure of Critical Theory," *German Studies Review* 162, 1978, pp. 125–138.
[47] *op. cit.*
[48] Thomas F. Pettigrew, "Prejudice," in Thomas F. Pettigrew et al. (eds.), *Prejudice*, Cambridge, Mass., 1982, p. 16.
[49] Part 2 discusses the evaluations of this explanation.

paranoia" which was manipulated to serve as the basis of a mass delusional system. He (and others) have remarked on the likeness between Sartre's portrait of the antisemite and the ideal-type "authoritarian personality," although it appears both were independently developed.[50] Adorno's analysis may be complemented by that of Langmuir[51] who shows how certain groups became victims of material and psychic exploitation. This confirmed their inferiority and rendered them vulnerable to chimeric accusations which served to externalize the fears of their accusers.

Since both Sartre, and Horkheimer and Adorno, begin with Marxian assumptions, they also conclude that antisemitism will only be ended by going beyond a class society to a classless state (Sartre), a society liberated from domination and violence (Horkheimer and Adorno): "In other words, once utopia was achieved, antisemitism would take care of itself."[52]

[50] Adorno, *op. cit.*, p. 971; Mufid J. Hannush, "Adorno and Sartre: A Convergence of Two Methodological Approaches," *Journal of Phenomenological Psychology* 4, 1973, pp. 297–313.
[51] Part 2.
[52] Jay, *op. cit.*, p. 149.

ROSEMARY R. RUETHER

The Theological Roots of Anti-Semitism[*]

It has sometimes been said that anti-Semitism is essentially pagan, not Christian. This view would have it that the Christian opposition to the Jews was benignly theological. Virulent anti-Semitism entered the picture only when the Christian community was assimilated into the gentile world and took over a preexisting, non-Christian "pagan hate" for the Jews.[1] This thesis is misleading (especially since it is based on a theological stereotype of the "pagan").

Rather, we must recognize Christian anti-Semitism as a uniquely new factor in the picture of antique anti-Semitism.[2] Its source lies in the theological dispute between Christianity and Judaism over the messiahship of Jesus, and so it strikes at the heart of the Christian gospel. It was this theological root and its growth into a distinctively Christian type of anti-Semitism that were responsible for reversing the tradition of tolerance for Jews in Roman law.

Jesus' own teachings took a somewhat more radical, but not entirely different, form from that of the contemporary school of Hillel. It was the school of Hillel that declared, for example, that the whole of the Law can be summed up in the command to love one's neighbor.[3]

But while there was a similarity in content, there was a difference in style between Jesus and the scribal schools that led to an overestimation of the difference between them. Jesus was an itinerant prophet preaching to the *'am ha'aretz* on the roads and hillsides in a way that rejected the barrier

---

[*] Edited and abridged from: Rosemary Ruether, *Faith and Fratricide: The Theological Roots of Anti-Semitism* (New York: Seabury Press, 1974).
[1] Edward Flannery declares that the sources of Christian anti-Semitism are either pagan hate or a misreading of Christian hermeneutics under the pressure of social competition. He denies that there is any root of anti-Semitism in the "legitimate anti-Judaism of orthodox Christian doctrine" (*The Anguish of the Jews*, New York, 1964, pp. 60–61); see also G. Baum, *Is the New Testament Anti-Semitic?*, New York, 1965. p. 328 n. 40.
[2] Simon, *Verus Israel*, Paris, 1948, 250ff.
[3] *Sab.* 31a (C. J. G. Montefiore, *A Rabbinic Anthology*, London, 1938, p. 173).

between the observant and the unwashed. While the Pharisees conducted their ethical interpretation in a carefully conservative manner that preserved the outer form, Jesus' spiritualizing of the halakah was iconoclastic toward the outward form. Doubtless this was the setting of the controversies between himself and the scribal class.

More importantly, however, Jesus set his demand for righteousness in the context of messianic proclamation. Jesus probably did not identify himself originally with the Messiah. This would actually have been meaningless prior to the messianic revolution itself. Rather, he declared that he was the definitive prophet of a coming Son of man whose Kingdom was soon to be established by God (Mark 8:38; Luke 9:26; 12:8–9). Inclusion in this Kingdom *then* rests on how people respond to Jesus' word *now*. This would raise the question in the minds of the hearers as to "who he was."

It is probable that Jesus' own self-understanding came increasingly to approximate that of the Messiah at the end of his life.

His final Jerusalem mission, therefore, created a swiftly mounting élan of ecstatic expectation that this act would coincide with God's dramatic incursion into history, overthrowing the reign of evil powers and establishing the reign of blessedness for God's elect. But this élan resulted instead in the rapid denouement of his own death. When, instead of the expected miracle, Jesus was hustled away from the Mount of Olives where he was encamped with his followers, quickly tried by the political Sanhedrin and the Roman powers, and executed in the common death by crucifixion of an insurrectionist, the disciples were faced with a decisive choice about the truth of that expectation which they had followed with mounting hope up to the point of this reversal. Either Jesus was not the vehicle of the messianic Advent of God, and they and he had been wrong, or else his rejection by the Roman powers, with the cooperation of the Jewish colonial leaders, was a hostile assault by the "enemies of God" which did not cancel Jesus' messianic identity.

For the dominant Jewish religious consciousness, including those "crowds who heard him gladly" – i.e., hoped that he was to be the one who would establish the Kingdom – this settled the matter. Jesus was not the Messiah. For Judaism had never heard anything about a dying Messiah. True, there was the idea of the suffering prophet, but this was not identified with the Messiah.[4]

---

[4] For the idea of the suffering prophet in first-century Judaism, see H. A. Fischel, "Martyr and Prophet," *Jewish Quarterly Review* 37, 1946/47, pp. 265 ff. and 363 ff.

But for the disciples, who had staked everything on the truth of his message, it was an intolerable shock. Yet they, too, shared the assumption that such an end was incompatible with messianic identity, and so they scattered in dismay.

But then an extraordinary experience overtook this frightened band. The objectivity of this event can never be verified. He was not dead, but still alive!

The disciples began to search the Scriptures to affirm their faith that this redemptive event was indeed the real meaning of the ancient prophecies. In many places they found confirmation of this faith. Of particular importance were the parts of the prophet Isaiah (especially 42:52–53) which told of a rejected prophet whose suffering and death made atonement for Israel. Shortly before his death Jesus himself had linked his fate with this prophecy.

But who are the enemies of the messianic prophet? Who are those enemies who attack and almost defeat the king in the Psalms? And who are the enemies who lead the suffering prophet to the slaughter and "make his grave with the wicked?" Are they not precisely those same enemies against whom the prophets themselves are constantly railing – that stubborn taint of unbelief which has ever refused the message of repentance which God has sent through his messengers? It is the official leadership, the priests and scribes, who represent this tradition of apostasy in Israel. They are the ones who have ever resisted the Holy Spirit and killed the prophets.

With this interpretation of the Scriptures, the disciples were ready to renew Jesus' messianic mission to Israel, now preaching that salvation is to be found only through his name. Those crowds in Jerusalem and Judea who had once heard him gladly would be told that this is the real meaning of his message.

Israel might still be saved if it recognized quickly that this is the real meaning of the prophecies. They should know, too, that the official leadership could not be trusted to interpret the Scriptures correctly because they are the heirs of those who had always rejected the prophets.

But the real clash between Christianity and the Pharisaic teachers was not over spiritualizing interpretations of the temple or the Law or even the belief that Jesus was the Messiah. Rather, the crux of the conflict lay in the fact that the Church erected its messianic midrash into a *new principle of salvation* .

Christianity is no mere "new patch" put on an old garment, or a new wine poured into old wine bottles. It demands a whole new "garment" and "container" of this new wine (Luke 5:3 ff.). This was the crux of the incompatibility of Christianity and the Jewish religious tradition, as interpreted by the schools. It resulted in the rapid expulsion of the Church from the womb of its mother religion with hard blows on the backsides of its ejected preachers (Matt. 10:17; Mark 13:9; Luke 21:31; John 12:42; 16:2; 2 Cor. 11:24).

But this inability of Christian preaching to convert the core of the synagogue itself was complemented by an unexpected turn of events. Gentiles were attracted to Christianity and began to come in great numbers. These Gentiles came from the circle of "God-fearers," attracted to Jewish ethical and monotheistic principles, who gathered around the synagogues, but who drew back from full proselyte status. For this circle of Judaizing Gentiles, Christianity provided everything that attracted them to Judaism, without those practices which they did not want to accept.

The Church, then, found itself with a paradox which its first preaching had not anticipated. Rejected by Judaism, it found its fertile missionary field among the Gentiles.

Yet the Church adapted its midrash rather rapidly to accommodate this development. By the second decade of the Church's mission, this Petrine church had already reached the point where its first midrash (that Jesus is the stone the builders rejected who has become the cornerstone of the community of salvation) had been expanded to include the idea that God was carving out for himself a people *from among the Gentiles.* This, too, was declared to have been known and continuously predicted by the prophets.

This new exegesis is expressed in the frequent correlation between the "unbelieving Jew" and the "believing Gentile." The Jewish leaders reject and kill Jesus, but the first believer is a Roman centurion at the cross (Mark 15:39). The success of the Samaritan mission added the stories about "the good Samaritan," in contrast to "the faithless Jew" (Luke 10:33; 17:16; John 4:40–42).

Israel is ranked with the Gentiles and the kings of the earth who are arrayed against God and his Anointed (Acts 4:25–27), whereas the Gentiles have become the "people."

The idea that apostate Israel not only is unbelieving toward the gospel, but actually tries to kill the great Messenger of God, his forerunners, the prophets, and his disciples, is of central importance to this argument. This theme provides the essential "story line" of all the Gospels, including that of John, as well as the book of Acts. What does this mean? Recent historical studies have shown that the Jewish authorities could have had, at best, a subsidiary relation to the death of Jesus.[5] Yet the Gospels elaborately play down the responsibility of the Romans, while erecting the theme that "the Son of man must suffer many things, and be rejected by the elders and the chief priests and the scribes, and be killed" into a text of key dogmatic importance. It is repeated in solemn threefold sequence in all three Gospels. The Gospel of John is built on the same story line, that "the Jews" are characterized by a desire to "kill" Jesus. The book of Acts repeats the same story line for the mission of the Church. Here, too, rejection by the synagogue constantly takes the form of "plots" by the "Jews" to "kill" the apostles.

We find an extraordinary need in the Gospels to shift the blame for the deaths of Jesus and his disciples from Roman political authority to Jewish religious authority. Modern historians usually explain this as due to the exigencies of the gentile mission. Since the Christian were now preaching to the Gentiles, they wished to play down any hostility of the gentile government.[6] But it is important to note that the shift is not merely from Roman to Jewish authority, but from *political* to *religious* authority. It is important to the Gospel tradition to throw the blame for the deaths of Jesus and his disciples not merely upon Jewish (much less gentile) political authorities, but specifically upon the head of the Jewish *religious* tradition and its authority. This suggests that the purpose of this shift was not merely one of apologetics toward the Gentiles, but one, first of all, of polemic toward the Jewish religious tradition.

Why is it necessary to emphasize that the Jewish religious tradition not only rejects the gospel, but tries to kill its messengers (including its "forerunners," the prophets)? We would suggest that this theme in the Christian tradition developed from the crucial need to make religious sense out of the crucifixion itself, i.e., to provide a dogmatic necessity for the fact that the Prophet-King-Son of man is not only to be unheard by an unbelieving people, but that *it was predicted that he should be killed* by them. This is accomplished by reading back into Jewish history a pattern of an apostate Israel which has always rejected the prophets and killed them. The best text for this was Isaiah 53 where the suffering servant is actually said to have died, but the theme of suffering in the Psalms can also be read as though it

---

[5] Paul Winter, *On the Trial of Jesus,* Berlin, 1961; also Ernst Bammel (ed.), *The Trial of Jesus,* Naperville, Ill., 1970, and Samuel G. F. Brandon, *The Trial of Jesus,* New York, 1968.
[6] B. S. Easton, *Early Christianity: The Purpose of Acts and Other Papers,* London, 1955, pp. 33–118.

referred to the actual death of the messianic king.[7] The recent innovation by Herod of erecting memorial tombs to the prophets, in imitation of the Greek practice of erecting memorial tombs to the heroes, is read in the Gospels as evidence that Jewish religious authority admits that they have always killed the prophets and are trying to expiate this crime.[8]

The primary materials for studying the attitudes toward the Jews in the Church Fathers are the *adversus Judaeos* writings. These writings are remarkable for their preservation of the archaic testimonies tradition. As such, they represent a continuous tradition of christological and anti-Judaic midrashim on the Old Testament, which was the earliest form of Christian theologizing. As we have seen, this method preexisted and is the hermeneutical basis of the New Testament. This tradition continues in the Church Fathers as an expanding collection of themes and proof texts designed to prove, on the one hand, Christology, and, on the other hand, the reprobation and "blindness" of the Jews.

Jewish history as a trail of crimes. The reprobation of the Jews is based, finally, on the assertion that they rejected Jesus as the Christ. But, as in the New Testament, the Church Fathers projected this final act of apostasy backward and constructed a view of Jewish history as a trail of crimes. They wanted to show that this was not a recent and forgivable misstep on the part of the Jews: they have ever been apostate from God. So the rejection and murder of Christ is the foreordained conclusion of the evil history of a perfidious people. As in the New Testament, with the death of Christ, the Jewish people are said to "fill up the measure of their sins."[9] The core of this theme is still that of killing the prophets.

But this list of the crimes of the Jews has been considerably, expanded in the Church Fathers. The Jews are not only prophet killers, but idolaters, law breakers, and sinners of every description. This proclivity for vice and idolatry is usually presumed to have begun with their stay in Egypt. . . . Chrysostom typifies the life of the Jews in Egypt by saying that they "built

---

[7] Barnabas Lindars, *New Testament Apologetic: The Doctrinal Significance of Old Testament Quotations*, Philadelphia, 1961, pp. 88 ff.

[8] Douglas R. A. Hare, *The Theme of Jewish Persecution of Christians in the Gospel According to Matthew*, Cambridge, 1967, pp. 83–84, 137–141. Hare cites Joachim Jeremias's study, *Heiligengräber in Jesu Umwelt*, Göttingen, 1958, pp. 118–21, for the view that Herod was the originator of such tombs and the rabbis probably opposed them; cf. Hans Joachim Schoeps, *Die jüdischen Prophetenmorde*, Uppsala, 1943.

[9] Chrysostom uses the same phrase (*Or. C. Jud.* V, 9 [*PG* 48, 898]) reading Dan. 9:24, where seventy weeks are given to "put an end to sin" as though this meant seventy weeks were given to "fill up the measure of the sins" of the Jews to the point of final reprobation, i.e., Matt. 23:32.

a brothel in Egypt, made love madly with the barbarians, and worshipped foreign gods," a statement which he incorrectly ascribes to Ezekiel.[10]

Other crimes are also brought in to extend this picture of Jewish sinfulness. The Jews are said to have ever been blasphemers against the Name of God (Isa 52:6: "On your account My Name is continually reviled among the Gentiles").[11] They have always been rebellious and resisted the Spirit (Isa. 64:2: "All day long I stretch my hands to a disobedient and gainsaying people").[12] They were gluttons (Ex. 32:6: "This people sat down to eat and drink and rose up to play"),[13] sensualists (Deut. 32:15: "Jacob waxed fat and began to kick"),[14] and adulterers (Jer. 5:8: "They became furious, wanton steeds. They neighed each one for his neighbor's wife").[15]

Perhaps the most extraordinary theme in this repertoire of sins is the charge that the Jews were infanticides and sacrificed their children to demons. Psalm 106:37 (a standard source for the patristic "catalogue of crimes") was the basis for this idea. Chrysostom, in his sixth sermon, draws particularly on this and other sources to portray Old Testament people as inveterate debauchers and idolators who "sacrificed their sons and daughters to demons." Chrysostom repeatedly speaks of the Jews as "godless, idolators, pedicides, stoning the prophets, and committing ten thousand horrors" (*Or. C. Jud.* 6,2). In his fifth sermon, he also declares that they were cannibals, eating their own children (*Or. C. Jud.* 5,6: Deut. 28:56 and Lam. 4:10).

The "two peoples" in the Old Testament. The hermeneutical method for proof-texting this tale of crimes supposedly characteristic of the Jews in Old Testament times consists of splitting the right hand from the left hand of the prophetic message. The prophetic dialectic of judgment and promise is presumed to apply, not to one people, the Jews, but to two peoples, the Jews and the future Church.

This turns the Jewish Scriptures which actually contain the record of Jewish self-criticism, into a remorseless denunciation of the Jews, while the Church, in turn, is presented as totally perfect and loses the prophetic tradition of self-criticism! This also means that the heroes of the Old

---

[10] Cf. Ezek. 16:31; 23:3; Chry. *Or. C. Jud* VI,2 (*PG* 48,906).
[11] In the LXX translation: Rom. 2:24; Just. *Dial.* 17; Ter. *Adv. Jud.* 13.
[12] Rom. 10:21; *Ep.* Barn. 12,4; Just. Dial. 24.
[13] Just. *Dial.* 20; Ps.-Nys. *Test.* 4.
[14] Chry. *Or. C. Jud.* I,2 (*PG* 48,846).
[15] Ibid., I,7 (*PG* 48,853).

Testament become the lineage of the Church, while the Jews are read as a people who never accepted or responded to their prophetic leaders and teachers.

The election of the gentiles. The heart of the *adversus Judaeos* tradition is the proof of the election of the gentile Church and its inheritance of the election of the rejected Jews. This idea in the Church Fathers most often is presented as an antithesis between "the Jews" and "the nations," i.e., the Gentiles. The Jews are that people that has never heard the prophets and is finally cast off for rejecting the Messiah. A new people, the believers from "among the nations," has taken their place as the elect people of God. There is little attempt in the patristic tradition to maintain the idea of a Jewish remnant in the Church as the stem into which the Gentiles are "ingrafted." The relationship becomes primarily one of substitution. The reprobate, unbelieving Jews are cast off, and the believing gentile people take their place.

The prophets foretold that Jewish election was temporary and provisional only, and that the Jews were finally to be rejected. Essentially, there is one covenant, *promised* to Abraham, *foretold* by the prophets, and *fulfilled* in the gentile Church, who accepted the Messiah promised to Israel. The Jews assume the status of a people on probation who fail all the tests and finally are flunked out.

The Reprobation of the Jews

As signs of their rejection, Jewish Law has been revoked by God, and they are perverse for continuing to observe it. Their cultic center is destroyed. The temple, the priesthood, the sacrificial system have all been terminated. The Jews celebrate the festivals illegitimately in the Diaspora, for God decreed in the Law that these festivals were to be observed only in the temple in Jerusalem. Judaism, as a vehicle of valid worship of God, has been terminated with the destruction of the priesthood and the temple. Jews are renegades from God in continuing to maintain the festivals outside this assigned context.

The spiritual fulfillment of the law. The Christian argument against the Law included not only the idea that the Mosaic Law was abrogated, and so Christians do not have to observe it, but also that it was spiritually fulfilled. The Christians do not observe its outward form, but its true inward meaning. Christians, not Jews, are the true "Law keepers." They are the ones from whom God has removed the "hearts of stone" (outward observance) and given "hearts of flesh" (inward spiritual obedience).

The prophetic commandment to "circumcize your hearts, not your flesh" is taken to mean that the real meaning of circumcision is repentance. The Christians, who are the repentant ones, are the truly circumcized, the "circumcized of heart," while the Jews, who are "puffed up" in their vain, fleshly claims about "carnal" circumcision, are "uncircumcized of heart."[16]

Christological fulfillment of the scriptures. The christological interpretation of the Old Testament is basic to the *adversus Judaeos* tradition and Christian theology generally. Much of the anti-Judaic writings concern themselves with the demonstration of the christological meaning of the Old Testament against the Jews. The manifestations of God are said to be actually revelations of the Father through the Son, or the Logos. The plural in the Genesis creation story ("Let us make man in our image," Gen. 1:26), the three men who appear to Abraham (Gen. 18:2), and other passages are said to be revelations of the Trinity.[17] Not only the general promise of Jesus as the Messiah, but every detail of his life, passion, death, resurrection are said to be revealed explicitly in the Old Testament.[18]

The Jews are said to be incapable of understanding or interpreting their own Scriptures or even finding God in them. The Jews are "blind," "hard of heart," and a "veil lies over their eyes." All this prevents them from seeing the inner meaning of the text, i.e., its christological meaning. But Jewish blindness is also a function of Jewish "literalism." Jews are "carnal men," as distinct from the Christian "spiritual men."

Judaizing and anti-judaism: the sermons of John Chrysostom. In the Christian Roman Empire of the fourth century, a new development in the relationship of Christians to the synagogue took place. The Christian "Judaizer" was of a different character than the militant Jewish Christian convert who sought to proselytize the synagogue in the earlier period. The Judaizing Christian was a Christian, not necessarily of Jewish background, who was attracted to Jewish rites and traditions, while remaining within the mainstream Church, which now had become the official imperial

---

[16] Deut. 10:16; Jer. 4:4; 9:26; Rom. 2:25–29; Gal. 5, etc.; *Ep.* Barn. 9, 1–5; Just. *Dial.* 24; Ter. *Adv. Jud.* 3; Cyp. *Test.* I, 8; Ps.-Nys. *Test.* 11; *Dial.* A.Z. (Frederick C. Conybeare, *Expositor* 45, 1897, pp. 460–462); Chry. *Or. C. Jud.* II, 1 (*PG* 48,857); Aph. *Dem.* 11; Jak. Serug. *Hom. C. Jud.* II; *Dial.* T.-A. II, 8; *Dial.* S.-T. (*PL* 20, 1172–74); Isid. *C. Jud.* II,16.

[17] *Dial. J.-P.* (*PG* 5,1178– 79). Typical patristic trinitarian exegesis of the O.T. ist found in *Dial.* A.-Z. (Conybeare *op. cit.*, pp. 304ff.); Just. *Dial.* 56–65; Isid. *C. Jud.* I, 1–4; *Dial.* Z.-A. bk. I passim; *Dial.* S.-T. (*PL* 20, 1167ff.); *Did. Jak.* 58 (*Pat. Orient.* 13, pp. 10ff.); *Dial.* T.-A., foll. 79–113.

[18] Cf. Cyp. *Test.* II,9–30; Ps.-Nys. *Test.* 2–9; Isid. *C. Jud.* I,7–62; *St. Silv.* (*PG* 121, 122–35).

religion. The Judaizing Christians came to the synagogue, not to convert it, but because they saw it as the roots of their own Christian practices.

Such Judaizing Christians practiced circumcision as well as baptism, followed dietary laws and rites of purification, observed the Sabbath as well as Sunday, and participated in Jewish fasts and feasts, such as New Year, the feast of Tabernacles, and the fast of Yom Kippur. They continued to date Easter by the Jewish calculations of Passover and celebrated the Pasch on 15 Nisan, regardless of the day of the week on which it fell. They also associated with the synagogue in other ways. They appealed to the Rabbis as charismatics who were regarded as gifted exorcists and healers. Since many Christians attended only the liturgy of the Word in the Church, it was easy to substitute the similar service of the synagogue on occasion for regular worship. The clapping and good fellowship of the synagogue appears to have contrasted favorably with growing pomp and long rhetorical sermons of the Church. Some of this Judaizing movement had a superstitious element to it, such as the amulets worn especially by the women.[19] But it is evident that the movement as a whole was not superstitious, but rather a sincere, if eclectic, emotional attraction which continued the identification of Christian traditions with their Jewish foundations. Officially, the Rabbis disapproved of such assimilation without full commitment. But, in practice, the synagogue tolerated the Judaizing Christians as "semiproselytes" much as they had previously tolerated the "God-fearing pagan," as a "stranger within the gates."[20]

The history of the Church's response to Judaizing is one of continued effort to separate Christian from Jewish practices, but with a tradition that stubbornly continued to remind the Christian of his Jewish roots.

The sermons of John Chrysostom are easily the most violent and tasteless of the anti-Judaic literature of the period we have studied. The Christians listening to Chrysostom should do everything in their power to hunt down the misguided Judaizers, just like hunters tracking wild animals, and persuade them by any method to abandon their evil fraternizing with Christ's murderers. Even if one must drag them into one's house by force and eat in front of them to make them break their godless fast, this is better

---

[19] Orig. *Hom. in Jer.* 12,13; Jerome, *Comm. in. Matt.* 33,6; cf. Marcel Simon, *Verus Israel: Etude sur les relations entre chrétiens et juifs dans l'empire romain,* Paris, 1964, pp. 373–382; Salo W. Baron, *A Social and Religious History of the Jews* II, New York, 1952, pp. 188–189.

[20] Simon, *op. cit,* pp. 391–393; Jean Juster, *Les juifs dans l'empire romain* I, Paris, 1914, pp. 277 ff; Bernhard Jacob Bamberger, *Proselytism in the Talmudic Period,* New York, 1968, pp. 134–140.

than to allow them to fast with the Jews on Yom Kippur (Chry. *Or. C. Jud.* VI,7; *PG* 48,916).

In these sermons, Chrysostom never actually tells his people to do any violence to the Jews themselves or their synagogues, although he is very free to declare that he "hates them," that "God hates them," all the prophets "hate them," and the holy martyrs "hate them." He even talks metaphorically about the Jews as "fit for slaughter:" What is evident is that the Jews, for Chrysostom, never appear as "brothers," potential brothers, or even as human beings. His evangelical concern is only for the Judaizers. The Jews themselves, in Chrysostom's sermons, have passed beyond the pale of humanity altogether into the realm of the demonic.

These sermons were preached in an excitable, faction-ridden Hellenistic city, where the Jews had been the subject of communal violence before, especially during the Jewish Wars. Such sermons as these gave the blessings of the Church's greatest preacher, "the Golden-mouthed," to what was now a government-sanctioned destruction of Jewish civic status and an increasing tendency for religion to become the vehicle for popular violence against the Jews. On the other side of the Jewish and Judaizing population, there was a pagan and gentile-Christian population, happy to attack this minority group who had lived in their own communally-governed section of the city since Hellenistic times. In the early fifth century, waves of violence broke out against the Jews in Antioch, with the first recorded Christian charge of Jewish "ritual murder." The great synagogues of the city were destroyed. Simon Stylites, the famous saint, intervened to prevent the governor from making reparations to the Jews. Eruptions of communal violence against the Jews continued to characterize Christian Antioch in the fifth and sixth centuries, until, in a final effort at mass conversion and an outbreak of massacre, the Jews were expelled from the city altogether.[21]

Theologically, Christians and Jews in patristic times had positions that were mutually exclusive, each claiming to be the sole legitimate heir of the biblical faith. Jews were no more tolerant of Christians than Christians were of Jews, although the Jewish view of "the nations" allowed Jews to coexist with Christians and with peoples of other faith, provided they let the Jews be themselves, whereas Christian universalism could allow for no such place for the non-Christian. By the same token, the Jew could tolerate a Judaizing Christian in the synagogue, although not a proselytizing

---

[21] Carl Kraeling, "The Jewish Community in Antioch," *Journal of Biblical Literature* 51, 1932, pp. 130 ff.

Christian in the synagogue, while the Christian could not tolerate a Judaizing Christian in the Church. Nevertheless, the Christian view did allow for a place for the Jews to continue to exist. The Jew was allowed to exist, indeed commanded to exist in the Christian era, not as one with a legitimate vehicle of religion in his own right, but in the negative space of divine reprobation and as an eventual or ultimate witness to the "truth" of the Church. Anti-Christianity was an extrinsic and defensive need for the synagogue, which was over as soon as the Church was organized outside the walls of the Jewish community. For Christianity, anti-Judaism was not merely a defense against attack, but an intrinsic need of Christian self-affirmation. Anti-Judaism is a part of Christian exegesis. Anti-Christianity is not properly a part of Jewish exegesis. The anti-Judaic arguments grew to a fixed standpoint between the apostolic period and the fourth century. These arguments were repeated over and over again in every Christian sermon, biblical commentary, or theological tract that touched on the Jews in some way. And since the Church continued to claim Jewish history and the Jewish Scriptures as its own history and scripture, and to understand itself as the heir to the election of Israel, it was difficult to preach or teach anything without touching on the Jews in some way. In the first third of the fourth century, Christianity was transformed from a persecuted faith into the established religion of the empire. What had previously been the hostile tradition of an illegal sect toward its parental faith now became the official creed of the civil religion of the Christian Roman Empire. In less than fifty years, Orthodox Christianity elevated itself from a position of toleration to that of the exclusive religion of the empire. By the reign of Theodosius I (378–95), the faith and practices of pagans and heretics became illegal. Their temples and churches were destroyed or confiscated. Their very existence was proscribed.[22]

Judaism was the only dissenting and non-Christian faith that was to remain legal in Christendom. Its status, both as a pariah religion and as a religion tolerated minimally in this pariah status, was unique.

Christian theology, while it decreed misery for the Jews as their historical status before God, did not advocate extermination. On the contrary, the official view of the Church guaranteed the ongoing existence of Judaism. Although the vituperations of clerics and theologians often fell into language that suggested that the Jews should be killed, the official theory excluded the "final solution" as an option here and now. Judaism was to exist until

---

[22] Stanley Lawrence Greenslade, *Church and State from Constantine to Theodosius*, London, 1954.

the end of time, but as an empty religion that had lost its elect status and inner spiritual power. It was to continue to exist in a pariah status in history, both to testify to the present election of the Church and to witness the final triumph of the Church. At the return of Christ, Jews would either finally acknowledge their error or else be condemned to final damnation. The Church should seek the conversion of Jews here and now, but also prevent the influence of Judaism on Christians. The Church felt called upon to enforce this status of reprobation in the form of social "misery," but the "final solution" could not be executed by men, but lay in the hands of God at the time of the final eschatological drama. The legislation of Christian emperors and Church councils on the status of the Jew in Christian society reflects the effort to mirror this theological theory in social practice.

Between 315 and 439 C. E. (from the reign of Constantine to the promulgation of the Theodosian Code), this view of the Jew was enforced through a steadily worsening legal status.

The rule of thumb for this development, as J. E. Seaver and James Parkes have summarized it, is as follows: the trend was always one of worsening status (until this trend was actively reversed by a counterdevelopment in the Enlightenment); a right, once lost to the Jews, was never permanently recovered, while the restrictions decreed against them were constantly reaffirmed and extended.[23]

The *Corpus Juris Civilis* issued by Justinian in 534 C. E. discarded over half of the more than fifty laws dealing with the Jews found in the Theodosian Code.[24] The Justinian Code further depressed the status of the Jews by discarding many laws protecting their civil and religious rights, while retaining and extending their restrictions.

With the Arab conquest, a new era began for Spanish Jewry that was to last for six hundred years. Moslems were by no means without their own laws which inferiorized both Jews and Christians. But relatively speaking, Jews had broader opportunities for advancement in Moslem than in Christian lands. Neither mass massacres, mass expulsions, nor forced conversion take place in orthodox Moslem areas.

---

[23] James S. Seaver, *The Persecution of the Jews in the Roman Empire*, University of Kansas, 1952, p. 56. The original ms. of this thesis (Cornell, 1947) is more extensive and contains both the Latin and Mr. Seaver's English translation of the legal texts. See also James Parkes, *The Conflict of the Church and the Synagogue*, London, 1934, p. 199.

[24] Parkes, *ibid.*, pp. 245–55.

Spanish Jewish history ends with a phenomenon which approaches racial anti-Semitism. Here we see a formally Christianized Jewish community which is nevertheless hunted down by the Inquisition for being secretly "Jewish." The "laws of purity of blood," which became general in Spanish society by the sixteenth century, were purely racial. They excluded the Jew from public and Church leadership, regardless of whether he was a secret Judaizer or the most sincere Catholic. Those who aspired to positions in public life or the Church had to display their genealogical charts to the Inquisition to prove that they had no hidden Jewish ancestry. Such laws remained on the books in Catholic religious orders, such as the Jesuits, until the twentieth century. They are the ancestor of the Nazi Nuremberg laws. They also present us with the ambivalence of the Christian demand for the Jew's "conversion." The individually converted Jew could be assimilated. The mass converted Jewish population, however, was still perceived as a separate "Jewish" community in an ethnic sense. All the diabolism attributed to "Judaism" was still popularly perceived as attached to the "Jew," in this way. Moreover, baptism, even if forced, automatically canceled all the anti-Judaic legislation and thus overthrew the barriers to Jewish advancement in Christian society. Thus, in Spain in the sixteenth century, we have a dress rehearsal for the nineteenth-century European experience. The Jewish community, made to assimilate *en masse*, then is perceived as a shocking invasion of Christian society, and barriers previously thrown up against them on religious grounds are now reinstituted on racial grounds.[25]

With the rise of the Islamic Empire, the role of the Jews in Gaul took on a new character. The Syrians, who had monopolized trade, were now cut off as Christians in an Arab land. In Gaul, economic institutions had deteriorated to the primitive level. The Jews remained the one go-between who could carry on some modicum of international trade between Europe and the Near East. Thus, in this period, they become uniquely identified as merchants.

The Jewish community prospered in the towns of France and Germany at the end of the Dark Ages, thanks to its ability to play the middleman in reviving commerce. But the theological image taught by the Church to the Christian populace was preparing a terrible revenge for this temporary escape from repression.

---

[25] Yitzhak Baer, *A History of the Jews in Christian Spain*, vol. 2 (From the Fourteenth Century to the Expulsion), Philadelphia, 1966; see also Cecil Roth, *A History of the Marranos*, Philadelphia, 1947.

From the Crusades to Emancipation: The Age of the Ghetto

In the high Middle Ages, the Church's struggle to reassert the theologically required status of "misery" upon the Jews was rewarded a thousandfold. The medieval period ended with the Jewish community reduced to political servitude, social ignominy, and ghettoization, economic ruin, vulnerability to violence from below, and arbitrary exploitation and expulsion from above, until finally the Jewries of England, France, Spain, Portugal, and much of Germany had been disseminated, expelled, or forced to practice their religion in hiding. Above this whole development, there reigned the theological image of the Jew, both shaping developments and then serving as the explanation and excuse for them, the image itself growing constantly more evil, until it culminated with the virtual identification of the Jew with the Devil. How this development took place is an exceedingly complex story with many of the connecting points of different factors uncertain, although the overall trend is ever downward. We can do no more than make the barest summary of the various elements here.

The great turning point of Jewish status in the Western Middle Ages, a turning point itself expressive of the success of the Church's indoctrination of popular religious hatred for the Jew, was the Crusades.

The Crusader's path was converted into the path of commerce. The trade routes which had been pioneered by Jewish traveling merchants since the rise of Islam now became unsafe for Jewish merchants, for Jewish caravans found on the routes to the East would automatically be slaughtered by Crusaders. So the rise of the Crusades corresponds to the expropriation and retreat of the Jew as merchant, who had kept the trade routes between Europe and Asia open during the Dark Ages.[26]

The pogroms of the Crusades were met with stoic heroism by the Jewish communities of the Rhineland. Refusing the baptism offered at sword's point by the Crusaders, they regularly submitted to death or committed mass suicide rather than be baptized. A martyr ethic was forged

---

[26] The economic theory of anti-Semitism, according to which each major wave of repression corresponded to the expropriation of a major area of the economy pioneered by Jews, was developed by William Roscher, "The Status of the Jew in the Middle Ages from the Standpoint of Commercial Policy," *Historia Judaica* 6, 1944, pp. 13–26 (trans. Solomon Grayzel). Frederick Schweitzer, in his one-volume *History of the Jews Since the First Century* A.D., New York, 1971, follows a version of this thesis, pp. 165–84. Guido Kisch criticizes the thesis on the grounds that it cannot explain the character of fanaticism of medieval anti-Semitism which must be viewed from the psychology of theological negation: *The Jews in Medieval Germany: A Study of their Legal and Social Status*, Chicago, 1949, pp. 320–22.

in European Jewry. The Christian doctrine of the Trinity was regarded as polytheism and its view of Jesus' divinity as idolatry.

This resistance of the Jews to baptism was inexplicable to Christians. Christian theology had deprived Jews of inner spirituality and defined them as people of mere legalism and "carnality." This encounter with Jewish faith then could not bring about repentance in Christians. It resulted instead in a compensatory wave of new anti-Judaic myths to justify this gratuitous slaughter of an unoffending group of people. The myths of ritual murder, well poisoning, and host profanation arose in the wake of Crusader violence to provide an image of the Jew as an insidious plotter against Christianity and to justify fanaticism.[27] These libels had not existed before. They arose as a reaction and an attempt to justify the violence of the Crusades, after the fact.

The Crusades also showed the Christian masses the vulnerability of the Jewish community, something they had not realized before. Now they saw that this prosperous group, seemingly under the protection of powerful princes, actually could be attacked by any mob with impunity. The weak forces of law and order were helpless against such mob violence. After this lesson had been learned, the pogroms never ceased for many centuries. The Crusades also helped to redefine the political status of the Jew. It was a crime to kill a Jew, placed under the king's peace. But since the prince protected the Jew, the Jew himself was now forbidden to bear arms. In a chivalric society, this worked to redefine the status of the Jews as serfs.

This political redefinition of the Jews as personal serfs of the prince only became clearly defined when it interacted with ecclesiastical law, which, in the early thirteenth century, was systematically working to reduce all Jewish social privileges.

The canonical legislation of the Church in the thirteenth century effected a systematic social degradation of the Jew. The Church struggled to reimpose all the old canonical and imperial anti-Judaic legislation back to Constantine. The Jew is always to be under, not over, Christians. In addition to this theological degradation of the Jew to the status of servitude, Christian society was to be rigidly protected from Jewish "contamination." Any social contact, living together, eating together, sexual relations, personal conversation, especially on religious matters, was to be prevented, lest Jewish "unbelief" contaminate Christian faith. This notion of "Jewishness" as a kind of contagion that one might catch by any kind of association

---

[27] Leon Poliakov, *The History of Anti-Semitism I: From the Time of Christ to the Court Jews*, New York, 1965, pp. 50–64.

was to become a virulent source of notions such as "well poisoning." It also provided the stock imagery of racial anti-Semitism, which was always to depict the presence of the Jews as a kind of dangerous or insidious "contagious disease." The final expression of the Church's effort to segregate the Jew from any social contact with Christian society was the ghetto and the wearing of Jewish dress, conical hat, and "Jew badge" (usually a yellow circle, symbolic of the Jew as betrayer of Christ for "gold," an image which fused religious with economic anti-Semitism). These regulations were passed at the Fourth Lateran Council (1215), although the Church only succeeded in enforcing them universally after the Council of Basel (1434).[28] These marks had the effect of making Jewish ignominy visible and singling the Jew out for physical attack as never before, destroying further the ability of the Jew to travel the open roads as a merchant.

Finally, the Talmud itself was declared illegal. Successive inquisitions condemned it, despite the defense put up against Christian accusations by talmudic scholars.[29] The Talmud and Jewish works were burned publicly in France in the mid-thirteenth century, bringing to an end an important center of talmudic scholarship.

The final element that shaped the status of the Jew in medieval society was the economic one. Deprived of normal participation in agriculture, first by their inability to hold Christian servants and then by outright prohibition of landowning; trade constricted by the new dangers of hostility; and most crafts closed off by the religious character of trade guilds – the Jew had no place in medieval economy except moneylending. Unfortunately, moneylending had no place in the Church's concept of economy.

In popular thought, Jewish usury was excusable, either because the Bible allowed one to give money at interest to the "stranger," or else because the Jews were damned anyway, so it made no difference if they sinned. However, the Jews had come to be understood as property of the prince, which automatically meant that their money was his personal property also. To rob a Jew was to rob a prince. To kill or convert a Jew was to deprive a prince of his property. The moneymaking capacity of the Jews became the personal assets of the princes. On these grounds, the princes protected Jewish usury, granted Jews rights of residence, prevented mobs from attacking them, and even prevented the Church from converting them! The Jews were changed from free economic actors into subjects of

---

[28] *Ibid.*, p. 65. Also Solomon Grayzel, *The Church and the Jews in the Thirteenth Century*, New York, 1966, pp. 59–71.

[29] Poliakov, *op. cit.*, pp. 33 ff.

the economic policy of the princes. They became the personal usurers of the princes.

This role as royal usurers of the princes allowed the Jews to survive, but only on the most precarious basis. Socially, they were degraded as figures of ignominy in every town. Protected from attack by the princes, they became the objects of boiling hatred which the exploited classes felt against both the political power and the economic exactions of the rulers. Since the Jews were the buffers and expressions of both of these kinds of power between the princes and the people, this hatred became diverted on to the Jews.

At any point, they could be ruined and expelled when popular protest, often taking the form of charges of ritual murder and other religious charges, made things too hot for the prince, forcing him to accede to the demands of townsmen or nobles against whom the feudal prince struggled for power. The Jews were caught in the middle of this power struggle and ultimately became its victims.[30]

The expulsions of the Jews from Spain and Portugal in the fifteenth century reflect the mingling of religious fanaticism with a new concept of nationalistic absolutism. The expulsions of the Jews from England in 1290, from France in 1390, and from most German cities in the mid-fourteenth to sixteenth centuries also had economics as their sub-theme, although the charges brought against them usually featured trumped-up accusations of ritual murder, host profanation, and the like.

As the Jewish role as moneylender was being broken in a Christian society (which was also expropriating this role for itself, often in a much more exploitative way), religious fanaticism grew all the more virulent. The late Middle Ages became not only the age of the ghetto, but the age of the Devil. The outbreak of the Black Plague in the mid-fourteenth century, which took the lives of a third of the population of Europe, and other factors unhinged the mind of Europe.Everywhere witches, devils, and death danced together through a cloud of sulfur and ashes, and the mingled figure of all these evils was stamped by the mythical face of "the Jew." The fact that Jews were prominent as physicians, especially to the princes, and the more hygienic character of Jewish life occasionally spared it somewhat from the ravages of the plague, only added to the paranoia. It was believed that a conspiracy of Jews and lepers had poisoned the sources of water with magically cursed bags of excrement and menstrual blood, which, through secret tunnels, flowed through all the wells of Europe. Again we see the

---

[30] James Parkes, *The Jew in the Medieval Community*, London, 1938, pp. 339–382.

image of the Jew as an insidious disease secretly poisoning the life systems of Christian Europe, an image which was to be revived in such potent form in racial mythology. All over Europe, pogroms broke out against the Jewish community, adding the corpses of the slaughtered to those dying from the plague.[31] The image of the Jew deteriorated in the minds of Christians to that of a deformed monster, with horns, tail, cloven hoofs, and sulfuric odor to betray his fundamentally diabolic character. At the moment when drama, woodcuts, and printing were enormously increasing the range of popular communication, it was this image of the Jew that was stamped on the popular minds of Europeans, and it remained the basic image of the Jew up to its use by Nazism.[32]

The "Middle Ages" for Judaism coincides with Christendom itself! Legal disabilities of Jews in Western society lasted from Constantine to the nineteenth century, when the liberal revolution dissolved the legal structures of Christianity as the established state religion. The age of the ghetto lasted, for Jews, into the nineteenth century in western Europe and into the twentieth in eastern Europe. The French revolutionaries disbanded the anti-Judaic laws in France in 1789, and Napoleon carried this revolution with him during his wars of conquest. But during the reaction and restoration, anti-Jewish restrictions were reinstated in many places. It was only between 1848 and 1870 that the ghetto was disbanded and full citizenship attained generally in western Europe. All disabilities were not dropped in Germany until the Weimar Republic! In eastern Europe, the pogroms of the late nineteenth and twentieth centuries mingled the old religious with the new racial charges against Jews. The ghetto was dissolved with the Russian Revolution, but for much of eastern Europe, the world of the ghetto was swept away, not by emancipation but by the Holocaust![33]

When we realize the continuation of the medieval status of the Jew down into the modern period, the imagined discontinuity between medieval anti-Judaism and Nazism narrows to uncomfortable proximity. We begin to realize that what Nazism revived was not a long-dead set of attitudes and practices, but a world only recently dissolved in the West, still maintained in the East, whose myths were still live, glowing embers easily fanned into

---

[31] Contemporary documents on the accusations against the Jews at the time of the Black Death are found in Jacob Rader Marcus, *The Jew in the Medieval World*, New York, 1972, pp. 43–48.

[32] Poliakov, *op. cit.*, pp. 123–54. Also Joshua Trachtenberg, *The Devil and the Jews*, New Haven, 1932; and Salo W. Baron, "Demonic Alien," *Social and Religious History of the Jews*, vol. 9, pp. 122ff.

[33] For a summary of these developments, see Schweitzer, *op. cit.*, pp. 185–280.

new flames. Moreover, the very processes of the emancipation, the arguments on which it was based, the price it demanded of Judaism revivified
anti-Judaism in new forms, translating the basis for contempt from theological to nationalist and then racial grounds. Where the Middle Ages was
intolerant of the religious alien, the modern state was intolerant of the
person of alien national identity. It had no place for Jewish self-government,
such as was possible in the medieval corporate state. The Jew in the modern
state became the representative of the "outsider" to nationalist identity. But
the same stereotypes, the same set of psychological attitudes were preserved in this change of theoretical grounds. Philosophical liberalism provided the theoretical basis for emancipation, but at the same time suggested
the basis for this transition from religious to nationalist anti-Semitism.
Protestant theology and biblical studies absorbed and deepened this cultural anti-Semitism.[34]

The price of emancipation was also seen as one of cultural assimilation.
Most liberals actually thought of this as paving the way for Jewish conversion to Christianity. All liberals took it for granted that ghetto Judaism
represented a bad moral, spiritual, and intellectual condition. Talmudic
Judaism, as the religious basis of the self-governing Jewish community,
must be relinquished. The price of emancipation was the destruction of
Jewish self-government and autonomous corporate identity. It was this
autonomous corporate identity, possible in the medieval corporate state,
which had allowed the Jews to keep a sense of peoplehood within Christian
society. It was this sense of autonomous corporate identity and peoplehood which the modern nationalist state could not tolerate and which
became the basis of modern anti-Semitism. Now Jewish identity in an
ethnic sense was seen as intrinsically evil. It must be dissolved so the Jew
could become a "German," or else it was seen as indissolvable, and so the
Jew must be expelled. In any case, the Jew must pay for emancipation by
ceasing to be a Jew in a corporate sense.

To be sure, the Jews themselves wanted emancipation too. They wanted
full access to modern cultural and economic life and were ready to pay for
this by sacrifice of their political autonomy.

Jews were offered an ideology of emancipation which was itself based on
a rationalist version of anti-Judaism.[35] The anticlerical deists rejected

---

[34] See D. C. Smith, *Protestant Attitudes Toward Jewish Emancipation in Prussia*, New Haven,
Yale University, Ph. D. thesis, 1971, esp. chap. 3.

[35] Jacob Katz, *Out of the Ghetto: The Social Background of Jewish Emancipation*: 1770–1870,
Cambridge, Mass., 1973, pp. 57–79. Smith, *op. cit.*, chap. 2 and passim.

Christianity also for the religion of reason which must supersede it. But, in either case, what was hated in biblical revealed religion was stereotyped as "Jewish", while all positive values of spirituality, rationality, and universality were the characteristics of Christianity or philosophy that were antithetical to "Judaism."

For liberals, what was "wrong" with the Jews was regarded as cultural. Jews could be emancipated if they ceased to be Jews culturally, becoming secular or, as most liberals secretly expected, Christian. For conservative Christians, what was wrong with the Jews was intrinsic to Jewish "character." Bigotry, immorality, legalism, carnality, materialism, and lack of inner spiritual or ethical principles were regarded as intrinsic traits that expressed the "nature" of the Jews.

Since Judaism was not a religion, according to either Christian rationalist or Christian romantic theories, Judaism came to be defined in this tradition of thought in nationalist, quasi-racial terms. Judaism was said to be, not a religion, but the laws of a nation. Jews were not a religious group, but a foreign nation. The antithesis of Judaism and Christianity was translated into an antithesis between Jews and Europeans, or Jews and Germans.[36]

It was not until the advent of racist anthropology in the late nineteenth century that this view received its full-blown racial theory. But the grounds for a secular translation of anti-Judaism into racial anti-Semitism were laid in the philosophy of the Enlightenment and then deepened in the philosophers of Romanticism.[37]

The processes of emancipation coincided with traumatic changes in European society in the revolutionary era which dissolved the old Christian order for secular, liberal industrialized society. Thus the processes through which Jews entered mainstream society also created a traumatic reaction in those classes – clerics, landholders, and lower-middle-class artisans – who were deeply threatened by the new secular industrial society. The secular Jews were hardly the creators of these new forces. Indeed, they formed only about one percent of the population in Germany and France, and only a small part of them were actually secularized, and even fewer were leaders in the commerce and culture of the new society. Yet they were concentrated in urban areas and in professions that made them highly conspicuous. As the beneficiaries of secularism, the secular

---

[36] Smith, *Protestant Attitudes*, pp. 74ff.; also Nathan Rotenstreich, *The Recurring Pattern: Studies in Anti-Judaism in Modern Thought*, London, 1963: on Kant, Hegel and Toynbee.
[37] George Mosse, *The Crisis of German Ideology: Intellectual Origins of the Third Reich*, New York, 1964, pp. 88–107.

Jews became the symbolic representatives of the dissolution of Christendom. Secular Jews came to be fantasized as a kind of "insidious disease," flowing into the veins of "Christian Europe," sapping its spiritual, moral, and economic energy. They were imagined to be the creators and secret managers of all the forces represented by the new secular industrial state. The traditional stereotype of the Jew as "carnal man," which mingled religious and economic anti-Semitism, ever conspiring against both the faith and the wealth of Christendom, was brought into play to create the new myth that everything which these threatened groups hated in the new society was intrinsically "Jewish."[38] Even socialists, especially Christian socialists, bought into this myth by identifying the Jews with capitalism, while conservatives identified Jews with the forces of scepticism, secularism, and democracy that were dissolving the old order, religiously and socially. Contrary as these two positions may appear, they often made common cause with each other in the anti-Semitic parties that arose in the late nineteenth century.[39] The infamous *Protocols of the Elders of Zion* was a chief instrument of this myth. Produced by the Russian secret police in the late nineteenth century, its roots lay in Russian anti-Judaic mysticism. It built the ancient Christian claim that the Messiah whom the Jews expect is the Anti-Christ into a fantasy wherein a Jewish secret government, in existence since the time of Christ, plots the overthrow of Christendom and the establishment of the reign of the Devil over the world in the last age of world history. The *Protocols* thus provided a clear link between Christian anti-Judaism and modern anti-Semitism.

Nazism arose as the final repository of all this heritage of religious and secular anti-Semitism, making Jews responsible for capitalism and communism simultaneously! The racial theory was new, but the stereotypes of hatred were old. The mythical Jew, who is the eternal conspiratorial enemy of Christian faith, spirituality, and redemption, was being shaped to serve as the scapegoat for all the things in secular industrial society which the middle class had created and now feared and hated for their dissolution of traditional religion, culture, social hierarchy, and life style. But the middle class could not challenge this new society without challenging the basis of their own wealth, and conservatives did not want to liquidate the economic

[38] *Ibid.*, pp. 126 ff. and passim.
[39] James Parkes, *Anti-Semitism*, Chicago, 1963, pp. 20–44; also Peter G. J. Pulzer, *The Rise of Political Anti-Semitism in Germany and Austria*, New York, 1964; and Paul W. Massing, *Rehearsal for Destruction. A Study of Political Anti-Semitism in Imperial Germany*, New York, 1949.

affluence of this society – only its social results. So the way to be against modern society without upsetting bourgeois power was to do so in a purely ideological way, diverting all the pent-up fear and unrest of the dissolution of Christendom onto the Jews. European society was primed to undergo a gigantic "purge" of the dangerous infection that it felt was threatening its inner health, wealth, and wisdom. The mythical Jew had long been fashioned in Christian history to serve as the symbol of this "disease" from which the Christian must purge himself in order to save himself. Under the slogan "the Jews are our misfortune", mass paranoia again gripped the soul of the European heartland, but in the language of racism and deliberately engineered by gangsters of mass communication.

JACOB KATZ

Anti-Semitism Through the Ages*

Having followed the evolution of anti-Jewish attitudes in modern times, we must ask whether this inquiry has yielded an answer to the question that launched it. That question may be restated as follows. The Jewish emancipation granted in the European countries, beginning at the end of the eighteenth century, presupposed the disruption of the ideological web that supported the prevailing anti-Jewish attitude. That web seemed to be intimately interwoven with the traditional Christian outlook, which contained a negative image of Jews and Judaism, in particular of their religious beliefs and morality. The acceptance of Jews as members of the modern state and society seemed, on the other hand, to indicate that the whole complex of Christian reservations against Jews had been abandoned. How, then, could anti-Jewish agitation re-emerge in the last decades of the nineteenth century, sustaining itself on images and prejudices apparently obsolete for a century and more?

The answer arrived at in the course of our inquiry can now be summarily stated. First, it is true that Christianity had lost its former hold on people's minds and its determining influence on state and society. The state and its agencies ceased to be institutionally linked to the Church, and the dynamics of society were no longer governed or controlled by Christian convictions. The leading elites operating in both these frameworks now were under the influence of more secular forces. Still, the recession of Christian influence was not tantamount to its eclipse. Even in its dogmatic version, Christianity was not entirely defunct. It still provided the universal discourse and spiritual atmosphere for some in society, for whom the traditional conception of the role of the Jew in history remained valid. The negative image attached to the word *Jew* thus retained its ideological

---

* Edited from: Jacob Katz, *From Prejudice to Destruction: Anti- Semitism, 1700–1933* (Cambridge, Ma.: Harvard University Press, 1980).

moorings. It could at least live on latently and if occasion arose be pointedly actualized. This indeed happened with the emergence of the anti-Semitic movement in the nineteenth century. As documented in the course of our inquiry, there was a whole series of strictly orthodox Christians between the leaders and precursors of the anti-Semitic movement: Stöcker, Rohling, Vogelsang, and others, not to mention the intermediaries like de Bonald and des Mousseaux in France, Julius Stahl and Herman Wagener in Prussia, and Sebastian Brunner in Austria, who, before the outbreak of the anti-Semitic movement, served as a kind of bridge between the traditional hatred of the Jew and its modern metamorphosis.

The second variety of Christian backing for modern anti-Semitism is found among those who were unconcerned about the dogmatic truth of Christianity. They nevertheless sustained religion as a component of nationalism, presenting Christianity as the only possible guarantee for personal or public morality, or they adhered to it for other not strictly religious reasons. Christianity of this kind, even if thoroughly diluted, was found to retain the doctrine of Christian superiority over Judaism, and this was easily transformed into overt anti-Semitism. Such more or less transparent connections between anti-Semitic arguments and their Christian background are found abundantly in the works of men like Glagau, Istoczy, Drumont, and others. Not Christians in the strict denominational or dogmatic sense, these men were sufficiently immersed in Christian tradition to draw upon it in substantiating their theories and strengthening their convictions. The thesis of the moral insensibility of Jews, their putative drive for world domination and the like, even if fostered by contemporary stimuli – the social distance between Jews and Christians and the actual economic success and political advancement of Jews – was clearly derived from traditional Christian concepts of Jewish mentality and Jewish messianic aspirations.

In a broader sense, modern anti-Semitism turned out to be a continuation of the premodern rejection of Judaism by Christianity, even when it renounced any claim to be legitimized by it or even professed to be antagonistic to Christianity. The wish to base anti-Semitism on grounds beyond the Jewish-Christian division remained in fact a mere declaration of intent. No anti-Semite, even if he himself was anti-Christian, ever forwent the use of those anti-Jewish arguments rooted in the denigration of Jews and Judaism in ealier Christian times. In historical perspective at least, Christianity always appeared as the higher religion – an evaluation apparent even in the thinking of thoroughly secularized anti-Semites like Voltaire, Bruno Bauer, and Eugen Dühring.

Such paradoxical combinations should not be too much of a surprise; they are in the nature of rationalistic secularization. Rationalism was capable of demolishing the intellectual structure of the traditional world-view while maintaining the underlying emotional layers and even the basic conceptual configurations, and modern anti-Semitism can be seen as a case of secularization on a grand scale. For it was the image of the Jew that was inherited from Christianity that determined the secular perception of the Jew. The difference was that on the cognitive level this perception had to be supported by reasoning derived from the newly evolved systems of thought. It was this composite character of modern anti-Semitism – an absolute archaic image covered by a layer of justifications – that made it an irrational phenomenon inaccessible to overt, logically oriented argumentation.[1]

The evidence that the anti-Jewish notions of the pre-emancipatory Christian era were carried over into post-emancipatory anti-Semitism is not found only in the domain of ideological justification. The social situation of the recently emancipated and grudgingly accepted minority provoked the animosity of the majority because of the pariah status the Jewish community had had before emancipation, when it had lived at the margin of Christian society. The term "pariah," suggested by Max Weber for a description of the Jewish status in medieval society, though it does not exactly accord with its original Indian connotation, well characterizes the situation of the Jews. It hints at ritualistically secured socioeconomic separation, combined with social degradation. The pariah status implies, or at least explains, the Jew's image in Gentile eyes, which assumed in the course of time an increasingly sinister and even diabolical character. The socially degraded Jew, close physically but remote culturally, was held capable of perpetrating any deed and committing any crime. At times, in Gentile eyes, the Jews ceased to be human at all.[2]

During the period under consideration here – that is, from the emergence of the idea of Jewish emancipation in the last decades of the eight-

---

[1] Secularization does not mean here simply the removal of some domain of life from the scope of religion, but rather the retaining of its emotional appeal even in that domain's secular metamorphosis. See Hermann Lübbe, *Säkularisierung. Geschichte eines ideenpolitischen Begriffs*, Freiburg, 1965.

[2] The use of the term pariah in the Jewish connection has been often taken exception to – for no good reason in my opinion, if one is careful not to equate it with its original meaning in the Indian context. See Salo W. Baron, *Social and Religious History of the Jews*, New York, 1952, I, 23–25, 297; Werner J. Cahnman, "Pariahs, Strangers and Court-Jews: A Conceptual Clarification," *Sociological Analysis* 35, 1974, pp. 154–166.

eenth century to its full implementation in the Western countries a hundred years later – the Jew was conceived of as a former pariah who had
moved from the margin of society to its very center, where he occupied, or
at least competed for, positions formerly the property of others. This
perception, though often exaggerated and distorted, was no mere product
of the imagination. Emancipation, whether formally completed at one
stroke as in France or acquired only gradually and amid more or less
prolonged wrangling, as in Germany, Austria, and Hungary, meant the
expansion of the living space of the Jews, physically, economically, socially, and intellectually. From the beginning of the emancipation, Jews
settled in streets, towns, and districts where they had been previously
excluded. They gained access to occupations and sources of livelihood
outside those allotted to them in former generations.

Professions open to them, such as medicine and law, now attracted more
Jews, not fewer. Moreover, the historical and sociological forces that were
instrumental in securing the relative preponderance of Jews in various
branches of the economy and public affairs continued to be active. Jews
continued to play a conspicuous role in banking, at the stock exchange,
and in management of the press. The great warehouses [department stores]
introduced in the last decades of the nineteenth century were a Jewish
commercial innovation publicly demonstrating the Jew's role in the process of modernization. For those who regretted the passage of a more restful
way of life, or felt economically and otherwise threatened by the new
developments, this very process was a thorn in the flesh. Given the basic
tenet of anti-Semitism, that Jews comprised an alien and pernicious element in society, the concentration of vital public functions in Jewish hands
must have been intolerable to them.[3]

They now aspired to be admitted to social circles, to join clubs, lodges,
and societies, or simply to frequent cafes, restaurants, theaters, and the like
that had hitherto been both inaccessible and of no interest to them. At the
same time, having acquired the language of the larger society and adopted
the basic elements of its culture, they began to take part in its intellectual
and artistic life. A great many Jews became patrons of culture, at times
constituting an important part of the theater audiences and the readership

---

[3] On the economic situation of German Jewry: Werner E. Mosse, "Die Juden in Wirtschaft
und Gesellschaft," in: W. E. Mosse (ed.), *Juden im Wilhelminischen Deutschland 1840-1914*,
Tübingen, 1976 pp. 57–113. On the romantic longings, see Fritz Stern, *The Politics of
Cultural Despair*, Berkeley, 1961.

of books and periodicals. The gifted among them became themselves active in intellectual and artistic creativity.

Anti-Semites wished to perpetuate the inferior position of Jews or even reinstitute some features of their pre-emancipatory situation. Thus, even if they negated the Christian motives responsible for the creation of the situation, anti-Semites still took it as the basis of their operation. There is a patent historical continuity between the two phases of the Jewish predicament.

The word "responsible," used in the previous paragraph, has a moralistic ring: applied deliberately, it transfers the subject of anti-Semitism from the domain of history to ethical accountability. It implies that Christianity is accountable for all the enormities of modern anti-Semitism, including its culmination in the Holocaust. There are historians and theologians who have accepted this verdict and drawn conclusions from it.

The historian who seeks to assess the question of responsibility cannot content himself with a recital of the fact while withholding moral judgment. Once he becomes involved in the question of responsibility, he is no longer dealing with the facts alone. He is, rather, concerned with determining the causal connection between events. He must pay attention to what might seem to contradict his judgment. The most powerful argument that has been adduced, by Christian apologists as well as by anti-Semitic ideologues, to acquit Christianity of the charge of having fostered anti-Semitism, is the fact that anti-Jewish sentiments and even atrocities existed in Hellenistic Alexandria, as well as in the Roman world long before Christianity. The application of the term *anti-Semitism* to these ancient phenomena gave additional weight to this reasoning. If animosity against Jews in antiquity was basically the same as in Christian and modern times, then anti-Semitism could not be attributed to a factor that emerged only later. The only permanent feature that was present in all the three phases, the pre-Christian, the Christian, and the modern, was the Jews themselves. Thus, it was easy for the anti-Semitic pundits to conclude that because of their hateful character and behavior the Jews were the cause of their own misfortune throughout their extended history.[4]

---

[4] This argument was formulated by Ignatz Klinger and has been reiterated by many: Friedrich Rühs, *Über die Ansprüche der Juden an das deutsche Bürgerrecht,* Berlin, 1816, pp. 6–12; Jakob Friedrich Fries, *Über die Gefährdung des Wohlstandes und Charakters der Deutschen durch die Juden,* Heidelberg, 1816, pp. 3–4; Bauer, *Die Judenfrage,* pp. 4–5. The idea has been well summarized by Hans Paul Bahrdt as the anti-Semitic apology: "Soziologische Reflexionen über die gesellschaftlichen Voraussetzungen des Antisemitismus in

Irrespective of the issue of responsibility, I regard the very presence of the unique Jewish community among the other nations as the stimulus to the animosity directed at them. The responses to this stimulus, however, have varied from time to time and from place to place, and insofar as these variations relate to each other chronologically, one can speak of a history of anti-Semitism. It is by comparing the modes and expressions of anti-Jewishness of different ages and by tracing the impact of former modes and expressions on their later mutations that the measure of historical responsibility can be assessed. The history and characteristics of ancient anti-Semitism in this sense becomes relevant for the appraisal of its Christian and modern variants. Elements of the ancient anti-Jewish tradition we have up to now encountered only as they have been transmitted through the channel of its Christian sequel. If the ancient phase of anti-Semitism is to be compared with the later phases, it will have to be viewed in its own historical context.[5]

In the ancient world also, Gentiles expressed animosity toward the Jews living among them; it went beyond the wonted tension between ethnic groups competing for the means of livelihood, political influence, and the like. Jews were singled out by Hellenists and Romans for acrimony and contempt, because of their strange rituals, circumcision, Sabbath observance, and dietary laws. The adherence to these religious prescriptions strengthened the social isolation of the Jewish community, of which one of the main elements was the absolute prohibition on intermarriage with members of other groups. The fact is, of course, that Jews entered the world of Gentiles first through contact with their neighbors and conquerors in their own land and then as Diaspora minorities committed to a religiously sanctioned exclusiveness unparalleled in the ancient world. Unlike other nationalities, Jews refrained from taking part in the religious exercises of their neighbors, condemning and ridiculing them as the outrageously sensual rites of the spiritually blind. This exclusiveness height-

---

Deutschland," in Werner E. Mosse (ed.), *Entscheidungsjahr 1932. Zur Judenfrage in der Endphase der Weimarer Republik,* Tübingen, 1966, p. 136.
5 There is abundant literature on anti-Semitism in ancient times. The definitive study remains that of Isaak Heinemann, "Antisemitismus", Supplement 5, "Pauly-Wissowa," in *Real-Encyclopaedie der klassischen Altertumswissenschaft,* Stuttgart, 1929, pp. 3–43. The relevant source material has recently been compiled and annotated in Menahem Stern, *Greek and Latin Authors on Jews and Judaism,* Jerusalem, 1976, vol. 1. A summary and analysis can be found in Ralph Marcus, "Antisemitism in the Hellenistic-Roman World," in Koppel S. Pinson (ed.), *Essays on Antisemitism,* 1946, pp. 61–75. See also Jan Nicholas Sevenster, *The Roots of Anti-Semitism in the Ancient World,* Leiden, 1975.

ened their own social cohesion and was probably instrumental in securing them a better chance for group survival in an alien and hostile environment. At the same time, this very guarantee of their survival elicited or intensified a peculiar brand of social animosity which, because of some similarity to its modern counterpart, has been accorded the name *anti-Semitism*. The first stimulus to the animosity in both cases has been the social cohesion and compactness of the Jews. As a reaction to it, the complex of imaginary notions about the Jewish mentality and other characteristics arose. Some aspects of ancient and modern anti-Semitism are similar, but a close examination reveals differences, most of which can be attributed to the Christian anti-Semitism that operated during the extended period separating modern anti-Semitism from its ancient counterpart.

That Christian anti-Semitism – that is, the stigmatization of Jews on the basis of Christian doctrines and world views – is no simple continuation of its ancient precursor is patently clear. To the previous charges, Christian animosity added indictments that arose out of the religious conflict between Judaism and Christianity, which was focused on the rejection of the Christian Messiah by the Jews; this carried with it the charge of deicide. All the other charges against Jews, including those current already in the ancient world, such as their hatred of the Gentiles and their moral insensibility toward strangers, now appeared combined with their religious guilt and their putative abandonment by God. The condemnation of Jews thus gained a quasi-metaphysical dignity unprecedented in the ancient world. This religious sanctioning of anti-Semitism then had its social consequences. Linked as it was to the central tenets of Christianity, with its all-pervasive influence, the hatred of Jews spread throughout society. Ancient anti-Semitism may have had a religious tinge produced by the Jewish contempt of the pagan gods. Still, it could not equal its Christian counterpart in emotional intensity, in the depth and breadth of its social expansion.

On the other hands, Christian anti-Semitism, transcending its pagan antecedent quantitatively and qualitatively, had redeeming features. Its condemnation was not unqualified; it kept open an escape hatch for Jews who would accept Christianity. The very toleration of Jews by the Church, otherwise fanatically exclusive toward heretics and the adherents of other religions, was warranted by the belief in the ultimate conversion of the Jews at the end of days. Pagan anti-Semitism lacked any such qualification of its condemnation of Judaism. The consistent adherence to the definition of the Jews as the enemy of mankind left no room for tolerating them. At times, this led to theoretical recommendations for the total destruction of the Jewish people; practically, it resulted in their being persecuted when their religious nonconformity became especially provoking. If such hostile reactions remained an exception, and Jews as a rule were left unmolested, even welcomed and at times privileged, it was because of the marginal nature of anti-Semitic theory in the world view of antiquity. The Jews' nonconformity and exclusiveness may have been an irritant, but the objection to Jewish existence did not assume the character of a principle. The latent animosity needed some special occasion to become socially or politically activated.[6]

Modern anti-Semitism combined the worst features of both its ancient and Christian antecedents. Emerging in the wake of Christian anti-Semitism, it inherited its mental and social pervasiveness. A measure of reserve toward Jews, oscillating between a sense of uneasiness and outright animosity, remained even where the intellectual texture of the Christian world view had worn thin. Yet Christianity's weakening hold implied also the dissolution of the Christian conception of the Jew's role in the history of mankind, from which the vindication of their presence in the midst of Gentile society as well as the anticipation of their future conversion to Christianity derived. The vision of the ultimate Jewish conversion was replaced by the expectation of the Jews' acculturation and assimilation in the not too remote future. The Christian belief in the spiritual efficacy of conversion – the cleansing of the converted Jew of all his supposed vices and shortcomings – as well as the acceptance, as an article of faith, of the certainty of the universal conversion of Jews in the future was sustained in face of a contradictory reality. Its rationalistic substitute, however, the expectation of Jewish assimilation, was open to empirical verification. The scrutiny of Jewish behavior in the decades following the emancipation, to see whether Jews were undergoing their expected metamorphosis, was the overt aspect of this verification.[7] It was, at the same time, a manifestation of latent anti-Semitism. For if Jewish integration had to be vindicated by observable facts, the conclusion could only be that Jews, as individuals and

---

[6] Menahem Stern, op. cit., p. 183; Sevenster, op. cit., pp. 11–12; Salo Wittmayer Baron, *A Social and Religious History of the Jews*, New York 1952, I, pp. 230–33, II, pp. 100–101. The difference between ancient anti-Semitism and its Christian version has been much discussed in the literature cited in n. 4. My own view is close to that of Edward H. Flannery, *The Anguish of the Jews*, New York, 1965, pp. 22–24.

[7] The study of the extent of integration of the Jews is a recurring motif among most of the anti-Semitic authors whose writings I have examined for this work. Striking examples are Paulus, Treitschke in Germany, Drumont in France, and Istoczy in Hungary.

certainly as a collective, continued to retain some of their characteristic features. As the fundamental badness of the Jewish personality had been taken for granted, it followed that the continued existence of the Jews in the Gentile world was indefensible.

This conclusion had its theoretical basis in the racial theory, which, from the 1860s, assumed a quasi-scientific garb. The premises were that races were distinctively different, that their differences vitally influenced human history, and that there was a necessary confrontation between the Semitic and Aryan races. Originally, these hypotheses were only employed intellectually, for historical and linguistic research. But unfortunately the confrontation between the Semite and the Aryan coincided with the traditional distinction between the Jew and the Christian; everything that had been said about the Jew was now applied to the Semite, and the contrary was always said about the Aryan. Thus the condemnation of Jews and Judaism was transferred from its original religious-historical framework into a supposedly scientific context. Thence it was transferred again to the public arena. In this nineteenth century, there were no political-social applications of the racial theory except to the Jews; even in regard to the Jews, the theory was not of prime importance. It did not create the contrast between the Jews and the rest of society, nor the criticism of Judaism by its detractors. This criticism, with its numerous arguments and justifications, amounted to the metamorphosis of the anti-Jewish tradition, which the racist theory now endowed with an explanation derived from ideas of the nature of peoples and the historical laws that govern them. Thus, the theory was not the cause of the situation but only its ideational accompaniment. Thoughts of eliminating the Jews arose among unrestrained anti-Semites long before the racial theory emerged. The theory simply helped these thoughts to crystallize into a clear idea – this idea was realized with the extermination of Jews by the Nazis.

Of course, it took the mentality of the Nazis, combined with the special historical circumstances under which they operated – both unpredictable in advance – to act upon the principles inherent in the situation.[8] The principles themselves, in more or less pungent terms, have been made explicit by the ideologues of the anti-Semitic movement in the late nine-

---

[8] I dealt with the problem of predicting the Nazi coming in my article "Was the Holocaust Predictable?", *Commentary* 59, 1979. Dühring, in particular, has long been recognized as a harbinger of Hitler. But at the Chemnitz Congress, Glagau referred to Dühring as a secluded scholar whose views on the Jewish question "deviated from what is practical or possible to implement." *Schmeitzner's Internationale Monatsschrift*, 1883, II, p. 288.

teenth century and by some of their earlier precursors. Still, it is only through the prism of hindsight that the anti-Semitism of the nineteenth century appears as a harbinger of the Hitlerite catastrophe. The anti-Semites of that time, especially the more radical among them, were demagogues who eschewed responsibility for the implementation of their ideas as well as for whatever impact they might have on other peoples' thoughts and actions. Hitler was taken by most of his contemporaries for such a demagogue. Who could surmise that he possessed the diabolic determination he did, and, a considerable further step, that he would also acquire the necessary power to carry out his will?

The anti-Semitic movement of the nineteenth century, which culminated in the Nazi period, stands revealed as the product of a peculiar constellation of historical circumstances. It consisted of the overt reaction to Jewish emancipation in countries where the millennial Christian resentment against Jews and Judaism remained a latent but mighty force. This constellation was a unique one – as every constellation depending on many factors always is – having no chance to recur in the same way a second time. Indeed, even if all the factors that constituted the constellation were to reappear, the situation would be different, for it would include the inevitable reaction to the consequences of the first constellation. The attempt to foresee the future on the basis of its analogies with the past is a futile undertaking.

What the historian can do, beyond the critically controlled reconstruction of the past, is to assess the extent to which the elements involved in a past constellation of events are still operative in the present and how the reactions to its consequences seem to shape up – without pretending to know what new combination may emerge out of these and other unapprehended elements.

The reactions to the culmination of anti-Semitism in the Holocaust are evident both in the Gentile and the Jewish world. As to the first, one conspicuous reaction was the heart-searching of theologians and intellectuals, spurred by Jules Isaac, who have tried, with modest success it is true, to influence the Vatican to delete some of the most offensive anti-Jewish passages of the Catholic ritual. The criticism of these Christian thinkers concerning the anti-Jewish attitude of the Church is more far-reaching than their criticism of ritual. It touches on the whole Christian tradition, demanding a radical revision of the Gospels' portrayal of Christianity emerging against the background of a deteriorated and God-forsaken Judaism. Although supported by the results of modern historical research, which might justify a change on the basis of historical facts, it is doubtful whether such a revision is at all possible theologically. It has been cogently argued by critics of the trend to eradicate anti-Semite inferences that such a revision would subvert the whole doctrinal edifice of Christianity. It has also been pointed out that the presentation of Christian doctrine even by the most sophisticated modern theologians retains the idea of Christian superiority, implying a concomitant negative evaluation of Jews and Judaism. It is more probable, therefore, that the revisionary trend, seeking a rehabilitation of Judaism within the framework of Christianity, will remain an esoteric exercise restricted in its impact to an intellectual elite.[9]

Shifts in the relations between religious groups like Christians and Jews are not the result of actions planned by intellectuals. As modern society has undergone considerable secularization since the anti-Semitic movement of the nineteenth century, the anti-Jewish predilections of Christianity may have died down in spite of the continuous doctrinal negation of Judaism. Whether this can be taken as a sign of the impending demise of anti-Semitism is, however, highly doubtful, even if the continuing decline of Christianity could be taken for granted; for anti-Semitism has simultaneously been weaning itself from its Christian roots. It has certainly survived the paralyzation of Christianity as an organized religion in Soviet Russia and in the other Communist countries of Eastern Europe.

In his day, Schopenhauer had theorized that, because of the peculiar cohesion of its adherents, Judaism would endure even if its rival, Christianity, should completely disappear.[10] The validity of this theory is still untested. For, even where Christianity has declined, the residue of its anti-Jewish aspects has persisted, and thus Jewish cohesion and the inimical reaction to it have continued to feed off each other. This is certainly true for those countries where anti-Semitism has become virulent, reaching the dimensions of a movement and allowing the millennial Christian resentment to metamorphose into its modern form. It is less true of those countries to which Jews immigrated only in the age of secularization, and where they could become citizens with equal rights and unlimited opportunities for advancement.[11] Still, even in these countries, they remained a nonconforming minority of exceptional cohesion. Nor is there any guar-

---

[9] Rosemary Rüther, *Faith and Fratricide: The Theological Roots of Antisemitism*, New York, 1974; Charlotte Klein, *Theologie und Antijudaismus: Eine Studie zur deutschen theologischen Literatur der Gegenwart*, Munich, 1975.

[10] Arthur Schopenhauer, *Sämtliche Werke, Parerga und Paralipomena*, Wiesbaden 1961, II, p. 280.

[11] On the difference in status of American Jewry following the struggle for emancipation, see Benjamin Halpern, *The American Jew: A Zionist Analysis*, New York, 1956.

antee that the memory of their pariah existence before emancipation will not affect their status in the future.

Zionism has aimed at a radical change, prompted by the conception of anti-Semitism as inherent in the Jews' status as a minority. But, though successful in establishing a Jewish state, Zionism has not achieved its ultimate goal, the elimination of the Diaspora. Instead of relieving Jews of their minority status, the state of Israel has added to their exceptionality – Jews who have not emigrated there are identified not only with their own country, but with Israel. Israel itself, as a newcomer on the international scene, owing its existence to most peculiar historical circumstances, is a target of constant attack. In the ideological expression of these attacks, anti-Semitic motives are routinely intermingled. These attacks inevitably affect the situation of Diaspora Jewry, which for better or worse is associated with the state. Thus, even where in their relations with Gentile society Jews are free of any discrimination, they may still feel themselves under attack and suspicion because of their connection with the state of Israel. Where, on the other hand, anti-Semitism, nourished by local stimuli, has survived, its expressions are colored by reactions to the Jewish state. Since anti-Jewish animosity has always trailed the path of Jewish history, and the last phase of it is characterized by the creation of the Jewish state, the new metamorphosis is hardly surprising. Whether this recent variant of anti-Semitism is the aftereffect of bygone revulsions or the portent of new ones is a question that imposes itself on our mind.

Jean Paul Sartre

What is an Anti-Semite?*

If a man attributes all or part of his own misfortunes and those of his country to the presence of Jewish elements in the community, if he proposes to remedy this state of affairs by depriving the Jews of certain of their rights, by keeping them out of certain economic and social activities, by expelling them from the country, by exterminating all of them, we say that he has anti-Semitic *opinions*.

This word *opinion* makes us stop and think.

But I refuse to characterize as opinion a doctrine that is aimed directly at particular persons and that seeks to suppress their rights or to exterminate them. The Jew whom the anti-Semite wishes to lay hands upon is not a schematic being defined solely by his function, as under administrative law; or by his status or his acts, as under the Code. He is a Jew, the son of Jews, recognizable by his physique, by the color of his hair, by his clothing perhaps, and, so they say, by his character. Anti-Semitism does not fall within the category of ideas protected by the right of free opinion.

It has become evident that no external factor can induce anti-Semitism in the anti-Semite. Anti-Semitism is a free and total choice of oneself, a comprehensive attitude that one adopts not only toward Jews but toward men in general, toward history and society; it is at one and the same time a passion and a conception of the world. No doubt in the case of a given anti-Semite certain characteristics will be more marked than in another.

Since the anti-Semite has chosen hate, we are forced to conclude that it is the *state* of passion that he loves.

How can one choose to reason falsely? It is because of a longing for impenetrability. The rational man groans as he gropes for the truth; he knows that his reasoning is no more than tentative, that other considerations may supervene to cast doubt on it. He never sees very clearly where

---

* Edited and abridged from: Jean Paul Sartre, *Anti-Semite and Jew*, trans. by George J. Becker (New York: Grove Press, 1948).

he is going; he is "open"; he may even appear to be hesitant. But there are people who are attracted by the durability of a stone. They wish to be massive and impenetrable; they wish not to change.

The anti-Semite has chosen hate because hate is a faith; at the outset he has chosen to devaluate words and reasons. How entirely at ease he feels as a result. How futile and frivolous discussions about the rights of the Jew appear to him. He has placed himself on other ground from the beginning.

Never believe that anti-Semites are completely unaware of the absurdity of their replies. They know that their remarks are frivolous, open to challenge. But they are amusing themselves, for it is their adversary who is obliged to use words responsibly, since he believes in words.

The anti-Semite readily admits that the Jew is intelligent and hard-working; he will even confess himself inferior in these respects. This concession costs him nothing, for he has, as it were, put those qualities in parentheses.

He considers himself an average man, modestly average, basically mediocre.

He has made himself an anti-Semite because that is something one cannot be alone. The phrase, "I hate the Jews", is one that is uttered in chorus; in pronouncing it, one attaches himself to a tradition and to a community – the tradition and community of the mediocre.

There is a passionate pride among the mediocre, and anti-Semitism is an attempt to give value to mediocrity as such, to create an elite of the ordinary. To the anti-Semite, intelligence is Jewish; he can thus disdain it in all tranquillity, like all the other virtues which the Jew possesses.

To this end he finds the existence of the Jew absolutely necessary. Otherwise to whom would he be superior?

The degree of integration of each anti-Semite with this society, as well as the degree of his equality, is fixed by what I shall call the temperature of the community. Proust has shown, for example, how anti-Semitism brought the duke closer to his coachman, how, thanks to their hatred of Dreyfus, bourgeois families forced the doors of the aristocracy. The equalitarian society that the anti-Semite believes in is like that of mobs or those instantaneous societies which come into being at a lynching or during a scandal. Equality in them is the product of the non-differentiation of functions. The social bond is anger; the collectivity has no other goal than to exercise over certain individuals a diffused repressive sanction. Collective impulses and stereotypes are imposed on individuals all the more strongly because none of them is defended by any specialized function. Thus the person is drowned in the crowd, and the ways of thinking and

reacting of the group are of a purely primitive type. Of course, such
collectivities do not spring solely from anti-Semitism; an uprising, a crime,
an injustice can cause them to break out suddenly.

We begin to understand that anti-Semitism is more than a mere "opinion" about the Jews and that it involves the entire personality of the
anti-Semite.

Facile talkers speak of a Jewish will to dominate the world. Here again, if
we did not have the key, the manifestations of this will would certainly be
unintelligible to us. We are told in almost the same breath that behind the
Jew lurks international capitalism and the imperialism of the trusts and the
munitions makers, and that he is the front man for piratical Bolshevism
with a knife between its teeth. There is no embarrassment or hesitation
about imputing responsibility for communism to Jewish bankers, whom it
would horrify, or responsibility for capitalist imperialism to the wretched
Jews who crowd the rue des Rosiers. But everything is made clear if we
renounce any expectation from the Jew of a course of conduct that is
reasonable and in conformity with his interests, if, instead, we discern in
him a metaphysical principle that drives him *to do evil* under all circumstances, even though he thereby destroy himself. This principle, one may
suspect, is magical. On the one hand, it is an essence, a substantial form,
and the Jew, whatever he does, cannot modify it, any more than fire can
keep itself from burning. On the other hand, it is necessary in order to be
able to hate the Jew – for one does not hate natural phenomena like
earthquakes and plagues of locusts – that it also have the virtue of freedom.
Only the freedom in question is carefully limited: The Jew is free *to do evil*,
not good; he has only as much free will as is necessary for him to take full
responsibility for the crimes of which he is the author; he does not have
enough to be able to achieve a reformation.

Thus the Jew is assimilable to the spirit of evil. His will, unlike the
Kantian will, is one which wills itself purely, gratuitously, and universally
to be evil. It is *the* will to evil. Through him evil arrives on the earth. All
that is bad in society (crises, wars, famines, upheavals, and revolts) is
directly or indirectly imputable to him. The anti-Semite is afraid of discovering that the world is ill-contrived, for then it would be necessary for him
to invent and modify, with the result that man would be found to be the
master of his own destinies, burdened with an agonizing and infinite
responsibility. Thus he localizes all the evil of the universe in the Jew. If
nations war with each other, the conflict does not arise from the fact that
the idea of nationality, in its present form, implies imperialism and the
clash of interests. No, it is because the Jew is there, behind the govern-

ments, breathing discord. If there is a class struggle, it is not because the economic organization leaves something to be desired. It is because Jewish demagogues, hook-nosed agitators, have seduced the workers.

Anti-Semitism is thus seen to be at bottom a form of Manichaeism. It explains the course of the world by the struggle of the principle of Good with the principle of Evil. Between these two principles no reconciliation is conceivable; one of them must triumph and the other be annihilated.

[The anti-Semite] seeks in historical events the signs of the presence of an evil power. Out of this spring those childish and elaborate fabrications which give him his resemblance to the extreme paranoiacs. In addition, anti-Semitism channels revolutionary drives toward the destruction of certain men, not of institutions. An anti-Semitic mob will consider it has done enough when it has massacred some Jews and burned a few synagogues. It represents, therefore, a safety valve for the owning classes, who encourage it and thus substitute for a dangerous hate against their regime a beneficent hate against particular people. Above all this naive dualism is eminently reassuring to the anti-Semite himself. If all he has to do is to remove Evil, that means that the Good is already *given*.

But that is not all, and now we touch on the domain of psychoanalysis. Manichaeism conceals a deep-seated attraction toward Evil.

His [the anti-Semite's] business is with Evil; his duty is to unmask it, to denounce it, to measure its extent. That is why he is so obsessed with piling up anecdotes that reveal the lubricity of the Jew, his appetite for money, his ruses, and his treasons. He bathes his hands in ordure.

His behavior reflects a curiosity fascinated by Evil, but above all, I think, it represents a basic sadism.

The anti-Semite is well aware of this individual weakness of the Jew, which hands him over to pogroms with feet and hands bound – indeed, he licks his chops over it in advance. Thus his hatred for the Jew cannot be compared to that which the Italians of 1830 felt toward the Austrians, or that which the French of 1942 felt toward the Germans.

It is *fun* to be an anti-Semite. One can beat and torture Jews without fear. At most they can appeal to the laws of the Republic, but those laws are not too rigorous.

There is in the words "a beautiful Jewess" a very special sexual significa-tion, one quite different from that contained in the words "beautiful Rumanian," "beautiful Greek," or "beautiful American," for example. This phrase carries an aura of rape and massacre. The "beautiful Jewess" is she whom the Cossacks under the czars dragged by her hair through the streets of her burning village.

A destroyer in function, a sadist with a pure heart, the anti-Semite is, in
the very depths of his heart, a criminal. What he wishes, what he prepares,
is the *death* of the Jew.

To be sure, not all the enemies of the Jew demand his death openly, but
the measures they propose – all of which aim at his abasement, at his
humiliation, at his banishment – are substitutes for that assassination which
they meditate within themselves. They are symbolic murderers. Only, the
anti-Semite has his conscience on his side: he is a criminal in a good cause.
It is not his fault, surely, if his mission is to extirpate Evil by doing Evil.

The portrait is complete. If some of those who readily assert that they
detest the Jews do not recognize themselves in it, it is because in actual fact
they do not detest the Jews. They don't love them either. While they would
not do them the least harm, they would not raise their little fingers to
protect them from violence. They are not anti-Semites. They are not
anything; they are not *persons*. Since it is necessary to appear to be
something, they make themselves into an echo, a murmur, and, without
thinking of evil – without thinking of anything – they go about repeating
learned formulas which give them the right of entry to certain drawing
rooms.

Many people are anti-Semites in the way Cousin Jules was an Anglo-
phobe, without, to be sure, realizing the true implications of their attitude.
Pale reflections, reeds shaken by the wind, they certainly would not have
invented anti-Semitism, if the conscious anti-Semite did not already exist.
But it is they who with complete indifference assure the survival of
anti-Semitism and carry it forward through the generations.

We are now in a position to understand the anti-Semite. He is a man who
is afraid. Not of the Jews, to be sure, but of himself, of his own consciousness, of his liberty, of his instincts, of his responsibilities, of solitariness, of
change, of society, and of the world – of everything except the Jews. He is a
coward who does not want to admit his cowardice to himself; a murderer
who represses and censures his tendency to murder without being able to
hold it back, yet who dares to kill only in effigy or protected by the
anonymity of the mob: a malcontent who dares not revolt from fear of the
consequences of his rebellion. In espousing anti-Semitism, he does not
simply adopt an opinion, he chooses himself as a person. He chooses the
permanence and impenetrability of stone, the total irresponsibility of the
warrior who obeys his leaders – and he has no leader. He chooses to
acquire nothing, to deserve nothing; he assumes that everything is given
him as his birthright – and he is not noble. He chooses finally a Good that is
fixed once and for all, beyond question, out of reach; he dares not examine

it for fear of being led to challenge it and having to seek it in another form. The Jew only serves him as a pretext; elsewhere his counterpart will make use of the Negro or the man of yellow skin. The existence of the Jew merely permits the anti-Semite to stifle his anxieties at their inception by persuading himself that his place in the world has been marked out in advance, that it awaits him, and that tradition gives him the right to occupy it. Anti-Semitism, in short, is fear of the human condition. The anti-Semite is a man who wishes to be pitiless stone, a furious torrent, a devastating thunderbolt – anything except a man.

Let us recall that anti-Semitism is a conception of the Manichaean and primitive world in which hatred for the Jew arises as a great explanatory myth.

We have demonstrated that anti-Semitism is a passionate effort to realize a national union *against* the division of society into classes. It is an attempt to suppress the fragmentation of the community into groups hostile to one another by carrying common passions to such a temperature that they cause barriers to dissolve. Yet divisions continue to exist, since their economic and social causes have not been touched; an attempt is made to lump them all together into a single one – distinctions between rich and poor, between laboring and owning classes, between legal powers and occult powers, between city-dwellers and country-dwellers, etc., etc. – they are all summed up in the distinction between Jew and non-Jew. This means that anti-Semitism is a mythical, bourgeois representation of the class struggle, and that it could not exist in a classless society. Anti-Semitism manifests the *separation* of men and their isolation in the midst of the community, the conflict of interests and the crosscurrents of passions: it can exist only in a society where a rather loose solidarity unites strongly structured pluralities; it is a phenomenon of social pluralism.

The authentic Jew who thinks of himself as a Jew because the anti-Semite has put him in the situation of a Jew is not opposed to assimilation any more than the class-conscious worker is opposed to the liquidation of classes. On the contrary, it is an access of consciousness that will hasten the suppression of both the class struggle and racism. The authentic Jew simply renounces *for himself* an assimilation that is today impossible; he awaits the radical liquidation of anti-Semitism for his sons. The Jew of today is in full war. What is there to say except that the socialist revolution is necessary to and sufficient for the suppression of the anti-Semite? It is for the Jew *also* that we shall make the revolution.

Part 2: Dimensions / Effects

HELEN FEIN

Dimensions of Antisemitism:
Attitudes, Collective Accusations, and Actions

Definition and Dimensions of Antisemitism

Although it has been one of the most persisting and deadly currents in western civilization, antisemitism has received little sustained attention nor any continuing theoretical discussion among social scientists except as it can be discerned in the individual as an attitude. Waves of interest and interdisciplinary discussion involving sociologists since 1938[1] most often reflected contemporary demands to evaluate events rather than attempts to develop new or exploit existing social-scientific theory. Yet, attitude research rests upon an implicit theory which we will explicate and discuss along with recent findings.

To begin with, we need a conception of the elements or levels of antisemitism to postulate how attitudes might relate to action hypothetically. I propose to define antisemitism as a persisting latent structure of hostile beliefs toward *Jews as a collectivity* manifested in *individuals* as attitudes, and in *culture* as myth, ideology, folklore, and imagery, and in *actions* – social or legal discrimination, political mobilization against the Jews, and collective or state violence – which results in and/or is designed to distance, displace, or destroy Jews as Jews. (Herein, it is assumed that Jews are people who are socially labeled as Jews as well as people who identify themselves as Jews, regardless of the basis of ascription.)

This definition is compatible with the explicit or implicit definition of antisemitism used by most survey researchers, but differs radically from

---

[1] Isacque Graeber and Steward Henderson Britt (eds.), *Jews in a Gentile World: The Problem of Anti-Semitism*, Westport, Conn., 1942. Charles H. Stember, *Jews in the Mind of America*, New York, 1966. Melvin M. Tumin, *An Inventory and Appraisal of Research on Anti-Semitism*, New York 1961. Leonard Dinnerstein, *Anti-Semitism in the U.S.*, New York, 1971. Talcott Parsons, "Postscript to 'The Sociology of Modern Anti-Semitism'," *Contemporary Jewry* 1, 1980, pp. 31–38.

that of Langmuir and (less radically) from Weil's usage herein. Langmuir would restrict the term antisemitism to chimeric assertions about Jews, arguing that "the endurance and intensity of xenophobic hostility against Jews does not mean that it has been different in kind – in basic nature and causes – from xenophobia directed against other major groups, including Jewish xenophobia against other groups." I do not assume there is a difference in the social and psychological dynamics of stereotyping and prejudice or hostility against Jews and others. I do, however, assume that the recurrence or continuity of hostility against the Jews, the interaction of its causes (nicely analyzed by Langmuir), and the recurring use of attitudes, accusations, and myths justifying or reinforcing hostility toward Jews as a collectivity as grounds for political mobilization against Jews (which has led to recurring violence) demand a specific explanation.[2] What is needed are both specific theories of antisemitism relating the development of an ideology justifying Jew-hatred to dominant ideologies, organizations and social structure,[3] and more general explanations of how hostility, discrimination, mobilization, and violence against Jews and comparable minorities are related to the political and economic roles they play; the latter is discussed in Part 3. Each type of theory enables us to probe the adequacy of the other.

Weil discriminates traditional (i. e., Christian) and modern nationalistic or political antisemitism from hostility based on intergroup conflict involving Jews which he would not label as antisemitism (nor would Langmuir), where it is free from expressions of prejudice, stereotypy, and hostility; nor would I. Weil further discriminates among types of expressed antisemitism, believing that social, religious, and economic antisemitism is of little import while political antisemitism is of substantive concern; my previous comments and observations in Parts 3, 4, and 5 herein indicate why I oppose *a priori* or premature judgments about the significance of types of antisemitism.

My definition differs from previous definitions first in its discrimination of levels – intra-individual, cultural, and social or institutional – without any assumption of how they are related. Tumin distinguishes forms (or levels) only *within individuals:*

---

[2] Comments about specific researches in the introductions to Part 3, 4, and 5 illustrate the usefulness of discriminating the grounds of accusation but also show how xenophobic and realistic hostility may feed or lead to more psychopathic or chimeric accusations justifying destruction of the Jews.

[3] see Introduction, Part 1.

We mean by anti-Semitism – to offer a minimal and enumerative kind of definition – that sentiment or action which maligns or discriminates against persons called Jewish on the ground that, being Jewish, they possess certain undesirable features. We make a distinction here among three forms of reaction: inner feelings, or prejudice, withdrawal or maintenance of distance from, and the active exclusion of, or discrimination against[4].

Simpson and Yinger, on the other hand, define antisemitism as action: "Anti-Semitism may be defined as any activity that tends to force into or to hold Jews in an inferior position and to limit their economic, political, and social rights."[5]

Secondly, the definition differs from previous usage of some scholars who distinguish antisemitism as an historically-specific ideology, restricting the term to the social movement labeled antisemitic by Wilhelm Marr in 1879 and to its heirs; some distinguish between "racial", "Christian", "socialist" and other varieties of antisemitism, and still others distinguish between antisemitism and anti-Judaism. I use the term antisemitic to denote belief or behavior oriented toward Jews as a collectivity which is intended or serves to *distance, displace, or destroy Jews qua Jews*, not distinguishing whether the ideological justification of attack is anti-Judaic, anti-capitalist, or antisemitic by its own profession. My assumption is that there is no reason why the attackers' justifications should define the phenomenon to be explained in a scientific explanation. The alleged justification or ideology is not an explanation of an antisemitic movement or behavior but an example of the data to be explained.

Thirdly, the definition excludes instances in which interest-groups, social classes or status groups (among whom there are large proportions of Jews) view their interests as endangered because of the programs, ideologies, actions, or social policies instigated by other interest-groups, social classes, ethnic or status groups, *unless Jews are attacked as a collectivity.*[6]

---

[4] Melvin M. Tumin, "Anti-Semitism and Status Anxiety: A Hypothesis," *Jewish Social Studies* 4, 1971, p. 309.

[5] George E. Simpson and Milton Yinger, *Racial and Ethnic Minorities*, 4th ed. New York, 1972, p. 253.

[6] In that competition and conflict between classes and groups over the distribution of resources and opportunities is a regular characteristic of social life in multi-ethnic societies, there is no special reason to classify actions which affect the interest of people as workers, consumers, owners, taxpayers, or residents of particular neighborhoods as antisemitic simply because those workers, consumers, owners, taxpayers, or residents include many Jews. Thus, controversies over housing regulations, the price of kosher meat, licensing criteria, U.S. "affirmative action" programs and quotas to enlarge participation of racial minorities which may affect the interests of individual Jews as tenants, consumers, producers, or competitors are not inherent instances of antisemitism, nor are they necessarily

What most researchers seem to assume is a positive relationship between attitudes and action, or that "ideology-in-readiness and ideology in words and action are essentially the same stuff."[7]

Their scales assess "ideology-in-readiness" or attitudes – prejudgments, cognitions, stereotypes, social distance, and self-prediction. The terms attitude, stereotype, and prejudice are often used interchangeably but it is useful to begin by discriminating and relating them. An attitude involves "a mental and neural state (2) of readiness to respond, (3) organized (4) through experience, (5) exerting a directive and/or dynamic influence on behavior."[8] Three dimensions of attitudes are conventionally discriminated in analysis: cognitive (knowing), affective (feeling), and conative (doing) components. Public opinion surveys tap cognition about Jews – what people think they know – by agreement with factive statements about Jewish characteristics, including themes from antisemitic propaganda. We know what people say they will do – not what they do – from their responses to social distance scales which ask how close one is willing to get to Jews: would one admit them into one's country, neighborhood, workplace, or family; would one vote for a qualified Jew for public office, marry a Jew. (Similar questions are asked on more recent surveys about other minorities to put social distance towards Jews in a comparative perspective.) Affect is evaluated by positive or negative judgments of what are seen as Jewish traits and generalized judgments of Jews: are Jews more/less/as honest as other businessmen, do they have too much power, are they as loyal as other citizens? Sometimes, respondents are asked to rank feeling about Jews and other groups at the same time. Negative stereotypes are also cognitions expressing affect. Antisemitic attitudes are inferred from cumulative agreement with generalized negative stereotypes and judgments and expressed desire to avoid Jews in certain relationships.

Antisemitic attitudes were most often labeled prejudices. Langmuir reviews the history of attitude research and criticizes past usage of racism and antisemitism as explanations. He also challenges the use of prejudice as a catch-all concept; it presumes norms of rationality in evaluating our

---

instances of "racism" although they affect the interest of non-White minorities. If class or status-group conflicts divide people on ethnic lines, they may become reinforced or surcharged by antisemitic charges (or charges of antisemitism) and especially prone to polarization and violence.

[7] Theodor W. Adorno, et. al., *The Authoritarian Personality,* New York, 1950, p. 5.

[8] William J. Mc Guire, "The Nature of Attitudes and Attitude Change," in Gardner Lindzey and Elliot Aronson (eds.), *Handbook of Social Psychology,* vol. 3, Reading, Mass., 1969, p. 142.

experience to which most of us don't usually adhere, evades the question of the validity of perceptions and stereotypes in general, and is ahistorical or tempocentric. Studies of prejudice, he asserts, fail to discriminate between the "psychopathologically prejudiced persons and mere conformists;" nor have such studies "explained the dynamic relation between them."

Langmuir presents a unique analysis of the structure and function of assertions about out-groups, discriminating realistic, xenophobic, and chimeric assertions which is illustrated by analysis of assertions about Jews. According to Langmuir, realistic assertions may correspond to realistic perceptions of Jewish behavior experienced in contact and/or competition. Hostile but realistic assertions about groups may be produced by the "self-fulfilling prophecy,"[9] in which the dominant group casts the minority or out-group in roles that evoke behavior confirming its expectations. When minority group members succeed in terms of the values and norms of the dominant group, "in-group virtues" are construed by a double-standard to be "out-group vices."[10] Langmuir then proposes an explanation of why certain oppressed and exploited groups (such as Jews and Blacks) become culturally defined as "fundamentally inferior."[11]

Such stigmatized out-groups are singularly susceptible to chimeric assertions. Both xenophobic and chimeric assertions attack all Jews for the alleged violations of some, but chimeras are accusations based on fantasy, Langmuir says, "figments of the imagination, monsters which ... have never been seen and are projections of mental processes unconnected with the real people of the outgroup." However, chimerical accusations against Jews – the myth of ritual murder, pollution of the host, well-poisoning, world-conspiracy – differ from chimerical assertions against Blacks; the usual charge against Jews is of aggression while Blacks are charged with incapacity or deviation from white norms.

Uniting both assertions and the ideologies justifying Jew-hatred is the *collective accusation.* In thematic analysis of three classics of Jew-hatred –

---

[9] Robert K. Merton, *Social Theory and Social Structures.* 2nd ed. Glencoe, Ill., 1957. pp. 421–424.

[10] *ibid.* pp. 426–430.

[11] One may also view Jews and Blacks as pariah castes (see discussion, Introduction to Part 1) and/or potential subjects for exploitation and oppression because they were both excluded from the sanctified western Christian universe of obligation determining reciprocity and inclusion in the community. See Helen Fein, *Imperial Crime and Punishment: British Judgment on the Massacre at Jallianwala Bagh 1919-1920,* Honolulu, 1977, pp. 9–14; George M. Frederickson, *White Supremacy: A Comparative Study in American and South African History,* Oxford, 1981, pp. 70–79.

Martin Luther's *About the Jews and Their Lies* (1543), Edouard A. Drumont's *La France Juive* (1885) and Adolf Hitler's *Mein Kampf* (1925–1927),
and Norman Cohn's analysis of the spurious "Protocols of the Elders of
Zion" *(A Warrant for Genocide*, 1969),[12] one finds several repeated accusations elaborated in different times and places:

1) the Jew is a betrayer and a manipulator (perhaps labeled as the Judas
   image);
2) the Jew is an exploiter personifying usury or modern capitalism (the
   Shylock image);
3) the Jew is a skeptic, an iconoclast, a revolutionary, undermining faith
   and authority (the Red Jew);
4) the Jew is non-human or a diabolic-murderer, poisoner, polluter (the
   demonologic image);
5) the male Jew is a sexual aggressor and pornographer and the Jewish
   woman is a seducer (the lecherous Jew).

The first three types of accusation might be either xenophobic or realistic,
but the fourth is clearly chimeric. Ruether, Langmuir, and Katz show how
these accusations have developed and changed over the last two millenia.

   The fifth accusation, of sexual rapacity and sensuality (attributed to
Jewish men and women, respectively) seems based on projection of the
desires of the dominant Christian community and parallels the "sexual
racism"[13] found in Black-White race relations and imagery in the western
world, raising both the sexual attractiveness of the "Jewess" to Gentile men
and the dangers Jewish men pose to Gentile women. This is a specifically
European image not noted in the United States where, historically, id
stereotypes incorporating sensuality have been projected onto Blacks, and
superego stereotypes (of cunning and egotism) have been projected on
Jews.[14] Only when united with the Nazi race ideology did this last
accusation lead to the prohibition against sexual union and close social
interaction between Jews and Gentiles as *"Rassenschande"* (institutionalized

---

[12] Martin Luther, "Von den Juden und ihren Lügen," in *Werke*, Bd. 53, Weimar, 1920 (1543).
Edouard A. Drumont, *La France Juive*, 14th ed, Paris, 1885. Adolf Hitler, *Mein Kampf*,
trans. by Ralph Mannheim, Boston, 1971 (1927). Norman Cohn, *Warrant for Genocide:
The Myth of the Jewish World-Conspiracy and the Protocols of the Elders of Zion*, Boulder,
Colo., 1969.

[13] Charles H. Stember, *Sexual Racism*, New York, 1978. Winthrop D. Jordan, *The White
Man's Burden: Historical Origins of Racism in the United States*, London, 1974. pp. 18–21,
69–86.

[14] Gordon Allport, *The Nature of Prejudice*, Cambridge, Mass., 1954, pp. 199–200.

in the Nuremberg laws in 1935). Ordinarily, sexual racism makes the woman of the subjected minority more desirable, not less.

A rudimentary paradigm for analysis of collective accusations is based on these questions:

1. What is *the Jew* accused of?
2. What is this attributed to? (Possibilities include religion, culture, race or innate essence, experience.)
3. Can their behavior/nature be changed? (This is logically related to the basis of attribution.)
4. Who is the accuser?
5. What events/acts/contexts are said to instigate the accusation?
6. What are the expressed (or implicit) punishment/policies advocated to redress Jews' behavior?

The attribution of Jewish violations to an intrinsic or racial quality in the late nineteenth century reinforced the earlier antisemitism of Christian origin and justified categorical elimination of the Jews. The new chimera or accusation of a Jewish world-conspiracy became, as Cohn asserts, "A Warrant for Genocide" (1969) leading to Nazi murders before the Holocaust.

The collective accusation is an example of what Neil Smelser labels "hostile beliefs" which are used to mobilize hostile behavior.[15] Collective accusations serve as "sanctions for evil,"[16] authorization of collective violence against the other who has been previously excluded from the "universe of obligation,"[17] and a means of dehumanization.[18]

Attitude research on antisemitism does tap belief in accusations about Jewish loyalty, power, and trustworthiness which stem from the first two classes of accusations enumerated (the Judas and Shylock images), and the range of xenophobic assertions about Jews. Survey researchers have not sought to tap belief in chimeric assertions about Jews, nor discriminated which cognitions simply reflect conventional stereotypes without hostile

---

[15] Neil J. Smelser, *Theory of Collective Behavior*, London, 1963, p. 226.
[16] Nevitt Sanford and Craig Comstock (eds.), *Sanctions for Evil: Sources of Social Destructiveness*, San Francisco, 1971.
[17] Fein, 1977, *op. cit.*, pp. 112–115.
[18] Herbert C. Kelman, "Violence without Moral Restraint: Reflections on the Dehumanisation of Victims and Victimizers," *Journal of Social Issues* 29, 1973, pp. 25–61. Israel W. Charney, *How Can We Commit the Unthinkable? Genocide: The Human Cancer*, Boulder, Colorado, 1982. Leo Kuper, *Genocide: Its Political Use in the Twentieth Century*, New York, 1981.

affect, and which are usually or intrinsically hostile accusations which
justify violence or discrimination against Jews. Weil, Wuthnow and Quinley and Glock[19] also recognize that not every negative stereotype and/or
dislike of Jews is necessarily hostile or of political import. Thus, it must be
kept in mind in evaluating attitude research on antisemitism – as on other
questions – that what we find depends in some measure on what is asked
and on the assumptions inherent in definition, indexing, and evaluation of
antisemitism. Most sophisticated researchers do not draw conclusions on
the basis of response to single questions alone.

Explanations of the Origin of Antisemitic Attitudes

Since the impact of attitudes is often taken for granted, many researchers
assume an explanation of why people hold antisemitic attitudes is an
explanation of antisemitism. The explanation of individual differences in
attitudes towards Jews and minorities most common since World War II is
socialpsychological, stemming from *The Authoritarian Personality*[20] (here-
after TAP). There are several grounds to suspect the theoretical adequacy
of its explanation. One may concur with Shils that TAP over-simplified the
concept of authoritarianism and anti-authoritarianism ideologically, equating anti-authoritarianism with anti-fascism and anti-fascists with democrats, failing to recognize left-wing authoritarians among the anti-fascists.[21]
One may question whether learning experiences (in childhood and adulthood) and the social contexts in which people form attitudes do not better
account for prejudices and ethnocentrism than early childhood experiences account for them. Altemeyer concurs "with the recent statement of
one of the original Berkeley researchers [N. Sanford] that 'rightist authoritarianism . . . owe(s) less to early childhood experiences than the authors
of TAP supposed.'"[22] Despite these grounds for doubt, the psychodynamic roots of "authoritarianism" (as conceived in TAP) as an explanation
of prejudice is still popular. Yet, the most consistent finding among researchers is the lack of predictive power of the F scale, the primary tool
developed in TAP to measure authoritarianism. Quinley and Glock de-

[19] Frederick Weil, herein. Robert Wuthnow, herein. Harold E. Quinley and Charles Y. Glock, *Anti-Semitism in America,* New York, 1979, p. 195.
[20] Adorno, *op. cit.*
[21] Edward A. Shils, " 'Right' and 'Left'," in Richard Christie and Marie Jahoda (eds.), *Studies in the Scope and Method of 'The Authoritarian Personality',* Glencoe, Ill., 1954.
[22] Bob Altemeyer, *Right-Wing Authoritarianism,* Winnipeg, 1981, p. 49.

clare that "no evidence is found that psychological theories of prejudice, including those which attribute prejudice to 'authoritarian personality,' contribute significantly to the explanation of contemporary anti-Semitism."[23] Altemeyer, reviewing scores of empirical studies, concludes that "the major conclusion in TAP that authoritarianism is highly related to prejudice – is still unconfirmed, long after it has been assimilated into our culture."[24]

The most prevalent alternative explanation is that of the cognitive theorists who relate prejudice to faulty generalization or learning. Both schools thus presume contemporary prejudice is primarily a function of *individual* vulnerability. However, another body of research on prejudice explains the retention of ethnic stereotypes as a product of intergroup relations and conflict rather than of individuals' dispositions.[25]

Recent American surveys consistently show that the better-educated strata and age groups are less prejudiced.[26] The effect of education is usually attributed to the development of better cognitive skills, knowledge about group differences, and universalistic values, all making people more immune to group stereotyping and collective accusations. However, a contradictory relationship between antisemitism, age, and education was found in one study of Blacks; "it is not the less educated and the old who are most inclined toward intolerance against Jews but precisely the reverse

---

[23] Quinley and Glock, *op. cit.*. p. 188; see also pp. 47–49, 87.

[24] Altemeyer, *op. cit.*, p. 33.
   The lack of confirmation of the relationship between authoritarianism and prejudice (assuming the former to be measured by the F scale) may be related to the changing distribution and social acceptability of prejudice, when we take into account the distinctions *among* prejudiced personalities remarked upon by Adorno et al. They distinguished between the conventionally and psychopathologically prejudiced, observing that people adopt ideologies because of conformity to social groups to which they belong – "there is a situational factor and a personality factor," see Adorno *op. cit.*, p. 10. However, they failed to explore how cultural norms and social cognition of particular groups could evoke, reinforce, and produce prejudice or non-prejudicial attitudes among the conventionally prejudiced; it is the conformists who are the potential or latent conformers to a democratic anti-prejudicial norm. Thus, if conventional respondents no longer turn up among the conventionally prejudiced on surveys because the authoritative trend set by opinion-leaders is against prejudice, we would find little or no relationship between scores on the F scale and expressions of prejudice on surveys. The implication is that personality structure is scarcely relevant for the prediction and social control of prejudice.

[25] Walter G. Stephan, and David Rosenfeld, "Racial and Ethnic Stereotypes," in Arthur G. Miller (ed.), *In the Eye of the Beholder: Issues in Stereotyping*, New York, 1982, pp. 97–98.

[26] Quinley and Glock, *op. cit.*. Gregory Martire and Ruth Clark, *Anti-Semitism in the United States: A Study of Prejudice in the 1980s*, New York, 1982, pp. 114–117.

– the young, educated Black."[27] The author attributes this to greater militancy and anti-White attitudes among the younger Blacks and their rejection of dependency on Whites.[28]

Furthermore, a positive relationship between education and tolerance or lack of antisemitism was not generally the case in the past. It was not found uniformly in American studies before 1960;[29] Weil[30] also shows that this has not been found uniformly in past European surveys and considers explanations of this. It appears that the effect of education depends on the specific climate of values and political culture dominant during the period. This is consistent with Merkl's finding[31] that among a sample of early Nazis, the party members expressing antisemitism were more educated than those showing no evidence of prejudice. However, Weil concludes that now "education seems to be acquiring an ability to reduce anti-Semitism, which it did not always and everywhere possess."

Another issue dividing researchers is the effect of traditional Christian beliefs on antisemitism. The Christian roots of antisemitism explicated by Ruether[32] lead us to expect that traditional Christians inculcated with the anti-Judaic myth will be more apt to accept antisemitic beliefs; Quinley and Glock show this to be the case: people believing in traditional Christian dogma are also more likely to accept traditional antisemitic stereotypes and accusations.[33]

This is largely based on Glock and Stark[34] which showed how U.S. churchgoers holding a set of orthodox and particularistic conceptions of Christianity blaming Jews were more apt to express antisemitism than other Christians. Similarly, Silbermann's study of German antisemitism also showed people expressing Christian religious hostility toward Jews were more likely to express antisemitic stereotypes than other Germans.[35] It should be noted that others, such as Martire and Clark, conclude that most of the positive relationship between Christian religious conviction

---

[27] Ronald T. Tsukashima, *The Social and Psychological Correlates of Black Anti-Semitism*, San Francisco, Ca., 1978, p. 114.

[28] See also Quinley and Glock, *op. cit.*, pp. 70–71.

[29] Tumin, 1961, *op. cit.* pp. 28, 40, 67, 69.

[30] Weil, herein.

[31] See Part 4.

[32] Part 1 herein.

[33] Quinley and Glock, *op. cit.*, ch. 6.

[34] Charles Y. Glock and Rodney Stark, *Christian Beliefs and Anti-Semitism*, New York, 1966.

[35] Alphons Silbermann, *Sind wir Antisemiten? Ausmaß und Wirkung eines sozialen Vorurteils in der Bundesrepublik Deutschland*, Köln, 1982, pp. 51–52.

and/or fundamentalism and antisemitism (or, rather, the greater likelihood Christian fundamentalists would be prejudiced) could be ascribed to education, race, and age.[36] These differences in interpretation may also be attributed to theoretical differences over the primacy of social influences, differences in the refinement of discriminating which aspects of Christian belief mediate the relationship, and the age of the data.

The Wuthnow survey of recent measures of American antisemitism illustrates and discusses the responses of researchers to some of the questions raised by Langmuir. How can we tell whether negative feeling is associated with cognitions of Jews which may or may not be realistic assertions? This concerns questions like: Do Jews control or play an important part in the movie industry? Do Jews feel as close to Israel as to the U.S.? Other questions are clearly questions of negative affect such as the judgment that Jews have too much power. The findings surveyed by Wuthnow, as in other recent surveys in the United States,[37] consistently show a substantial decline in antisemitism and readiness to discriminate against Jews and other minorities in the U.S. since the 1930s. A substantial minority (about a third of Americans) harbor negative images of Jews, and charges and negative feelings have increased somewhat since the 1970s; however, the American ideal norm is predominantly against group discrimination, affirming that individuals should be treated on their own merits.

Weil, comparing Austria, France, the Federal Republic of Germany, and the United States, herein, concludes that there has been an overall reduction of antisemitism and trends are encouraging, because "education seems to be acquiring an ability to reduce anti-Semitism, which it did not always and everywhere possess. . . ." Differentiating between political antisemitism (stereotypes and evaluation of Jews that have the potential for being elaborated by ideologies, movements, and parties) and non-political antisemitism, Weil estimates about one out of five Americans and French nationals showed signs of political antisemitism in 1970 whereas about two of five West German and Austrian nationals exhibited political antisemitism then. Although there has been a marked decline in political and non-political antisemitism in the Federal Republic of Germany, there is an identifiable cluster of adherents to national-socialist ideology among the population. However, this does not appear to be related to contemporary antisemitism, nor does expression of political antisemitism distinguish

---

[36] Gregory Martire and Ruth Clark, *op. cit.,* pp. 73–75.
[37] *ibid.* and Quinley and Glock, *op. cit.*

partisans of one mainstream party from another. Non-political antisemitism was only slightly higher in the Federal Republic of Germany than in Austria or in the U.S. in 1970 (shown by about one-third of the samples in the latter states), but markedly lower in France where only one in ten French nationals was estimated to have shown signs of this in 1970.

The strong post-World War II American decline has been related to the repudiation of racism and ethnocentrism by the intellectual elite and the growing acceptance of the norm of non-discrimination and tolerance in public life, as Jews, Catholics, and Blacks gained or demanded entry into previously closed organizations and sectors of American life. This trend has also been related to a transmutation of American nationalism based on a multi-ethnic identity with objects of threat lying outside the polity, rather than locating the enemy within.[38] Changes in the U.S. since the 1960s show that the growth of tolerance toward dissidence and diversity is largely a function of age. While before 1964 there was little difference in the expression of antisemitism in the U.S. between people of different ages, there has been a negative relationship between age and antisemitism (and toleration) since then:

> The overall decline in anti-Semitism since 1964 is not primarily the result of changes in the views of individuals; rather it is the result of generational change. In 1964 older adults tended to be highly anti-Semitic. Their dying and replacement by today's young adults has resulted in lower levels of anti-Semitism, since young people today tend to be relatively unprejudiced. . . . Since 1964, Americans have been led by young adults to an increasing tolerance of a variety of life-styles and beliefs. . . . this general tolerance for diversity is strongly tied to tolerance of Jews in particular – indicating that the increasing acceptance of Jews is, in part, a reflection of the more general trend toward increasing acceptance of social pluralism.[39]

How Do Attitudes on Antisemitism Influence Behavior?

What, one may ask, is the longer-term significance of such a change in attitudes? Because relevant research is less than fifty years old and most studies are of the United States, we can not yet assess how trends in public opinion on antisemitism are related to antisemitic behavior in a comparative context or against longer-term historical trends. Before making implications from attitude surveys, we need to consider some tentative presuppositions about how attitudes are related to behavior and assess their plausibility now. These are:

---

[38] Parsons, *op. cit.*
[39] Martire and Clark, *op. cit.*, p. 5.

1) Antisemitic attitudes are consistently and positively related to anti-semitic behaviors; a decline in prejudice should lead to a decline in anti-semitic acts and anti-Jewish discrimination and social distance from Jews.

2) A decline in antisemitic behavior, social distance, and discrimination should lead to a decline in prejudice.

3) There is no necessary connection between feelings and behavior about Jews first, because there is no necessary relation between feelings and behavior, and second, because the same cognitions and stereotypes may logically have different behavioral implications depending on the situation. (E. g., perceptions of the enormity of Jewish power may lead people in one epoch to fear Jews and join against them in antisemitic movements as self-defense, and in another epoch to accommodate and negotiate with them if it is in their self-interest.)

Assuming 3) is correct, one might infer that assessing popular attitudes has no prognostic value because (i) attitudes do not determine behavior; (ii) decisions are usually made by elites, discrete sets of individuals, not the masses; (iii) the persistence of antisemitic attitudes among a large minority indicates elites could justify antisemitic policies if they choose to draw on this constituency; and (iv) there is usually sufficient disagreement about the goals of public policy to justify more than one choice.

4) However, one might draw the alternative inference that expressed antisemitic attitudes (as reflected in surveys) enable us to assess the relative prevalence of hostile beliefs about Jews at any point in time. The perception of such hostility by elites or decision-makers may be one of the parameters affecting policy. If this is so, surveying the balance of negative and positive stereotypy or prejudice against Jews enables one to detect the shift of limits. (This position ignores the question of how intensely different constituencies respond on this question, and what their relative significance is to elites; neither question is answered by survey research.)

The first assumption is the easiest to reject as it is, but represents a specific example of the general question of the relation of attitudes to behavior. Generally, there is no clear theoretical reason to expect people to do what they say; behavior may be governed by more than one attitude toward the object and the situation, expectations of sanctions and social judgments of significant others for discrimination, and role-specific norms. Researchers regularly find that "prejudice is a poor predictor of discrimination. . . . The same act over time and in different social contexts changes its meaning, that is, its social definition."[40]

---

[40] Howard J. Ehrlich, *The Social Psychology of Prejudice*, New York, 1973, p. 14.

> For example, behavior toward a Negro female physician may be directed primarily by one's attitude toward Negroes, toward females, toward physicians, toward any two of these characteristics, or toward all three simultaneously.[41]

Although prejudice has also been the major explanation of racial discrimination in the American social-scientific literature, there has been little theoretical attention to, or empirical analysis of, alternate explanations, and few recent scientific studies of discrimination in actual (rather than constructed) situations.[42]

The second assumption, that a decline in social distance and discrimination should produce and/or be concomitant with a decline in prejudice against Jews, parallels findings in ethnic and race relations in the U. S. since 1945.[43] Since attitudes serve an adaptive function, changes in the status and roles played by minority-group members, increasing equal-status contacts between groups, should increase favorable perceptions of minorities. The increasing acculturation of American Jews, their participation in higher education as teachers and students, and their preponderant distribution in whitecollar and professional occupations (which expanded during that period) has increased social interaction with other middle-class Americans, reducing their visibility as a distinctive "other."[44] Some qualifications must be recalled in projecting the future, however.

A decline in actual social distance does not always lead to more positive feelings and evaluations, but may reinforce stereotypes, when members of different groups who conceive themselves as equal or conceive of the other as unequal but achieve different rates of success, encounter each other in situations that reiterate the inferiority of one group. (This has occurred in some instances of school desegregation between Whites and Blacks and in some unsegregated school settings between Christians and Jewish teenagers).[45] Further, greater interaction with minority-group members caused by eliminating discrimination in employment may lead to increased competition by enlarging the number of competitors, making the new competitors more visible. This may increase the likelihood that the older status-groups occupying (or seeking to inherit) positions will find anti-minority prejudice and ideologies stigmatizing the new contenders a useful

---

[41] *ibid.*, p. 17.
[42] Joe R. Feagin and Douglas Lee Eckberg, "Discrimination: Motivation, Action, Effects, and Context," *Annual Review of Sociology* 6, 1980, pp. 1–20.
[43] Thomas F. Pettigrew, "Prejudice," in Thomas F. Pettigrew (ed.) *Prejudice*, Cambridge, Mass., 1982, pp. 26–29.
[44] Charles H. Stember, *Jews in the Mind of America*, New York, 1966, pp. 13–21.
[45] Stephan and Rosenfeld, *op. cit.*, pp. 120–127. Quinley and Glock, *op. cit.*, pp. 90–92.

tool to justify closing the gates. It may serve to express their resentment and keep the new contenders out. Similarly, groups which confront Jews principally in the market-place as a middleman-minority may be more likely to have their prejudices reinforced.

To this point, we have been talking about parallel changes in attitudes of the dominant group or mass public in the U.S. towards Jews, Blacks, and other minorities, noting the parallels and ignoring how these groups regard each other. Conflicts of interest and ambivalent perceptions of each other by Blacks and Jews in the U.S. (which have sometimes obscured their longer-range interests, values, and alliance) have been related by observers to antagonistic social roles in which they encountered each other in competitive arenas – schools, the professions, businesses, and housing – as well as ideologies and values adduced to support or attack issues in contention, e. g., "affirmative action." The consistent finding that there is more acceptance of antisemitic stereotypes among Blacks than Whites in the U.S. (which is best accounted for by the roles Jews play in ghetto-based marginal businesses) may cause observers to overlook the fact that there is also greater rejection of discrimination against Jews by Blacks than by Whites in the U.S.[46] Most Black antisemitism can be accounted for by negative experiences or perceptions of Blacks of Jewish businessmen and landlords; although the majority of Blacks hostile to Jews whom they perceive as economically exploitative are hostile to all Whites in these roles, they are also more likely to confront Jews in these roles in urban ghettos because Jews were more apt to go into marginal businesses.[47] One might view this as support for Langmuir's position that realistic hostility based on the information and concepts available to the person making judgments should not be labeled antisemitism. Quinley and Glock note that Blacks also expressed spontaneous, favorable judgments of Jews, recognizing that Jews, as victims of discrimination and persecution, have identified with and supported rights for Black Americans more than other groups of White Americans did. Thus, while attitude surveys can be helpful in clarifying the bases of beliefs, summary descriptions of findings may further distort these beliefs. People concerned about Black antisemitism were less apt to note the increased expression of anti-Black prejudice among Jews during the same period, Hentoff pointed out.[48] This, too, often could be attributed to realistic hostility and conflict as discussed in the Introduction to Part 3.

---

[46] Martire and Clark, op. cit. pp. 6, 11. Quinley and Glock, op. cit., ch. 4.
[47] see Part 3.
[48] Nat Hentoff (ed.), Black Anti-Semitism and Jewish Racism, New York, 1970.

Unfortunately, we lack data on how other minority groups view Jews and view each other.

The third position, that antisemitic attitudes may and do have different behavioral implications in different situations, is theoretically consistent with attitude research but has seldom been examined in historical situations. Looking at one of the key stereotypes of Jew-hatred, the exaggeration of Jewish power and its cohesion (woven into the myth of the Jewish world-conspiracy), one may observe that notorious antisemites have concluded critical alliances with Jews in situations where it served their interests. Given belief in Jewish power, role theory tells us that a political actor will be more likely to collaborate with Jews than an actor not subscribing to this stereotype when rewards for collaboration are positive and there are no negative costs or sanctions to consider; however, the same actor might be more likely to discriminate against or destroy Jews when the rewards for such acts are greater than the costs. The variables to consider, then, in predicting behavior are power, interests, resources, and sanctions as well as attitudes.

Historically, cases from the interwar years can certainly be adduced to support this. Perceptions of Jewish influence and united response led Mussolini to adopt a foreign policy sympathetic toward Jews internationally during the 1920s (when Italian domestic policy was non-discriminatory), and to turn toward categorical discrimination against them in 1938 when he sensed collective Jewish interest internationally was antifascist.[49] An exaggerated view of Jewish influence over the Allies was a critical element in Rumania's turn-about in 1942, when the same antisemitic government that had sanctioned discrimination and massacres of Jews in 1941 refused to deport its Jews to Auschwitz in 1942.[50] East European governments, with which Jewish parties actively collaborated in the 1920s to assure Jews' rights and to protect their group and class interests, later systematically excluded Jews from participation and power (and/or were indifferent to violence and discrimination against them) in the 1930s.[51]

This very selective culling of examples leads us to conclude there is no linear relationship between antisemitic attitudes and antisemitic behavior.

---

[49] Meier Michaelis, *German-Jewish Relations and the Question of the Jews in Italy, 1922–1939,* London, 1978.

[50] Helen Fein, *Accounting for Genocide: National Responses and Jewish Victimization During the Holocaust,* New York, 1979, p. 75.

[51] Bela Vago, "The Attitude toward the Jews as a Criterion of the Left-Right Concept," in Bela Vago and George L. Mosse (eds.) *Jews and Non-Jews in Eastern Europe 1918–1945,* New York, 1974, pp. 24, 26, 36, 41.

What alternative relationships could we expect? Related to this question is that of the interaction between the antisemitic political actor and the anti-antisemitic actor. What kind of resistance will antisemites elicit? Indeed, what can we say about the anti-antisemitic political actor? Firstly, can we isolate such an actor or sector of public opinion? Secondly, how critical is anti-antisemitism to an integrated set of political attitudes or ideology? Can we predict individual behavior merely from survey results showing the absence of prejudice any better than we could from results showing evidence of prejudice?

Regarding stereotypy and perceptions of Jewish power (trust, loyalty), opinion analysts usually differentiate those subscribing to negative antisemitic percepts of Jews, those denying them, and the uncertain or neutral; however, most analysts in their interpretations stress only the change in the number (or percent) of antisemitic subscribers. Yet, the remainder varies reciprocally (after subtracting the antisemitic respondents) between those subscribing to positive stereotypes (or rejecting negative ones) and the neutral or indifferent. What weight in interpretation do we give each?

The successful execution of "the Final Solution" can be used as a case-study of the effects of public indifference and organized hatred. Reviewing research on German attitudes and behavior toward Jews before and during the Holocaust, Kershaw[52] asserts that the proportion of Germans approving antisemitic measures did not grow but the increase of the indifferent sector was marked and critical under National Socialism. Weil argues herein the critical variable was not popular antisemitism but indifference and hostility to liberal democracy.

Can we assume that the execution of antisemitic programs depends on the growth in the number of antisemites or the decline in resistance to antisemitism (anti-antisemitism)? How we estimate the weight of the indifferent, neutral, and/or those with "weak" or mixed attitudes depends on which assumption we choose.

Another attempt to discover an anti-antisemitic public is to study polls longitudinally and deduce an evolving pattern of commitment to non-discrimination that is paralleled by responses to questions of race discrimination. Were one to show this sector not only views Jews with sympathy but has a positive commitment to non-discrimination, we could typify them as principled anti-antisemites. What can we infer about their behavior? The principled anti-antisemite (following the same line of reasoning about political actors) would be no more likely to collaborate with Jews

---

[52] See Part 4.

than with other groups, but would be more likely than antisemites to defend them against discrimination or destruction, regardless of the positive incentives by other political actors (parties, organizations, movements, the state) to injure them. This is the plausible supposition waiting to be tested.

To this point, we have been viewing public opinion on antisemitism additively, the measurement and addition of individuals' tendencies to think, view, and feel about the Jews. A theoretically enriched lens, I suggest, would be to see that this expression of attitudes reflects the inclusiveness of the community corresponding to the nation-state: who is included within the circle of trust as a full member of the community, and who can be excluded. Thus, the percentage willing to exclude a Jew, a Black, or any minority member from the guarantees of citizenship or equal access to opportunities (or to discriminate against them) is an index of the exclusion of the other from the universe of obligation[53] at a given point in time. This enables us to discern longitudinal trends among Americans, French, Germans; is it optional, permissive, or mandatory to grant minorities equal rights and access? Both the dominant tendency and the size and stability of the "anti-antisemitic" or "anti-discriminatory" faction are elements in assessing whether antisemitism is defined as a politically permissible option or as illegitimate within the political culture. The sizeable decline and persistence of the drop in antisemitism in U. S. public opinion since the 1940s, which parallels the increase in visible participation and status of Jews in American life and simultaneous legislative enactment of anti-discrimination laws, supports the view that discrimination against Jews in public life is not a permissible option in the U. S., although hostile accusations and negative stereotypes are still prevalent among a sizeable minority. Racial discrimination also elicited majority disapproval after the pressure of the civil rights movement triggered federal legislation and intervention. Viewing the sum of poll responses as indices of the political consensus in democratic states assumes that changes in public opinion are more likely to be responses to social change than their cause.

To sum up: It appears that our second assumption is supported from the American data; a decline in actual social distance and discrimination has been accompanied by a decline in expressed prejudice against Jews since World War II, lending credence to Merton's conclusion[54] that attitudes toward out-groups are a product of their place in the social structure. Thus,

---

[53] Fein, 1979, *op. cit.* p. 3.
[54] Merton, *op. cit.*

modifying the social structure, rather than education of the dominant groups, has led those among the latter more responsive to new attitudes to reject the older hostile stereotypes of Jews.

A brief review of historical experience shows we can not accept as false the third assumption, that "there is no necessary connection between feelings and behavior about Jews;" antisemitism may have different behavioral implications in different situations. However, the prevalence of violence against Jews following the successful political organization of antisemitism before and during the Holocaust[55] suggests the critical term is *necessary* connection; instead, one might propose that antisemitic beliefs and culture are more likely to enable antisemitic movements to gather support and disarm opponents into collaboration or inaction, than are anti-antisemitic beliefs and culture, leading to discrimination, expulsion, or destruction of the Jews.

We might inquire of what use attitudes surveys are in estimating future possibilities. The answer to this depends on the political context; both the third and fourth positions are plausible in different contexts. Within democratic societies in which public opinion is a parameter politicians do take into account, attitude research is a useful tool to tap the prevalence and distribution of hostile beliefs about Jews and other minorities. Yet when surveyors cite multidimensional indices aggregating conventional folk agreeing with stereotypes without passion, traditionalists seeking to maintain their own social distance, and pathologically hostile potential followers of antisemitic movements, and do not discriminate among the anti-antisemites, it is of limited values. This suggests the need for greater discrimination in conceptualizing, executing, and reporting such surveys.

---

[55] See Part 4.

GAVIN I. LANGMUIR

Toward a Definition of Antisemitism

Whatever most who now use the term "antisemitism" mean by it, they do not use it in its original and explicitly defined sense, and I will argue that as presently used it impedes rather than aids understanding of hostility against Jews.[1] "Antisemitism" was invented about 1873 by Wilhelm Marr to describe the policy toward Jews based on "racism" that he and others advocated. Although elements of the racist theory can be traced back to the eighteenth century, if not earlier, the theory itself was only fully elaborated in the latter half of the nineteenth. It proclaimed that humans were divided into clearly distinguishable races and that the intellectual, moral, and social conduct and potential of the members of these races was biologically determined. As elaborated in the Aryan myth it maintained that Jews were a race and that, not only were they, like other races, inferior to the Aryan race, but also that Jews were the most dangerous of those inferior races.

If that meaning of "antisemitism" is clear, the falsity of the Aryan myth on which it depends is now obvious. Contemporary biologists no longer believe there are distinct racial boundaries between humans, only differences in the relative commonness of certain hereditary traits, for every marriage circle is a potential race.[2] And since any man and woman who are not sterile can breed, marriage circles or patterns of intercourse are decided, not by biological processes, but by geographic or cultural proximity as determined by geographic and cultural barriers. Hence racial boundaries are no more distinct than cultural or geographic boundaries. Jews, who

---

[1] This is a revised version of my "Prolegomena to any present discussion of hostility against Jews," *Social Science Information* 15, 4/5, 1976, pp. 689–727; Italian translation in *Comunità* 181, 1979, pp. 212–57. The original article left the meaning I attributed to "antisemitism" implicit. The revision is intended, among other things, to make my definition explicit. I want to dedicate it, with great affection, to the pioneering scholar and sensitive human who first commissioned it, Léon Poliakov.

[2] Leslie C. Dunn, "Race and Biology," *Race, Science and Society,* New York, 1975, pp. 41, 53. See also Michael Banton, *Racial and Ethnic Competition,* Cambridge, England, 1983.

have lived in so many regions and cultures, certainly do not collectively constitute a race, even though some Jews may have some hereditary physiological traits which distinguish them from some other groups of the European population.

The greatest weakness of the Aryan myth, however, was not the belief that large human groups could be sharply differentiated according to hereditary biological traits, but the conviction that biological inheritance explained cultural differences, a conviction obvious in the confusion of language and biology involved in the concept of "Semitism." Since cultural and geographic proximity or barriers have affected patterns of intercourse, there have indeed been some obvious correlations between distinctive physiological and distinctive cultural traits, for example, in Chinese civilization. But where that has occured, these traits have been connected contingently, not necessarily. Knowledge of such a historical correlation does not predict the mental or cultural potential of the offspring of such groups who are raised in a markedly different culture.

And if a necessary correlation cannot be demonstrated by history, even less can it be demonstrated by biology. Recent advances in genetic biology and behavioral biology have made it clear that our present knowledge of the relation between gross physiological characteristics and the functioning of the brain is minimal, that our understanding of the relation between the brain and mental processes is extremely limited, and that mental adaptation to environment is apparently constrained but not determined by our genetic inheritance. Hence it is impossible to infer the mental or cultural potential of large groups from biological data. Although some people still insist that it is possible to establish a statistical correlation between some gross physiological characteristics, such as pigmentation, of large groups and their mental and cultural potential, assertions of this kind have been so persuasively criticized as to seem worthless. Not only have the biological distinctions used been elementary or dubious, not only have the criteria used to measure mental and cultural performance and potential been recognized as crude and culturally biassed to an unknown but vast degree, but it is now obvious that the strong biases of the most prominent proponents of such theories dictated their theories, controlled their empirical research, and led them into major fallacies and even fraud.[3]

---

[3] The vigour of the debate indicates the subjectivity of any convinced assertions on the issue. See for example: Arthur Robert Jensen et.al., *Environment, Heredity, and Intelligence*, Cambridge, Mass. 1969; Hans Jürgen Eysenck, *The IQ Argument*, New York, 1971; Luigi Luca Cavalli-Sforza and Walter F. Bodner, *The Genetics of Human Evolution*, San Fran-

Since the best present knowledge so obviously invalidates the Aryan theory, it follows that we cannot use "racism", the central and false concept of that myth, to explain the hostility towards Jews – or blacks – displayed by the propagators of the myth. The Aryan myth was *their* (false) rational-ization of their hostility, but since we do not believe that biological differences were the cause of their hostility, "racism" cannot be *our* ex-planation of the myth or of their hostility.

We may, of course, use "racism" to refer to those relatively recent historical beliefs, utterances, and actions which maintain, without empir-ical foundation, that racially different peoples necessarily have different mental or cultural potentials, and we may call those who hold such ideas racists. In that sense, the terms are convenient labels, like "Zoroastrian", to denote certain historical beliefs and those who have held them, and no confusion will arise if the terms are only used taxonomically to denote those historical beliefs. But only a genuine racist, only someone who believes that biological differences were the fundamental cause of such hostility, can use racism as an explanatory category – and that conclusion can only be derived from biology, not social science.

Despite the biological propensities of early anthropologists,[4] "race" is not a term proper to the social sciences. Social scientists use the term either as it is defined by contemporary biologists or in their descriptions of the thoughts of the people they study. In the latter case "race" refers not to a process of nature but to an artifact of human consciousness which, like phlogiston or centaurs, may have no existence outside the mind of the people studied. And if the best contemporary biological knowledge forces social scientists to accept that someone who rationalized his hostility by "race," for example, Alfred Rosenberg, was wrong in his beliefs about "race," then they must conclude that the biological fact of race (so far as it is a fact) did not cause Rosenberg's beliefs and hostility. They must then look to other features of human nature, such as irrational or wishful thinking, which fall within the purview of their own disciplines, to explain why Rosenberg was so hostile to Jews and embraced that error about "race."

cisco, 1971; R. H. Herrnstein, "IQ", *Atlantic Monthly* 228, 3, 1971, pp. 44–64; S. Scarr-Salapatek, "Unknowns in the IQ Equation," *Science* 174, 1971, pp. 1223–38; Leon J. Kamin, "Heritability Analysis of IQ Scores: Science or Numerology?," *Science* 183, 1974, pp. 1259–66; Stephen J. Gould, *The Mismeasure of Man*, New York, 1981; Melvin Konner, *The Tangled Web: Biological Constraints on the Human Spirit*, New York, 1982; Howard Gardner, *Frames of Mind*, New York, 1983; Richard Charles Lewontin, Steven Rose, and Leon J. Kamin, *Not in Our Genes*, New York, 1984.
4 See Léon Poliakov, *Le mythe Aryen*, Paris, 1971, pp. 150–89, 263–82.

And as they develop their explanation of such hostility, they should use terms that distinguish their own explanation clearly from the rationalizations they are trying to explain. To typify and explain the process that produced the erroneous thought of believers in the Aryan myth as "racism" is to confuse a symptom with a cause, a confusion that enables the Aryan myth to contaminate our scientific thinking.[5]

I have laboured this point at some length because what has been said about "racism" applies equally to "antisemitism." In its original meaning, "antisemitism" is as erroneous an explanation of hostility toward Jews as the racism from which it emerged in 1873. And in its present use, "antisemitism," like "racism," has given hostages to the Aryan myth.

Of course, because of Hitler, the term has been transvalued. Not only are Jews good in their own eyes, but they are now seen as no worse than, or as good as, anyone else by many others in the West. Consequently, "antisemitism" is now understood as a highly pejorative term both by Jews and many non-Jews – which is what makes the charge of "antisemitism," loosely defined, so useful a weapon in political discourse. So long as memories of the Final Solution remain vivid, the use of that special term of dark origin implies that there is something unusually and uniquely evil about any serious hostility toward all Jews.

But the common use of "antisemitism" now to refer to any hostility against Jews collectively at any time has strange implications. Although it transvalues the original meaning of the term and rejects the categorization of Jews as a race, it nonetheless carries over from the Aryan myth the implication that hostility toward Jews is an enduring (if now bad) reaction of non-Jews to some unique and unchanging (if now good) characteristics of real Jews. It also implies, in agreement with that myth, that the hostility which engendered Hitler's Final Solution was not different in fundamental nature, only in intensity and the technology applied, from the riots in ancient Alexandria in the first century of the common era or from any other hostility Jews have ever had to face. The usage thus implies that

---

[5] Despite the careful distinctions which Pierre Louis van den Berghe makes to avoid that pitfall in his valuable book, *Race and Racism*, New York, 1967, it seems to me that he comes very close to falling in because he, as a social scientist, decided to use "race" with the meaning given it by the racists he was studying and to treat "racism" as a unitary phenomenon sufficiently distinct to be susceptible of a separate, general, socio-anthropological explanation. Conversely, Christian Delacampagne uses so broad a conception of "racisme" to develop his fascinating argument that he can locate its emergence among the Greeks in antiquity: *L'invention du racisme*, Paris, 1983; revised edition, *Racismo y occidente*, Barcelona, 1983.

there was nothing uniquely evil in quality about the Final Solution, only a quantitative difference.

In fact, there have been such obvious changes in some characteristics of hostility against Jews that scholars have felt the need to make some distinctions, typically by adding adjectives to "antisemitism." Thus Hannah Arendt and many other historically minded scholars have distinguished between religious and racial "antisemitism." But those adjectives only distinguish secondary characteristics of the hostility; they do not imply a fundamental difference in its nature. Although the adjectives distinguish different historical rationalizations for the hostility, the noun "antisemitism" still implies a constancy in the basic cause and quality of hostility against Jews at any time. That implication may be expressed negatively when looking at non-Jews or positively when the focus is on Jews. Thus one book traces "anti-Semitism" from the first century to the present and defines it as "actions and attitudes against Jews based on the belief that Jews are uniquely inferior, evil or deserving of condemnation by their very nature or by historical or supernatural dictates."[6] Jacob Katz puts it positively: "I regard the very presence of the unique Jewish community among the other nations as the stimulus to the animosity directed at them."[7]

Like the Aryan myth, this conception of "antisemitism" depends, I would argue, on the fallacy of misplaced concreteness or illicit reification, in this case on the unproven assumption that for centuries, and despite innumerable changes on both sides, there has been a distinctive kind of reaction of non-Jews directed only at Jews that corresponds to the concept presently evoked by the word "antisemitism." What makes that fallacy attractive to many people, I would suggest, is their prior assumption that, whether by divine choice or otherwise, there has always been something uniquely valuable in Jewishness, because Jews have always incorporated and preserved uniquely superior values. They then assume that the resolute and enduring expression of those unique values by Jews has aroused a correspondingly unique type of hostility against them as bearers of that unique quality throughout their existence.

Such a perspective might fairly be called ethnocentric; and, not surprisingly, those who accept it have not felt any need to examine non-Jews carefully to see whether the quality of their hostility to Jews has in fact been

---

[6] Paul E. Grosser and Edwin G. Halperin, *Anti-Semitism: The Causes and Effects of a Prejudice*, Secaucus, N.J., 1979, p. 5.

[7] Jacob Katz, *From Prejudice to Destruction*, Cambridge, Mass., 1980, p. 322.

unique and unchanging. Yet the quality of hostility against Jews cannot be determined by premises about Jews, for it is a characteristic of the mentality of non-Jews, not of Jews, and it is determined, not by the objective reality of Jews, but by what the symbol "Jews" has signified to non-Jews. Moreover, the kind of hostility evoked has not been directed only against Jews.

✳

There is, of course, another well-known definition of "antisemitism" which is not based on Jewish history yet implies that there has been something unusual about hostility toward Jews. Social psychologists and sociologists have defined antisemitism as an expression of ethnocentrism or "ethnic prejudice," or simply "prejudice." Since their disciplines, influenced by anthropology with its tendency to cultural relativity, involved a wider perspective on social conflict than historical study of a specific conflict, they were more prepared to see antisemitism as unique in historical detail but not in nature, to recognize that antisemitism was similar to the unusual hostility of whites against blacks in America and to the hostility faced by other groups which had never been categorized as races by the racists.[8] Yet although that broadening of perspective brought a major advance in the understanding of antisemitism, it also presents problems.

"Ethnic prejudice" has the advantage that it is a term of social science which receives its definition from the theories of the social sciences, not from the rationalizations of racists or the presuppositions of the victims of such hostility. And while the concept clearly includes in its purview those beliefs which have been termed "racism", it recognizes that false beliefs about race and about groups which have never been considered races may be identical in basic nature and etiology. It frees us to recognize that, despite differences in the concrete detail of their historical expression, attitudes toward a variety of groups may be manifestations of a single basic phenomenon or process.

Yet if "racism" is too misleading and restrictive in its connotations, the problem with "ethnic prejudice" as presently defined is that it is too inclusive. Some of the better known definitions may indicate the problem.

Ethnocentrism is based on a pervasive and rigid ingroup-outgroup distinction; it involves stereotyped negative imagery and hostile attitudes regarding outgroups, stereotyped positive imagery and submissive attitudes regarding ingroups, and a hierarchical, authori-

---

[8] Gordon W. Allport's classic, *The Nature of Prejudice,* Cambridge, Mass., 1954, indicates the extent of that broadening of perspective.

tarian view of group interaction in which ingroups are rightly dominant, outgroups subordinate.[9]

Prejudice is a pattern of hostility in interpersonal relations which is directed against an entire group, or against its individual members; it fulfills a specific irrational function for its bearer.[10]

We use the term prejudice to refer to a set of attitudes which causes, supports, or justifies discrimination.[11]

Ethnic prejudice is an antipathy based upon a faulty and inflexible generalization. It may be felt or expressed. It may be directed toward a group as a whole, or toward an individual because he is a member of the group.[12]

Our theory leads us to propose that what appears at first glance to be discriminations among men on the basis of race or ethnic group may turn out upon closer analysis to be discriminations on the basis of belief congruence over specific issues.[13]

We shall define prejudice as an emotional, rigid attitude (a predisposition to respond to a certain stimulus in a certain way) toward a group of people.[14]

Prejudice is a negative attitude toward a socially defined group and toward any person perceived to be a member of that group.[15]

The fundamental weaknesses of all these definitions is most obvious in the last one: almost any form of intergroup hostility – including that all-too-normal component of history, war – involves prejudice. Hence any hostility against Jews collectively can still be defined as "antisemitism." Thus Glock and Stark have defined antisemitism as "the hatred and persecution of Jews as a group; not the hatred of persons who happen to be Jews, but rather the hatred of persons *because* they are Jews."[16] Yet I, for one, would be reluctant to assert that the hostility which, for example, many French people felt toward Germans between 1870 and 1945, differed only in

---

[9] Daniel J. Levinson, "The Study of Ethnocentric Ideology," in Theodor W. Adorno, Else Frenkel-Brunswik, Daniel J. Levinson, and R. Nevitt Sanford, *The Authoritarian Personality,* New York, 1950, p. 150.

[10] Nathan Ward Ackerman and Marie Jahoda, *Anti-Semitism and Emotional Disorder,* New York, 1950, pp. 3–4.

[11] Arnold M. Rose, "The Roots of Prejudice," *Race and Science,* New York, 1961, p. 393.

[12] Allport, *op. cit.,* p. 9.

[13] Milton Rokeach, *The Open and Closed Mind,* New York, 1960, p. 135.

[14] George E. Simpson and J. Milton Yinger, *Racial and Cultural Minorities,* 4th ed., New York, 1972, p. 24.

[15] Richard D. Ashmore "Prejudice: Causes and Cures," in Barry E. Collins (ed.), *Social Psychology,* Reading, Mass., 1970, p. 253.

[16] Charles Y. Glock and Rodney Stark, *Christian Beliefs and Anti-Semitism,* New York, 1966, p. 102.

intensity and overtness of expression from that directed against Jews and blacks in the same period. I do not wish to abandon the insight that the kind of hostility symbolized by Auschwitz differed in more than intensity from that symbolized by Sedan, Verdun, or the Swastika on the Eiffel Tower.

The theories of "ethnic prejudice" were originally developed primarily to deal with the hostility against Jews and blacks that seemed the archetype of racism, and they therefore suggested that this was an unusual kind of hostility. But "ethnic prejudice" rapidly came to refer to hostility against other groups, thereby diluting the unusual quality of "ethnic prejudice." A major reason for that extension was that the fundamental criterion underlying most definitions was cognitive performance about specific groups, the presence of a failure of learning as measured by some unstated standard, the maintenance of a "faulty and inflexible generalization" about a group, to use Allport's language. Indeed, that criterion is implicit in the term chosen from common usage, prejudice; to prejudge is to make a judgment without knowledge or without adequate knowledge. But by what standard is a generalization about groups to be considered faulty?

Thinking in terms of categories is inevitable and essential for human action, and no one has had perfect knowledge about something as intangible, complex, and ill-understood as "groups." The problem for the people who invented the term "ethnic prejudice" was, therefore, to find some standard by which they could assess generalizations about groups and distinguish between those which were so faulty as to be abnormal – as to indicate prejudice – and those which manifested only the normal, inevitable amount of prejudgment.

The standard the social scientists used was primarily their own standard of rationality,[17] their own knowledge of social groups and their own judgment – frequently as liberals or members of the groups which were the objects of such hostility – as to which generalizations were most faulty and dangerous. That almost unconscious decision was ironic since social scientists spend much of their lives disagreeing with each other about the nature of groups and the effect of membership on an individual's conduct. But a more serious problem is that the presenticentric, ethnocentric, and egocentric quality of that standard makes it historically, culturally, and socially biassed. People of different periods or contemporaries who had not had the same opportunity to acquire information about groups, to assess the reliability of that information, and to learn how to think analytically about

---

[17] Howard Shuman and John Harding, "Prejudice and the Norm of Rationality," *Sociometry* 27, 1964, pp. 353–71; the article accepts the validity of the norm of rationality.

abstractions would almost inevitably seem prejudiced in the eyes of these social scientists. Imagine applying the standard to medieval people!

To escape that dilemma, some scholars, such as Levinson, Allport, Jahoda, and Yinger, have emphasized that the generalizations must be not only faulty but also inflexible or rigid. The people who express faulty generalizations must also manifest an unwillingness to modify them when confronted with new information which implies that they are faulty. While the faults of the generalizations may simply reflect lack of social opportunity to know better, the inflexibility with which they are held suggests a refusal to learn, a psychological inhibition – as is implied in Ackerman and Jahoda's definition. It is this approach which underlies the whole conception of the prejudiced personality developed in *The Authoritarian Personality*.

The weakness of this solution is that either it necessitates an unacceptable psychological reductionism or else it has to face the very objections it was designed to overcome. In the first case, let it be assumed that people who hold their generalizations inflexibly do so because of some psychological weakness. Hence, if one could examine some people psychologically, determine which psychological problems they have, and observe which kinds of their statements about groups were psychologically connected with their psychopathology, then one could infer that these generalizations were faulty because the people were psychologically blocked and could not learn. It would then follow that the generalizations of other people with the same psychopathology could be assumed to be prejudiced. This approach, however, involves the assumption that a psychological assessment of people makes possible a decision about the *truth* of their assertions, an obvious reductionist fallacy.

That fallacy was so obvious that most social scientists who emphasized a psychological explanation of "prejudice" sought to avoid it. They argued instead that it was possible to show a clear correlation between the more extreme and apparently rigid faulty generalizations which were objectively invalid and some psychopathological conditions. Yet any such correlation still depends upon a prior judgment about the falsity of generalizations about groups and hence upon some standard of objectivity which is not culturally or socially biassed, and that was just what was missing.

The reason this approach seemed plausible at all was because it was used within a society with a relatively uniform educational system and a highly developed system of mass communications so that the researchers were able to assume that any firmly maintained generalizations that deviated drastically from their own standard of rationality could not be explained by variations in cultural influence on cognitive performance and could, therefore, be considered to be inflexible rather than merely faulty. Yet that was only an assumption, and an assumption, moreover, which overlooked the difference between non-rational and irrational thought and encouraged the tendency to impute psychological weaknesses to those who disagreed notably with the social scientists' values and ideas about groups. Furthermore, it overlooked the problem that this approach could not be applied to study of earlier periods or of contemporary societies with markedly different cultures or subcultures.

A very different solution to the problem of distinguishing rigidity in beliefs from mere error was to disregard the specific content of people's belief about groups and examine the structure of the way they thought in general. Regardless of the truth of their specific assertions, do people form their beliefs in different ways according to their personality? This was a major hypothesis of *The Authoritarian Personality,* and it was further developed by Milton Rokeach in *The Open and Closed Mind.* He designed a "Dogmatism" scale which measured, he believed, the difference in the extent to which people reacted to new information on the basis of its intrinsic merits or on the basis of such cognitively irrelevant factors as personal insecurity or fear of social authorities.

One problem with Rokeach's approach, however, is that it is difficult to assess dogmatism in the abstract without reference to assertions on specific subjects. And since the items in his Dogmatism scale refer to universal problems and current issues, the assessment of the responses relied considerably on Rokeach's judgments about the correct or psychologically indicative answers, so that the problem of cultural bias may still be present. Were Rokeach's scale applied to earlier cultures, it would be discovered that most of them were highly dogmatic – even though we, using the criterion of Auschwitz, might judge them much less "prejudiced". There is also the problem of disagreement about non-rational values and the fact that peoples and cultures are selectively dogmatic, that Calvinists were highly dogmatic theologically while being highly flexible in economic matters. Rokeach's approach does not pay enough attention to the phenomena of historical change, social differentiation, and mental compartmentalization. And for just that reason, it is of little help in determining which people will make dogmatic negative assertions about which groups. There may, indeed, be a dogmatic refusal to make such assertions.

Confronted with these difficulties in finding any standard of objectivity which would distinguish between prejudiced and merely erroneous generalizations about groups, and which would be value-free, some scholars who did not favour a psychological explanation of "prejudice" solved the problem by cutting the Gordian knot. In order to eliminate socio-cultural bias, they simply abandoned the effort to distinguish between faulty and valid generalizations about outgroups. Instead, they considered as "prejudice" any negative attitudes toward groups or toward individuals because they were members of groups, and also any discriminatory actions against groups and individuals as members. The definitions of Rose and Ashmore are examples of this approach, and its peculiar implications are apparent from Ashmore's definition of "prejudice reduction" as "any move toward perceiving, evaluating, and responding to members of the group in question as individuals."[18]

Not only negative but also positive evaluations of groups are, by implication, "prejudice". Absence of "prejudice" only occurs when all evaluations of groups are given up and individuals relate to other people simply as individuals. But from this extremely nominalistic and anarchic perspective, in this never-never land of individuals with personal but no social qualities, in this view of humanity which overlooks the importance of non-rational thought for values, any evaluation of people's conduct as members of social collectivities is impossible or illegitimate. The concept of prejudice is so broadened as to be useless for analyzing the social reality with which everyone, including social scientists, must deal.[19]

It might seem that "ethnic prejudice" is even more useless a concept than "racism" because, if it recognizes that the kind of hostility manifested against "races" has also been directed against people who constitute a cultural but not a racial group, and therefore avoids the trap of "racism," it fails to set limits to that widening of perspective and avoidance of the errors of racists. Yet that is not the case, for "ethnic prejudice" avoids the flagrantly erroneous implications of "racism", and, as I shall try to indicate, the work done by those who have defined it has been immensely valuable and indicates a way to avoid some of the dilemmas just discussed.

※

Serious study of intergroup hostility – as opposed to detailed descriptions of particular examples – began in the 1920's, perhaps partly in reaction to

---

[18] Collins, *op. cit.*, p. 255.
[19] Robert Alan Levine and Donald Thomas Campbell, *Ethnocentrism*, New York 1972, provides an exhaustive survey of theories relevant to "ethnocentrism" which illustrates how diversely and broadly that term has also been used.

the carnage between 1914 and 1918. Anthropologists developed the concept of xenophobia, the idea of an instinctive hostility toward strange – little known and differently constituted – outgroups; and the invention of the social distance scale by E. S. Bogardus in 1928 provided a way of measuring relative hostility toward different outgroups. In the same period, people began to speak of "race prejudice," but the theoretical basis for the recent conception of "ethnic prejudice" only appeared in 1938 when John Dollard linked the historical, anthropological, and sociological study of intergroup hostility with Freudian insights into irrationality and aggression; and only after 1950 did the term "prejudice" become fairly standard, largely replacing its competitor, "ethnocentrism."

Bogardus and Dollard focussed on hostility against blacks in the United States, but work on prejudice rapidly came to concentrate heavily on hostility toward Jews, because of the Nazi persecutions. Most of the early fundamental work, including *The Authoritarian Personality,* appeared in the *Studies in Prejudice* sponsored by the American Jewish Committee. The participation of European Jewish exiles familiar with Freud also strengthened the conjuncture between American social psychology and Freudian thought. By 1954, however, when Gordon Allport summed up the work of this early school in *The Nature of Prejudice,* the danger to Jews had diminished radically, and sociologists and psychologists in the United States concentrated again on the domestic scene and particularly on the flagrant problem of "prejudice" against blacks, although "prejudice" against Jews (or "antisemitism") remained a major topic, and increasing attention was paid to "prejudice" against other groups in America.

How did the analysts of "prejudice" up to 1954 understand the hostilities they examined? Many, often conflicting, definitions and theories of "prejudice" were formulated, but the hallmark of the original conception was its *cognitive definition* of prejudice as faulty and inflexible beliefs about outgroups and its *psychopathological* explanation of those cognitive errors. Since much of Nazi thought seemed patently irrational, and since those who rigidly held the most indisputably invalid ideas about Jews and blacks also contradicted themselves, manifested an obsession with Jews and blacks, and showed other symptoms of abnormality, psychological explanations seemed in order and were soon found, aided by the rising prestige of Freudian thought.

One of the more influential, if not the most valid, of these explanations was the oedipal theory about hostility against Jews. It is of interest here because it served to make the character of hostility against Jews unique. Implied in Freud's *Moses and Monotheism* (1939), developed by Rudolph

M. Loewenstein in 1951, and accepted by Norman Cohn in 1969,[20] the oedipal theory – inevitably distorted in summary – proposes that Christians, (believing or acculturated) identify with Christ the punished Son, associate Jews with the distant, punishing Father of the Old Testament, and hate Jews as father figures (disguised as sibling rivals) and ideal targets for the displacement of hostility resulting from personal failure to resolve the oedipal situation. If the oedipal theory had what some might consider the advantage of making hostility against Jews unique, it was not accepted by most psychologically oriented investigators because diagnosed oedipal conflicts also correlated with prejudice against blacks, and because no single psychological diagnosis correlated with all instances of prejudice.

All psychological explanations did, however, rely heavily on the Freudian concept of displaced aggression, the displacement of hostility or projection of guilt onto a socially provided target, a scapegoat; and that displacement was interpreted as a sign of some psychic weakness or mental ill-health. While this explanation was developed to explain the most manifestly hostile, it was also applied in weakened form to explain the far greater numbers of people who were not patently neurotic or psychopathic and were only mildly hostile toward Jews and blacks. Because of some personal weakness, these people felt a need to conform closely to the values of their own group and to reject outgroups.

This early conception of "ethnic prejudice" presented it as something psychologically and socially abormal, as the expression of psychopathological, authoritarian personalities, as a reflection of individual psychological problems. And just as Auschwitz could not be explained by any real threat Jews had posed to Germans, so this conception sharply distinguished ethnic prejudice from "normal" or "rational" hostility occasioned by real differences in values and real competition for scarce goods. The early school also insisted that prejudice might be directed against any culturally distinguishable outgroup, not just against those labelled as races.

Since 1954, work on "prejudice" has concentrated heavily on the most pervasive hostility in American society, that against blacks, in part because of black militancy. And it may be no accident that, when looking primarily at themselves rather than at Germans, American social scientists have focussed primarily on the mass of the moderately hostile, have stressed the normality of "prejudice" under prevailing conditions, and have explained

---

[20] Rudolph M. Loewenstein, *Christians and Jews*, New York, 1951; Norman Cohn, *Warrant for Genocide*, New York, 1969. In the revised edition of his book, Chicago, 1981, Cohn has abandoned this explanation.

it, not as irrationality, but primarily as a failure of socially organized learning. While recognizing that general psychological factors such as anxiety can affect learning in general, this optimistic school has deemphasized the role of psychopathology – of displacement, projection, and scapegoating – in favour of an analysis of something which could be reorganized by social planning, the social conditioning of learning. While this school has continued to use a *cognitive definition* of prejudice, it has also given a *cognitive explanation* of how faulty generalizations are acquired.

Milton Rokeach, for example, argued that people were intolerant of Jews and blacks because the hostile persons "knew" that Jews or blacks had different values from their own. They believed so because, as a result of institutionalized discrimination or ghettoization, Jews and blacks were kept at a distance and socially presented as symbols of discongruent values. But if the hostile persons could only learn that individual Jews or blacks in fact shared some of their fundamental values, hostility would diminish sharply, and these outgroup members would seem preferable to members of their ingroup who disagreed about these values. If only they could meet, some of the best friends of these hostile persons would be Jews or blacks. Thus, although Rokeach asserts that general anxiety leads some people to be dogmatic, to use their belief systems as a defence mechanism and close their minds to alternative possibilities, what he analyzes primarily is cognitive behaviour, social learning, leaving the whole question, for example, of why there was institutionalized discrimination against Jews and blacks out of consideration.

The tendency toward a purely cognitive explanation becomes marked in *The Tenacity of Prejudice* by Gertrude J. Selznick and Stephen Steinberg.[21] According to them, individual psychopathology plays no significant role in most people's acceptance of anti-Jewish and anti-black stereotypes. The single factor that correlates most clearly with routine "prejudice" in America – and with ignorance of democratic norms – is lack of a genuine education in the social sciences and humanities, in other words, a failure of social training of cognitive abilities. And in recent work on aggression in general,[22] not only is there almost no concern with "prejudice", but psychopathological explanations of aggression are almost completely neglected or rejected, and aggression is explained by social modelling, by observation of the rewards and punishments of imitating the conduct of others. Hence prejudice is but one aspect of learned behaviour.

---

[21] Gertrude J. Selznick and Stephen Steinberg, *The Tenacity of Prejudice*, New York, 1969.
[22] *E. g.*, Albert Bandura, *Aggression*, Englewood Cliffs, N.J., 1973.

Thus, in contrast to earlier work, recent analyses of "prejudice" emphasize cognitive explanations of cognitive behaviour over psychopathological explanations; they concentrate their attention on "normal" patterns of hostility; and they explain the "normality" of "prejudice". Yet part of the phenomenon escapes them. Rokeach admitted that, in different investigations, between two and twenty percent of his subjects responded primarily to racial or ethnic identifications, not to beliefs, and he wondered why these people responded so differently from the bulk of his subjects. Similarly, Selznick and Steinberg acknowledge that individual psychopathology, not educational deprivation, may explain the rabidly hostile who create and disseminate prejudiced stereotypes.

There are clearly two broad conceptions of "prejudice" in the work of social scientists. The earlier school viewed prejudice in terms of the beliefs and conduct of a distinct minority of the population composed of markedly psychopathological people who actively created and sustained negative, faulty beliefs about outgroups, whereas later work has viewed prejudice as the beliefs and conduct of the much larger group of social conformists who readily learn and accept the socially provided negative stereotypes.

If both schools seem to be talking about the same phenomenon, "prejudice," that is because both have used similar questionnaires or other devices for self-reporting. The items in these instruments are designed to elicit reactions to assertions that liberal social scientists, Jews, and blacks have considered to be indicative of prejudice; and the items range from the most flagrant errors and the most vehement advocacy of discriminatory policies to assertions whose evaluation is much more judgmental. Both the abnormally hostile and mere conformists will assent to many or most of these items so that the line drawn between the psychopathological and the conformists – and even those who view the outgroup objectively but disagree on values or goals – will be purely statistical. While these techniques make it possible to demonstrate that there is a continuum from highly hostile to highly favourable attitudes, they do not distinguish between different kinds of hostility, between psychopathological, conformist, and realistic hostility.

Both schools, therefore, face certain problems. Although they provide two different kinds of explanation for "prejudice", so that their findings taken together do suggest two – or three – different kinds of hostility, they cannot distinguish between the two because both schools use the same cognitive criterion to define assertions as prejudice or stereotypic. In the second place, if there is indeed a difference between psychopathologically prejudiced persons and mere conformists, these schools have not explained the dynamic relation between them; they have not shown how the assertions and the conduct of each have affected the other. And thirdly, they have provided no such dynamic explanation because they have only examined "prejudice" horizontally or synchronically: they have only examined carefully people in contemporary societies in which the stereotypes are already deeply rooted in the culture. Lacking a strong historical foundation, they cannot explain, other than by very superficial references to history, how the negative stereotypes became so culturally rooted or why particular groups became primary targets for prejudice.

Despite these problems, the work of both schools represents a huge advance in systematic analysis of a wide range of attitudes toward groups, and it has posed the problems which must be overcome if there is to be further advance. Intuitively, the distinction between the psychopathologically prejudiced and the social conformists seems highly valid. Moreover, Rokeach's effort to distinguish between the form of thought and the content of specific assertions seems very promising. If only one could find the right handle, one feels that most of the discrete findings would fall into place.

It is perhaps here that an historian's perspective can be helpful for, as we have suggested, a principal problem of the work on prejudice has been the presenticentric and ethnocentric character of the principal standard used to identify instances of "prejudice:" the application of the standard of a modern, highly informed knowledge of group characteristics – often by a member of the outgroup in question – to decide which generalizations are so faulty and rigid as to satisfy the principal defining criterion of prejudice. Yet a knowledge of medieval history, for example, would suggest that many of the fourteenth-century European peasants who believed that Jews committed ritual murder were not psychopathological, that they would have been abnormal if they had not so believed, and that they were not peculiarly dogmatic or conformist given the standards and opportunities of their periods. For it was not they who had initiated the accusation; they merely accepted what the social authorities on whom they relied, who were much better educated, had told them; and they had no way to verify the accusation personally. That insight would suggest that there is a crucial distinction between the content of an assertion and the people who assert it, that an assertion which performs one function for some people may perform a different function for others. If this is so, we should perhaps pay less attention to the grammatical meaning of stereotypes and more to their contextual function.

Directly or by implication, recent definitions of "prejudice" link verbal artifacts (*e. g.*, grammatical assertions made about Jews which modern observers can judge to be true or false regardless of who has uttered them) with the emotional states and physical behaviour of those who uttered them. More than that, study of prejudice has relied primarily on analysis of verbal behaviour in an artificial situation: as has often been observed, research has relied heavily on the technique of selfreporting, on people's responses to the questionnaires and interviews of the researchers. And if only some definitions of prejudice are explicitly based on verbal behaviour (faulty generalizations), almost all are so based implicitly because the phenomena referred to in the definitions (patterns of hostility, discrimination, sets of attitudes) have been established on the basis of verbal behaviour because of the research techniques. Even greater has been the reliance on verbal behaviour out of context in statements about historical prejudice (*e. g.*, the "antisemitism" of Tacitus). Yet it has long been observed with puzzlement or satisfaction that there often seems to be a great difference between what people say about outgroups in an artificial context and what they actually say and do when confronted personally with clearly identifiable members of the outgroup in a normal context.[23]

The difference between what people say in an artificial and a normal context has often been explained by hypothesizing that social norms which oppose discrimination or violence have inhibited people from doing what they would like to have done.[24] Yet whatever the merit of that explanation, it leaves the obvious problem that verbal behaviour as elicited and interpreted by the analysts of prejudice is not a reliable predictor of normal external – to say nothing of internal – behaviour. That failure, I would suggest, is a result of the fact that analysts of "prejudice" have taken verbal behaviour out of context, divided it into fragments, rearranged it, and placed their own interpretation on it.

Verbal communication, the technique humans have developed far beyond any other beings, is our best technique for understanding and empathizing with other people engaged in situations and conduct of any complexity. Yet a dictionary understanding of individual words and a syntactical understanding of phrases and sentences will not enable us to understand a speaker's intention unless we can also recognize the function the speaker wants those sounds to fulfil. And function can only be discov-

---

[23] Richard T. LaPiere, "Attitudes vs. Actions," *Social Forces* 13, 1934, 230-37.
[24] *E. g.*, Gunnar Myrdal, *An American Dilemma*, New York, 1944; Bruno Bettelheim and Morris Janowitz, *Social Change and Prejudice*, New York, 1964.

ered by a recognition of the context or structure within which that verbal behaviour occurs, as Freud, Wittgenstein, and the semioticists have emphatically insisted in very different ways. Moreover, as poetry and William Empson[25] would remind us, apparently declaratory statements may serve more than one function at a time.

If the primary function of verbal behaviour is to communicate with and influence other humans, the primary question to ask about assertions some of whose words refer to outgroups is: what is their function? What is the person who makes the assertion trying, consciously or subconsciously, to communicate? And is that intention realized by the recipient? As soon as we ask these questions, we become aware of a striking and hitherto unrecognized characteristic of many definitions of "prejudice:" they say what prejudiced assertions are *not,* but they do not say what they *are.*[26] To say that assertions are faulty, rigid, inflexible, emotional, and pejorative does not tell us what kind of communication they themselves intrinsically are.

The definitions which follow are an effort to distinguish between assertions referring to outgroups on the basis of their intrinsic structure when viewed in context, and thereby to discover their intended function. The approach resembles that of Rokeach: we will try to distinguish the form of these assertions from their specific content. But we will not examine the form of people's whole belief systems about a variety of subjects; we will analyze only the form of assertions which contain verbal references to outgroups and imply a negative evaluation. And we will not try to define their form by some external criterion such as "dogmatism;" we will try to isolate formal characteristics intrinsic to the assertions – or vehicles of communication – themselves. Then we will interpret the intention or function of assertions with these different formal characteristics.

> Realistic assertions about outgroups are propositions which utilize the information available about an outgroup and are based on the same assumptions about the nature of groups

---

[25] William Empson, *Seven Types of Ambiguity,* 3rd ed. New York, 1955, p. 3: "I propose to use the word in an extended sense, and shall think relevant to my subject any verbal nuance, however slight, which gives room for alternative reactions to the same piece of language."

[26] John Harding, Harold Proshansky, Bernard Kutner, and Isidor Chein, "Prejudice and Ethnic Relations," in Gardner Lindzey and Elliot Aronson (eds.) *The Handbook of Social Psychology,* 2nd ed., vol. 2, Reading, Mass., 1968–69, p. 6: "Consequently, it seems most useful to us to define prejudice as a failure of rationality *or* a failure of justice *or* a failure of human-heartedness in an individual's attitude toward members of another ethnic group."

and the effect of membership on individuals as those used to understand the ingroup and its reference groups and their members.

Xenophobic assertions are propositions which grammatically attribute a socially menacing conduct to an outgroup and all its members but are empirically based only on the conduct of an historical minority of the members; they neglect other, unthreatening, characteristics of the outgroup; and they do not acknowledge that there are great differences between the individuals who compose the outgroup as there are between the individuals who compose the ingroup.

Chimeric assertions are propositions which grammatically attribute with certitude to an outgroup and all its members characteristics which have never been empirically observed.

All three of these kinds of assertions may obviously be used to justify hostility toward an outgroup and discriminatory treatment of it and its members; and when they are so used, we may speak of realistic hostility, xenophobia, and chimeria. It is also obvious that these three kinds of hostility may be expressed by only a few individuals or by many people; and we would therefore say that realistic hostility, xenophobia, and chimeria only become socially significant when they are widespread and influence social policy. For reasons which I hope will become apparent, I would reserve use of the term "antisemitism," if it should be used at all, for socially significant chimeric hostility against Jews.

Let us look at each kind of assertion more carefully. By realistic assertions used to justify hostility I mean little more than that the person who makes them is trying to understand the reality of the outgroup and its members and is using all readily available information and all the conceptual tools that he or she would use to analyze the ingroup, its subgroups, and their individual members. Since groups (including Jews) do have different values and do compete for scarce goods, these assertions may provide the basis for hostile attitudes and actions. But by realistic hostility I mean that an effort to analyze the outgroup and its members objectively without wishful or fearful thinking has preceded the negative evaluation or advocacy of discrimination.

The most obvious characteristic of xenophobic assertions (e. g., "Jews are Christ-killers") is that they equate all people labelled as members of an outgroup with the actions of some members which have been considered a threat to the ingroup. All Jews are the same and do what those Jews did; individual Jews are no more than bearers of the outgroup's characteristics. In this way, the group is presented as the fundamental reality of which its members are no more than expressions. Yet a group of any size such as "the Jews" cannot be tangibly experienced: for centuries no one has been able to encounter "the Jews" as a whole or all individual Jews. The concept of "the Jews" or of any large outgroup is an abstraction. And what xenophobic assertions do is to make the abstraction more real than any individual components.

How then is the abstraction constituted? The characteristics ascribed to it are those ascribed by the ingroup to some members of the outgroup, *e. g.*, to some Jews whose real, observed conduct has been interpreted as a threat to the ingroup. Xenophobic assertions thus fit the "kernel of truth" theory of prejudice; and here it is well to remember that, so long as it was safe to do so, Jews readily asserted that they had killed Christ,[27] and Jews indeed engaged disproportionately in moneylending in the middle ages. Yet if we think of Jews as Christ-killers or moneylenders, it is obvious that these were not the only characteristics of the Jews who were involved in such threatening conduct, much less of Jews who were never involved in those threatening situations. Nor, in those threatening situations, were Jews the only element; very obviously, many more kinds of people and many more factors were involved in producing those situations than some Jews. A xenophobic assertion is neither a genuine effort to provide a realistic description of the outgroup nor a genuine attempt at causal explanation of the threatening situations to which the assertion alludes.

Although, because of its grammatical meaning, an individual xenophobic assertion may appear to be intended as a description of the outgroup, examination of all xenophobic assertions about an outgroup, *e. g.*, "the Jews," indicates that they are far from including, or assuming knowledge of, all that was known about Jews or that might have been inferred about them with certainty. Xenophobic assertions have a different function which becomes obvious when we stop focussing obsessively on the outgroup and examine other obvious properties of these assertions.

An obvious formal feature of these assertions is that they link the abstraction of the outgroup label with another abstraction denoting a social menace, whether a threat from without or an internal weakness of the ingroup, which causes anxiety in the speaker, *e. g.*, "the Jews" with the persecution of Christians, indebtedness, lack of control of scarce goods, national disunity, international peril. A xenophobic assertion affirms the existence of a social peril which can be connected with the existence of the outgroup because some of its members have in fact been involved in the

---

[27] James Parkes, *The Conflict of the Church and the Synagogue*, New York, 1961, pp. 46, 80; Bernhard Blumenkranz, *Juifs et Chrétiens dans le monde occidental 430–1096*, Paris, 1960, pp. 45, 169–71, 269–70.

events considered threatening. Within a xenophobic assertion, the meaning of the outgroup label is supplied and delimited by grammatical connection with some threat, not by the empirical characteristics of the outgroup. The subject of a xenophobic assertion is not the outgroup; it is a felt social menace.

Less obvious but more striking is the fact that there is no mention or implicit recognition of the range of individual variation within the outgroup by a modifying adjective such as "some," even though the person who makes the assertion may be well aware that there are marked differences. Yet all members of the ingroup know from their most immediate experience that it is possible, even inevitable, to discriminate a wide range of individual variation within every group they have ever experienced: within the family and peer groups, at work, in the army – even among their animals, their cattle or dogs. They know that they have never been in or observed any group in which individual variation was not obvious, discussed, and important. Yet the people who make xenophobic assertions refuse or are unable to utilize that fundamental understanding of reality in their assertions. Why?

The reason for the absence of any reference to variation or to inoffensive characteristics of "the Jews" is that xenophobic assertions are not intended to function as empirical descriptions of Jews, and that the abstraction does not refer primarily to Jews. If we look at a set of xenophobic assertions which refer grammatically to an outgroup such as "the Jews," it becomes apparent that these assertions refer to a subset of a larger phenomenon; they draw attention to conditions which are believed to menace the ingroup, but only to those menaces in which some Jews have been noticeably involved. The abstraction "the Jews" does not function to signal descriptive statements about real Jews; it serves as a symbol for the kind of threat; and the outgroup label will not serve as an unambiguous symbol of the danger if individual variations and various positive qualities are attributed to "the Jews."

If we expand our horizon and look at all sets of xenophobic assertions made by an individual about various outgroups, we realize that they embrace most of the social conditions which the individual feels to be a serious menace to himself and to any reference group with which he may unreservedly identify. It then becomes even more obvious that the outgroup labels are employed in these assertions not to signal a description of the outgroups but to identify felt threats. Xenophobes are not talking about real people but about something much more intangible, their sense of danger, of chaos.

Why is there this apparent contradiction between the manifest meaning of these assertions when viewed in isolation and their intended function? At least two interpretations seem possible. The most obvious is that these assertions are made by people who feel threatened but know so little about social conditions, especially the more complicated, that they lack the concepts to deal with them. They try to communicate their alarm and call for help, but they understand so little that they can only point to some concrete actions and some salient real people and use them as symbols of the much broader menace.

In the assertions of such people, the name of the outgroup has a double function. On the one hand, by pointing to one salient example of humans engaged in the menacing conduct, the speaker avoids the necessity of describing the complex menacing condition; on the other hand, because the overgeneralization of the collective term implies that more people are engaged in this menacing conduct than anyone has concretely observed, the collective term serves to symbolize all the people who thus endanger the speaker's community, all the actions and conditions which he does not understand but believes exist. And the more the symbolic sense of the outgroup label dominates, the more a xenophobic assertion becomes a tautological cry of alarm about a complex and ill-understood menace, e. g., the usurers ("the Jews") are undermining society by their usury.

A further interpretation is suggested by the failure to employ the fundamental human awareness of individual variation. Xenophobic assertions may not be just a reaction to an ill-understood menace but also a refusal to try to understand. Many people who are well aware of the complexities of social reality and have considerable information about an outgroup may nonetheless make xenophobic assertions, so that their assertions seem a willful refusal to try and understand. In some instances, of course, informed people make xenophobic assertions which they do not believe in order to inhibit understanding among the people they are addressing, whom they wish to manipulate. But when the assertions are not cynically hypocritical, their function would seem to be to short-circuit any genuine effort on the speaker's part to understand either the outgroup or the menace. Apparently the consciousness of menace is so great that the anxiety provoked makes objective thought impossible even for these relatively well-informed people. They seem to feel so immediately threatened that they are incapable of expending time and energy on indecisive examination of empirical complexities. Instead, they relieve their tension in one of two ways, or both: by inappropriate but immediate action and by repressing consciousness of some of the most deeply threatening causes of the menace.

Although the repression or destruction of members of the outgroup may have little effect on the basic menace, the action of attacking them is nonetheless one immediate way to reduce, at least temporarily, the tensions caused by the menace, both by expending the increased adrenalin, so to speak, in immediate action and by distracting attention from other deeper dimensions of the menace through concentration on immediate practical action. This kind of incitation and action is the weaker of the two forms of scapegoating. Some people, who are linked by their group label to people who have indeed been involved in the menace, are attacked as if their disappearance would end the menace.

But xenophobic assertions and action can also function to repress consciousness of those elements of the menacing condition which cannot be readily manipulated such as the complexity of economic exchange. And, of much greater importance for the maintenance of social identity and cohesion, they can function to inhibit awareness of those elements of the menace whose recognition would weaken belief in the values and unity of the ingroup and undermine the self-esteem of its members, for example, recognition of a discrepancy between the stated values of some or all members of the ingroup and their actual behaviour. Obsessive focussing on very partial, but manipulable and external, components of the menace distracts attention from more intimately threatening aspects, from weaknesses of ingroup organization and similarly menacing conduct of its own members.

According to this interpretation, the xenophobic assertion that "Jews are Christ-killers" reflects awareness that Jesus' death was a consequence of the refusal to believe of most of the people who should have been most able to understand his message, a refusal which undermined and threatened the convictions on which Christians relied for their eternal salvation and on which the Christian community was based. Significantly, that assertion only appeared about 90 C.E. in the fourth gospel when it had finally become clear that most Jews were not going to believe that Jesus was divine and had been resurrected. By asserting that "the Jews" had killed Christ because they were stubbornly blind to truth, Christians were able to avoid any effort to understand the real characteristics of Jews and hence any more penetrating explanation of why some people believed in Christ and others did not, which might have opened the jaws of chaos.[28] Thereby

---

[28] Peter L. Berger, *The Sacred Canopy*, New York, 1969, p. 51: "Every human society is, in the last resort, men banded together in the face of death."

"the Jews" became the symbol of the fundamental and much more complex problem of unbelief in general. The various expressions of the concept of Jewish Christ-killers identified the fundamental menace – that Christ might be only a dead human and that Christian belief was lifeless. And through that xenophobic assertion or expression of alarm, not only was awareness of that most frightening menace repressed, but as accusation the charge enabled many Christians through many centuries to release their tensions or repress their own doubts by attacking Jews.

Viewed in this way, some familiar characteristics of xenophobic assertions become more comprehensible. The typical habit of referring to the outgroup in the singular, to "the Jew" instead of "the Jews," can be seen as a consequence of the fact that the abstraction functions primarily as a symbol of menace and refers only secondarily and syntactically to real humans; and the abstraction can only so function if the plurality of meanings with which "Jews" can be connected is blocked out so that one Jew is identical with all others. That need to repress awareness of individual variation, also explains such familiar xenophobic expressions as "some of my best friends are Jews" or "he is a Jew but . . . ." Since the abstraction "the Jews" has only the remotest connection with the diversity of real Jews, any close relations with individual Jews which do not confirm the sense of menace will force the xenophobe to redefine those individuals as exceptions who do not fit within the abstraction, as not being *real* Jews.

Another characteristic of xenophobes and their assertions is that they seem to contradict themselves. Yet that apparently illogical and psychopathological behaviour becomes understandable when we realize that the abstraction is not used logically and empirically but is intended to symbolize ill-understood and unconnected menaces. If someone says both that the clannish Jews only look after their own and that the pushy Jews are taking over our welfare institutions, it may seem a contradiction, but it permits people to express both the fear that "we are not attractive or impressive enough for those people to want to join us" and the fear that "we are losing control of institutions vital to our well-being." There is only contradiction if we mistake xenophobic assertions for empirical or causal propositions.

We may deal with chimeric assertions much more briefly. We have introduced the neologism, "chimeria," because "prejudice" has such a wide range of meanings in common usage, and because we wish to make a distinction which is not recognized in the social scientists' conception of "ethnic prejudice." The Greek root of chimeria makes it a fitting companion to xenophobia, but, more importantly, the ancient use of chimera to refer to a fabulous monster emphasizes the central characteristic of the phenomenon we wish to distinguish from xenophobia. In contrast to xenophobic assertions, chimeric assertions present fantasies, figments of the imagination, monsters which, although dressed syntactically in the clothes of real humans, have never been seen and are projections of mental processes unconnected with the real people of the outgroup. Chimeric assertions have no "kernel of truth." This is the contrast which distinguishes the hostility that produced Auschwitz from that manifested against Jews in ancient Alexandria.

The clearest example is the assertion that Jews commit ritual murder. Had ritual murder occurred, that conduct would have been so corporeal that it could have been directly observed. But not only do we have no satisfactory evidence that Jews ever – to say nothing of a habit – committed ritual murder; a careful examination of the evidence makes it apparent that those who initiated the accusation had never observed that conduct themselves.[29] Moreover, not only are we sceptical of the assertion; many contemporaries were equally sceptical even though they did not have the benefit of Freudian insights into irrational processes.

A much less obvious example, because it is about an incorporeal quality not susceptible of direct observation and is still widely believed, is the chimeric assertion that blacks are innately inferior in mental potential to whites – an allegation strangely resembling assertions about the mental inferiority of females as compared with males.[30] When we assess this example, it would be well to bear in mind that, until the development of modern historical methods and knowledge, even those who did not believe that Jews habitually committed secret ritual murder could not decisively disprove it. And even now it is impossible to prove that no Jews ever committed a ritualized murder, for it is remarkably difficult to establish the negative proposition that physically possible conduct has never occurred.

In the case of the assertion about blacks, the difficulty of proving or disproving it is even greater because what is alleged is so intangible. We

---

[29] see Gavin I. Langmuir, "Thomas of Monmouth: Detector of Ritual Murder," *Speculum* 59, 1984, pp. 820–46; and "The Knight's Tale of Young Hugh of Lincoln," *Speculum* 47, 1972, pp. 459–82.

[30] The same might be said of assertions about sexual appetite, emotionality, or lack of courage. Since women are not by any biological definition a race and participate in the same culture as males, perhaps nothing is more indicative of the human propensity, even in the most intimate relations, to exploit others who are enduringly different than male xenophobic and chimeric assertions about females. An analysis of male attitudes to women according to the hypotheses presented here would be most interesting.

can observe particular acts or performances in a particular setting, but not "intelligence." Indeed, it seems probable that there is no such single entity or characteristic, but rather different types of mental activities each of which may be more or less developed in each individual. Nor can we observe what is "innate" in a group of individuals.

It has so far been impossible to estimate with any precision the extent to which an individual's mental performance is determined by genetic endowment and what by his or her environment. Even if environmental factors could be held constant in comparisons of individuals, which presently seems impossible, we have no knowledge of how genes are connected with the specific mental activities examined by "intelligence" tests. Specific purely biological information about an individual cannot yield anything but the grossest predictions about an individual's future mental activities, primarily negative assessments of the potential of biologically highly abnormal or physically damaged individuals. To determine an individual's biological potential for any particular mental activity with any precision is, therefore, impossible. And it is even more impossible to predict the mental potential of a group. Not only are the complexities to be considered vastly increased, but what is designated as a group is not stable. No one can predict with whom its present members and their descendants will breed, what conditions the progeny of those unions will face, or how they will react to them.

Since no one thus far has been able to devise any techniques of research based on sound theory that could decide objectively whether there is any difference in the innate mental potential of a group, and since the question itself may be meaningless because based on erroneous reifications of mental ability and of groups, ethnocentric assumptions, and ignorance of biology, any unhesitating assertion that blacks as a group are thus inferior has no kernel of truth and attributes to all blacks a characteristic they have never been observed to possess.[31]

In fact, of course, the accusation against blacks arose without the help of modern biological knowledge and sophisticated techniques of intelligence testing. It initially depended simply on the observation that blacks then could not – or did not want to – perform certain mental and physical acts that were highly valued in white culture. But that observed contrast provided no kernel of truth about innate abilities because it was susceptible of radically different interpretations, depending on the attitude of the interpreters. Many whites, especially Christians who believed that man-

---

[31] See above, n. 3.

kind descended from Adam and Eve, held that the differences were the result of different geographic and historic conditions and would disappear in a common environment; and those who held that view were encouraged by the ability with which blacks were adapting to the radically different and degrading conditions brutally imposed on them by whites, progress which seemed obvious evidence of the mental potential of blacks. Many others were uncertain. All too many whites, however, moved by self-interest, ethnocentrism, and fear, proclaimed that blacks were innately inferior in mental potential to whites. And although that was something they had never observed nor could observe, they asserted it with as much conviction as they did the indisputable fact of the existence of people with darker pigmentation.

Chimeric assertions thus attribute with certitude to outgroups characteristics which have never been empirically observed. Another characteristic of chimeric assertions, which sharply distinguishes them from xenophobic assertions, is that they apply to all real individuals who can somehow be identified as members of the outgroup. Here we may think of the Nuremberg laws and their consequences. Because the fantasy attributes a quality to the outgroup which is unobserved and unobservable – whether because of a conscious conspiracy of secrecy or an unconscious conspiracy of nature – no observable conduct of individual members can prove that they do not have that quality, that they are exceptions. To the contrary, they may be all the more dangerous because their alleged menace is so well camouflaged.

Chimeric assertions come in two types. The examples we have just given are of the stronger and more easily recognizable type in which the fantasy attributes qualities to the outgroup and all its members which they have never demonstrably possessed, and which few if any other people known to the ingroup have been believed to possess. Hence the attribution of these qualities makes the members of the outgroup seem inhuman or subhuman monsters who fall outside the norm of humanity of the ingroup.

The weaker type of chimeric assertions are difficult to detect because they seem similar to xenophobic assertions in that they seem to have some connection, however remote, with observable reality, some "kernel of truth." An example would be the situation in which a badly damaged body was found in a society in which many people committed brutal homicide; and although no evidence whatsoever connected Jews with the crime, they were nonetheless accused. Since there was no verifiable knowledge that any Jews had participated in any way in the menacing occurrence, the assertion would be chimeric. Yet if it was known that Jews had in truth

occassionally killed Christians, the assertion would have a surface plausibility – particularly since it would function to deny that any members of the
ingroup were guilty. So long as one looks at single assertions of this kind
about a specific event, they have an air of plausibility because some Jews
could indeed have committed the crime. But the chimeric nature of the
assertion becomes obvious when such individual assertions are stated as a
generalization: if Jews are present, all brutal murders where the killers are
unknown are committed by Jews.

One reason why such chimeric assertions seem more plausible than
either the stronger form or xenophobic assertions is that when such an
assertion is made about a specific event, it may be hard to distinguish
between the statement as an assertion and the statement as an hypothesis. Since the crime could have been committed by Jews, that could be an
acceptable hypothesis to investigate; yet if their guilt is asserted with
complete conviction without any investigation, it is a chimeric assertion. It
may be difficult to decide whether an assertion is an hypothesis or a
chimeric assertion, but if it is immediately followed by incitation to action
or by action against members of the outgroup, its chimeric nature can be
recognized.

In contrast to xenophobic stereotypes, chimeric assertions use the abstraction of the group label primarily to point to all members of the outgroup. Since the attributed quality is unobservable, its attribution cannot
be contradicted by any observation of differences between individual members. Moreover, since chimeric assertions allege conduct that can be committed by any living member, these assertions function to incite attacks
against any and all members of the outgroup much more directly and forcibly than most xenophobic stereotypes, since the latter often refer to past
conduct and permit exceptions of individuals as not real members of the
outgroup. Chimeric assertions are thus the stronger of the two forms of
scapegoating because of their greater potential for inciting immediate action against present evils by attacking all members of the outgroup, and because the conduct attributed to the scapegoat has no empirical relation to it.

The initial or originating function of chimeric assertions would seem
to be to express the awareness of individual members of the ingroup of a
menace within themselves, their awareness at some psychic level that there
are threatening cracks in their personality between their imagination or impulses and the social values they have internalized, their feeling that they
are not comfortably integrated either with their society or within themselves. Chimeric assertions, I would suggest, function to relieve the resulting tension – the fear or guilt – by expressing its existence openly in a

socially acceptable form, by presenting the interior conflict as a social problem, a struggle between the ingroup and its acknowledged enemies. Thereby, the microcosm of the individual psyche is harmonized with the macrocosm of socially acknowledged realities, the sense of separation from society with its values is diminished, and the individual may obtain social approval for his struggle to support those values against evil. And since, as with xenophobic assertions, the symbolization refers the menace syntactically to manipulable, concrete, external agents, it can serve to release tension temporarily by inciting immediate, if inappropriate, action, and it can distract attention from the real, internal, and more threatening causes and thereby reduce consciousness of their internality.[32]

Since no aspect of the study of prejudice has received more attention from the psychologically minded than the processes of displacement and projection in the individual psyche, there is no need to elaborate this last point. It is worth emphasizing, however, that xenophobic assertions seem to be reactions to ill-understood menaces to social organization, while chimeric assertions seem to be reactions to ill-understood menaces to individual psychic integration, which suggests that xenophobia may be explained largely in terms of social developments, whereas the origin of chimeria is to be sought primarily in individual development.

It may be noted that we have spoken thus far of the verbal or other behaviour of members of the ingroup and said little about the characteristics of members of the outgroup. Yet for xenophobic and chimeric assertions to function, there must be an identifiable outgroup which is believed to be a threat. Although the verbal behaviour we have been examining is not intended to function as an empirical description of outgroups, some awareness of the outgroups existence is necessary for the outgroup label to serve as a symbol of social and personal menace. In the case of xenophobic assertions, it needs to be known that an outgroup exists and that some of its members have been involved in certain conduct that threatened the ingroup; and in the case of chimeric assertions, it is necessary to know that there is a socially and culturally distinguishable outgroup with different values. Moreover, for either kind of assertion to incite to tension-relieving action, there must be humans recognizable as members of the outgroup who can be discriminated against or destroyed.

All this can occur, however, without any of those physiological differences which are so important in racist theories. Despite the general ten-

---

[32] This formulation seems compatible both with psychoanalytic interpretations and with social learning theories.

dency of humans to share scarce goods with as few people as possible and to use any discernible difference, however irrelevant or meaningless, as a line to defend against outsiders, an outgroup is not an aggregation of people with long noses, dark skins, or other physical characteristics. What identifies people originally as members of a group are the social and cultural characteristics which integrate them as a group and make them a social force or resource and a potential threat. And it is on the basis of those characteristics that the informed governing elite of the ingroup will identify and evaluate an external group in order to deal with it realistically. So long as members of the external group do not reside within the society of the ingroup, any physiological distinctiveness of the members is entirely secondary to the political, military, religious, etc., significance of the group.

Yet what may be true of external or international relations becomes less true when members of the outgroup move and live within the society of the ingroup, in other words, when the outgroup is a minority within the society of the ingroup. In this case, not only may social authorities want to be able to identify individual members for police or other purposes, but other members of the ingroup may wish to be able to recognize them in order to avoid them, and those predisposed to incite tension-relieving action by xenophobic or chimeric assertions will need to be able to point to the individuals to be attacked and to use them as symbols of social and personal menace.

Hence, when a subordinated group of socially and culturally distinguishable people within a society is the object of xenophobia and chimeria, there may be pressure to ensure that, in addition to any differences in religion, names, residential patterns, social conduct, and economic and legal status, the individual members shall also be physically distinguishable from members of the ingroup. If, as in the case of blacks in America, a physical difference has always paralleled the social and cultural differences, the physiological difference will simply be increasingly emphasized as a symbol of the other differences. But if, as in the case of Jews, no perception of physiological difference accompanies the original consciousness of cultural and social differences, then the possibility of physical differentiation may be created by commanding the individual members of the outgroup to wear distinguishing clothes or to carry cards of identity or by developing a physiological stereotype based on characteristics which distinguish some members of the outgroup from many members of the ingroup.

In any case, whether individual members are distinguishable by cultural or physiological differences, recognition of their empirical reality will be repressed by the symbolic significance of their label, *i.e.,* the sight of

identifiable Jews will only bring the significance ascribed to "the Jews" to
mind. Real Jews will be selectively perceived by some members of the
ingroup simply as physical symbols of social and personal menace, thereby
completing the confusion between syntax and experience, between symbol
and reality.

✳

The definitions proposed and their interpretation seek to distinguish rather
than to relate three phenomena, and the phenomena are presented in a
temporal vacuum. Yet realistic, xenophobic, and chimeric assertions are
obviously related, and obvious questions remain. What relation, if any, is
there between these three kinds of assertions? How are these assertions
related to the people who utter them and the occasions on which they utter
them? Can the same kind of assertion perform different functions for
different people and at different times? Are some people merely initiators
and some merely bearers?

Most psychological and sociological studies of "prejudice" have attempted to explain why some poeple in contemporary societies are more
prejudiced than others; and they have examined societies in which stereotypes are already deeply imbedded in the culture; yet lacking anything but
the shortest temporal perspective, they have been unable to explain how
the stereotypes got there. Can we now construct a dynamic model, however schematic, to describe how belief in chimeric assertions – in the
inhumanity or subhumanity of some outgroups – developed in a society
from which it was previously absent?

The moment we pose that question, we realize that there is no necessary
relation between xenophobia and chimeria. If we think about European
culture and its extensions outside of Europe from 500 to the present, it is
obvious that many or most Europeans have made frequent xenophobic
assertions about many groups within their society and about most external
societies with which they have come in contact. There is, therefore,
nothing unusual about xenophobic hostility against Jews.

Like every other major group, Jews have unique characteristics, a unique
history, and their own particular goals. It is also true that Jews have
maintained a very distinctive identity for millenia. And since they have for
centuries maintained their identity as a minority within a larger society and
refused, or not been allowed, to assimilate, it is not surprising that the
xenophobia against them has been millenial and often intense. Yet the
endurance and intensity of xenophobic hostility against Jews does not
mean that it has been different in kind – in basic nature and causes – from

xenophobia directed against other major groups, including Jewish xenophobia against other groups. There therefore seems no good reason to
distinguish xenophobic hostility against Jews from that directed against
other groups by giving it a special term, "antisemitism."

"Antisemitism" implies that there has been something peculiar about
hostility against Jews, something more than a matter of duration and
intensity. Of course, for Jews, any hostility against them is of particular
importance just because it is directed against them and their values, but that
is a value judgment, not an objective argument about humanity in general.
Nonetheless, as the Final Solution indicated all too clearly, Jews do seem to
have been the object of an unusual hostility; and provided that we refuse to
regard xenophobia against Jews as peculiar, it can indeed be argued on
objective grounds that Jews have also been the object of an unusual, if not
unique, form of hostility for which a special term may seem in order. In
addition to xenophobic hostility, Jews have been a primary target for
socially significant chimeric hostility.

If we look for chimeric assertions of any frequency which have been
general in European culture, we realize that they have been directed above
all against Jews and blacks, save for those directed for a short period against
the individuals labelled as witches. If xenophobia is so common a human
reaction to outgroups that objectivity is the exception, socially significant
chimeria has neither been continually present nor been directed against
many outgroups and is obviously dependent on peculiar historical circumstances.

If we leave the case of witches aside, then chimeria seems to have been
directed primarily against outgroups whose members, whatever their
other characteristics, have had certain cultural or physiological characteristics which the vast majority of them would not or could not change. These
characteristics, however, only became of fundamental significance to the
ingroup when it desired to exploit the outgroup and was able to do so
decisively. Moreover, socially significant chimeria against Jews and blacks
only emerged after the ingroup had made them almost completely powerless and heavily exploited minorities within the society of the ingroup. It is
also important to notice that while control was initially imposed to permit
one kind of exploitation, once it was firmly established and that kind of
exploitation was well developed, other kinds of exploitation followed.

To deal with these historical characteristics of chimeria and to explain
why only certain outgroups became objects of chimeria and scapegoats *par
excellence* and why they came to be seen as inhuman or subhuman, we need
to introduce the concept of the self-fulfilling prophecy. W. I. Thomas

formulated the invaluable theorem that "if men define situations as real, they are real in their consequences;" and Robert K. Merton then formulated this definition: "The self-fulfilling prophecy is, in the beginning, a *false* definition of the situation evoking new behaviour which makes the originally false conception come *true*."[33] I would like to modify Merton's definition for our purposes as follows: the self-fulfilling prophecy is, in the beginning, a motivated definition of an outgroup as inferior in one fundamental way that is accompanied by treatment which evokes new behaviour in members of the outgroup that seems to corroborate and strengthen the original judgment of inferiority.

This definition assumes that the ingroup's control of the outgroup is sufficiently great so that the members of the outgroup are forced to conform in important ways to the expectations of the ingroup. The operation of the prophecy is directly dependent on the extent to which the ingroup can ensure that, in its transactions with the outgroup, the exchanges will be highly favourable to the ingroup – to paraphrase Michel Crozier's modification of Robert Dahl's definition of power.[34] The greater the ability of the ingroup to exploit members of the outgroup as a group, the more effective the self-fulfilling prophecy. And at its extreme, in the case of powerless and heavily exploited minorities within the ingroup's society, the operation of the prophecy can make it seem true that the drastically exploited outgroup falls outside the ingroup's normative definition of humanity and may be treated accordingly.

The self-fulfilling prophecy can operate decisively in intergroup relations whenever the exchanges are so favourable to one group that members of another are forced to modify basic forms of conduct in order to survive. Yet its effect will vary dramatically depending on the kind of exploitation, the original nature of the exploited group, the form of control which permits the original exploitation, and the relation between the original characteristics of the exploited group and the character of the initial exploitation.

There appear to be two main forms of exploitation, ideate or psychological and material or physical; and they may combine in different patterns. Thus the original, ideate, religious exploitation of Jews by Christians was followed by economic, political, and physical exploitation, whereas the original exploitation of blacks as physical labour was followed by sexual, psychological, and ideological exploitation. It would seem that even if one

---

[33] Robert K. Merton, *Social Theory and Social Structure*, 2nd ed. Glencoe, Ill., 1957, p. 423.
[34] Michel Crozier, *La société bloquée*, Paris, 1970, p. 34.

form of exploitation originally predominates, it leads to the other so that both are combined in the fully developed form. In other cases, however, the ideate and the material are combined in the initial exploitation, or the combination occurs so quickly, that it is difficult to distinguish a single initial basis.

In Japan, people otherwise genetically and culturally indistinguishable from the majority of Japanese were concerned with the slaughter of animal products, activities which were related to the Shinto concept of religious pollution. The introduction of Buddhism and its fusion with Shintoism in the eighth and ninth centuries greatly strengthened the belief in the impurity of those activities and of the people who performed them. Those who engaged in those socially needed but religiously impure activities, the Eta, were exploited both physically and psychologically so that they became a rigidly segregated, endogamous, impoverished caste of untouchables with a subculture of its own. The belief developed among other Japanese that the Eta were foreigners of a different culture and race who had been introduced into Japan; and Japanese continued so to believe long after the abolition of the legal status in 1871, and long after the religous basis had been seriously undermined.[35]

In caste societies in which cultural norms of religious impurity brand groups of occupationally specialized people as pariah outcastes, it may be difficult or impossible to decide whether the original basis of exploitation was economic or religious. Indeed, all exploitation may necessarily have both a material and an ideate dimension, even though we do not have to treat the ideate as always or merely a rationalization of economic relationships. Yet in European culture and its extensions, no socially needed physical or occupational activity, except perhaps sexual intercourse, was considered religiously polluting – although fighting and supplying credit nearly came to be so viewed. And so far as there was an occupational caste sharply defined by the purity-impurity continuum, it was not the lowest classes but the superior caste of the priesthood (and to a much lesser extent the nobility). Religious deviation was, however, considered seriously polluting regardless of occupation. Thus physical exploitation was not directly linked with the concept of religious pollution, and psychological exploitation was not directly linked with occupation. Exploitation could therefore be predominantly psychological in origin without being initially physical (Jews), or predominantly physical in origin without being initially psychological (blacks), however much that might change thereafter.

---

[35] George A. De Vos and Hiroshi Wagatsuma, *Japan's Invisible Race*, Berkeley, Ca., 1967.

Exploitation affected different kinds of outgroups within western societies differently. We may divide exploited groups in western societies into three broad categories. In the first, the people exploited, *e. g.*, peasants, have belonged to the same society and had broadly the same culture, including religion, as their exploiters, in other words, they have been a class within the broadest reference group of the exploiters; and they have been distinguished only by the fact of their exploitation. Any individuals thus exploited who were able to escape the legal and economic constraints of their occupation ceased to be people who could be thus exploited. In this case, the self-fulfilling prophecy operates to maintain but not increase exploitation. It operates to retard exit from the exploited class because the deprival of opportunities available to the exploiters makes the exploited seem inferior in other ways than the character of their occupations. We may think of the exploitation of agricultural or industrial workers which has evoked distinctive behaviour other than occupational and produced a class subculture which marked upwardly mobile members and retarded their access to higher occupations. Yet if an individual can escape that economic and legal status, although cultural lag may retard his or her ascent, it will not mark him or her as a person to be forcibly returned to that original status. Moreover, since downwardly mobile members of superior classes may slip into the exploited class, no sharp line distinguishes the exploiters occupationally and culturally from the exploited. In this case, although the self-fulfilling prophecy affects whole classes of people, it does not determine the fate of their individual members.

In the second category, the people exploited did not originate within the society of the exploiters and therefore differed markedly at the outset in cultural characteristics from the exploiters. Their exploitation was consequently associated with a difference in cultural characteristics which identified the exploited as members of an outgroup in relation to the whole society or the most extensive reference group of the exploiters. Thus both the legal and economic constraints of their exploitation and their marked cultural difference identified individual members as people to be exploited. Individuals who sought to escape that occupational exploitation were therefore culturally recognizable as strangers and as people to be exploited. Yet if their exploitation was not related to particular features of their cultural difference but only to the fact of difference, and if none of the differences were unchangeable, then here also, although the self-fulfilling prophecy operated to maintain the outgroup, to evoke new distinguishing behaviour, and to retard the exit of individuals from the outgroup, it did not operate to increase control, exploitation, and enduring differentiation.

We may think of the slave societies of antiquity and the early middle ages, when captives in war of many different cultures were the main source of the most heavily exploited kind of labour.[36] Exploitation and compelled changes in behaviour were very severe at the outset and then diminished as the exploited abandoned their cultural distinctiveness and gradually merged with the less severely exploited and then the higher classes of the society. Since these societies made slaves out of diverse peoples, including some of their own, the outgroup of slaves had no distinctive common culture, and no single characteristic of cultural difference marked all members of the outgroup and indicated who should be exploited in this fashion. Moreover, no great significance was then attributed to cultural difference in general. Polytheistic tolerance of religious pluralism minimized the importance of religious difference; and at least in Mediterranean Europe, long familiarity with a range of physiological differences which did not clearly parallel lines of exploitation diminished the significance even of physiological differences as independent indicators of who should be exploited.

If slaves were initially considered as legally dead, as dead as their compatriots killed on the battlefield, as things rather than humans, their humanity remained as self-evident as the humanity of the unconquered members with whom slave societies had diplomatic or commercial relations. And since slaves could abandon their original culture and assimilate that of their masters, they were increasingly treated as humans: they acquired some legal protection, were freed, lost more of their cultural distinctiveness, and gradually became indistinguishable. Because none of their distinguishing characteristics were permanent, the exploited lost the signs which independently designated them as people to be thus exploited. In this case, the self-fulfilling prophecy, which had operated in full force at the beginning of the exploitation, only acted thereafter to retard the decrease in exploitation – which nonetheless continued to descrease until the only way to see who should be thus exploited was to see who was in fact being so exploited.

The fate of the third category was very different. Here the people exploited did not originally belong to the same society as the exploiters and hence differed in cultural characteristics. But, in contrast to the mere fact of difference, what identified them as people to be exploited were particular

---

[36] Although, significantly, members of the ingroup might also be punished by being made slaves or given an almost identical status.

characteristics, whether cultural or physiological, peculiar to those particular outgroups; and those characteristics, moreover, were ones which
most members would not or could not change. Even though members of
the outgroup assimilated many of the characteristics of the ingroup culture,
their distinctiveness remained patent. The self-fulfilling prophecy could
therefore operate in full force to produce an increase in distinctive behaviour – and exploitation – for members of such outgroups remained clearly
marked as people to be exploited regardless of where they were found or
what they were doing.

In this case, the self-fulfilling prophecy operates through what I will label
the institutionalization of an outgroup status of fundamental inferiority in
contrast to the institutionalization of a contingent or conditional inferiority
in the case of the first two categories. The prerequisite for the institutionalization of a status of fundamental inferiority is that the original exploitation
of members of the outgroup and the judgment that they are inferior are
directly associated in the minds of members of the ingroup with the
particular and unchanging characteristics which distinguished that outgroup from other outgroups.

Thus early Christians judged that Jews were fundamentally inferior
because of their uniquely informed disbelief in Christ and were therefore to
be exploited to demonstrate the Christian monopoly of saving truth. And
although other peoples had disbelieved and persecuted Christians, this
judgment that Jews were inferior was inextricably associated with the
enduring adherence to Judaism (despite long knowledge of Christianity)
which distinguished Jews – save for those who abandoned Judaism and
association with Jews – from all other populations and all members of the
ingroup. In the case of blacks, the judgment that they were so fundamentally inferior in culture that they could be exploited as physical labour was
inextricably associated with enduring physiological characteristics which
distinguished them – save for some of the offspring of sexual unions with
members of the ingroup – from all other populations and all members of
the ingroup. Hence, so long as the judgment of inferiority and the exploitation continued, individual members of the outgroup could not escape
designation as people who were unchangingly or fundamentally inferior
and should therefore be exploited whenever possible.

For that reason, both exploitation and control of these outgroups could
be maintained and increased to a degree impossible in the case of classes or
polycultural slaves; and the self-fulfilling prophecy could therefore operate
with maximum efficiency. Members of such outgroups could be efficiently
excluded from most social roles of prestige or of significant authority over

members of the ingroup. Consequently, powerless as they were, they were denied the opportunity to demonstrate their potentials and forced to adapt their conduct in basic ways to comply with the demands of the ingroup. Typically excluded from military service, the right to carry arms, or the exercise of political authority, and barred from education, trades, and professions, members of the outgroups had to develop different techniques of self-preservation such as marginal occupations, postures of submissiveness, bribery, flattery, and other forms of ingratiating behaviour, as well as avoidance of responding to violence with violence for fear of merciless reprisals (the *Judenrat* being an extreme example). That adaptation produced not only new genuine characteristics of the outgroups but also new judgments by the ingroup that the outgroups were indeed fundamentally inferior.

Political exclusion, moreover, was accompanied immediately or gradually by economic specialization. When political control of the outgroup was firmly established, members of the outgroup were restricted to one or a few occupations which the ingroup considered inferior or degrading. And since the changing needs of the exploiters, not the original characteristics of the exploited, determined to which inferior but necessary activities the outgroup was assigned, the enforced occupational specialization of the outgroup bore no necessary relation either to the original characteristics of the outgroup or to the original way in which it was exploited.

When the self-fulfilling prophecy had operated to that extent, the institutionalization of a status of fundamental inferiority changed to the institutionalization of a status of essential inferiority, a status considered appropriate to people who were inferior, not in some particular characteristics, but in essence, by nature. The transition occurs when the conduct of an outgroup which had been the basis for the original judgment of inferiority ceases to be the sole or principal justification for exploitation and is seen as merely one major symptom of a much deeper, essential inferiority that can be recognized through its several specific manifestations but is itself too intangible to be observed directly.

As a result of the self-fulfilling prophecy, the outgroups had acquired several new cultural and social characteristics which the ingroup interpreted as further evidence of inferiority. Yet there was no necessary relation between those different forms of conduct save that the ingroup's self-fulfilling prophecy had imposed them on the outgroup. Consequently, the additional "inferior" characteristics of the outgroup could not be understood as an obvious consequence of the original fundamental inferiority; nor, conversely, could the original conduct be seen as the cause of the later inferior conduct – at least not without a damaging evaluation of the ingroup's conduct. Hence both the original voluntary conduct and the later imposed conduct were understood as expressions of, as caused by, a deeper essential inferiority that infected all conduct; and any subsequent indications of inferiority could easily be attributed to that intangible essence. Jews were not inferior because they did not believe and killed Christ; they disbelieved and killed Christ because of their essentially inferior nature which was also manifest in their clannishness, avarice, and cowardice. Blacks were not inferior because of their ignorance of western technology and culture but because of a natural inferiority which was also manifest in their laziness, cowardice, and sexual promiscuity. With the institutionalization of a status of essential inferiority, xenophobic hostility against an outgroup reaches a peak of intensity and opens the way for a new kind of hostility.

The outgroup and its individual members have now become identified and labelled by their enduring, original, distinctive characteristics, by their new adaptive characteristics, by their concentration in demeaning occupations, and by physical segregation. They have also become so powerless that, not only can they not demonstrate their potentials, but they cannot even act so as to disprove totally false ideas about their conduct. Harshly exploited and controlled, surrounded by xenophobic stereotypes which use the outgroup label as a symbol of social menaces, and assigned a status as essentially but intangibly inferior beings, the outgroup and its individual members become ideal targets on which to project chimeric assertions, ideal scapegoats in the strongest sense.

If some individuals in the ingroup now make chimeric assertions, particularly of the weaker form which can be confused with hypotheses about specific events, the grammatical meaning of their assertions will receive a hearing from many xenophobes who are predisposed to believe additional evil about the outgroup which confirms their own feeling that the outgroup is a social menace. But worse, some social authorities with the same outlook may trust those who make chimeric assertions as fellow members of the ingroup and, on the basis of the assumed reliability of their testimony, take official action against members of the outgroup. Some judges may condemn members of the outgroup for specific crimes; and other social authorities, more sceptical but also more cynical, may find it advantageous to support accusations they themselves do not believe or turn a blind eye to unofficial actions such as lynchings. Thereby, the chimeric accusations gain social confirmation and spread more rapidly as rumour. The stage is now set for chimeric assertions of the stronger form about inhuman conduct, about a general conscious conspiracy or an unconscious conspiracy of nature or biology.

Finally, in addition to the already socially significant xenophobia and chimeric rumours, both kinds of chimeric accusations come to be used in literature, art, and other cultural media, where their function of symbolizing social and psychic menace makes them peculiarly valuable. Thereby, they become deeply rooted in the culture, an almost unavoidable element in social indoctrination, and an influence on social policy. The essential inferiority produced by the self-fulfilling prophecy has acquired monstrous lineaments. The monster may in fact be a combination of the chinks in the social armour protecting the members of the ingroup and of the psychic cleavages within individual members, but for many in the ingroup those threatening fissures leading from cosmos to chaos will have been reassuringly located, localized, externalized, and concretized so that they may be attacked directly, immediately, and brutally.

Chimeria has become socially significant. However personal and individual in origin, chimeric assertions are now widely accepted and affect social policy. Yet it is crucial to recognize that the existence of socially significant chimeria does not mean either that all members of the ingroup believe the chimeric assertions or that all those who do believe them use them to perform the same function that they perform for those who initiated them or for those who accept and propagate them as originally intended. Precisely because of the discrepancy between what a chimeric assertion means manifestly according to common language and what those who originate them are trying to communicate, chimeric assertions can function differently and have different psychological implications for different people.

Once the self-fulfilling prophecy about outgroups with enduring characteristics has produced the institutionalization of a status of essential inferiority, with its inevitable accompaniment of widespread xenophobia, xenophobes can listen to the assertions invented by people prone to chimeria and reinterpret them to serve their own needs. Unable themselves to verify whether some members of the outgroup have indeed been observed to display the chimerically asserted conduct, many xenophobes will take in the manifest grammatical meaning of chimeric assertions, accept them on social authority as empirically valid, and repeat and use them as xenophobic assertions, so that they now function to express what xenophobes feel as social, not personal psychic, menaces. That duality of function of chimeric assertions is the reason why modern questionnaires which rely on the artificial technique of self-reporting are poor indicators of psycholog-

ical differences. Poor, but not completely inefficacious, because the xenophobes most likely to believe chimeric associations readily will be those
whose individual psychology makes them resonate unconsciously to the
latent, primary function of chimeric assertions.

                                    *

The need to define antisemitism and the definition toward which I have
been moving should now be clear. Taken literally, "antisemitism" is most
misleading and thoroughly contaminated with the erroneous presuppositions of the racists. I have sought to demonstrate that neither the theories of
"racism" nor those of "ethnic prejudice" enable us to distinguish what has
been unusual about some hostility toward Jews. Yet "antisemitism" is still
used, as it was by racists, to refer to any hostility at any time against Jews
collectively, and to imply that there has always been something special
about that hostility. That usage depends on a value judgment about Jews
but is no longer based on any theory which would distinguish the quality
of hostility against Jews from that directed against all other major groups –
including hostility expressed by Jews against others. Objectively, it is
therefore meaningless or platitudinous. If it is to have any importance for
objective thought, not merely for feeling and political rhetoric, it must be
demonstrated that Jews have in fact been the object of a kind of hostility
different from that which all major groups confront.

   The theory I have advanced does identify an unusual quality of hostility toward Jews: there has been socially significant chimeric hostility, the
acceptance by large numbers of relatively normal people of beliefs that
attribute to Jews characteristics and conduct that have never in fact been
observed or empirically verified. If "antisemitism" is meant to refer to an
unusual hostility against Jews, then that hostility can be termed "antisemitism." It might be argued that since socially significant chimeria has not been
directed only against Jews, there is no reason to give it a special name when
directed against Jews. Nonetheless, socially significant chimeria is an ab-
erration that has seriously affected very few groups but has afflicted them
terribly. The use of a special name to designate the peculiarly horrifying
example which marked European culture for seven centuries and killed
millions of victims during the Final Solution therefore seems justifiable.[37]

---

[37] For a sketch of the historical formation of antisemitism which uses the concepts developed
    here and explains why I place the emergence of antisemitism in the thirteenth century, see
    my "Qu'est-ce que 'les Juifs' signifiaient pour la société médiévale?" in Léon Poliakov
    (ed.), Ni Juif ni Grec, Paris, 1978, pp. 179–90 or "Medieval Antisemitism," in Henry

Yet if we continue to use that literally most misleading term, we, as social scientists, should free "antisemitism" from its racist, ethnocentric, or religious implications and use it only for what has been, objectively, an unusual kind of human hostility directed against Jews. And if we do so, we may then be able to distinguish more accurately between two very different kinds of threats to Jews. On the one hand, there are situations in which Jews, like any other major group, were or are confronted with realistic hostility, or with that well-nigh universal xenophobic hostility which uses the real conduct of some members of an outgroup to symbolize a social menace. On the other hand, there were or may still be those situations in which Jewish existence has been or is much more seriously endangered because real Jews have been converted in the minds of many into a symbol that denies their empirical reality and justifies their total elimination from the earth.

Friedlander and Sybil Milton (eds.), *The Holocaust: Ideology, Bureaucracy, and Genocide*, Millwood, N. Y., 1980, pp. 27–36.

ROBERT WUTHNOW

Anti-Semitism and Stereotyping*

In the years during and immediately following Hitler's dictatorship in Europe, the problem of anti-Semitism seemed both obvious and important to students of human behavior.

A second reason for acquiring an understanding of anti-Semitism is that it has occupied an important place in the history of modern culture. It can even be argued that a full understanding of the nature of Western civilization requires some familiarity with the role that anti-Semitism has played in the development of this civilization. History also shows that anti-Semitism has been subject to recurrent cycles of ebb and flow. Because it currently appears to be neither particularly visible nor virulent, it cannot be assumed that anti-Semitism is strictly a problem of the past that will not erupt again in America or in some other part of the world.

Finally, there is substantial evidence that anti-Semitism continues to be characteristic of at least a sizable minority of the American public. The time-worn stereotypes that have served as rationalizations for discrimination and hostility toward Jews over the centuries have by no means been eradicated. As we shall see presently, the most recent studies show that there are still many Americans who cling to these traditional stereotypes and who overtly express negative feelings about Jews. These attitudes and feelings generally have not resulted in blatant aggression.

For each of these reasons it is useful to understand the nature and causes of contemporary anti-Semitism. This chapter reviews evidence on the extent and nature of contemporary anti-Semitism in America, indicates what the trends in anti-Semitism have been in recent years, identifies those sectors of the population that are most likely to register anti-Semitic attitudes and feelings, discusses the main theories that have been offered to explain why people cling to anti-Semitic beliefs, and briefly considers some of the proposals that have been suggested for combating anti-Semitism.

---

* From: Arthur G. Miller (ed.), *In the Eye of the Beholder*, Praeger New York, 1982, pp. 137–187, abridged.

Recent Trends in Attitudes Toward Jews

Some perspective on contemporary attitudes toward Jews can be gained by comparing them with evidence from earlier surveys and polls. Information from national polls, although of varying comparability, has been available since the advent of public opinion polling in the late 1930s. This material affords some assessments of trends in attitudes toward Jews over a period of four decades.

It will simplify the examination of these trends if the period for which evidence is available is divided into two parts: from the late 1930s until the early 1960s, and from the early 1960s to the present. Trends in attitudes toward Jews during the first period were relatively unambiguous, and have been discussed in detail in Charles Herbert Stember's book *Jews in the Mind of America*.[1] The trends during the second period are less clear, and require a more careful examination of what the polls have shown.

The First Period: Trends Through the Early 1960s

Because of the events in Europe, a number of public opinion surveys in the United States conducted between 1938 and the end of World War II included questions aimed at measuring public attitudes toward Jews. In 1962, Stember replicated many of these earlier questions in a national survey, making it possible to examine any changes that might have occured. As shown in Table 4.8, the comparisons revealed that a consistent and dramatic reduction in negative attitudes and feelings about Jews had taken place.

In the late 1930s close to 50 percent of the public felt that Jews had too much power in the United States, but by the early 1960s this figure had dropped 30 percentage points. In the earlier period nearly a quarter of the public suspected Jews of controlling finance. By the latter date hardly anyone held this view. As to Jewish loyalty, questions were not asked, as they have been more recently, about Jewish ties with Israel, but some efforts were made to determine whether the public believed Jews to be involved in international conspiracies of a radical or Communist nature. This view had been widely disseminated in Nazi propaganda, and occasionally had been advanced by the media in the United States in connection with several highly publicized conspiracy cases. In the late 1930s about a fourth of the public held this view of Jews. By the early 1960s these attitudes had not disappeared entirely, but hardly anyone still believed that Jews were a threat to the country, and fewer than one in five thought Jews were more involved in radical politics than non-Jews.

---

[1] New York, 1966.

Table 4.8
Trends in Attitudes Toward Jews, 1938–1962

	Percent
Jewish power	
Do you think Jews have too much power in the United States? (percent "yes")	
1938–1946 (average of 14 polls)	47
1962	17
Jews have too much power in finance.	
1938–1944 (average of 4 polls)	21
1962	3
Jewish loyalty	
In your opinion, what nationality, religious or racial groups in this country are a menace to America? ("Jews")	
1940–1946 (average of 9 polls)	19
1962	1
Do you think Jews tend to be more radical in polities than other people?	
1938–1940 (average of 6 polls)	28
1962	17
Stereotypes and feelings	
Percent who said Jews have objectionable qualities	
1940	63
1962	22
Percent who regarded Jews as a race	
1946	42
1962	23
Jewish businessmen are less honest than other businessmen	
1938–1939 (average of 4 polls)	46
1962	18
Discriminatory attitudes	
Would you vote for a Jew for president who was well qualified for the position? (percent "yes")	
1937	49
1959	72
If a candidate for Congress should declare himself as being against the Jews, would this influence you to vote for him or to vote against him? (against)	
1945	31
1964 (Selznick & Steinberg)	58
I definitely would not marry a Jew	
1950	57
1962	37
Percent saying it would make a difference to them if a prospective employee were Jewish	
1940	43
1962	6

Source: Adapted form *Jews in the Mind of America* by Charles Herbert Stember, tables on pp. 50–209. © 1966 by the American Jewish Committee. Published by Basic Books, Inc., New York. Reprinted by permission.

Equally dramatic declines in anti-Semitism between the late 1930s and early 1960s were evidenced in data on stereotypes and negative feelings. For example, a survey in 1940 showed that nearly two-thirds of the sample mentioned characteristics of Jews that were regarded as objectionable. In the 1962 poll, by comparison, only 22 percent mentioned objectionable qualities. A replication of an earlier question asking about the honesty of Jewish businessmen also demonstrated a dramatic shift in the proportion of the public subscribing to this view, from nearly half to less than one-fifth.

Stember's comparisons also show consistent reductions in the proportion of the public favoring discriminatory attitudes toward Jews. For example, the proportion of the public saying it would vote for someone who was Jewish for president increased from about half to nearly three-quarters. Increases also occured in the number of people who said they would vote against someone who was a self-declared anti-Semite. Other questions having to do with intermarriage, employment, housing, and college admissions also showed declining support for discrimination. While the proportion disapproving of intermarriage between Jews and non-Jews was still sizable, support for discrimination in hiring, housing, and college admissions had shrunk virtually to nothing.

The Second Period: Trends Since the Early 1960s

The trend in attitudes and feelings toward Jews since the early 1960s are more difficult to assess. In part this is because no survey such as Stember's has been done to replicate earlier polls exactly and, thereby, to provide reliable indicators of trends. A number of polls have asked questions about attitudes toward Jews, but often the wording of the questions is sufficiently different to make precise comparisons impossible. The other difficulty is that even the most reliable evidence does not point uniformly toward a single trend, as did the data for the period prior to the 1960s. Table 4.9 summarizes the results of questions asked since the early 1960s that give some basis for drawing inferences about trends in attitudes toward Jews.

The issue of Jewish power has been raised in at least seven polls since 1962. The wording of the questions has varied, from ones that ask straightforwardly whether people think Jews have too much power in the United States to ones that ask whether various groups have too much, too little, or about the right amount of power. Even those that have been worded exactly the same do not yield estimates of trends that are beyond dispute. For example, the 1962 and 1964 questions were worded identically, yet the results suggest that a dramatic reduction in negative sentiment somehow took place during this two-year period. The 1975 and 1976 Yankelovich questions were also worded identically but show widely differing results. Some caution must be exercised, therefore, in drawing inferences about trends.

The results seem to indicate the following: if anything, there was a modest *increase* in the proportion of the public that felt Jews have too much power between the early 1960s and the mid-1970s. This conclusion is evident from comparing the 1962/64 results with the Yankelovich results of the mid-1970s (these are the questions that were worded most comparably). Allowing for the fact that the Yankelovich figures may have been inflated by virtue of having been obtained from a question that also asked about the power of a number of groups other than Jews, the differences suggest a significant increase between the earlier and the later years. The average of the 1962 and 1964 figures is 14 percent, while the average of the 1975 and 1976 figures is 32 percent. The CPS figures are from differently worded questions. They indicate that absolute levels of negative sentiment about Jewish power may not have been as high as the Yankelovich figures would suggest. But these figures also indicate a relative increase in anti-Jewish sentiment for the period 1972–1976 (from 13 percent to 17 percent). Even a comparison between the 1976 CPS figure and the average of the 1962/64 figures suggests a modest rise in negative sentiment (from 14 percent to 17 percent).

The main finding that does not support the idea of an increase is the 1978 Response Analysis figure. It is possible that suspicion of Jewish power declined substantially between 1976 and 1978. But a more likely explanation of the discrepancy between the 1978 and the 1976 figures concerns the Response Analysis survey itself. Whereas the other surveys were drawn from carefully designed samples of the U.S. population, the Response Analysis study was drawn from telephone directories and conducted by telephone without the usual attempts to reach nonrespondents. It is quite likely, in other words, that the study contained sampling biases. More important, it was done shortly after the telecast of "Holocaust" and most of the questions asked were about the Holocaust. The question about Jewish power (which followed these other questions) probably elicited fewer negative responses than it might have under other conditions.

If the balance of evidence on attitudes toward Jewish power points to an upward trend in negative sentiment, the same cannot be said about attitudes toward Jewish loyalty. Here the evidence is remarkable for the stability it reveals. Both in 1964 and in various studies conducted between 1974 and 1978, the proportion agreeing that Jews are more loyal to Israel than to the United States has stood at about 30 percent. The reason this

Table 4.9
Trends in Attitudes Toward Jews, 1962–78

	Percent
Jewish power	
Do you think Jews have too much power (influence) in the United States? (percent "yes")	
1962 (Stember)	17
1964 (Selznick & Steinberg, 1969)	11
1972 (CPS)	13
1975 (Yankelovich)	37
1976 (Yankelovich)	26
1976 (CPS)	17
1978 (Response Analysis)	12
Jewish loyalty	
Jews are more loyal to Israel than to the United States. (percent "yes")	
1964 (Selznick & Steinberg)	30
1974 (Harris)	33
1974–1976 (average of 5 Yankelovich polls)	29
1976 (Harris)	30
1978 (Harris)	29
Stereotypes	
Jews have objectionable qualities. (percent "yes")	
1962 (Stember)	22
1974 (Harris)	31
Jewish businessmen are not as honest as other businessmen. (percent "yes")	
1962 (Stember)	18
1964 (Selznick & Steinberg, 1969)	28
1974 (Harris)	18
Feelings	
"Feeling thermometer" scores indicating dislike	
1964 (CPS)	9
1968 (CPS)	8
1972 (CPS)	5
1976 (CPS)	10
Discriminatory attitudes	
Would vote for a Jew for President	
1967 (Gallup)	82
1978 (Gallup)	82
Do you approve or disapprove of marriage between Jews and non-Jews? (percent approving)	
1968 (Gallup)	59
1972 (Gallup)	67
1978 (Gallup)	69

stability seems remarkable is that attitudes toward Israel itself have fluctuated dramatically with changing political conditions in the Middle East. The two facts taken together suggest that views of Jewish loyalty may be only weakly associated with opinions of Israel.

Information on other stereotypes has been less abundant than might be expected. Two questions that provide comparisons over time are Stember's 1962[2] question about objectionable qualities of Jews and Harris's similarly worded question in 1974.[3] Judging strictly by the percentages mentioning negative qualities, it appears that there may have been an increase in negative stereotyping. But care must be exercised in drawing this conclusion, because the two questions were not worded exactly the same. Nor is it clear how much the responses may have been affected by interviewer probing or related questions. A comparison of the specific kinds of qualites mentioned (such as aggressiveness and clannishness) suggests that the content of anti-Jewish stereotyping may have remained much the same. The evidence, therefore, gives no indication that volunteered stereotypes have declined or become less negative since the early 1960s, but it is difficult to know with certainty whether they have become more negative, as the data may suggest at first glance.

The only stereotype question that was worded exactly the same in two studies is the one about Jewish businessmen being less honest than other businessmen. In both the Selznick and Steinberg study in 1964[4] and the Harris study in 1974,[5] respondents expressed this stereotype by disagreeing with a statement denying any differences between the ethics of Jewish businessmen and other businessmen. The results indicate a substantial decline in the proportions disagreeing. The Stember study in 1962 included a related question that asked people whether they thought Jewish businessmen were "more honest or less honest" than other businessmen, and found fewer who thought they were less honest than in the Selznick and Steinberg study. But even the Stember figure suggests that there has, at least, been no increase in the prevalence of this stereotype.

The evidence on trends in feelings toward Jews presents an interesting contrast to the trends in stereotypes. This evidence is limited to that obtained from the CPS national election survey's "feeling thermometer."

---

[2] op. cit.

[3] Louis Harris and Associates, Inc., *A Study of Attitudes Toward Racial and Religious Minorities and Toward Women*, National Conference of Christians and Jews, New York, 1978.

[4] Gertrude J. Selznick and Stephen Steinberg, *The Tenacity of Prejudice*, New York, 1969.

[5] op. cit.

The data show that the proportions of the public who said they disliked Jews declined between 1964 and 1972. But between 1972 and 1976 these proportions increased, such that the percentage expressing dislike for Jews in 1976 was even somewhat higher than it had been in 1964.

A more detailed examination of these changes (see Figure 4.1) shows that there was also a substantial decline between 1972 and 1976 in the frequency of positive feelings toward Jews. This proportion was smaller in 1976 than it had been in 1964. The largest increase between 1972 and 1976 was in the proportion expressing no feelings toward Jews either way.

What may have caused this shift in feelings between 1972 and 1976 is a question that needs to be addressed in further research. The shift itself must be treated with some caution, however, since it is based on responses to a single survey question.

Overall, judging from the various sorts of available evidence, it appears that the 1960s marked a continuation of earlier trends away from negative attitudes and feelings about Jews. The two exceptions to these trends appear to have been an increase in negative sentiments about Jewish power

Figure 4.1

"Feeling Thermometer" Ratings of Jews, 1964–76

(national sample, age 21 and over, non-Jews only)

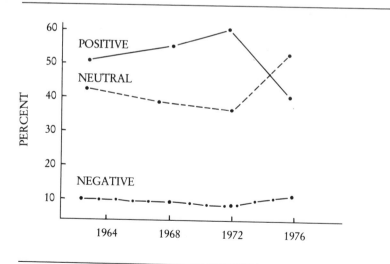

Source: Adapted from Center for Political Studies. National Election Surveys 1964–1976, University of Michigan.

and relative constancy in attitudes about Jewish loyalty toward Israel. But specific stereotypes, general feelings, and discriminatory attitudes all appeared to decline as far as negative sentiments were concerned. The trends during the 1970s suggest that anti-Semitic feelings may no longer be on the decline, and may have increased. Discriminatory attitudes and opinions of Jewish loyalty appear to have remained about the same during the 1970s, while opinions of Jewish power and feelings about Jews appear to be tinged with more suspicion and dislike at the end of the 1970s than they were in the early 1970s.

Summary

It is too soon to determine whether the trends in attitudes toward Jews during the 1970s represent something appreciably new or simply the culmination of longer-range trends. The longer-range trends are easier to evaluate. Since the late 1930s there has been a dramatic reorientation of public opinion toward Jews. Perhaps the best way of summarizing the force of this reorientation is to compare three composite profiles of public opinion toward Jews – in the late 1930s, in the early 1960s, and in the late 1970s.

In the late 1930s there were many who manifested no hostility or prejudice toward Jews. But at most they represented only about half the American public. The other half opposed hiring Jewish employees, thought Jewish businessmen were dishonest, regarded Jews as having too much power, said they would not vote for a Jew for president, and considered the persecution Jews were experiencing in Europe as being their own fault. Up to two-thirds of the public were against allowing more Jewish exiles to emigrate to America, said they would object to their son or daughter marrying a Jew, and regarded Jews as having objectionable traits. One in every five Americans considered Jews a menace to American society. About one-fourth expected there would be a widespread campaign against Jews in the United States; one in eight said they would support such a campaign.

By the early 1960s the picture had altered considerably. The dominant view was now one of tolerance rather than bigotry. Only one-third said they would object to marrying a Jew, and less than one-fourth thought Jews were dishonest, had objectionable traits, or had too much power. Virtually no one supported discrimination against Jews as far as housing, hiring, or college admissions was concerned, and hardly anyone still held the view that Jews were a menace to society. The only negative stereotypes that still received acceptance by large minorities of the public had to do with Jewish aggressiveness and clannishness.

As of the mid-1970s to late-1970s, public attitudes toward Jews continued to be overwhelmingly favorable in comparison with the attitudes of several decades before. Whereas the majority view during World War II had been to regard Jews as a race that had brought persecution on itself, the vast majority in the 1970s were aware of the history of Jewish persecution and only a few blamed it on the Jews themselves. The majority also regarded Jews as being honest, philanthropic, talented, and intelligent. Only about one-fourth of the public held negative attitudes about Jewish clannishness and Jewish aggressiveness. Over 80 percent said they would vote for someone who was Jewish for president, if that person was qualified. The core of consistently negative opinion and overt dislike toward Jews had shrunk to only about 10 percent of the population. Still, there were larger numbers – between one in four and one in three – who questioned the power and loyalty of Jews, who disapproved of intermarriage between Jews and non-Jews, and who subscribed to mildly negative stereotypes about Jews.

The Question of Interpretation

Once the factual evidence on trends and contemporary attitudes and feelings toward Jews has been considered, difficult questions of interpretation remain. First, there is the question of truth content. If a large number of Jews say they would support Israel even if this meant opposing U.S. policy, does saying that Jews are more loyal to Israel than to the United States necessarily constitute anti-Semitism? Or is it anti-Semitic to say that Jews are clannish when historically their very survival has required their sticking together? Consider the following. A study of prejudice among high school students in several schools containing large numbers of Jewish students found that non-Jewish students tended to regard their Jewish counterparts as clannish. But the study also found that Jewish students were indeed more likely to associate with Jews than with non-Jews, and that their parents put pressure on them to date Jews rather than non-Jews (as did Christians' parents to date Christians; Glock et al., 1975[6]). Were the non-Jewish students responding to fact or displaying prejudice?

An argument used frequently in justification of considering attitudes like the above as signs of anti-Semitism is to say that these attitudes are stereotypes. A stereotype is an overgeneralization that attributes to an entire group characteristics that may be true only of some of its members.

---

[6] Charles Y. Glock, et. al., *Adolescent Prejudice*, New York, 1975.

To say that "Jews" are clannish fails to recognize that some are and some aren't. To say that "Jews" are more loyal to Israel than to the United States denies the fact that a majority may be more loyal to the United States than to Israel, or may hold dual loyalties. Frequently stereotypic thinking develops in the absence of true information. One hears an anecdote about Jews being clannish or disloyal, and jumps to the conclusion that all Jews are this way. Evidence to the contrary may be dismissed as the exception proving the rule.

Unfortunately, the kind of evidence supplied by public opinion polls is seldom detailed enough to tell whether a person is genuinely manifesting stereotypic thinking by subscribing to a statement about Jews. Faced with the choice of having to agree or disagree with a statement about Jews (such as "Jews are more loyal to Israel than to the United States"), a person who knows that *some* Jews are like this may agree rather than imply by disagreeing that *no* Jews are like this (or earn the interviewer's displeasure by refusing to answer). What such a person means to say is that there is a probability of Jews being as the statement says, and, although this probability may not be high, it is perhaps higher than among non-Jews. Survey questions seldom provide for this degree of complexity. If the statement in question contains an element of truth, respondents are forced to deny this element of truth in order to avoid appearing prejudiced.

It is also the case, though, that the kinds of statements used to measure prejudice are typically more than mere probabilistic statements of fact. Usually they reflect an extreme view or one with clearly negative connotations. For example, the statement that Jews are more loyal to Israel than to the United States carries deeper connotations than one that merely describes Jews as willing to support Israel in opposition to official U. S. policy. Some of the survey questions typically employed also ask for evaluations to be made, rather than for mere agreement or disagreement (for example, Jews having *too much* power or *disapproving* of intermarriage with Jews). Questions phrased in these ways presumably tap into sentiments that are genuinely anti-Semitic. Yet there is no guarantee that even such questions provide infallible indicators of anti-Semitism.

Because any single survey question is likely to fall short of capturing the complexity of the public's views, careful studies of prejudice have generally been on scales that combine responses to a number of questions to measure anti-Semitism. In their study *The Tenacity of Prejudice,*[7] for example,

---

[7] *op. cit.*

Selznick and Steinberg combined responses to 11 stereotype questions to form an index of anti-Semitism.

Having a scale to measure anti-Semitism also makes it easier to assess the meaning of particular survey questions. For example, Selznick and Steinberg found that people who thought Jews were more loyal to Israel than to the United States were also more likely to agree that Jews have irritating faults, are dishonest, wield too much power, and so on. In other words, some who question Jewish loyalty are responding simply to the element of truth contained in the statement, but the overriding tendency is for this view to go along with other negative ideas about Jews. Among those in the study who subscribed to the other 10 stereotypes about Jews, 90 percent thought Jews were more loyal to Israel than to the United States, whereas on the average only 30 percent held this view. However, some of those who manifested no other signs of anti-Semitism still questioned Jewish loyalty (among persons agreeing with none of the other 10 items, for example, 5 percent agreed with the statement about Jewish loyalty). In short, some persons agreed with the statement, presumably because it bore an element of truth, even though they held no negative sentiments about Jews.

What can be inferred, then, from the survey evidence we have reviewed? Some assistance may be obtained from the Selznick and Steinberg study.[8] In their sample (based on a national poll conducted in 1964) about three-quarters of those who held the view that Jews are more loyal to Israel than to the United States seemed to be persons who could be classified as anti-Semitic, judging from all the various questions the authors had at their disposal. The other one-quarter were not. If the meaning of this item has stayed roughly the same, these figures suggest that a reasonable inference to draw from the fact that 29 percent of the public now subscribes to this view would be that no more than about 21 percent could be classified as anti-Semitic if more extensive information were available.

Extrapolating in the same manner from other questions in the Selznick and Steinberg study suggests that about 24 percent of the public may be responding in an anti-Semitic way when they deny that Jewish business-men are as honest as other businessmen; between 15 percent and 24 percent may be reflecting anti-Semitism in responses to questions about Jews having too much power (depending on which poll is used). These figures seem consistent with the findings (discussed earlier) showing that between one-fourth and one-third of the public volunteered things they

---

[8] *op. cit.*

disliked about Jews when asked to do so in the 1974 poll. They are higher, however, than the proportion (10–12 percent) that characterizes its overall feelings toward Jews as dislike.

Whether these particular extrapolations are accurate can be questioned. The general point worth remembering is that everyone who agrees with a particular survey question cannot be classified as anti-Semitic, especially if the question contains an element of truth. At the same time, responses to stereotype questions cannot be discounted simply because they contain a factual dimension.

A second question of interpretation is illustrated by the "fully-only" problem. The question is basically whether the 10 percent who say they dislike Jews (or the 25 percent who say things that may reflect negative attitudes toward Jews) constitutes a significant enough number to elicit concern ("fully 10 percent") or whether it is such a small proportion as to be negligible ("only 10 percent"). A satisfactory answer to a question such as this requires a great deal of knowledge about the history and character of prejudice, social conditions, and the role of prejudice in social life. Even those who claim such knowledge may arrive at different assessments. At minimum, the answer given will depend on several considerations.

First, what is being evaluated. A statistic showing that 10 percent of the public has cancer will be taken more seriously than one showing that 10 percent has sore throats. If "dislike Jews" conjures up images of concentration camps, pogroms, and synagogue burnings (actual or potential), any proportion clearly will be regarded more seriously than if "dislike Jews" is considered bland, natural, or inconsequential.

Second, what implicit comparisons are being made. Four options are possible: comparisons with the past, comparisons with other social groups, comparisons with an idealized state of affairs, and comparisons with what is considered reasonably attainable. Comparisons with the past typically lead to inferences that current levels of anti-Semitism are relatively benign. Comparisons with other social groups are more difficult to make, since various such comparisons are possible. As the survey evidence has shown, Jews tend to elicit more dislike than Protestants or Catholics, but less dislike (generally) than blacks. Comparisons with an idealized state of affairs are most likely to inflate the seriousness with which anti-Semitism is regarded. Many who have studied it have likened it to a disease that should be eradicated completely. As long as 10 percent of the population is afflicted, there is cause for concern. Comparisons with what is reasonably attainable tend to produce mixed evaluations.

Those making these comparisons readily admit the unlikelihood of eliminating prejudice completely, but hold to the conviction that it probably can still be reduced. Present levels of anti-Semitism, in their view, may not be high, but are perhaps higher than necessary. There is no reason why one, rather than all, of these comparisons should not be made. Knowing and using all the available options is likely to produce the most balanced assessment.

Third, who is doing the evaluating. Admittedly this is a touchy question, but it is one that must be confronted openly. An investigator who has devoted years of his or her life to the study of prejudice may be more inclined to emphasize, rather than minimize, the seriousness of the problem. The same may be said of a funding agency that has poured thousands of dollars into studying the problem. By the same token, someone who belongs to an ethnic group or social stratum accused of being prejudiced may discount the seriousness of the problem altogether. The victims of prejudice are also likely to be deeply divided over its importance: some will wish to ignore it entirely, while others will exaggerate its effects. Perhaps the main thing to be said is that both caution and introspection need to be exercised in interpreting statistics on anti-Semitism.

A third question concerns the balance between positive and negative stereotypes. What is the significance of the fact that positive images of Jews are subscribed to by a ratio of two to one, compared with negative images? This question can be addressed from three quite different perspectives. The first suggests that the positive images serve as a counterbalance to the negative images. The second says the positive images provide no counterbalance, and may even be detrimental. The third stresses the ambivalence illustrated by the joint presence of the two. Those who adopt the first view readily admit the truth content of stereotypes. They recognize that Jews, like any group, have likable and unlikable qualities. They are less concerned about the public's criticism of the latter as long as it also acknowledge the former. The second view tends more to regard stereotyping of all kinds as faulty thinking. From this perspective, negative images are problematic independently of whatever positive images may be held, and the positive images reflect a simplistic tendency to see Jews as a monolithic category rather than a heterogeneous population. The third view derives from the observation that negative and positive stereotypes often resemble each other, differing only in the evaluation attached to a perceived characteristic, such as Jewish ambition or the Jewish presence in business. According to this view, simultaneous but discrepant evaluations indicate an ambivalent orientation toward Jews. Ambivalence is an unstable attitude based on an exaggerated, if not irrational, assessment of desirable and undesirable qualities. When fear and fascination are present, unpredictable behavioral responses, including hostility and discrimination, can result.

Of the three views, the last has been least supported empirically. Those who hold negative images of Jews usually are not the same persons who hold positive images. If there is any ambivalence, therefore, it is at the cultural level rather than at the individual level. The second view has been emphasized in many empirical studies. These have shown the undesirable consequences of negative stereotypes, particularly at the interpersonal level when hostility or avoidance is manifested. The effects of positive stereotypes have been largely ignored in these studies. The first view gives perhaps the most balanced overall assessment of the relation between stereotypes and the larger position of Jews in the society. It is clear that positive as well as negative relations have been cultivated between non-Jews and Jews.

Finally, there is the question of what moral significance should be attached to stereotypes and negative feelings. Here again, different positions have been taken and it is difficult to determine which is more appropriate, since the arguments rest more on conceptions of value and propriety than on observations of fact. One argument holds that people have the right to think and feel what they please, as long as their thoughts and feelings do not infringe on the rights and freedoms of others. According to this view, prejudice does not afford cause for particular concern unless it results in discrimination. In the case of anti-Semitism, the relatively privileged status that Jews have acquired in American society is pointed to as evidence that prejudice should not be considered a problem of moral significance.

An opposing argument – and this is probably the most commonly shared view among social scientists who have studied prejudice – is that stereotypes and ill-feelings are intrinsically subject to moral reproach. According to this view all expressions of disapproval should be eradicated, and a culturally relative attitude of tolerance and acceptance should be engendered even toward groups whose life-styles and values may be radically different from prevailing cultural standards. Falling somewhere in between these opposing views is the argument that social criticism should be upheld and encouraged, even toward minority groups, as long as the criticisms stem from thoughtfully held value positions, are applied justly, and are not in violation of civil liberties.

The three views are well illustrated in the different arguments that have been presented concerning the right of openly prejudiced groups, such as the American Nazi party, to hold demonstrations. According to one view, these groups need not elicit serious concern because their activities (thus far) have not resulted in any overt aggression toward Jews or other minorities. According to a second view, the open display of prejudice is itself damaging, and should be actively opposed. Others hold the view that these groups' rights to speak out should be protected, but that their arguments should be scrutinized to determine if they are accurate and fair.

It should be fully apparent from these many views and considerations that the facts alone do not yield definitive inferences about the nature and extent of contemporary anti-Semitism. The evidence from polls and surveys provides a basis for interpretation, but the interpretation itself depends on additional considerations of perspective and evaluation. It is possible to lay out the main perspectives from which some choice must be made, but not to dictate what that choice should be. What social scientists have attempted to do is provide evidence on the relative magnitude of stereotypes and feelings that may serve as crude indicators of anti-Semitism, and to develop theories explaining variations in the occurrence of these stereotypes and feelings. Once this evidence has been provided, the problem of interpretation remains, but presumably can be addressed from a more informed perspective.

The Social Location of Negative Attitudes

As a first step toward explaining why people hold negative attitudes toward Jews, social scientists have attempted to learn who these people are and how they differ from people who do not harbor hostility toward Jews. Research has generally focused on the following social distinctions: education, occupation, age cohort, religion, and race.

Education

Of all the social differences that appear to distinguish people who hold negative images of Jews and people who reject such images, educational differences appear to have the most decided effect. Quinley and Glock[9] write in their overview of the Berkeley research, for example, that education is the "key factor" in explaining anti-Semitism. The higher a person's level of education, the less likely that person is to express negative attitudes or feelings toward Jews. In Selznick and Steinberg's national survey in

---

[9] Harold E. Quinley and Charles Y. Glock, *Anti-Semitism in America,* New York, 1979.

1964,[10] for example, 52 percent of those who had received only grade school education scored "high" on the study's index of anti-Semitic stereotypes; by comparison, only 15 percent of those who had graduated from college scored high on the index. The only major exception to this pattern in the Selznick and Steinberg study was that the college-educated were more likely than the less educated to defend social club discrimination against Jews. Overall, the effect of education appeared to be one of increasing tolerance and sophistication as far as attitudes toward Jews were concerned.

Whether education is as strongly associated with attitudes toward Jews in the late 1970s as it was in the mid-1960s was examined in an unpublished report by Lipset and Schneider.[11] Using data from the 1974 Harris poll,[12] they constructed an index of anti-Semitic stereotyping that, though containing questions different from those asked in the Selznick and Steinberg study, would classify respondents according to relative degrees of stereotyping in a manner comparable with the earlier research. This index, it turns out, is related just as strongly to education as Selznick and Steinberg's index had been. Lipset and Schneider concluded that education is still one of the most powerful factors affecting anti-Semitism, and that the rise in overall levels of education in the United States constitutes a significant reason for the reduction of anti-Semitic stereotyping that has occured over the past several decades.

These conclusions pertain to anti-Semitic stereotyping. The relationships between education and other perceptions of Jews are less simple. For example, Lipset and Schneider show that persons with college and postgraduate degrees are more likely than persons with high school educations to say that Jews have too much power. They suggest that persons with higher levels of education may have more contact with Jews or may be more aware of the kinds of power that Jews actually have than persons with lower levels of education.

The relationships between education and feelings about Jews also differ from the relationships between education and stereotypes. The ratio of negative to positive feelings on the CPS "feeling thermometer" was higher among persons with lower levels of education than among persons with

[10] op. cit.
[11] Seymour M. Lipset and William Schneider, *Antisemitism and Israel: A Report on American Public Opinion,* unpublished Manuscript, Stanford University, Department of Sociology, 1979.
[12] op. cit.

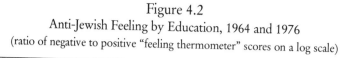

Figure 4.2
Anti-Jewish Feeling by Education, 1964 and 1976
(ratio of negative to positive "feeling thermometer" scores on a log scale)

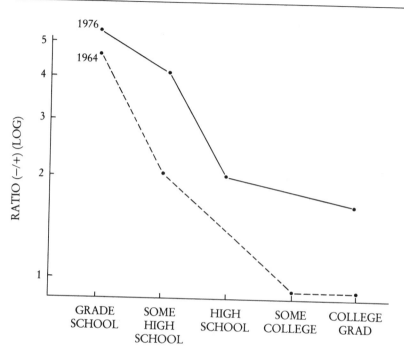

Source: Adapted from Center for Political Studies. National Election Surveys 1964–1976, University of Michigan.

higher levels in both 1964 and 1976. But the differences between the less-educated and the more-educated were significantly smaller in 1976 than in 1964 (see Figure 4.2). This was due to the fact that feelings among the grade-school-educated had remained virtually unchanged while feelings among the college-educated had become substantially less positive than they had been in 1964. These changes suggest that the power of education as a force against prejudice may have diminished somewhat as the numbers of persons obtaining higher levels of education have increased. This is a relative decline. Overall, education remains strongly associated with the tendency to reject negative images of Jews.

Occupation and Income

Since levels of education are closely associated with differences in occupation and income, investigators have sought to discover whether anti-Semitism also varies according to occupation and level of income, and whether it is these differences or the differences in education that are actually responsible for differences in anti-Semitism. Studies such as those of Selznick and Steinberg and Lipset and Schneider[13] have generally shown that anti-Semitism is lower among white-collar workers than among blue-collar workers, and that it decreases with rising levels of income. However, these differences usually disappear or are substantially reduced when level of education is controlled. Accordingly, most investigators have come to regard characteristics intrinsically associated with education, such as greater cognitive sophistication or different cultural values and tastes, as the principal factors leading to a reduction of anti-Semitism, rather than the sheer fact that educated people may have higher incomes or more secure jobs.

Age Cohort

Age differences have been of particular interest to researchers investigating anti-Semitism, since lower levels of prejudice among the young would provide further evidence that anti-Semitism was declining, whereas any substantial tendency for the young to hold higher levels of anti-Semitism might signal a trend toward increasing anti-Semitism. Judging from the trends that have been examined already, we would expect the young to be less prejudiced than the old. This is generally what studies have shown. In Selznick and Steinberg's study,[14] for example, 59 percent of those in the survey who were 55 or older scored high on the anti-Semitism index, compared with 31 percent of those 35 or younger. Since levels of education tend to be higher among the young than among the old, Selznick and Steinberg also controlled for education, and found that the differences attributable to age, though reduced, were still significant. Lipset and Schneider found that similar differences were evident among white respondents in the 1974 Harris data.[15]

Another use that has come increasingly to be made of data on age differences concerns the role of cohorts. Social scientists have suggested that a cohort of people born during roughly the same interval of time may

---

[13] Both *op. cit.*
[14] *op. cit.*
[15] *op. cit.*

respond to events in a way that differs from that of another cohort born at a different time. In the case of anti-Semitism, the cohort of people who were young during World War II, for example, might well be expected to have different attitudes toward Jews than a cohort of people who had matured before the war or another cohort that was not born until after the war.

Cohorts become particularly useful for studying changes in attitudes. Lacking data on changes in particular individuals' attitudes over a period of time, it is possible to make estimates of such changes by comparing the attitudes of a "birth cohort" (that is, a group of people born during a particular period) at one time period with the attitudes of that same birth cohort at a later time. For example, it would be possible to compare the "feeling thermometer" scores given in 1964 by people who had been born between 1900 and 1919 with those given in 1976 by people born during that period. The differences would provide an estimate of how much the attitudes of this particular cohort of people had changed between 1964 and 1976. By examining changes in the attitudes of cohorts, it is possible to determine whether trends have occurred because people's attitudes have actually changed over time, or simply because older people have died and have been replaced by new cohorts of younger people.

An illustration of a cohort analysis is shown in Table 4.11, which compares the "feeling thermometer" responses of four cohorts of people given in 1964 and again in 1976. They are a "prewar" cohort who had reached maturity before the start of World War II, a "World War II" cohort who matured during the war, a "Cold War" cohort who matured after World War II, and a "Sixties" cohort who matured during the countercultural unrest of that decade. It will be recalled that the overall trend in "feeling thermometer" scores between 1964 and 1976 was one of increasing negativity toward Jews. The data in Table 4.11 reveal more clearly how that change came about. The prewar cohort showed virtually no change in its feelings toward Jews. In both 1964 and 1976 it was the most negative of all the cohorts. The feelings of this group, it appears, had developed at a time when anti-Semitism ran high in American culture, and even at these later points these feelings remained relatively negative.

In comparison, the cohort that matured during World War II was least disposed to hold negative feelings toward Jews in 1964, but its feelings became markedly more negative by 1976. The Cold War cohort (which matured immediately following World War II) scored almost as low on negative feelings in 1964 as the World War II cohort. But by 1976 its feelings had become considerably more negative. Indeed, its feelings had become slightly more negative even than those of the prewar cohort. What appears to have happened in these two cohorts was that increasing distance from World War II led to an increase in anti-Semitism. Having been socialized during or immediately following the war, these cohorts probably were keenly aware of the effects of anti-Semitism, and may have adopted artificially positive feelings toward Jews. With age and with the declining salience of anti-Semitism as an issue in American culture, however, these cohorts gradually abandoned their positive feelings toward Jews and became neutral or negative.

Table 4.11
Feelings Toward Jews by Cohort, 1964–76

| Cohort | Birth Year | Ratio of Negative to Positive Feelings | | |
		1964	1976	1976 ÷ 1964
Pre-World War II	1900–1919	.25 (406)	.28 (560)	1.12
World War II	1920–1927	.09 (250)	.18 (258)	2.00
Cold War	1928–1939	.13 (346)	.30 (353)	2.31
Sixties	1940–1943	.16 (101)	.19 (172)	1.19

Source: Center for Political Studies. National Election Surveys 1964–1976, University of Michigan.

Finally, the cohort that matured during the 1960s showed relatively low levels of negative sentiment, and these levels remained virtually constant between 1964 and 1976. It is impossible to know precisely why its feelings remained relatively constant, but the turbulence of the 1960s (including the civil rights movement) may have been an important factor. This cohort's feelings probably were rooted less in the memory of World War II than those of the older cohorts and, therefore, may have been less subject to change with increasing distance from the war. Instead, the strong sentiments against racial prejudice and in support of other civil rights and libertarian attitudes to which this cohort was exposed as it matured during the 1960s may have prevented its feelings toward Jews from shifting in a negative direction.

Religion

Research on the relationship between religion and attitudes toward Jews has shown that negative attitudes generally are more likely to be found among Protestants than among Catholics, among members of conservative or evangelical churches and sects than among members of theologically liberal denominations, and among persons firmly committed to traditional religious beliefs than among persons less committed to such beliefs.

The differences between Catholics and Protestants, while relatively small, have been documented consistently by virtually every major study of anti-Semitism. For example, the Selznick and Steinberg survey[16] in the mid-1960s found that 36 percent of the Protestants scored "high" on anti-Semitism, compared with 32 percent of the Catholics. Stember found similar differences in his review of the earlier polls on anti-Semitism.[17]

Comparisons between Catholics and Protestants are not entirely meaningful, though, since there are many different Protestant denominations. The more conservative of these denominations tend to manifest considerably more readiness than the more liberal denominations to subscribe to negative attitudes toward Jews. For example, Selznick and Steinberg distinguished Unitarians, Congregationalists, and Episcopalians from other denominations, and found that the former scored significantly lower on their measure of anti-Semitism than the latter, even when differences in education were controlled.[18] Lipset and Schneider's analyses of the 1974 Harris data found much the same denominational patterns, with Episcopalians scoring lowest on anti-Semitism and Baptists and sects scoring highest (correcting for differences in education).[19]

Denominational differences of this sort have led to speculation that persons more committed to their religious beliefs and practices might be more negative toward Jews than the less religiously committed. One of the most careful examinations of the relationship between religiosity and attitudes toward Jews was conducted in the mid-1960s by Charles Y. Glock[20] as part of the Berkeley project on anti-Semitism in America. The study showed that orthodox religious belief is not necessarily a source of anti-Semitism. But orthodoxy does tend to nurture three kinds of orientations that produce anti-Semitism: particularism – the view that only Christians are saved; historic anti-Semitism – the tendency to blame Jews for the

---

[16] op. cit.
[17] op. cit.
[18] op. cit.
[19] op. cit.
[20] Charles Y. Glock and Rodney Stark, *Christian Beliefs and Anti-Semitism*, New York, 1966

death of Christ; and religious hostility – the idea that Jews belong to a false religion and will reap God's punishment as long as they do. These orientations reinforce one another, and lead those who hold them to adopt negative attitudes of a more secular nature about Jews.

Race

A final background factor that has been included routinely in research on the social sources of anti-Semitism is race, particularly differences between the attitudes of blacks and whites. Given the fact that prejudice tends to occur more among persons with lower levels of education, it might be assumed that blacks, on the whole, would be more prejudiced toward Jews than whites would be, since average levels of education among blacks are lower than among whites. This assumption has been confirmed only for certain kinds of anti-Semitism. Most research has found that blacks are somewhat more inclined than whites to agree with stereotypes about the economic characteristics of Jews. For example, Selznick and Steinberg[21] found that 40 percent of the blacks in their sample thought Jews control international banking, compared with only 28 percent of the whites. They found similar differences on stereotypes dealing with aggressiveness and dishonesty in business. The same patterns were evident in the 1974 Harris survey.[22] Forty-eight percent of the blacks, compared with 34 percent of the whites, agreed with the statement "When it comes to choosing between people and money, Jews will choose money." Blacks were also more likely to agree that "Most of the slum owners are Jewish" (37 percent versus 20 percent), and that "Jewish businessmen will usually try to pull a shady deal on you" (33 percent versus 19 percent).

On stereotypes of a less economic character, blacks are usually no more inclined to agree than whites are. In the Selznick and Steinberg study, for example, there were virtually no differences between blacks and whites on agreement with stereotypes about Jews sticking together too much or having too much power. Similarly, in the Harris study blacks were no more likely than whites to say that Jews feel superior to other groups, are irritating, or are too ambitious.

The difference between blacks and whites on economic stereotypes appears to be primarily a function of economic contact between blacks and Jews. Selznick and Steinberg were able to demonstrate this fact by showing that high scores on an index of economic anti-Semitism were much higher

---

[21] *op. cit.*
[22] *op. cit.*

among blacks than among whites, among those who had contact with Jews in their work, whereas there were relatively small differences among blacks and whites who had no work contact with Jews. The effect of work contact was to increase economic anti-Semitism among blacks but to reduce it among whites. For noneconomic anti-Semitism, work contact produced a reduction among both blacks and whites.

Summary

Research has located anti-Semitism primarily among the lower classes, particularly among those with lower levels of education. The effects of other social variables on anti-Semitism, in comparison with the effects of education, tend to be small and partly a function of educational differences. There is also an overlap between the kinds of people who have been found to be more anti-Semitic according to other variables and the less well-educated. Members of religiously conservative denominations and older people, for example, also tend to be people with lower levels of education. In sum, education looms as an important factor for explaining and under-standing variations in anti-Semitism.

But what is it about education that causes differences in prejudice? Is it that the educated have values that militate against prejudice? Are they taught not to be prejudiced? Or do they have more opportunities and fewer frustrations, so that they can afford not to be prejudiced? These questions require an examination of the theories that have been put forth to explain anti-Semitism and the evidence that has been gathered to test these theories.

Theories of Anti-Semitism

The main theories that have been advanced to explain why some people are more inclined than others to exhibit anti-Semitic stereotypes and feelings include contact, authoritarianism, cultural values, and cognitive sophistica-tion. These theories have enjoyed different degrees of success when subjec-ted to actual research tests.

Contact

One of the earliest and simplest theories of anti-Semitism stresses lack of contact as the principal cause of ill-feelings between Jews and non-Jews. Since Jews constitute slightly less than 3 percent of the U.S. population and are concentrated largely in a few urban areas, it has seemed reasonable to believe that absence of contact might be a factor in explaining anti-Semitism. This theory rests on the assumption that the more people interact, the

more they will come to like one another. For many years this generalization was proclaimed as one of social science's basic "laws" of human
behavior. Not only did it seem to be supported by a great deal of evidence,
but it also squared intuitively with ideas about people fearing the unknown
and favoring that with which they are familiar.

Like most "laws" of human behavior, this generalization has had to be
severely qualified in light of closer attention to the facts. As social scientists
began to examine the relationship between contact and feelings more
carefully, they rediscovered the wisdom of another ancient maxim: familiarity breeds contempt. Sometimes conflict and hatred, rather than good-
feeling, result from social interaction. Thus a modified "law" was formulated: the more people interact with one another, the more they will come
to like one another, *unless* they come to hate one another!

This important stipulation must be applied to the contact theory of
anti-Semitism. Most research has verified the assumption that contact
between Jews and non-Jews is associated more with positive feelings than
with negative feelings. But there are some important exceptions. As noted
earlier, for example, contact between blacks and Jews seems to contribute
to negative stereotypes about Jewish economic characteristics. This fact is
consonant with the results of studies examining the effects of contact
between blacks and whites on racial prejudice. When contact occurs
between equals, as among friends, it usually reduces prejudice; but when it
occurs between persons of unequal status, as between employers and
employees or between persons of discrepant socioeconomic standing, it is
likely to increase levels of prejudice, especially on the part of the subordi-
nates.

A second qualification that must be made as far as the contact theory of
anti-Semitism is concerned is that the interaction has to be relatively close.
It is not sufficient merely to be in the same context with Jews. Being in the
same context can actually increase prejudice. This is because of the "truth
content" problem discussed earlier. No ethnic group is entirely free of
unlikable qualities. Persons casually acquainted with its members are more
likely to be aware of this than anyone else. If they do not cultivate personal
friendships across ethnic lines, their perceptions are likely to remain at the
level of generalizations and criticisms.

This is clearly illustrated in Glock et al., *Adolescent Prejudice*.[23] The
study included teen-agers from three high schools. In the first nearly half
the students were Jewish. In the second about one-fourth were Jewish. In

---

[23] *op. cit.*

the third there were virtually no Jews. The anticipated result was that anti-Semitism among non-Jewish students would be lowest in the first school because of greater contact and familiarity with Jews, and highest in the third school, where such contact was precluded. The study found just the opposite to be the case. Anti-Semitism among non-Jews was highest in the school with the most Jewish students, next highest in the second school, and lowest in the school with virtually no Jews. In all three communities, however, students who listed Jews among their close friends were, as expected, less likely to harbor negative stereotypes than students who did not cultivate such friendships.

Why were ill-feelings greater in the contexts with larger numbers of Jewish students? The reasons were difficult to establish precisely, but two factors seemed to be at work. One was that non-Jews seemed to be envious of the academic success of the Jewish students. In the settings with larger numbers of Jews, accordingly, stereotypes about Jewish aggressiveness and conceit were espoused with greater frequency. Second, both Jewish and non-Jewish parents in these settings put more pressure on their children not to date outside their own religious group, because dating of this sort was a clear possibility. This pressure was associated not only with anti-Semitism on the part of the teen-agers in general but also with perceptions of Jewish clannishness.

Authoritarianism

A second theory that has been advanced to explain differences in prejudice, and in anti-Semitism particularly, stresses personality factors. The research conducted by T. W. Adorno and his colleagues in the late 1940s, leading to the publication of *The Authoritarian Personality*,[24] was heavily influenced by Freudian psychoanalytic theory and sought to explain anti-Semitism as a product of impaired psychological functioning. Anti-Semitism was held to be but one element in a complex of attitudes that the authors character- ized as "authoritarian" and attempted to measure with the "F-scale" (F for fascism). The attitudes constituting this authoritarian orientation included rigid adherence to conventional, middle-class values; submissive, uncrit- ical attitudes toward idealized moral authorities; a tendency to condemn and reject violators of conventional values; opposition to the subjective and imaginative; superstition and stereotypic thinking; a preoccupation with power relations, strength, and toughness; generalized hostility; a tendency

---

[24] Theodor W. Adorno, et al., *The Authoritarian Personality*, New York, 1950.

to believe that wild and dangerous things go on in the world; and an exaggerated concern with sexuality.

In simplest terms, the authoritarian personality theory attributes anti-Semitism and other forms of prejudice to a particular style of psychological functioning. Frustration, anxiety, ambivalence, and rigidity combine to produce aggressive behavior and stereotyped attitudes toward Jews, minority groups, or other convenient scapegoats. Prejudice and discrimination provide an emotional outlet for the pent-up anxieties that the authoritarian person cannot otherwise express.

The Selznick and Steinberg study paid careful attention to the relationship between the F-scale and anti-Semitism.[25] They had assumed, in fact, that this relationship would prove important, both as an explanation of anti-Semitism in its own right and as an explanation for the greater preponderance of anti-Semitism among members of the lower classes, it might be supposed, would be more subject to frustration and anxiety, and therefore more likely to vent aggression through prejudice and discrimination. What they found was that authoritarianism seemed not to be rooted in childhood upbringing or frustrating relationships with parents, as the initial theory had suggested, but in factors associated more with the subject's own style of cognitive functioning. Using various pieces of evidence showing the importance of differences in values and styles of thinking, Selznick and Steinberg argued that authoritarianism should not be regarded as a personality style produced by repressed childhood training or subsequent frustration, but that it should be regarded more as a measure of rigid, simplistic thinking.

The study of adolescent prejudice by Charles Y. Glock and his colleagues[26] also explored various measures of authoritarianism, frustration, and anxiety to determine whether these factors might be important to the understanding of anti-Semitism among teen-agers. Their findings were even more damaging to the authoritarian personality explanation than those of Selznick and Steinberg. Using a measure of authoritarianism that had been extensively tested in previous research to ensure against response-set bias and other difficulties of interpretation, they found no relationship at all between authoritarianism and anti-Semitism. Nor did they find any relationship between anti-Semitism and other personality scales designed to measure frustration or lack of self-esteem. Although the investigators cautioned that the lack of relationships may have been due to unseen flaws

[25] op. cit.
[26] op. cit.

in the scales themselves, they suggested that there seemed to be little support for the idea that anti-Semitism among teen-agers is rooted in frustration or impaired psychological functioning.

It is important not to misinterpret what researchers have concluded about the overall value of the authoritarian personality theory. They have not argued that authoritarianism doesn't exist or that it has no bearing on prejudice. At least some of the research has shown positive relationships between measures of authoritarianism and measures of anti-Semitism. What researchers have taken issue with primarily is the idea that prejudice is a response to deep frustrations and anxieties in the emotional or motivational makeup of individual personalities. They have suggested, instead, that authoritarianism is a way of thinking, a cognitive style, that people learn, not because it is needed to cope with psychological problems but because people are exposed to a subculture in which these ways of thinking predominate.

Cultural Values

A third theoretical approach has attempted to explain prejudice as a product of creeds, values, and ideologies. This approach regards anti-Semitism as but one element of a broader cultural ethos composed of unenlightened values. It claims that people are anti-Semitic because they are exposed to a subculture in which prejudice, bigotry, and anti-democratic values flourish. Anti-Semitism, therefore, need not satisfy deep-seated psychological anxieties to be adopted; it is passed on from one generation to another as part of a normal outlook on life, and will be perpetuated unless other values are introduced to combat it.

In the Selznick and Steinberg study, cultural values loomed as one of the most powerful predictors of variation in anti-Semitism.[27] Another indication that anti-Semitism is rooted in a general climate of intolerance is the fact that persons who are anti-Semitic tend to hold intolerant attitudes toward other minority groups as well. In the Selznick and Steinberg study, anti-Semitic respondents also tended to score high on measures of racial prejudice and anti-Catholic prejudice. In the 1976 CPS "feeling thermometer" responses the same patterns were evident. Among persons who disliked Catholics, 35 percent also disliked Jews, whereas only 9 percent of those who said they liked Catholics disliked Jews. And among those who disliked blacks, 25 percent disliked Jews, while only 6 percent of those who said they liked blacks disliked Jews.

---

[27] op. cit.

The general point is that anti-Semitism is not an isolated form of intolerance, but is part of a larger subculture of anti-democratic values. To understand why people are anti-Semitic, therefore, one must understand the mechanisms by which this general anti-democratic subculture is maintained.

One such mechanism is parental influence. Within an intolerant subculture it is only natural for parents to pass along intolerant values to their children, and for their children to learn these values as part of their childhood socialization. Research has shown that children pick up prejudiced language from their parents at an early age. Some research also suggests that parents may communicate intolerant values with increasing frequency as children grow older. For example, prejudiced teen-agers in the adolescent prejudice study were likely to say that their parents had put pressure on them to date and to associate only with members of their own race and religion. This tendency appeared to increase as teen-agers matured, apparently because parents become more concerned that their children might enter into interracial or interreligious romances.

Another mechanism by which an intolerant subculture is maintained is peer pressure. A characteristic of all subcultures is that persons holding similar values interact with one another, thereby maintaining and mutually reinforcing the values of their subculture. The effect of such interaction on anti-Semitism was also documented in the adolescent prejudice study.

A third mechanism that reinforces intolerant values is what social scientists have termed "localism." Localism refers to the degree to which persons' interests are oriented to their familiy, immediate friends, and local community. It contrasts with cosmopolitan interests of a more national or international scope. Social researchers have investigated the effects of localism and cosmopolitanism on prejudice and other forms of intolerance. In a study of North Carolina church members, for example, Wade Clark Roof[28] showed that "locals" were significantly more anti-Semitic, racially prejudiced, and politically conservative than "cosmopolitans," even when differences in education were taken into account.

Roof's study also demonstrated that part of the relationship between traditional religious commitment and intolerance was attributable to the fact that religiously committed persons also tended to be locally oriented, and that religious participation reinforced intolerance when people were locally oriented, but not when their outlooks were cosmopolitan. The

---

[28] Wade Clark Roof, *Community and Commitment: Religious Plausibility in a Liberal Protestant Church*, New York, 1978.

effect of localism, it appears, is to shield people from the influence of the larger culture. It serves, in effect, as a protective cognitive barrier around the traditional folk cultures in which intolerance flourishes.

The primary factor that weakens commitment to a subculture of intolerant values appears to be education. It exposes people to democratic ideals that they may not have learned from their parents or peers, and broadens their interests so that they come to be more tolerant of cultural diversity. As levels of education have risen, tolerance and civil libertarian values have also become more prevalent. The extent of the change has been documented by a replication of Samuel Stouffer's study *Communism, Conformity, and Civil Liberties.*[29] In 1954, Stouffer found that 89 percent of the public thought an admitted Communist should not be allowed to teach in a college or university. By 1977 this figure had dropped to 57 percent. Other comparisons showed that support for removing a book by a Communist from the public library had dropped from 66 percent to 42 percent, willingness to deny the right of speech to a Communist had declined from 68 percent to 42 percent, and intolerance of atheists on each of these measures had also declined (from 84 to 39 percent for teaching; from 60 to 39 percent for books; and from 60 to 38 percent for speaking). In short, not only anti-Semitism but also the subculture of intolerance in general has eroded significantly over the past several decades.

The other main body of research concerning anti-Semitism and values has been that focused on the effects of political ideology. A major study by Lipset and Raab, *The Politics of Unreason,*[30] examined the role that right-wing extremism has played in American politics and its effects on attitudes toward Jews and other minority groups. The study showed that not only has there been an anti-democratic subculture in the United States, but that its fears and prejudices have been exploited repeatedly by archconservative political groups. Anti-Semitism has been nourished as part of the ideologies of such groups. People who have found themselves dispossessed by social change (the "once-hads") have been particularly susceptible to these appeals. These movements have emerged periodically in response to economic and political upheavals. Their successes have been limited as far as mainstream politics is concerned, but they have been an important force in the periodic rekindling of anti-Semitism.

---

[29] Samuel A. Stouffer, *Communism, Conformity, and Civil Liberties,* New York, 1955.
[30] Seymour M. Lipset and Earl Raab, *The Politics of Unreason: Right-Wing Extremism in America, 1790–1970,* New York, 1970.

Extremist left-wing movements have traditionally avoided anti-Semitism as part of their ideologies. However, Lipset and Schneider[31] note that anti-Semitism appears to be gaining ground among younger political liberals. Young people (under 40) who voted for George McGovern in the 1972 presidential election, for example, were as anti-Semitic in the 1974 Harris survey as younger people who voted for Richard Nixon. They also expressed more sentiment against Israel. By comparison, older people who voted for McGovern were significantly less anti-Semitic than older people who voted for Nixon.

Lipset and Schneider suggest that two developments, in particular, have probably contributed to the new mood of anti-Jewish feeling among younger liberals. The first was the Black Power movement, which separated the more militant left, among both young blacks and young whites, from the more moderate liberals who had supported the civil rights movement. Jews had been associated with the latter, and therefore came under attack from the former. The anti-Jewish sentiments held by younger blacks have already been discussed. The second appears to have been Israel. Although liberals have generally expressed greater support for Israel in public opinion polls than conservatives have, these differences have been small (and sometimes reversed) among younger people. The reason has been a feeling, especially on the part of younger liberals and radicals, that Israel has exploited Palestinians and that the United States has used Israel to advance imperialist objectives against Arab countries.

Both of these ideologies are of recent origin, and may be of limited duration. But they illustrate a more general point about the relationship between values and anti-Semitism: its volatility. While there has been a general erosion of anti-democratic values in American culture, attitudes toward Jews are influenced by other values and interests. These have been subject to greater fluctuation that depends on short-term political and economic events.

Cognitive Sophistication

The leading theory of prejudice that has been advanced on the basis of recent research views anti-Semitism as a function of differences in levels of cognitive sophistication. Anti-Semitism, according to this theory, consists principally of faulty habits of thought. These habits are characterized by simplism, overgeneralization, and fallacies of logic. They reflect early childhood training and inadequate exposure to the educational process.

---

[31] *op cit.*

Education, if effective, arms individuals against simplistic thinking and reduces their inclination to accept anti-Semitism and other stereotypes. It also exposes individuals to the historical, social, and cultural sources of differences between minority and majority groups, and teaches about the harmful effects of prejudice and discrimination.

The cognitive perspective on prejudice contrasts sharply with that represented by the authoritarian personality research. The two begin by raising different questions about prejudice. The authoritarian personality theory asks why people *adopt* prejudice, and suggest that they do so because they have deep-seated psychological needs that must be fulfilled. Cognitive theory asks why people *abandon* prejudice, and suggests that they will do so only if they are exposed to educational influences that jar them out of traditional habits of thought. In other words, cognitive theory assumes that prejudice is sufficiently prevalent to be learned naturally, and to become a natural way of thinking without having to fulfill any particular personality needs.

Cognitive theory also contrasts with theories stressing cultural values, although this distinction is less pronounced. In some respects, cognitive theory subsumes theories emphasizing cultural values, since exposure to enlightened, libertarian values presupposes a certain degree of cognitive sophistication. The difference is primarily one of emphasis. Those who stress the importance of cultural values emphasize the importance of specific ideas, such as democracy and liberalism, in inhibiting prejudice. Those who stress the importance of cognitive sophistication attach more emphasis to the style or form of one's thought, apart from its specific content. Thus, sophisticated modes of thought inhibit tendencies to over-generalize, help one to make more accurate social distinctions, and lend themselves to more complex views of history and of society, which in turn reduce tendencies to engage in anti-Semitic stereotyping.

The effectiveness of cognitive theory for explaining variations in anti-Semitism has been demonstrated in various research studies. For example, the Selznick and Steinberg study found a strong relationship between a scale measuring "simplism" (tendencies to reduce complex social problems to simple solutions) and anti-Semitism.[32] Similarly, the adolescent prejudice research found strong relationships between anti-Semitism and various cognitive measures, including simplism, intellectual orientations, and academic achievement. Other studies that have focused on different variables have also tended to stress the importance of cognitive sophistication. For

---

[32] *op. cit.*

example, Lipset and Raab's study of political extremism found that "monism" (seeing things through a single perspective) was a common theme in many extremist movements.[33] Or, to take another example, Roof's study of the effects of localism stresses that localism is essentially a narrowed perspective that prevents persons from recognizing the complexity of social life.[34]

Rethinking Anti-Semitism

The finding that anti-Semitism appears primarily to reflect a style of thinking rather than a need-induced personality formation has led social scientists to reexamine the cognitive components of prejudice. This work has resulted in some important modifications in the way prejudice is defined. These modifications suggest ways to overcome some of the difficulties of interpretation that were discussed earlier. They are also aimed at providing more effective means of combating prejudice. Essentially they revolve around a distinction between the perceptual and the explanatory components of attitudes toward Jews.

The perceptual component refers to the attitudes that are perceived as being characteristic of Jews. It refers particularly to perceptions of differences between Jews and non-Jews. For example, Jews may be perceived as being relatively powerful, intelligent, ambitious, wealthy, dishonest, clannish, pushy, religious, hard-working, greedy, and so on. Both positive and negative characteristics are likely to be perceived. Perceptions of this nature are to be evaluated primarily in terms of truth content. Research might show, for example, that there is some truth to the idea that Jews are relatively wealthy compared with other minority groups; it might show that the idea of Jews being relatively dishonest is completely false. Stereotyping, therefore, may be defined as a perception that is either untrue or overexaggerated. A group difference, for example, may in fact exist, but not exist to the extent or as universally as it is perceived.

The explanatory component of anti-Semitism refers to the fact that people generally not only perceive group differences, but also adopt implicit or explicit explanations to account for these differences. A perception of Jewish clannishness, for example, can be explained as a racial quirk, or it can be explained as a product of historical circumstances. The importance of the explanatory component, apart from perceptions, should be evident from this example. An explanation stressing racial quirks is likely

---

[33] op. cit.
[34] op. cit.

to lead to quite different feelings and actions than one stressing historical conditions.

In attempting to explain why people harbor negative feelings toward Jews or engage in discriminatory acts toward them, both perceptions and explanations are likely to be important. A false or overexaggerated perception of some negative characteristic is likely to reinforce ill-feeling and discrimination. So is an explanation that focuses on racial, genetic, or other immutable group traits rather than on broader social forces. Even a mistaken perception of Jewish characteristics is less likely to lead to hostility or hatred if it is properly explained. All the more so for negative characteristics that may in fact exist: ill-feelings can perhaps be avoided simply by denying the existence of these characteristics, but a more effective means of avoiding ill-feelings would probably be to acknowledge their existence and to seek an accurate explanation.

Proposals for Combating anti-Semitism

How can anti-Semitism be curtailed, eliminated, or at least prevented from increasing? Different proposals have been put forth, including programs involving the schools, the churches, the media, and the courts. Not everyone agrees on the most effective methods of fighting anti-Semitism. Nor is there consensus that the problem is serious enough to warrant special attention. Those who have studied the problem most carefully, however, agree that it should continue to be monitored, and that the results of existing knowledge about the sources of anti-Semitism should be applied in whatever ways possible to combat it. This knowledge, as we have seen, points primarily to methods involving cognitive skills.

One of the most recent, and perhaps the most thorough, reviews of the state of current knowledge about anti-Semitism is Quinley and Glock's *Anti-Semitism in America*.[35] In the final chapter of their volume they set forth the following recommendations:

1. People should be taught to recognize anti-Semitism in themselves and in others.

2. People should be taught that prejudice is morally wrong.

3. Instruction should be given in principles of equality, democracy, freedom of speech, freedom of religion, and other civil liberties.

---

[35] *op. cit.*

4. The social and cultural differences both among Jews and between Jews and non-Jews should be openly discussed, and efforts made to teach about the historical reasons for these differences.

5. Instruction in the use of rules of logic and inference should be provided, especially with reference to understanding social phenomena.

Proposals of the kind set forth by Quinley and Glock place special emphasis on the role that schools could play in combating anti-Semitism. Many schools, in fact, have initiated courses to teach about prejudice, discrimination, and minority groups, or have included segments on these topics within social studies curricula. Still, there is evidence that schools have often placed instruction about prejudice among their lowest educational priorities or have failed to examine carefully what the most effective ways of teaching about prejudice might be. It is clear that more experimentation is needed to develop effective instructional packages. It is also clear, however, that the schools should continue to provide instruction about prejudice even in the absence of such experimentation.

Summary

The main points of this chapter may be summarized as follows:

1. The latest public opinion polls indicate that at least one-fifth, and perhaps as much as one-third, of the American public harbors negative attitudes and feelings about Jews.

2. When compared over time, the polls show dramatic reductions in anti-Semitic stereotypes and feelings since the 1940s.

3. Research on the social location of anti-Semitism has found it to be relatively more common among the uneducated than among the educated; among the old more than among the young; among Protestants, members of theologically conservative denominations, and the religiously committed more than among Catholics, members of liberal denominations, and the less committed; and among blacks more than among whites, but only on stereotypes about economic characteristics of Jews.

4. Theories seeking to explain anti-Semitism have focused on contact, authoritarianism, cultural values, and cognitive sophistication. The leading theoretical approach to anti-Semitism in recent years has stressed the role of cognitive functioning. According to this approach, anti-Semitism is rooted principally in faulty habits of thought. These consist of simplism, overgeneralization, and fallacies of logic. They are strongly influenced by the extent of exposure one has had to the educational process.

5. The importance of cognitive factors as determinants of proclivities to engage in anti-Semitism has produced an interest in specifying more carefully the cognitive components of prejudice. A useful distinction is that between the manner in which group differences between Jews and non-Jews are perceived and the manner in which these differences are explained.

6. The main proposals that have been put forth for combating prejudice have focused in recent years on cognitive skills; churches, community groups, volunteer associations, the performing arts, and particularly the schools have been urged (with some success) to reexamine the content of their programs and teaching with an eye to eradicating stereotypes about Jews.

FREDERICK WEIL

The Extent and Structure of Anti-Semitism in Western Populations since the Holocaust

In analyzing anti-Semitism in Western societies, it is important to distinguish among various types of hostility to Jews, for if the form is incorrectly specified, it is possible to misunderstand the phenomenon. Therefore, it will be appropriate to begin by making a few preparatory theoretical remarks.[1] We may consider three main forms of hostility to Jews: (a) "traditional" folk prejudice and religious defamation, (b) "modern" nationalistic racism and ethnocentrism, or political anti-Semitism, and (c) hostility bred of direct intergroup conflict, mostly over material goods, but sometimes also over political goals, particularly where Jews sought or gained assimilation into national societies. These three forms may be briefly characterized in the following manner.

Traditional anti-Semitism originated in the defamation arising from the conflict between the early Christian Church and the Jewish community, and from their mutual efforts to maintain boundaries between their adherents. From this beginning, a number of prejudices and stereotypes entered folk conceptions of the Jew by the middle ages, due more to the latter's segregation from gentile society than from any direct conflict between the groups.

This "traditional" anti-Semitism is different from the political anti-Semitism connected to the ethnocentric aspects of modern nation-building and the insecurities arising among population groups displaced in the process of industrialization. Rather, modern anti-Semitism is secular and relies on somewhat different stereotypes than those of medieval folk culture[2] – although the residue of "traditional" anti-Semitism left the Jews especially susceptible to being singled out as scapegoats by popular demagogues.

Finally, it makes sense analytically to distinguish the conflictual aspects of intergroup tensions from the prejudicial aspects (recognizing, of course, that they may not be empirically separate). For while conflict free of prejudice tends to be resolvable by

---

[1] Some of the following arguments are developed further in Frederick D. Weil, *Anti-Semitism in the Context of Intergroup Relations: a Comparative Historical View*, paper presented at the Annual Meeting of the American Sociological Association, Detroit, September 1983.

[2] Joshua Trachtenberg, *The Devil and the Jews: The Medieval Conception of the Jew and its Relation to Modern Antisemitism*, New Haven, 1943.

bargaining and mediation, conflict overlaid with prejudice tends to resist such resolution. Thus, it may not be best to analyze "traditional" or "modern" anti-Semitism most centrally in terms of intergroup conflict,[3] but rather, in terms of prejudice, stereotyping, and scapegoating. This is not to argue, as we will see, that anti-Semitic prejudice is the direct cause of all persecution or discrimination – prejudice is often the direct cause of Jews being *selected* as targets at times when targets were sought for other reasons – but only that conflict is not necessarily a more important cause. One might, for instance, compare the nature of tensions between Jews and gentiles during the period of urbanization and industrialization to tensions among distinct gentile groups in the same period (say, different ethnic groups in the United States or Austria). One could argue that it was the *overlay* of prejudice, and not simply the conflict of interests, which made the tension so sharp and some problems in intergroup relations so intractable.[4]

Now, of course, "traditional" and "modern" anti-Semitism are themselves historical, not abstract types, but as with most such historical types, one may find residues of earlier forms during later periods. One could argue that from roughly the Jewish Emancipation to the aftermath of the Holocaust, one finds a declining influence of traditional forms and a growing predominance of modern or political forms, as Western society became increasingly secularized, as industrialization progressively wiped out the largely rural reservoirs of traditional beliefs, and as the mass population became ever more politicized in the processes of nation-building and class conflict. Nazi policy itself accelerated the decline of traditional forms, since it further undermined their social sources.[5] However, the Holocaust, together with the decisive defeat of Nazism, cauterized the further growth of radical political anti-Semitism: in defeat, Nazism's main effect was to discredit "modern" anti-Semitism in its nationalistic and racialist forms. Thus, we should not expect to find large pockets of radical political anti-Semitism in most Western societies since 1945 – and in former Axis countries, overt expressions of political anti-Semitism should be particularly delegitimated to the extent that liberal democratic political cultures have been popularly embraced.

We should expect to find three primary residues of anti-Semitism in Western societies since the Holocaust, corresponding to those outlined above. (1) Low levels of traditionalist anti-Semitism are most likely cen-

---

[3] cf. Hans Rosenberg, *Große Depression und Bismarckzeit*, Berlin, 1967; Reinhard Ruerup, *Emanzipation und Antisemitismus*, Göttingen, 1975.
[4] But see the important analysis of black and white ethnic success rates in the United States by Stanley Lieberson, *A Piece of the Pie: Blacks and White Immigrants Since 1880*, Berkeley, 1980, which in some respects bridges this distinction.
[5] David Schoenbaum, *Hitler's Social Revolution: Class and Status in Nazi Germany, 1933–1939*, Garden City, NY, 1963.

tered in the relatively small sectors least touched by industrial development and secularization. Similarly, since most Established Christian churches have now officially rejected or moderated religious anti-Semitism, the latter has been pushed to the fringes of the Christian world – especially in Western Europe, although less so in the United States due to the importance of dissenting churches here.[6] (2) Political anti-Semitism now most likely takes a low-grade form which asserts that Jews have too much influence or that they have divided national loyalty, but not that they are betrayers of the nation or diluters of the racial blood – and Jews are no longer so easily made scapegoats for political and economic problems. And (3) hostility based on intergroup conflict should appear primarily in areas where Jews still reside and interact with gentile populations. Thus, for instance, one is unlikely to find a great deal of intergroup conflict in West Germany, where few Jews live, although the residues of anti-Semitic prejudice may remain; and one may find higher levels of intergroup conflict in the United States, but levels of prejudice are likely to be lower due to the lack of historical "traditionalism" and the long history of democratic politics.[7]

*

In this article, I examine the extent and structure of anti-Semitism in four Western societies: West Germany, the United States, France, and Austria, with the main emphasis on the first two. I will address the following questions:

> To what extent does a radical anti-Semitism similar to that of the Nazis still exist in West Germany and Austria?
>
> If anti-Semitism has declined in those countries, what is the source of this decline, and how do present levels compare with those in countries like the United States and France, which have longer histories of liberal democracy, but which have seen substantial degrees of anti-Semitism in their histories?

---

[6] "Established" and "dissenting" are used in the traditional sense: the former refers to the Catholic Church and those now or recently recognized as "national" churches, and the latter refers to the non-Established churches and sects. In this respect, as Seymour Martin Lipset, *The First New Nation,* New York, 1963 has argued, American culture is strongly affected by the fact that it is a nation of (religious) dissenters. (See also reflections of this pattern in the survey evidence in Charles Y. Glock and Rodney Stark, *Christian Beliefs and Anti-Semitism,* New York, 1966 and Harold E. Quinley and Charles Y. Glock, *Anti-Semitism in America,* Second Edition, New Brunswick, 1983.

[7] Ben Halpern, *The American Jew: A Zionist Analysis,* New York, 1956.

What sectors of society are most prone to hold anti-Semitic views, and are there indications that such views are likely to become politically mobilized? And are other groups more likely than Jews to become targets of discrimination, scapegoating, prejudice, or hostility based on conflict?

1. Anti-Semitism and Popular Support for Liberal Democracy

There seems little doubt that the Holocaust was the greatest of the Nazi crimes as well as the greatest tragedy to befall Jews in millenia of anti-Semitism. The causes of the Holocaust cannot be fully examined here, but one can argue that the systematic mass murders were possible only as the actions of (1) a modern secular state, and (2) a state radically opposed to liberal democracy. The Church never had the will to engage in genocide,[8] and hostile populations never had the ability to conduct more than incomplete pogroms. And liberal democracy, while in power, has seemed everywhere to provide decisive protection against such extremes (despite its deficiencies in protecting against lower levels of popular prejudice and discrimination, which have been noted since nineteenth century writers like Tocqueville and Marx). Moreover, with the destruction of liberal-democratic civil rights, and especially under conditions of political repression, the full support of the population was not even necessary for such mass murder – nor does it seem to have existed in Nazi Germany.[9] Rather, one can argue, the causal sequence between popular anti-Semitism and the destruction of the Holocaust was indirect: a sufficient segment of the population was indifferent or hostile to a liberal democratic regime form, and after this regime was suspended, the new state was able to commit crimes which the population itself could not. Thus, while secularized and even political anti-Semitism within the population were (and are) serious matters, their most extreme effects depended on the attainment of power by a group radically commited to the persecution and destruction of the Jews – even if their mass base of support was not built directly on this

---

[8] Salo W. Baron, *A Social and Religious History of the Jews*, Second Edition, Volumes I–XVII, New York, 1952–80; James Parkes, *The Conflict of the Church and the Synagogue: A Study in the Origins of Antisemitism*, New York, 1969 [1934] and *The Jew in the Medieval Community: A Study of his Political and Economic Situation*, New York, 1976 [1938]; Rosemary Ruether, *Faith and Fratricide: The Theological Roots of Anti-Semitism*, New York, 1979.

[9] See, e.g., Rainer C. Baum, *The Holocaust and the German Elite*, Totowa, NJ, 1982, on the question of "moral indifference"; and Marlis G. Steinert, *Hitler's War and the Germans*, Athens, Ohio, 1967, on evidence from Nazi opinion surveys.

intention.[10] If this argument is correct, then an examination of the political realm and the factors that shape it is an important prelude and adjunct to our analysis of popular political hostility and less malignant social and economic ethnocentric prejudices.

Although I stress the importance of the political realm, it is only possible here to highlight a couple of factors in Western political culture since 1945; and I will concentrate mainly on West Germany, since it had farthest to go in the establishment and legitimation of liberal democratic values.[11] However, even the United States, which experienced no regime change, moved considerably closer toward its liberal democratic ideals in this period.[12]

I. Most West Germans have come to accept the defeat of National Socialism, and there is almost no public support for its revival, at least not in its old colors. In surveys from 1953 to 1977, the number of respondents who said they would welcome or were indifferent to a new Nazi party fell almost by half (to 7 percent and 14 percent, respectively).[13] However,

---

[10] I develop this argument at greater length in Frederick D. Weil, "The Imperfectly Mastered Past: Anti-Semitism in West Germany Since the Holocaust," *New German Critique* 20, 1980, pp. 135–153; see also Karl Dietrich Bracher, *The German Dictatorship*, New York, 1970; Rainer M. Lepsius, "From Fragmented Party Democracy to Government by Emergency Decree and National Socialist Takeover: Germany," in Juan J. Linz and Alfred Stepan (eds.), *The Breakdown of Democratic Regimes: Europe*, Baltimore, 1978, pp. 34–79; Eva Reichmann, *Hostages of Civilization: The Social Sources of National Socialist Anti-Semitism*, Boston, 1951.

[11] Gabriel Almond and Sidney Verba, *The Civic Culture*, Princeton, 1963, and *The Civic Culture Revisited*, Boston, 1980; Sidney Verba, "Germany: The Remaking of Political Culture," in Lucien W. Peye and Sidney Verba (eds.), *Political Culture and Political Development*, Princeton, 1965; Ralf Dahrendorf, *Society and Democracy in Germany*, Garden City, NY, 1969; David P. Conradt, "Changing German Political Culture," in Almond and Verba (eds.), *op. cit.*, 1980, pp. 212–272; Frederick D. Weil, *Post Fascist Liberalism: The Development of Political Tolerance in West Germany Since World War II*, Ph. D. dissertation: Harvard University, 1981.

[12] Tom W. Smith, "General Liberalism and Social Change in Post World War II America: A Summary of Trends," *Social Indicators Research* 10, 1980, pp. 1–28 and *Atop a Liberal Plateau? A Summary of Trends Since World War II*, paper presented to the Midwest Association for Public Opinion Research, Chicago, November 1982; James A. Davis, "Communism, Conformity, Cohorts, and Categories: American Tolerance in 1954 and 1972–73," *American Journal of Sociology* 81,3, 1975, pp. 491–513 and "Conservative Weather in a Liberalizing Climate: Change in Selected NORC General Social Survey Items, 1972–78," *Social Forces* 58, 4, 1980, pp. 1129–1156; Clyde Z. Nunn et al., *Tolerance for Nonconformity*, San Francisco, 1978; John L. Sullivan et al., *Political Tolerance and American Democracy*, Chicago, 1982; Frederick D. Weil, "Review of Sullivan", et al., "Political Tolerance and American Democracy," *American Journal of Sociology* 89, 4, 1984, pp. 963–66.

[13] Full citations of the sources of these and other survey results reported here may be found in Weil, *op. cit*, 1980 and Weil, *op. cit.*, 1981 and in the notes to Table 1, below.

about a quarter or a third of the population still refuses to find the historical Nazi regime all that bad, although there is a long-term trend toward rejection. Thus, the percentage of West Germans agreeing that "National Socialism was a good idea badly carried out" rose from 47 percent in 1945–46 to 55 percent in 1947–48, where it remained until 1968; but by 1977 it dropped to 26 percent. Likewise, 38 percent of the West Germans asked in a 1964 survey denied that the national socialist state had been "an unjust state (Unrechtstaat), a criminal regime (Verbrecherregime)," but this figure dropped to 25 percent in 1979. Similarly, most observers agree that radical right movements pose little serious threat to most other Western European and North American liberal democracies at the moment.[14]

Most West Gemans have also come to accept the Nazis' responsibility for committing war crimes, but most do not accept any theory of collective guilt. Thus, the opinion that Germany alone was responsible for starting World War II rose from 32 percent in 1951 to 62 percent in 1967. However, until the late 1960s, a growing majority of West Germans came to favor "drawing a line" (Schlussstrich ziehen) on the past and enforcing a statute of limitations on war crimes – the numbers rose from 34 percent in 1958 to 67 percent in 1969 – but from then, opinion began to level off or even reverse, falling slightly to 62 percent by 1978. It seems that the TV film "The Holocaust" reinforced this trend, for public opinion changed twelve points in three months, dropping to 50 percent in 1979 in favor of retaining a statute of limitations. On the other hand, the West Germans compared favorably to Austrians in this respect, for in a 1976 survey, 83 percent of the latter favored a statute of limitations on prosecuting Nazi war crimes – and 85 percent favored "drawing a line" and releasing convicted war criminals.

The same long-term trends are observable regarding the post World War II international settlement. The expectation that Germany might be reunified in the near future fell from 71 percent in 1946 to 13 percent in 1976 (and 1981). West Germans also gave up hope that the former German lands now east of the Oder-Neisse line would one day be returned to Germany.

---

[14] Seymour Martin Lipset and Earl Raab, *The Politics of Unreason,* Chicago, 1978; Seymour Martin Lipset, *Political Man,* Second Edition, Baltimore, 1981(a) and *The Revolt Against Modernity,* paper presented at the conference "Modernization vs. Traditional Values," sponsored by the Council on Religion and International Affairs, Carnegie Center for Transnational Studies, Cold Spring Harbor, NY, (October 1980), 1981(b), Christopher T. Husbands, "Contemporary Right-Wing Extremism in Western European Democracies: A Review Article," *European Journal of Political Research* 9, 1981, pp. 75–99.

In 1953, 66 percent believed they would be returned, but by 1970 only 11 percent thought so. Indeed, with the coming of Brandt's Ostpolitik and the general thaw in East-West relations in the late 1960s and early 1970s, large majorities became willing to formalize the international status quo by recognizing the existing borders. Support for recognition of the Oder-Neisse line as the (East) German-Polish border and of the German Democratic Republic itself both rose from about one West German in ten in the 1950s to two out of every three in the early 1970s. It is probable that this turning away from "national" problems greatly helped open the way for West Germans to turn their attention to their "social" problems.[15]

II. An overwhelming majority of West Germans has come to support the Bonn government, and smaller, but rising numbers of West Germans also support civil liberties in concrete cases. Neo-fascist parties have only once attained more than 2 percent of the vote in a national election since 1945 (4 percent in 1969), and communist parties have not attained more than 2 percent of the vote since 1949, when they received 6 percent; and voting turnout has risen from just under 80 percent in the first federal elections in 1949 to stabilize at over 90 percent in the last several elections. While voting statistics are not good measures of "deep" democratic beliefs, they do indicate a high level of popular legitimation. More revealing have been answers to survey questions of this sort: "Do you think it is better for a country to have *one* party in order to have the greatest possible unity, or *several* parties so that the different opinions can be freely represented?" In 1950 only 53 percent chose a multiparty system and a full 24 percent said "one party", while in 1979 the democratic alternative received 90 percent support and only 4 percent said "one party." Support for the present constitution also rose from 30 percent in 1955 to 70 percent in 1978.

Respect for civil liberties has also grown, but to a lesser extent. Thus, in answer to the abstract question, "which of the four freedoms do you personally consider most important – freedom of speech, freedom of worship, freedom from fear, or freedom from want?" the number saying "freedom of speech" rose from 26 percent in 1949 to 58 percent in 1970; and concrete tolerance for a communist party's right to exist rose from 34 percent in 1950 (after dropping to 28 percent in 1957, during the period when the West German Communist Party was banned) to 45 percent in

---

[15] Dahrendorf, op. cit.; Gebhard Ludwig Schweigler, *National Consciousness in Divided Germany*, Beverly Hills, 1975; c.f. A. J. P. Taylor, *The Course of German History*, New York, 1962; also see the *Journal fuer angewandte Sozialwissenschaften* 2, 1976, for similar results in Austria.

1979. Indeed, by the 1970s West Germans were expressing higher levels of political tolerance in opinion surveys than were Americans in allowing a range of unpopular non-conformists to speak publicly.[16] Cross-national studies indicate that the populations of Italy and Austria – also post-fascist democracies – have also moved closer to the average for Western countries in their adherence to liberal democratic norms.[17]

While this short excursus does not examine the root causes of democratization and liberalization, it should serve to indicate that the political orientations of West Germans and the citizens of other post-fascist regimes have largely converged with the rest of the liberal democratic camp. Perhaps West Germans have not repudiated the Nazi past to an extent which an outside observer might think fit, but still, they have begun to accumulate a backlog of democratic tradition which is often thought to have prevented several older democracies from collapsing in the Great Depression.

2. Trends in Popular Anti-Semitism since the Holocaust

West German opinions on politically motivated crimes against the Jews have followed much the same trends as opinions on National Socialism. The crimes have become increasingly delegitimated, but the guilt (or its consequences) has been more and more rejected. In 1949 and 1958 West Germans were asked whether "persons who commit anti-Semitic actions in Germany today should be punished by a court or not," and the proportion answering "yes" rose from 41 to 46 percent; this figure rose to 78 percent when the same question was asked in 1960, but with the word "anti-Semitic" changed to "anti-Jewish" (judenfeindlich).[18] Thus, roughly comparable questions show a definite trend toward willingness to condemn political anti-Semitic crimes.

On the other hand, as was the case for opinions on National Socialism, West Germans have increasingly rejected collective responsibility for past

---

[16] An atheist, a communist, a neo-Nazi: see Frederick D. Weil, "Tolerance of Free Speech in the United States and West Germany, 1970–79: An Analysis of Public Opinion Survey Data," *Social Forces* 60, 1982, pp. 973–993.

[17] Almond and Verba, *op. cit.*, 1963 and *op. cit.*, 1980; Samuel Barnes, Max Kaase et al., *Political Action: Mass Participation in Five Western Democracies*, Beverly Hills, 1979; Edward N. Muller et al., "Support for the Freedom of Assembly in Western Democracies," *European Journal of Political Research* 8, 3, 1980, pp. 256–88.

[18] In 1970, the population of Hessen was asked their opinion on a statement regarding speech rather than actions, "one should not publicly abuse the Jews, of course, but prison is too hard a penalty for anti-Semitic remark": 60 percent agreed and 32 percent disagreed.

Nazi crimes. Thus, while 65 percent of respondents to a 1949 survey believed that Nazi propaganda had been effective in intensifying anti-Semitic feelings in Germany, much smaller numbers were willing to admit that they themselves had been so affected: 21 percent said they were sympathetic to this propaganda (27 percent found it "repugnant") and only 7 percent report reacting favorably to seeing Jews wearing yellow Stars of David (50 percent found the sight bad). Twelve years later in 1961, a number of surveys were conducted during the trial of Adolf Eichmann, who was sentenced to death by an Israeli court for mass murder. While 67 percent of the West Germans surveyed favored the death sentence or life at hard labor (15 percent urged consideration of mitigating circumstances), a majority also agreed with this statement in connection with the trial: "I personally had nothing to do with it and don't want to hear anything more about it" (59 percent). And 88 percent of the respondents to a 1961 survey denied that they "as a German feel at all guilty (mitschuldig) for the extermination of the Jews," while only 8 percent acknowledged any sense of collective guilt at all. However, large majorities have maintained that many Germans did not know at the time what was happening to the Jews – 72 percent in 1961 and 77 percent in 1979. And while 31 percent of West Germans in 1949 disagreed that "Germany has an obligation to make reparations to the still living German Jews," 46 percent in 1966 agreed with the demand, "the reparations to the Jews should finally be ended; they have already gotten too much." Thus, there has been rising tendency to reject collective guilt or responsibility for past (proven) crimes. Here again, however, the West Germans compared favorably to Austrians: 76 percent of the latter in a 1973 survey rejected the statement that "Austrians in particular should stand up for the Jews because Austrians were involved in crimes against the Jews during the Hitler period."

This does not in itself mean, however, that anti-Semitism is rising in West Germany: on the contrary, it has steadily declined since the early 1950s – although there are indications that it may have risen in the early 1950s. Some of these trends can be seen graphically in Figure 1. The apparent rise in anti-Semitism in the early 1950s is visible for the open-ended question, "what is your overall view of Jews?" and for the *perception* that anti-Semitism was rising. Since that time, the latter question and most other indicators of anti-Semitism – and in some cases, ethnocentrism – have declined: This is true for the opinion that Germans are, or are for the most part, "more capable and gifted than other peoples," for an unwillingness to marry a Jew, for the opinion that Jews incite hatred or sow discord, and for the question, "would you say that Germany is better off without

Figure 1
Trends in Ethnocentrism and Anti-Semitism in West Germany

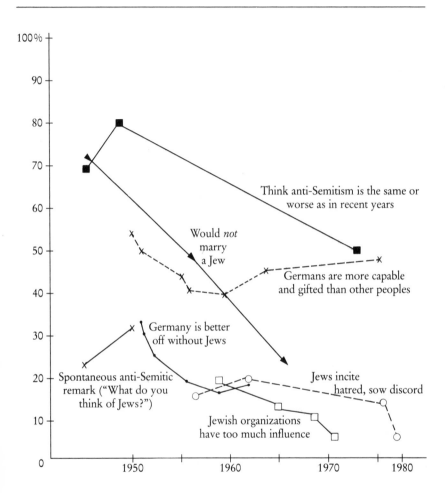

Jews?" The same downward slope is also visible for the most clearly political expression of anti-Semitism for which there are trend data – that Jews or Jewish organizations exercise too great an influence on national politics.[19] Very similar results were obtained from a 1965 sample of elites

---

[19] This last question was generally asked with a list of potentially overly-influenced groups, and Jews were virtually always perceived as the least or almost least objectionable (the trade unions were most often seen as too powerful). Additional figures shown in Table 1 appear to deviate from this trend because of variations in question wording.

(100 each doctors, lawyers, Catholic clergy, and Protestant clergy): 11 percent of the combined sample responded that the Federation of Jews in Germany had too much political influence, but significantly, 16 percent of the doctors and 18 percent of the lawyers, as against only 3 percent of the Catholic and 6 percent of the Protestant clergy, gave this anti-Semitic response. Considering that the clergy may have an interest in saying that another religion does not have too much influence, the fact that other elites are somewhat more anti-Semitic than the general population does not bode well for West German political culture.[20]

Some of these data can be compared to similar questions from other countries: in some cases there are comparable trend lines, while in other cases there are simply isolated data points. A selection of survey results is shown in Table 1, comparing West Germany with the United States, France, and Austria. The questions in Part 1 of Table 1 generally concern political anti-Semitism, which I have argued is the most serious form. On the question whether Jews have too much power, we see that the West Germans are by no means the most anti-Semitic. When this question has been asked in a list with other groups, Jews have also been near the bottom in the United States and France; and when the question was asked in the U.S. without a comparative list, the "too influential" response dropped from nearly half the population in the late 1930s (after rising to well over half in the mid-1940s) to 17 percent in 1962 and 11 percent in 1964. However, while both the United States and West Germany show downward trends of anti-Semitism on this question (there is only one data point for each of the other two countries), it should also be noted that levels seem to have risen during the post-1974 economic squeeze caused by rising oil prices.[21]

It may be argued (as Lipset and Schneider[22] do) that the question of Jewish power is not a pure measure of anti-Semitism, since it contains an evaluative or empirical component – whether Jews have proportionately

---

[20] Dahrendorf, op. cit.; Wolfgang Zapf, Wandlungen der deutschen Elite. Ein Zirkulationsmodell deutscher Fuehrungsgruppen 1919–1961, Munich, 1965.

[21] Seymour Martin Lipset and William Schneider (Anti-Semitism and Israel: A Report on American Public Opinion, manuscript for the American Jewish Committee, 1978), however, point out that neither Jews nor Israel were seen as the chief causes of America's economic or political problems connected with the oil price rise – rather, the oil companies, the Arab nations, and the President were held mainly responsible – but that large numbers still believed that Jews and Zionist organizations were among the groups with too much influence on American Middle Eastern politics.

[22] op. cit.

more power than their share of the population. The questions of willingness to vote for a Jewish candidate of one's own party and, to a lesser
extent, of questionable Jewish loyalty or "nationality" do not suffer from
this objection.[23] On these questions, West German responses are considerably more anti-Semitic than those of Americans, but they are *not* more
anti-Semitic than those of other Europeans. Roughly the same holds true
of the less clearly political questions of Jewish power in business, whether
there are too many Jews in the country, and whether Jews cause trouble
(sometimes, with their ideas) – although there are not comparable data for
all countries.

Very approximate estimates of political anti-Semitism in these four
countries can be made on the basis of the data in Part 1 of Table 1: estimates
for rates of change and 1970 levels are shown in the left-hand panel of
Table 2.[24] The 1970 estimates reinforce our earlier impression that the
West Germans express somewhat higher levels of political anti-Semitism
than the Americans, but middling levels for Europeans – or more precisely,
a good deal higher than the French, but somewhat lower than the Austrians. Indeed, since the French sample estimate for 1970 is as low as the
American, one could argue that what emerges is a distinction between
post-fascist and long-term liberal democracies: that twenty-five years after
the defeat of Nazism, the after-effects of political anti-Semitism were still
visible. However, all countries show a long term reduction in political
anti-Semitism in the postwar period, with the declines in Europe steeper
than in the United States[25] – and indeed, if these trends are carried out into
the 1980s, we might estimate that West German levels approach those of
the Americans, while the French are somewhat lower and the Austrians
somewhat higher. It must be re-emphasized, however, that the data are far
too sparse for these to be regarded as more than very rough approxima-
tions, and that the extrapolations into the 1980s are especially uncertain
lacking further recent data.

I have argued that economic and social anti-Semitism are less dangerous
to Jews than political anti-Semitism, and for that reason, although there are
more available data, these aspects will be reviewed more briefly: some of

---

[23] Jews themselves have always claimed a "national" component in their own identity, but in
the modern period, whose hallmark in this respect is nationalism, charges of disloyalty are
central to political anti-Semitism.

[24] A technical footnote in Table 2 explains the calculation procedure. Estimates were also
calculated for the mid-1980s, but because of the uncertainty that the trends shown would
continue, they were not considered reliable and are not shown in Table 2.

[25] It was perhaps equally steep in America in the late 1940s and the 1950s.

Table 1
Trends in Anti-Semitism in Four Western Countries
Part 1: Political Anti-Semitism

1. Do Jews have too much power (% Yes)

Yr	37-38	46	49	50	52	56	60	61	62	63	64	66	67	68	69	71	73	74	75	76	77	78	79	81	82
US	41	55	–	–	34	–	–	–	17	–	11	–	–	–	–	–	–	–	37	26	19	–	17	20	–
BRD	–	–	–	–	–	–	–	–	–	20	18	13	–	–	9	6	–	18	–	–	–	–	–	–	–
A	–	–	–	–	–	–	–	–	–	–	–	–	–	–	–	–	–	–	–	–	–	28	–	–	–
F	–	–	–	–	–	–	–	–	–	–	–	–	–	24	–	–	–	–	–	–	–	–	–	–	–

2. Do Jews have too much power in business? (% Yes)

Yr	37-38	46	49	50	52	56	60	61	62	63	64	66	67	68	69	71	73	74	75	76	77	78	79	81	82
US	47	43	–	–	–	–	–	47	–	26	–	–	–	–	–	–	–	–	–	–	–	–	–	33	–
BRD	–	–	–	–	–	–	–	–	–	–	–	–	–	–	–	–	–	–	–	–	60	–	–	–	–
A	–	–	–	–	–	–	–	–	–	–	–	–	–	–	–	–	–	–	–	–	–	54	–	–	–
F	–	–	–	–	–	–	–	–	–	–	–	–	–	–	–	–	–	–	–	–	–	–	–	–	–

3. Would vote for Jew in own party (% No)

Yr	37-38	46	49	50	52	56	60	61	62	63	64	66	67	68	69	71	73	74	75	76	77	78	79	81	82
US	46	–	–	–	49	–	22	23	–	17	–	–	13	–	8	–	–	–	–	–	–	–	–	–	–
BRD	–	–	–	–	–	45	–	–	–	–	–	–	–	–	–	–	–	–	–	–	–	–	–	–	–
A	–	–	–	–	–	–	–	–	–	–	–	–	–	–	–	–	–	–	–	–	–	–	–	–	–
F	–	–	–	–	–	–	–	–	–	–	50	–	–	–	–	–	–	–	–	–	24	–	–	–	–

4. Questionable Jewish loyalty/nationality (% Yes)

Yr	37-38	46	49	50	52	56	60	61	62	63	64	66	67	68	69	71	73	74	75	76	77	78	79	81	82
US	–	–	–	–	–	–	–	–	–	–	30	–	–	–	–	–	34	26	–	27	–	29	29	30	–
BRD	–	–	–	–	–	–	–	–	–	–	–	–	–	–	–	–	–	55	–	–	–	–	–	–	–
A	–	–	–	–	–	–	–	–	–	–	–	–	43	–	–	–	–	–	–	–	–	–	–	–	–
F	–	43	–	–	–	–	–	–	–	–	–	19	–	–	–	–	–	–	–	–	–	9	–	–	–

5. Are there too many Jews in the country? (% Yes)

Yr	37-38	46	49	50	52	56	60	61	62	63	64	66	67	68	69	71	73	74	75	76	77	78	79	81	82
US	–	–	–	–	–	–	–	–	–	–	–	–	–	–	–	–	–	–	–	–	–	–	–	–	–
BRD	–	–	–	37	29	–	–	–	18	–	–	–	–	–	–	–	–	–	–	–	–	–	–	–	–
A	–	46	–	–	–	–	–	–	–	–	–	–	–	–	–	21	–	–	16	–	–	–	–	–	–
F	–	–	–	–	–	–	–	–	–	13	–	–	–	–	–	–	–	–	–	–	–	–	–	–	–

6. Jews cause trouble (sometimes: with their ideas) (% Agree)

Yr	37-38	46	49	50	52	56	60	61	62	63	64	66	67	68	69	71	73	74	75	76	77	78	79	81	82
US	–	–	–	–	–	–	–	–	–	10	–	–	–	–	–	–	–	–	–	–	–	–	–	10	–
BRD	–	–	–	–	–	–	–	–	–	–	–	–	–	–	–	–	–	29	–	–	–	15	9	–	–
A	–	–	–	–	–	–	–	–	–	–	–	–	–	–	–	–	–	–	–	–	–	–	–	–	42
F	–	–	–	–	–	–	–	–	–	–	–	–	–	–	–	–	–	–	–	–	–	–	–	–	–

Sources: Doris Bensimon and Jeannine Verdes-Leroux, "Les Français et le Problem Juif. Analyse secondaire d'un sondage de l'IFOP," *Archives de Sociologie des Religions* 29, 1970, pp. 53–91; Dieter Bichlbauer and Ernst Gehmacher, "Vorurteile in Österreich," *Kölner Zeitschrift für Soziologie und Sozialpsychologie* 24, 4, 1972, pp. 734–746; Hazel Gaudet Erkine,

```
        37-
Yr      38 46 49 50 52 56 60 61 62 63 64 66 67 68 69 71 73 74 75 76 77 78 79 81 82
```

7. Can tell a Jew just by looking? (F: Are Jews a separate race?) (% Yes)

```
US    - - - - - - - - - - 43 - - - - - - - - - - - - - -
BRD   - - - - - - - - - - - - - - - - - - 45 - - - - - -
A     - - - - - - - - - - - - - - - - - 38 - - - - - - -
F     - - - - - - - - - - - 7 - - - - - - - - - - - - -
```

8. Are Jews being punished today by God for killing Jesus? (% Yes)

```
US    - - - - - - - - - - 20 - - - - - - - - - - - - 12 -
BRD   - - - - - - - - - - - - - - - - - 28 - - - - - - -
A     - - - - - - - - - - - - - - - - - - - - - - - - -
F     - - - - - - - - - - 8 - - - - - - - - - - - - - -
```

9. Would you marry a Jew (or: let your child) (% No)

```
US    - - - 57 - - - - 37 - 56 - - - 21 - - - 61 - - - - 42 -
BRD   - - 70 - - - - 54 - - - - - 29 - - - - - - - - - - -
A     - - - - - - - - - - - - - - - 35 - - 37 - - - - - -
F     - - - - - - - - - - - 37 - - 16 - - - - - 16 - - - -
```

10. Have contact with, know Jews (% Yes)

```
US    - - - - - - - - - - - 84 - - - - - - - 49 - 46 - 80 -
BRD   - - - - - - - - - - - - - - - - - 32 - - - - - - -
A     - - - - - - - - - - - - - - - - 40 - - - - - - - -
F     - - - - - - - - - - - 23 - - - - - - - - - - - - -
```

Key: US = United States; BRD = West Germany; A = Austria; F = France.

"The Polls: Religious Prejudice, Part 2: Anti-Semitism," *Public Opinion Quarterly* 29, 4, 1965–66, pp. 649–664; Dr. Fessel, 1976 (survey); George H. Gallup (ed.), *The Gallup International Public Opinion Polls: France 1939, 1944–1975*, New York, 1976, and *The International Gallup Polls Public Opinion 1978*, Wilmington, 1980; Hyman and Wright, *op. cit.;* Institut für Demoskopie Allensbach, Jahrbücher; Bernd Marin, "Ein historisch neuartiger 'Antisemitismus ohne Antisemiten'? Beobachtungen und Thesen am Beispiel Österreichs nach 1945," *Geschichte und Gesellschaft* 5, 1979, pp. 545–569, and Marin, *op. cit.*, 1983; Martire and Clark, *op. cit.;* Gary T. Marx, *Protest and Prejudice: A Study of Belief in the Black Community*, New York, 1967; Quinley and Glock, *op. cit.;* Geraldine Rosenfeld, "The Polls: Attitudes Toward American Jews," *Public Opinion Quarterly* 46, 1982, pp. 431–443; Roland Sadoun, "Le Problem Juif," *Sondages: Revue Française de l'Opinion Publique* 29, 2, 1967, pp. 69–90; Sallen, *op. cit.;* Selznick and Steinberg, *op cit.;* Silbermann, *op. cit.;* *Sondages*, 31, 1–2, 1969, p. 114; Charles Herbert Stember, *Education and Attitude Change*, New York, 1961, and *Jews in the Mind of America*, New York, 1966; Hildegard Weiss, "Antisemitismus: Inhalte und Ausmaß antijüdischer Einstellungen in der Wiener Bevölkerung I, II, & III," *Journal für angewandte Sozialforschung* 17/3, pp. 13–26, 17/4, pp. 12–22, 18/1, pp. 9, 16, 1977–78.

Table 2
Trends in Anti-Semitism in Four Western Countries:
Summaries from Table 1

	Political Anti-Semitism		Social and Religious Anti-Semitism	
	Mean percent Change/Year	% of Population Anti-Semitic: 1970 est.	Mean percent Change/Year	% of Population Anti-Semitic: 1970 est.
United States	− .69	22%	− .37	34%
West Germany	−1.81	37	−1.99	40
Austria	− .97	42	.67	36
France	−1.62	22	−1.35	10

Note:
The estimates in this table are derived from the data in Table 1 ("Political Anti-Semitism" from items 1–6 and "Social and Religious Anti-Semitism" from items 7–9). Because the original data were so sparse, one should probably not make too much of differences less than half of a percentage point in the rates of change, or differences less than ten percentage points in the 1970 estimates.

Technical Notes:
Statistics were used as a guide in calculating these estimates, but no attempt was made to assess their statistical validity because the data were so irregular. The mean percentage change per year was calculated from regression slopes of trend data in Table 1, weighted according to statistical significance as follows:
    for $p < .01$, weighted × 3
    for $p < .05$, weighted × 2
    for $p > .05$, weighted × 1
    for only 2 data points, weighted × 1
The 1970 estimates are averages of (a) regression estimates, and (b) estimates calculated from weighted average slopes, if only one data point available.

these data are shown in Part 2 of Table 1 and in Table 3. In general, most of the questions which measure probable behavior showed some easing of economic and social anti-Semitism in West Germany; but trends in prejudicial stereotypes were more ambiguous. Thus, a declining number of respondents said they would not shop in a Jewish store if the same goods were cheaper there (25 percent in 1949, 14 percent in 1974); and a declining number also said they would not marry a Jew, but here prejudice was higher than that in the United States and France at the same time – but not more than in Austria. Other questions which elicited decreasingly anti-Semitic responses included the perceptions that Jews are industrious, peace-loving, helpful, and artistically talented: and West German opinions here were generally more philo-Semitic than those of Austrians. Questions which showed rising levels of economic and social anti-Semitism include

Table 3

Ethnocentrism: Group Stereotypes

	West Germans																						Austrians
	Self	Germans	Jews	Jews	Jews	Jews	Jews	Guest-Workers	Guest-Workers	Turks	Yugoslavs	Italians	Italians	Blacks	Blacks	Japanese	Japanese	British	British	Americans	Americans	Russians	Jews
	1957	74	49	60	61	65	74	64	71	75	75	64	75	72	75	61	70	62	58	62	70	58	73
Intelligent	–	90	–	–	–	–	46	8	9	–	–	23	–	36	–	–	57	–	–	–	28	–	–
Industrious	46	92	–	52	–	–	71	22	43	–	–	24	–	35	–	–	80	28	24	26	21	–	52
Peace-Loving	–	77	–	–	14	–	53	15	27	–	–	–	–	–	–	–	19	–	–	–	8	–	–
Helpful	41	71	–	–	25	22	59	30	41	–	–	56	–	48	20	–	–	–	44	47	–	13	27
Not Clean (–)	–	6	–	–	–	–	27	–	–	–	–	–	–	–	–	–	–	–	–	–	–	–	21
Would not Marry (–)	–	–	70	–	54	–	–	–	–	82	62	56	–	–	80	67	–	–	–	–	–	–	35
Devout	21	–	–	–	–	–	45	–	–	–	–	–	70	–	–	–	–	29	16	20	–	16	79
Cowardly (–)	–	28	19	–	–	15	38	–	–	–	–	–	–	–	–	–	–	–	–	–	–	5	20
Artistically Talented	–	73	39	–	–	–	69	–	–	–	–	–	–	33	–	–	–	44	–	–	–	–	40

Sources: Institut für Demoskopie of Allensbach, Jahrbücher; Marin, *op. cit.*, 1979.

the opinions that Jews do not like physical work and will avoid it, that they are cowardly, and that they keep others out of business – in these cases, the West Germans are more anti-Semitic than the Americans or Austrians. There was a small decline in the opinion that Jews are intelligent, and Jews are seen much more often in West Germany as using shady business practices and dirty tricks than in the U.S.

Following the same procedures as those above for political anti-Semitism, estimates for 1970 levels of social and religious anti-Semitism were calculated for the questions in Part 2 of Table 1 (except question 10) – and the same cautions must be observed here to an even greater degree since the data are much sparser still. The results are given in the right-hand panel of Table 2. Here we see that the French appear to express the least non-political anti-Semitism, and the West Germans somewhat more than the Americans and Austrians. However, such anti-Semitism may be declining fastest in West Germany (but the rate of change for the European countries is based exclusively on the question of willingness to marry a Jew – not by itself a very good measure of anti-Semitism).

One can argue that since the Holocaust, ethnic prejudice has acquired new objects in West Germany, the migrant Guest Workers. In various surveys, West Germans have been asked their views of a number of characteristics of certain ethnic groups and other nationalities, and for some of these characteristics, self-anchoring responses about the respondent himself or "the Germans" are also available (see Table 3). The only groups seen in a consistently worse light than the Jews are the Guest Workers (and their constituent groups, Turks, Yugoslavs, and Italians) and the Russians. The Americans, British, Japanese, and even Blacks are sometimes seen as having better, sometimes worse, qualities than the Jews. The Guest Workers, and each important group of Guest Workers for whom there are data, are considered less intelligent, less industrious, less helpful, and less clean than the Jews. Moreover, more West Germans would not marry a Turk, Yugoslav, or Italian (but also not a Black or Japanese) than would not marry a Jew.[26] In comparison, samples of Eastern Europeans held more negative stereotype of Jews than of Americans, Blacks, or Gypsies, in that order.[27]

There are other indications that potential political prejudice exists against Guest Workers, at least in a reduced or latent state. West Germans

---

[26] However, it should be noted that most of these latter data come from different time points.
[27] Radio Free Europe/Radio Liberty, *Stereotypes Projected to Jews, Blacks and Gypsies by East Europeans and Austrians*, mimeograph, 1980.

see the presence of Guest Workers as an increasingly serious problem, and this seems recently to have become a majority opinion. 32 percent of the respondents in 1964 and 36 percent in 1971 saw them as a "serious problem for us;" 55 percent of the respondents in a 1975 survey fully agreed (an additional 28 percent partially agreed) that "it is to be feared that in the future the Guest Workers will become a serious problem for us;" and 50 percent in 1980 feared that there would be increasing tension between Guest Workers and Germans in the next year or two. And by 1982, fully 82 percent of West German respondents said that there were too many Guest Workers in the Federal Republic (as compared to 18 percent saying too many Jews in 1963). However, according to our analysis thus far, there is no reason to look for West German exceptionalism on this point. Every western, industrialized country has migrant workers (of internal and external origin) who form an underclass willing to do work spurned by middle-income workers, and each of these countries faces at least some economic uncertainty for the future. The populations of all of these countries have shown antagonism or prejudice towards their migrant workers; for instance, 62 percent of French respondents said there were too many North Africans in a 1966 survey. Nor have we seen evidence that any radical ethnocentric political movement imminently threatens to acquire a significant degree of power in West Germany – or indeed, in most other Western democracies.

3. The Structure of Anti-Semitism in Western Countries since the Holocaust

Studies in the United States have established that certain structural factors in the American population are associated with higher levels of anti-Semitism.[28] Their findings can be used as a benchmark against which to compare the structure of anti-Semitism in West Germany and other countries. In particular, the better educated are much less anti-Semitic than the worse educated in the U.S., and no other measure of social status (e. g., income, occupation) can account for this relationship. Moreover, a good portion of falling levels of anti-Semitism in America is due to rising levels of formal education in the population. Age, too, plays an important role. In general, the young in America are less anti-Semitic than the old; and older

---

[28] Gertrude J. Selznick and Stephen Steinberg, *The Tenacity of Prejudice*, New York, 1969; Lipset and Schneider, *op. cit.*; Gregory Martire and Ruth Clark, *Anti-Semitism in the United States. A Study of Prejudice in the 1980s*, New York, 1982.

liberals are less anti-Semitic than older conservatives (but ideology plays no role among the young).

Most studies of anti-Semitism in West Germany reveal patterns for age and education similar to the American studies. In the most comprehensive recent empirical study in West Germany,[29] it was found in 1974 that those with a university degree were a full 35 percentage points less anti-Semitic on a general scale than were those with just a grammar school education (Volksschule ohne Lehre), and that those under 30 were 18 percentage points less anti-Semitic than those over 55. In Austria, too, the younger are considerably less anti-Semitic than the old; but in France age seems to have little effect on anti-Semitism. We may speculate that the younger generations in West Germany and Austria are less anti-Semitic than the old because they did not grow up under a fascist regime, while there is little difference between generations in France because there was no regime change (except the wartime Vichy regime) – but this does not satisfactorily explain the existence of a generation gap in the United States. I believe the factor of a regime change played an important role here, but clearly, other factors must also be adduced.

This result reinforces the importance of interpreting such findings in a comparative framework. In related research, I have shown that the effect of education on political anti-Semitism is not universal as generally thought,[30] but rather, varies considerably across time and place. While the better educated are more liberal in certain countries and in certain historical periods for certain values, they are not more liberal under other conditions:[31] The question here is what factors determine education's effects

---

[29] Herbert A. Sallen, *Zum Antisemitismus in der Bundesrepublik Deutschland*, Frankfurt, 1977; Alphons Silbermann, *Sind wir Antisemiten? Ausmaß und Wirkung eines sozialen Vorurteils in der Bundesrepublik Deutschland*, Cologne, 1982.

[30] E. g., Herbert Hyman and Charles Wright, *Education's Lasting Influence on Values*, Chicago, 1979.

[31] Since this is true, the psychodynamic interpretation of education's effects can be rejected (see, e.g., Theodore Adorno, et al., *The Authoritarian Personality*, New York, 1950; Lipset, op. cit., 1981(a); cf. Melvin Kohn, *Class and Conformity*, Homewood, Ill., 1969). This interpretation may be valid under some historical and cultural conditions, but it is not universal. It was not possible to assert this on the basis of data from a single country because one could argue that students with certain psychological predispositions might seek more education than others (Walter T. Plant, "Longitudinal Changes in Intolerance and Authoritarianism for Subjects Differing in Amount of College Education over Four Years," *Genetic Psychology Monographs* 72, 1965, pp. 247–87); but they cannot be expected to choose their country or historical period – at least not as a result of their psychological predisposition. The interpretation that education's effects simply reflect class interests must also be rejected since these effects remain strong even when class variables are

on political anti-Semitism. Selznick and Steinberg[32] postulated that education's liberalizing effects in the United States represent the influence of the "official," Enlightenment culture: this hypothesis was expanded and applied cross-nationally to the U. S., West Germany, France and Austria. The results showed that this effect varied according to two determinants of Enlightenment culture: the length of time a country had had a liberal democratic regime form, and the degree either of "traditionalism" or of religious pluralism in the country. Thus, education had the strongest effect of reducing political anti-Semitism in the United States, a long-term liberal democracy with a small traditional sector and important religious pluralism: the weakest effect in Austria, a short-term liberal democracy with a large traditional sector and a religiously homogeneous population; and a middling effect in West Germany and France, which are mixed cases in this respect. This conclusion is reinforced by findings for Eastern European samples that education had no effect, or a reversed effect, on anti-Semitic attitudes there.[33] And previous research[34] showed that education's effect on tolerance of political opposition may have grown in West Germany since the late 1960s, and I argued that this was due to the lag in institutionalization of liberal values (through the school system) in a post-fascist democracy. Thus, there is reason to think that as more time passes in West Germany and Austria since their transitions to liberal democracy, education is likely to attain a stronger influence in reducing political anti-Semitism – and tolerance will become more firmly structurally grounded in the dominant institutions of socialization. These findings are illustrated in Table 4.[35]

Most studies also indicate that other peripheral segments of Western societies tend to be the most anti-Semitic, just as they tend to be least politically tolerant or liberal: those in rural areas, the petty bourgeoisie and sometimes workers (especially if they are not in the unions), those in the peripheral regions (e. g., the American and German south), and as pointed out, the old and poorly educated. These demographic patterns bear some similarity to the sociological base of support for the Nazis in the 1920s and

---

controlled. Thus, it may be concluded, the effect of education on postlutical anti-Semitism must be interpreted as a form of socialization.

[32] *op. cit.*

[33] Radio Free Europe/Radio Liberty, *op. cit.,* pp. 17–18.

[34] Weil, *op. cit.,* 1981; Weil, *op. cit.,* 1982.

[35] Full analyses and discussion are given in Weil, forthcoming "The Variable Effects of Education on Liberal Attitudes: a Comparative-Historical Analysis of Anti-Semitism Using Public Opinion Survey Data."

Table 4
The Effect of Education on Anti-Semitism in Four Western Countries

Jews Have Too Much Power (% Yes)

	USA				BRD		France	Austria
	1945	1952	1964	1981	1966	1974	1969	1976
Non HS Grad	59%	38%	19%	25%	13%	19%	19%	23%
HS Grad	61	32	7	21	14	16	26	33
College Grad	53	26	5	17	14	8	23	29
Total	58%	34%	12%	20%	13%	18%	24%	28%
Gamma	-.08	-.21	-.47	-.15	.04	-.23	.10	.20

Would Vote for Jew in Own Party (% No)

	USA				BRD	France
	1952	1960	1969	1981*	1960	1966
Non HS Grad	51%	32%	15%	46%	45%	51%
HS Grad	46	18	4	34	42	47
College Grad	43	17	3	23	44	41
Total	49%	22%	8%	34%	44%	50%
Gamma	-.15	-.32	-.60	-.33	-.05	-.18

Questionable Jewish Loyalty/Nationality (% Yes)

	USA			BRD	France	Austria
	1952*	1964	1981	1974	1966	1968
Non HS Grad	13%	41%	37%	58%	20%	42%
HS Grad	12	23	27	51	18	41
College Grad	10	11	24	41	17	34
Total	12%	30%	28%	55%	19%	40%
Gamma	-.11	-.58	-.32	-.19	-.06	-.09

* Question formulation differs substantially from others in the series for country.

1930s.[36] However, studies of the United States since World War II also conclude that while anti-Semitism is more prevalent among peripheral

---

[36] See the on-going debates on this topic in, e. g., Juergen W. Falter, "Wer verhalf der NSDAP zum Sieg?", *Aus Politik und Zeitgeschichte* 14, B28–29, pp. 3–21 and "Waehlerwanderungen vom Liberalismus zu (rechts-) extremen Parteien. Ein Forschungsbericht am Beispiel des NSDAP-Aufstiegs 1928–1933," in Lothar Albertin (ed.), *Politischer Liberalismus in der Bundesrepublik Deutschland*, Goettingen, 1980; Lipset, op. cit., 1981 (a); Richard F. Hamilton, *Who Voted for Hitler*, Princeton, 1982; Frederick D. Weil, "Review of Richard Hamilton, Who Voted for Hitler?", *Social Forces* 63, 1, 1984; Thomas Childers, *The Nazi Voter: The Social Foundations of Fascism in Germany, 1919–1933*, Chapel Hill, 1983.

segments of American society, and that while it is tied to certain identifiable clusters of authoritarian values, anti-Semitism in *not* an important part of any conservative political movement which has succeeded in gaining a mass following – from the McCarthyites to the John Birchers to the new Christian Right, and from Goldwater to George Wallace to Reagan.[37] Indeed, Lipset[38] is at least partly correct in his contention that recent economic difficulties in Western societies have not resulted in greater political and ethnocentric reaction because the demographic reservoirs of reaction have largely been drained by the same processes of modernization against which they traditionally protested. I would argue, however, that one should be cautious about reaching too optimistic conclusions based on the reactionary potential of declining population segments, since future dislocations which effect currently *powerful* groups could perhaps produce similar political reactions.

On the other hand, disturbing patterns of political anti-Semitism can be found in surveys from the last period of mild political radicalization in West Germany during the late 1960s when the neo-fascist National Democratic Party (NPD) nearly cleared the 5 percent hurdle required for representation in Parliament in the 1969 federal elections. For, while only 11 percent of the respondents with an opinion in a 1969 survey believed that "the Jews once again have too much power and influence here" (19 percent thought it was partly true, and 69 percent did not believe it), this position was taken by 36 percent of those who said they would vote for the NPD and 23 percent of those who welcomed the NPD's electoral gains, by 18 percent of those who said their economic situation had worsened in the past year,[39] 16 percent of refugees or expellees from the East, 15 percent of those who were dissatisfied with the performance of the government, 14 percent of those who favored outlawing the West German Communist Party, and – significantly – by 17 percent of those who favored an end to war-crimes trials and 20 percent of those who thought that "the Guest Workers harm us more than they help [nuetzen] us."

Do these findings mean that political anti-Semitism is still flourishing in West Germany? There are three questions here: (a) Is political anti-Semitism widespread? (b) Is it increasing or decreasing over time? (c) Can we identify a coherent political anti-Semitism connected to a radical polit-

---

[37] Selznick and Steinberg, *op. cit.;* Lipset and Raab, *op, cit.;* Martire and Clark, *op. cit.*
[38] op. cit. 1981 (a) and op. cit., 1981 (b).
[39] See also Klaus Liepelt, "Anhänger der neuen Rechtspartei: ein Beitrag zur Diskussion über das Wahlreservoir der NPD," *Politische Vierteljahresschrift* 2, 1967, pp. 237–71.

ical ideology in the general public? The first and second questions have already been largely answered in the negative. In order to answer the third question, a factor analysis was conducted of a set of ideological questions on the 1969 survey just cited.[40] Three factors summarizing the responses were extracted, which can be identified as Main-Stream Partisanship, National Socialist Ideology, and Voelkische Ideology. The results showed that a national socialist ideology did indeed continue to exist as an identifiable cluster of opinions at this time – although only a very small segment of the population still adhered to it – and that anti-Semitism was one important element of this cluster, along with prejudice against the Guest Workers and concern for issues remaining from the historical Nazi regime (war crimes and the statute of limitations). But this ideology was *not* related to main-stream politics in West Germany or to a milder kind of patriotic or voelkische ideology (the two other factors). Nor were sympathy with the neo-fascist NPD or anti-communism major components of this traditional national socialist ideology, since neither loaded strongly on this factor. This finding supports Niethammer's argument that the West German neo-fascism of the 1960s had a different character than the Nazism of the 1920s–1940s, since it was no longer strongly connected to racialist theories but rather rested mainly on anti-communism.[41]

Thus, a coherent, radical politicized anti-Semitism appears to have become something of an historical relic in West Germany: once this historical national socialist ideology is taken into account, contemporary West German neo-fascism hardly appears to contain an anti-Semitic component. Nor are the followers of any of the mainstream parties distinguished from any others by a stronger adherence to political anti-Semitism. In contrast, the adherents of the right-wing third party in Austria (the FPÖ) express considerably higher levels of political anti-Semitism on almost all survey questions.[42] However, in France, higher levels of political anti-Semitism are generally not associated with the voters of any of the mainstream parties except the Communist Party.

---

[40] Factor analysis is a statistical technique which can summarize a number of responses, showing which go together and which are separate, and the "factors" can be interpreted as the underlying or latent structure of the data. (However, since the factors can only summarize the questions which have been asked, they should not be interpreted to mean that other factors might not exist.).

[41] Lutz Niethammer, *Angepaßter Faschismus. Politische Praxis der NPD*, Frankfurt, 1969.

[42] Bernd Marin, "Umfragebefunde zum Antisemitismus in Österreich 1946–1982: SWS-Meinungsprofile aus: Journal für Sozialforschung 23, 1983," in John Bunzl und Bernd Marin, *Antisemitismus in Österreich. Sozialhistorische und soziologische Studien*, Innsbruck, 1983; Dr. Fessel survey of 1976.

4. Contemporary Anti-Semitism in Perspective

We are now in a position to summarize and draw a number of conclusions from our analysis. We have reviewed the available evidence concerning anti-Semitic currents in the populations of several Western countries, and the central points were these:

A distinction must be made for the modern period between political anti-Semitism and other forms, mainly social, economic, and religious. Although the latter forms have been irritating and sometimes damaging to the life-chances and living conditions of Jews, only political anti-Semitism has been truly dangerous.

Radical political anti-Semitism was probably *not* widespread among the German population prior to the Nazi rise to power, nor was it likely prevalent during their rule.[43] The Holocaust was therefore *not* the direct result of popular anti-Semitism but rather of the attainment of power of a radical movement, an event which must be explained in other terms – mainly, the weakness of liberal democratic orientations. Thus, there was no reason to expect, nor did we find, that the postwar West German population is radically politically anti-Semitic. They are more anti-Semitic than the American population, but they occupy a middling position among other European nations.

Trends in the absolute levels and structures of anti-Semitism in all countries examined are encouraging: there has been an overall reduction in anti-Semitism, and the structures which support this reduction are strengthening. In particular, education seems to be acquiring an ability to reduce anti-Semitism, which it did not always and everywhere possess; and new generations are expressing less prejudice and, to some extent, less hostility to Jews than older generations. Moreover, political anti-Semitism is not connected to the mainstream party systems of any of the countries except Austria (but the Austrian Freedom Party is quite a small third party) and to some extent France (the French Communists are mildly more anti-Semitic),

---

[43] See Steinert, *op. cit.*, for evidence regarding opinion surveys conducted for the Nazi regime; see Paul W. Massing, *Rehearsal for Destruction: A Study of Political Anti-Semitism in Imperial Germany*, New York, 1949; Peter G. J. Pulzer, *The Rise of Political Anti-Semitism in Germany and Austria*, New York, 1964; Uriel Tal, *Religious and Anti-Religious Roots of Modern Antisemitism*, Leo Baeck memorial lecture, no. 14, New York, 1971 and *Christians and Jews in Germany: Religion, Politics, and Ideology in the Second Reich, 1870–1914*, Ithaca, NY, 1975; Ruerup, *op. cit.*; Rosenberg, *op. cit.*; Bracher, *op. cit.*, for evidence regarding not only the successes but also the limitations of pre-Nazi German anti-Semitism.

but instead is restricted to marginal political movements which have little
following.

The main reason for this change in the structural basis of anti-Semitism
in West Germany is that the latter's political culture has converged to a
very great extent with that of countries with much longer liberal democratic traditions. Institutions of socialization have largely "caught up" with
the post-1945 regime change (there is evidence that they lagged in this), and
both schools and the direct experience of liberal democratic practice are
now socializing new generations in greater ethnic and religious tolerance.
And on the negative side of the same coin, political anti-Semitism has
declined because of its connection to the old, discredited historical Nazi
regime; and it is only weakly tied to mass-based neo-fascism. It was not
possible to investigate Austria's political culture as thoroughly here, but we
have found that declines in political anti-Semitism were more sluggish
there. Considering the extent of decline in the United States and France,
however, it seems reasonable to suggest that the reduction of anti-Semitism
in these countries and West Germany is also related to the general liberalization from the 1950s to the mid-1970s.

A final reason for this decline is the reduction of the traditionalist sources
of anti-Semitic prejudice: on the one hand, the Churches have moderated
many of their views, and on the other hand, the religious and traditional
sectors have declined as a proportion of Western populations.[44] This
further reduction in traditional anti-Semitism affects the possible future of
political anti-Semitism, since anti-Semitic prejudice often conditioned the
selection of targets for modern nationalistic ethnocentrism.[45]

For these reasons, tensions which arise between Jews and gentiles are
more likely than in the past to be manifested as simple intergroup conflict
and be reduceable by negotiation and mediation, and Jews are less likely to
be selected as scapegoats for problems they had little to do with creating. It
was not possible to investigate intergroup conflict directly with the data
available, but a number of indirect inferences may be permissable. In
countries where few Jews still live – above all, West Germany – there is

---

[44] There has been much less decline in American than European Christian religiosity, but the
former was never as important a source of anti-Semitism as the latter. See, however, the
debate in Glock and Stark, *op. cit.*, 1966 and *op. cit.*, 1973; and Russell Middleton, "Do
Christian Beliefs Cause Anti-Semitism?," *American Sociological Review* 38, 1973, pp.
33–52, and "Response," *American Sociological Review* 38, 1973, pp. 59–61.

[45] Jacob Katz, *From Prejudice to Destruction: Anti-Semitism, 1700–1933*, Cambridge, Mass.,
1980.

probably insufficient contact between Jews and gentiles for much conflict to exist; but if contact is not responsible for the decline in prejudice there, anti-Semitism has declined for other reasons which we have explored. In countries where many Jews live – above all, the United States – a certain amount of what appears to be anti-Semitic prejudice is probably actually intergroup conflict. (This would be true, for instance, of certain recent conflicts between Jews and Blacks over racial quotas, or between Jews and foreign-policy liberals over Israel.) Such a situation is more auspicious for the reduction of hostility to Jews, since the resolution of conflict is a more straightforward task in liberal democracies than the deconstruction of prejudice. The roles of contact and conflict are perhaps more complex, however, in Austria where many of the resident Jews are transients from the Soviet Union to Israel and other Western countries, and in France where a good many Jews are recent, culturally foreign immigrants from North Africa – but it is not possible to take these factors into account in this short article.

The problem of anti-Semitism has not disappeared in Western countries since the Holocaust, but considering the evidence we have seen, it seems reasonable to believe that renewals of anti-Semitism in the foreseeable future are unlikely to be as severe as those of the turn of the century – let alone as dangerous to Jews as those of the Nazi period. At the same time, however, the danger does continue to exist that scapegoats will be sought during crises. I have suggested that levels of hostility to certain groups need not necessarily be high in normal times for tragedy to result from a crisis if that prejudice is mobilized by a radical political movement. Unfortunately, the likely target of scapegoating may simply have shifted away from Jews to other ethnic minorities – especially the foreign workers in Europe and foreign workers and Blacks in America. On the other hand, studies have shown reductions in racial prejudice in the United States and Europe: perhaps one's best hope is that intergroup tensions can be confined to matters of conflict – which can be mediated – rather than prejudice, which is little susceptible to rapid reduction, especially during a crisis.

Harold E. Quinley and Charles Y. Glock

Christian Sources of Anti-Semitism*

For centuries, Christianity was a principal force behind the segregation and persecution of Jews. It was the official religion of much of the Western world, and its followers displayed little tolerance or mercy toward those not accepting Christian teachings. To many Christians, furthermore, Jews were not just religious heretics, but Christ-killers. They were held personally responsible for the Crucifixion of Jesus and believed to have brought down upon themselves the wrath and vengeance of God. In murdering the Redeemer, they had supposedly sealed their fate and that of their children for eternity. This charge of deicide served as the inspiration for the medieval segregation of Jews and for the bloody pogroms – officially sanctioned massacres – that have recurred throughout Western history.

The Christian roots of anti-Semitism are thus strong; Jews have been stigmatized as religious heretics, defilers, and murderers. Indeed, such images have been so powerful that they have often been invoked even when religious issues have not been directly at issue. Adolf Hitler – who otherwise had little to say about religion – found it convenient to evoke Christian symbols in justifying the confinement and execution of more than six million Jews.

While all this is true of the past, what is its relevance in America today? Heretics are not being burned at the stake, and no respected Christian leader refers to the Jews as "accursed." It is an age of *rapprochement* between Jews and Christians, a time of mutual acceptance and even of cooperation. American history is not without examples of religiously inspired prejudice and bigotry, of course, but over time the nation has learned to live with its religious differences reasonably well. The differences have made necessary a quest for ways to minimize disagreement and to emphasize the values of religious tolerance and pluralism.

---

* From: Harold E. Quinley and Charles Y. Glock, *Anti-Semitism in America* (New York: Free Press, 1979, Chapter 6).

Americans are thus understandably puzzled when it is suggested that they are religiously prejudiced. Religious intolerance is admitted to exist in the backwoods – or perhaps within certain untutored sections of the country – but not among the majority of Christians.

It is certainly true that Americans do not actively persecute one another on religious grounds and that Christian and Jewish religious bodies now work with one another openly and positively in a variety of ways. Yet there remain reasons to doubt that Christians are entirely free from anti-Semitic prejudice. Once a social pattern becomes deeply entrenched within a culture, it does not easily die out. In the past Christianity was a prominent source of anti-Semitism, and it seems unlikely that there are no remaining vestiges of this legacy. Further, while the official position of Christian churches is one of tolerance, this does not mean that such a norm will necessarily be observed by all church members or, indeed, by all church leaders. Numerous examples can be cited of discrepancies between an institution's formal norms and the informal practices of its members.

Because such doubts were entertained, it was decided to make religion a subject of special investigation in the series of studies on anti-Semitism in America. If anti-Semitism is nourished by certain interpretations of Christian faith or by some forms of Christian worship, this fact ought to be known so that remedial steps might be taken. By the same token, if modern Christianity proves to be a positive force helping people to transcend their old prejudices, this too should be understood so that it can be made even more effective.

As reported earlier, three studies were undertaken to explore the interconnections between religion and anti-Semitism. One study involved the participation of a sample of 3000 church members residing in the San Francisco Bay Area. A second study, designed to assess whether the findings from the Bay Area study would hold true for the adult population of the country as a whole, involved 2000 interviews with a sample of that population.[1] A third study focused on clergy rather than laity and was based on 1580 questionnaires completed by a sample of Protestant pastors serving parishes in the state of California.[2] The results of the two studies of laity were highly concordant. Consequently, this report on the findings is

---

[1] The full report of these studies is contained in Charles Y. Glock and Rodney Stark, *Christian Beliefs and Anti-Semitism*, New York, 1966.

[2] The report of this study is in Rodney Stark, Bruce D. Foster, Charles Y. Glock, and Harold E. Quinley, *Wayward Shepherds: Prejudice and the Protestant Clergy*, New York, 1971.

restricted to the more comprehensive of the two lay studies – the one based on Northern California churchgoers – and the study of clergy.

Christian Beliefs and Anti-Semitism: A Model

The basic propositions tested in these three studies can be stated rather simply (see Figure 6-1). They are that certain interpretations of Christian faith are conducive to producing religiously based hostility toward Jews, and that this religious hostility makes those who harbor it especially prone to secular anti-Semitism.

FIGURE 6-1.
Causal Sequence: Orthodoxy to Anti-Semitism

Orthodoxy

Particularism

Hostile Image of Historical Jew

Hostile Image of Modern Jew

Secular Anti-Semitism

Source: Rodney Stark et al., *Wayward Shepherds*, New York, 1971, p. 12.

The beginning of this postulated causal chain is orthodox Christian belief, a commitment to those doctrines which historically have been central to the Christian religion. These include beliefs in an omnipotent, all-knowing

God who imposes certain requirements on man; in Jesus Christ as the Son of God, sent to earth so that men could be forgiven for their sins and receive the blessing of eternal life; and in the existence of Hell, to which those who turn their backs upon such Christian beliefs will be sent.

As will be seen, not all church people today – clergy or laity – accept these doctrines in such literal terms. Those who do, it was predicted, would be especially likely to be caught up in the second link in the chain leading to anti-Semitism, a disposition to see Christian truth as the only religious truth and to view all other faiths as fallacious and misguided.

The importance of such a particularistic religious orientation is that it may lead to hostile feelings toward those not accepting traditional Christian doctrines. If only right-thinking, orthodox Christians are saved, non-Christians are by definition damned. This imputation can extend to Buddhists, Hindus, Satanists, or other religious outsiders. Historically, however, Jews have been a special object of Christian invectives, and in this country Jews are by far the largest and most conspicuous non-Christian group. For these reasons, if hostile feelings flow from particularistic religious conceptions, it is likely that they will most often be directed against Jews. This can take the form of *hostility toward historical Jews* – the renegades from the Christian faith and the crucifiers and revilers of the Son of God. It can also take the form of a *hostility toward the modern* Jew – the heretic and the nonbeliever in essential Christian truths. That *particularistic* Christian belief does lead to religious hostility toward both historical and modern Jews are the next links in the postulated causal chain.

The final link in the causal model is the crucial one – the linkage between religious hostility toward Jews and *secular anti-Semitism*. The idea here is rather simple and straightforward, namely, that ideas have consequences. It is proposed that people who maintain hostile attitudes toward Jews on religious grounds will be especially vulnerable to hostile secular stereotypes of Jews. In effect, if it is believed that Jews are heretics or out of favor with God, it is a small step to also believing that they are wicked or evil in other ways as well.

Christianity and Religious Hostility Toward Jews

This causal sequence provided the theoretical framework used to investigate and explain the existence of anti-Semitism among American Christians. In order to determine its accuracy, it was necessary to devise ways to measure the various critical components of the theory – orthodoxy, particularism, religious hostility toward Jews, and secular anti-Semitism.

Orthodox christianity

The measurement of commitment to orthodox Christian belief was approached through asking respondents to express their degree of acceptance of such traditional articles of Christian faith as belief in God, the divinity of Jesus, the devil, life after death, and the Biblical accounts of Jesus' miracles. It was discovered that there are considerable differences in what church people believe about these central tenets of Christianity. The differences are illustrated in Table 6-1, which shows the proportion of Protestant and Roman Catholic laypersons and Protestant clergy who responded in an orthodox way to a sample of the questions asked. The range is from 86 percent of Roman Catholics who expressed unequivocal belief in the divinity of Christ to 38 percent of Protestant laypersons who acknowledge without qualification the existence of the devil. On most questions the majority give orthodox responses, but the majority is rarely overwhelming, and it is clear that there are many Christian church members and clergy who do not subscribe to traditional tenets of faith.

Table 6-1.

Christian Laypersons' and Protestant Ministers' Acceptance of Orthodox Religious Beliefs.

	Laypersons		Protestant
	Protestants	Catholics	Ministers
"I believe in God and I have no doubts about it." (percentage agreeing)	71%	81%	67%
"Jesus is the Divine Son of God and I have no doubts about it." (percentage agreeing)	69	86	61
"There is life after death." (percentage accepting as completely true)	65	75	79
"The Devil actually exists." (percentage accepting as completely true)	38	66	41
100% (N) =	(2,326)	(545)	(1,580)

Source: Adapted from Charles Y. Glock and Rodney Stark, *Christian Beliefs and Anti-Semitism,* New York, 1966, pp. 5, 7, 12; and Rodney Stark, Bruce D. Foster, Charles Y. Glock, and Harold E. Quinley, *Wayward Shepherds: Prejudice and the Protestant Clergy,* New York, 1971, pp. 17, 19, 23.

That there is variation made it plausible to develop a summary measure of it. To this end, an index of orthodoxy was constructed based on lay answers to the questions asking them about the existence of a personal God, the divinity of Christ, the authenticity of Biblical miracles, and the existence of the devil. In the construction of the index, a respondent received a score of 1 for each of these belief questions on which he or she expressed certainty about the truth of the Christian position. Respondents received a score of 0 for each item on which they acknowledged doubt or disbelief about the orthodox response. Thus a person could score as high as 4 by being certain in his faith on all four items, or as low as 0 by reporting doubt or disbelief on all four. Following the same procedure, an index of orthodoxy was also constructed for Protestant clergy.

Table 6-2.

Orthodox Religious Beliefs of Laypersons and Protestant Ministers.

	Percentage Scoring High in Religious Orthodoxy			
	Laypersons		Protestant Ministers	
United Church of Christ	4%	(141)	7%	(137)
Methodist	10	(381)	6	(350)
Episcopal	14	(373)	19	(204)
Disciple of Christ	18	(44)	a	
Presbyterian	27	(457)	24	(225)
Lutheran Church in America	43[b]		39	(86)
American Lutheran Church		(195)	59	(115)
American Baptist	43	(76)	65	(144)
Missouri Synod – Lutheran Church	66	(111)	89	(131)
Southern Baptist	88	(76)	95	(167)
Sects	86	(247)	–[a]	
Catholic	62	(500)	–	

[a] None included in this study.
[b] Figure is for L. C. A. and A. L. C. combined.
Source: Adapted from Glock and Stark, *Christian Beliefs and Anti-Semitism*, p. 13; and Stark *et al.*, *Wayward Shepherds*, p. 33.

Table 6-2 reports the proportion of laypersons and clergy who scored 4 on the orthodoxy index; that is, respondents who gave an orthodox response to each of the four items included in the index, and therefore can be considered highly orthodox. In this table results are presented not only for Protestants taken as a whole but also broken down to show the figures for members of different faiths. Overall, Roman Catholic laymen are much more likely to score high on orthodoxy than Protestants. The figure for total Protestants, however, masks great variations by denomination. At the one extreme are the members of the United Church of Christ, where only 4 percent score as highly orthodox. At the other extreme are the Southern

Baptists and sect members, where respectively 88 percent and 86 percent score as highly orthodox. This variation by denomination also holds true, as can be seen, for Protestant clergy. (Catholic priests, it will be recalled, were not surveyed in these studies; thus there is no figure for the degree of their orthodoxy.)

Particularism

The main interest in these inquiries lay not with religious orthodoxy *per se*, of course, but with the consequences it has for other beliefs in the causal chain leading to secular anti-Semitism. The first of these, it will be recalled, was religious particularism – the belief that one's own religion is the only true one and that all others are false and even pernicious. Particularism can be viewed as a kind of religious chauvinism. It is a dismissal of all religious perspectives different from one's own.

Within Christianity, particularistic attitudes have historically centered on the question of salvation: Who will and who will not receive God's grace and be rewarded with eternal life. One traditional answer has been that one must accept Jesus Christ as savior in order to be so saved. In recent years, this definition has been liberalized in many denominations so that salvation is a possibility for Jews, Moslems, and other non-Christians.

However, as has been observed already in the discussion of orthodoxy, the gap between official pronouncements and individual attitudes – whether among the clergy or the laity – is often a large one. So it is with religious particularism. Two-thirds of the Protestant laypersons and half of the Catholics agreed that a belief in Jesus Christ as savior was "absolutely necessary" for salvation. Among Protestant clergy, this figure reached 69 percent. The majority of Christians clearly continue to hold beliefs that would condemn non-Christians to damnation (as well as those Christians not accepting Jesus as the Son of God).

As above, this "total" statistic is something of a fiction, varying greatly from denomination to denomination. Among Protestant laity, the percentage holding to such a belief ranges from a low of 38 percent among United Church of Christ to a high of 97 percent among Missouri Synod Lutherans and Southern Baptists. Among clergymen, the figures similarly vary from 29 percent of the United Church of Christ ministers to 97 percent among Missouri Synod Lutherans and 99 percent among Southern Baptists. The belief that non-Christians are damned is thus virtually unanimous in some churches, while a minority viewpoint in others.

Since these denominational distributions correspond with those found above for orthodoxy, it seems likely that orthodoxy and particularism are closely linked (as the model suggested they would be). In fact, they are. Among clergy and laity alike, an orthodox theological world view leads to the belief that those rejecting Jesus Christ as the savior of mankind are personally doomed.

The potential importance of such particularistic attitudes for anti-Semitism lies in what they may imply for how persons of the Jewish faith are responded to. In the past, particularist beliefs have led to a missionary zeal to convert those not believing in orthodox Christian truths and, of frequent occasions, to the persecution of those rejecting such conversion. Christianity today has lost much of its previous fervency but perhaps not all of its righteousness. Orthodox, particularistic Christians may continue to have feelings of hostility toward nonbelievers and, because of their visibility, especially toward Jews.

Images of the Historical Jew

Undoubtedly the most pernicious and sinister of all Christian images is that of Jews as Christ-killers – the murderers of Jesus Christ, the Christian Redeemer. The principal source of this epithet is a passage in the Book of Matthew describing the trial of Jesus before the Roman Procurator of Judea, Pontius Pilate. According to Matthew's account, Pilate thought Jesus to be innocent of any wrongdoing and sought to avoid his execution. A long-standing Jewish custom allowed a condemned prisoner to be pardoned at feast time, and Pilate gave the Jewish multitude the choice of releasing Jesus or another prisoner, Barabbas, who had been found guilty of murder and sedition. Instead of Jesus, however, the crowd was per-suaded by their priests and elders to pardon Barabbas. When Pilate protes-ted Jesus' innocence, the Jewish multitude cried out, "His blood be on us, and on our children."

The charge that Jews are collectively responsible for the execution of Jesus has been repeated through the centuries and has been used to justify continued Jewish persecution. In a 1939 pastoral letter, for example, Conrad Gröber, the Roman Catholic Archbishop of Freiburg, Germany, wrote that the Jews were entirely responsible for the Crucifixion of Christ and that "their murderous hatred of Him has continued in later cen-turies."[3] Bishop Hilfrich of Limburg echoed this viewpoint, adding that

---

[3] Pastoral letter of January 30, 1939, *Amtsblatt für die Erzdiözese Freiburg,* February 8, 1939, quoted in Guenter Lewy, "Pius XII, the Jews, and the German Catholic Church," *Com-mentary,* February 1964, pp. 23–35.

for their murder of God the Jews have been under a curse since the original Good Friday.[4] Such religious attitudes were fairly typical of the German Roman Catholic hierarchy – and to a lesser extent of Protestant church leaders – at the time. In this country much the same charges were being made by Father Charles E. Coughlin and revivalist preachers such as Gerald B. Winrod and Gerald L. K. Smith.

Following the destruction of European Jewry, the Roman Catholic Church and most of the major Protestant churches recanted their previous positions on this issue. They denounced the doctrine of Jewish guilt for the Crucifixion and taught that all mankind is responsible for the death of Jesus. Today only a few denominations – most notably the Missouri Synod Lutherans and Southern Baptists – have failed to condemn the age-old charge of deicide.

Official church actions, however, can hardly be expected to change people's minds overnight. Indeed, research has shown that most Protestants remain completely unaware of their denominations' official pronouncements and that in many issue areas Catholic openly rejected their church's stands (such as in relation to birth control).[5] Thus it was felt that some church members might continue to hold Jews responsible for the Crucifixion, even though their church's official teachings were otherwise.

The presence among contemporary Christians of a belief that Jews were responsible for the Crucifixion was explored somewhat differently in the lay and clergy studies, although both studies confirm that such a belief continues to be widely held. In the lay study, which dealt with the subject more comprehensively, an effort was made to assess not only Matthew's account of Jewish responsibility for the Crucifixion but also the themes that Pilate tried to prevent the execution and that the Jewish multitudes, stirred up by their priests and elders, forced the Crucifixion to be carried out.

Seventy-nine percent of the laity (Catholics and Protestants alike) agreed that Pilate "wanted to spare Jesus from the cross." Forty-seven percent of the Protestants and 46 percent of the Catholics acknowledged that "a group of powerful Jews wanted Jesus dead." When given a choice of choosing the Romans, the Greeks, the Jews, the Christians, or none of these as the group most responsible for crucifying Christ, 58 percent of the Protestants and 61 percent of the Catholics chose the Jews.

---

[4] Quoted in Lewy, "Pius XII."
[5] Charles Y. Glock, Benjamin B. Ringer, and Earl R. Babbie, *To Comfort and to Challenge*, Berkeley, 1967, and Andrew M. Greeley, *The Denominational Society*, Glenview, Ill., 1972.

At least as an historical interpretation, it is evident from these figures that many Christians continue to hold Jews responsible for the Crucifixion. Further, many of them assign questionable or evil motives to the Jewish rejection of Jesus. When asked why the Jews rejected Christ as the Messiah, 44 percent of the Protestants and 39 percent of the Catholic supported the assertion that the Jews "couldn't accept a Messiah who came from humble beginnings," 21 percent of Protestants and 16 percent of Catholics charged that "the Jews were sinful and had turned against God."

Protestant clergy were asked only the question about which group was most responsible for crucifying Christ, but the option "all mankind" was added to those made available to the laypersons. Given that option, the majority of clergy – 54 percent – chose it, but 32 percent still chose the Jews. Thus, even among clergy there is a substantial minority who blame the Jews for Christ's death.

Hostile Religious Conceptions of the Contemporary Jew

The persistence of specifically religious, as distinct from secular, hostility toward Jews was also investigated with respect to the modern Jew. Is it believed that Jews today continue to bear the stigma of their rejection of Jesus? To measure this dimension of belief two propositions were put to the lay and clerical respondents. The first suggested that Jews are still to be blamed for the Crucifixion: "The Jews can never be forgiven for what they did to Jesus until they accept Him as the true savior." In the lay study, 33 percent of the Protestants and 14 percent of the Catholics agreed with this statement, while another 27 percent and 32 percent, respectively, were uncertain in their beliefs. All together, then, 60 percent of the Protestants and 46 percent of the Catholics at least acknowledge the possibility that Jews are unforgiven for their treatment of Jesus. Clearly, for many Christians the Crucifixion remains a salient point of reference in their judgment about Jews.

The second statement was even more strongly worded. It asked, in effect, whether the contemporary Jew is "cursed by God:" "The reason the Jews have so much trouble is because God is punishing them for rejecting Jesus." To agree with this statement is tantamount to viewing the mistreatment of Jews today as divinely ordained. It was accepted by 13 percent of the Protestants and 11 percent of the Catholics in the lay study. If we add to these figures those who were uncertain in their views, 39 percent of the Protestants and 41 percent of the Catholics allowed the possibility that Jews were under God's curse.

Many rank-and-file church members thus hold hostile religious images of Jews. Considerably fewer clergy subscribe to such images, although the number, particularly with respect to the view that "the Jews can never be forgiven for what they did to Jesus until they accept Him as the true savior," is not insubstantial. Nineteen percent of the clerical respondents agreed with this statement, while another 6 percent were uncertain of their position. On the more strongly worded statement – that Jews are being punished for rejecting Jesus – 8 percent agreed, with another 4 percent uncertain.

Feelings of religious hostility toward Jews thus also exist among the clergy, albeit at a lower level than among the laity. The anomalous nature of these attitudes can be better appreciated if they are compared with the way in which Americans characteristically think about other ethnic or population groups. With very few exceptions, judgments are made about them in contemporary terms and not from the perspective of past history. For example, the atrocities of the Romans is virtually never considered in presentday conceptions of modern-day Italians, or the vicious raids of the Vikings in thinking about Scandinavians. Those are simply past events holding little relevance to contemporary values or beliefs. Even an occurence as recent and as murderous as World War II is today of small consequence to the images held of our former adversaries. The Germans and the Japanese of contemporary times are seldom equated with the hated enemies of forty years ago.

To make such judgments of Jews is thus a rare and peculiar practice. Even if Jewish leaders were active agents in the execution of Jesus some 2000 years ago, it is odd that Americans would consider this fact to have any bearing on their evaluations of Jews today.

Orthodoxy, Particularism, and Religious Hostility

But are these tendencies among Christians attributable to their religious beliefs? More specifically, is religious hostility toward the contemporary Jew a product of an orthodox and a particularist vision of Christian faith? The answer is yes, but not absolutely. Not all Christians whose faith is highly orthodox and particularistic exhibit religious hostility. In turn, not all Christians whose faith is other than orthodox and particularist are entirely free of such hostility. There exist, however, rather strong tendencies for the beliefs and hostility to go together.

Among Protestant laity, 86 percent of those who are highly orthodox and highly particularist, and who attributed Christ's death to the Jews feel that Jews still cannot be forgiven for rejecting Jesus. In contrast, only

1 percent feel this way among those low on both orthodoxy and particularism and who did not blame the Crucifixion on the Jews. Fewer Catholics than Protestants harbored a negative religious image of the modern Jew in the first place, and thus the actual percentage differences for them are smaller. However, a majority of Catholics holding the negative image scored high on particularism and orthodoxy and also blamed the Jews for the Crucifixion.

The same pattern of relation holds for Protestant clergy. Among clergy who are highly orthodox and highly particularist, and who attribute the Crucifixion to the Jews, 89 percent agreed either that the Jews can never be forgiven until they accept Christ or that the Jews are being punished by God or both. In comparison, such agreement is only 18 percent among non-orthodox, nonparticularist clergy who reject an image of the Jews as responsible for Christ's death.

As a consequence of these patterns, anti-Jewish feelings are found largely within those denominations where religious views of an orthodox and particularist nature are most commonly taught. In the clergy study, 69 percent of the Southern Baptists and 53 percent of the Missouri Lutherans agreed that Jews would remain unforgiven until they accept Christ as savior, as contrasted with only 3 to 4 percent of the United Church of Christ, Methodist, and Episcopalian clergy. A similar range of opinions was found among laypersons. Eighty percent of the Southern Baptists and 70 percent of the Missouri Synod Lutherans agreed that the Jews remain unforgiven. Among members of the United Church of Christ, Methodists, and Episcopalians, the figures were respectively 10, 12 and 11 percent.

In summarizing these findings, it must be pointed out exactly what is involved in the holding of such beliefs. To consider Jews to be unforgiven and an object of God's punishment is an unmistakably hostile attitude. It represents a highly damaging conclusion – one that is almost certain to affect the holder's general feelings toward Jews. To entertain such notions is thus a form of religious bigotry and prejudice.

From the perspective of traditional Christianity, this judgment may seem unfair or overly harsh. For conservative Christians it is often an article of faith that Jews – a group not accepting Jesus as the Son of God – remain unforgiven and unsaved; it may not seem that such a position involves any hostility or prejudice. This argument, for example, was made by the Reverend Wayne Dehoney, then president of the Southern Baptist Convention, in criticizing the results just reported. He was quoted in *Newsweek* magazine:

> Christians do believe that all Jews who reject Christ as the Messiah are therefore lost from
> God's redeeming love – as are all men of all races who have not personally responded to
> God's grace through faith in Jesus Christ. This is not racism; this is the Christian doctrine
> of personal salvation.[6]

A similar position was taken by a Missouri Synod Lutheran minister respondent in the clerical study:

> I feel sorry for all Jews who have rejected Jesus and thus have no God. There is only one
> God (Father-Son-Holy Ghost). "He that knoweth not the Son honoreth not the Father,"
> said Jesus. The unrepentant Jew is unsaved. God loves the Jews and chose them, and my
> Savior is a Jew. But they have chosen to reject Him. What more could they have wanted
> from the Messiah?

While such statements might seem perfectly reasonable from an orthodox point of view, they amount to a demand that Jews renounce their own religious convictions and heritage and accept Christianity; if they do not, they will be punished for eternity.

Christian Beliefs and Anti-Semitism

The first four stages of the model have thus been substantiated. A commitment to an orthodox and particularistic version of Christian faith does indeed lead to the holding of hostile religious feelings toward modern-day Jews. It does so through a cognitively related chain of beliefs; once certain basic assumptions are made about religious reality, it follows logically that Jews will be viewed as religious outsiders or heretics.

It is time now to present evidence on the final and most controversial step in this model. The central purpose of these investigations was to determine whether religious convictions play any part in contemporary anti-Semitism. It was thought that people who held hostile religious conceptions of Jews might tend also to develop anti-Jewish feelings of a more general or secular nature – simply put, that people who disliked Jews on religious grounds would easily fall prey to disliking them in more secular ways as well.

Anti-Semitism among Church Members

A long battery of questions was included in the study of laity for the express purpose of measuring various forms of secular anti-Semitism. These items included most of the same belief statements considered in

---

[6] Wayne Dehoney, letter to the editors of *Newsweek*, May 23, 1966, in response to a story on
    "Christian Beliefs and Anti-Semitism."

earlier chapters, as well as questions designed to measure the respondents' feelings toward interacting with Jews and their potential reaction to Jews under certain hypothetical conditions. Since little difference was found among these various indicators of anti-Semitism, attention here will be limited to anti-Semitic beliefs.

First, how anti-Semitic in their beliefs are churchgoers? Are the values of Christian brotherhood reflected in a greater acceptance of Jewish people? Or do the religious feelings outlined above produce greater hostilities toward Jews? Speaking generally, the level of anti-Semitism found among church members is about the same as that found among the general public. The proportion of respondents in this study accepting negative stereotypes of Jews was almost identical to that in the national study cited in Chapter 1. For example, 33 percent of the Protestants and 29 percent of the Catholics agreed that it was true or somewhat true that "Jews are more likely than Christians to cheat in business." Thirty-one percent and 26 percent, respectively, felt that "Jews, in general, are inclined to be more loyal to Israel than to America." And 57 percent and 55 percent agreed that "Jews want to remain different from other people, and yet they are touchy if people notice these differences."

Such figures indicate that church members are not much different from anyone else when it comes to anti-Semitic prejudice. In the national study it was estimated that a third of the American people were highly prone to hold anti-Semitic beliefs; in the present study the figure was set at 33 percent for Protestants and 29 percent for Catholics.[7] Again, it should be pointed out that such percentages do not refer to the virulent form of anti-Semitism associated with Nazi Germany or with certain hate groups in this country. Anti-Semitic feelings of this type are relatively rare in present-day America. These figures do, however, refer to individuals who are highly disposed to stereotype Jews in negative ways, including stereotypes of an overtly belligerent and hostile nature.

Anti-Semitism can thus be found within the churches as well as outside of them. This in itself is hardly a surprising finding; there are few knowledgeable observers who believe that organized religion is entirely free from prejudice. To what extent, however, are such anti-Semitic beliefs a product of distinctly religious convictions rather than of something else?

---

[7] Catholics have often been the objects of religious prejudice themselves, and this apparently contributes to their somewhat lower levels of anti-Semitism. Catholics, however, do not appear to be any more tolerant than Protestants or atheists. About a third of each religious group, for example, would not allow an atheist to teach in a public high school.

Previously, four distinct sets of Christian beliefs were identified, and their causal connections demonstrated. Orthodoxy was seen to produce a particularistic world view in which only right-thinking Christians were subject to salvation; theological beliefs of this nature, in turn, were associated with hostile religious images of both the historical and modern Jew. Upon examination, *all four of these religious beliefs were found to be strongly associated with secular anti-Semitism.* Indeed, taken together, they prove a powerful predictor of secular anti-Semitism. This is indicated in Table 6-3, which combines these four dimensions of Christian belief into a single composite index of "religious bigotry." As this table indicates, the respondents' anti-Semitism varies in direct relation to their positions on this measure. Among Protestants, the proportion of anti-Semites ranged from 10 percent among those low in religious bigotry to 78 percent among those high on this dimension; among Catholics, the range was from a low of 6 percent to a high of 83 percent. These variations are among the greatest of any encountered in the studies in this series. Moreover, these variations are sustained when such controls as age, education, and socio-economic background are taken into account. That is to say, whether persons are young or old, educated or uneducated, rich or poor, the more the religious beliefs are subscribed to, the greater the anti-Semitism.

Table 6-3.

Percentage of Christian Laypersons Scoring High in Anti-Semitic Belief at Each Level of Religious Bigotry Index.

Percentage scoring high and medium high on index of anti-Semitic belief	Index of Religious Bigotry						
	Low 0	1	2	3	4	5	High 6
Protestants	10% (216)	15% (233)	28% (206)	37% (146)	46% (159)	57% (124)	78% (97)
Catholics	6% (31)	17% (54)	19% (78)	39% (59)	40% (33)	58% (21)	83% (6)

Source: Adapted from Glock and Stark, *Christian Beliefs and Anti-Semitism,* p. 136.

It is important to recognize, however, that the process through which this occurs is not directly from orthodox and particularist belief to secular anti-Semitism. Believing that salvation is possible only through Christ, for example, does not lead believers directly to be disposed to accept the additional belief that Jews are more likely than Christians to cheat in business. Rather, what the religious beliefs do is generate hostility to Jews as religious outsiders. For those believing that Jews are damned on religious grounds, it is apparently a small step to believing that Jews are also avaricious, unethical, clannish, and unpatriotic.

The significance of the linkage of Christian orthodoxy and particularism to secular anti-Semitism should not be underestimated. A large proportion of churchgoers in this country are orthodox and particularist in their religious outlooks, and in this respect *most Christians are susceptible to such religious sources of anti-Semitism.* It is not a small or deviant perspective in Christianity that contributes to anti-Semitic sentiments among people; it is the theological convictions of a large part of the religious mainstream of America.

Anti-Semitism among Protestant Ministers

Anti-Semitism among Protestant ministers is less prevalent than among Protestant laity. For example, while 53 percent of the Protestant laity agreed that it was at least somewhat true that "Jews were more likely than Christians to cheat in business," only 10 percent of the California ministers answered this way. Similarly, while 31 percent of the laity accepted the possibility that Jews were more loyal to Israel than to America, only 19 percent of the ministers agreed. Overall it was estimated that 17 percent of the Protestant clergy surveyed were anti-Semitic, as against 33 percent of the Protestant laity.[8]

This difference is attributable in part to the fact that clergymen, on the average, are better educated than lay persons. When clergy are compared with laity who have had more than a college education, which most clergy have had, the difference in anti-Semitism rates is considerably less – the clergy's 17 percent is measured against 22 percent for highly educated Protestant laity. However, among lay persons it was found that, to a large extent, the lower anti-Semitism of the more-educated was the result of their being less likely than the less-educated to subscribe to orthodox and particularist beliefs. When the more-educated did subscribe to such beliefs, they were as likely as the uneducated believers and considerably more likely than uneducated nonbelievers to be anti-Semitic.

---

[8] These two studies were based upon slightly different samples, of course, and the two estimates are thus not drawn from comparable populations. If anything, however, the lay sample (based upon the San Francisco Bay Area) should comprise more disproportionately unprejudiced respondents than the clergy sample (based upon the state of California as a whole).

Besides being less anti-Semitic, clergy also differ from laity in that their religious convictions are less likely to produce anti-Semitism. Among highly educated Protestant laity, for example, 86 percent are anti-Semitic of those who are highly orthodox particularists and feel some religious hostility toward Jews. Only 9 percent are anti-Semitic among those without the religious convictions and the hostility. Among clergy, the range is from 9 percent to 47 percent. Thus among both laity and clergy it is clear that religious convictions are a source of anti-Semitism, but the relation is considerably stronger for laity than for clergy. This is attributable to the clergy's greater ability than laity, while believing in the eternal damnation of the Jews, not to permit this to spill over into secular anti-Semitism.

That the links in the causal chain leading from religious convictions of the kind specified to anti-Semitism are not inexorable affords some promise that the chain can be broken without asking people to abandon their religious convictions. It would appear, however, that the clergy who are able to do this for themselves are not helping their parishioners to follow suit. Such clergy may well proclaim that Christian doctrines of love, brotherhood, compassion, and forgiveness erase any potential for prejudice contained in their Christian convictions. For themselves this may indeed hold true. The evidence suggests, however, that relatively few of the laity whose religious convictions are conservative are receiving the message.

Summary

The model set forth at the beginning of this chapter proved to be accurate. The acceptance of orthodox Christian beliefs leads to a particularistic religious orientation in which only right-thinking Christians are seen as saved and all others are damned. These views, in turn, are associated with hostile feelings toward Jews – which have both a historical dimension (Jews being held responsible for the Crucifixion) and contemporary effects (Jews being condemned for their rejection of Jesus as savior). Such religious beliefs, finally, are associated with secular forms of anti-Semitism. Christian laypersons and ministers holding these religious conceptions are disproportionately prejudiced in their attitudes toward Jews.

The churches today, then, may not openly preach anti-Semitism, and their official position may be one of reconciliation and rapprochement. In reality, however, orthodox Christianity continues to serve as an agent of anti-Semitic prejudice in America. It does so by introducing a set of cognitive assumptions that provide people with reasons to dislike Jews. Not everyone who accepts these assumptions draws from them the same hostile conclusions about Jews, but the majority of theological conservative churchpeople do make such connections. Thus, despite the liberalization of American religion, Christianity continues to have a strong impact upon what people think about Jews. Indeed, of the various factors examined in the entire series of studies, religious beliefs were second only to a lack of education as a primary source of anti-Semitic prejudice among Americans.

Part 3: Comparative Contexts

HELEN FEIN

Anti-Jewish and Anti-Minority Discrimination, Ideology, and Violence in Comparative Contexts

The Ecology of Antisemitism among World Civilizations

Another sociological approach to antisemitism – whether one focuses on discrimination, myths, and ideology, or political anti-Jewish mobilization, violence, and persecution – is to examine how it is related to the influence and diffusion of different civilizations, the state of political economy and group integration, and the presence, status, and visibility of the Jews themselves.

When one scans the record of modern antisemitism visually,[1] one immediately observes how much correspondence there is between the ecology of antisemitism and the orbit of western Christian civilization, and that it grew more in the late-developing nation-states of central and eastern Europe than in nation-states which had been consolidated earlier. Pogroms and anti-Jewish accusations also emerged in the nineteenth and (especially) the twentieth century in the mid-East and North Africa where the influence of Islam, Christian proselytism, and western colonialism (and its negation in nationalism) converged. Looking at a longer time-span, one may observe that, although there were Jewish communities for over a thousand years in China and India, antisemitism was unknown in both civilizations: Jews were assimilated in China eventually, and as a group were integrated into the caste-system of Indian society. Although Japan lacked an indigenous Jewish population, antisemitism was a modern European import to Japan, assimilated by the elite in their drive to master modernity after the Russo-Japanese war. In part, they responded to their experience with Jewish bankers during that war who eagerly assisted them to fight Czarist Russia, then engaged in persecuting its Jews. Japanese army officers imbibed the fraudulent *Protocols of the Elders of Zion* after the Russian revolution in the course of their collaboration with the anti-revolutionary

---

[1] Martin Gilbert, *Jewish History Atlas*, New York, 1976.

White Army.[2] Their experiences supported the contemporary European myth of Jewish bankers and Jewish world-power propagated by the *Protocols*.[3] In terms of Langmuir's typology of assertions (Part 2), their belief in Jewish power was a realistic assertion based on their experience. That power could be viewed as helpful or threatening. Later on, these officers conceived of a plan to exploit Jewish refugees in Japanese-ruled areas prior to World War II to enhance Japanese world power by giving them self-rule.[4] This was meant to establish links to the U. S. government through American Jewry. Although the "Fugu plan" was not actualized, the governing Japanese military did protect the Jews caught in the Japanese orbit during World War II; they segregated and concentrated them but did not deport them. This indicates the difficulty of assuming antisemitic (or other) attitudes are unified. It also supports the proposition (3) discussed in the Introduction to Part 2 that the behavior of people holding negative stereotypes of Jews is not predictable, especially when they hold no negative feeling toward them.

Turning toward Islamic civilization, we find general agreement that discrimination against non-Muslims is intrinsic to Islam. Jews and Christians are a recognized outgroup as "people of the book ... *dhimmis*, or tolerated infidels, whose lives were to be protected by the secular power under Islamic law in exchange for their accomodation to civil discrimination, ritual subordination, powerlessness, and oppression."[5] Although the actual status of Jews in the Arab world has varied in different epochs from being a privileged and prosperous class to a degraded and impoverished one, their rise – and the duration of their privileges – was a function of the extent of *toleration* at all times.

The rise of Arab antisemitism[6] in the twentieth century has most often been related to the Arab conflict with Jewish nationalism and Israel rather

---

[2] Tetsu Kohno, *Debates on the Jewish Question in Japan*, Amherst, Mass., (pamphlet), 1983, pp. 7–12.

[3] Ben Ami Shillony, "Anti-Semitism Without Jews: the Anti-Jewish Ideology of Japan During World War II," (Hebrew) *Zion* 46, 2, 1981, pp. 125–145; David Kranzler, "Holocaust: Japanese Policy Toward the Jews 1938–1941," *Forum on the Jewish People, Zionism and Israel* 34, 1979, pp. 63–84.

[4] Marvin Tokayer and Mary Swartz, *The Fugu Plan*, New York, 1979.

[5] Helen Fein, *Accounting for Genocide: National Responses and Jewish Victimization During the Holocaust*, New York, 1979, p. 5; Hamilton A. R. Gibb and Harold Bowen, *Islamic Society and the West: A Study of the Impact of Western Civilization on Muslim Culture in the Near East*, Vol. I, New York, 1971, p. 227; Jehoshafat Harkabi, *Arab Attitudes to Israel*, Jerusalem, 1972, pp. 218–223; S. D. Goitein, *Jews and Arabs: Their Conflicts Through the Ages*, New York, 1964, pp. 62–89.

[6] Discussed in Part 5.

than to any characteristic of Jews in the Islamic states or indigenous conflict therein. However, there is extensive evidence of the earlier ritualized degradation and powerlessness of Arab Jews in North Africa, Iran, and Yemen.[7] The intense religious hostility of certain Islamic sects who defined Jews as unclean and polluting indicates that Jews were not simply strangers, a discriminated minority, but had become a *pariah caste* in certain places.[8] Jews especially (but also Christians) maintained their morale by messianic expectations in a reaction, as Weber proposed (Part 1) that was typical of pariahs.[9] The colonization of the mid-East enabled Arab Jews to raise their aspirations and (under the French) gain special privileges which evoked the resentment of the Muslim majority. Muslims saw that the Jews – and other *dhimmis* – had violated the contract and no longer accepted their powerlessness. Competition among *dhimmi* communities in the nineteenth century instigated Christians to propagate antisemitic libels which led to violence against Jewish competitors.[10] Stillman also observes that fierce economic competition between the Christian minority and Jews in the Levant instigated the Christians to ally themselves with Arab Muslims and to introduce western antisemitism in the Arab world.[11] It was not only the conflict with Israel but the transfer of power to the majority which led to more discrimination and violence against Jews after 1945.[12]

Roles of Jews in Multi-Ethnic Empires and Plural Societies

Yet, how do we explain the distinctive role played and high status often enjoyed by Jews and other minorities in Muslim (Ottoman) and other empires? Armstrong in "Mobilized and Proletarian Diasporas" (herein) surveys the range of medieval and modern history to explain how and why Armenian, Jewish, and Chinese diasporas (among others) have served multi-ethnic empires so well, viewing the Jews as the "archetypical diaspora." To compensate for the lack of a homeland to which immigrants drawn from "situational diasporas" may return, "the religious myth defines a substitute homeland for the archetypical diaspora." Mobilized

---

[7] Bernard Lewis, *The Jews of Islam*, Princeton, N.J., 1984; Albert Memmi (ed.), *Jews and Arabs*, Chicago, 1975; Bat Ye'or, *The Dhimmi: Jews and Christians under Islam*, Rutherford, N.J., 1985.

[8] See discussion of caste, Part 1.

[9] Ye'or, *op. cit.,* pp. 154–155.

[10] Lewis, *op. cit.,* pp. 147–148.

[11] Norman A. Stillman, *The Jews of Arab Lands: A History and Source Book*, Philadelphia, 1979, pp. 109–110.

[12] Memmi, *op. cit.,* pp. 19–29.

diasporas are exploited by the dominant ethnic elite in pre-modern multi-ethnic polities which rely on them to supply skills the dominant group lacks. Armstrong goes on to consider how different diasporas coexist in the same empire (comparing the Russian and the Ottoman Empires), and which situations lead toward hostility and/or violence toward the diaspora: suspicions of loyalties to a foreign homeland and uneven modernization which engenders competition with members of the dominant group. It appears that the status of Jews and Armenians in both the Ottoman and Russian empires was inversely related: as one group declined (perhaps because it was seen as less loyal), the status of the other increased as the elite began to rely on them more.

The nineteenth-century massacres and the annihilation of the Armenians in 1915 in the Ottoman Empire show that Christian minorities were as vulnerable to collective violence as were Jews under Islam: both minorities were excluded from the dominant group's universe of obligation, the circle arising from relationship to sacred authority.[13] The dominant Islamic community may coexist in a non-violent symbiosis with the minority or turn violently against them, to expel or annihilate the non-Muslim minority if it comes to be seen as a threat, a foreign entity, or agent of a foreign power.[14]

Although there is a vast body of literature on ethnicity, the *political* relationships of Jews to multi-ethnic states has not been discussed extensively. Salo W. Baron proposed, observing the experience of Jews in multi-ethnic societies, that national states based on homogeneity are less likely to tolerate Jews than states based on many nationalities or heterogeneity.[15] From this, one might hypothesize that the more heterogeneous the peoples in a state are, the less likely is antisemitism. The one known study whose data can be reanalyzed to test this hypothesis does not support it. When one relates political antisemitism in 1936 to population homogeneity (classing nations as homogeneous if three-fourths of their people spoke the same language and belonged to the same church), one finds 6 of 10 more heterogeneous states but only 1 of 9 more homogeneous states had highly

---

[13] Helen Fein, *Imperial Crime and Punishment: British Judgement on the Massacre at Jallianwala Bagh, 1919-1920,* Honolulu, 1977, pp. 7-10.

[14] See Harold Paul Luks, "Iraqui Jews During World War II," *Wiener Library Bulletin* 30, 43-44, 1977, pp. 30-39 and Harvey E. Goldberg, "Rites and Riots: The Tripolitanian Pogrom of 1945," *Plural Society* 8, 1, 1977, pp. 35-54 for instances of the latter.

[15] Salo W. Baron, "Changing Patterns of Antisemitism," *Jewish Social Studies* 38, 1, 1976, p. 15.

successful antisemitic movements at that time.[16] Thus, the more hetero-geneous states were more, not less, antisemitic.[17]

Multi-ethnic states often are labeled plural, divided or segmented, so-cieties but should be distinguished from them. Within pre-modern plural societies (such as Poland before the twentieth century), Jews often enjoyed high collective or corporate status, endowed as a group with corporate rights of self-governance. Yet, the very structure of plural societies is conducive to collective violence and genocide when circumstances change:

> In the plural society, racial or ethnic or religious differentiation is elaborated in many different spheres. There is generally inequality in the mode of political incorporation . . .
>
> The plural society, in its *extreme* form, is characterized by a superimposition of inequalities . . . And issues of conflict tend also to be superimposed along the same line of cleavage and inequality. These structural conditions are likely to be conducive to genocidal conflict. They aggregate the population into distinctive sections, thereby facilitating crimes against collectivities.[18]

In modernizing or modern states, plural societies are especially prone to conflict as groups use the political arena to resolve class conflicts and status disparities. Minorities which have often played the role of "middlemen" – merchants, bankers, administrators, servants of the dominant class – are especially prone to victimization in such societies.

Jews (and Other) Middleman-Minorities

Middleman-minority theory seeks to explain (1) why certain minorities play such roles, (2) what effects such roles have on others' responses to them and how this reinforces the minorities' cohesion, (3) under what circumstances hostility towards the minority group emerges, and (4) what accounts for the forms it takes. Zenner's paper (herein) is the most compre-hensive review of the state of this theory today.

Middleman-minority theory encompasses a range of groups and class situations from pre-modern societies to advanced capitalism: we may cull from this body which theories best pertain to the Jews historically with least bias. Middleman-minorities are enlisted by dominant national elites to fill status gaps in their societies: expanding trade patterns in a world-

---

[16] Fein, 1979, *op. cit.*, pp. 44–45, 88.

[17] Heterogeneity of peoples was more characteristic of newer states emergent after 1878 than older states. See the discussion in the Introduction to Part 1 of the uses of antisemitism in such states, and Fein, 1979, *op. cit.*, pp. 85–86.

[18] Leo Kuper, *Genocide: Its Political Use in the Twentieth Century*, New Haven, Conn., 1981, pp. 57–58.

market especially creates the need for skilled intermediaries not found in a feudal economy. Jews were enlisted to develop pre-modern "pariah capitalism" because they were stigmatized outsiders; thus, they might acquire wealth without power or "weak money," as G. Hamilton puts it:

> This phenomenon of weak money may be outlined as follows: a ruling elite allows and even promotes a well-defined status group to generate and accumulate wealth in order to prey upon or profit from this wealth. Moreover, the ability of the elite to extract the wealth is a function of its capacity to define and keep the commercial group in a state of political and social subjugation. One way to accomplish this end is to "ethnicize" commercial class positions; for the more abject and marginal the commercial group, the more vulnerable it is to a vast variety of predatory squeezes. In order to create this wealth and in order to maintain their style of life, the elite grants economic privileges to pariah groups. The more these pariah capitalists want to be granted commercial privileges the more susceptible they must be to elite extractions. The more indispensable pariah commerce becomes to the elite, because of revenues and luxury goods, the more the elite must maintain rigid social boundaries and the means to squeeze out revenue. Thus monetary resources possessed by the commercialists not only serve to enrich the elite but also serve to maintain high levels of social and political subjugation for the pariah group.
>
> Thus the phenomenon of pariah capitalism is a prime example of a situation where those who possess monetary resources do not have high status, where those who control the means of production do not obtain political power. Instead, such possession and control indicate low status and political dependence.[19]

Class conflicts between the peasants and nobility and national conflicts may be easily displaced upon the pariah group because they are the most visible representatives of the ruling class. Further, minority characteristics engendering hostilitiy – solidarity, special cultural attributes, a "dual ethic" or alleged double-standard of obligations to minority and dominant-group members – are reinforced by their economic position and the hostility of the dominant group.

Comparisons are most often drawn between the role of Jews in eastern Europe and overseas Chinese in east Asia.[20] These groups were pushed or pulled from their states of origin by persecution and/or demographic pressures, drawn to new lands by the dominant elite's need for a commercial class to whom they had no attachment. The minority had transnational contacts and abilities which allowed them to fill the status gap between the dominant elite and the peasantry. Both minorities reacted to discrimina-

---

[19] Gary Hamilton, "Pariah Capitalism," *Ethnic Groups* 2, 1978, pp. 1–15.

[20] D. Stanley Eitzen, "Two Minorities: The Jews of Poland and the Chinese of the Philippines," *Jewish Journal of Sociology* 10, 2, 1968, pp. 221–240; Willem Frederik Wertheim, "The Trading Minorities in Southeast Asia," in Willem Frederik Wertheim (ed.), *East-West Parallels: Sociological Approaches to Modern Asia*, Chicago, 1964; Maurice Freedman, "Jews, Chinese and Some Others," *The British Journal of Sociology* 10, 1959, pp. 61–70.

tion and hostility by reinforced group solidarity, maintaining their special cultural attributes which, in turn, reinforced their cohesion, and instigated or justified the dominant group's hostility. Further, the restrictions imposed by the dominant group upon both minorities may have caused group members' behavior to resemble the stereotypes propagated by the dominant group, an example of the "self-fulfilling prophecy" described by Merton.[21] Violence against the Chinese in the era of pre-modern nation-states was most often related to their rulers' fear of their revolt, whereas violence against the Jews was related to the revolt of other subordinated classes and national groups and justified by the anti-Judaic myth and accusations of chimerical crimes. Where popular violence or state discrimination against Chinese minorities have been justified in the modern world, rulers usually created an anti-Chinese ideology or myth as in Thailand and Malaysia[22], or identified the local Chinese as enemies of the state, agents of the People's Republic as in Indonesia and Vietnam, indicating the need for an ideology of collective accusation to justify violence.

The greatest discrimination against Chinese and Jews arose after national independence when native classes reigned unchecked by colonial powers. This confirms the dependence of middleman-minorities on elites remarked upon by Armstrong and Blalock.[23] Modern ideologies of nationalism usually define the high economic status of minorities specializing in such roles as illegitimate,[24] assuming majority rule means that wealth and status should correspond to the power stemming from their number. Middleman-minorities have been charged with both failure to assimilate and assimilation; competition from majority-group members desiring to oust them from their places and competition by the minority seeking positions occupied by majority-group members may provoke both charges. Since 1945, national independence has led to the flight and/or expulsion of diverse middleman-minorities in response to state discrimination, collective violence, and movements to replace non-native middle classes; these victims include Jews in North Africa, Indians in Uganda, and Chinese in Malaysia, Indonesia, Vietnam, and the Philippines.

Most sociologists seek to create generalized theories to explain the role of a number of groups or actors in a similar position – "middleman

---

[21] Robert K. Merton, *Social Theory and Social Structures*, 2nd ed. Glencoe, Ill., 1957, pp. 426–430.
[22] Mahathir Bin Mohammed, *The Malay Dilemma*, Kuala Lumpur, Singapore, 1970.
[23] See Zenner herein.
[24] As Mohammed, *op. cit.*, did in Malaysia.

minorities," the middle classes, elites. Andreski's "An Economic Interpretation of Antisemitism"[25] is an exemplary but not altogether successful attempt to specify sociological theory to explain the variable intensity of antisemitism. Andreski hypothesizes how antisemitism is related to the numbers, wealth, economic and cultural division of groups and their complementarity, and shows how his propositions are related to the historical processes generating modern antisemitism. Andreski himself limits the scope of his theory by stressing that it can not explain German antisemitism which, he asserts, came from above.[26]

What is singular in Andreski's work is that it offers us clear, testable propositions which may be confirmed, disconfirmed, and revised. He proposes that

> If we take Europe in the 20th century we see that the differences in the intensity of antisemitism roughly correspond to the ratios of the Jews to the total populations . . . As an approximate rule, there is a critical ratio which is most conducive to popular persecutions, and which seems to lie around 10 per cent.[27]

In a study of the success of the Final Solution[28] the success of national antisemitic movements up to 1936 was related to Jews' size and status in different nations:

> The median percent Jews constituted of the population was almost ten times larger in high anti-Semitic states than in low ones (4.85%:0.5%) and median visibility (in the city with the most Jews) was almost five times (11.5%:2.5%) higher in high than in low states. However, neither the perception nor the salience of the Jews was a simple function of their size, as their unfortunate history in Germany alone testifies. Jews were no less visible in Sofia than in Vienna, but not stigmatized in Sofia as they were in Vienna. One of the factors distinguishing Bulgaria from the state of Austria-Hungary was that the role of the middleman in Bulgaria was most often performed by Greeks and Armenians rather than by Jews.[29]

The relative size and visibility of Jews was positively related to the success of national antisemitic movements up to 1936, but accounted for little over one-third of the variation in their likelihood of success. These findings are in accord with Andreski's theses and indicate its limitations.

If we relate Andreski's and Armstrong's theories and Zenner's review to the main-stream of sociological theory, we find three major lines of theory

---

[25] Summarized in Zenner.
[26] See Part 4 for research on this point.
[27] See Zenner herein.
[28] Fein, *op. cit.*, 1979, discussed in Introduction, Part 4 herein.
[29] *Ibid.*, p. 89.

which advance different expectations to explain the intensity of antisemitism in different times:

1) The more ethnic group membership and socio-economic status coincide, the fewer cross-cutting associations there will be, and the greater is the probability for polarization of issues on ethnic lines resulting in conflict. The more polarized the parties in conflict are, and the more statuses are superimposed, the more likely it is that conflict will be violent.[30] Therefore, the more the Jews are restricted to middleman-minority roles (and/or the more these roles are monopolized by the Jews), the more antisemitism can be expected.

2) The more groups play distinct socio-economic roles in the class structure, the more complementary they are and the less basis there is for conflict. When minorities enter or aspire to obtain new positions previously held by dominant-group members, and/or dominant-group members try to find places in niches occupied by and/or controlled by minorities, competition between dominant and minority-group members emerges. The more competition there is involving Jews, the more antisemitism there will be. (This is compatible with recent findings, challenging the expectations of Marxists and modernization theorists, that the less ethnic concentration/ segregation and the more intergroup competition there is, the more are groups likely to mobilize on ethnic lines.)[31]

3) Middleman-minorities exercise distinct *political* as well as economic functions for the elite. As an intermediary stratum between the elite and the masses, they serve the elite as a scapegoat in crises. This enables the masses to ventilate and displace their hostility against the ruling elite, thus protecting the latter.[32] The security of middleman-minorities or "mobilized diasporas" depends on the security of the dominant elite. Challenges to elite position stemming from mobilization of lower strata, uneven modernization, or external threats associated – really or symbolically – with the minority will lead to attacks against the minority. Thus, the intensity of antisemitism cannot be explained by the role played by Jews but by challenges to the role of the elite.

These theses are not contradictory in terms of the history of antisemitism, however, for they specify different types and contexts of conflict

---

[30] Ralf Dahrendorf, *Class and Class Conflict in Industrial Society,* Stanford, Cal., 1957, pp. 172–172; Kuper, *op. cit.,* pp. 57–58.

[31] Susan Olzak, "The Economic Construction of Ethnicity," a paper presented at the 78th Annual Meeting of the American Sociological Association, August 31–September 4, 1983, Detroit.

[32] Hubert Blalock, *Toward a Theory of Minority Group Relations,* New York, 1967, pp. 82–83.

which may instigate protagonists to attack the Jews and mobilize antisemitism. The third thesis most often refers to pre-modern states and empires and is consistent with the data presented by Armstrong and the experience of the Jews in eastern Europe from the 17th to the 19th century.[33]

The first and second thesis both predict conflict, but *different* forms of antagonism; complementarity based on an ethnic division of labor may turn into *inter-class* conflict, while competition based on free and unrestricted rivalry among individuals may lead to *intra-class* conflict, if the latter can be transformed into a struggle between ethnic or other status groups by ideological assertions that one group is an illegitimate or unfit competitor. The antagonist who exploits antisemitsm or other prejudice may be moved by economic self-interest and/or fear of loss of status.[34] Instances where Jewish assimilation and competition provoked antisemitism as in Spain in the 15th century[35] and Germany in the late 19th century[36] are cases of inter-class conflict where the competitor was stigmatized as illegitimate by the original or revised version of the anti-Judaic myth. The third thesis may refer to either of the two class situations, as all class situations are also political situations. The 1648 Chmielnitsky massacres in which the Jews, serving the Polish overlords, where slaughtered by Ukrainians in revolt against these overlords, represent the first type of situation (based on complementarity), whereas the 1492 expulsion of Jews from Spain[37] represents the second. To comprehend both cases, one might propose that any conflict involving Jews in which they are perceived as a collectivity may, given the tradition of antisemitic collective accusation (myth, libel, and ideology) lead to antisemitic mobilization.

These theses might be tested by comparing cases across a range of parallel historical situations to determine how well they explain them. To this point, these theories have neglected the difference in the prevalence, intensity and timing of violence experienced by different middleman-minorities. Ideology is usually interpreted sociologically as a secondary or derivative phenomenon. But it was the antisemitic myth and tradition of

---

[33] See also the related discussion, in Part 5, of antisemitism in the Soviet Union, a state in which Jews are not a middleman-minority but likely to be in the professional/technical elite.

[34] Everett C. Hughes, "Dilemmas and Contradictions of Status," in Lewis A. Coser and Bernhard Rosenberg (eds.), *Sociological Theory*, New York, 1964.

[35] Salo W. Baron, *Social and Religious History of the Jews*, Vol. X, New York, 1965, pp. 167–220.

[36] Norbert Kampe, "Jews and Antisemites at Universities in Imperial Germany (1)," *Leo Baeck Institute Yearbook* 30, 1985, pp. 357– 394.

[37] Which Armstrong discusses herein.

collective accusation against the Jews[38] which made Jews available as pariahs, and it is the persistence and transformation of this myth and tradition of collective accusation which has been used to mobilize violence against them.

Ideology and social structure may be viewed as independent or interacting elements in theory. Collective accusations and collective violence against minorities most often occur in plural societies based on ethnic stratification and/or segregation. Ideologies of collective accusation and charges of crime – real or chimerical – by a minority-group member provide a trigger to justify collective violence against the subordinated group which is perceived by the dominant group as a just punishment; the alleged crime of the minority-group member is attributed to their group collectively, justifying their punishment to avenge or expiate the crime against the dominant group.[39]

> Departing from Durkheim, one could say that the "function" of punishment is to produce new crime, and the "function" of crime is to legitimate punishment. What kinds of findings are explained by this insight? Reviewing the research on collective violence, that is, violence directed against groups, or arbitrarily selected members of groups, because of membership in a racial, ethnic, or religious group, one notes that with surprising regularity a crime is alleged to have been committed by a member of the group before he (or they) is attacked . . . What better justifies punishment than crime?[40]

Often race riots have been preceded by real or perceived challenges to the structure of domination by the underdogs. But,

> collective violence is not always preceded by the victims' challenge to the structure of accomodation. Pogroms against Jews have traditionally been incited by charges of ritual murder or desecration of the host, charges propagated until modern times within societies in which Jews were characterized by the dominant churches as guilty of the greatest crime of history, deicide. That such crimes as ritual murder, based on the false assumption that Jews needed Gentile blood for baking Passover matzoh, were spurious did not mean that alleged violators in a climate of hysteria could not be found to confess to them. Among societies in which such beliefs were shared, there was both a perceptual ground and, often, a collective tradition of pogroms which enabled governments to foment such pogroms purposefully. Otto Dahlke describes how such charges against the Jews were sanctioned by the Russian government in Kishinev in 1903 to divert attention from indigenous sources of unrest.[41]

---

[38] See Ruether, Part 1.
[39] Emile Durkheim, The *Division of Labor in Society*, New York, 1933; Fein, 1977, *op. cit.*, pp. 1–19.
[40] *Ibid.*, p. 13.
[41] *Ibid.*, p. 14; Otto Dahlke, "Race and Minority Riots: A Study in the Typology of Violence," *Social Forces* 30, 1952, pp. 419–425.

Dahlke, comparing the Kishinev pogrom of 1903 and the Detroit riot of 1943, showed how the traditional ritual murder legend was invoked in the former but does not show any similar single charge, myth, or accusation against Blacks in Detroit. The latter were the target of generalized police hostility (also reciprocated by the Blacks) and preexisting prejudices by Southern and foreign-born Whites in Detroit. It was direct competition between Blacks and Whites for space and resources in Detroit that triggered the riot; no comparable competition between Jews and other Russians in Kishinev has been noted. Chimerical accusations provide a trigger which authorities may invoke or explosit at their discretion.[42]

The dissimilarities in the causes and mobilization of violence in these two instances illustrate the range of attackers' and instigators' motives. Both the social structure of ethnic domination, challenges to its stability, internal crises, and the ideology and mobilization of collective violence need to be accounted for to explain anti-minority outbreaks; in the case of the Jews, the antisemitic collective accusation, whether based on the anti-Judaic myth or clad in modern dress as racial antisemitism, has been the underlying paradigm to justify destroying them. Zenner[43] also observes how similar ideologies are used to mobilize and justify anti-minority violence, especially against the overseas Chinese in Asia.

Collective accusations against Jews may be more likely in conflicts in which Jews are involved, but collective accusation displacing blame on to them also occurs in conflicts in which they figure only symbolically; the exterminatory antisemitism of the Nazis (Part 4) was based on a totally chimeric and demonic symbolization. Antisemitic accusations may be injected in conflicts in states virtually without Jews: since World War II, it has been consistently used in the Soviet satellites[44] most recently in Poland 1982, when the ruling communist elite was challenged by mass opposition represented by the Solidarity movement. Whether it "works," serves the

---

[42] Attributions frame both cognitions and accusations. Walter Zenner ("Middleman Minorities and the Diffusion of Anti-Semitism," paper delivered at the meeting of the American Ethnological Society, Toronto, May 10, 1985) relates an illustration of what Poliakov, *op. cit.*, calls "antisemitism in the pure state" in the accusation of the *fripiers* – Parisian old-clothes merchants labeled as Jews because this was considered a Jewish occupation – of merchant's son in 1652. Exploited outgroups are most easy to frame by collective accusations of chimerical crimes (see Langmuir, Part 2), but on occasions, elites seen by authorities as too powerful may also be framed by accusations of crimes that never occured, as were the Knights Templar in France (Norman Cohn, *Europe's Inner Demons: An Enquiry Inspired by the Great Witch Hunt*, New York, 1975, pp. 75–98).

[43] Zenner, *op. cit.*

[44] Paul Lendvai, *Anti-Semitism Without Jews*, Garden City, N.Y., 1971; see also Part 5.

social function for which it was intended, in the absence of intergroup conflict involving Jews or just in the absence of Jews, is open to question. In this instance, it was denounced by the opposition and did not divert collective antagonism to the government.

To test the role of ideology and the role of social structure in precipitating antisemitism, we need careful comparison of the incidence, timing and intensity of violence and discrimination against Jews in different states and eras, discriminating the political-economic roles they have played, the structure of group competition and complementarity, and the diffusion of the antisemitic myth as variables. Then we may test our conclusions against similar studies of other middleman-minorities perceived as outsiders who have been subjected to traditional collective accusations and of minorities immune from such hostile accusation.

John A. Armstrong

Mobilized and Proletarian Diasporas[*]

The recent revival of interest in the historical dimension of social and political development necessarily entails a concern for types of polities which have been outside the mainstream of political science as a discipline. Both the older institutionalism and newer systems approaches have tended to take the nation state and the coincidence of polity and society for granted.[1] Political scientists specifically concerned with areas outside Europe and its overseas descendants have been more sharply aware that multiethnic composition is nearer the norm than the exception for major polities. Historically, however, multiethnicity has been still more clearly the norm, even in European polities. Consequently, an extended longitudinal framework is almost essential for adequate comparative investigation of the multiethnic polity. One of its most significant components, the diaspora, constituting a distinctive collectivity – perhaps even a separate society – can hardly be understood except in historical perspective. Much of the literature on contemporary diasporas appears to consider them to be anomalies, or at least very transitory. Some diasporas are indeed the result of contemporary social and economic forces. A deeper historical perspective suggests, on the other hand, that other types of diasporas, like multiethnic polities themselves, are the norm rather than the exception.

The first purpose of this article is to suggest a typology of the more significant types of diasporas. A typology constitutes, by itself, a limited step toward further theoretical development. In elaborating the kind of

---

[*] From: *American Political Science Review* 70, 1976, pp. 393–408.
[1] Even historical studies of nationalism pay scant attention to diasporas. See for example Carleton J. H. Hayes, *The Historical Evolution of Modern Nationalism,* New York, 1931; Friedrich Meinecke, *Weltbürgertum und Nationalstaat,* Munich, 1911; Hans Kohn, *The Idea of Nationalism,* New York, 1944; and Salo W. Baron, *Modern Nationalism and Religion,* New York, 1947. Recent social science discussions like Richard A. Schermerhorn, *Comparative Ethnic Relations,* New York, 1970 and Cynthia H. Enloe, *Ethnic Conflict and Political Development,* Boston, 1973 deal only in passing with mobilized diasporas.

typology suggested here, one can hardly avoid examining data and making assumptions which have further, though more tentative, theoretical implications. Second, therefore, I offer a partial explanation of the changing position of the major types of diasporas within multiethnic polities. This explanation is based on close study of a wide range of historical data, a small part of which is cited by way of illustration. The present essay, however, is an exploration, not a verification. Consequently, its propositions, while (I hope) logically interrelated and not in conflict with existing secondary data, are designed primarily as hypotheses for further investigation.[2]

In the sense in which I use the term, "diaspora" applies to any ethnic collectivity which lacks a territorial base within a given polity, i.e., is a relatively small minority throughout all portions of the polity. Obviously this category embraces numerous ethnic collectivities such as widely dispersed hunting or pastoral nomads and certain semitribal groups like Gypsies. Since, however, the concern of this article is the major ways in which diasporas have interacted with the multiethnic polity, it focuses on two types: the *proletarian diaspora*, essentially a disadvantaged product of modernized polities; and the *mobilized diaspora*, an ethnic group which does not have a general status advantage, yet which enjoys many material and cultural advantages compared to other groups in the multiethnic polity. Because the mobilized diaspora has a much longer and more complex history, most of the article will be devoted to it, with the emergence of the proletarian diaspora considered primarily as a contrast to the mobilized diaspora.

Even the preliminary definitions just advanced suggest that my consideration of diasporas rests on two theoretical positions. The first, derived in part from the work of Frederik Barth and his associates, stresses the significance of boundaries among collectivities which cannot be defined by geographical partition.[3] Clearly, a diaspora is something more than, say, a collection of persons distinguished by some secondary characteristic such

---

[2] I am completing a monographic study on the German diaspora in the Russian Empire and the beginnings of its replacement by the Jewish diaspora. This work will employ in a limited context both quantitative and nonquantitative data to test some of the hypotheses advanced here. The study will appear in a book edited by Jeremy Azrael for the American Association for the Advancement of Slavic Studies Collaborative Research Project on Nation-Building and National Integration in the USSR. Since considerable amounts of data on Russia are cited in this and in previous studies I have published, I have documented here only the most important assertions about the Russian multiethnic polity.

[3] Frederik Barth (ed.) *Ethnic Groups and Boundaries*, Bergen, 1969.

as, for example, all persons with Scottish names in Wisconsin. For the mobilized diaspora, which has often constituted for centuries a separate society or quasi-society in a larger polity, the factors making for stable identification require especially close examination.

Consideration of the factors leading to persistence of the mobilized diaspora also rests on assumptions derived from exchange theory. In contrast to many subordinate ethnic groups (including, nearly always, proletarian diasporas), the mobilized diaspora is apt to have an elite which is more sophisticated in calculation of advantages and in symbol manipulation than is the elite of the dominant ethnic group. Because it assumes that both participants in an interaction may improve their positions, although the more powerful (in the present study, the dominant ethnic elite) achieves the better terms, an exchange model appears most appropriate. Only (as happens infrequently) when one participant (the mobilized diaspora) is coerced by the superior physical force controlled by the dominant ethnic elite, must the exchange framework give way to a conflict model.[4]

Utilization of the exchange framework requires two important qualifications. In the first place, rational calculation of the terms of exchange has been limited to elite members. While I do not attempt to examine elite decision making, the historiographical consensus does provide reasonably strong evidence that mobilized diaspora elite members, and members of dominant ethnic group elites, have in fact calculated the costs and benefits involved in their interactions. It is less easy to show that elites have represented the interests of their co-ethnic masses; but, as will appear later, there is evidence that mobilized diaspora masses identify with their elites in terms of perceived life chances. A second qualification relates to the derivation of the exchange model from economics, where values accruing to participants can ordinarily be expressed quantitatively. At this stage of our knowledge about mobilized diasporas, such calculations are completely unfeasible. Consequently, the exchange model used here is only a heuristic device; and the propositions derived with the aid of the model, because they refer to tendencies rather than precise parameters, constitute only weak hypotheses.

---

[4] See especially Robert Curry, Jr. and L. L. Wade, *A Theory of Political Exchange*, Englewood Cliffs, N. J., 1968, pp. ix ff.; and Peter Blau, *Exchange and Power in Social Life*, New York, 1964, pp. 151 ff. On the uses of conflict theory in ethnic relations see Schermerhorn, *op. cit.*, p. 44.

Boundary Maintenance in Mobilized Diasporas

Examination of the boundary-maintenance mechanisms which have enabled mobilized diasporas to persist leads one to conclude that the category contains two subtypes with considerably different characteristics. Because the Jews are commonly considered the model for all diasporas, I shall refer to the first subcategory, in which they fit, als the *archetypal diaspora*. The second subcategory may be termed the *situational diaspora*. As these terms imply, the superficial difference between the two subcategories is the completeness and permanence of the diaspora condition of the first, or archetypal, as compared to the partial and temporary conditions as a diaspora of the situational ethnic group. The most important situational mobilized diasporas have been the Germans, throughout Eastern Europe, and the Chinese, dispersed over broad areas of Southeast Asia. In both cases the situational diasporas were fragments of far larger, compact ethnic masses constituting two of the world's great societies. The considerable degree of individual movement between the situational diaspora and its great society homeland suggests that the diaspora condition was perceived as a transitory phenomenon. In contrast, for millennia, Jews (and groups like the Parsees) did not constitute compact majorities anywhere.

At the level of historical "reality," the superficial distinction based on attachments to homelands is harder to maintain. The obvious case of the recent formation of a Jewish homeland immediately comes to mind. More important than this isolated instance is the fact that, by the criterion of possession of a territorial base, a large majority of mobilized diasporas occupy an intermediate position. The case of the Armenians, second only to the Jews in historical importance, is instructive. As late as 1915, two-thirds of the Armenian ethnic group continued to live in Eastern Anatolia and the central Transcaucasus, although Armenians probably constituted the majority in only restricted portions of these regions. Even after the unprecedented Turkish holocaust during World War I, one-third of all Armenians have continued to live in Soviet Transcaucasia. As early as the thirteenth century, however, it was clear to observers like Marco Polo that the dispersed segment of the Armenian ethnic group was behaving like an archetypal diaspora.[5] The basic reason was that the compact settlement area had not only been subjugated for centuries by foreign conquerors, but

---

[5] Speros Vryonis, *The Decline of Medieval Hellenism in Asia Minor and the Process of Islamization from the Eleventh Century through the Fifteenth Century*, Berkeley 1971, p. 235.

John A. Armstrong

had suffered an equally long period of economic and cultural eclipse compared to the affluence and vitality of the Armenian diaspora.

The major significance of the different relations of situational and archetypal diasporas to their "homelands," however, lies in the dimension of ethnic *myth* rather than external historical reality.[6] In both cases the myth of the homeland is crucially important, but the two forms of myth are sharply distinguished. In turn, the different forms of ethnic myth crucially influence two other boundary-maintaining mechanisms: *communications specialization* and *role specialization*. This complex of factors is decisive not only for maintaining the stable boundaries of the mobilized diaspora, but for the latter's exchange relationship with dominant ethnic elites.

The situational diaspora's myth is relatively close to the familiar "modern" myth of nationalism. Diasporas such as the Eastern European Germans (prior to 1945) and the Overseas Chinese resembled modern nations in their belief (not utterly unfounded) that they were parts of larger ethnic collectivities which had achieved distinctively superior levels of secular civilization.[7] For most, like the Chinese, attachment to a peculiar religion has been very weak. Because of its syncretic nature, the Chinese belief system readily accommodated to Thai and Burmese Buddhism, and considerable numbers of Chinese even converted to Islam in Malay regions.[8] German peasant settlers in Russia and Hungary kept their Protestant religion and rarely intermarried with neighboring Orthodox peasants. In the mobile society of metropolises such as St. Petersburg, however, numerous upper-class Germans intermarried and made the relatively slight denominational transition from Lutheranism to Orthodoxy.[9] Moreover,

---

[6] "Myth" refers to an integrated set of beliefs emphasizing the historical continuity and peculiar identity of a group. Since the myth has strong affective connotations, group members commonly resist efforts to subject it to critical analysis; none of these features implies, of course, that the myth is either true or false.

[7] See especially Richard J. Coughlin, *Double Identity: The Chinese in Modern Thailand*, Hong Kong, 1960, pp. 121, 160. Indians in East Africa and Malaya and Lebanese in West Africa also probably should be considered situational mobilized diasporas; Indians in Africa are convinced of their cultural superiority, according to Pierre L. Van den Berghe, *Race and Ethnicity*, New York, 1970, pp. 277, 293–94.

[8] Coughlin, *op. cit.*, pp. 78, 192; Victor Purcell, *The Chinese in Southeast Asia*, London, 1951, p. 59; *The New York Times*, September 16, 1974. The Chinese maintain intense family (ancestral) identification; this appears closer to identification with a superior culture than with religion in the usual sense.

[9] Fervent Lutherans did protest, but the extent of their concern and the numerous cases they cite are in themselves evidence of the tendency of the German diaspora to assimilate religiously. It had before it, of course, the frequent example of marriages and conversions to Orthodoxy among Lutheran royal families.

the situational diaspora myth of cultural superiority was rarely – until a very recent period – associated with the typical nationalist claim for *political* unification of all members, diaspora and homeland, of the ethnic group. The German diaspora in the Russian Empire (perhaps to a lesser extent in Poland-Lithuania and Hungary) was explicitly averse to political attachment to its great society.[10] The very concept of political attachment of the Southeast Asian Chinese to the Chinese Empire was, except for transitory incidents noted below, unrealistic until very recently. As will become apparent, the situational diaspora's rejection of ethnic political unification has not saved it from the suspicions of the dominant elites of their multiethnic polities; these elites have less frequently suspected archetypal diasporas, lacking any realistic connection to a homeland, of disloyalty.

Deprived of a great society to which to attribute cultural superiority, the archetypal diaspora has found a more intense focus of distinctiveness in its peculiar religion. This has been true for intermediate groups like the Armenians or the Greeks of the Ottoman Empire as well as for more obviously archetypal diasporas like the Jews and the Parsees. In each case, moreover, the religious myth, although perhaps predominantly otherworldly, has had a significant territorial focus. The Iranian shrines of the Indian Parsees, the Greek Ecumenical Patriarchate in the Phanar district of Istanbul, and of course the city of Jerusalem, provided territorial foci for the myth of ethnic identity during the long centuries when these religious centers had very restricted practical relation to the life of the diasporas. The manner in which the Gregorian Catholicosate of Echmiadzin has increased in significance as the symbolic center of Armenian life, although transferred in fact from one alien polity to another, is a still better illustration of how the religious myth defines a substitute homeland for the archetypal diaspora. Moreover, precisely because the myth is religious, its ability to maintain the crucial element of endogamy is stronger among archetypal than among situational diasporas.

Communication networks, as Karl Deutsch has shown, constituted a major basis for *modern* ethnic identification.[11] Distinctive communication

---

[10] It is precisely this rejection of political ties with the homeland which distinguishes mobilized diasporas, as I conceive them, from minorities like English-speaking Canadians in Quebec, who can be more aptly categorized as outposts of a dominant ethnic group.

[11] Karl W. Deutsch, *Nationalism and Social Communication*, Cambridge, Mass., 1953. Deutsch suggested the importance of communications networks for modern ethnic identity in an earlier work, "Medieval Unity and Its Economic Conditions for an International Civilization," *Canadian Journal of Economic and Political Science* 10, 1944, pp. 18–35.

patterns connected to religious and cultural myths have been significant for mobilized diasporas for centuries. All mobilized diasporas have sought to maintain their peculiar languages for internal use. Situational diasporas, with some access to cultural resources of their great societies, have generally been more successful: thus most Germans in Russia continued to speak German, and most Overseas Chinese speak some form of Chinese.[12] This linguistic distinctiveness is more necessary for maintaining *secular* myths, whereas the archetypal diaspora can rely on sacral resources. However little this diaspora actually uses the linguistic vehicle of its religion, the sacral language constitutes a vital element of the myth. Moreover, while adopting alien languages for the vast majority of communications, the archetypal diaspora usually maintains two important restrictions. First, the written word, with its exceptionally strong sacral implications, remains in the group's original alphabet, which is often very different from those of surrounding ethnic groups.[13] For example, while employing Arabic, Persian, Romance, or Germanic dialects, Jews have continued to write in the Hebrew alphabet; one Armenian script is used for two very different dialects. Moreover, borrowed linguistic elements which offend the central religious elements of the myth are avoided. Thus medieval Spanish Jews were more receptive to Arabic than to Latin, regarded as a specifically ecclesiastical vehicle of a hostile church; and they purged the dialects they did accept (Yiddish and Ladino) of words with specific Christian connotations.[14]

Although some measure of linguistic peculiarity is important for the mobilized diaspora, it cannot avoid accommodating to a considerable extent to the linguistic patterns of its environment if the diaspora is to maintain material and cultural advantages in the multiethnic polity. The

---

[12] Coughlin, *op. cit.,* pp. 140–41, 144, 158; W. L. Cator, *The Economic Position of the Chinese in the Netherlands Indies,* Chicago, 1936, pp. 19, 29, 35; Guy Hunter, *South-East Asia – Race Culture, and Nation,* London, 1966, pp. 44 ff.; G. William Skinner, *Chinese Society in Thailand,* Ithaca, 1957, p. 169.

[13] See especially Matthias Mieses, *Die Gesetze der Schriftgeschichte: Konfession und Schrift im Leben der Völker,* Vienna, 1919, pp. 67 ff.; Istvan Hajnal, "Le Rôle Social de l'Ecriture et l'Evolution Européenne," *Revue de l'Institut de Sociologie* (Brussels), IV, 1924, pp. 32 ff.

[14] Max Weinreich, "The Reality of Jewishness versus the Ghetto Myth," in *To Honor Roman Jakobson,* The Hague, 1967, III, 2209; *Language in Sociocultural Change: Essays by Joshua A. Fishmann,* Anwar S. Dil (ed.), Stanford, 1972, pp. 297 ff.; Stephen Sharot, "Minority Situation and Religious Acculturation; A Comparative Analysis of Jewish Communities," *Comparative Studies in Society and History* 16, 1974, 340, 347; Yitzhak Baer, *A History of the Jews in Christian Spain,* II, Philadelphia, 1966, Abraham A. Neuman, *The Jews in Spain,* I, Philadelphia, 1942.

tension between maintaining at least symbolic attachment to its own language, and the practical employment of other languages, leads diaspora members to acquire unusually strong linguistic skills. In Southeast Asia the Chinese quickly acquired a minimum command of the colonial powers' languages; even in Thailand the Chinese have been far ahead of the dominant ethnic group in mastering English.[15] In nineteenth-century Russia, Germans constituted a disproportionate element of the Asian consular service skilled in Oriental languages, just as Armenians are very numerous among Soviet Orientalists. For most archetypal diasporas, transmission of the archaic sacral language required some type of formal training in communications skills. It was a short step from the study of the sacral language to the essential study of more utilitarian languages and then, through the broadening circle of cultural contacts, to a structured educational experience.

The combination of linguistic skills and their relation to broader patterns of communications specialization has probably contributed more than the diasporas' myths themselves to their occupational role specialization. In turn, it is just this specialization which has made mobilized diasporas so useful as modernizing or proto-modernizing elements. Apart from purely linguistic skills, the network of personal and family relations (buttressed by the latent threat of diaspora community sanctions) were highly effective premodern devices for facilitating long-distance commerce. Thus Spanish Jews were indispensable for international commerce in the Middle Ages and Armenians controlled the overland trade between Europe and the Orient as late as the nineteenth century. Because of their special skills, dominant ethnic elites have often calculatingly assigned advantageous roles to mobilized diaspora members. Thus, in seventeenth-century Java, the Dutch rulers pragmatically calculated that the Chinese should be allowed to substitute a poll tax for military construction labor because they were more productive "in merchant services, agriculture, lime-burning, tailoring and other ways."[16] Two centuries earlier the Ottomans had exempted Armenian and Jewish diasporas from the "boy tax" (children forcibly recruited for the Janissaries) for very similar reasons.[17] More generally, dominant elites have retained military leadership and formal governing roles, while leaving despised but lucrative commercial roles to the mobi-

---

[15] Skinner, *op. cit.*, p. 169; Coughlin, *op. cit.*, p. 153.
[16] Cator, *op. cit.*, p. 13.
[17] Hamilton A. R. Gibb and Harold Bowen, *Islamic Society and the West*, I, Part 2, London, 1950, p. 223.

lized diasporas. In these role allocations the implicit exchange relationship is often based on the economist's principle of relative advantage. For example, Lebanese Christians began to occupy middleman roles, which the dominant Ottoman elites despised, in eighteenth century Egypt, and more recently have acted as a mobilized diaspora in West Africa. In Lebanon itself, although native Christians are dominant in middleman roles such as banking and mercantile activities, the small Armenian diaspora community has, through its *relatively* greater skills in industrial development, provided 18 per cent of capital investment in large industry, 43 per cent in minor manufacturing.[18] Indeed, the case for referring to these diasporas as "mobilized," thus implying that they have a certain modernizing potential, does not rest on their specialization in middleman roles. Situational diasporas have often been directly involved in transmitting innovative economic techniques – e.g., Saxon miners in Eastern Europe and Chinese exploitation of gold and tin mines in Borneo and Malaya.[19] Perhaps archetypal diasporas are less inclined to provide the heavy manipulative labor in geographically isolated settings which mining entails. But, as a historian of seventeenth-century Istanbul writes: "Only the (Jewish, Armenian, and Greek) minorities, less hampered by religious imperatives (than Moslems), are capable of starting an adaptation to new conditions, all the more naturally since it is to them that the foreigners (possessing new techniques) turn."[20]

Dynamics of Interaction Within the Multiethnic Polity

The typology presented in the preceding section required some discussion of the interaction of mobilized diaspora and dominant ethnic elite, but emphasized the internal development of the diaspora itself. Significant aspects of this development very frequently have taken place long before the diaspora's incorporation in a given multiethnic polity. Hence, in a sense, the special qualifications of the diaspora appear to the dominant elite

---

[18] Loretta Kh. Ter-Mkrtichian, *Armiane v Stranakh Arabskogo Vostoka*, Moscow 1965; Eugen Wirth, "Damaskus-Aleppo-Beirut: Ein geographischer Vergleich dreier nahöstlicher Städte im Spiegel ihrer sozial und wirtschaftlich tonangebenden Schichten," *Die Erde* 97, 1966, p. 180.

[19] Roger Portal, *L'Oural au XVIIIe Siècle*, Paris: Institut d'Etudes Slaves, 1950, pp. 65, 99; F. Ia. Poliansky, "Promyshlennaia Politika Russkogo Absoliutizma vo Vtoroi Chetverti XVIII v. (1725-1740 gg.)," *Voprosy Istorii Narodnogo Khoziaistva SSSR*, 1957, p. 106; Cator, *op. cit.* pp. 139 ff.

[20] Robert Mantran, *Istanbul dans la Second Moitié du XVIIe Siècle*, Paris, 1962, p. 510.

as "given" factors, and this elite may not even be aware of the extent to which (in the long run) these diaspora skills may be strengthened or weakened by the exchange relationship. In the following set of propositions, therefore, one must be careful to distinguish between short-run advantages, usually perceptible to both the diaspora and to the dominant elites, and long-run advantages which may be discernible (if at all) only to the outside observer.

(1) Within the multiethnic polity, the mobilized diaspora is temporarily indispensable for the dominant ethnic elite. Much of the reasoning behind this proposition, particularly the analysis of diaspora skills, has already been presented. But it is important to stress the other side of the exchange relationship: the paucity of skills among the dominant ethnic elite, which often consists almost entirely of warriors, landlords, and perhaps priests of the dominant religion. As a Turkish nationalist, Ziya Gökalp, plaintively expressed it, "the poor Turks inherited from the Ottoman Empire nothing but a broken sword and an old-fashioned plow."[21] As long as they *were dominant,* however, the elites of the major ethnic group could acquire from others the skills they needed. Among diaspora technical skills prized by dominant elites, medicine has always ranked very high. As an early student of the question wrote, Jews (but the generalization could also be applied to Germans, Chinese, or Armenians) acquired medical skill because it was highly transferable: "The study of philosophy did not afford a prospect of earning a living and at that period jurisprudence afforded the least prospect of all (moreover, at first the latter was valid only in one's homeland, since other laws prevailed elsewhere); but the study of medicine was a cosmopolitan one which, *mutatis mutandis,* could be utilized everywhere."[22] In fact, medicine often acted as the entering wedge for Jews and other diasporas to secure access to a broader range of skilled professions.

In addition to their technical role specialization, the diasporas' communications skills have been especially prized by dominant elites who rarely possess either the multilingual ability or the more subtle understanding of diverse communication patterns required to deal effectively with a multiethnic population. Thus the first Arab caliphs found it necessary to employ Christian secretaries for civil administration; as late as the fourteenth

---

[21] Quoted by Uriel Heyd, *Foundations of Turkish Nationalism: The Life and Teachings of Ziya Gökalp,* London, 1950, p. 74.
[22] G. Wolf, "Zur Geschichte jüdischer Ärzte in Österreich," *Monatsschrift für Geschichte und Wissenschaft des Judentums* 13, 1864, pp. 196–97; cf. Guido Kisch, *Die Prager Universität und die Juden,* 1348–1848, Mährisch-Ostrau, 1935, p. 36.

century the Egyptian Coptic minority monopolized the secretarial roles.[23] Even where diasporas have been excluded from formal administrative position, they nearly always occupy (Spain, Ottoman Turkey, Russia, and the colonial empires of Southeast Asia) the quasi-administrative roles of tax farmers. In the nineteenth-century Ottoman Empire, it is said, there was an Armenian banker behind every high official, indispensable for providing the surety bond which permitted the official to be entrusted with revenue collection.[24]

(2) Within the multiethnic polity, the mobilized diaspora depends for security on the dominant ethnic elite. Among the upper stratum of mobilized diasporas, at least, there has been considerable awareness of the mutual dependency between diaspora and dominant elite. Faced with the terror of the Inquisition, late fifteenth-century Jews came close to identifying with the Ottoman power. "You do not know who the Turk is. If God will favor us, that is, conversos (unwilling converts to Christianity), the Turk will be in Castile within a year and a half ... The Turk is called the Destroyer of Christianity and the Defender of the Jewish Faith," wrote an Istanbul Jew.[25]

Perhaps the most articulate legitimization for adherence to a multiethnic polity was advanced by the Baltic German situational diaspora as a rearguard stand against both Russian und German nationalism. An 1870 editorial, appropriately entitled "About the Situation," idealizes the recent past:

> When we looked to the East, we saw a strong overlord whose arm protected us from disorder and preserved for us the blessings of peace. Further, we saw a broad field in which our sons and younger brothers had always been able to make a way and a position for themselves with slight effort and where a gracious monarch regarded us with great and well-earned trust. We saw a great empire, whose institutions we knew little of, except that none equalled ours in autonomy and enlightenment appropriate to the times.[26]

---

[23] Dominique and Janine Sourdel, La Civilisation de l'Islam Classique, Paris, 1968, p. 370; A. S. Tritton, The Caliphs and Their Non-Muslim Subjects, 2nd ed., London, 1970, p. 72; cf. H. Montgomery Watt, Islam and the Integration of Society, Evanston, 1961, p. 121, on the persistence of crypto-Zoroastrians (i. e., what are today known as "Parsees") in the civil service of the caliphs.

[24] Avedis K. Sanjian, The Armenian Communities in Syria under Ottoman Dominion, Cambridge, 1965, p. 36. On the ubiquity of Chinese tax farmers, see expecially Purcell, op. cit., p. 664.

[25] Baer, op. cit., II, 347.

[26] "Zur Lage," Baltische Monatsschrift 19, 1870, 8; cf. Hans Rothfels, Reich, Staat und Nation im deutsch-baltischen Denken, Halle, 1930, pp. 226 ff.

The note of personal loyalty to the sovereign is frequent in mobilized diaspora commentaries; but allegiance to a dominant elite perceived as embodying a superior ideal of supranationalism is not confined to traditional fealty. For example, Chinese diasporas in Southeast Asia and the Indian middleman minorities of East Africa strongly identified with colonial elites against indigenous nationalist movements, with little regard for the nominal source of these elites' authority.

(3) From the internal standpoint, the delicate balance of forces maintaining a mobilized diaspora's position within the multiethnic polity is most apt to be upset by a sharp overall rise in social mobilization. Such evidence as is available strongly suggests that widespread deprivation in a stagnant traditional social order does not incite strong antidiaspora activity *even* among dominant ethnic elements engaged in direct competition with diaspora middlemen. It would be difficult to find a recent independent polity as stagnant as late nineteenth-century Morocco. Yet excellent impartial studies testify to the good relations between Jewish and Moslem traders and artisans in the same occupations. "In sum, each asks only to perpetuate a lazy indifference which time has in some manner sanctified. In this rural life, stupefying for the mind but subjected to the quest for daily bread, economic contacts sufficed, perhaps, to engender a climate of mutual comprehension and collaboration between Moslems and Israelites."[27] In the common situation of specialized occupational roles, stable division of roles between the dominant and the diaspora ethnic groups appears to be readily accepted. Thus the Hungarian gentry, throughout much of the nineteenth century, seems to have been satisfied with the arrangement whereby Magyars owned estates, ruled, and commanded, while Jews occupied the liberal professions as well as middleman roles.[28] A similar mutual satisfaction apparently prevailed between dominant Thais and the Chinese diaspora up to the 1930s.

Hungary and Spain, are, however, classic instances of ouster of Jewish diasporas from favorable positions as the result of *mobilization* of lower strata of the dominant ethnic group. Accompanying a general increase in territorial and occupational mobility was awareness that advantages en-

---

[27] Pierre Flamand, *Un Mellah en Pays Berbère: Demnate,* Paris, 1952, p. 141. See also Roger LeTourneau, *Fès avant le Protectorat,* Casablanca, 1949, pp. 186, 448; H. Z. Hirschberg, "The Jewish Quarter in Moslem Cities and Berber Areas," *Judaism* 17, 1968, p. 406; Joseph Goulven, *Les Mellahs de Rabat Salé,* Paris, 1927, presents a somewhat less favorable picture. Cf. Mantran, *op. cit.,* p. 65.

[28] Robert A. Kann, "Hungarian Jewry during Austria-Hungary's Constitutional Period (1867–1918)," *Jewish Social Studies* 7, 1945, pp. 357–86.

joyed by the diasporas were not "inevitable" but could be altered to the apparent advantage of the dominant ethnic group. While not discounting such influences as the anti-Judaism of the Spanish Church, the principal authorities in late medieval Spain stress the importance of lower strata attacks on Jews in a situation of expanding opportunities, while the elite – including bishops and religious-military orders – was eager to protect the Jews because of their economic value.[29] As Américo Castro trenchantly puts it:

> Finally, a day would come when the Catholic Sovereigns had an urgent need for the "common people" to further their militant imperial enterprises, and with it would come at last the annihilation of the two castes (Moslems and Jews) who no longer possessed any possible defenses . . . the lower strata of Christian society began to rise in the ranks and the way became clear for them to govern those who had formerly dominated them as *grandes de Castille* without being Christians.[30]

The passage just quoted implies that the position of the dominant elites themselves, closely identified with the mobilized diasporas through symbiotic activity, conversion, and sometimes intermarriage, was insecure. As larger elements of the dominant ethnic population became politically and economically mobilized, the "impurity" of the upper stratum threatened to become a ground for drastic turnover in elites. In other words, the *terms of exchange* had become distinctly less favorable for the dominant ethnic elite. The diaspora had not effected this change; but it could in a sense "compensate" for it by becoming a sacrifice ("shock absorber" is Blalock's term)[31] to divert populist animosity from the elite. As a result, the latter frequently turned to scapegoating, thus essentially altering its relation with the diaspora from *exchange* to *coercion*. Just as Ferdinand of Aragon sanctioned the Inquisition to quiet populist rumors assailing his Jewish ancestry, Sultan Abdul Hamid preferred to turn violently on the Armenian diaspora rather than to risk being identified with it in rising Turkish public opinion as he was in fact by descent. There are some indications that similar motivations lay behind the anti-Chinese measures taken by the Thai elite (with its considerable Chinese ancestry) after the revolutionary

---

[29] See especially Neuman, *op. cit. I*, p. 182; Baer, *op. cit.*, p. 25; Fernand Braudel, *La Méditerranée et le Monde Méditerranéen à l'Epoque de Philippe II*, 2nd ed., Paris, 1966, II, 29. Cf. Weinreich, *op. cit.*, III, p. 2201, for a description of the similar situation in the medieval Rhineland.

[30] Américo Castro, *The Spaniards*, Berkeley, 1971, pp. 502, 570.

[31] Hubert H. Blalock, Jr., *Toward a Theory of Minority-Group Relations*, New York, 1967, p. 81. On p. 79 Blalock appears to agree with my point that a mobilized diaspora is relatively secure in a traditional social order.

upheavals of the 1930s.[32] In a very similar way, the slow, uneven process of modernization in Russia has made antidiaspora tactics attractive to very different kinds of dominant ethnic elites. No one would deny that Alexander III was sincerely anti-German; but his weak son, Nicholas II, took anti-German measures at the outbreak of World War I partly to divert attention from the notorious German atmosphere of his Court. More recently, Soviet leaders with Jewish in-laws (including Stalin, Khrushchev, and Brezhnev) have probably been motivated to some degree by fear of too close identification with the disliked diaspora.[33]

Dynamics of the International Context

By definition, multiethnic polities belong to James Rosenau's category of highly penetrated systems in which domestic developments are extraordinarily dependent on extrasystemic conditions.[34] These polities have operated in an international environment geographically or chronologically remote from the modern Western model of impenetrable nation states. Consequently, the numerous treatments which depict mobilized diasporas exclusively as *victims* of intrasystemic forces ignore the crucial effects of international *politics* upon the exchange relation between diaspora and dominant ethnic elite.

---

[32] Coughlin, *op. cit.*, pp. 128, 168; Purcell, *op. cit.*, p. 169.

[33] John A. Armstrong, "Soviet Foreign Policy and Anti-Semitism," *Soviet Jewry, 1969* (Academic Committee on Soviet Jewry, 1969), pp. 65–69. I do not pretend that the explanation of internal factors presented above is adequate to explain all cases of persecution of mobilized diasporas, especially those involving recent anti-Semitism. Ernst Nolte in *Three Faces of Fascism*, New York, 1966, emphasizes quite rightly the importance of the search for scapegoats after military defeat (in Weimar Germany and late nineteenth-century France; he might have added Turkey after defeats in 1876–78 and 1915–19). Still, it can be argued that *one* significant factor in all three of these countries was the highly uneven pace of modernization, which made it profitable for elites of premodern origin to condone scapegoating by discontented members of their ethnic group. More directly contrary to my interpretation, at least on the surface, is the important study by Bruno Bettelheim and Morris Janowitz, *Dynamics of Prejudice*, New York, 1950, which attributes increases in anti-Semitic attitudes in both Germany and the United States to *downward* mobility. Of course outbreaks of anti-Semitism occasionally occur in successfully modernized countries, despite what I contend is the generally favorable position of the vestigial mobilized diasporas there. Unfortunately, such an ingrained historical prejudice is hardly likely to disappear merely because of economic and social transformations. It is not surprising that when anti-Semitism does occur in a modernized society the causes are different from those in slowly modernizing multiethnic societies. Apart from the hideous Nazi exception, however, dominant elites in Western modernized societies *have* succeeded in preventing the *attitudes* Bettelheim and Janowitz note from resulting in catastrophic *behavior*.

[34] James N. Rosenau, *The Scientific Study of Foreign Policy*, New York, 1971.

(4) In the external relations of the multiethnic polity, the mobilized diaspora is as indispensable (and as transitory) as it is for the internal interests of the dominant ethnic elite. Two basic factors account for the importance of the mobilized diaspora in external relations. In the premodern period, international commerce, although small in terms of the overall economic activity of the large multiethnic states, was indispensable to rulers. Luxury items were needed to nurture dominant elite loyalties and some military items (including the technological innovations mentioned earlier) had to be imported. Consequently, the activity of the mobilized diasporas was vital when the polity was expanding territorially, and retained considerable defensive significance even during stagnation. For example, in the late sixteenth century Sephardic Jews, through their contacts with European traders, contributed significantly to the Saadian dynasty's revival of Moroccan power, just as earlier their long-range commercial contacts had strengthened Moslem and Christian monarchies in Spain. Other refugee Sephardic Jews and Armenians from Kaffa in the Crimea extricated the Ottoman Empire sufficiently from Venetian commercial domination to enable the Empire to reach the pinnacle of its power.[35]

The situations just mentioned are excellent illustrations of the point made earlier, that the dominant elite of a given multiethnic polity customarily takes the skills of its mobilized diaspora as a given, since they were acquired under other regimes. The case of the Armenians shows how complicated this competition for diaspora skills can become. Apparently the Armenians began to be a mobilized diaspora during the early Middle Ages, when they occupied a precarious but profitable position between the Byzantine Empire and Moslem states. A few centuries later, in 1590, Shah Abbas recognized the importance of Armenian skills by forcibly transplanting their major center for transit trade, Julfa, to New Julfa, a suburb of his Persian capital. However, he was not the only ruler to profit from this drastic move. By breaking up the homeland center of Armenian commerce, Abbas set in motion a new dispersion which fructified the Armenian diaspora in the rival Ottoman Empire as well as in Poland and even in the Moghul Empire.[36] Two centuries later, the Tsar harvested many of the

[35] Gaston Deverdun, *Marrakech,* Rabat, 1959, p. 453; Halil Inalcik, *The Ottoman Empire: The Classical Age, 1300-1600,* London, 1973, p. 129; Moise Franco, *Sur l'Histoire de Israélites de l'Empire Ottoman dequis les Origines jusqu'à Nos Jours,* Hildesheim, 1973 – reprint of 1897 ed, p. 57.

[36] Sanjian, *op. cit.,* p. 48; V. A. Baiburtian, *Armianskaia Koloniia Novoi Dzhulfy v XVII Veke,* Erevan, 1969, *Istoricheskie Sviazi i Druzhba Ukrainskogo i Armianskogo Narodov,* Kiev,

long-term benefits of increased Armenian dispersion (and the heightening of skills which accompanied it) by incorporating the remaining Armenian centers on the Transcaucasus trade route. The Russian government recognized its potential, although wholly unearned advantage, by conceding to the Armenian mercantile elite exemption from tariffs on the route from Persia to Leipzig. A few years later Prussian finance minister Friedrich von Motz sought a treaty with Russia to enable Prussian trade to penetrate Asia with the aid of the Armenian "commercial people" under Russian protection.[37]

The example just cited suggests that the commercial advantages accruing to multiethnic empires from their mobilized diasporas could provide leverage in international negotiations. But mobilized diasporas have often been more directly involved in foreign policy. Perhaps the most striking example is the way in which the Phanariot Greeks maintained de facto direction of Ottoman foreign policy for one hundred fifty years. The key move occured when "in the later seventeenth century the Phanariot Greeks gradually ousted the renegades and Levantines who had hitherto served as interpreters in dealing with foreign embassies."[38] The office of Grand Dragoman (created in 1669) soon became equivalent to permanent head of the Ottoman foreign office. One Grand Dragoman even acquired the formal title of Minister of Secrets (ordinarily the Greeks prudently left these honorific posts to Moslems) and acted as chief Turkish delegate at the Carlowitz peace conference.[39] In the neighboring Russian multiethnic empire, German diaspora diplomats were so influential that not until the 1880s did a Tsar (Alexander III) order all diplomatic correspondence to be conducted in Russian. As late as 1914 one indispensable diplomat of German origin was still reporting home to St. Petersburg in French, since he simply did not know Russian. Just five years later, the new Bolshevik elite found the polyglot Polish Jew, Karl Radek, equally indispensable for foreign negotiations.

(5) Dominant ethnic elite perceptions of mobilized diaspora disloyalty tend to negate the value of the diaspora for external relations. The very character-

---

1965, pp. 101 ff., 122 ff.; R. L. Abramian, *Armianskie Istochniki XVIII V. ob Indii*, Erevan, 1968.

[37] Valentin Wittschewsky, *Russlands Handels-, Zoll- und Industriepolitik von Peter dem Grossen bis auf die Gegenwart*, Berlin, 1905, p. 57; Hermann von Petersdorff, *Friedrich von Motz*, Berlin, 1913, II, p. 323.

[38] Bernhard Lewis, *The Emergence of Modern Turkey*, London, 1961, p. 87.

[39] *Ibid.*, Steven Runciman, *The Great Church in Captivity*, Cambridge, England, 1968, p. 364; Gibb and Bowen, *op. cit.*, p. 236.

istics which originally made the diasporas valuable have tended, over considerable time periods, to arouse the suspicions of the dominant elites. Groups which partially escaped the control of absolute monarchs, groups whose co-ethnics lived under rival sovereigns, groups which carried on constant intercourse across frontiers could hardly avoid arousing distrust. For more xenophobic elites – the fifteenth-century Spanish monarchs and latter-day Soviet elites – simple distrust of "cosmopolitans" has been sufficient to damn the Jewish diasporas. Yet it is remarkable how long and well a more sophisticated elite like the Ottomans trusted their Jewish subjects; most Eastern European elites were equally tolerant of German diaspora contacts.

(6) *The most potent source of the dominant ethnic suspicion of the mobilized diaspora is the existence of its "homeland" outside the dominant elite's territorial control.* This proposition requires careful qualification. As was discussed in the preceding section, a sharp rise in social mobilization with concomitant populist pressures is *the most* important factor jeopardizing a mobilized diaspora. *That* danger arises, however, only when a dominant elite's interest in utilizing a diaspora has eroded and the alternative of scapegoating affords a short-run advantage. In contrast to this "cynical" calculation, real suspicion that a diaspora has transferred its loyalty to the occupants of its homeland pervades the dominant elite itself.

It is important to distinguish the positions of the *situational* and the *archetypal* diasporas. For the former, much depends on the political activity of its great society. Probably German disunity is the basic reason that Eastern European German minorities were rarely distrusted by dominant elites (although often denounced for their overbearing manner by lesser figures) until the formation of the Second Reich. After that, for understandable reasons, it was all downhill for the diaspora Germans until the expulsions at the end of World War II. The Southeast Asian Chinese, on the other hand, while never suffering as extreme a reversal, have been intermittently distrusted precisely because the polity of the great Chinese society, while *choosing* isolation, at all times possessed considerable potential for imperialist intervention. Thus Spanish suspicion that a haughty mandarin mission was preparing to oust Spain from the Philippines led to the brutal massacre which terminated a local Chinese uprising in 1603. A factor behind the Dutch decision (1854) to suppress the Borneo mining *kongsis* was their sending envoys to the Emperor of China.[40] More recent suspicions, associated with the attraction Sun Yat-Sen exerted in the 1920s

---

[40] Purcell, *op. cit.*, p. 591; Cator, *op. cit.*, p. 157.

and the Chinese Peoples Republic in the 1960s have induced equally harsh reactions from new indigenous elites in countries like Indonesia.

One might suppose that the vastly lower power *potential* of the archetypal diasporas' homelands would correspondingly reduce the dominant elites' suspicions. At times this has indeed been the case. Generally the religious nature of the archetypal diaspora myth, with its transcendental element, has induced diaspora members to accommodate to the curses and revilings of the ethnic groups among which they live. Even when the dominant elite protected the diaspora from serious physical harm, it eventually reinforced the diaspora's ignominious position by formally excluding it from positions of power and by enforcing residential segregation and sumptuary laws. This happened in sixteenth-century Istanbul, despite the Jews' exceptionally favored position. It is not surprising that messianic movements became noticeable among them about that time.[41] Since, however, recovery of the Jewish homeland was not then within the realm of practical politics, the movements aroused little concern among the dominant Ottoman elite which, moreover, had rather less need for diaspora services as the Empire became more homogeneously Moslem in population and more stagnant in economic and military affairs. The sharp decline of the Jews in the Ottoman Empire is, however, one of the few instances of a diaspora's being largely displaced in an *unmodernized* context without extreme coercion by the dominant ethnic elites.

More often, as Karl Deutsch has noted, a minority "with links to the domestic system and some particular links to the international or foreign input" will eventually react to persecution by loosening its ties to the multiethnic polity.[42] In other words, the dominant ethnic elite's suspicions tend to be self-fulfilling. The Phanariot Greeks' loss of their influential position in the Ottoman Empire is a good example of this interaction. Soon after acquiring their extraordinary influence in foreign negotiation, Phanariot elites began to dream of recreating the Byzantine Empire. At first they regarded partnership with the dominant but declining Moslem elites as the only feasible tactic. By the latter part of the eighteenth century, however, revival of an Orthodox Empire sponsored by Russia attracted those Phanariots who were too impatient to endure the humiliating terms which

[41] Gibb and Bowen, *op. cit.*, I, Part 2, pp. 217, 241; Lewis, *op. cit.*, p. 454; Haim Nakoum (former chief rabbi), "Jews," in *Modern Turkey*, Elliot Mears (ed.), New York, 1924, p. 87; Uriel Heyd, "The Jewish Communities of Istanbul in the Seventeenth Century," *Oriens* 6, 2, 1952, p. 308ff.

[42] Karl W. Deutsch "External Influences on the Internal Behavior of States," in *Approaches to Comparative and International Politics,* Robert Barry Farrell (ed.), Evanston, 1966, p. 12.

the Ottoman elite exacted from its Christian junior partners. Eventually the first wave of modern nationalism induced the Greeks to strike for independence at a time when the Ottoman elite was gravely concerned with Russian and other European Christian encroachments. The result was nearly catastrophic for the Phanariot diaspora: "The Turks were no longer prepared to trust the Orthodox. With the holocaust at the Patriarchate the old dispensation was ended."[43] The long period of Phanariot access to top policy making terminated in 1821 with the execution of two successive Grand Dragomans. "The chief beneficiaries were the Armenians, already well established as money-changers and bankers; better trusted than the Greeks, better educated than the Jews, they moved into many positions previously held by both . . ."[44]

Incipient independence for the Greek homeland entailed destruction of Greek diaspora ascendancy. The position of the Armenians provides a still sharper illustration of the sensitivity of dominant elites to the attraction exerted on diasporas by their homelands. Although the Armenian diaspora (particularly in India) resented Persia more than the Ottoman Empire during the sixteenth and seventeenth centuries, the location of the sacral center, Echmiadzin, in the Persian domains worried the Ottoman elite. Even earlier, the latter had maneuvered to secure control of the diaspora by inventing the title of "patriarch" for the Gregorian Bishop of Bursa and bringing him to Istanbul. Gradually the cultural center of Armenian life gravitated there. Far into the nineteenth century Ottoman leaders referred to the Armenians as the "loyal *millet*," i.e., the most loyal of the non-Moslem minorities. But continued concern with the religious attraction of Echmiadzin led the Ottomans to make repeated efforts to encourage rival Armenian religious centers in their own territory (Jerusalem and Cilicia). The threat became greater when Echmiadzin and the surrounding Transcaucasian homeland passed from the stagnating Persians (who, in any event, as Moslems could not easily pose as champions of an Armenian ethnic revival) to the dynamic Christian Russian Empire. The Russian government, while encouraging the Gregorian Church, moved quickly to place it under the supervision of St. Petersburg officials. By the 1830s the Armenians had acquired the status of a significant secondary mobilized diaspora within the southern borderlands of the Russian Empire, both commercially (as noted earlier) and in governmental and military posts

---

[43] Runciman, *op. cit.*, p. 406.
[44] *Ibid.*; Lewis, *op. cit.*, pp. 87, 455; Bernard Lewis, *Islam in History*, London, 1973, p. 135.

concerned with its Oriental subjects.[45] A more recent Armenian analysis provides a good indication of the way in which sophisticated diaspora elites have been able to comprehend the delicate balance of exchange relation with the dominant elite:

> The position of the Armenian authorities at the capital was obviously influenced by the Porte's apprehensions of, the hostility to Russia ... (since control of all ecclesiastical institutions by the Echmiadzin Catholicos) would surely be construed by the Porte as tantamount to placing them under Russian authority. This was a contingency that the Armenian leaders at Constantinople felt must be avoided at all costs if the security of the empire's Armenian *millet* was to be safeguarded.[46]

Unfortunately for the Armenian diaspora, its internal conflicts prevented the solution of replacing Echmiadzin church authority by that of the Cilician center. Still more dangerous was the coincidence between the rise of a Russian-sponsored threat to the Ottoman Anatolian frontier and the birth of modern nationalism in both the Turkish Moslem dominant ethnic group and among the Armenians themselves. All of these developments came to a head in 1876 when the Ottoman and Russian Empires clashed militarily. Massacres of the Armenians during that period were succeeded twenty years later by worse atrocities, and in 1915 (once again under the threat of Russian invasion) by the near-final "solution" of genocide.

Succession of Mobilized Diasporas

(7) In a multiethnic polity where slow mobilization of the dominant ethnic group results in a persistent need for mobilized diaspora skills, diasporas will tend to succeed one another in advantageous positions. The preceding discussion of the factors which jeopardize mobilized diasporas has contained many hints that, as one's position declined, another arose in some polities to provide the middleman and communication skills the dominant elite continued to need. Indeed Proposition 7 can be deduced (although not rigorously) from Propositions 1, 3, 4, and 5: if a diaspora is indispensable for both internal and external purposes, yet is incapacitated by factors (increased mobilization among the dominant ethnic group, growing dominant elite suspicion of the diaspora's external connections) largely independent of the elite's continuing need for these skills, it is at least probable that that elite will turn to a more trusted mobilized diaspora if one is available.

---

[45] Louise Nalbandian, *The Armenian Revolutionary Movement*, Berkeley, 1963, pp. 27, 43, 71, 133; Lewis, *op. cit.*, 1961, p. 350.

[46] Sanjian, *op. cit.*, p. 242.

A possible alternative, of course, for the dominant elite is to forego the advantages which *any* mobilized diaspora could contribute. The sixteenth-century Spanish elite's reaction is often considered the paradigm of this alternative. Having massacred or expelled the Jewish diaspora and the important Moslem communities, the Spanish elite itself resolutely renounced the skills they had supplied. As Américo Castro has written:

> An essential requisite to be a counselor of the emperor was that he be the son or grandson of *labradores*, that is, of peasants, farmers, or people who tilled the soil . . . In sum, the ideal was that the ancestor of a counselor of His Imperial Majesty, the lord of half the world, should be illiterate, that he should lack even the elementary knowledge or technical experience to be a bricklayer, muleteer, tailor, or itinerant salesman. By no means should he be a physician, pharmacist, or – an hidalgo! Neither the status of the hidalgo nor one's patent of nobility guaranteed beyond the shadow of doubt that the royal counselor was free from Jewish or Moorish ancestry . . . Since the Jews had a reputation for being the most intelligent and learned men, they (Spaniards) purposely chose to appear ignorant and illiterate on the surface to avoid the risk of being earmarked as Jews.[47]

No doubt there is an element of rhetorical exaggeration in Castro's generalization. Much indirect evidence suggests that there was indeed a continuing need for diaspora skills in Spain, and the downward course of Spanish power during this period is incontestable.[48] Still, one should be on guard against exaggerating the importance of the rejection of diasporas. After all, unusual tolerance for diasporas did not prevent a strikingly parallel decline of the Ottoman Empire. After his magisterial examination Fernand Braudel concluded that basic conditions of economic growth had turned against the large imperial polities by the end of the sixteenth century.[49] On the whole, however, the Spanish course is hardly one which sophisticated dominant ethnic elites will wish to emulate.

While some tendencies toward succession of mobilized diasporas appear in other polities,[50] the experiences of the Russian and the Ottoman Empires are clearest and historically most significant. Consequently, a tabular juxtaposition of these experiences, bringing out the striking similar-

---

[47] Castro, *op. cit.*, pp. 550–52.
[48] *Ibid.*, p. 591; Fernand Braudel, *Capitalism and Material Life, 1400–1800*, London, 1973, p. 24
[49] Braudel, *1966, op. cit.*, II, p. 46. The Spanish kingdom was obliged to import Flemish and Burgundian administrators from its outlying possessions and (more or less surreptitiously) French merchants and artisans (forty thousand in Madrid alone by 1655) to assume specialized roles Spaniards could not fill.
[50] Notably in nineteenth-century Hungary, where Jews replaced the urban German diaspora in many occupations with the tacit acquiescence of the Magyar elite, which regarded Jews as more assimilable, Kann, *op. cit.*, pp. 371 ff.

ity of successive but chronologically remote stages in the dynamics of diaspora-dominant elite interaction in the two multiethnic Empires, is suggestive. The comparison is especially significant because the Ottoman Empire made little progress toward economic and social modernization, while the Russian polity eventually did achieve modernization, although in an exceptionally protracted, uneven manner.[51] The comparison does, however, suggest two important differences: (a) the tendency of the interval between successions of mobilized diasporas to decrease in the successfully modernizing polity (Russia); and (b) the diminishing importance of successive mobilized diasporas in such a polity. In the Ottoman case, intervals are uneven in a random way which may reflect the dominance of "extraneous" or chance factors. The Russian case, on the other hand, suggests a chronological telescoping of the dynamic variable (diaspora succession) as modernization proceeds.

A recent monograph reveals that Lenin himself recognized that Jewish mobilized diaspora skills were essential to replace Russian bourgeois defectors – to "sabotage the saboteurs."[52] Some of these defecting specialists were in fact Germans, although the Germans had been declining as a diaspora for several decades prior to the Revolution. For example, German capital pioneered in textile manufacturing in Russian Poland, but during the last decades of Tsarist rule, Jewish capital became increasingly significant there.[53] Jews had operated the highly important grain and timber trades in the western parts of the Russian Empire for a century and were extremely important in central banking by 1914.[54] The very intensity of attacks on Jews (largely perpetrated by lower strata of the dominant Russian ethnic group directed by its elite in a classic example of scapegoating) aroused Jewish eagerness to acquire overtly powerful positions after the Revolution: "There can be little doubt that the thirst for power had been exacerbated by centuries of drought and that Jews were determined to drink deeply of the sweet waters of power."[55] By the 1920s Jewish membership in Soviet policy-making bodies was roughly comparable (one-

---

[51] I have analyzed the social implications of the pace of Russian modernization in "Communist Political Systems as Vehicles for Modernization," in *Political Development in Changing Societies*, ed. by Monte Palmer and Larry Stern, Lexington, 1971, pp. 135 ff.

[52] Zvi Y. Gitelman, *Jewish Nationality and Soviet Politics*, Princeton, 1972, p. 23.

[53] Ezra Mendelsohn, *Class Struggle in the Pale*, Cambridge, England, 1970, p. 17; cf. Suchev Bernhard Weinryb, *Neueste Wirtschaftsgeschichte der Juden in Russland und Polen*, Breslau, 1934.

[54] Gitelman, *op. cit.*, p. 76.

[55] *Ibid*, p. 116.

fourth to one-half of the total) to German proportions in the Tsarist governing elite of the eighteenth and nineteenth centuries. Probably Jews were even more important in the liberal professions. But the constant insecurity of their position, in contrast to the widely accepted superiority of the Russian German diaspora prior to Alexander III, is indicated by the fact that the small portion of the Jewish group which acquired influential posts was obliged to renounce (and actively attack) the major elements of its diaspora culture.

As I have shown elsewhere,[56] officially sponsored anti-Semitism, like the secret setting of employment quotas, undermined the Soviet Jewish position at least by 1942. This chronology irrefutably demonstrates that the internal dynamics of the Soviet system, particularly the rapid replacement of the cosmopolitan Old Bolshevik elite by lower-strata Russians imbued with popular prejudices, was the main factor at the start of the anti-Semitic campaigns. Certainly the dramatic establishment of a Jewish homeland in 1948 could not have been the instigating force. Nevertheless, certain indiscreet (though thoroughly understandable) demonstrations of Jewish attachment to the concept of Israel (e. g., Madame Polina Molotov's declaration to Minister Golda Meir – "I am a Jewish daughter"), like the Armenian or Greek responses to Ottoman humiliations during the preceding century, exacerbated dominant elite suspicions. Although the crescendo of accusations and arrests during 1949–53 was not completely sustained by Stalin's successors, the position of Jews as an influential diaspora in the USSR was ended. In their place, but to a much more restricted degree (mainly in foreign commerce and on the southern borderlands) were installed Armenians – whose homeland, with the religious center of Echmiadzin – lay securely under Soviet control.

(8) In polities (whether or not multiethnic) where social and economic modernization has proceeded rapidly and evenly, mobilized diasporas do not perform indispensable activities and are generally not subject to discrimination. The greatly diminished position of the Armenian diaspora, as compared to its German and Jewish predecessors in the Russian polity, suggests that as modernization proceeds, mobilized diaspora skills become less significant, Even in a slowly, unevenly modernizing polity like the Russian, the dominant ethnic group (and some others) eventually provide the communications and technical role specialists once provided by diasporas. Western polities rapidly accomplished this phase of modernization decades ago. In such societies, vestigial diasporas may continue to be

---

[56] John A. Armstrong, *The Politics of Totalitarianism*, New York, 1961, chapter 11.

Comparative Succession of Mobilized Diasporas

	Ottoman Polity			Interval Scale (Years)	Russian Polity		
	Principal Diaspora	Secondary Diasporas	Dates		Dates	Principal Diaspora	Secondary Diasporas
	Catholic Levantines	*Greeks* (few *Jews* and *Armenians*)	1453–	0	1710–	*German* (mainly Baltic; slowly declining after 1881)	*Jews* and *Armenians* (by mid-nineteenth century)
	Jews (mainly Sephardic; high point in midsixteenth century then slow decline due to cultural and economic factors without coercion)	*Greeks* (ten times more numerous than *Armenians* in Istanbul, but latter most important in Syria)	1490–	100			
	Greeks (mainly Phanariot; sharp decline after nationalist uprising)	*Jews* (major residual position); *Armenians* (rapidly rising in Istanbul); *Lebanese* (becoming important in Egypt)	1650–	200	1919–	*Jews* (declining after 1942)	*Armenians* (rising after mid-1950s)
				300	1952–	*Armenians* (limited, slightly declining after 1964)	*Jews* (highly jeopardized residual position)
	Armenians (rapidly declining after 1876)	*Jews* (modest recovery after 1880, as most trusted); *Greeks*; *Lebanese*	1821–	400			
			1919	500			

represented somewhat disproportionately in certain middleman roles, but never predominate in a broad range of crucial roles as they have in traditional or slowly modernizing multiethnic polities. Not only does a well-educated portion of the dominant elite possess considerable communication skills, but it is generally strong enough to enforce universal adoption of its language (or occasionally a bilingual compromise) by means of standard educational requirements. Influenced by the universalist values of the dominant elite, members of the dominant ethnic group appear to accept diaspora colleagues (even though they may be perceived as competitors) in much the same way that dominant ethnic occupational competitors did in a stagnant traditional society like nineteenth-century Morocco.

Proletarian Diasporas

The proposition just offered concerning the position of mobilized diaspora members in successfully modernized societies – despite the numerous exceptions which spring to mind [57] – is important for understanding the critical differences between the position of the mobilized and the proletarian diaspora. Before exploring this dichotomy, qualification is necessary. At all times and places, large portions of mobilized diasporas, like members of proletarian diasporas, have occupied disadvantageous roles in the occupational structure. The *luftmenschen* of the Jewish Pale were far from exceptional. A large proportion of even the relatively prosperous Armenian community of Istanbul was occupied in such menial work as porterage. But even the worst-off members of these diasporas had before them the symbol of upward mobility provided by their co-ethnics: "the Jewish journeyman by no means considered himself permanently a wage earner. As he saw it, were he compelled to suffer the insults of his master one day, the next he himself might become an employer, the master of his own shop. For such changes in status were fairly common practice."[58] Lacking such an upwardly mobile reference group, proletarian diasporas have, on the contrary, consisted of a nearly undifferentiated mass of unskilled labor.[59]

---

[57] See footnote 33 above.

[58] Mendelsohn, *op. cit.*, p. 9.

[59] Stephen Castles and Godula Kosack, *Immigrant Workers and Class Structure in Western Europe*, London, 1973, p. 310; John A. Jackson, *The Irish in Britain*, London, 1963, pp. 79, 81. It is true that at times specific proletarian diasporas have tended to take unskilled jobs in particular economic branches, but these are almost always characterized by greater job

Lack of even the prospect of access to advantageous *occupational roles* is accompanied by low *communication skills.* Only 67.9 per cent of one group of Algerians studied recently in France could read or write in the dominant language, which is hardly surprising since 68.3 per cent could not read or write Arabic. Oral communication is almost as difficult; in Switzerland pidgin Italian has become known as the "slave language" because it is the only vehicle for communication among the diverse proletarian diaspora workers as well as between them and their dominant ethnic employers.[60] Here is a typical case of what Joshua Fishman calls "diglossia," i.e., the division of linguistic codes between those perceived (by both the dominant ethnic group and the proletarian diaspora) as appropriate for "high" purposes and those reserved for "low" purposes.[61] Clearly their low communication skills reinforce the low perceived status of the proletarian diaspora members in addition to lowering their performance. Moreover, communication limitations make it difficult for a proletarian diaspora to maintain an identifying *myth.* Even the predominantly Polish and Italian proletarian diasporas in France in the 1940s learned to speak French very imperfectly. Because of this linguistic obstacle, combined with less tangible communications barriers, a high proportion abandoned the practice of their Catholic religion, even though it is the faith of the dominant ethnic group. For Moslem workers in Western Europe, religious tradition apparently serves more as an added barrier to assimilation (especially through intermarriage) than as an identifying myth.

Given the circumstances of the proletarian diasporas, it is difficult to envisage their relations with dominant ethnic elites in terms of exchange theory. One viewpoint is that the appropriate framework of analysis is strict conflict theory (usually Marxist-Leninist), based on the assumption that the dominant ethnic elites are able to manipulate values in such a way that the proletarian diasporas lose absolutely as well as relatively.[62] In purely material terms, this contention has been strongly debated.[63] Neither side of the debate appears to have looked at the crushing *material* circum-

---

turnover and geographical mobility than roles occupied by the dominant ethnic group, and by less status mobility.

[60] Castles and Kosack, *op. cit.,* pp. 182, 191.

[61] Joshua Fishman, *Sociolinguistics,* Rowley, 1970, p. 78.

[62] Castles and Kosack, *op. cit.,* especially p. 476.

[63] Charles P. Kindleberger, *Europe's Postwar Growth: The Role of Labor Supply,* Cambridge, Mass., 1967, pp. 204 ff; Pierre Grandjeat, "Les Migrations de Travailleurs en Europe," *Cahiers de l'Institut International d'Etudes Sociales,* I, Cahier 1, Paris, 1966, pp. 62 ff.; Arnold M. Rose, *Migrants in Europe,* Minneapolis, 1969, pp. 150 ff.

stances in the areas of, say, Turkey or Morocco where the diasporas originate. The enormous *cultural* and *psychic* impoverishment of the proletarian diasporas can, however, scarcely be questioned. Equally important in any conclusion concerning the undesirability of the process of formation of proletarian diasporas in modernized societies is the matter of relative deprivation. The degraded condition of the diasporas can hardly fail to arouse destructive animosities between them and the dominant ethnic groups when the cultural and physical appearance gap between the groups is also wide.

(9) *In polities where economic and social modernization has proceeded rapidly and evenly, proletarian diasporas tend to become progressively more distant culturally and in physical appearance from the dominant ethnic group, and to suffer more discrimination.* American readers are familiar with the concept of successive waves of immigrants taking over the least desirable housing and starting at the bottom of the occupational ladder. Unquestionably this process, in the United States, has entailed increasingly greater perceived cultural differences between proletarian diasporas and the dominant ethnic group. What is not so often recognized is that the modernized European polities have experienced a very similar succession of proletarian diasporas. After the first centuries of the Roman imperium, slave diasporas did not constitute a major source of labor in Europe (or for that matter in Islamic and other major civilizations of the medieval and early modern eras): Modernization began, therefore, with local, homogeneous, unskilled labor supplies:

> The standard stable partnership is between a poor region with regular emigration and an active town ... The origins of the new citizens in a lively town like Metz or Constance for example (the latter from 1367 to 1517) could equally well be marked on a map. In each case it would disclose a wide area associated with the life of the town ... (that) spoke its dialect ... (The town) left the lowly tasks to new arrivals (from this region). Like our over-pressured economies today, it needed North Africans or Puerto Ricans at its service, a proletariat which it quickly used up and had quickly to renew. The existence of this wretched and lowly proletariat is a feature of any large town.[64]

---

[64] Braudel, *op. cit.*, 1973, pp. 380–81. Braudel's generalization is supported by the ingeniously compiled statistics presented by Roger Mols, *Introduction à la Démographie Historique des Villes d'Europe du XIVe au XVIIIe Siècle*, Louvain, 1955, II, 379 ff. Cf. Nathan Glazer and Daniel P. Moynihan, *Beyond the Melting Pot*, 2nd ed. Cambridge, Mass., 1970, p. 10: "The classic heterogeneity of great cities has been limited to the elite part of the population ... not, as in the United States, the masses."

By 1788 "foreigners," i.e., French-speakers like the Auvergnat water-carriers and Savoyard sawyers, performed the menial tasks of Paris. Most labor was still recruited from northern and eastern regions with *dialects* as well as standard speech similar to Parisian, however. A little later, the less desirable urban roles (and those in migratory agricultural labor) were assumed by Bretons (often Celtic-speaking) and persons from countries adjoining France.[65] As modernization (and prosperity) increased, however, these quasi-native elements resisted the painful dislocation involved in long-distance migration. By the twentieth century, southern Italians and Poles were, consequently, moving into the less desirable roles of the Parisian occupational structure. Together these groups comprised 52 per cent of all foreigners in France by 1936, and 53 per cent a decade later.[66] It was not until the 1950s "postindustrial" period that *bidonvilles* for non-European workers became noticeable. Half a million non-Europeans entered France during 1955–62 alone. By the 1970s over a million North Africans were in France, compared to ninety thousand in 1936.[67]

In some respects the British experience was less gradual because reliance on the culturally distinct Irish for mobile, heavy labor began in the early nineteenth century, declined for nearly a century after the first industrial booms were over, then turned sharply upward during World War II. As late as 1966, there were 350 000 Irish workers as compared to 500 000 from the Commonwealth (mostly non-white).[68] Although friction between natives and nonwhite immigrants was evident sooner in Britain, France, contrary to characteristically optimistic forecasts, was not immune. As recently as 1969 one French observer concluded that:

> Sure of our own nationality, which has resisted all kinds of attacks and has so valiantly digested all kinds of bastardization, we have developed as one of our national characteristics a sort of tolerant, individualistic and chauvinistic indifference to foreigners, which will persist in this thoroughly bourgeois era because it is essentially based on self-assurance.[69]

The signs of latent animosity, related to cultural distance, should have been apparent by then. For example, in the late 1940s, a French sample ranked North Africans (who at that time were mostly French citizens) with

---

[65] Braudel, *op. cit.*, 1973, pp. 380–81; Louis Chevalier, *La Formation de la Population Parisienne du XIXe Siècle*, Paris, 1949, pp. 21, 165, 210.

[66] Alain Girard and Jean Stoelzel, "Français et Immigrés," *Institut National d' Etudes Démographiques*, Cahier No. 19, Paris 1953, p. 19.

[67] Castles and Kosack, *op. cit.*, pp. 296, 432.

[68] Rose, *op. cit.*, p. 24.

[69] *Ibid*, p. 115.

Germans as "least liked." Moreover, on the operationally critical question of whom respondents would most object to as sons-in-law, 70 per cent (as compared to 45 per cent for Germans) indicated North Africans.[70] With astonishing rapidity this latent hostility became manifest between 1968 and 1975, with North Africans engaging in radical labor activities and French extremists lynching Algerians.[71]

Some writers have stressed the postcolonial aspects of the succession of proletarian diasporas. While it is true that France and Great Britain have drawn on former colonies, a very similar progression has occurred in West Germany, despite German lack of a colonial empire.[72] The first cycle of replacement of local, German workers in unskilled labor (during the late nineteenth century) did draw on culturally – although not legally – alien Poles from eastern Prussia, but Poles from the Russian and Austro-Hungarian Empires were also attracted. By 1910 virtually the same proportion (four per cent) of the German labor force was foreign as in West Germany in 1965. Nevertheless, as in France and Britain, a striking change in the ethnic makeup of this four per cent has occurred. By 1973 more than half of the immigrant workers had come from such culturally distant countries as Yugoslavia and Greece, including nearly 30 per cent from Moslem Turkey.[73]

Politics has played an important part in promoting the succession of proletarian diasporas in successfully modernizing polities, just as it has been significant in the succession of mobilized diasporas in the slower or unsuccessful multiethnic polities. Within the international framework, preservation of a stable equilibrium since 1945 has been a crucially necessary condition for the recruitment of labor from progressively more remote regions. From the standpoint of internal politics, the progression has been largely the result of *non-decisions.* Certainly Western European governments have facilitated migration and in a few instances (Franco-Algerian agreements) have actively promoted it. In general, however, it has been undirected market forces which have shaped the nature of labor

---

[70] Girard and Stoelzel, *op. cit.,* pp. 37, 41.

[71] Edward R. F. Sheehan, "Europe's Hired Poor," *The New York Times Magazine,* December 9, 1973; cf. *The New York Times,* May 2, 1973, and Jean-Paul Sartre's editorial article in *The New York Times,* March 11, 1973.

[72] The poor excuse for a colonial empire which the Second Reich cherished produced no significant labor export; in a sense, of course, the Ostarbeiter compelled to work in Germany during World War II constituted a temporary proletarian diaspora.

[73] Castles and Kosack, *op. cit.,* p. 19; Kindleberger, *op. cit.,* p. 177; Rose, *op. cit.,* p. 24; *The New York Times,* November 24, 1973.

migration. In spheres where polities have the capacity to initiate policies, failure to act may be just as political as positive action. The feasibility of controlling the succession of proletarian diasporas – at least up to the present – is demonstrated by the experience of the Soviet-bloc polities. Since the late 1960s the economy of the German Democratic Republic has exerted almost as strong an attraction on foreign unskilled labor as that of the German Federal Republic. Considerable reservoirs of underutilized labor exist in Poland and the Balkan Soviet-bloc countries. Nevertheless, foreign employment in East Germany has been limited to the magnitude of several tens of thousands, ordinarily workers recruited for specific contract projects.[74] The situation within the multiethnic USSR (which may well determine GDR policy on migration as well) is more critical. Rapid industrialization with prodigal use of labor, low productivity in agriculture, and a sharply declining reproduction rate among European ethnic groups is straining the resources of the Soviet dominant ethnic areas. In contrast, Soviet regions most distant geographically and culturally (the Moslem-culture republics of Central Asia and the Caucasus) have very high reproduction rates and underutilized labor forces. Nevertheless, there has been no migration of unskilled labor from these regions to the cities of Russia and the Ukraine, which continue to recruit predominantly from the adjacent Slavic rural regions. Moreover, while the subject is treated with great reticence in Soviet publications, there are some indications that this restraint represents a definite policy decision.[75]

(10) There is a reciprocal relation between modernization and diasporas: (a) In polities where modernization is rapid and even, mobilized diasporas tend to become vestigial and their members are advantaged; whereas proletarian diasporas become increasingly important and their members are deprived. (b) In multiethnic polities where modernization is retarded, mobilized diasporas are temporarily advantaged as a group, but are successively discarded and their members are deprived; whereas proletarian diasporas are vestigial, and their members are no more deprived than the lower strata of the dominant ethnic group. This lengthy proposition can be derived from Propositions 7, 8, and 9. It also sums up the conclusions of this article. That *both* tempos of modernization lead to severe discrimination against ethnic groups may

---

[74] *The New York Times,* July 11, 1972, on increased Polish and Rumanian export of contract labor to *West* Germany, despite *East* German opposition.

[75] John A. Armstrong, "The Ethnic Scene in the Soviet Union," in *Ethnic Minorities in the Soviet Union,* Erich Goldhagen (ed.), New York, 1968, p. 7.

seem like another of the bitter ironies of history. But the ten propositions I have advanced are not intended to be commandments. The saving note, if there is one, is recognition of the autonomy of politics which *might* be able to create frameworks in which both patterns of discrimination are avoidable.

WALTER P. ZENNER

Middleman Minority Theories: a Critical Review[*][1]

Introduction

In recent years, social scientists have given much attention to interethnic relations and the problem of racism as it refers to dominant Europeans, and conquered or otherwise subordinated nonwhite proletarians and peasants. Much less stress has been given to that subtler racism which affects stigmatized groups of middle economic position. Yet these ethnic groups have been the objects of some of the most violent attempts at "final solutions" of conflicts in this century. The question of the relationship of economic class to ethnicity is crucial to an understanding of the precarious social position of these "middle-level" groups.

Here, a review of various theories and other explanations of this phenomenon will be made. It will draw on social and economic history, sociology, and anthropology. Since many of the theories started as explanations of anti-Semitism, attention must be given to Jewish history, although these theories have a much broader relevance than the sociology and ethnology of Jewish groups. For a long time, analogies have been drawn between the socioeconomic roles of the Jews in Europe and other groups, notably East Asians in East and South Africa, Lebanese in West Africa, and the Chinese in Southeast Asia.[2] This analogy forms the basis of the "middleman minorities theory" which generally seeks to explain the

[*] From: R. S. Bryce-Laportes (ed.), *Sourcebook on the New Immigration*, New Brunswick, Transaction Books 1980, pp. 413–425.
[1] The research for this paper was done with the aid of Faculty Research Fellowship 020–725A from the Research Foundation of the State University of New York. I would like to thank Thomas A. Barker, Maurice N. Richter, Jr., Werner Cahnman, George Gmelch, Robert Jarvenpa, and the participants in the Culture, Ethnicity, and Class Seminar at the University of Albany, as well as anonymous reviewers for their comments and encouragement.
[2] Howard Becker, *Through Values to Social Interpretation*, Durham, 1950. Max Weber, trans. *Ancient Judaism*, Glencoe, 1952 and Willem Frederik Wertheim, *East-West Parallels*, The Hague, 1964.

economic specialization of certain minorities who occupy strategic niches in the commercial and industrial life of certain countries, and the hostility these minorities evoke. Explanations are sought for anti-Semitism and similar prejudices in cultural and structural features of the minorities' situation, with particular emphasis on the economic roles which the minorities occupy. (While "middleman minority theories" are discussed here without special reference to the problems of American immigration, the various theories reviewed are relevant to the American context. The theories do pertain to any discussion of economic competition between new immigrants and veteran residents in general, and in the context of a capitalist job market or business situation in particular. They also have something to say about the problems of middle class professionals.)

Proof that such prejudices are caused by the economic position of the victims would affirm middleman minority theories, just as affirmation of similar consequences among other middleman groups throughout the world would strengthen the plausibility of this kind of explanation of anti-Semitism. Systematic data retrieval on trading and similar groups is in its infancy. Thus, while the different middleman minority theories suffer from weaknesses and inadequacies which will be pointed out in this review, they are still useful as propositions for use in further study.

In defining these ethnic minorities, the term "middleman" is derived from the roles of trader and broker in commerce. Voltaire, in 1761, referred to the Jews as "these wandering brokers," while Kant conceived of the Jews as "a whole nation of merchants;" both epitomized the "middle-man" or "marginal trading" minority-type.[3] But even the Polish and German Jews of the eighteenth century were not merely traders. In addition to trade and commerce, one finds that members of the "middle-man minorities" include labor contractors, rent collectors, moneylenders, craftsmen, government officials, and even truck farmers.

This lack of clarity is no different from that of other areas of comparative research in which there should be applied hypotheses and theories which have been developed to various minorities, rather than try to develop a "synthetic" definition to cover all cases.[4]

There are, of course, several examples of "trading minorities" which are cited by the "middleman minority theorists," and which may be seen as

---

[3] See two articles in Jacob Katz (ed.), *The Role of Religion in Modern Jewish History*, Cambridge, Mass., 1975; Jacob Katz, "Religion as a Uniting and Dividing Force in Modern Jewish History," and Lewis Feuer, "Response."

[4] Igor Kopytoff, "Types of Religious Movements," in *Symposium on New Approaches in the Study of Religion*, Seattle, 1964.

"proto-typical." Besides the Jews, these include Parsis in India, Armenians and Greeks in the Balkans and Asia Minor, overseas Chinese and Indians, the Syro-Lebanese in West Africa and Latin America, and Scots in sub-arctic Canada and southern Africa. All of these groups have had their successful traders, although some have not faced persecution. Two other groups are the Japanese Americans[5] and mixed-bloods (for example, mestizos in Middle America; mulattos in the West Indies).[6] The main characteristics which these minorities share include involvement in a money economy and occupying a position between the dominant elite and the poor. The economic position alone does not suffice to explain host hostility against the minority. In this paper, most of the examples will be drawn from groups within which trade is a major occupation.

Economic Position: Status Gap and Complementarity

The specialization of these groups as "middlemen" can be explained as an adaptation to particular economic conditions. Many have pointed to circumstances where a dominant elite, whether conquerors, colonists, or feudal lords, is disinclined to enter the commercial sphere, and the indigenous peasantry does not possess the skills necessary to undertake such activities.[7]

This condition has been labeled a "status gap" in which the other status holders do not challenge those who come to occupy these roles and which is a state of complementarity rather than competition.[8]

The situations which bring about such a status gap are several. Blalock's label of "peasant-feudal" for this setting is simplistic and misleading,[9] but he has specified the kinds of situations which produce such complementarity.

---

5 See Ivan Light, *Ethnic Enterprise in America*, Berkeley and Los Angeles, 1972 and Edna Bonacich, "A Theory of Middleman Minorities," *American Sociological Review* 38, 1973, pp. 583–94.
6 Hubert Blalock, *Toward a Theory of Minority Group Relations*, New York, 1967.
7 Wilhelm Roscher, "Die Stellung der Juden im Mittelalter betrachtet vom Standpunkt der allgemeinen Handelspolitik," *Zeitschrift für die gesamte Staatswissenschaft* 31, 1875, pp. 503–26; Abraham Leon, *The Jewish Question: A Marxist Interpretation*, 3rd ed., New York, 1970; Becker, *op. cit.;* Irwin Rinder, "Strangers in the Land," *Social Problems* 6, 1958, pp. 253–60; Stanislav Andreski, "An Economic Interpretation of Anti-Semitism," *Jewish Journal of Sociology* 5, 1963, pp. 201–213 (Reprinted in *Elements of Comparative Sociology*, London, 1964); Tamotsu Shibutani and Kian Kwan, *Ethnic Stratification*, New York, 1965; Richard Alonzo Schermerhorn, *Comparative Ethnic Relations*, New York, 1970; Blalock, *op. cit.*
8 Andreski. *op. cit.*
9 Blalock. *op. cit.*, p. 82.

These include the needs by a conquering or colonist elite for intermediaries with the native population, the introduction of a new technology, and the incorporation of a territory into the world market economy. The same type of situation may arise if those who have previously fulfilled these tasks have either been expelled or have removed themselves.

Several "strategies" may be followed in filling the "status gap." Outside skillholders may be "imported" or the skills may be "adopted" by training members of the society in the new skills.[10] "Importation" takes various forms, such as slaves and indentured labor, contract labor, and the encouragement of outside entrepreneurship, either individual or corporate. While individual enterprise is most commonly associated with the "middleman minorities," all of these imported skillholders share a common characteristic, in that all segment the economy along "insider-outsider" lines, whether it is the "split-labor" market created by low-paid foreign workers,[11] or a monopoly on the sale of imported goods.

Importation of skillholders in the short run has advantages, such as far fewer prerequisites for training and demands for fewer accommodations. Since the imported skillholder is relatively isolated, the host society and its rulers appear free to decide to what degree they wish to accommodate to him.[12] While Hirsch concentrates his attention on groups employed by the ruling elite, his statements have wider application. Examples include the medieval and Renaissance Jewish merchants and moneylenders invited to immigrate to such communities as the cities on the Rhine in the eleventh century, or Mantua and Venice in the fifteenth and sixteenth centuries.

In "adopting" skills, societies often turn to those elements which are either *declassé* or otherwise degraded. Displaced from their warrior trade, the samurai are an example of this type, having helped Japan acquire modern skills in the nineteenth century. These groups have "little to lose and much to gain."

In the case of commercial middlemen, there are political implications to their group membership. If they are "indigenous," it is presumed that their loyalties lie within the boundaries of the state and with the dominant ethnic group. They would reinvest their capital locally and add to local power. If they are foreign, it is assumed that "their interests were linked

---

[10] Abraham Hirsch, "'Importing' and 'Adopting' Skills," *Human Organization* 24, 1965, pp. 124–27.

[11] Edna Bonacich, "A Theory of Ethnic Antagonism: The Split-Labor Market," *American Sociological Review* 37, 1962, pp. 547–59.

[12] Hirsch, *op. cit.*

primarily to those of the emerging poles of development, what in time would be called metropoles."[13]

In dealing with the "importing" or „adopting" strategies, the filling of the gap is viewed from the ruler's outlook, but it can be seen as well from the perspective of „native" and "foreign" skillholders, where the situation may be one of competition rather than complementarity. In the creation of a money economy, such as that of medieval Europe, Jews may first fill intermediary roles, only to be displaced by a new native bourgeoisie.[14] Conversely, foreign and minority middlemen may displace native traders, as a national economy is encapsulated into the "world economy" in a dependent position. "Minority" traders with extensive foreign ties may have competitive advantages over the natives.[15]

Strangers and Trade

Questions of determination of stranger, pariah, or sojourner status or advantage, and others at a more basic level, cannot be answered without examining the relationships of economics to questions of group and self-identity.

Even in the beginnings of craft specialization, there is a connection between "strangeness" and dealing with outgroups.[16]

In the fairly simple horticultural societies of the African East Horn, it has been suggested that itinerant craftsmen have a low status because (a) they depend on trade and bargaining for their living rather than agriculture or herding; (b) varying demand for their products forces a higher degree of mobility on them than on others; (c) they "socialize" natural products (cotton into cloth; iron ore into iron objects);[17] (d) they are a symbolic reflection of landlessness in a landed society.[18] This is so, despite a lack of major linguistic or cultural differences in other aspects.

---

[13] Immanuel Wallerstein, *The Modern World System*, New York and London, 1974, 1, p. 151.

[14] See Roscher, *op. cit.*; Wilhelm Roscher "The Status of Jews in the Middle Ages from the Standpoint of Commercial Policy," trans. by Howard Becker, *Historia Judaica* 6, 1944; and Wertheim, *op. cit.*, p. 84.

[15] Wallerstein, *op. cit.*, p. 151.

[16] Werner Cahnman, "Socio-Economic Causes of Anti-Semitism," *Social Problems* 5, 1957, pp. 21–29; and Brian Foster. "Ethnicity and Commerce," *American Ethnologist* 1, 1974, pp. 437–48.

[17] C. R. Hallpike, "Some Problems in Cross-Cultural Comparison,": in Thomas O. Beidelman (ed.), *The Translation of Culture*, London, 1971.

[18] Ronald A. Reminick, "The Evil Eye Belief among the Amhara of Ethiopia," *Ethnology* 13, 1974, pp. 270–92.

In the transformation of simple agrarian societies into complex urban-agrarian ones, trade is often associated with the appearance of foreign merchants; thus, the alien may symbolize the replacement of monetary exchange for reciprocal transactions.[19]

The outsider has advantages in monetary dealings precisely because he does not face the same kinds of demands for reciprocity which confront the members of the insider groups. This reduces the stress of commerce which threatens the "folk" moral order and which, in turn, is threatened by the moral demands of traditional society. His "opportunism" and mobility aid him in keeping "objectivity." "The ethnic difference has the effect of reducing the conflict inherent in face-to-face commercial transactions."[20]

But, as Foster writes of Thailand: "Tension and conflict arising from commerce are not eliminated by traders belonging to a different ethnic group from the people surrounding them. The tension is simply shifted from the interpersonal level to another level of social structure on which there are mechanisms for dealing with it. Shifting the conflict to the level of interethnic relations is made possible by the police power of the state."[21]

The "stranger" is attractive in certain intimate roles (from moneylender to courtier) precisely because he is socially distant. He treats loans and transactions as purely commercial. He is not as likely to enter the competition for authority and prestige because as a stigmatized stranger he is excluded.[22]

Cultural Attributes of Middlemen

There is agreement that the success of certain groups in trade and other middleman roles is not simply a function of being strangers to their clients, but a product of their special aptitudes, residues of past experiences, and present ways of life. It is noteworthy that the groups most generally cited as "middleman minorities" have had their origins in the "old civilizations" of Asia and the Middle East, namely Indians, Chinese, Armenians, Syrians, Jews, and Greeks, even though some of these groups had been predomi-

---

[19] Leon, *op. cit.*, pp. 134–35; and Elliot P. Skinner, "Strangers in West African Societies," *Africa*, 33: 4, 1963, pp. 307–320.

[20] Foster, *op. cit.*, p. 442. See also Shibutani and Kwan, *op. cit.*, p. 191 and Georg Simmel, *Soziologie*, Leipzig, 1908, pp. 685–91.

[21] Foster, *op. cit.*, p. 443.

[22] Simmel, *op. cit.*, pp. 685–91; Werner Cahnman, "Pariahs, Strangers and Court Jews – A Conceptual Classification," *Sociological Analysis* 35, 1974, pp. 155–66; Lawrence Rosen, "Muslim-Jewish Relations in a Moroccan City," *International Journal of Middle East Studies* 3, 1972, pp. 435–49; and Foster, *op. cit.*

nantly peasant prior to migration.[23] These special characteristics are viewed as independent variables.

The two opposing views of Sombart and Weber represent two poles in the consideration of the economic role of middleman minorities. Sombart sees the Jews as rational capitalists par excellence, while Weber sees Judaism as supporting a nonmodern "pariah capitalism."[24]

Most authors follow Weber's opinion that Jews and other minority middlemen were not the foremost "midwives" of modern capitalism, although they do so for different reasons.[25] However, even those who accept Weber's basic reasoning may be close to some of Sombart's interpretations; for instance, Bonacich[26] accepts Weber on the limits of pariah capitalism, but attributes a rational future-time orientation to these minority members. Thus, the following listing of elements and patterns attributed to middleman minorities is not internally consistent.

Social scientists have claimed that middleman minorities have the following traits:

(a) rational "economizing" behavior, including price cutting and frugality;[27]

(b) future-time orientation[28] and high achievement motivation;[29]

(c) intellectual, rational orientation to religion and life, marked by restraint and self-control;[30]

(d) economic activity viewed as necessity, not as means to salvation;[31]

(e) "ritualistic" segregation of group, including ban on outgroup marriage and restrictions on eating with outsiders;[32]

(f) a double standard of morality towards ingroup and outgroup members (as opposed to scrupulous fairness to all), including over- and under-pricing;[33]

(g) high group morale and self-esteem, as well as sublimation of feelings of vengeance in the face of rejection by others;[34]

---

[23] Bonacich, 1973, op. cit.
[24] Werner Sombart, The Jews and Modern Capitalism, trans. 1951, and Weber, op. cit.
[25] For example, see Leon, op. cit., p. 182.
[26] Bonacich, 1973, op. cit.
[27] Sombart, op. cit., pp. 148, 206–07.
[28] Bonacich, 1973, op. cit.
[29] David C. McClelland, The Achievement Motive, New York, 1953.
[30] Sombart, op. cit., pp. 222–38.
[31] Weber, op. cit., p. 345.
[32] Weber, ibid., pp. 336–55.
[33] Weber, ibid., p. 344 and Becker, op. cit., p. 110.
[34] Bonacich, 1973, op. cit., and Weber, op. cit., pp. 403–04.

(h) tendency towards frequent migration (Sombart's "Saharaism");[35]
(i) strong attachment to former homeland;[36]
(j) perpetuation of "separatist complex," including continued teaching of a foreign language and/or religion.[37]

Various authors have stressed that the separate culture of the minority is reinforced by the minority situation, either because it has an economic payoff,[38] or because it is reinforced by host hostility.[39] Leon[40] very strongly maintains that the occupational ethos to which the group adapts may become a crucial part of its culture. In his Marxist view, the Jewish "people-class" became so adapted to being moneymen during the feudal period that, if a Jew became a feudal landlord or peasant, he would be forced to convert to Christianity. In modern times, when the niche to which the Jews had accommodated became obsolescent, they either tended to assimilate or were squeezed out.

Strangers, Entrepreneurship, and the State

Weber and Sombart were primarily concerned with a problem which is only touched on here – the role of various ethnic groups and religious groups in facilitating the " 'take-off' of a society into the developed world." Weber's view that the Jew could not provide the model for the society can be accepted by looking at the culture of the host society, rather than the minority.

Eisenstadt[41] argues that, if a group like the Puritans or the samurai is viewed as a secondary elite, it is more likely to be integrated into the society and will have much greater influence in transforming the society. On the other hand, if a large part of the capitalist class in society is composed of members of a despised "strange" minority, this may make trade and commercial enterprise a despised occupation and prevent the develop-

---

[35] Sombart's "Saharaism," *op. cit.*, p. 328.
[36] Bonacich, 1973, *op. cit.*
[37] Weber, *op. cit.*, p. 353; Cahnman, *op. cit.*; Bonacich, *ibid.*, and Sheldon Stryker, "Social Structures and Prejudice," *Social Problems* 6, 1958, pp. 340–54.
[38] Abner Cohen, *Customs and Politics in Urban Africa*, Berkeley and Los Angeles, 1969, pp. 141–60 and Walter P. Zenner, *Syrian Jewish Identification in Israel*, Ann Arbor, 1965.
[39] Edna Bonacich, "Reply to Stryker," *American Sociological Review* 39, 1974, p. 282.
[40] Leon, *op. cit.*, pp. 82–7, 139–40.
[41] Shmuel Noah Eisenstadt (ed.) *The Protestant Ethic and Modernization*, New York, 1968, p. 15.

ment of capitalism, as occurred in Poland.[42] This suggests again that it is the host society rather than the minority alone which determines the influence of the minority.

Related to this are the services which the middleman minority provides the ruling elite. Minority members are likely to serve the elite as taxpayers, farmers, personal retainers, and the like; in turn, the state provides minority members with protection, except when the service which the elite requires is that of scapegoat.[43]

The state may encourage the "separatism" of the minority. This was certainly true of the medieval and early modern Christian and Muslim states which treated religious minorities differently from members of the majority religion.[44] In West Africa, European colonial governments created split-labor from outside, and they controlled "stranger groups" through designated "tribal" leaders. Such policies often gave "stranger" groups a sense of extraterritoriality.[45]

One recent theory, known as the "sojourner hypothesis," strives to explain the economic success of these minorities, their persistence in modern industrial as well as agrarian societies, and the hostility towards them in terms of their own attributes and relationships to both emigrant community and host society.[46] According to Bonacich, the "stranger" quality of those groups which become "middleman" minorities is derived from their continued attachment to their homeland and their desire to return to it.

To Bonacich, middleman minorities start as immigrants who do not plan to settle permanently in the host country, thus contrasting strongly with both natives and permanent settlers. The economic effects of this strong attachment to the homeland are (1) thrift and a future-time orientation, since they need to plan their return, and (2) the selection of occupations which provide them with liquid resources and do not tie them to the place of sojourn. In fact, liquidity and the attachment to the homeland are the defining attributes of this minority type, rather than trade or any other particular occupation.

---

[42] This viewpoint is expressed by S. Andreski in two articles: "Methods and Substantive Theory in Max Weber," in Eisenstadt (ed.), *ibid.*, p. 60 and Andreski, *op. cit.*

[43] Blalock, *op. cit.;* Lewis Coser, "The Alien as a Servant of Power: Court Jews and Christian Renegades," *American Sociological Review* 37, 1972, pp. 547–59; Cahnman, 1974 and Foster, *op. cit.*

[44] Stryker, 1958, *op. cit.;* Salo W. Baron *Social and Religious History of the Jews,* 2nd ed. New York, 1967; and Leon, *op. cit.*, pp. 133–93.

[45] Skinner, *op. cit.;* and Cohen, *op. cit.*, pp. 9, 141–50.

[46] Bonacich, 1973, *op. cit.*

Since the sojourner remains attached to his homeland, he maintains a high degree of ethnic solidarity, which gives him economic advantages over natives and permanent settlers against whom he discriminates. For instance, the fellow ethnic is favored as an employee. The economic success and refusal to assimilate also arouse host hostility which, because of the high morale of the sojourning minority, further reinforces group solidarity.

Bonacich has extended the range of middleman minority theory from preindustrial to industrial societies, much as Sombart tried to do, but by using a Weberian framework. While she has framed reasonably clear, usable hypotheses, her thesis is weakened by the essential vagueness of her terms, several of which must be refined.

Still, while her definition of "middleman minorities" stretches out very far, and while her hypotheses do not necessarily apply to all such groups, they are operational and can form part of our armory of propositions in studying minorities, whether Gypsies or Jerbans. However, Bonacich's effort to find an objective definition and correlatives for "sojourning" do demonstrate the difficulties for finding cross-cultural and cross-national definitions of "alienness."

Ethnic Solidarity and "Objective" Visibility

Edna Bonacich is not alone in seeing the social networks and ethnocentrism of the minority as a factor in its success. Still, it is the task of the social scientist to specify the level and form of social organization.[47]

Middlemen minorities do not simply favor all "coethnics" equally in the network of jobs. Generally, family, kin, and compatriots from the same locale are favored over those farther removed. The *Mans* who have been successful in the Chinese restaurants of London are all members of one Hong Kong single lineage village,[48] and various varieties of local and language and ritual groupings of Jews:[49] all served a similar purpose in providing the basis for patronage in obtaining job placement or business contacts.

---

[47] Cohen, *op. cit.;* James L. Watson, *Emigration and the Chinese Lineage,* Berkeley and Los Angeles, 1975; and John North, *North for the Trade,* Berkeley and Los Angeles, 1972.

[48] Watson, *ibid.*

[49] See two articles by Walter P. Zenner, *op. cit.,* and "Syrian Jews in Three Social Settings," *Jewish Journal of Sociology* 10, 1968, pp. 101–20.

While favoritism towards kinsmen and compatriots is viewed as a form of precapitalist particularism, it is evident at the upper reaches of high finance and multinational corporations.[50]

Of course, some ethnic groups have greater solidarity in maintaining monopolies over lines of trade or particular occupations than others.[51] In general, however, the informal organization and ethnic solidarity of a group, whether an elite or a middle-status group, helps it maintain morale and may aid its members' economic success.

Groups which exhibit extreme "sojourning" behavior, like the Ibadi Jerbans, will maintain such separation. Their families are completely segregated from the host environment.[52] The often celibate Chinese laundrymen,[53] and the London Chinese restaurant workers, left their families at home,[54] although in the latter case, the British immigration laws forced these "sojourners" to become immigrants and thus become subject to acculturation.

One would expect that such a "separatist complex" would be manifested mainly by first-generation immigrants. Later descendants of immigrants would be more likely to show signs of assimilation and acculturation, unless there were institutional and situational bars.

Variations may occur, however, even among first-generation immigrants, one may find breaks with the "sojourning" pattern, such as individuals who intermarry. For instance, an immigrant or sojourning group of males is more likely to intermarry or carry on sexual contacts with local women than those importing brides. This would provide the stage for considerable offspring identifying with the local population. Whether or not this occurs depends on how distant the immigrants are from the homeland. In an age where the trip from Hong Kong to London is less than twenty-four hours, absolute distance is less relevant than during an earlier period.[55]

Ideological bars (for example, religious, caste, or racial prohibitions) to contact and assimilation should be examined. Some groups, like orthodox

---

50 Abner Cohen, *Two Dimensional Man*, Berkeley and Los Angeles, 1974, p. 99 and Pierre Michel Fontaine, "Multinational Corporation and Relations of Race and Color in Brazil: The Case of Sao Paulo," *International Studies Notes* 2, 4, 1975, pp. 1–10.

51 Abner Cohen has presented this thesis in two publications: *Custom and Politics, op. cit.,* and *Two-Dimensional Man, op. cit.,* pp. 94–98.

52 Russell Stone, "Religious Ethic and the Spirit of Capitalism," *International Journal of Middle Eastern Studies* 5, 1974.

53 Paul C. P. Siu, "The Sojourner," *American Journal of Sociology* 58, 1952, pp. 34–44.

54 Watson, *op. cit.*

55 *Ibid.,* p. 144.

Jews or Hindus, may have more of these in the tradition than other groups. Learning the *lingua franca* of the country is necessitated by the nature of commercial activity, although many in the immigrant group can escape this. Related to the very phenomenon of perceived alienness, avoidance of involvement in local politics may or may not be related to occupation.

In general, Bonacich and her predecessors exaggerate the middleman group's exclusivity and overstress its unity. They often fail to note the importance of assimilation, self-hatred, and similar phenomena. While "middleman minorities" appear to be more unified and less downtrodden than other minorities, they also are affected by low esteem. In addition, changes in the general political environment may require a strategy of imitation rather than separation.

Bonacich implies that the ethnic solidarity and failure to assimilate is a factor in arousing host hostility, while others[56] see visibility as preventing assimilation and arousing hostility. In fact, it is difficult to disentangle these factors. It is important to realize that what matters is perception of the separateness, whether in terms of visibility or of group solidarity, rather than the actual behavior of the minority. "Elite," "middle-status," and "low-status" groups may all utilize strategies which heighten their visibility or lower it, and others may try to heighten the perception of separation as well.[57] In light of this, whether we consider a particular group of traders as "strangers" or as "native bourgeoisie" must be investigated in terms of the mutual perceptions of those participating in the social field.

Host Hostility

The economic position of middleman minorities, and their visibility and presumed solidarity, are all seen as factors in arousing the hostility of others towards them over and above simple xenophobia. There is general agreement that here we have a case of "class conflict reinforced by ethnocentrism."[58] Two motifs which appear in various combinations in models explaining host hostility are the "scapegoat" explanation and the "rational kernel of truth" hypothesis. The different theories may also emphasize a generalized host hostility, the "resentment of the clientele" or the "competition of native middlemen."

---

[56] D. Stanley Eitzen, "Two Minorities: Jews of Poland and Chinese of the Philippines," *Jewish Journal of Sociology* 10, 1968, pp. 221–40; Andreski, 1963, *op. cit.*, and Stryker, 1958, *op. cit.*
[57] Cohen, 1974, *op. cit.*, pp. 90–118.
[58] Shibutani and Kwan, *op. cit.*, p. 196.

Blalock presents a series of propositions which see the middleman group as used by the elite to displace the attacks of the masses and to stabilize the society:

(a) A foreign or visible group filling the "status gap" is more suited to fulfill the scapegoat role than are former peasants or mixed bloods.

(b) Since the distinctive group is less assimilable, it serves the elite as a buffer and preserves the triadic relationship of elite, minority, and masses.

(c) In times of prosperity and tranquility, there is an economic coalition between elite and middleman minority, with the latter group enjoying high economic status without political power; in times of stress, the elite will form a coalition with the masses and blame the minority for troubles.[59]

(d) The middleman group serves as an ideal scapegoat during time of stress because it is the apparent source of frustration; it is politically impotent and yet visible, and sufficiently similar to the elite in position and function to serve as its stand-in. Its visibility is perpetuated through its own solidarity, adaptive skills, and the reinforcement given to these through host hostility.[60]

Blalock presents a rather static picture of elite-minority-mass relations. He writes as if political power can be separated from economic power, which is overly simple. He also does not give sufficient weight to the service which the minority may serve as a source of income, in the form of taxes or even bribes, for the elite. One may argue that the elite will support the minority in times of prosperity, when it gains monetarily from such support, but will abandon the minority when it becomes impoverished.[61]

Applying her "sojourning hypothesis" to industrial, as well as feudal and colonial societies, Bonacich also stresses hostility coming from the clientele of the minority. Whereas Blalock focuses on the "scapegoating" function, she sees the conflict between the minority and the masses as realistic. In her analysis, she does not distinguish situations where the conflict is primarily between clients and shopkeeper from those stressing labor or commercial rivals, but sees them as operating simultaneously.

---

[59] See also G. Lenski, *Power and Privilege*, New York, 1966, pp. 243–48; Foster, *op. cit.;* Ellis Rivkin, *The Shaping of Jewish History*, New York, 1971; and Wertheim, 1964, *op. cit.*, pp. 53–57.

[60] Blalock, *op. cit.*, pp. 82–83.

[61] Leon, *op. cit.*, pp. 159–60 and Baron, *op. cit.*, pp. 198–202.

Bonacich also perceives kernels of truth in the charges that these minorities either refuse citizenship in the host country or have "dual loyalties," and that they "drain the host country of its resources" by sending remittances home, not building the productive capacity of the host country. The latter charge of extracting profits is made against multinational companies and native bourgoisie, as well as minority traders.

The nationalism which underlies such charges is considered by Stryker[62] to be an important "political motif" that distinguishes situations where minorities which maintain a separate culture face much hostility from those where they do not.

Skinner[63] suggests that nationalism in Africa played a similar role in heightening hostility to the "strangers" (Africans from other regions), but that it was primarily a reaction to the separatism which was encouraged during the colonial period. However, he does make it clear that competition between the "strangers" and the locals for jobs has been an important factor in this hostility.

Because of the synthetic nature of her article, Bonacich obscures the differences which exist between situations where the leading opponents of the minority are clientele from those where they are competitors. She assumes that it is the more "efficient organization" of the minority which establishes and maintains a monopoly, when, in circumstances such as absolutist Germany of the eighteenth century, minority entrepreneurs may be brought in to break the monopolistic powers of native bourgeois guilds.[64] Similarly, native guildsmen in sixteenth-century Padua wished to oust the Jewish craftsmen, but the University of Padua opposed this, preferring competition to monopoly.[65]

Bonacich correctly sees rational motivation behind much of the host hostility, but she leans toward an acceptance of the hostile views of the opponents of the middleman minorities. For her, the commercial competitors are only one of several factors in the conflict between the minority and the majority; for others, they are the "prime opponents."[66]

---

[62] Stryker, 1958, op. cit.

[63] Skinner, op. cit.

[64] Selma Stern, The Court Jew, Philadelphia, 1950; Frederick Abbott Norwood, The Reformation Refugee as an Economic Force, Chicago, 1942, and Coser, op. cit.

[65] Brian Pullan, Rich and Poor in Renaissance Venice, Oxford, 1971, p. 528.

[66] Andreski, 1963, op. cit.; Ber Borochov, Nationalism and the Class Struggle, New York, 1937, pp. 184–85; Leon, op. cit.; and Mordecai Lahav, Sotziologia shel Toldot HaGolah HuYehudit Le'Or HaMarxism, Marhiva, 1951, pp. 57–59.

The potential rivals may be members of other ethnic groups, as between Christians and Jews in Syria,[67] and Scots, Jews, and Indians in the Central African "kaffir trade."[68] Thus, the Roscher distinction[69] between "native" and "foreign" traders must be examined carefully in each situation.

The Marxist interpretations emphasize the rivalry between different types of producers. To Leon[70] anti-Semitism originates in the "antagonism toward the merchant in every society based principally on use-value." In feudal society, it is the hostility of the landowner to the moneyman who "exploits" the modes of production but does not "create" them. The landowner is the client of the merchant for luxury goods, for which he must yield part of his surplus. While remaining hostile, merchants and lord develop a bond of necessity, a situation of complementarity, and antagonistic cooperation.[71]

Leon does not assume that it is the unassimilable nature of the middleman minority which produces antagonism; rather he lays stress on a change from complementarity to competition.

Andreski's[72] interpretation presents a quite sophisticated analysis of one instance when competition replaced complementarity and created mass anti-Semitism. His analysis allows for such sociopsychological features as prejudice and perception of group difference as playing significant causal roles. When Andreski speaks of a movement, he does not necessarily deny the preexistence of the prejudice on which the movement is based, but only that the prejudice has become active.

Andreski's thesis is as follows:

Strong popular movements against a nondominant minority are stimulated by (a) "the conspicuousness and indelibility of the distinguishing marks"; (b) "the coincidence of cultural and religious and racial dividing lines"; (c) "general poverty, and particularly, the process of impoverishment"; (d) "the ratio of the minority to the majority, and particularly, the process of increase of this ratio"; (e) "the minority's share of the total wealth, and particularly, the process of growth of this share"; (f) "the extent to which economic complementarity is absent"; and (g) "the absence of common foes." Andreski's introduction of demographic factors is

---

[67] Waterbury, *op. cit.*, p. 69.
[68] F. Dotson and Lilian Ota Dotson, *The Indian Minority of Zambia, Rhodesia and Malawi*, New Haven, 1968, pp. 78–86.
[69] Roscher, *op. cit.*
[70] Leon, *op. cit.*, p. 71.
[71] See also Rivkin, *op. cit.*, and Lahav, *op. cit.*, p. 46.
[72] Andreski, 1963, *op. cit.*, pp. 201–13.

significant. The larger the ratio of the minority to the majority of the total population, the more the points of friction. The proportion of minority members to majority members that is needed to stimulate the animosity of the majority is about ten percent, he writes.

Andreski does not indicate if this ratio is for key urban centers and the capital city or the country as a whole. Considerations of proportions of minority members should take the location of the minority into account. For instance, a concentration of a minority population in the capital city may give rise to an antiminority mass movement in the capital and credence to such sentiment elsewhere.

The factor of control of wealth in a constricting economy relates with particular sharpness to the situation of middleman minorities in general.[73] Andreski's concern with the direction of control of wealth, impoverishment, and enrichment is acute. He suggests that the minority must achieve some economic success, since a "mass movement aiming at spoliation needs prospect of booty of some size." He does not deny the possibility that at this crisis the minority may be on the wane.

Andreski's effort at stating elegant propositions, including relatively precise ratios of minority to majority, involves him in a somewhat garrulous effort to differentiate Polish anti-Semitism from Hitlerite anti-Semitism. It is also noteworthy that Andreski makes no assumptions about the actual solidarity of the minority group or its failure to assimilate. In fact, his stress on increasing competition between the two groups would support Duker's suggestion that anti-Semitism thrived on assimilation. One would suppose that, as members of the majority and the minority seek similar positions in the socioeconomic hierarchy, they would compete more with each other than before. Thus, a "final solution" is more desired than the assimilation of minority members.[74] With the modifications indicated, Andreski's interpretation should be applied to cases of host hostility besides pre-World War II Poland.

In a recent exchange between Stryker and Bonacich,[75] the factors accounting for the absence of host hostility were briefly reviewed. Both reemphasized the situation of complementarity, as it may have existed in pre-British India with its "emphasis on the small scale locality group" as

[73] Rivkin, op. cit.
[74] Abraham G. Duker, "Acculturation and Integration: A Jewish Survivalist View," in Judd L. Teller (ed.), Acculturation and Integration: A Symposium, New York, 1965; and Wertheim, op. cit.
[75] Sheldon Stryker, "A Theory of Middleman Minorities: A Comment," American Sociological Review 39, 1974, p. 281; and Bonacich, 1973, op. cit.

one where there was absence of conflict. In turn, Bonacich suggests that these minorities "indeed arouse the hostility" of competing classes, but these classes must have sufficient power for such hostility to surface. She denies that there was an absence of hostility towards the Parsis, but only that such hostility did not surface.

The degree of separateness is another variable in determining host hostility. Stryker[76] suggests that, after their emigration to Protestant countries, the Huguenots did not face intense anti-Huguenotism because they lacked a "separatist complex" despite their economic position. But Protestant refugees did face opposition from local residents who resented their competition.[77] However, Portuguese immigrants in Brazil did go through a period of acute host hostility during the 1890s, including instances of violence. This campaign did peter out, in part, because Portuguese origin is hardly an indelible stigma in a Portuguese-speaking country where many claim such an origin.[78]

In dealing with host hostility, one must examine whether particular hostile acts are channeled towards the minority alone (for example, the Tsarist pogroms of prerevolutionary Russia; Amin's expulsion of Asians from Uganda), or towards all the "haves" (for example, the October Revolution; the Cambodian evacuation of cities in 1975). While Marxist class conflict would obviously have a crippling effect on a prosperous middleman minority, it may involve different imagery and activity. This, of course, should not be assumed since ethnocentrism may be disguised.

Other Sources of Antiminority Ideology

So far, in considering this set of socioeconomic theories, one cannot fail to notice some repeated criticisms. The categories by which the minority is distinguished from majority members, as found in social scientific writing, are often vague. These theories do not answer questions of why particular groups have been singled out for genocide and expulsion. The concepts of "stranger" and "sojourner" and "native bourgeoisie" are too vague to help us. While the "middleman minority" theories tend to focus on the minorities, the sources of this distinction lie in the majority, with certain groups playing a major role.

---

[76] Stryker, 1958, *op. cit.*

[77] Norwood, *op. cit.*

[78] June E. Hahner, "Jacobinos vs. Galegos: Urban Radicals vs. Portuguese Immigrants in Rio de Janeiro in the 1890s," *Journal of Interamerican Studies and World Affairs* 18, pp. 125–54.

In the previous sections, the clientele and labor and business competitors were seen as possible sources of hostility. Competitors, particularly commercial ones, are often those most hostile to the minority. Since the banner of antiminority sentiment is often outspokenly anticommercial, its origin must be sought in groups other than rival tradesmen. Lenski[79] suggests that the priests in agrarian societies may be such a group. Groups among the priests often were the main social critics in those societies.

In modern societies, intellectuals often take over this function, especially that alienated segment of the intelligensia which is likely to become the leadership of revolutionary cadres and who provide revolutions with a counter-ideology. To overthrow a regime, they must form coalitions with others, since by themselves they are too weak.[80] In any case, whether clergy or intelligensia are advocates of an old tradition of reciprocity, that is, an ethos of *noblesse oblige,* or are opponents of bourgeois Philistinism or exponents of a radical egalitarianism, they are antagonistic to the moneymen.

The degree to which the minority becomes the "scapegoat of revolution,"[81] of course, will depend upon the needs of coalition-building, the proportional position of the minority, and the type of revolution which the particular ideologists advocate. If xenophobia, however, is added to the vulnerability of a minority and to hatred of the "worshippers of Mammon," a potent mixture indeed has been created. Attacks against the minorities may be either sincere or cynical. A controversy has arisen as to whether the Portuguese Inquisition was a "cynical" instrument of power, designed to eliminate members of a class and to enrich itself, or a sincerely "fanatical" court ferreting out "judaizers" and other heretics.[82]

Opposition to the middleman minorities could develop independently. Indeed, much of the socioeconomic interpretation of antiminority sentiment which has been discussed here is written *as if* antiminority ideology is developed independently. That this is not always the case has been demonstrated amply with regard to European anti-Semitism.[83] The anti-Jewish

---

[79] Lenski, *op. cit.,* pp. 264–66.
[80] *Ibid.,* pp. 70–71.
[81] Judd Teller, *Scapegoat of Revolution,* New York, 1954.
[82] Herman P. Salomon, "The Portuguese Inquisition in the Light of Recent Polemics," *Journal of the American Portuguese Cultural Society* 5, 1971, pp. 19–28, 50–55 and Wertheim, *op. cit.,* pp. 79–82.
[83] Norman Cohn, *Warrant for Genocide,* London, 1967; Leon Poliakov, *The History of Anti-Semitism,* New York, 1974.

ideology, which included a villainous stereotype of the Jew as a devil and/or moneyman, persisted in European countries even after Jews had been expelled. In England and France, certain economic roles have been identified with Jews, including the second-hand clothing trade and usury; thus, anyone involved in these was identified as a "Jew" of sorts.

European "anti-Semitism in the pure state" has been carried by non-European traders or by Asian intellectuals who have studied abroad. A sobriquet such as "Jews of the East" applied to the Chinese in Southeast Asia is such a transfer. A pamphlet entitled "The Jews of the East," allegedly written by King Rama VI of Thailand, was written during a period when the Thais and other non-Europeans were undergoing extensive westernization, including the beginning of studies abroad and mission school education. It was also a period when anti-Semitism was endemic in most European countries, including the colonial powers. Anti-Semitism is not the only ideology which is imported for use against middleman minorities. The "Yellow Peril," anti-Communism, or antiwesternism can all serve this purpose.

Obviously, the hostility between these minorities and their hosts is the product of particular social conditions. If it were only a stereotype it would be shortlived, as was the anti-Semitic outbreak against the fripiers of Paris.[84] Nevertheless, Bonacich's query as to why host hostility against "sojourning" middleman minorities is often so intense must be answered by an examination of both the stereotypes which are projected onto the minority in question, and the objective conditions. If the label used carries with it overtones of conspiracy and diabolism, it will be more potent than without such connotations.

The State of Middleman Minority Theory

So far, the theories reviewed here present a useful set of hypotheses which are of value in comparing minorities cross-culturally and cross-nationally, including ethnic groups whose specialties are not strictly in trade, such as the Japanese-Americans, one of Bonacich's key examples. One could further extend many of the hypotheses to groups which are not "middlemen" in any sense of the word. Bonacich's "sojourning" concept could be applied to "guest workers" in Europe who are "sojourners" of a very proletarian variety. One could even use her formulation in contrasting dissimilar groups such as Gypsies and Jews.

---

[84] Poliakov, *op. cit.*, pp. 196–97.

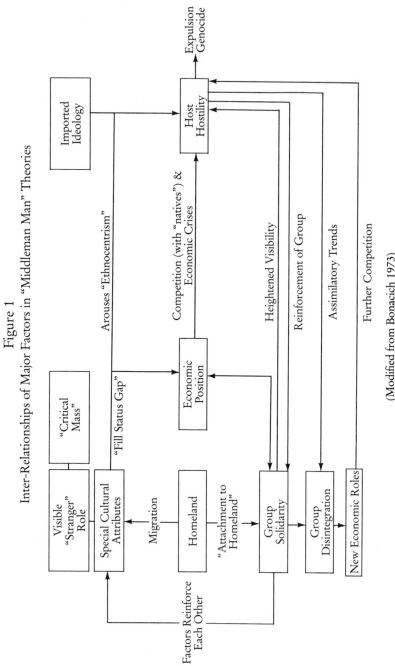

Figure 1
Inter-Relationships of Major Factors in "Middleman Man" Theories

(Modified from Bonacich 1973)

Such stretching of a theory has the effect of vitiating other aspects. Weber's interest in discovering the link between modern capitalism and the "economic ethic" of particular religions is lost when one substitutes abstractions such as "liquid occupation" for specific occupations like peddler and shopkeeper. There is a difference between a truck farmer and a merchant. We must be careful to ground our abstractions in ethnographic and historical detail, of the type provided by Waterbury and A. Cohen.[85]

At present, minority theory in general, and middleman minority theory in particular, provides useful questions and tentative answers. In my view, this type of socioeconomic explanation is insufficient to explain all aspects of the situation of these groups. As many exponents of these theories realize, attention must be paid to the specific historical circumstances of each group. The symbols used in uniting subgroups for effective economic activity and for mobilizing masses of people for antiminority action are often grounded in a long history.

In this evolution, the mythical Jew is often as important as the real Jew. This applies as well to those who become "Jews" by extension. Even the descriptions of Jews and others by Sombart (and to a lesser extent Weber and Becker) seem imbedded in the imagery of the myth.[86] Thus, even the sociologist must pay attention to the phenomenology of the stereotype. And, comparativists must deal more sensitively with internal variation within the minority in terms of occupation, subgroup organization, and tendencies towards assimilation and separation, as well as majority group perceptions of the minority.

Much more systematic comparison must be done. Some can be "controlled comparisons" like Skinner's contrast of Thai and Indonesian Chinese, or Eitzen's comparison of Philippine Chinese with Polish Jews,[87] even though the latter did not use the middleman minority framework explicitly. Stryker[88] has attempted a more ambitious comparison of three groups, although his published article is reduced from a longer manuscript. Not only must we compare whole minority groups with each other, but particular role types, such as the moneylender, the courtier, and the artisan, must be compared across cultural lines. Coser, Cahnman, and

---

[85] Waterbury, *op. cit.*, and Cohen, 1969, *op. cit.*

[86] Sombart, *op. cit.*; Weber, *op. cit*; Becker, *op. cit.*; and E. Shmueli, " 'The Pariah People' and Its 'Charismatic Leadership'," *Proceedings of the American Academy for Jewish Research* 36, 1968, pp. 167–247.

[87] G. William Skinner, *op. cit.*, and Eitzen, *op. cit.*

[88] Stryker, 1958, *op. cit.*

Zenner[89] have discussed the role of the Court Jew in a comparative perspective.

Systematic comparison which makes use of recent ethnographic and historical data can help steer us away from the stereotypes which have pervaded social scientific writing on this subject from the days of Marx and Weber. This effort at review of previously published work is only the beginning.

---

[89] Coser, *op. cit.;* Cahnman, 1974, *op. cit.* and Walter P. Zenner, "Jewish Retainers as Power Brokers in Traditional Societies," paper presented at the Annual Meeting of the American Anthropological Association, San Francisco, 1975.

Part 4: Impacts On The Holocaust

HELEN FEIN

The Impact of Antisemitism on the Enactment and Success of "The Final Solution of the Jewish Question"

We turn in this part from generalized and comparative theory to empirical analyses of a specific antisemitic movement – the *Nationalsozialistische Deutsche Arbeiterpartei* (NSDAP), and of the way the persecution of the Jews was related to popular, party, and elite opinion, and types of antisemitism. Merkl examines the role and intensity of antisemitic prejudice in the NSDAP based on a computerized re-analysis of autobiographies of early party members gathered in Germany in 1934 by a Columbia University sociologist.[1] Kershaw examines how the persecution of the Jews was related to German public opinion, using diverse sources.

Merkl's analysis shows us how the Nazi party attracted and promoted antisemites, reinforcing their world-view. Fully two-thirds of the respondents were antisemites by their own report, and the majority of these were preoccupied with the question of Jewish conspiracy or possessed by *Judenkoller*, raving about the Jews. We can not infer with certitude that the other third were not antisemitic – they might also have been indifferent towards antisemitism, taking it for granted – as they were not presented with specific questions to frame their responses as in a public opinion survey. Merkl also observes: "There is no telling how many of them deliberately omitted this theme, either because they anticipated a negative reaction from an American readership, or because in their social circles there was a sense of shame attached to talking about such phobias." Those who presented their antisemitism spontaneously in their self-reports often used it as a totalistic explanation of German defeat in the war, social revolution, moral disintegration, and depression, which parallels the explanation offered by Hitler in *Mein Kampf* and by the spurious *Protocols of the Elders of Zion*.[2] Antisemitism was far more prevalent than xenophobia

---

[1] Theodor Abel, *Why Hitler Came to Power*, Englewood Cliffs, N.J., 1938.
[2] Norman Cohn, *Warrant for Genocide: The Myth of the Jewish World-Conspiracy and the Protocols of the Elders of Zion*, New York, 1969.

and fear of the outside world and more pathological – personalized and paranoid – than was hatred of Marxism, the most general target of hostility. Respondents who were predominantly anti-Marxist usually also came from antisemitic backgrounds. Perhaps of more portent, the paranoid antisemites already held more and higher party offices than other party members in this sample by 1934 (the time the autobiographies were written). Yet, while the majority of these early Nazis then expected the movement to lead to a national renaissance, economic recovery, and a new social order, few (4.7%) of them expected Europe to be freed from Jews or Marxism.[3]

Can their prejudice be explained in terms of general propositions or hypotheses accounting for antisemitism? Based on their reports, it can not be accounted for by rural background, downward mobility, unemployment, poverty, or lack of education. Contrary to expectations relating prejudice to lack of education,[4] Merkl found party members "with no evidence of prejudice turn out to be the least educated..."

The impact of authoritarian child-rearing on the later development of antisemitism, prejudice, and authoritarianism among these early Nazis is difficult to assess because of Merkl's confused conception of authoritarianism[5] and of authoritarian child-rearing – confusing emotional and economic deprivation and wellbeing[6]. The most prejudiced and paranoid party members recalled severe disciplinary relationships with their fathers. These correspond to the childhood genesis of the ideal-type "authoritarian personality" constructed by Adorno et al.[7] discussed in Part 2. Since such families also propagated the ideals of *völkisch* antisemitism which their sons assimilated at home and in school, their prejudices may also be explained as a function of social learning. These predispositions were usually latent

---

[3] Peter H. Merkl, *Political Violence under the Swastika: 581 Early Nazis,* Princeton, N.J., 1975, p. 469.

[4] See discussion Part 2.

[5] Merkl concludes: "Authoritarianism does not seem strongly related to antisemitism or xenophobia" (p. 465). He considers Adorno's model as dubious, although the impact of child-rearing on later attitudes was clear (p. 715). Part of the problem of making any definitive inferences from this study is Merkl's faulty conceptualization and measurement of authoritarianism which was equated with attitudes to authority (pp. 489–491), assuming that any hostility to authority was anti-authoritarian, overlooking the fact that hostility to conventional authority was completely compatible with submitting to Hitler's authority; Adorno had specified how authoritarianism produced "authoritarian aggression" and hostility to specific authorities (Theodor Adorno et al., *The Authoritarian Personality,* New York, 1950).

[6] Herein.

[7] *Op. cit.*

when a wave of *Judenkoller* began in 1918–1919 as German defeat was blamed on the Jews. Thus, the evidence is consistent with several theories of antisemitism showing how crises will be interpreted in terms of underlying paradigms of blame-casting, including psychoanalytic, cognitive, group conflict, and social learning theories.

Given the self-selection of the sample of NSDAP members analyzed by Merkl, one can not deduce from this that any hypothesis about the genesis of antisemitism is confirmed or disconfirmed. Several more recent and systematic studies of Nazi party members, leaders, and voters attempt to establish how well class, occupation, age, sex, region and urbanism account for joining and voting for the party.[8] Such studies approach the question of motives for joining or voting for the party indirectly, given their limitations of data, and seldom provide evidence to assess how important antisemitism was to joiners and voters. Hamilton, in a recent review of the question "Who voted for Hitler?", observed how much patterns of NSDAP support in the German countryside were related to religious group leadership: it was less successful in Catholic rural areas where the priests opposed the NSDAP than in Protestant rural areas. He reports some evidence of the successful use of antisemitism in the Protestant countryside, where the causes of economic problems could be attributed by the Nazis to Jewish middlemen, especially cattle-traders.[9]

By contrast, Allen's study of Thalberg,[10] a middle-sized Protestant city, in which the few Jews were highly integrated along class lines, showed the local NSDAP did not make much use of antisemitic appeals, presumably because they believed they would not work. The major theme of the NSDAP in Thalberg and in larger cities was opposition to Marxism, the threat of which, exaggerated by the media, led to a bandwagon effect among conservatively-inclined voters.

Since there were other antisemitic parties competing for the voters' choice in Germany in 1928 and 1933, the willingness of German voters to vote for any and all of such parties showed that antisemitism certainly was no deterrent to large numbers of German voters. Given the importance of

[8] Michael H. Kater, *The Nazi Voter: A Social Profile of Members and Leaders, 1919–1945*, Cambridge, Mass., 1983; Thomas Childers, *The Nazi Voter: The Social Foundations of Fascism in Germany*, Chapel Hill, N.C., 1983; Richard Hamilton, *Who Voted for Hitler?*, Princeton, N.J., 1982.
[9] *Ibid.*, p. 604.
[10] William S. Allen, *The Nazi Seizure of Power*, Chicago, 1965.

the young, vigorous cadres of the NSDAP in local mobilization[11] drawing out potential voters, and the attraction of the NSDAP to rabid anti-semites,[12] it appears that antisemitism had a cumulative effect on different levels: in recruiting new members into the NSDAP, sustaining the enthusi-asm of activists in their daily work, sometimes mobilizing voters, and reinforcing solidarity within the party.

We may ask: What elements of antisemitism evoked identification among voters and party-members? Drawing on Langmuir's typology,[13] we find that all types of collective accusations against the Jews were used – with realistic (related to intergroup conflict), xenophobic, and chimerical assertions. These included crude economic appeals (relying on the image of the Jew as the exploiter), cultural and religious hostility (based on xenophobia), and the myth of Jewish world-conspiracy – the twentieth-century chimera – which "explained" German defeat, depression, and world revolution. Based on this case, it is not difficult to differentiate between types but it is hard to conclude any type of collective accusation against Jews poses no danger. In a personal and cultural crisis (as NSDAP members show in the selection by Merkl herein), belief in any type of collective accusation, regardless of the realism of its cognitive content, may be exploited by movements whose ideology could justify annihilation of the Jews.

It was not the conception or type of antisemitism (about which classes and groups differed), but the very centrality of "the Jewish question," Karl Schleunes asserts, that instigated the need for a "Final Solution."

> The fact that there was no widespread agreement on what might comprise a solution to the Jewish problem rested ultimately on lack of agreement about the nature of the Jewish problem itself. To many of those who supported Hitler before 1933 the Jewish problem was an economic one. The exclusion of Jewish competition would undoubtedly have been satisfactory to the vast majority of his lower-middle-class followers. . . To other groups, such as his own SA, the Jew offered a target for venting their addiction to violence. . . The factional struggle for control over Jewish policy was not resolved until late 1938, after the SS had clearly emerged with the most effective proposals for a solution. Then, and only then, did Hitler commission it to prepare a coordinated policy toward the Jews. . . It was the Jew who helped hold Hitler's system together – on the practical as well as the ideological level. The Jew allowed Hitler to ignore the long list of economic and social promises he had made to the SA, the lower party apparatus, and the lower middle classes. . . An ideological retreat on the Jewish issue in these circumstances was impossi-

---

[11] Described by Allen, *ibid.*
[12] See Merkl herein.
[13] See Introduction, Part 2.

ble. . . This solution, which Hitler had created for himself, made the Jewish problem and the promise of its solution a functional necessity.[14]

Without offering any evidence, Schleunes uncritically accepts the conventional wisdom that lower-middle class voters put Hitler in office which the analysis of Hamilton[15] tends to disconfirm.

How, one may ask, was the "Jewish problem" perceived by the German public? Kershaw's survey of German sources – the Gestapo, the SPD – contrasts with our contemporary reliance on disinterested public-opinion research institutes (non-existent in the Third Reich) and shows the everyday behaviors of Germans that might register support, opposition, or apathy toward racial discrimination against Jews between 1933 and 1939, including shopping in Jewish stores, negotiating with Jewish cattle-dealers, supporting Jewish employers (thus undermining the boycott movement), helping Jewish neighbors during the Kristallnacht pogrom as well as direct verbal criticism of discrimination, deportation, and visible violence. Kershaw further discriminates opposition to the means (rather than the end-goal) of exclusion of the Jews and the diversity of sources and lack of articulation and reinforcement of the opposition.

In contrast to popular rejection of violence against Jews during Kristallnacht (1938), overt German public responses to the deportation and annihilation of the Jews were nil: "The Jews were out of sight and literally out of mind." Local applications to the authorities for Jewish apartments demonstrates how many people were aware they had been (or were soon to be) seized. Knowledge of the *direct* mass murder of the Jews in the East by the *Einsatzgruppen* "was fairly widespread," but reports of automated murder by gassing in mobile vans and extermination camps appear to have been less widely circulated.

Kershaw's conclusion complements the findings of Merkl and Schleunes about the relative importance of antisemitism among different constituencies. It shows the critical significance of disinterest or the absence of anti-antisemitism[16] rather than the growth or intensification of antisemitism in accounting for German indifference to the annihilation of the Jews. A minority among the German public were virulent antisemites, but a larger number were passive antisemites, accepting the need to exclude the Jews. Those whose value system was opposed to discrimination, whether

---

[14] Karl A. Schleunes, *The Twisted Road to Auschwitz: Nazi Policy toward German Jews, 1933–1939*, Urbana, Ill., 1970, pp. 257–261.

[15] *Op. cit.*

[16] See also discussion Part 2.

based on liberal-humanitarian or Christian values, were another minority. The Nazi propaganda machine did not succeed in transforming this diverse public into a mass of virulent Jew-haters, but it did succeed in depersonalizing Jews: ". . . Depersonalization increased the already existent widespread indifference of German popular opinion and formed a vital stage between the archaic violence of the pogrom and the rationalized 'assembly-line' annihilation of the death camps."

Kershaw also addresses the question of the "function" of the destruction of the Jews for the regime and the Nazi movement which has been a question of much dispute. His conclusions differ somewhat from those of Schleunes previously cited:

> . . . one can speak of antisemitism functioning as an integrating element. But this was mainly within the ranks of the Nazi Movement itself, above all within the SS. . . The energies galvanised within the Movement in the so-called "years of struggle" could not simply be phased out from 1933, and were necessary to retain the dynamism of Nazism and prevent it from sagging into stagnation. This more or less aimless energy could be manipulated and channelled, as in 1935 and 1938, into attacks on the Jews, and the "Jewish Question" could function, too, in giving ideological purpose to the "enforcement agency" of the regime and the broad mass of the German people. . . Popular support for National Socialism was based on ideological norms which had little in essence to do with antisemitism and persecution of Jews. . .

Lastly, Kershaw remarks on how the absence of expressed elite and institutional opposition (especially citing the church hierarchies) made possible the destruction of the Jews. His conclusion complements that of *Accounting for Genocide*[17] showing how much it was the lack of resistance in German-occupied and/or German-allied states that enabled the "Final Solution" to succeed and vitiated the mobilization of resistance that might have checked it. German allies and self-governing satellites in the "colonial zone" could assent or fail to consent to anti-Jewish discrimination and deportation of the Jews. Such states (assuming their will to resist anti-Jewish discrimination) could utilize their freedom to deny official cooperation, thwarting or postponing a direct threat to their Jews. In German-occupied states, native bureaucracies (used to implement German orders) might resist and resign, delay, or subvert the execution of orders. When confronted with the deportation of Jews, clerical protests justified other citizens turning from dissent to resistance or disobedience to unjust authority.

---

[17] Helen Fein, *Accounting for Genocide: National Responses and Jewish Victimization During the Holocaust*, New York, 1979.

The actions of social authorities – church leaderships especially – did not merely reflect but defined the situation, instigating actors to avert or stop deportations in the colonial zone, and to inhibit collaboration and subvert raids in the command zone. We do not know whether either private appeals or public protest would have had any direct effect in the SS zone where there was least warning time. But news of church condemnation – however conveyed – might have at least impeded the efficiency of the operation by demoralizing the chain of accomplices. Now we know how many of Hitler's orders were averted, subverted, or countermanded – extermination of tubercular Poles, mass deportation of the Dutch, catching the Jews of Denmark, burning of Paris, destruction of Germany. The order to exterminate the Jews was not checked because it was already taken for granted that getting rid of the Jews was a legitimate objective. Those who did not agree had learned to perceive that the "Jewish problem" was caused by the Jews (and hence would disappear if they did) and inhibited redefinition of the situation to avoid dissonant perceptions and avoid costs of involvement.[18]

The success of prewar antisemitic movements predisposed many states to cooperate with the German drive to annihilate the Jews, regardless of how free they were to resist. Where prewar political antisemitism had been legitimated, church leaders whose protests might have justified resistance to collaboration and/or giving direct aid to the Jews were more likely to say nothing publicly, or to say nothing before it was too late. (Although some might like to account for their silence as a response to antisemitic beliefs of their parishioners, this was often a circular relationship, for it was often their support for prewar antisemitic movements and/or indifference to them that enabled such movements to grow.)

In Germany itself, Kershaw concludes, there was no popular demand for the annihilation of the Jews. (This conforms to Weil's observations[19] about the Germans' prewar attitudes and post-war feelings about National Socialism.) But given Germans' acquiescence in the Jews' exclusion from society, which reinforced their depersonalization and the lack of resistance of the churches and German elites,

dynamic hatred of the masses was unnecessary. Their latent antisemitism sufficed to allow the increasingly criminal "dynamic" hatred of the Nazi regime the autonomy it needed to implement the "Final Solution."

To this point, we have not examined how the specific grounds used by Hitler to justify antisemitism may have instigated the annihilation of the

---

[18] *Ibid.*, pp. 91–92; on the latter point see *ibid.*, Chs. 3–6; see also Christopher R. Browning, *The Final Solution and the German Foreign Office*, New York, 1978, pp. 5–7, 178–186 on the extent of opportunism moving German bureaucrats who volunteered their cooperation.

[19] Part 2.

Jews. Since World War II there has been extensive recognition of the role of racism in justifying exploitation and degradation of some groups by others and, finally, the Holocaust. Mosse shows how European racism, which culminated in the Holocaust, focussed all negative values and devalued body images on the stereotype of the Jew, reinforcing earlier accusations.[20] Yet Nazi racism went far beyond the main genres of racism which claim to demonstrate group superiority and inferiority, serving to justify domination, by dehumanizing the Jews, ultimately justifying their annihilation rather than exploitation. But political antisemitism of the nineteenth and twentieth centuries was not always based on racism, nor was nineteenth century racism always antisemitic, Katz notes;[21] according to this view, racism was a mode of rationalization. If Nazi racism was, as Mosse asserts, a "scavenger ideology," one must show how these scavengers chose and selected justifications to destroy their prey, and why these worked so well: the tradition of collective accusation and Jew-hatred was there to tap. "As Hitler once candidly confessed to Rauschning, 'If the Jew did not exist, we should invent him.'"[22] Goldhagen asserts that

> Anti-semitism served the Nazis not only as a rallying banner in their ascent to power; it continued to perform essential functions in the Nazi regime during its tenure of power... Of the latent functions that the image of Jewry performed in the Nazi system, the most important was that of embodying the Evil and the Profane of this world... The Nazi regime linked the whole of the newly proclaimed realm of the taboo to the Jews. .... Another of the latent functions of such anti-Semitism performed in Nazi Germany was that of bridging the gulfs dividing the German social classes... [in terms of manifest functions] we shall show how the Nazi leaders used anti-Semitism with conscious purposefulness to achieve political ends, namely, to divert popular embitterment caused by the decline of German fortunes in the war and to weaken the morale of German enemies.

However, ideology may be a cause of action as well as an effect at the actors' end-in-view. There are many explanations relating the Holocaust to Hitler's world-view and the Nazi ideology, which integrated antisemitism, racism, geopolitical Social Darwinism, and anti-communism. I have elsewhere proposed that the annihilation of the Jews, Gypsies, and less than perfect Germans was a latent function of the legitimating myth of Aryan destiny chosen by the Nazi elite as a political formula to take over

---

[20] George L. Mosse, *Toward the Final Solution: A History of European Racism*, New York, 1978.

[21] Part 1.

[22] Erich Goldhagen, "Pragmatism, Function and Belief in Nazi Anti-Semitism," *Midstream*, December 1972, pp. 52–62.

the state.[23] Racism implied that the victims could not escape by working out a symbiotic relationship with their oppressors, substituting accomodation to exploitation for annihilation; nor could they convert and be assimilated. How racism sanctioned murder indirectly is often overlooked. Early twentieth-century racism drew the idea from eugenics that selective *breeding* of the population (and conversely, inhibiting reproduction) was a social or state responsibility. This goal was also accepted in the U.S.A., embodied in laws regulating reproduction of the insane and the mentally defective before it was radically applied in Germany in 1939, when Hitler signed a secret order authorizing the killing of defective, mentally ill, and institutionalized German children and adults.[24]

> But the program did not serve only to eliminate Germans. It was also a prototype for future mass extermination. Jews, Poles, and Czechs in concentration camps interned as political prisoners, foreign workers in Germany who became unable to work, and Poles institutionalized in insane asylums were also killed. The same staff that developed the gas chambers for the special killing centers within Germany developed the massive installations at Auschwitz, and many members of the staff transferred to extermination camps. The gassing of German children . . . was halted by Hitler's edict in response to protests by Germans . . . The gassing of German Jews was never stopped; few Germans felt any need to remark or protest their absence.[25]

Thus it was this conjunction of ideologies guiding the totalitarian state (which legitimated its power by invoking the Aryan myth) that justified the state in deciding who shall live and who shall die, who shall be born and who shall be aborted.

After the Jews, the Gypsies were categorically defined, segregated, concentrated, and annihilated by Nazi Germany. Just as we cannot explain how well the "Final Solution of the Jewish Question" achieved its goal of annihilating the Jews without understanding the origins and success of prewar antisemitism, we can not understand how the Gypsies were murdered in German-controlled states in World War II without understanding how the Gypsies had been excluded from the European Christian universe of obligation and the prevalence of violence, discrimination, and prejudice against them over the centuries.[26]

---

[23] Fein, *op. cit.*, pp. 8, 20–25.
[24] Frederic Wertham, *A Sign for Cain,* New York, 1966; Stephan L. Chorover, *Genesis and Genocide,* Cambridge, Mass., 1979, ch. 5.
[25] Fein, *op. cit.*, p. 26.
[26] Donald Kendrick and Grattan Puxon, *The Destiny of Europe's Gypsies,* New York, 1972.

PETER MERKL

Dimensions of Nazi Prejudice*

National socialism is in itself an *outré* subject and, after Auschwitz and
Nazi aggression in World War Two, few aspects of it could be more *outré*
than its cultivation of hatred toward the Jews, toward other nations, and
toward any other objects of Nazi hostility. These hatreds, moreover, were
not just personal quirks or the incidental byproducts of the Nazi struggle
for power. They were a rather wellunderstood functional prerequisite of
the revolutionary Nazi movement and of the totalitarian regime that
followed. Our examination of Nazi ideology, more than any other part of
this study, has shown how little the Nazi movement was motivated by
shared, constructive goals of any kind. Instead, the movement owed its
solidarity and dynamic drive to the skillful manipulation of fears and
hatreds which were rather common in Weimar society and, for that matter,
elsewhere in the Western world and in Eastern Europe. Antisemitism, in
particular, was Adolf Hitler's Big Lie which attracted hundreds of thousands to his cause. The hatreds of the lost war and the social malaise of a
disintegrating class society added to the store of hostilities the Nazis could
manipulate.

Once the movement had propelled its leaders into absolute power, the
built-in hatreds and the collection of haters they had attracted began to
have the potential power of one of the major industrial nations of the
world. The hatreds took on a life of their own, as autistic fantasies of hatred
began to turn into actual policies of an increasingly well-armed government. German rearmament made it possible for the Nazi leadership to
prepare for its war of aggression, the collective acting-out of the fantasies of
revenge for long-forgotten humiliations. Totalitarian control made it possible to act out the anti-Communist and anti-Socialist hatreds in Germany.
And the combination of the initially successful imperialistic drive to the

---

* From: Peter Merkl, *Political Violence under the Swastika* (Princeton, N. J.: Princeton
University Press, 1975).

east with totalitarian control made possible the slaughter of millions of European Jews. As Hannah Arendt has persuasively pointed out, none of these acted-out hatreds fulfilled any rational purpose or followed any vital necessity except for the warped logic of hate-filled minds.[1] The empirical material of the Abel collection, of course, gives us few clues to the function of prejudice for the movement and the regime. Instead it allows us to document the presence of extraordinary amounts of prejudice and hatred in the respondents, a feature which still has to be fully acknowledged in much of the literature.[2] It further permits us to ascertain different degrees of prejudice and to relate them to the background, socialization, and other attitudes and behavior of the respondents.

Our scale begins with the respondents whose *vitae* contain no evidence of their prejudice. There is no telling how many of them deliberately omitted this theme, either because they anticipated a negative reaction from an American readership or because in their social circles there was a sense of shame attached to talking about such phobias. In a manner of speaking, all the other cases can be considered those without a sense of shame about their prejudice. A truly prejudiced person, according to Gordon Allport, implicitly tends to assume that everybody shares his prejudice. Many Nazis are known to have regarded the United States of the early thirties as a country with plenty of antisemitic prejudice. We can safely assume that a considerable number of those who give no evidence of prejudice were indeed not "truly prejudiced" in this sense and had other motives for joining the NSDAP. This may have been true especially with some of the younger, more naive respondents. It is hard to imagine a reasonably perceptive, mature person who would join the NSDAP without being fully aware of its chief issue.

The next entry on the scale is that of mild verbal projections and clichés such as we would expect among Nazi social gatherings. We can assume that persons of weak prejudice would use the language of prejudice in a perfunctory way to establish rapport with their fellows.[3] From this weak motivation there is a huge step to the severity of *Judenkoller*. A good

---

[1] *The Origins of Totalitarianism,* new. ed., New York; 1966, pp. 423–429, 452.
[2] Books which clearly tackle the pivotal role of the hatreds and phobias in Nazi policy, such as Karl A. Schleunes, *The Twisted Road to Auschwitz,* Urbana, Chicago, London, 1970, are still rather in the minority.
[3] See especially the interpretation of the use of prejudiced language in popular agitation to establish rapport between the demagogue and his audience by Leo Lowenthal and Norbert Guterman, *Prophets of Deceit,* New York, 1949.

Peter Merkl

FD-62: Shadings of Antisemitism

	Number	Per cent
No evidence	146	33.3
Mild verbal projections, or party clichés	63	14.3
Sudden *Judenkoller* from cultural shock, 1918	84	19.1
Sudden *Judenkoller* from economic, personal crisis	38	8.6
Relates alleged episodes with Jews	43	9.8
Relates episodes with sexual angle	9	2.0
Preoccupied with "the Jewish conspiracy" (implying counter-threats)	57	12.9
	440	100.0

one-fourth of the respondents report rather clearly how under the impact of a personal crisis or the cultural shock of 1918 they suddenly became virulent antisemites. As the word *Judenkoller* indicates, these choleric explosions signify considerable intensity and a kind of rupture in the continuity of the respondent's mental life. Great inner tensions, but not necessarily a pronounced prejudice, may have been present for years prior to the sudden outbreak. "Coming out" as a raving antisemite would release the tensions and focus them on the object of the displacement. Afterward, the restored balance is rationalized with a reinterpretation of the respondent's life which may take the form of a personal anecdote with which he explains his prejudice to himself and to others. The content of these alleged episodes usually involves primary elements such as good faith, personal honesty, decency, sexual probity, or parent-child relations, rather than the broader stereotypes of conspiracy or grand economic manipulations.

The anecdote-teller is a confirmed, self-rationalizing antisemite, but he is still a person relatively at a static balance between his displacement and his rational self. He can leave his scapegoat alone except for symbolic vilifications. At the last point in our scale, however, there is no longer even a sense of balance between the person and his sickness, but the dynamic disequilibrium of paranoia. Cornered by his surging fears of "the conspiracy" and of personal persecutions, the paranoid is a dangerous man. He has become a "political antisemite" who feels compelled to take political action against the object of his displacement. He will lash out at his imagined tormentors, plot counter-conspiracies against their alleged conspiracy, and go around propagandizing to warn people about the fancied menace. There are many stories about the distribution of handbills and attaching of posters and stickers on walls, park benches, and places of public convenience. The sight of these dirty old men (and women) peddling their social pornography would be rather ridiculous, if the consequences had not been so chilling.

Social Background of Prejudice Groups

There are considerable age differences among the prejudice groups. By far the youngest group, with nearly half of its members born after 1901, are those who indulge only in mild verbal projections. The next-youngest group are those whose *vitae* give no evidence of prejudice. The relative youth of these two groups tends to confirm our speculation that naive young respondents may indeed have stumbled into the Nazi movement without strong antisemitic motivation. By far the oldest groups are the *Judenkoller* groups, with more than half born in the prewar generation (before 1895) and a good three-fourths before 1902. This suggests that the choleric outbreak tended to occur at a mature age – about 30 or even later. We have already mentioned the significance of passing the age of 30 in German society. The cholerics may well tend to be men who had failed to pass from young adulthood to middle age in a creditable way. The other two groups are more evenly distributed by age.

As for the size of the community of residence, the no-evidence and mild verbal groups tend to be more rural, while the three most prejudiced groups are heavily metropolitan, especially from Berlin, which housed nearly half of the paranoids. Rural-urban migrants figure prominently but not unexpectedly among both the choleric and the paranoids, while most of the anecdotes are told by respondents who never moved from where they were born.

By occupation, the choleric tended to be military-civil servants or business and professional people – in other words, respondents particularly vulnerable to the defeat and red scare of 1918. Military-civil servants were also prominent among the story-tellers, while business and professional respondents had more than their share of the paranoids. The farmers and the workers were the least antisemitic. White-collar workers and women tended to limit themselves to the milder verbiage, but they also tell anecdotes and, in the case of the white-collar workers, included a disproportionate number of paranoids.

Does prejudice relate to downward social mobility, as some American research has suggested?[4] Respondents in social decline indeed stand out

---

[4] Bruno Bettelheim and Morris Janowitz, *Dynamics of Prejudice*, New York, 1950, pp. 59 and 150; and Gordon W. Allport, *The Nature of Prejudice*, Cambridge, Mass. 1954, pp. 209, 216–219.

among the choleric and the paranoid. However, the upwardly mobile from a farm background more than match their *Judenkoller* and those moving up from a city background are every bit as paranoid, and tell many anecdotes to boot. We have already encountered the choleric rural-urban migrants, who probably overlap with the farm climbers, two paragraphs earlier. There may well be enough of a rupture of conscience, or of maladjustment, in rural-urban migration to create the inner tensions for the choleric outbreak and the displacement. The city climbers, the reader will recall from part one, tended to be in the forefront of all Nazi activities. They show the most evidence of prejudice, while the least evidence is found among those who never tried to rise above the station of their fathers.

Some of these motives also come out in the varying interpretations of the vaunted *Volksgemeinschaft* (solidarism) by the prejudice groups. The most choleric were the solidarists from below, followed, naturally, by those claiming national solidarity against the outside world. The choler of the former may well have been related to the wrath of the social underdog against his "betters." The most likely to tell anecdotes, however, were respondents who had either no class consciousness at all or very strong and unsolidaristic class feelings. Their fathers tended to be workers or high military and professional people. The most paranoid were the solidarists from above, who may well have felt particularly threatened by the Socialist and trade-union movements and by the erosion of their own status. The paranoids, indeed, tended to have military-civil servants or high military and other professional persons as fathers. Economic crisis, as such, seems to have little bearing on the intensity of prejudice. The largest incidence of *Judenkoller* and of anecdote-telling was among respondents who suffered no unusual economic strictures. Those who became unemployed or whose businesses failed before 1929 tended to show no great evidence of preju-dice. The casualties of the depression of 1929–1932, to be sure, had more than their share of mild verbal projections and slightly more paranoids than the average for the whole sample. But even here the relationship between the self-initiated friction and true external, economic causation of prejudice remains obscure.

Is antisemitic prejudice a function of the decay of a particular faith, or of secularization? The Protestants of the sample are noticeably more preju-diced than either the Catholics or those who state no religious affiliation. But they stand out chiefly for mild verbal projections and for their paranoia. The Catholics more often have *Judenkoller* and, particularly often, indulge in prejudicial anecdotes. The latter tendency probably is related to the well-established German Catholic tradition of telling nasty anecdotes about the priesthood. If anecdote-telling thrives in Catholic areas, paranoia seems to be most common in evenly mixed areas.

Is formal education an antidote to prejudice? Not exactly. Those with no evidence of prejudice turn out to be the least educated, while the paranoids and those using only mild verbiage have the highest number with *Abitur* or even university study. The choleric tend to have attained a secondary school education *(mittlere Reife)*. When we pit ideology against pragmatism in their political understanding, however, there is a clear progression from the slighter to the more extreme forms of prejudice. The more intense the prejudice, the more ideological the cast of mind, particularly of the "low, ideological" sort, although there are surprising numbers of highly intelligent people among the paranoid.

Antisemitism in the Nazi Party

It is interesting to find out how the intensity of prejudice in our sample relates to the holding of party offices and to the partisan activities the respondents engaged in. Was intense prejudice an advantage or a hindrance in a party career? We can imagine that the heaviest antisemites might have been an embarrassment to the party. The evidence is somewhat ambiguous. The groups with the fewest party offices (53–54%) were the anecdote-tellers, the choleric, and those with no evidence of prejudice. Respondents who engaged in mild verbal projections, by contrast, held many offices at the local level, a fact that ties in with their perfunctory use of the party clichés of antisemitism. By far the most office-holding group (70.2%), however, were the paranoids, of whom 38.6% held offices such as special organizers of functions, speakers at rallies, *Ortsgruppenleiter*, higher-level offices, or legislative mandates. The prominence of the political antisemites in this area in spite of their patent mania clearly heralded the course of the Third Reich.

The relationship of prejudice to stormtrooper membership, on the other hand, is somewhat at variance with the pattern of office-holding in the party. To be sure, the mild-verbal and the paranoid group held the highest percentage of members here, too, while more than half of the choleric and the anecdote-tellers never became stormtroopers. But this time those who gave no evidence of prejudice are also highly involved, and rival even the paranoids in their percentage of men who graduated from the SA to the SS. We have to remember that the original function of the stormtroopers was to act not against the Jews but rather against the paramilitary formations and raiding parties of the extreme left. It was only at a rather late stage and mostly after Hitler came to power that stormtrooper violence began to turn on Jewish fellow-citizens.

The patterns of office-holding in the SA and SS further confirm this impression. Here most ranks up to the *Sturmfuehrer* and *Sturmbannfuehrer* levels turn out to be held by respondents who give no evidence of prejudice. Even the mild-verbal group has no more stormtrooper ranks than the choleric (32%). Only the paranoids are once again heavily represented in the higher level offices.

The partisan activities tell a similar story. The paranoids were the most heavily involved in street fighting and meeting-hall brawls, often "day and night." The next heaviest fighters were the mild-verbal and the no-evidence groups. The cholerics and anecdote-tellers were noticeably less involved, especially in "day-and-night" fighting at the peak time, 1931–1932. Instead they stood out for proselytizing and electioneering. The story-tellers were still a good step ahead of the cholerics in fighting and behind them in proselytizing. Here, it would appear, they reveal themselves as having gone a step beyond *Judenkoller* toward the fighting stance of the paranoid political antisemites.

The anecdote-tellers also have a slight edge over the cholerics in getting a sense of personal integration out of the struggle itself. To be sure, neither group comes close to the disproportionate numbers of no-evidence and paranoid respondents for whom this sense of integration from the struggle is the chief satisfaction in the party. The cholerics and the story-tellers instead tend to feel uplifted by the thought of striving for utopia and, among the cholerics only, by the Hitler cult. The mild-verbal group tends to be gratified by the classless comradeship in the movement and not much more by the struggle itself than the cholerics and story-tellers.

The upshot of this and the preceding comparisons is, then, that there is a rather important difference here in the degree of political mobilization of the various prejudice groups. If it is chiefly those with no evidence of prejudice and the paranoid, and perhaps to a limited extent the mild-verbal group, who are driven by a deep inner need for the political struggle, then the strong prejudice of the choleric and the anecdote-tellers may indeed be an inhibiting factor on political activity other than proselytizing. As *Judenkoller* and facetiousness turn into paranoia, however, prejudice evidently drives people into violent and aggressive political actions – which explains the consistently leading role of the paranoids in office-holding and in stormtrooper violence. The no-evidence group participated without inhibition in stormtrooper activities but evidently held few offices in the NSDAP precisely because of its lack of prejudice. The party was dominated by the political antisemites and even the mild-verbal group seems readily to have followed their maniacal leadership.

Childhood and Prejudice

The genesis of strong prejudice is a fascinating topic which deserves detailed exploration with clinical methods. The Abel *vitae*, unfortunately, allow only broad categories of childhood settings to be compared and, for obvious reasons, they tell more about adolescence than about childhood. Respondents who grew up in poverty show the least prejudice. Those with a disciplinarian upbringing and the orphans, on the other hand, have the highest number of paranoids and fewer respondents who exhibit no prejudice. Here the theories of the "authoritarian mind" of a disturbed father-son relationship seem obviously to apply.[5] Of the economically well-off childhoods, the freewheeling are high in prejudice, especially in *Judenkoller*, while the sheltered are among the least prejudiced of all the groups. Considering the importance attached to freewheeling childhoods in some cultures, including our own, this is a startling discovery. The break-down-like *Judenkoller*, moreover, is about the last consequence we would expect of a freewheeling childhood unless, of course, we view this freeewheeling permissiveness, from a conservative point of view, as self-destructive.

The influences of the parents, especially the father, follow predictable lines. The least prejudiced by far are the children from an unpolitical home environment, followed by those from a nationalistic or patriotic environment. The most prejudiced, as we would expect, are the children of *voelkisch* or antisemitic parents, who also supply the largest percentages of aggressive paranoids and of the mildly verbal, as well as more than their share of tellers of prejudiced anecdotes. Most of the choleric, however, come from nationalistic or militaristic homes where they may well have learned to identify closely with the glories of the empire that disintegrated in 1918.

Their reported school environments follow similar lines. Those who report an influential *voelkisch*, antisemitic, or Nazi teacher, or conflict with Jewish fellow-students, are the most prejudiced and include the largest numbers of paranoids and story-tellers. Students in a nationalist school environment are more likely to engage in mild verbal projections or to have *Judenkoller*.

---

[5] It has become customary to speak of "an ambivalence toward the parents" rather than of authoritarian childhood influences. See for example, Allport, op. cit. p. 374.

We have no record in most cases of when or at what ages the prejudice began, but we can look into the ages at which strongly prejudiced persons became politicized or militarized, or joined the NSDAP. Stage two (militarization) respondents who were under 18 or over 35 tend to be the most antisemitic, with emphasis on *Judenkoller* and anecdotes. The paranoids are most frequent among those who were militarized between 26 and 35. Regarding stage three (politicization), those who entered it under 26 tend to be paranoids and to tell anecdotes, while those over 25 are more often victims of *Judenkoller*. With respect to the age of joining the party, finally, those under 21 and between 40 and 50 have the most paranoids. The cohorts who joined after the age of 35 tend to have suffered more than their share of *Judenkoller*. The general impression is one of the very young and the middle-aged joining forces in prejudice.

To account for the very young, we need only crosstabulate antisemitism with the youthful postures to find that the paranoids heavily tend to be classified as "hostile militants" in the first 25 years of their lives. To account for the older semesters, and their *Judenkoller*, we can look back in Weimar history to 1918–1919. The choleric, it turns out, experienced the cultural shock of 1918–1919 far more often (82.5%) than any other prejudice group, and mostly in the form of shock at the "moral disintegration" of German postwar society or of shock at the new Weimar elites in society and government. For many respondents, perhaps as many as one-seventh of the sample, their *Judenkoller* outbreak and the cultural shock of 1918–1919 are the same. The consequences of this choler on the political development of respondents also show up in our statistics, in the age intervals of the transition from the middle stages to stage four, the NSDAP. The choleric were faster than any other group in moving along the ladder of extremist escalation. There must have been a massive *Judenkoller* wave throughout Germany in 1918–1919.

It stands to reason that a person of strong antisemitic prejudice may also express other hostile feelings. However, we could just as easily argue that one kind of displacement obviates the need for other displacements. Let us examine the relevant crosstabulations. When we look at the list of objects of hostility, the large group of anti-Communists and anti-Socialists are the lowest in prejudice, with 37.4% showing no evidence of it, even though they are not far below the average in the number of paranoids. The highest and most severe prejudice prevails among those who habitually link the Jews to their anti-Marxism and who also have the largest shares of paranoids, cholerics, and anecdote-tellers. Respondents who vent their spleen on "reactionaries," Catholics, and liberals generally make only mild verbal projections, but they also tell anecdotes. The Nazis with the all-embracing hate-list are the second most prejudiced group and stand out in particular for their *Judenkoller* and their story-telling. Except for anti-Marxism, then, there is little evidence that one displacement makes others unnecessary.

The relationship between the respondents' prejudice and their attitude toward their political enemies, presumably the Communists and other antagonists of their fights, gives an added dimension to this. The cholerics are prone to calling their political enemies subhuman, rodents, and the like, in a clear demonstration of parallel displacements. The paranoids, logically enough, prefer to call them traitors or an abstract conspiracy, another parallelism. The story-tellers and, less often those giving no evidence of prejudice, finally, tend to express a liking for their political enemies and a desire to win them over which obviously could not be parallel to any antisemitic feelings they had.

Regarding their other ethnocentric feelings, nearly a fourth of the sample gives no evidence of either prejudice. The paranoid antisemites exhibit a very strong hatred of aliens and "alien forces" in Germany (xenophobia). All of the other, more prejudiced groups show more than their share of this phobia. The story-tellers, paranoids, and cholerics also tend to stress the inferiority of other nations, while the mildly verbal group more often stresses the hostile foreign nations outside (chauvinism). Again the displacements appear to be clearly parallel except for the not unrealistic perception of Germany's wartime enemies as hostile. The primary objects of ethnocentric displacement are aliens in Germany and the obverse of a flattering national self-image, "inferior foreign breeds."

The Prejudiced Personality

In spite of the tempting topic, we have to content ourselves with rather limited indications of the prejudiced personality, because of the limitations of the data. Let us take a look at the whole configuration of each case and at a few attitudes and aspects revelatory of personality. First of all, there is the formative influence or experience distinguishing each case. The mildly verbal group stresses the experience of youthful comradeship and of social or economic humiliations. The cholerics, as we would expect, tend to be influenced by *Fronterlebnis*, educational or literary influences, or alleged encounters with Jews or aliens. The anecdote-tellers, of course, report encounters with Jews or aliens, as well as educational experiences, even more often than the cholerics but they also tell stories of social or economic humiliation. The paranoids, finally, relate alleged encounters, the defeat and revolution of 1918–1919, and the experience of youthful comradeship as their formative experiences.

The social settings of party membership also tell something about the personality of the respondent. The fully mobilized paranoid, it turns out, was less likely than members of the other prejudiced groups to have any family members save rather distant ones in the party. He was a loner. The spouses of cholerics, by way of contrast, were often members too, and the mildly verbal group tended to have practically their whole family in the NSDAP. The tellers of prejudiced anecdotes are a link to the paranoids, many with distant relatives and more than their share of whole families in the party. The general impression is that the paranoids were loners whose pseudopolitical obsessions were their whole lives. Interestingly, respondents who give no evidence of prejudice and who, as will readily be recalled, were quite involved in the fighting and far less in party offices also tend to be loners. After all, a person who joins an antisemitic movement just for the sake of fighting and without showing any antisemitic prejudice is psychologically rather marginal, too. By contrast, the choleric married to a party member and the mildly verbal conformist whose whole family were Nazis seem socially well-integrated. The lack of social integration of the anecdote-tellers is also documented by their extraordinarily high rates of political friction reported in family or school (25%), and of political boycotts or firings (36.4%).[6]

How did these people view themselves? Their dominant ideological motives tended to be antisemitism with all the groups of heavier prejudice, beginning with the cholerics. Small proportions of the paranoids also were Nordic-German romantics or revanchists, the two themes which were also dominant among the mildly verbal groups. In their attitudes toward political violence, those who were physically involved were rather low in prejudice (56–61%) and differed strikingly depending on whether they were sadists or masochists. The sadistic bullies who were biased heavily tended to be paranoid antisemites, while the prejudiced masochists more often inclined toward verbalisms, *Judenkoller*, or anecdotes. Sadism obviously inclines the violent to all-out mobilization and paranoid aggression, while masochism holds them back. Perhaps the impact of the war, which removed the inhibitions against violence, also accounts for the

---

[6] Oddly enough, the paranoids report not nearly as much political friction in any of these settings in spite of their fears of persecution. Their political mobilization evidently made them less likely to cause friction with their environment since they had a good outlet for their self-representation, their political roles.

mobilization of prejudice. Most cholerics incline toward the realistic acceptance of violence as the price of victory. Respondents who express a dislike for or regrets about the violence are even more restrained in their prejudice than the masochists who, as the reader may recall, are characterized by their self-pity and guilt feelings in connection with heavy participation in fighting.

Our final measure is of the pathology of each case in terms of its most abnormal feature. Respondents showing an extreme degree of leadership cult, group conformity, and masochism or insecurity are among the least prejudiced. The cholerics and anecdote-tellers, and most of all the paranoids, by way of contrast, show a high degree of irrationality and a lack of balance in their accounts. Nearly one-sixth of the sample falls into this combination of strong prejudice and irrationality. Some of the cholerics and the mildly verbal also show a high degree of cultural shock.

Examples of Antisemites

It is difficult to select among the wide variety of antisemitic respondents some that could be called typical. The real genesis of their prejudice tends to remain obscure in any case, even though the presentation may include an attempt to make it plausible. Quite frequently, a respondent's account invites all kinds of speculation about what really happened or how much he (or she) ever understood his own development.

A "typical" case of social decline is an aristocratic country judge's son, born 1893, who had an upper-class education and held an officer's patent until he literally fell off a horse, ruining his officer's career (no. 139). His accident did not stop him from fighting with the Free Corps and the vigilantes in Berlin. After the war he became in turn an agricultural trainee, commercial trainee, insurance representative, accountant, public employee, and, after many intervals of unemployment, a taxi driver in the years 1928 to 1932. His inherited money was lost in the inflation as a consequence of a bad investment with a company by which he was employed. Even the taxi business did not yield enough to support his wife and two children, and he supplemented his income as a doorman and caretaker for a public agency. His political involvement, he claims, grew from the idle conversations of taxi chauffeurs waiting for customers.

The idle sitting-around at taxi stands, caused by the bad economic situation, led to constant political discussions among the chauffeurs [and other idlers there]. Since there was many an old soldier of like mind in the company I worked for, we soon went about systematically influencing our Marxist colleagues. The conduct of the Jews in the west of Berlin and the fact that 80–90% of the customers were Jews was a great support for our undertaking.

The respondent joined the party only years later when renting two rooms of his flat to a party local. Thus far, this account creates a superficial impression of a kind of "taxicab theory of antisemitism" in which the envied, well-to-do customers are equated with the Jews by the down-and-out hack drivers. Even at that, we can surmise that the antisemitic angle was one of the few effective lines to use in the conversion of "the Marxist colleagues." As it happens, this respondent wrote two *vitae*, one accounting for his military and economic career, the other about his political development. In the latter, he wrote, among other things, how he viewed the role of prejudice in his political life: "I felt a strong aversion toward anything Jewish since I had been in school. It was reinforced by my father's views and *pushed me gradually* and under deteriorating economic circumstances into political activity, though not immediately with a political party. In particular a political feud in the [company] where I worked in 1923 stirred up my interest in politics." (italics supplied)

There is no reason to doubt the respondent's assertion that it was his prejudice that drove him into politics, although we might accord his father a more prominent role. In any case, it is worth noting that it took a great deal of economic strictures and, in the end, something of a *quid pro quo* in the rental of his rooms to the NSDAP to make this warped soul crawl out from under his rock and join a party. Quite probably, there were many more such antisemites who remained, as he should have, aloof from politics.

Another respondent of the same age, born 1893 (no. 24), was a commercial employee who volunteered for the war. He served with enthusiasm, and soon as an officer, until he was wounded in 1918. Convalescing from his wounds and "a stomach ruined by the diet of the trenches" in a South German spa during the darkest days of the war, he suddenly experienced *Judenkoller:* "Without any influence from any other source, an insight came into my life which was decisive for my later development as a Nazi. I became an antisemite because of what I was witnessing daily." And he describes the promenade area of the spa, Bad Kissingen, with two rows of benches, one for the military convalescents, the other for the guests of the spa.

[In the one row,] miserable, undernourished, shot-up soldiers in their old deloused uniforms. Many of them were so weak from their wounds and privations that they barely existed . . . on the miserable hospital food. In the other row, the guests were chattering, constantly eating fruit or cakes, the ladies in elegant robes, high modern boots . . ., diamonds on their hands and around their fat necks, with arrogant, un-German conduct which bore no relation to the hard times, laughing and joking indecently. The gentlemen of this exquisite society were well-nourished . . . and very busy. Stock quotations were flying through the air. . . . The guests were at least . . . 85% Jews.

The respondent stresses that he had never been an antisemite before "although I had always had a barely conscious racial aversion to Jews." The collapse and revolution further politicized his "barely conscious racial aversion" and turned it against all the economic and political abuses he could pin on the Jews. While he does not identify the politics of his parents or other early influences, it is a safe guess that here, too, a modicum of prejudice antedated his experiences in Bad Kissingen. He shows no awareness of the logical gap between the individual examples alleged by him and the global sweep of political antisemitism.

A case of *Judenkoller* without antecedents or earlier prejudice, but with an authoritarian upbringing in poverty, is that of a locksmith born in 1889 (no. 263), who felt a great urge to roam through the German countryside and a hatred for the city. A soldier in peacetime and in the war as well, he took the German defeat and the "revolution" very hard:

> The partisan squabbles took an even greater hold of the people. The Jews had laid such a foundation and they had managed to prepare all this inner corruption behind the façades. Wherever you looked, wherever you went to talk to people, you found Jews in the leading positions.
>
> And so I was seized by such a tremendous hatred that once, in 1922 at a war invalids' meeting, I launched into the open struggle against the Jews without realizing in my innermost mind the consequences to which their regime was to take us. I began to search. I bought books that threw some light on the Jewish way of life and its goals. I studied Freemasonry and discovered that, according to the documents handed down, this terrible war had long been prepared and planned. Although they tried to tell us that the war was our fault, I suddenly realized that it was all a game of intrigues, a net of lies without equal in world history.

The *Judenkoller* here had turned into paranoid delusions of global conspiracy. The respondent was unemployed for years and very lonely until, in 1932, he joined the brown movement, where he developed a peculiar fixation on the martyrs and casualties of the struggle.

Another respondent born about 1891 (no. 192) tells about being spanked repeatedly by his father, a loyal domestic servant with Jewish families for nearly half a century, for showing hostility toward his father's employers. The son's complaints soon were transmuted from the hostility of Jean Genêt's play *The Maids* to the corrosive envy of an employee of a Jewish textile businessman in Frankfurt. By 1924, his hostilities had become focused so specifically on "the Jewish question, capitalism, Freemasonry, and Jesuitism" that "these questions became the content of my life."

He began to propagandize for his new beliefs and soon lost his job because of the conflict between the "dirty thinking and actions of my boss and my blood-related feelings." His wife shared his prejudice and, with plenty of time on their unemployed hands, they soon discovered the Nazi party together.

His wife, born 1896 (no. 193), also wrote a *vita* in which she disclosed that her innkeeper parents, like her husband's father, were rural-urban migrants. One of eight children, she was also very strictly raised but, as she relates, also with kindness and justice. In spite of the resistance of her father to her early and lively interest in politics, she became very well-informed and aware of the significance of the war, "regretting that I was not a boy who could go out and defend the fatherland." She was very upset about "the collapse of a skilfully undermined system which already carried the seeds of its own subversion. . . . The German people was led by a horde of criminals who in turn were led by the wire-pullers of the International, the Jews." Her two brothers joined the SA in 1923–1924, and the girls in the family were strongly attracted by Hitler's *Mein Kampf* and other Nazi literature. The respondent participated in demonstrations and shouting slogans in the streets "until we were hoarse." In 1929 she attended the big party rally in Nuremberg, where she first encountered her great and glorious leader of the years to come.

Some antisemitic respondents are physically so aggressive that we need not be in the least surprised about the direction taken by the Third Reich. A high Prussian civil servant, born 1885 (no. 28), was so outraged by defeat and revolution that he went from one rally of the left to the next to heckle and harass prominent Socialists, republicans, and revolutionaries. In close cooperation with the Kapp *putsch*, he proposed to suppress the general strike with armed force. In November 1918, he attempted to call a mass meeting against the revolution and, subsequently, he founded innumerable nationalistic organizations for civil servants, officers, and Catholics, mostly as fringe groups of the DNVP. His aggressive hatreds included not only Marxists, "the *Reichstag*, the red headquarters," the "treasonous and godless Social Democrats," but also the Center party and the Catholic church, that "imperialist world power," and the Democrats (DDP), "all Jews." His antisemitism he describes as "an instinctive aversion for the Jewish race" which in 1919 turned into a mania. He relates: "Whenever a Jew was carrying on impertinently on the elevated or on the train and would not accept my scolding without further impertinence, I threatened to throw him off the moving train . . . if he did not shut up immediately." This sociopath of a civil servant also threatened Marxist workers with a gun and with his boot during the Kapp *putsch,* according to his own account. His egomania evidently drove him to create evernew fringe groups in which he could play the cock of the walk. As soon as he was no longer in the center of things, he would stage major provocations, get into trouble with the law, or simply lose interest in the group. "I always took it to be a weakness of my political enemies in the civil service that they let me get off so easily every time," he wrote with the innocence of the sociopath who is asking to be restrained. Apart from a court trial for disturbing the peace, two disciplinary proceedings, and denials of promotion, he seems to have met his match only once: he was beaten up by Communists, he claims, in a fracas that cost him a few teeth and his gold watch. He joined a *Nationalso-zialistische Freiheitsbewegung* briefly in 1924 and was a *Kreisleiter* until he lost interest and resigned. In 1930, he once more worked for the NSDAP as a secret mole burrowing in the bureaucratic warren, and joined officially in 1932. On coming to power, the party promoted him to the rank of *Oberregierungsrat* and gave him a position in the Prussian Ministry of Commerce.

Another respondent illustrates the curious ambivalence of some anti-semites who like Adolf Eichmann[7] not only had friendly social contact with Jews but at times even showed some interest in or identification with Jewish groups and symbols. A banker's apprentice, born 1897 in an occupied area (no. 438), he began his political activities in 1920 by heckling at SPD, DDP, and Center party rallies "whenever nationalistic principles were denigrated under the eyes of the French." He attributes such denigration in particular to Jewish speakers. After his expulsion from the occupied area in 1923, he remained aloof from politics until the presidential election campaign of 1925. He propagandized in a Catholic association for Hindenburg until that group threw him out "in a tumultuous session on election day, after I had announced my vote." He lost his bank job for undisclosed reasons and returned deeply disgruntled to his home town:

> My hatred for the Jewish bankers and stockbrokers was all that remained. I tried to penetrate deeper into the Jewish character. Getting together with the Jews, Kahn and Mohr, who had gone to school with me, I learned that some so-called Hitler boys were carrying on in Germersheim and bothering the chosen people. One night in the summer of 1926, Mohr lifted my disguise with a rash remark in front of my younger brother. I decided to take up the fight against these two Jews. . . . I joined the young leaders of the

---

[7] See for example, Hannah Arendt, *Eichmann in Jerusalem,* New York, 1963, pp. 28–33, 38–42, 56–65. Eichmann was born in 1906 and had been in the *Wandervogel* and in a quasi-military youth organization before joining the NSDAP and SS in mid-1932.

NSDAP local in Germersheim and right after a lecture . . . about the "world vampire of Judaism," I signed up with enthusiasm. I'll make no secret of the fact that I was regarded upon entry at first as a spy for Kahn. But I soon convinced my new comrades otherwise by intensively distributing copies of the *Eisenhammer*. . . .

This stalwart "fighter against Jews, Freemasons, and the Black [Catholic] International" evidently employed the familiar mechanism of trying violently to dissociate himself from what might seem to the public, including his own brother, a friendly association. As in so many cases of prejudice, there is a curious mingling of private and public motives.

There is a certain plausibility about outbreaks of *Judenkoller* among military-civil servants under the impact of defeat and revolution or of small businessmen when economic crisis strikes. Few people are mentally so stable that we cannot picture them going through a breakdown in which "my hatred against the Jews grew by leaps and bounds, and I became certain that the Jews are Germany's misfortune" (no. 523, born 1886). What requires explanation is not the private breakdown and use of scapegoats, but their translation into public political action. Let us examine some of the paranoids who turned their private manias into activist careers.

A good many of the paranoids are simply *voelkisch* partisans from the earliest times. A typical case is a druggist, born 1888 (no. 11), who was already in the antisemitic Retail Clerks Union (DHV)[8] before the war upon the advice of his boss. Following the war, in 1922, he joined the *Deutschvoelkische Freiheitsbewegung*, held a local office in it, and soon switched to the NSDAP and the SA. He says very little about his beliefs but rather describes how his drugstore was boycotted by Communists, and Socialists and denied deliveries by "a certain industrial enterprise in town." He also fails to indicate whether, as a stormtrooper, he engaged in any demonstrations or fighting. "Our National Socialism was purely a matter of sentiment *(Gefuehlssache)*," he states after indicating a good deal of proselytizing and of "ruthless action" for the cause in earlier years.

Another such activist was an executive of a shipping firm, born 1898 (no. 12), who joined the *Schutz-und-Trutzbund*[9] in response to the "betrayal of the German front by the new rulers" and Jewish war profiteers.

---

[8] On the *voelkisch* character of the DHV, see also Iris Hamel, *Voelkischer Verband und nationale Gewerkschaft*, Frankfurt, 1967.

[9] On the rise of the postwar antisemitic movement including the counterrevolutionary *Schutz-und-Trutzbund*, see especially Uwe Lohalm, *Voelkischer Radikalismus, Geschichte des Deutschvoelkischen Schutz- und Trutz-Bundes 1919–1923*, Hamburg, 1970, especially chapters 2, 4, and 5.

He spent much of the republican era abroad, away from "the alien racial elements now abroad in Germany," but in contact with like-minded people in Holland, where he also read *Mein Kampf.* In 1929, the campaigning against the Young Plan not only brought him back to sign the petition, but also enlisted him in the NSDAP. He became a stormtrooper and Nazi speaker "although my firm had nearly 60% foreign and especially Jewish customers." He undertook to proselytize and organize party cells among the "red sailors" of the Rhine shipping traffic and claims to have been in an *SA Sturm* where executives, public prosecutors, businessmen, workers, and the unemployed were cooperating in perfect harmony. At the time he wrote his *vita,* the respondent was the political director of his local.

Another old antisemite, born 1886 (no. 271), was a civil servant who tells of his father's allegiance to such nineteenth-century political antisemites as Ahlwardt, Stoecker, Henrici, and the *Deutscher Antisemitenbund.* The respondent and his brother had been militant members of the DHV since 1912 and he was also in the *voelkisch Deutschsoziale Partei* of Hamburg and the *Deutscher Turnerbund.* The writings of Fritsch, Duehring, Claass, and Dahn, he asserts, convinced him of the pernicious role of Jews in recent German history from Stahl and Marx to the contemporary German press. The respondent seems to have suffered a *Judenkoller* in 1912 and then to have gone on to severe paranoia, which caused him to see Jews everywhere in the government and to agonize over the question of whether Jesus was a Jew. His account of his war and postwar experiences is an unbelievable jumble of such mutterings. The Freemasons and the Catholic Center party also receive their share. The respondent spent most of his Weimar years with the DNVP, feeling "inhibitions" about joining the NSDAP. Finally, in 1932, after three years of withdrawal from politics, he attended a Nazi rally and arrived at the sudden realization that "this was what I had been looking for since 1912." It is cases like these which dispel this writer's concern about the possibility that the Nazi party, in helping to collect the *vitae,* may have removed the more embarrassing cases.

Our last example is another civil servant, born in 1879 (no. 291), who grew up in an orphanage because of the early death of his mother and served in the military before and during the war. In his thirties he read H. S. Chamberlain's *Foundations of the Nineteenth Century* and "through a friend in the police, got to know the slums and criminal quarters of the big city, the breeding places of the corruption of the people *(voelkische Zersetzung).*" He was "highly aware, despite the outlawing of political activity among the soldiers, of the progress of Marxism and the corruption of the people. The call of Chamberlain in the great world struggle and the bugle call of Dietrich Eckart [a Nazi writer] after the war took me among the freedom fighters of Adolf Hitler."

In 1922, the respondent founded and led the Wuerzburg local of the NSDAP. "I was *Ortsgruppenleiter,* stormtrooper, and a soldier, but this time a political soldier." He participated in the beer-hall *putsch* and, during the outlawing of the party, was a candidate for the *Reichstag* on behalf of the *Nationalsozialistische Freiheitspartei.* After Hitler's release from prison, he helped to reconstruct the party and the SA in Lower Franconia.

He met Hitler many times and, in addition to Chamberlain, read *Mein Kampf* and the writings of Gottfried Feder. His deepest wartime impressions culminated in "the appearance of Negro divisions against our heroically fighting nation" and "the Germanic tragedy of the sons of our blood brothers, who emigrated to the United States, coming back to turn the fortunes of war against us." He ends his rantings with a flourish:

> A true follower of Hitler had to be determined to eliminate the consequences of the shameful Treaty of Versailles and thus to push open once more the door to life, which has been slammed on our people and its children; to vanquish the culture-destroying, godless, Jewish Marxism and Bolshevism again, and thus to banish the great menace in Europe – nay, in the world at large. This was a struggle not just for the existence of the German people, but of the white race in general.

This old fighter and early Nazi leader undoubtedly thought he knew what he was talking about and fighting for, even if his rantings made little sense then and now. There is a difference between the unserious talk of an American right-wing demagogue, such as Loewenthal and Guterman have analyzed in their book[10] and very similar rantings by the leaders of a popular mass movement about to come to power in a modern nation-state. The difference can be deadly indeed, even though the rantings are just as illusionary as those of the demagogue, who may be content to fleece his audience of gifts and contributions.

Ethnocentricity Aside From Antisemitism

Another and parallel prejudice is that against aliens or foreign nations. Our tabulation shows the distribution of xenophobic themes in the Abel sample. To begin with, there is a slight, if somewhat debatable, difference between respondents who show no prejudice and those who seem una-

---

[10] Especially in *Prophets of Deceit,* Loewenthal and Guterman, *op. cit.* See also the antisemitic rhetoric of no. 274 (born about 1892), a military-civil servant who undertakes to defend the assassination of Rathenau and other political *(Feme)* murders by rightwing zealots.

FD-71: Ethnocentricity Other than Antisemitism

	Number	Per cent
No ethnocentricity	220	46.0
Unconcerned about outside world, parochial	54	11.3
Foreign nations dangerous, hostile (encirclement)	47	9.8
Projective, likes others' nationalism, attributes economic envy, hostility to them	11	2.3
Scores foreign press criticism of Nazis	9	1.9
Venom against aliens in Germany	65	13.6
Anti-Catholic hatred (beyond political friction)	7	1.5
Vague reference to alien "international" forces, or conspiracy	25	5.2
Alien nations are inferior	40	8.4
	478	100.0

ware of the outside world. Then there are three categories of hostile perception of foreign nations, all of which we shall call chauvinistic. There are another three themes of xenophobia. There are some Protestant regions, especially in the north, where anti-Catholic prejudice was so strong as to be quite comparable in intensity to the hatred of aliens or Jews. Anti-Catholicism also was an important ideological motive among certain racist or *voelkisch* ideologues in Austria or other Catholic areas.[11] The theme of alien inferiority is simply the obverse of delusions of national or ethnic superiority. We will not go into as much detail on ethnocentricity as on antisemitism, because the former issue is more on the surface and requires little explanation. Nevertheless, it may be worth relating this prejudice to wartime experiences and attitudes.

The three generations differ slightly in their commitment to the different ethnocentric themes. The "youngest" attitude, represented by half its respondents in the postwar generation, is unconcern about the outside world. The next youngest exhibit no prejudice. The "oldest," by comparison tend to display the ideas of inferiority and superiority among nations. This group, as well as the chauvinists and xenophobes, has particular strength among the members of the war generation (born 1895–1901). The non-ethnocentric and the parochials are also noticeably more from rural and small-town areas. The highly mobile among cities tend toward xenophobia.

Which occupational groups were the xenophobes and which the chauvinists? To begin with, workers, farmers, and women are relatively free of

---

[11] See George Mosse, *The Crisis of German Ideology,* New York, 1964, pp. 159, 231, 257.

ethnocentricity. The most chauvinistic are the military-civil servants and, less so, the white-collar employees, who are more often xenophobic. Delusions of ethnic superiority are particularly popular with women and, less often, with military-civil servants and business and professional men. If it is a matter of the father's occupation, however, the children of military-civil servants tend to be far more often convinced of German superiority and more xenophobic than they are chauvinistic. It is as if there were a generational progression from chauvinism to xenophobia. The sons and daughters of high military or professional people or of artisans tend to be more chauvinist, but those of businessmen are balanced between the two, and those of farmers are more xenophobic.

Social mobility also has a bearing on the choice between the two or three alternatives. Respondents moving up from the farm and social decliners are not particularly ethnocentric. Those who never attempted to rise, by comparison, tend to be chauvinists. The upwardly mobile in the city, again, are xenophobes or obsessed with German superiority. This is somewhat surprising if we are inclined to think in terms of the ethnic tensions of the melting-pot of rural-urban migration. But integral nationalism evidently is more at home with the next generation that grows up in the urban environment. It is their burning social ambition which turns upon the alien or exalts their own national identity.

The different interpretations given to the vaunted *Volksgemeinschaft* also tell the story. Ethnocentricity is highest (71%) among those who call for national solidarity against the outside world and who, naturally, tend toward chauvinism and feelings of national superiority, often as a result of their *Fronterlebnis*. But it is also rather high (53.1%) among respondents of strong class-consciousness and the solidarists of the middle (48%), who take out their social frustrations on the aliens and on the inferiority of "lesser breeds." Ethnocentricity, by comparison, is much lower among the solidarists from below (22.8%) or above (43.2%), or among those innocent of class feelings (41.5%), who tend slightly toward chauvinism. The strongly class-conscious may hate the alien more because he cannot readily be fitted into their social scale of values, but the solidarists of the middle (mostly military-civil servants and white-collar workers) hate him simply because he is an alien.

Religion and education also add some significant differences. Protestant Nazis tend to be far less ethnocentric, but more chauvinistic than Catholics or those who failed to indicate their religion. Catholics are more convinced of the inferiority of other nations. The most xenophobic are those who state no religious affiliation. German education gives a doubtful demonstration of its humanistic character when we learn that the best-educated of the sample incline toward the belief in the inferiority of other nations. Thirty-seven and one-tenth percent of the respondents holding this belief completed their secondary education *(mittlere Reife)* and 17.1% have the *Abitur.*

War and Revolution

If we look for the dominant ideological motive of the ethnocentricity group, we learn that the antisemites and the Nordic-German romantics were also by far the most ethnocentric (56.8% and 55.8%). The antisemites were heavily xenophobic, and the romantics inclined toward visions of national superiority and toward chauvinism. The superpatriots shared this approximate balance between xenophobia and chauvinism, while the re-vanchists were heavily chauvinistic. These relationships are not unexpected, but they suggest that we should take a closer look at all the experiences that might contribute to the ethnocentricity of the respondents.

It is particularly interesting to observe whether certain contacts with foreign nationalities seem to have predisposed a respondent more toward chauvinism or toward xenophobia. Foreign birth or sojourn seems to produce chauvinism; borderland or occupation experiences more heavily relate to xenophobia. Both of the last-mentioned seem to result in a rather high degree of ethnocentrism, especially the experiences with the French occupation (71%) which we have found to be so potent a stimulus to Nazi involvement.

The ethnocentric groups also differ somewhat in their military service patterns. Those who never served, mostly the postwar generation, are noticeably less ethnocentric (38,6%) than the war and prewar generations. Those who served in peacetime, in particular, are the most ethnocentric (50%) and both rather chauvinistic and xenophobic. As for their war experiences, the most ethnocentric (76.6%) and especially chauvinistic group are the bitter-enders, with their hostility toward draft-dodgers and civilians in general. They are quite convinced of the inferiority of other nations but not nearly as xenophobic as, for example, those whose initial enthusiasm turned to disaffection with the war. Those who stress the egalitarian *Fronterlebnis* also tend to be chauvinists. The youthful victory-watchers, also tend to be more heavily chauvinistic than xenophobic.

In their reaction to the German defeat, the most ethnocentric (86.3%) are those who blame the *Kaiser* and the civilians. They are mostly chauvinistic or believe in the inferiority of other nations. Even respondents who blame Marxists and Spartakists for the German defeat more often are chauvinists rather than xenophobes. Only among those who reacted with diffuse emotion and who were also rather young are the xenophobes the prominent element. As for the revolution, however, the xenophobes clearly tend to blame international Bolshevism or the Jews. The territorial changes in the east, of course, may well have tended to blur the national status of some revolutionary leaders – Hitler himself did not acquire German citizenship until the early 1930s. The chauvinists tend to blame the Weimar parties, the Jews, or the Spartakists and mutineers for the revolution.

The direct impact of the occupation, by way of contrast, mostly made xenophobes out of those who were punished, jailed, or expelled by the French. Respondents who only express hatred or distaste for the occupation, on the other hand, were more often chauvinists. The question of whether the displacement went toward the aliens inside or toward the obvious enemy outside evidently was greatly influenced by actual conflicts and friction.

We are still unable to explain completely why some ethnocentrics insist on hating aliens rather than foreign nations, which would have followed more logically from the experience of international conflicts. One prevalent reason so far has been the parallel nature of antisemitism in various contexts to xenophobia. In their perception of the Weimar "system," too, those who view Weimar as the *Judenrepublik* rank high in xenophobia as well as in the belief in other nations' inferiority. But there are also other factors present. Respondents who raise the traditional anti-capitalistic objections to Weimar are just as xenophobic, and those who look beyond the regime of the "red and black" parties toward utopia are far more so. We must be dealing with an intense integral-nationalistic impulse here which probably interacts with other attitudes as well. Let us examine what other attitudes bear the highest interrelationship with xenophobia.

With regard to the objects of hostility, the strongest xenophobic impulse is found among respondents with the all-embracing hate-lists; 42.9% are xenophobes. The next most xenophobic group are respondents who vent their spleen on "reactionaries," Catholics, and liberals (24.6%), well ahead of the anti-Marxists (13.4%) and the antisemitic anti-Marxists (12.7%). If the all-embracing hate-list reflects the intensity of free-floating hostility or a high propensity for displacements, this would seem to be a typical feature of Nazi xenophobia. On the antisemitism scale, it will be recalled, the xenophobes most heavily tend to be paranoids, cholerics, or tellers of prejudicial anecdotes. In their attitude toward political enemies, the xenophobes are mostly physically aggressive or *outrés* who probably considered aliens also as "subhuman," rodents, immoral, etc. In their attitude toward authority, too, the xenophobes heavily tend toward hostility vis-à-vis the police and government authority.

In their level of political understanding, the xenophobes are mostly of the low-ideological type or of medium intelligence, which makes them considerably more ideological than any other group. Their formative experiences tend to be alleged encounters with Jews or aliens or an educational or literary experience. By comparison, those who believe in German superiority and the chauvinists also cite such alleged encounters but they are also strongly influenced by the war and by their *Fronterlebnis*. The attitudes toward violence of the xenophobes heavily emphasize attitudes of physical involvement, and more often masochism than sadism.

The pathology of xenophobia yields disproportionate numbers of irrational paranoids and of the insecure or masochistic. By comparison, the chauvinists and those who believe in German superiority tend to have much more often a severe case of cultural shock from the events of 1918–1919. In 1934, finally, the expectations of the xenophobes more than those of anyone else were set on empire and on totalitarianism within it. Here we obviously have a very important element of the Nazi attitude, a kind of core group even though its ideological profile is far from clear.

Dimensions of Hostility

At first glance, there may seem to be some duplication in the effort to measure Nazi hostility apart from antisemitism and ethnocentricity, not to mention the other ideological and attitudinal indicators. However, the importance of sorting out the various overlapping dimensions of the political culture of the Nazi movement suggests a strategy of overlapping measurements in the hope of winnowing out each motive by itself and its relation to the others. This measurement (FD-61) began as an attempt to inventory the hostilities of the respondents by their chief objects. Since crosstabulation requires a certain amount of consolidation, however, the emerging categories are less clear: Antisemites, anti-Marxists, anti-establishmentarians, and the all-embracing or intense leftover of hatred shall be the labels. The last-mentioned also includes motives of a more private sort, such as a hatred of particular individuals which has somehow become politicized.

By far the largest of our groups are the anti-Marxists, whose prominence raises the question whether and to what extent the Nazi movement was an

FD-61: Chief Objects of Hostility

	Number	Per cent
Jews, the "conspiracy"	53	12.5
Jewish Marxists, Communists	9	2.1
Socialists, Free trade union leaders	34	8.0
Communists	45	10.6
Marxists in general	190	44.7
Catholics, Church, Center party	19	4.5
Liberals, capitalists	33	7.8
Reactionaries	7	1.7
All of above	10	2.4
Others (personal hostilities)	24	5.7
	424	100.0

anti-Marxist movement. Historically there was an intense feeling of rivalry with Socialism among the more labor-oriented elements of the Nazi movement and a strong sense of opposition to Communism and Socialism among the bourgeois Nazis. But the *vitae* rarely show a case in which a passionate anti-Marxism could be cited the principal motif. There is frequently an eloquent expression of regret about how the Social Democrats alienated the German workingman from his fatherland and, on occasion, an expression of the desire to win him back from the "reds." There are also plentiful descriptions of fighting against Communists and *Reichsbanner* in the streets and meeting-halls, along with deprecatory remarks about these opponents. But no Abel respondent, with the possible exception of a Russian emigré or two, exhibits anything like the anti-Communist crusading spirit familiar from certain contemporary American groups and campaigns. Perhaps a real flesh-and-blood enemy does not lend itself as well to the manipulation of paranoid fantasies as does one that is either distant or a mere figment of the popular imagination. In any case, anti-Marxism as a crusade does not appear to have moved the respondents as deeply as did some of the other attitudes we discussed earlier in this section.

Social Background of Hate Groupings

How do the anti-Marxists and the other groups relate to the different Nazi generations? The anti-Marxists, of whom 39.9% belong to the postwar generation, are among the youngest. More than half of them were born after the turn of the century. Only the small group of the intense haters is that young. The oldest group are the antisemites. The youthfulness of the anti-Marxists suggests that their anti-Marxism had little to do with the prewar Socialist movement, but rather constituted a hostile reaction to the well-entrenched and powerful SPD and KPD of the Weimar years. Thus it contains strong elements of anti-establishmentarianism just as the older anti-reactionary attitude did. Many respondents, indeed, in spite of the occasional involvement of their own parents, considered the Socialist and labor movement an outdated legacy of the past or an obnoxious monopoly over union-controlled jobs or welfare benefits limited to holders of "red" party-member cards.

The anti-Marxists tended to live either in Berlin or in rural areas, as compared to the anti-reactionaries and intense haters who more often lived in large towns or other metropolitan areas. The anti-Marxists, furthermore, mostly lived in the place of their birth, or they might be highly mobile among cities, but they were not as often rural-urban migrants as were the antisemites and the anti-reactionaries. The borderland respondents also tended to be strong anti-Marxists because they considered the SPD an obstacle to ethnic unity and also because they felt betrayed by a Socialist government in Berlin. They were also anti-reactionary, a trait they shared with respondents from the occupied areas where the impact of foreign occupation seems to have loosed an avalanche of displacements on all kinds of targets other than the occupiers.

By occupation, the anti-Marxists tended to be workers, as we would expect them to be, but also women, and military-civil servants. Business and professional persons were more frequent among the antisemites or among the anti-reactionaries, who also had a greater share of white-collar workers and as large a proportion of military-civil servants. The disaffection and sense of rivalry with the Marxist labor movement was evidently their predominant motive. We can tentatively extend the inquiry into the preceding generation by looking at the occupation of the fathers. The anti-Marxists had mostly military-civil servants and workers as fathers, while the fathers of anti-reactionaries tended to be farmers or workers. There may well have been a working-class Tory tradition present here.

Many working-class Tories are upwardly mobile people who spurn the existing trade union movement because they feel that they can do better by themselves. Others again feel so well integrated into a hierarchic society that their shock at Socialist pushiness outweighs their interest in their own advancement. Our anti-Marxists tended not to attempt to rise above the station of their fathers and may have felt envious of the success of the Socialists and unionists as individuals in the Weimar Republic. Many were in social decline and may have resented successful Socialists all the more.

The anti-reactionaries, by comparison, were upwardly mobile and evidently more preoccupied with the capitalists, Catholics, and other established circles who may have been reluctant to accept them. The anti-reactionaries tended to be Catholics, which may explain their hostility toward the Catholic establishment. The anti-Marxists, by comparison, were mostly Protestants or respondents who failed to indicate their religion. Historically, winning the loyalty of the German worker in Protestant areas involved fighting the SPD, while in Catholic areas the *Sozialverein* and Catholic labor associations were often better-established than the SPD and the Free Trade Unions. Our data clearly bear this out.

The Reaction to Defeat and Revolution

The great shock of the year 1918 hit the various hate groupings quite differently. The cultural shock of the antisemites chiefly took the form of complaints about social and moral disintegration and shock at the press and the new Weimar elites. The anti-Marxists instead were shocked about the fall of the old order and the disparagement of the glories and military symbols of the empire, as well as about the new Weimar elites. To see this in the appropriate light, we have to remember how young they were at the time. Very few of them actually mourned the passing of a social order they had experienced only as children. The anti-reactionaries instead tended to complain about the absence of order and discipline.

Their reaction to the German defeat gives us a first clue to their motivation. Unlike the antisemites and anti-reactionaries, who tend to blame the defeat on the *Kaiser* and the civilians, the anti-Marxists heavily blame it on the Marxists and Spartakists. More than half of them, of course, had never served in the military and, of those who had been in the war, many became disaffected, but evidently they quickly changed their minds at the "Marxist excesses." There were many victory-watchers among them, too. Their reaction to the "revolution," moreover, was mostly to blame the Spartakists or mutineers, or unspecified rabble, or the Western powers. The anti-reactionaries instead tended to blame the Weimar parties, and the antisemites the Jews for the revolution. The motive of the anti-Marxists for becoming militarized (stage two) tended to be the shock of defeat and their sense of opposition to the red revolutionaries, certainly a plausible reaction.

Our second clue has to come from the youth-group background of the anti-Marxists, since so many of them were rather young at the time of defeat and revolution. The fathers of the anti-Marxist respondents tended to be militarists or *voelkisch*-antisemitic, while the anti-reactionaries, for example, more often had fathers of moderate political color or an unpolitical home environment. The anti-Marxists also report a *voelkisch*-antisemitic school and peer group environment and more than their share of orphans and childhood poverty.

As for their first youth group association, one in ten of the anti-Marxists turns out to have been in a Socialist or Communist youth group. A good many also joined *Jungdo*, or bourgeois groups, or were in a Free Corps or military training group before they turned 26. What they liked best about this first youthful association was its spirit of comradeship, marching and ideological direction, or just demonstrations. And what they liked the least were "un-national views" or the ideology and leadership of their group. It looks as if their dislikes and very likely their antisemitism led them to defect from their Socialist or Communist youth groups and to drift into the NSDAP. Quite a few, in fact, joined the Hitler Youth or the stormtroopers to begin with. As their motives for joining the NSDAP (stage four), indeed, many cite the "rough opposition" of the Communists, or the dynamic impression of the Hitler movement. Anti-Marxism seems to have been a convenient umbrella to cover a wide range of bourgeois or ex-Socialist youthful attitudes.

Ideological Attitudes and the NSDAP

Among the dominant ideological themes of the Abel group, anti-Marxism plays no role at all. When we cross it with these themes, in fact, most of those "without any ideology" turn out to be anti-Marxists. Hitler-worshippers, Nordic-German romantics, and solidarists, in this order, make up the bulk of the anti-Marxists. Relatively low on the antisemitism scale,[12] they are also the lowest in other forms of ethnocentricity. Only in their attitude toward authority do they exhibit an extraordinary amount of authoritarianism and of extreme leadership cult.

Their level of political understanding tends to be rather low and of the dimwit-romantic or low-pragmatic sort, as compared to the highly intelligent anti-reactionaries, or the low-ideological antisemites. This corresponds to the differentials in their formal education, of which the anti-reactionaries have the most and the anti-Marxists the least. The antisemites have quite a few members with a lot and quite a few with very little

---

[12] This is low only in relative terms. In absolute numbers the very large group of anti-Marxists still supplies more than half of the paranoids on that scale.

education. The expectations of the anti-Marxists in 1934 tended to be the dream of the totalitarian 1000-year Reich, with hints of purges and brain-washing. Their pathology indeed suggests special movement qualities for this direction: A high degree of leadership cult and of group conformity. These qualities also highlight their role in the Nazi party. The chief satisfactions of the anti-Marxists in the party, for example, tended to be the Hitler cult and the spirit of comradeship of the stormtroopers, as compared to the utopian consciousness exhibited by the antisemites and the anti-reactionaries. In contrast to these other groups, also, the anti-Marxists held only rather minor local offices in the party. They were far more heavily involved with the stormtroopers than were the antisemites and anti-reactionaries, and yet the latter two held the more important offices there at the *Sturmfuehrer* and *Sturmbannfuehrer* levels. The anti-Marxists did most of the fighting, while the antisemites concentrated more on proselytizing, and the anti-reactionaries on electioneering. This did not prevent the anti-Marxists from a masochistic attitude toward violence and yet a distinctly *outré* manner of referring to their political opponents. It is not unfair to say that the anti-Marxists were mostly the foot soldiers of the movement. Eugen Kogon in his *Theory and Practice of Hell* describes the typical SS guard in his concentration camp as a simple man with a few fixed ideas in his head. Such a fixed idea without much ideological underpinning was probably the stereotypical anti-Marxism we are examining here.

IAN KERSHAW

The Persecution of the Jews and German Popular Opinion in the Third Reich*

To what extent did antisemitism serve to integrate the German people and mobilise them behind the Nazi leadership during the Third *Reich?* That is the central question which this article seeks to answer. By examining dissent from and approval of various facets of the persecution of the Jews, it attempts to explore the spheres of penetration of Nazi racial ideology in the consciousness of "ordinary" Germans.**

The question of the significance of the "Jewish Question" for the "broad mass" of the German population in the Third *Reich* is a complex issue which has prompted frequent speculative generalisation but little system- atic exploration.[1] Alongside the apologetic, much heard in Germany since the end of the war, that the persecution of the Jews can be put down to the criminal or insane fixations of Hitler and the gangster clique of top Nazis around him in the face of widespread disapproval by the mass of Germans insofar as they knew and understood what was going on, exists the counter-generalisation, much favoured by Zionist historians and recently

* From: *Leo Baeck Yearbook* Vol. XXVI (1981), pp. 261–289.
** The author wishes to thank the Alexander von Humboldt-Stiftung for its financial support of the research on which this article is based.

[1] The only studies to date which have concerned themselves directly with the problem are: Marlis G. Steinert, *Hitlers Krieg und die Deutschen. Stimmung und Haltung der deutschen Bevölkerung im Zweiten Weltkrieg*, Düsseldorf 1970, pp. 236–263; Lawrence D. Stokes, "The German People and the Destruction of the European Jews," *Central European History* 6, 1973, pp. 167–191; Otto D. Kulka, " 'Public Opinion' in National Socialist Germany and the 'Jewish Question'," *Zion* XL, 1975 No. 3/4, pp. 186–290 (in Hebrew, documents in German and with an English summary); and Ian Kershaw, "Antisemitismus und Volksmeinung. Reaktionen auf die Judenverfolgung," in Martin Broszat und Elke Fröhlich (eds.), *Bayern in der NS-Zeit II. Herrschaft und Gesellschaft im Konflikt*, Munich-Vienna, 1979, pp. 281–348. In addition there is a useful unpublished contribution by Aron Rodrigue, *German Popular Opinion and the Jews under the Nazi Dictatorship*, University of Manchester B.A. thesis, typescript, 1978, of which there is a copy in the Wiener Library.

re-popularised by Lucy Dawidowicz,[2] of a German people thirsting for a
"war against the Jews," in which antisemitism, based on a centuries-old
tradition of persecution, played a central role in providing Hitler's support
from the German people and in motivating the popular adulation of the
Führer." According to this interpretation, the central role of antisemitism
in Hitler's ideology is echoed by its central role in the mobilisation of the
German people.

Far from emphasising a more or less spontaneous eruption of popular
antisemitism in the socio-psychological crisis of Weimar, contrasting interpretations have stressed the conscious manipulative exploitation of anti-
semitism, which thus functioned as a tool of integration and mass mobilisation by the Nazi régime, whether – according to a recent East German
study[3] – in the interests of imperialist finance-capital, or – following the
argument of a prominent West German historian – as the cementing
element which guaranteed the continuing ceaseless "negative" dynamic
diverting from the inevitable failures of socio-economic policy and holding
the antagonistic forces of the Nazi movement together.[4]

It seems time to confront such interpretations with as rigorous, full of
nuance and exhaustive an examination as possible of the empirical evidence
for the reactions of the German people to the anti-Jewish policies of the
Nazi régime.

Such a task is faced with a series of complicated questions of method
arising from the source material. Obviously, we cannot expect, in conditions of an ideological dictatorship and terroristic police state, open "first-
hand" comments of opinion adverse to the régime. Numerous expressions
of opinion can be found, but they are invariably reflected through the
distorting mirror of the records themselves, with their different inbuilt
biases.

The confidential "opinion" reports of the Nazi authorities themselves,
compiled at regular intervals to provide the régime with as clear a picture as
possible of the morale of the population and its reactions to policies and
propaganda, represent the most important category of material offering
such expressions of opinion. Despite the obvious difficulties of interpreta-

---

[2] Lucy Dawidowicz, *The War against the Jews 1933–1945*, Harmondsworth, 1977, esp.
pp. 77, 209–211.
[3] Kurt Pätzold, *Faschismus, Rassenwahn, Judenverfolgung*, Berlin 1975, pp. 28–32.
[4] Martin Broszat, "Soziale Motivation und Führer-Bindung des Nationalsozialismus," *Vier-
teljahrshefte für Zeitgeschichte* 18, 1970, pp. 392–409, esp. pp. 400ff.

tion,[5] such material, if used in a differentiated and critical way, can provide many insights into popular mentality and behaviour. Coupled with these "secret" sources, not intended for the public eye, the Nazi press itself – though hardly a reflection of freely expressed opinion – can through the tone of its commentaries give indications of popular reactions hostile to the régime, and can thereby augment the picture derived from the report material.[6] Further amplification is provided by the reported comments of individuals denounced and prosecuted by the Nazi *Sondergerichte* for expressing anti-régime opinions, and by anonymous letters of protest sent in to the various government offices. Apart from such evidence, largely to be found in the administrative records of the régime itself, two categories of material survive which allow a picture to be assembled from sources hostile to the régime. The records of the exiled political enemies of the Nazis, especially of the Social Democratic Party working from Prague, then Paris and finally London, were based upon first-hand reports smuggled out of Germany from all parts of the *Reich* before being assembled, digested, and circulated abroad. They are a rich source of information about socio-economic conditions under Nazism, and contain lengthy sections relating to the persecution of the Jews.[7] Finally, there are Jewish accounts – published memoirs but also the Wiener Library collection of "eye-witness reports", which provide a rich source, relatively little used with regard to relations between Jews and non-Jews in Nazi Germany.

All this evidence, from whatever source, is impressionistic and subjective. Statistical quantification of "public opinion" is totally lacking. The question of the representative nature of the evidence is therefore a key one, but one which there is no statistically sound method of answering. The only satisfactory way of proceeding is to allow the sources where possible to speak for themselves, and to cite sources which themselves seem representative in their comments of the vast mass of the surviving material in all its nuances. Despite difficulties of interpretation, the material, criti-

---

[5] For detailed discussion of the material and the problems of interpretation, see Martin Broszat, Elke Fröhlich and Falk Wiesemann (eds.), *Bayern in der NS-Zeit. Soziale Lage und politisches Verhalten der Bevölkerung im Spiegel vertraulicher Berichte*, Munich-Vienna, 1977, which also contains (pp. 427–486) a selection of reports dealing with the reactions of non-Jews in Bavaria to the "Jewish Question". See also Kershaw, *op. cit.*, pp. 283–285.

[6] See, for example, C. C. Aronsfeld, "Not All Germans are Guilty," *The Gates of Zion*, July 1954, for use of such material.

[7] 'Deutschland-Berichte der Sopade' (henceforth referred to as 'Sopade') 1934–1940, copies in the Wiener Library. Originals of the regional reports were consulted in the 'Emigration Sopade' collection of the Archiv der Sozialen Demokratie, Friedrich-Ebert-Stiftung/Bonn.

cally deployed, is highly suggestive of broad lines of interpretation of popular reactions to the persecution of the Jews.

Such reactions were necessarily conditioned to some extent by the geographical distribution of Jews, and by the traditional relationship between Jews and the non-Jewish population long before the Nazis appeared upon the scene. The heavy concentration of Jews in large cities meant that in extensive regions of Germany most people came in the normal course of their lives into no physical contact with Jews.[8] Outside the setting of the big city, direct contact took place mainly in spas, tourist centres, and in those farming districts where Jews continued to dominate the cattle trade. In many areas, therefore, the "Jewish Question" was from the beginning at most an abstract issue unrelated in any direct sense to the everyday lives of the population. This presented no barrier to the acceptance of racial ideas, but such ideas were inherently unlikely to serve as the motive force and provide the major appeal of Nazism in the many localities where the physical presence of Jews was negligible.[9]

Though the climate for Jews obviously worsened dramatically during the period of the Nazis' rapid rise to power, research has done much to counter and qualify the notion of a society driven by pathological hatred of the Jews, in which "generations of antisemitism had prepared the Germans to accept Hitler as their redeemer".[10] Though Hitler himself apparently regarded antisemitism as the most important weapon in his propaganda arsenal,[11] it seems in fact, far from being the main motive force in bringing Nazism to power, to have been secondary to the main appeal of the Nazi message. A contemporary Jewish assessment of the spectacular Nazi gains in the 1930 *Reichstag* election emphasized that millions of Nazi voters were in no sense antisemites, adding pointedly, however, that their rejection of antisemitism, on the other hand, was evidently not great enough to prevent them giving their support to an antisemitic party.[12] Analysis of the

---

[8] For the regional distribution of the Jewish population in Germany, see Esra Bennathan, "Die demographische und wirtschaftliche Struktur der Juden," in *Entscheidungsjahr 1932. Zur Judenfrage in der Endphase der Weimarer Republik.* Ein Sammelband herausgegeben von Werner E. Mosse unter Mitwirkung von Arnold Paucker, Tübingen, 1965, pp. 87–131.

[9] In the whole of Lower Bavaria, for example, there were only 293 Jews forming a mere 0 · 04 per cent of the population and concentrated almost entirely in four provincial towns – Kershaw, *op. cit.,* pp. 288–289.

[10] Dawidowicz, *op. cit.,* pp. 210–211.

[11] Hermann Rauschning, *Hitler Speaks,* London, 1939, pp. 233–234.

[12] Cited in Arnold Paucker, *Der jüdische Abwehrkampf gegen Antisemitismus und Nationalsozialismus in den letzten Jahren der Weimarer Republik,* 2nd edn., Hamburg, 1969, document 32, pp. 194–195.

ideological motivation of a selection of *Alte Kämpfer* in joining the NSDAP suggests antisemitism was decisive only in a small minority of cases.[13] And in his perceptive study of the rise of Nazism in Northeim in Lower Saxony, where the NSDAP polled almost double the national average in 1932, W. S. Allen reached the conclusion that the Jews of the town were integrated on class lines before 1933 and that people "were drawn to antisemitism because they were drawn to Nazism, not the other way round."[14]

Antisemitism cannot, it seems, be allocated a decisive role in bringing Hitler to power, though (given the widespread acceptability of the "Jewish Question" as a political issue, and one exploited not only by the Nazis) it did not do anything to hinder his rapidly growing popularity. The relative indifference of most Germans towards the "Jewish Question" before 1933 meant that the Nazis had a job on their hands after the takeover of power to persuade them of the need for active discrimination and persecution of the Jews. With what success the Nazis were able to transform latent anti-Jewish sentiment into active, dynamic hatred[15] is explored in the pages which follow.

Three areas have been selected for analysis. The first section concentrates on reactions to the stepped-up anti-Jewish campaign of the summer of 1935. In the second part the varying reactions to the November pogrom of 1938 are examined. The third section focuses on reflections of opinion during the period of deportation and extermination.

I. Boycott, Terror and Race-Laws: The Antisemitic Campaign of Summer 1935

In the spring and summer of 1935 the Nazis unleashed their second wave of anti-Jewish violence, which was gradually brought to a halt only by the promulgation of the hastily assembled racial laws at the Nuremberg Party Rally in September and by the growing proximity of the 1936 Winter Olympics. The level of intimidation and terror produced by *Einzelaktionen* of Party, NS-Hago, SA, SS and HJ units was higher than at any stage

---

[13] Peter Merkl, *Political Violence under the Swastika. 581 Early Nazis,* Princeton, 1975, pp. 33, 446 ff. and *passim.*

[14] William Sheridan Allen, *The Nazi Seizure of Power. The Experience of a Single German Town,* Chicago, 1965, p. 77.

[15] See Michael Müller-Claudius, *Der Antisemitismus und das deutsche Verhängnis,* Frankfurt a. Main, 1948, pp. 76–79, 119, 157 for the equivalent formulation: "statischer Haß – dynamischer Haß".

since the initial wave of antisemitic action following the seizure of power in 1933. In the context of a deteriorating economic situation and the need to avoid making gratuitous enemies on the diplomatic front, a relative calm had set in by the end of 1933 and lasted a full year until a new series of verbal tirades by rabid antisemites such as *Gauleiter* Streicher (Franconia), Kube (Kurmark) and Grohé (Köln-Aachen) and an intensified campaign of filth in the *Stürmer* set the tone for the renewed and heightened violence of 1935.[16]

The domestic and foreign consolidation of its position by the Nazi régime does not of itself explain the renewed violence against the Jews in 1935. It does, however, account for the régime's willingness to slacken its tight rein on the radical but nihilistic dynamism of the party's rank-and-file activists. Anti-Jewish violence provided not only an outlet for pent-up energies in the movement; it gave the Party activists an apparent *raison d'être* for their commitment to the movement in a period where the disappointment of many *Alte Kämpfer* was intense, where the Party's role in the new state seemed anything but clear, and where the emasculation of the SA's powers had left a sizeable army of activists without any obvious political function.

The agitation seems to have been galvanised through pressure from the *Gau* level and below, with the *Reich* leadership doing no more than allowing the wave of violence to run its course largely unchecked until the late summer, by which time it was becoming counter-productive. As in all antisemitic campaigns, a high level of manipulation was involved. *Gauleiter* Grohé of Köln-Aachen actually suggested in March and April 1935 that new boycott propaganda and an intensified attack on the Jews would serve as a useful ploy "to raise the rather depressed mood in circles of the *Mittelstand*",[17] and the new campaign of 1935 has been therefore interpreted as a conscious attempt to divert popular opinion from increasing dissatisfaction with socio-economic conditions in the Third *Reich* through focusing their anger and frustration on the Jew.[18] Undoubtedly there was an almost total lack of spontaneity in the anti-Jewish actions of the summer and, as Grohé's comments show, the second-tier Nazi leaders made claims for the diversionary and integrating role of antisemitism. It would be as well, however, not to press the point too far. It was less the *Mittelstand* or

---

[16] See Pätzold, *op. cit.*, pp. 194–195; and Uwe Dietrich Adam, *Judenpolitik im Dritten Reich*, Düsseldorf, 1972, p. 115 ff.

[17] Cited in Steinert, *op. cit.*, p. 57.

[18] See Pätzold, *op. cit.*, pp. 202–203, 231.

any other specific social group which was mobilised by the anti-Jewish campaign, than the Party activists (among whom were of course many members of the *Mittelstand*). The basic division was between the Party formations and the bulk of the population and, as the evidence presented below demonstrates, the anti-Jewish violence of the summer of 1935, far from diverting attention from discontent, actually helped to increase that discontent by providing widespread grounds for criticism of the Party and its affiliations. The anti-Jewish violence was therefore divisive rather than integrative in its effect. Primarily a release mechanism for the pent-up destructive energies of rank-and-file activists, the campaign alienated rather than won support for the Nazi Party.

The anti-Jewish campaign of 1935 had two main interlinked, though distinguishable features: the boycott of Jewish shops, firms and businesses carried out by terrorising the owners and harassing would-be customers; and the accompanying unprecedented level of public violence reflected in the high frequency of physical attacks on Jews and their property. Unlike 1933 there was no single one-day, nation-wide boycott, but the regional *Gau* organisations saw to it that every part of Germany experienced the Nazi Party's attempt to exclude the Jews from any trading contact with the rest of the population. Given the massive extent of the intimidation and coercion, it is remarkable how difficult the Nazis found it to break the ties between the Jews and their non-Jewish customers.

Reports from many parts of Germany, emanating from Nazi and non-Nazi sources, indicate how little the mass of ordinary Germans were persuaded by Nazi propaganda stressing the need to avoid trading with Jews. In Pomerania, for example, where the NSDAP had had some of its best results before 1933, the Gestapo office at Stettin reported in spring and early summer 1935 that a large proportion of the population – workers, better-off sections of the bourgeoisie, even *Beamte* and Party Members, and above all the rural population – were still shopping overwhelmingly in Jewish stores, saying they were cheaper, had a better range of choice, and that their "Aryan" employees would be out of a job if the Jews were bankrupted. In some places even an increase in patronage of Jewish shops was noted.[19] Reports from Baden in the South-West noted that Jewish shops were "overcrowded" and that people, undeterred by harassment and intimidation, were going where things were cheapest. In Mannheim, it was claimed, the boycott was a total failure, with Jewish departmental

---

[19] Robert Thévoz *et al.* (eds.), *Pommern 1934/35 im Spiegel von Gestapo-Lageberichten und Sachakten (Quellen)*, Cologne-Berlin, 1974, pp. 70, 82, 103–104 and see also p. 173.

Ian Kershaw

stores doing "splendid business."[20] Some months later the Munich *Polizei-direktion* saw the massive success of the annual sales at a leading Jewish clothing store in the city as a sign that many women still "had not understood nor want to understand the lines laid down by the *Führer* for solving the Jewish Question."[21] Reports from several areas mention demonstrative purchasing by some people in Jewish shops.[22] In many places there were reports of Nazi Party members and even functionaries purchasing their goods at Jewish shops.[23] One Jewish firm in Pirmasens had allegedly been making *Arbeitsdienst* uniforms at favourable prices for the "Aryan" concern which had farmed them out.[24]

The boycott problems of the Nazis were even greater among the rural population. Here, the main issue was the remaining dominance in many areas of the countryside of the Jewish cattle-dealer, the traditional middle-man and purveyor of credit for untold numbers of German peasants. Despite vicious intimidation and ceaseless propaganda, however, the Nazis found it an uphill struggle. As in the towns, where many people continued to shop, despite the pressure, where goods were cheapest and bargains most attractive, so in the countryside racial ideology was far less important than economic self-interest. Most peasants were unconcerned about the racial origins of the cattle-dealer as long as his prices were good and his credit readily forthcoming.

Reports from Pomerania repeatedly point out the special difficulties in persuading the rural population to end its dealings with Jews.[25] The authorities noted with disgust the basic pragmatism and blatant economic self-interest of the peasantry, as a result of which "the Party's long task of enlightenment is quickly brought to nothing."[26] In the Koblenz-Trier area the comments were even more forthright. The rural population allegedly showed little understanding for the "Jewish Question;" the boycott was largely rejected, and was a failure; Jewish activity in parts of the Mosel valley was unimpaired or even on the increase; and as the Gestapo sum-

---

[20] 'Sopade', 21st September 1935, p. A31; 16th October 1935, pp. A23–25. (The 'Deutsch-land-Berichte der Sopade, see n. 7, were compiled in two parts, Part A, 'Nachrichten und Berichte', Part B, 'Übersichten'. I cite exclusively from Part A and the pagination is prefixed by "A" as in the original.)

[21] Broszat, 1979, *op. cit.*, p. 458.

[22] Eg. 'Sopade', 21st September 1935, pp. A29–30, 36–37.

[23] See Franz Josef Heyen, *Nationalsozialismus im Alltag*, Boppard am Rhein, 1967, pp. 153–163; Rodrigue, *op. cit.*, pp. 19–20, Thévoz, *op. cit.*, pp. 103–104; Kershaw, *op. cit.*, p. 300.

[24] 'Sopade', 21st September 1935, pp. A32–33.

[25] Thévoz, *op. cit.*, pp. 103–104, 173, 177, 189–190.

[26] *Ibid.*, p. 73.

med up early in 1936, "the Jew is still a friend for many."[27] According to the Gestapo in Ulm, peasants and Jews in that area were still on "Du" terms.[28] In the Palatinate the mood among small wine growers was reputedly very poor in 1935 because the Nazis were driving out Jewish dealers and replacing them with "Aryans" who were unable to provide the same supply of credit.[29] Similar complaints were made in Bavaria. "Aryan" cattle-dealers had little capital and could not offer prices comparable with those of their Jewish rivals. The consequence was that the ousting of the Jewish cattle-dealers made remarkably little headway, and even as late as 1937 the Gestapo at Munich were forced to concede "shocking results" arising from their enquiry into relations of peasants with Jews: in Swabia alone there had been 1,500 cases of peasants trafficking with Jews in 1936/37, and although this had been put down to the lack of reliable "Aryan" dealers with sufficient capital, the real reason, claimed the Gestapo, was "the attitude of the peasants in which any sort of racial consciousness was missing."[30]

Economic interest predominated over ideology also among workers who felt the threat of unemployment if their Jewish employer were ruined. Enquiries into the overwhelmingly Jewish ownership of cigar factories in Lower Franconia in 1935 met the unanimous response that the population were glad to have work and did not ask whether the employer was an "Aryan" or a Jew. The relationship between the factories and the local population had been a wholly good one to date, and there had been no complaints at all about the employers.[31]

Tourist areas, too, were highly sensitive to the possible harmful effects of the boycott. Much criticism was levelled at the anti-Jewish notices posted at the entrance and exit of most villages. In some places, probably on grounds of the harmful economic consequences rather than the racially offensive nature of the notices, the wording was altered to express welcome to Jews, or the notices disappeared altogether.[32] Even Nazis pointed

---

[27] Staatsarchiv (StA) Koblenz, Abt. 441/28263, fols. 321, 423–427, 483–485, Regierungspräsident (RP) Koblenz, 4th December 1934, 3rd February 1935, 4th June 1935; Abt. 441/28264, fols. 143–147, RP Koblenz, 4th October 1935; Abt. 441/28267, fols. 61–63, Gestapo Koblenz, 5th March 1936; Abt. 441/35465, fols. 251, 379, Landrat (LR) Bad Kreuznach, 27th February 1936; LR Simmern, 28th February 1936; Heyen, *op. cit.*, pp. 134, 146.

[28] Paul Sauer, *Württemberg in der Zeit des Nationalsozialismus*, Ulm, 1975, pp. 156–157.

[29] 'Sopade', 16th October 1935, p. A21.

[30] Kershaw, *op. cit.*, pp. 300–301.

[31] *Ibid.*, p. 299.

[32] *Ibid.*, p. 302–303; 'Sopade', 21st September 1935, p. A36.

out the probable damaging effect of the anti-Jewish slogans along the Franconian "Romantische Straße" on the tourism of Rothenburg, Dinkelsbühl, Nördlingen and Ansbach, and with the massive extension of the notices – up to 1935 mainly a Franconian speciality – grave misgivings were also expressed in tourist areas such as Garmisch-Partenkirchen.[33]

Nazi racial propaganda played no great part in shaping the attitude and behaviour of the great many Germans who ignored intimidation to continue their economic relations with Jews in 1935. Their actions were determined wholly by material considerations and by economic self-interest. This meant, of course, that while there was no broad swell of opinion actively supporting Nazi measures, nor was there any notable sign of support for the Jews as Jews in the conflict. For some, doubtless, insofar as they rationalised their behaviour at all, continued patronage of a Jewish store was still compatible with the feeling that Jews exerted undue dominance on the German economy and that there was justification for the broad aim of removing them from that dominance. Nazi pressure on the boycott issue encountered therefore no solid principled objections and no opposition from any institutions, such as the Christian churches, which retained a good deal of influence over the formation of public attitudes. The consequence was, inevitably, that despite the lack of broad popular support, Nazi intimidation and propaganda did combine to reduce the economic viability of many Jewish concerns during the course of the summer. Although reports from all sides testify to the continued custom of Jewish businesses, there is no doubt that the terror was taking its toll and that trade in many areas was slackening alarmingly.[34] By 1936 Jews in some areas were even finding it difficult to get German undertakers to bury deceased members of their families.[35] The boycott had gone this far. By 1937 numerous Jewish businessmen had seen their customers driven away, had sold out or gone into liquidation, had emigrated or moved to larger cities where they could continue a shadowy existence for some time to come on the fringes of society, withdrawn, threatened, and persecuted.

The unprecedented degree of open violence which accompanied the "boycott movement," leaving a trail of demolition and the spectacle of Jews being publicly beaten up and maltreated by their tormentors, met with

---

[33] Kershaw, *op. cit.*, p. 302.
[34] 'Sopade', 21st September 1935, pp. A31–33; 16th October 1935, pp. A23–25, 36; Heyen, *op. cit.*, pp. 138–139, 142–143, 146; Thévoz, *op. cit.*, pp. 118, 151, 177, 182–183, 196; Rodrigue, *op. cit.*, pp. 17–18; Kershaw, *op. cit.*, p. 308.
[35] See Kershaw, *op. cit.*, p. 297; Heyen, *op. cit.*, p. 146.

widespread condemnation among non-Nazis. Much criticism undoubtedly arose from anger at the disturbance of the peace as such rather than out of direct sympathy for the Jews. The result was rather to be seen in growing antipathy towards the Nazi Party than in rejection of the anti-Jewish aims of the régime. Nevertheless, there is evidence, too, from Nazi sources as well as those hostile to the régime, of sympathy for the Jews and rejection on humanitarian grounds of the violence employed against them.

A report from Berlin which reached the exiled SPD leadership in Prague claimed that the population generally rejected the terror measures against the Jews. This source, which might have been expected to reflect a pro-worker bias, added that sympathy for the Jews was stronger in sections of the bourgeoisie than among workers. It concluded, however, with the pointed remark that those deliberately and ostentatiously patronising Jewish shops or going to Jewish doctors were doing so mainly to irritate the Nazis not to help the Jews.[36] Reports from Hesse, the Rhineland and North-West Germany concurred in their assessment that the primitive Jew-baiting was carried out only by small Nazi cliques and met with detestation among "decent" Germans: the spectacle of Jews being publicly beaten up by the SA before being taken into "protective custody" is said to have filled the people of Hannover with repulsion.[37] In the Palatinate, claimed the SPD's informant, as many as four-fifth of the population "without exaggeration" rejected the anti-Jewish campaign, though he added that only a few courageous individuals risked being dubbed *Judenknechte* and thereby becoming the target of Nazi terror themselves for retaining neighbourly contact with Jews. On the other hand, the "quite barbaric slogans" had been for the most part removed, parents were forbidding their sons and daughters to have anything to do with the anti-Jewish songs which were being sung in the Hitler-Youth, and the *Stürmer-Kästen*, the display-cases where Streicher's pornographic anti-Jewish newspaper could be seen in villages the length and breadth of Germany, were welcomed only in "the brutalised section of the SA."[38] The distasteful, "gutter" antisemitism of Streicher, disseminated through the *Stürmer*, met with much criticism even within the Party. Mass-meetings held by Streicher in Berlin and Hamburg in the summer of 1935 saw large numbers of the audience walking out in disgust, others unable to believe their ears at the base nature of the message, and a thinness of applause which was embarras-

---

[36] 'Sopade', 21st September 1935, p. A37.
[37] *Ibid.*, 21st September 1935, p. A36; 16th October 1935, pp. A28–29, 36.
[38] *Ibid.*, 16th October 1935, pp. A21–22.

sing to Streicher and his Nazi hosts.[39] People in Westphalia were saying that Hitler was allowing himself to be led on the road to misfortune by the mad Streicher, though this report admitted that there was no shortage of those in the SA and the NSDAP who were only too ready to be gripped by vulgar antisemitism *(Radauantisemitismus)*.[40]

Reports from Nazi authorities augment this picture of broad distaste and animosity towards the archaic and primitive methods of the anti-Jewish campaign. The Gestapo at Stettin regarded the harassment of customers entering Jewish shops as mistaken and only suited to cause disturbance in the population. It was also a fundamental error, thought the Gestapo, to send children around the streets of one Pomeranian town carrying anti-Jewish placards, which was rejected by the population at large and by most Party members.[41]

Popular opinion towards the methods of the anti-Jewish campaign was even more hostile in the Catholic South and West of Germany, and there are distinct indications here of objections to the treatment of the Jews on Christian or humanitarian grounds, which the Gestapo were only too ready to attribute to the active polemicising of the Catholic clergy.[42] The Gestapo in Aachen reported in early September 1935 that the treatment of the "Jewish Question" had provoked "the greatest indignation," since the Catholic mentality tended to value the Jews as human beings first and foremost and place little emphasis on the racial standpoint. The Catholic population was generally "extremely tolerant" *(weitgehendst duldsam)* towards Jews and rejected emphatically all measures affecting individual Jews. Outrages against the Jews, it was said, were condemned by the overwhelming majority of the population, and given the mood of widespread scepticism about the Nazi Movement could only do more harm than good.[43]

Violent outbreaks of *Judenkoller* were largely absent from the Catholic regions of Southern Bavaria until 1938. A notable exception occurred, however, with the riotous disturbances in the centre of Munich on the 18th and 25th May 1935, when anti-Jewish "demonstrations" took place among the crowds of Munich's busy shoppers. There was nothing spontaneous about the riots. They were the culmination of a long campaign, initiated

[39] *Ibid.*, 21st September 1935, pp. A37, 42–46.
[40] *Ibid.*, 16th October 1935, p. A30.
[41] Thévoz, *op. cit.*, pp. 70, 103–104.
[42] See Bernhard Vollmer, *Volksopposition im Polizeistaat. Gestapo-und Regierungsberichte 1934–1936*, Stuttgart, 1957, p. 197; Kershaw, *op. cit.*, pp. 309 ff.
[43] Vollmer, *op. cit.*, pp. 277, 296, 323.

and stirred up by no less a figure than *Gauleiter* Adolf Wagner, Minister of the Interior in Bavaria, who had used two employees of the *Stürmer* working in collaboration with sections of the Munich police force to instigate the action – carried out, as it transpired, by some 200 members of an SS camp near Munich. The response of the public, as the Munich police felt compelled to report, was wholly opposed to this sort of antisemitism, and with the mood in the city very heated, Wagner was forced to denounce in the press and on the radio the "terror groups" who were the cause of the trouble.[44] The distaste felt by the Munich public was more likely evoked by the hooliganism and riotous behaviour of the Nazi mob than by principled objections to antisemitism, for such primitive violence found condemnation deep into the ranks of the Nazi Party itself. Even *Gauleiter* Karl Wahl of Swabia – certainly no friend of the Jews – condemned what he called the "aping of Franconian methods."[45]

One feature of the campaign of 1935 was the prominence given by Nazi propaganda – with the *Stürmer* very much to the fore – to the question of "racial disgrace" *(Rassenschande)*, in which sexual relations between Jews and "Aryans" were contrived to be a central moral issue for the German people. The simulated pressure on this matter accorded neatly with the intensified concern of Nazi medical men and civil servants to come to a ruling on mixed "Aryan"-Jewish marriages, which came to form part of the Nuremberg Laws.[46] The public manifestation of the *Rassenschande* issue frequently took the form of "demonstrations" by Nazi mobs outside the homes of known "offenders," physical attacks on those Jews singled out by the Nazi press, and the parading through the streets and otherwise "unmasking" of those German girls who had allowed themselves to be "defiled" by Jews. The response of the population was, however, not all that the Nazis desired.

According to one report from Norden, a small town in North Germany, the threat to public order through anger among the population at a procession of girls from good bourgeois families through the streets of the town under accusation of having sexual relations with Jews was such that Kurt Daluege, head of the *Ordnungspolizei* was brought in personally from Berlin in order to calm things down. The population was on this issue,

---

[44] Kershaw, *op. cit.*, pp. 293–294; Broszat, *Bayern in der NS-Zeit*, pp. 442 ff.; Pätzold, *op. cit.*, pp. 216–221.
[45] Kershaw, *op. cit.*, p. 294.
[46] See Karl A. Schleunes, *The Twisted Road to Auschwitz*, Urbana-Chicago-London, 1970, pp. 118 ff.

commented the report, wholly against the Nazis.[47] In Breslau, reported an SPD informant, the rioters outside the homes of supposed *Rassenschänder* were always the same small mob. He claimed the Nazi pornographic propaganda in the local gutter press met with widespread revulsion among the people of the city. Particular displeasure was provoked by large placards bearing the names and addresses of German girl offenders being carried round. In one incident, in which a sizeable crowd gathered outside the home of an accused *Rassenschänder*, the problem and the whole persecution of the Jews, it was reported, was heatedly discussed. Comments such as: "the treatment of the Jews is a cultural disgrace," could be heard; a man who spat out in disgust at Nazi slogans was arrested; there were allegedly as many opponents as protagonists of the measures against the Jews in the crowd.[48]

Although there is overwhelming evidence for widespread unease and extensive indignation and disgust at the anti-Jewish terror of the Nazi mobs in 1935, it is clear that popular opinion was divided. Apart from intimidation, the sheer volume of anti-Jewish propaganda was beginning to make itself felt, and above all large sections of the population were effectively neutralised through their indifference to the problems facing the Jewish minority. The numerous regional reports reaching the exiled SPD leadership, though anxious where possible to demonstrate the lack of solidarity of the German people with the Nazi Party, felt forced to concede these points.

In Baden, it was said, popular attitudes about the anti-Jewish campaign ranged from enthusiasm to repulsion. However, although some "sharply rejected" the persecution, the majority of the population remained "completely apathetic" *(absolut teilnahmslos)*.[49] A report from Dresden described the general attitude of the population as at best one of indifference. People were saying, it went on, that some Jews at least deserved all they were getting for the way they had exploited earlier political circumstances for their own benefit, and where sympathy was expressed it was allegedly only for the less well-off Jews, who had no connections in high places. But generally, people did not get unduly "worked up" *(aufgeregt)* at "the goings-on" *(das Treiben)*.[50] Another report from Saxony admitted that the propaganda had not been without influence on many people, who

---

[47] 'Sopade', 21st September 1935, p. A35.
[48] *Ibid.*, p. A39.
[49] *Ibid.*, 16th October 1935, pp. A23–25.
[50] *Ibid.*, 21st September 1935, p. A37.

were now prepared to see the Jews as the cause of their troubles and had become their fanatical opponents.[51] In Bavaria, an SPD informant reported, the persecution found no active support in the population, but was not without effect. The propaganda was leaving its traces: people were losing their impartiality about the Jews and were beginning to say the Nazis were right in their struggle, though they were against its more extreme forms.[52] One report from Bavaria also spoke of the intensified anti-Bolshevik propaganda having an effect even among SPD-orientated workers and at the same time weakening the resistance to antisemitism. A former close colleague of the SPD informant had apparently asked whether comments that Goebbels had made in his speech at the party rally in September 1935 about the leading role of Jews in the Bolshevik leadership were correct, and thought that it had been a mistake to have so many Jews in leading positions in the German government.[53] One other ominous sign that, in the face of much instinctive repulsion at the inhumanity of the Nazis, antisemitism was gradually gaining ground in popular opinion was the fact that the *Stürmer,* despite the widespread distaste it provoked, was able to increase its circulation four-fold in the first ten months of 1935.[54]

Reactions to the racial laws, as to other aspects of the persecution of the Jews, were divided, though all the indications are that feelings about the legislation were far more muted and passive than towards more physical approaches to the "Jewish Question."

Reports reaching the SPD leadership stressed the negative response of the population to the laws, though this was almost certainly reflecting above all the response of former SPD sympathisers whose general attitude towards the Nazi régime was negative. Even so, reports from Berlin and from North-West Germany spoke of strong criticism and even "open rejection" of the laws in particular among the upper bourgeoisie *(besseres Bürgertum),* with sections of the *Mittelstand* showing apprehension because of possible repercussions for German trade abroad. Though there was said to be an almost uniform rejection of the *Rassenwahn* of Hitler and Streicher among the working-class, the report from North-West Germany did recount comments of a negative kind about the former dominance of Jews in the SPD and Jewish exploitation of workers, pointing out that Jews were finally learning what civil rights amounted to.[55] Another report, from

[51] *Ibid.,* 16th October 1935, p. A36.
[52] *Ibid.,* 21st September 1935, p. A31.
[53] *Ibid.,* 16th October 1935, p. A12.
[54] "How popular was Streicher?" (no author), *Wiener Library Bulletin* 5/6, 1957, p. 48.
[55] 'Sopade', 16th October 1935, pp. A10–11.

332 Ian Kershaw

Westphalia, indicated a mixed response to the laws even in Nazi circles, but added the significant comment that the worst feature of the previous situation had been the "legal uncertainty," which had gone too far even for the Nazis.[56] Such comments recur frequently in the confidential reports of the Nazi authorities and of the Gestapo in their assessment of responses to the racial laws. Among the most negative reactions, according to the Gestapo, were those encountered in Aachen, where the laws met with absolutely no enthusiasm among the Catholic population, and were greeted only in the expectation that they would bring the troublesome *Einzelaktionen* to an end, a hope also expressed in many other areas.[57]

On the basis of a wide range of Gestapo reports which were unavailable to the present writer,[58] the Israeli scholar O. D. Kulka divided reactions to the Nuremberg Laws into four categories: acceptance as an effective and lasting provision for social separation between Germans and Jews; criticism on ideological, religious and social grounds, as reflected in the attitudes of Christians, the liberal intelligentsia and the Left; opposition within the Party and SA to the "moderate" character of the laws; and lack of reaction to the laws arising from indifference to ideological and political matters.[59] Of these, the last category was probably the most typical one. A wide range of reports from Bavarian localities do not even mention the promulgation of the laws, and the reports of the *Regierungspräsidenten*, summarising opinion at the regional level, indicate only in the briefest terms that the legal regulation of the "Jewish Question" had been generally welcomed and had met with the approval of the population, not least in its contribution towards the elimination of "the recently prevailing intense disturbance." For this reason if for no other it was stated that "the population approves in every respect of the objective *(sachlich)* struggle against Jewry."[60] The lack of interest of the mass of Germans in the racial legislation was perhaps best articulated in the comments of an SPD informant from Saxony, who said the anti-Jewish laws were not taken very

---

[56] *Ibid.,* p. A30.
[57] Vollmer, *op. cit.,* pp. 285–286; see also *ibid.,* pp. 298, 323; Thévoz, *op. cit.,* p. 196; Kulka, *op. cit.,* pp. 265, 269, 271.
[58] Permission to work in the Institut für Marxismus-Leninismus in East Berlin and the Generalstaatsarchiv Potsdam was not granted; equally frustrating was the attempt made on two separate occasions to use the Gestapo materials in Rep. 90P of the Geheimes Preußisches Staatsarchiv in West Berlin, where the relevant reports were withdrawn until further notice until the staff of the archive had completed their editions of the material!
[59] Kulka, *op. cit.,* summary p. XLIII.
[60] Cited in Kershaw, *op. cit.,* pp. 297–298.

seriously: the people had other worries and were of the opinion that the entire to-do about the Jews *(Judenrummel)* was only staged in order to divert people from other things and to give the SA something to do.[61]

The promulgation of the Nuremberg Laws combined with the growing proximity of the Olympic Games to take much of the heat out of the antisemitic campaign before the end of the year, although sporadic acts of violence did not altogether cease. For almost three years, until the summer of 1938, it would not be going too far to claim that the "Jewish Question" was almost totally irrelevant to the formation of opinion among the vast majority of the German people. One sign of this was the evident lack of any overt reaction to the assassination, in February 1936, of a leading Nazi functionary in Switzerland, Wilhelm Gustloff, by a young Jew. The time was wholly inopportune for major retaliation against the Jews; Frick and Hess banned any prospective sallies against Jewish targets, and Germany remained quiet. Reactions to the murder of Gustloff show just how little interest there was in retaliatory action against the Jews. Though the Nazi press made the most of its windfall, the response in the population, apart from the usual ardent Nazis, was muted in the extreme. As one report sarcastically put it: "The deep sadness of the people for this co-fighter of Adolf Hitler expressed itself in total disregard."[62] The manipulation of "popular anger" in the "Jewish Question" is as blatant for its non-appearance in the case of Gustloff, as for its unleashed pogrom in the case of vom Rath, two and a half years later.

Nazi authorities were themselves more than well aware that they still had far to go before they could speak of a successful mobilisation of the people behind their racial policies. The Munich office of the Gestapo wrote in the summer of 1937 that the Catholic peasantry of Bavaria were "deaf to any discussion of the racial problem,"[63] and a few months earlier the SD had stressed, in a confidential report, the necessity of producing, "a popular mood of extensive hostility towards the Jews."[64] Some progress, from the Nazi point of view, had however undoubtedly been made. The nuanced reports reaching the exiled SPD leadership were already making the important distinction between the general rejection of the Streicher method of combating the Jews – primitive "pogrom antisemitism" – and

---

[61] 'Sopade', 16th October 1935, p. A36.
[62] *Ibid.,* 9th March 1936, p. A11 (Saxony). Reports from Bavaria, South-West Germany, and Silesia are couched in similar terms.
[63] Cited in Kershaw, *op. cit.,* p. 309.
[64] Document printed in Kulka, *op. cit.,* pp. 274–275.

the undoubted gains the Nazis had made in persuading the people that there was indeed "a Jewish Question," and thereby coloring their attitude towards the Jews as such. A report from Saxony, for example, noted that "a considerable proportion of the population is today convinced of the correctness of the National Socialist race doctrine and regards its application for the German people as a historical necessity, however regrettable the consequences unfortunately are for individual Jews and 'Aryans'."[65] Reports from a variety of regions added that antisemitism had undoubtedly acquired roots in broad sections of the population; that popular opinion took the view that Jews might be allowed to live in Germany, but without any positions of authority; that it was correct to deprive Jews of their civil rights and separate them from Germans; and that though not in agreement with the hard methods employed against them by the Nazis, people were of the opinion that "it doesn't harm the majority of Jews."[66] At the same time a report from Hesse pointed out that although the "Jewish Question" featured very little in political discussion, people had become "so brutalised that they do not feel the humanly degrading *(menschlich-niedrige)* aspect of antisemitism," with the exception of some sections of the bourgeoisie.[67] Three reports from Berlin summed up the general response of popular opinion to three years of Nazi propaganda and persecution: although one could in general say "that the racial question had not prevailed as a question of ideology *(Weltanschauungsfrage)*," the Jew-baiting had not been without influence on popular opinion, and attitudes had filtered through which earlier would have been rejected. "In general terms," concluded the Berlin reports, "one can say that the Nazis have indeed brought off a deepening of the gap between the people and the Jews. The feeling that the Jews are another race is today a general one."[68]

II. The Pogrom of November 1938

The background and course of the pogrom, and the horrific results it had for Jewish families, have been often and adequately described.[69] It was the only occasion during the Third *Reich* when the German public was confronted directly, on a nation-wide scale, with the full savagery of the

---

[65] 'Sopade', 11th February 1936, pp. A17–18.
[66] *Ibid.*, pp. A17–21.
[67] *Ibid.*, pp. A19–20.
[68] *Ibid.*, pp. A20–21.
[69] See, for example, Lionel Kochan, *Pogrom. 10 November 1938*, London, 1957 and Rita Thalmann and Emmanuel Feinermann, *Crystal Night*, London, 1974.

attack on the Jews. Never before and never again did the persecution of the Jews stand at the forefront of the public's attention as on the morning of the 10th November 1938, when the results of what Goebbels called the "spontaneous answer" of the German people to the murder of vom Rath were there for all to see.

Goebbels' claim was universally recognised as a ludicrous one, and it was abundantly clear that whole affair had been directed and orchestrated by the Party.[70] Most "non-organised" Germans knew nothing about the pogrom until they were confronted with the debris-laden streets the following morning. There were no signs of spontaneity, but willing cooperation and participation of the public did occur in some places, usually where radical antisemites had held leading positions in the local Party for some years and had been able successfully to poison the atmosphere against the Jews. In a number of small towns in Hesse, for example, where there was a history of violent antisemitism going deep into the *Kaiserreich,* party agents and provocateurs were able to whip up frenzied support from crowds of bystanders and spectators in anti-Jewish violence which began in parts of this region a day before the great pogrom was unleashed.[71] The participation seems to have been largely non-ideologically motivated. Sensation-mongers and rabble on the look-out for plunder were prominent, and where political motives existed they seem to have been framed in terms of populist resentment against supposed exploitation by the Jews.[72] In some instances young people and school children, not only those organised in the Hitler Youth, seemed to enjoy the spectacle and amused themselves by making fun of the sacred contents of the ruined synagogues.[73] In other cases accounts speak of "otherwise normal citizens" taking part in the mob violence,[74] and according to the postwar recollection of a rabbi from Düsseldorf, where the pogrom seems to have been carried out in particularly brutal fashion, even prominent "Aryan" citizens

---

[70] This was recognised even by the Nazi Party's Supreme Court in its investigations of murders committed during the pogrom. See Hermann Graml, *Der 9. November 1938. "Reichskristallnacht",* Bonn, 1953, p. 16: "Auch die Öffentlichkeit weiß bis auf den letzten Mann, daß politische Aktionen wie die des 9. November von der Partei organisiert und durchgeführt sind, ob dies zugegeben wird oder nicht".

[71] *Ibid.,* pp. 7–13.

[72] *Ibid.,* pp. 13–14.

[73] Wiener Library (WL), PIId528 (Potsdam); and see Kershaw, *op. cit.,* p. 329.

[74] WL, PIId15 (small, unnamed town in the Erzgebirge); and see PIId749 for Ulm, Mergentheim and Heilbronn in Württemberg.

such as doctors of the municipal hospital and presidents of the District Courts took part in setting the synagogue on fire.[75]

The evidence suggests overwhelmingly, however, that more typical reactions of the crowds which gathered to view the wreckage and destruction could be seen in the numbed bewilderment and destruction which the American Consul in Leipzig recorded,[76] and the silent disgust interspersed with muttered invectives condemning the barbarity of the action and expressing shame and horror at what had taken place, which Ruth Andreas-Friedrich observed in Berlin.[77] Jewish eye-witness accounts of the events of *Reichskristallnacht*, many compiled within days of the pogrom, abound with references to the kindness of "Aryan" and "Christian" neighbours and are anxious to point out the overwhelming rejection of the pogrom by the vast majority of the population, mentioning their sympathetic comments, their disgust and shame and their lack of participation in the actions, repeatedly attributed to a narrow group of fanatics. They leave no doubt of the widespread unpopularity of the pogrom.[78] Reports reaching the SPD leadership and other exiled left-wing groups were also unanimous about the sharp condemnation of the outrages by the great majority of the German people, and eye-witnesses recounted the unmistakable abhorrence and many expressions of sympathy for the Jews.[79] Though the exiled anti-Nazi groups were keen to illustrate a broad popular front against the régime, such comments concur wholly with those from all other sources. Even the Berlin Gestapo admitted that "the sympathies which the Communists accord the Jews found lively support in bourgeois and above all clerical circles."[80] Other reports from Nazi authorities leave no doubt that the *"Judenaktion"* was unreservedly acclaimed only among the extremists

---

[75] WL, PIId151.

[76] Jeremy Noakes and Geoffrey Pridham (eds.), *Documents on Nazism, 1919–1945,* London, 1974, pp. 472–474. See also the comments of the British Consul General in Frankfurt, cited in Hans Rothfels, *The German Opposition to Hitler,* London, 1961, p. 31 and of the British Chargé d'Affaires in Berlin, cited in Stokes, *op. cit.,* p. 175.

[77] Ruth Andreas-Friedrich, *Der Schattenmann,* Berlin, 1947, pp. 28–37.

[78] Eg. WL, PIId Nos. 8, 15, 40, 93, 291, 528, 574, 658, 749, 760; "B Scheme", nos. 5, 32, 36, 55, 66, 78, 84, 85, 87, 147; PIIIf Nos. 134, 183; and "Der 10. November 1938", a typescript of short reports by emigrants, collected in 1939 and 1940 by S. Brückheimer. "Eye-witness accounts" are extensively cited by Kershaw, *op. cit.* pp. 327–335 (with regard to the pogrom in Bavaria), and Rodrigue, *op. cit.,* pp. 32–37.

[79] See 'Sopade', 10th December 1938, pp. A44 ff; 'Deutsche Mitteilungen', 19th November 1938, 22nd November 1938, 7th January 1939, 25th February 1939 (copies in the Wiener Library).

[80] Printed in Kulka, *op. cit.,* pp. 279–282.

and fanatics even within the Nazi Movement.[81] Michael Müller-Claudius' subtly carried-out private survey of opinion among a small group of Party members suggested in fact that only about five per cent fully approved of the pogrom as against 63 per cent who displayed some form of disgust or anger, and 32 per cent who were reserved or indifferent in their comments.[82]

Unlike all other phases of the persecution of the Jews, the wealth of documentation for the November pogrom allows some rough differentiation of the nature of popular reaction in terms of geographical, confessional and class variants.

Much suggests the correctness, in broad terms, of the SD's observation that "the measures against Jewry experienced far stronger rejection in the South (with the exception of the *Ostmark*) and the West of the *Reich* (Catholic, more densely settled, overwhelmingly urban population) than in the North (Protestant, less densely settled, rural population)."[83] The more plentiful survival of evidence from South and West Germany, especially from Catholic regions, possibly distorts the picture somewhat, though lends support to the view that attitudes to the pogrom were particularly hostile and assistance for Jews most forthcoming in such areas. There are some indications that despite the ferocity of the pogrom in the large cities, the size and anonymity of the densely-populated city provided the maximum chance of safety for Jews and allowed non-Jews to risk actions which they would not have dared undertake in the more intimate social networks of small towns or villages. Several reports and also recollections of Jews suggest that antisemitic attitudes were at their most threatening in small towns,[84] and in rural districts the Jews were particularly isolated and exposed, though it must be added that many of the clearest demonstrations of sympathy and practical forms of assistance occurred in Catholic rural areas.[85]

Catholicism posed, of course, no automatic barrier against antisemitism. Sporadic violence against the "murderers of Christ" had formed part of the

---

[81] See the report from the RP of Lower Bavaria and the Upper Palatinate in *ibid.*, p. 277 and Broszat, 1979, *op. cit.*, p. 473.
[82] Müller-Claudius, *op. cit.*, pp. 162 ff.
[83] Bundesarchiv Koblenz (BAK), R58/1094, Fol. 109 (printed in Kulka, *op. cit.*, p. 286).
[84] PIId749 compares Stuttgart favourably with the position of Jews in Ulm, Mergentheim and Heilbronn; PIId15 and PIId40 mention the utterly friendless conditions in small towns in the Erzgebirge and near Cologne; much of the evidence in Graml, *op. cit.*, is taken from small towns in Hesse.
[85] See Kershaw, *op. cit.*, pp. 334–335.

traditional social scene in many Catholic areas of Germany and of other European countries. And Catholic Austria was singled out by the SD from those areas where the level of rejection of the pogrom was high. Vienna, in fact, where nine-tenths of Austrian Jews lived and which had its own long history of racial tension, seems to have been one of the few cities of the Greater German *Reich* where no traces of popular hostility to the pogrom are encountered.[86] In the *Altreich,* however, the Catholic "sub-culture" proved difficult terrain for the NSDAP before and after 1933. The relatively sympathetic attitude towards Jews in Catholic areas can not, for the most part, be put down to the direct lead given by the Catholic clergy, though there are not a few cases of priests speaking out openly and bravely against the pogrom and on behalf of the Jews.[87] Rather, the widespread rejection of the Nazi Party, above all for its assault on the Catholic Church itself, brought with it a rejection of many aspects of Nazi ideology and of the more unsavoury aspects of Nazi rule. And despite the reluctance of the hierarchy to take an open stance on the persecution of the Jews, and its silence in November 1938, the centuries-old teaching of 'love thy neighbour' stood for many Christians in total contradiction to Nazi inhumanity.

An SD report from Württemberg reveals similar attitudes among the Protestant population, which showed "human sympathy and religious solidarity" with the Jews and rejected the pogrom on the grounds that "the Jews are human beings too." Among members of the *Kirchlich-Theologische Societät,* a wing of the Confessing Church, copies of a text of Karl Barth, 'Salvation comes from the Jews,' was distributed.[88] In general terms, however, it seems clear that the inroads which Nazism had made into the Protestant Church by 1933, and the avidly nationalistic stance adopted even by clergy who became attached to the Confessing Church opened the door to Nazi racial ideas to a much greater extent than was the case in the Catholic Church. The Protestant Church in Württemberg was in an area much affected by liberal values, and was very conscious of its own identity – juxtaposed as it was with Catholic areas and having resisted a vigorous Nazi assault on its rights in 1934. In Northern and Eastern regions, the position of the Protestant Church was less defined and the attachment of much of the population far weaker than in the South-West.

Nazi attempts to break down the traditional value-system of Christianity and replace it with one based upon race-hatred highlighted some of the

---

[86] Rodrigue, *op. cit.,* pp. 35–36.
[87] See Kershaw, *op. cit.,* pp. 315.
[88] StA Ludwigsburg, K110 Nr. 44, SD-Stuttgart, 1st February 1939, fols. 2–4.

limits of totalitarian mobilisation facing the régime. Much evidence shows, too, that the Nazis encountered similar difficulties among sections of the bourgeoisie who were still influenced by liberal humanitarian values or by a sense of propriety and "cultural" dignity.

Again the strong liberal traditions in South-West Germany proved a barrier to the penetration of the Nazi message of hate. According to the Stuttgart branch of the SD, reporting under the heading of *Liberalismus*, "dyed-in-the-wool democrats showed special friendliness towards the Jews and sympathised very much with those Jews who were taken into custody." Rumours about suicides and deaths in concentration camps were set in circulation.[89] Examples abound in Jewish eye-witness accounts of sympathy, abhorrence, and shame expressed in particular by members of the bourgeoisie.[90] Motives for rejection of the pogrom were often mixed. Many who sympathised with much of what Nazism stood for obviously felt this was going too far. A feeling of "cultural disgrace" *(Kulturschande)* and damage to the German image abroad combined with anger at the senseless destruction of property and humanitarian feelings. One anonymous letter, apparently from a conservative bourgeois Nazi sympathiser and addressed to Goebbels, ended:

> "One could weep, one must be ashamed to be a German, part of an Aryan-*Edelvolk*, a civilised nation guilty of such a cultural disgrace. Later generations will compare these atrocities with the times of the witch-trials. And nobody dares to say a word against them, though 85 per cent of the population is angry as never before. Poor Germany, wake up properly before it is too late!"[91]

Similar comments were reported to the SPD by an informant in Saxony who, it was said, came from a middle-class background himself and had no contact with Social Democracy though he was well acquainted with businessmen, intellectuals and officers. He claimed he had not encountered a single person, even among higher civil servants and Party members, who "was not filled with disgust at this outbreak of a bestiality which one only knew in the darker epochs of mankind." He mentioned the humanitarian sympathy and assistance given so Jews, but also pointed out the economic-based anger about senseless destruction of property when the people were being exhorted to save their empty toothpaste-tubes and sardine-tins. He spoke of bitter criticism of Goebbels and of other leading Nazis and, in

[89] *Ibid.*, fols. 2–6.
[90] Eg. WL., B55 (Breslau); B66 (Munich), and see Kershaw, *op. cit.*, pp. 331–332 for evidence from Bavaria.
[91] Cited in full in Kershaw, *op. cit.*, p. 332.

contrast to earlier years, even of criticism of Hitler for his toleration of such misdeeds. His conclusion was that the régime had lost much support through the pogrom, "not least in the upper sections of the bourgeoisie which had been so sympathetic to National Socialism at the beginning."[92]

The SD summarised its own view of reactions to the pogrom among the bourgeoisie in the following style:

> "... The actions against the Jews in November were very badly received. Criticism varied in accordance with the attitude of the individual. Business circles pointed to the damage which had arisen through the actions, others criticised the legal measures, and the bourgeoisie, just freed from anxiety about war, pointed to the dangerous effects which could arise abroad. When then the reaction abroad expressed itself in vile inflammatory campaigns and boycott measures, these liberal-pacifist circles agreed with foreign opinion and labelled the measures taken as 'barbaric' and 'uncivilised' *(kulturlos)*. From a basic liberal attitude, many believed they had openly to stand up for the Jews. The destruction of the synagogues was declared to be irresponsible. People stood up for the 'poor repressed Jews'."[93]

Reactions in other sections of society are less easy to specify. There are numerous indications (though drawn mainly from Catholic regions) of rejection of the pogrom by peasants, both on grounds of Christian charity and common humanity and also through outrage at the senseless destruction of goods and property.[94] Materialistic reasons for condemnation could also be heard in workers' circles, and according to the Berlin Gestapo the underground KPD consciously and successfully played on such feelings in exploiting the popular resentment against the pogrom.[95] Workers, like other sections of the population, also responded negatively to the pogrom from less materialistic motives. Reports reaching the exiled SPD leadership from Berlin and from the industrial region of Upper Silesia spoke of embittered reactions in the factories and work-places and of direct assistance given to Jews by workers.[96]

There were few occasions, if any, in the Third *Reich* which produced such a widespread wave of revulsion – much of it on moral grounds – as the *Reichskristallnacht* pogrom. Kulka's view that "most did not denounce the atrocities against the Jews, but protested against the destruction of German property as being contradictory to the declared economic policy of the

---

[92] 'Sopade', 9th February 1939, pp. A1–2.
[93] BAK, R58/1094, fol. 109 (printed in Kulka, *op. cit.*, p. 286).
[94] See Kershaw, *op. cit.*, pp 332–335.
[95] Document printed in Kulka, *op. cit.*, p. 280.
[96] 'Sopade', 10th December 1938, pp. A46–48; see also 'Deutsche Mitteilungen', 22nd November 1938.

régime, stressing the need for avoiding waste of national wealth" is a far too sweeping generalisation, which can be countered by a great deal of evidence from Jewish as well as from non-Jewish sources.[97]

The clumsy alienation of German popular opinion through the pogrom seems to have persuaded the Nazi leadership that such a tactic should never again be tried, and that anti-Jewish measures should take a more "rational" course. Though, from the régime's point of view, the pogrom was successful in forcing the pace of solution to the "Jewish Question," the hostility which leading Nazis showed towards Goebbels, the instigator of the pogrom, may well have been influenced by the negative public response. Similarly, Hitler's announcement – against the pressure of the radicals – that there should be no public identification badge for Jews was possibly a veiled reflection of the negative reactions to anti-Jewish measures.[98] And a year later, following the attempt on Hitler's life in the Bürgerbräukeller in Munich in November 1939, on the anniversary of the pogrom, Rudolf Hess specifically prohibited a repetition in order to prevent any unrest in the first critical months of the war.[99]

The influence of popular opinion extended no further. This was in great measure a reflection of the conditions of extreme terror and intimidation in which people lived, and which were of themselves sufficient to deter any organised pressure of opinion on the régime. Reports of arrests and recrimination for pro-Jewish comments, assistance to Jews or criticism of Nazi actions abound in the sources.[100] Summarising the impressions of their reporters, the SPD leadership admitted

"that however great the general indignation might be, the brutalities of the pogrom hordes had increased their intimidation and consolidated the notion in the population that all resistance was useless against the unrestrained National Socialist power."[101]

Moreover, without support from above popular opinion was bound to remain inchoate and inarticulate. The one source this could – and arguably ought – to have come from was the leadership of the Christian Churches. Apart from much success in orchestrating popular opposition in the church struggle, the Churches came, in 1941, to lead a victory without

[97] Kulka, *op. cit.*, summary, p. XLIV.
[98] See Dietrich Orlow, *The History of the Nazi Party, vol. 2, 1933–1945*, Newton Abbot, 1973, pp. 250–251.
[99] *Ibid.*, p. 265 n. 8.
[100] Eg. WL., PIId760 (Berlin); PIId40 (near Cologne); PIId528 (Potsdam); Noakes and Pridham, *op. cit.*, p. 475 (Leizpzig); Kershaw, *op. cit.*, p. 335 (Lower Franconia).
[101] 'Sopade', 10th December 1938, p. A44 and see also p. A46.

parallel for public opinion in halting the "Euthanasia Action." It happened because the Churches made a public cause of concern their own. In the case of the Jews, the Churches took no such stance.

Despite the largely negative response to the pogrom, popular opinion on the "Jewish Question" remained in any case divided. It was the method rather than the aim of Nazi policy which people condemned. Just as the Nuremberg Laws of 1935 had been widely acclaimed in contrast to the condemnation of the primitive brutality of the *Einzelaktionen,* so in 1938 there was "approval," "understanding," and "satisfaction" shown at the draconian but "legal" measures taken to exclude Jews from Germany's economic life alongside the wide condemnation of the violent and destructive pogrom.[102] Despite the rejection of the archaic forms of "pogrom antisemitism," there was, therefore, extensive acceptance of the "rational antisemitism" whose victory was sealed by the public reactions to *Reichskristallnacht.*

Furthermore, dissent at the method of proceeding on the "Jewish Question" was also perfectly compatible with general approval of Hitler's leadership and of the main aims of German policy under Nazi rule. As an SPD observer in Berlin pointed out, the view continued to be expressed that the extremes of Jewish policy took place against Hitler's wishes. "Hitler certainly wants the Jews to disappear from Germany, but he does not want them to be beaten to death and treated in such fashion:" such comments could be frequently heard and, it had to be admitted, continued to carry weight.[103]

However negative the instant reactions to *Reichskristallnacht* were, the pogrom had no lasting impact on the formation of opinion. Reactions to events of major importance, whether of euphoria or of revulsion, gave way remarkably quickly to the sullen apathy and resigned acceptance which characterised the day-to-day existence of most Germans in the Third *Reich.* "Daily routine again already" ('Schon wieder Alltag'), the heading of the December report of the *Sopade,* summed it up neatly.[104] The "Jewish Question" was at the forefront of popular opinion on very few occasions during the Nazi dictatorship. The most spectacular occasion was *Reichskristallnacht.* But everything points to the fact that this event receded within a few weeks into the dim background of people's consciousness. It

---

[102] A point made by the SD in its annual report for 1938 – BAK, R58/1096, fols. 31–32; see also Steinert, *op. cit.,* p. 75.
[103] 'Sopade', 10th December 1938, p. A48.
[104] *Ibid.,* p. A1.

had not been something which concerned them directly, nor was it of continuing intensity, and it had been perpetrated on a tiny and basically unloved social minority. Increasingly from November 1938 the Jews were forced to emigrate or to retire wholly into isolation on the fringes of society. Either way, Germans saw less and less of Jews. The dehumanisation and social isolation of Jews after the November pogrom could, therefore, only increase the extent of the indifference of the German people towards their fate, an indifference which had been but momentarily disturbed by the atrocities of *Reichskristallnacht*.

III. Deportation and Extermination

Remarkable as it may sound, the "Jewish Question" was of no more than minimal interest to the vast majority of Germans during the war years in which the mass slaughter of Jews was taking place in the Occupied Territories of the East. The evidence, though it survives much more thinly than for the prewar period, allows no other conclusion. The depersonalisation of the Jew had been the real success of Nazi propaganda and policy. Coupled with the inevitable anxieties, pressures, and strains of the civilian population in war, encouraging a "retreat into the private sphere"[105] and concern for matters only of immediate and personal relevance, mainly day-to-day economic matters, and along with the undoubted further weakening in questions of moral principle which the war brought, it ensured that the fate of the Jews would be farther than ever from the forefront of people's minds after 1939.

During the first two years of the war mention of the "Jewish Question" hardly occurs in the opinion reports of the Nazi authorities. One account written by a rabbi towards the end of 1940 claimed that the "Jewish Question" had become less important during the war and that anti-Jewish feeling among the ordinary population had declined. He pointed to the active clandestine help which thousands of Jews living in their ghetto-like conditions still received daily from ordinary Germans.[106] Whether or not this account was over-generous to the state of German opinion, there is no doubt that conditions for Jews deteriorated sharply following the invasion of Russia in June 1941. The "Yellow Star" was eventually introduced to be compulsorily worn by Jews from September 1941, a whole range of vicious new restrictions in autumn reduced Jewish living conditions to a

---

[105] Steinert, *op. cit.*, p. 242.
[106] WL., PIIa625, cited by Rodrigue, *op. cit.*, p. 43.

level far beyond anything which had been previously experienced, and in the same months the mass deportations to the East got under way. This combination of anti-Jewish measures was one of the few short periods in the war when public reactions found a muted and distorted echo in the reports of the authorities.

According to the SD, the decree ordering the wearing of the "Yellow Star" was "welcomed by the overwhelming proportion of the population."[107] The decree, it was said, had met a long-cherished wish of large sections of the population, especially in areas where Jews were numerous, and many people were critical of the exceptions made for the Jewish wives of "Aryans," saying this was no more than a "half measure." The SD added that "for most people a radical solution of the Jewish problem finds more understanding than any compromise, and that there existed in the widest circles the wish for a clear external separation between Jewry and German *Volksgenossen.*" It was significant, it concluded, that the decree was not seen as a final measure, but as the signal for more incisive decrees with the aim of a final settlement *(Bereinigung)* of the "Jewish Question."[108] It seems difficult to accept such comments as they stand. The tone is reflective only of the overtly Nazi element of the population, and it is more than likely that the SD was in this case as in other instances interpreting comments made by Party members as reflective of general popular opinion. Understandably, those critical of the measures were far less open in their comments, though the SD reports themselves point out that "isolated comments of sympathy" could be heard among the bourgeoisie and among Catholics – the two groups most vociferous in their condemnation of earlier anti-Jewish measures – and "medieval methods" were spoken of.[109] The leading Nazi newspaper in Stuttgart castigated "cases of false pity and misapplied humanity towards the Jews" in early October 1941, and condemned passengers in a tramcar who had spoken up on behalf of a Jew wearing the "Yellow Star." Germans, commented the newspaper, had even been seen shaking hands with wearers of the star in the open streets.[110] A Jewish eye-witness described the sympathy and shame of Germans and the assistance given to Jews in Berlin, and the *Reich* Security Main Office (RSHA) passed a decree only a month after the introduction of the yellow

---

[107] Cited in Steinert, *op. cit.,* pp. 239–240.
[108] Heinz Boberach (ed.), *Meldungen aus dem Reich. Auswahl aus den geheimen Lageberichten des Sicherheitsdienstes der SS 1939–1944,* Neuwied, 1965, pp. 220–225.
[109] Steinert, *op. cit.,* p. 239.
[110] Cited in Rodrigue, *op. cit.,* p. 44.

star condemning the still existent friendly relations which had again come to light between Jews and Germans who "seem not to have grasped even the most elementary principles of National Socialism"[110a] and who were to be arrested whenever seen in contact with Jews.[111] Almost certainly, those still continuing such contact or condemning the recent measure were in a small minority, as were those openly lauding the public branding of Jews. For the majority of the population the decree introducing the "Yellow Star" passed without comment, and very likely without notice.[112]

The deportations, too, went apparently unaccompanied by much attention from the German population. Most reports confine their comments to a cold, factual account of the "evacuations" without reference to the reactions of the non-Jewish population. In one or two instances stereotype "approval," "satisfaction" or "interest" of the local population is registered.[113] Personal recollections, however, indicate some indignation among Germans, and in Berlin even a unique open protest and demonstration took place when it came to the deportation of the Jewish partners of mixed marriages in the months following the débâcle at Stalingrad, and was successful in preventing their transportation. According to Goebbels, it was still the bourgeoisie, especially intellectual circles, who were unsympathetic to the régime's anti-Jewish measures.[114]

Such expressions of approval or disapproval practically exhaust the evidence. For the rest, the silence is evocative. The lack of registered reaction to the deportations is almost certainly not a grotesque distortion of popular attitudes. Not only intimidation, but the widespread indifference towards the remaining tiny minority of Jews explains the lack of involvement in their deportation. And real interest, where it existed, was often based less on human concern than on the hope of material advantage. The *Kreisleitung* in Göttingen, where, as in many German towns the housing situation was catastrophic, was inundated with applications for apartments belonging to Jews when it was known that their deportation

---

[110a] For a particular account of Nazi directives to the press on inciting the German population against the Jews even during the final phase of the war, see G. Bording Mathieu, "The Secret Anti-Juden-Sondernummer of 21st May 1943," *Leo Baeck Institute Yearbook* 24, 1981, pp. 291–300 (Ed.)

[111] Cited in Rodrigue, *op. cit.*, p. 44.

[112] Marlis Steinert (*op. cit.*, p. 240) noted that in the report of the *Reichsfrauenführerin* for August and September 1941 comments on the decree were recorded for only two areas, Hessen-Nassau and Berlin.

[113] See Kershaw, *op. cit.*, p. 338.

[114] Louis P. Lochner (ed.), *The Goebbels Diaries,* London, 1948, pp. 196, 209, 225 (entries for 2nd, 6th and 11th March 1943); see Steinert, *op. cit.*, p. 254.

was imminent.[115] And a complainant in Fürth near Nuremberg wrote to the *Reichsstatthalter* of Bavaria in 1942 on behalf of the co-tenants of her apartment block protesting at the sequestration of Jewish property by the *Finanzamt* when so many were crying out for it: "Where is the justice and *Volksgemeinschaft* in that?" she lamented.[116]

Such obvious self-interest existed alongside the widespread passivity and emotionless acceptance of the deportations. There can be little doubt that strong reactions would have left their mark in the reports of the authorities. Such reports contain a mass of comment critical of the régime, and at the very same time as the deportations were going ahead and eliciting practically no response from the population, the force of angry and concerned popular opinion was bringing to a halt the removal of crucifixes from Bavarian schools and, of much greater significance, was compelling the régime to stop the gassing of thousands of mentally defective Germans in the "euthanasia programme." Compared with the popular interest in the film *I Accuse*, an attempted justification of euthanasia, the insidious antisemitic propaganda film *Der ewige Jude* was far less well attended than most films, according to a report from the *Kreisleitung* Kiel in December 1941.[117] A year later, a second disguised private survey of opinion carried out by Michael Müller-Claudius showed that whereas just less than a third of his selected group of Party members had been indifferent or non-committal about the "Jewish Question" following the pogrom of 1938, the figure was now 69 per cent.[118]

Most people probably thought little and asked less about the fate of the Jews in the East.[119] The Jews were out of sight and literally out of mind. But knowledge of atrocities and mass shootings of Jews in the East, mostly in the nature of rumour brought home by soldiers on leave, was fairly widespread. If most rumour was unspecific, eye-witness accounts of shootings and broadcasts from foreign transmitters provided material which was sufficiently widely circulated for Bormann to feel obliged in autumn 1942 to provide new propaganda directives to counter rumours about the "very sharp measures" taken against the Jews in the East.[120] Concrete details

---

[115] Document printed in Kulka, *op. cit.*, p. 287.

[116] Geheimes Staatsarchiv, Munich, in Reichsstatthalter 823.

[117] Steinert, *op. cit.*, p. 243; Stokes, *op. cit.*, p. 183 n. 64.

[118] Müller-Claudius, *op. cit.*, pp. 167–176.

[119] Kulka undoubtedly goes too far in his generalisation that "people were acquainted with the ultimate fate of the deported Jews" if by this he is inferring firm knowledge rather than vague surmise. Compare Stokes, *op. cit.*, pp. 180–181 and the sources cited there.

[120] Cited in Steinert, *op. cit.*, p. 252.

were often not known, but the awareness that dire things were happening to the Jews was sufficient to provoke anxiety about possible retaliatory measures of the enemy should Germany lose the war.[121] One SD report from Franconia in December 1942 stated:

> "One of the strongest causes of unease among those attached to the church and in the rural population is at the present time formed by news from Russia in which shooting and extermination *(Ausrottung)* of the Jews is spoken about. The news frequently leaves great anxiety, care, and worry in those sections of the population. According to widely held opinion in the rural population, it is not at all certain now that we will win the war, and if the Jews come again to Germany they will exact dreadful revenge upon us.[122]

Knowledge about the mass murder of Jews in the East was suddenly highlighted in April 1943 by Goebbels' attempt to exploit the discovery of Polish officers' graves at Katyn. The German propaganda about Katyn was widely rejected, especially in church circles and among "intellectuals." According to the SD it was being said that Germans had no right to condemn the Soviet atrocities "because on the German side Poles and Jews have been done away with in much greater numbers."[123] The Nazi Party Chancellory recorded similar sentiments expressed by members of the clergy in Northern Westphalia:

> "In combating the Jews in the East the SS had used similar methods of butchery. The terrible and inhumane treatment meted out to the Jews through the SS demands nothing short of God's punishment of our people. If these murders do not bring bitter revenge upon us, then there is no longer any divine justice! The German people has taken such blood guilt upon itself that it cannot reckon with mercy and pardon . . ."[124]

Similar comments were heard after the uncovering at Winniza in July 1943 of mess graves of Ukrainian victims of the Russian secret police.[125] Soon afterwards Bormann provided new directives for the Party banning all discussion of a future "total solution" *(Gesamtlösung),* and allowing only statements that Jews had been put "to appropriate labour assignment" *(zu zweckentsprechendem Arbeitseinsatz).*[126]

Comments about the murder of Jews refer almost invariably to mass shootings by *Einsatzgruppen.* The gassing, both in mobile units and then in the extermination camps, was much more secretly carried out and found

---

[121] See Kershaw, *op. cit.,* pp. 338–339.
[122] Cited in *ibid.,* p. 339.
[123] Boberach, *op. cit.,* p. 383; see Stokes, *op. cit.,* p. 186.
[124] Document printed in Kulka, *op. cit.,* p. 290.
[125] Stokes, *op. cit.,* p. 187.
[126] Cited in Steinert, *op. cit.,* p. 257.

little echo inside Germany, to go by the almost complete absence of comment in the documentary sources.[127] Even so, the silence was not total. Rumours did circulate, as two cases from the Munich *Sondergericht*, dating from 1943 and 1944 and referring to the gassing of Jews in gas-vans, prove. One of the accused claimed to have heard the rumour from a soldier.[128] Knowledge or even rumour about the extermination camps in Poland may have been more extensive in the Eastern regions bordering in Poland than in the West of Germany. According to a report of the *Gauleitung* of Upper Silesia in May 1943 the Polish resistance movement had daubed the slogan "Rußland-Katyn, Deutschland-Auschwitz" in public places of the Upper Silesian industrial region; "the concentration camp Auschwitz, generally known in the East, is meant," added the report.[129] An exhaustive search of extensive Bavarian materials, on the other hand, reveals no mention of the name of any extermination camp in the East.[130] There was some knowledge of the camps among leading members of the German Resistance and among Church leaders, and the extent of auxiliary services to the camps meant that total secrecy was a practical impossibility.[131] The extent of knowledge will, however, never be known. Lawrence Stokes's judicious, if inconclusive, assessment that "it may be doubted ... whether even rumours of Auschwitz as a Jewish extermination centre had circulated widely throughout Germany – and if they had, whether they were believed" is probably as far as one can take it.[132]

Despite an unceasing barrage of antisemitic propaganda, the last two years of the war saw the German population preoccupied less than ever with the "Jewish Question." By 1944 there were fewer than 15,000 Jews left in Germany,[133] and party propagandists reckoned that hundreds of thousands of young Germans now hardly knew "what the Jew is." Whereas the elder generation knew "the Jew" from their own experience, for the young "the Jew" was only a "museumpiece," something to look at with curiosity, "a fossil wonder-animal *(fossiles Wundertier)* with the yellow star on its breast, a witness of bygone times but not belonging to the present."[134] This was testimony at one and the same time to the progress

---

[127] See Steinert, *op. cit.*, p. 261; Stokes, *op. cit.*, pp. 184–185; Kershaw, *op. cit.*, pp. 340–341.
[128] *Ibid.*, p. 340.
[129] Document printed in Kulka, *op. cit.*, p. 289.
[130] Kershaw, *op. cit.*, pp. 340–341.
[131] Stokes, *op. cit.*, p. 184; Steinert, *op. cit.*, pp. 258–259.
[132] Stokes, *op. cit.*, p. 185.
[133] Steinert, *op. cit.*, p. 259.
[134] Cited in *ibid.*, p. 259.

of abstract antisemitism, and to the difficulty of keeping alive the hatred of an abstraction. Many people evidently found the stereotype antisemitic tirades less than relevant to their real lives, as was clear from SD reports in May 1943 of the wholly negative reactions, especially of "intellectuals" but also of workers and white-collar employees, to the antisemitic vitriol in a speech by the Leader of the Labour Front, Robert Ley.[135]

The depersonalisation of Jews found expression, too, in the files of letters sent to Goebbels suggesting, for example, that Jews be rounded up in cities threatened by bombing-raids, or that ten Jews be shot for every civilian killed in a raid.[136] Other references to Jews in the last war years, hardly less brutal and dehumanised in tone, saw the bombing-raids as revenge for German treatment of the Jews, and in one instance criticised the German government for its "clumsy" *(ungeschickt)* handling of the Jewish issue; by enclosing Jews in ghettos, it was said, the Germans would have retained "an effective threat and counter measure."[137] Comments attributing the allied air-raids to the revenge of the Jews show the unmistakeable traits of influence by Nazi propaganda linking the war to Germany's fight against a hostile Jewish world. And the hallmarks of antisemitic attitudes outlasted the Third *Reich* to be detected in varying degrees of intensity in three-fifths of those Germans in the American Zone tested by public opinion researchers of the occupying forces in 1946.[138]

Conclusion

Popular opinion on the "Jewish Question" formed a wide spectrum running from the paranoid Jew-baiters at the one extreme, undoubtedly a tiny minority; through a wide section of the population whose existent prejudices and latent antisemitism, influenced in varying degrees by the virulence of Nazi propaganda, accepted legal restrictions on Jews amounting to economic exclusion and social ostracism whilst rejecting the blatant and overt inhumanity of the Jew-baiters; and finally including another minority imbued with a deeply Christian or liberal-humanitarian moral sense, whose value-system provided the most effective barrier to the Nazi doctrine of racial hatred.

---

[135] *Aus deutschen Urkunden 1935–1945,* (unpublished collection of documents, copy in the Imperial War Museum, Department of Foreign Documents, London), pp. 68–69.
[136] Cited in Steinert, *op. cit.,* p. 260.
[137] Cited in Kershaw, *op. cit.,* p. 342.
[138] Anna J. Merritt and Richard L. Merritt, *Public Opinion in Occupied Germany. The OMGUS Surveys, 1945–1949,* Urbana, 1970, pp. 146f.

In its attempt to infuse the German people with a dynamic, passionate hatred of the Jews, the Nazi propaganda machine was less than successful. Except on isolated occasions when the "Jewish Question" directly confronted them, most obviously following the 1938 pogrom, Germans seldom had Jews on their mind. The constant barrage of propaganda failed to make the Jews the prime target of hatred for most Germans, simply because the issue seemed largely abstract, academic, and unrelated to their own problems. The result was, for the most part, widespread disinterest in the "Jewish Question." Amid the prevailing apathy and disinterest, however, the "dynamic" hatred of the few, whose numbers included some of the leaders of the Third *Reich* and among them the *Führer* himself, could flourish. "Dynamic" Jew-haters were certainly a small percentage of the population; but active friends of the Jews formed an even smaller proportion. Furthermore, even when opinion was widely antagonistic towards Nazi actions, as in November 1938, it was impossible to articulate it. No political party, interest group, trade union or church had made it its job before 1933 to combat openly the dangerous growth of antisemitism. After 1933 the task was incomparably more difficult – perhaps impossible. Divisions of opinion, including widespread latent antisemitism, were reflected in the churches themselves. But the reluctance of the church hierarchies, for whatever motives, to oppose the inhumanity towards the Jews in the 1930s at the same time as they were often vigorously and successfully combating Nazi anti-church measures, and their public silence in the early war years when at the same time they were exposing the horrors of the "euthanasia programme," prevented any possibility of antisemitism becoming an issue.

Where the Nazis were most successful was in the depersonalisation of the Jew. The more the Jew was forced out of social contact and into the ghetto, the more he seemed to fit the stereotypes of a propaganda which intensified, paradoxically, its campaign against "Jewry" the fewer actual Jews there were in Germany itself. Depersonalisation increased the already existent widespread indifference of German popular opinion and formed a vital stage between the archaic violence of the pogrom and the rationalised "assembly-line" annihilation of the death camps.

It would go too far to deny antisemitism any "objective function" of diverting from acute socio-economic problems and especially of translating pseudo-revolutionary energy into apparently realisable goals which in turn could keep alive the utopian vision of a German-dominated "New Order" in Europe. In this sense, perhaps, one can speak of antisemitism functioning as an integrating element. But this was mainly within the ranks of the Nazi Movement itself, above all within the SS. Antisemitism provided a common denominator, necessary in a movement which was so obviously a loose coalition of interests as the Nazi Party, and which after 1933 was devoid of any real active political role apart from indoctrination and social control. The energies galvanised within the Movement in the so-called "years of struggle" could not simply be phased out from 1933, and were necessary to retain the dynamism of Nazism and prevent it from sagging into stagnation. This more or less aimless energy could be manipulated and channelled, as in 1935 and 1938, into attacks on the Jews, and the "Jewish Question" could function, too, in giving ideological purpose to the "enforcement agency" of the régime – the SS – Gestapo – SD organisation. Party activists needed activity: and antisemitism went a long way towards providing the SA and, in practical terms, otherwise useless sections of the Party with something to do and at the same time binding them propagandistically more closely to the apparent "aims" of Leader and Movement.

In the light of the evidence assembled in this paper it would, however, be mistaken to translate this functionalist explanation to the relationship between the régime and the broad mass of the German people. There was certainly extensive manipulation of opinion and Nazi propaganda could claim some success. But the ideological function of antisemitism with regard to the mass of the population consisted at most in strengthening the German identity-feeling and sense of national-consciousness by associating the Jews with Bolshevism and plutocracy and otherwise caricaturing the non-German character of Jewry. Popular support for National Socialism was based on ideological norms which had little in essence to do with antisemitism and persecution of Jews, and which can be summed up most adequately by the sense of social, political and moral order embodied in the term *Volksgemeinschaft*, ensured by a strong state which would suppress conflict to ensure strength through unity. While Jews and other minority groups, it is true, found no place in the Nazi concept of this "people's community," their exclusion was hardly a leading feature of the hopes and aspirations of the millions who, in the chaos of the Depression, were prepared to entrust the building of this new Germany to Hitler.

The permanent radicalisation of the anti-Jewish policies of the régime can hardly be said, on the evidence we have considered, to have been the product of, or to have corresponded to, the strong demands of popular opinion. It led in 1935 and 1938 to a drop in prestige for the Party, which might even have had repercussions for Hitler's own nimbus had he been seen to have supported and sided with the radicals. The radicalisation of the negative dynamism, which formed the essential driving-force of the Nazi Party, found remarkably little echo in the mass of the population. Popular opinion, largely indifferent and infused with a latent anti-Jewish feeling further bolstered by propaganda, provided the climate within which spiralling Nazi aggression towards Jews could take place unchallenged. But it did not provoke the radicalisation in the first place.

In its policies against the Jews the Nazi régime acted not with plebiscitary backing but with increasing autonomy from popular opinion, culminating in extermination carried out by the SS and SD as a "never to be written glorious page of our history", as Himmler put it, whose secret it was better to carry to the grave.[139] The very secrecy of the "Final Solution" demonstrates more clearly than anything else the fact that the Nazi leadership felt it could not rely on popular backing for its extermination policy. And yet it would be a crass oversimplification to attribute simply and solely to the criminal ideological paranoia of Hitler, Himmler, Heydrich and a few other leading personalities of the Third *Reich* the implementation of policies which led to the death camps. The "Final Solution" would not have been possible without the progressive steps excluding the Jews from German society which took place in full public view, in their legal form met with widespread approval, and resulted in the dehumanisation of the figure of the Jew. It would not have been possible without the atmosphere of hostility which was met only by apathy and widespread indifference. And it would not have been possible, finally, without the silence of the church hierarchies, who failed to articulate what opposition there was to Nazi racial policies, and without the consent ranging to active complicity of other prominent sections of the German élites – the bureaucracy of the Civil Service, leading sectors of industry, and the armed forces. Ultimately, therefore, dynamic hatred of the masses was unnecessary. Their latent antisemitism sufficed to allow the increasingly criminal "dynamic" hatred of the Nazi régime the autonomy it needed to implement the "Final Solution."

---

[139] *International Military Tribunal*, vol. 24, pp. 145ff. (Doc. PS–1919); Hans Buchheim, et al., *Anatomie des SS-Staates*, Olten, 1965, vol. 1, p. 329.

Part 5: The Question Today

HELEN FEIN

Contemporary Conflicts: How Do Jewish Claims and Jewish Nationhood Affect Antisemitism?

In this section we inquire how the change in the status of Jewry since the establishment of the state of Israel and changes in the status of Jews in other states since the Second World War have changed antisemitism and the relationship of Jews with other collectivities and nations. Our selections focus on conflict situations – the stance of the USSR toward its Jews and world Jewry, and Arab attitudes toward world Jewry and Israel – and the potential for increase of antisemitism in the west.

While world Jewry as a collectivity is greater than Israel (including Jewish communities in democratic, authoritarian, and Soviet-bloc states) and is, at the same time, less inclusive than Israel (which contains Arab Muslims, Christians, and Druze), its image is often conflated with that of Israel, both among Jews and outside Jewry. This stems from many motives, but is made plausible by the organized material aid world Jewry has given Israel, the political support of Jewish defense organizations for Israel, and the predominantly positive identification of individual Jews in states throughout the world with Israel. "We are all Zionists now," it has been stated (or overstated) to summarize western Jews' self-conception. To understand the implications of this, one must recall the diversity of religio-political self-conceptions among Jews prior to World War II. The range of ideal-typical patterns of identity and consciousness may be illustrated in the following table.

One might also view this as a continuum of types of national identification related to education, acculturation, urbanism, and migration patterns of Jews. As Jews in eastern and central Europe became urbanized and confronted modernity from the late nineteenth to the mid-twentieth century, they tended to move away from the traditional, enclosed *shtetl* in which orthodoxy was the norm (B) and were more likely to become bourgeois nationalists (C) or, Zionists, Bundists, or socialists (D). Forms of religious identification also varied with social class and the degree of

Table 5:1
Types of Ideologies and Belief-Systems Among Diaspora Jews

Collectivity-Orientation:	Value-Orientation Predominant: Sacred	Secular
National	A. _____*	C. bourgeois nationalists (100% Americans, French, Hungarians, etc.) of Mosaic, Israelite, Jewish faith or origin
Supra-national	B. Traditional Orthodoxy	D. Zionist, Bundist (particularistic); Socialist (universalistic)

* This missing box is now filled in Israel by messianic nationalist movements such as the Gush Emunim.

modernity achieved. In the west, most Jews adhered prior to World War II to the compact Jewish notables, convened in a special Sanhedrin in 1806, made with Napoleon (fortifying the grant of citizenship during the French Revolution in [1791]). It mandated that they give up interests and claims as a collectivity for individual freedom and civil rights; as the deputy Clermont-Tonnère put it in 1789, "To Jews as individuals everything; to Jews as a distinct community, nothing." Here they became bourgeois nationalists, often super-patriots, affirming that their highest loyalty was to the state which made them citizens. Zionism was initially feared (in the early decades of the twentieth century) by some Anglo-American Jewish leaders, because it might reopen the question of Jews' identification and loyalty and endanger their civil rights in the west, if they raised collective claims on their behalf. Yet, in the post-World War II world, western Jews collectively and individually chose to go beyond this box (C), changing the compact on their own initiative, as they publicly supported Israel as the embodiment of Jewish peoplehood and as a nation-state, while they still claimed (and largely attained in the North Atlantic states) full civil rights and participation. This entailed going beyond rather primitive or simple-minded notions of loyalty (which had generated the double-bind of the "dual loyalty" charge) to assert they both had national, Israel-centered, and Jewish claims and obligations. These may be reconciled by (a) denying there is any conflict, since Israel and the democratic states have common interests, (b) ranking what is most important to each cause, (c) judging claims by transcendant universalistic norms of how states should behave, and (d) evaluating the claims and costs pragmatically in each situation to determine priorities.

However, democratic states are more apt to tolerate plural identifications than other states. The concerns of government about the loyalty or national identification of their citizens have raised special problems for Jews in authoritarian or totalitarian states demanding exclusive identification with the state, and/or which identified the state with one religious or ethnic group. The identification of Jews with Israel has been exploited to reinforce antisemitism with anti-Zionism in the Soviet Union,[1] although discrimination against Soviet Jews as a nationality or religious collectivity preceded the establishment of Israel. The Arab-Israeli conflict generated threats against Jews in most Arab states, and awakened fears which caused many Jews to flee since 1948[2] from the states of the mid-east and newly-independent nations of north Africa. Syria forbade its Jews, an isolated second-class minority, to leave but has protected them from collective violence. Other authoritarian and totalitarian regimes also threaten their Jewish minorities. The Jewish community of Ethiopia, known as Falashas or Beta-Israel (most of whom were evacuated by Israel from refugee camps in the Sudan by 1985), were forbidden to leave Ethiopia legally and were decimated by many causes, including conditions preceding the present revolutionary government's accession to power (1974): persecution and slaughter by other Ethiopians activated by fear of sorcery and traditional hostility toward the Jews; famine and terror from revolutionary and counter-revolutionary insurgents which have also killed other Ethiopians; and political and cultural marginality inducing Jews to convert so as to improve opportunities.[3]

Jews were also vulnerable to attack as Jews in some authoritarian Latin-American "national security" states (between 1976 and 1984) which used terror – torture and extra-judicial executions – against all citizens, especially in Argentina. Argentina has broadcast and tolerated antisemitic propaganda and instigated or tolerated physical attacks against Jewish property and community institutions during that period. Although antisemitism in Argentina preceded this period and has many ideological sources, it was counter-balanced by the democratic exercise of the free press as long as Argentinians enjoyed civil liberties. Since the Argentinian military have

---

[1] See Goldhagen and Nudelman herein.
[2] Hayyim J. Cohen, "Asia and Africa: Survey," in *The Yom Kippur War: Israel and the Jewish People*, New York, 1974, pp. 255–267.
[3] David Kessler, *The Falashas: The Forgotten Jews of Ethiopia*, London, 1982; Louis Rapoport, *The Lost Jews: Last of the Ethiopian Falashas*, New York, n.d.

consistently been shown to be more antisemitic than other Argentinians,[4] their use or toleration of violence against Jews is not surprising. The hostile myth of a Jewish conspiracy against Argentina which the military accepted was expressed, for example, in their interrogation and torture of an Argentine Jewish newspaper publisher, Jacobo Timmerman, arrested without charge in 1977 and freed in 1979.[5]

In the north Atlantic states, democratic governments tended to be more open to ethnicity and plural identification in the post-World War II years, although there were considerable differences among these states. Canada, Belgium, and the United States have been more accepting of ethnic political organizations and demands than France and the Federal Republic of Germany. In the U.S. and Great Britain, the status of Jews has visibly risen since 1945, as more joined the upper-middle classes based on education and were over-represented[6] in professional and intellectual elites[7].

Prewar goals of western Jewish communities to eliminate discrimination against Jews in employment, education, and housing have been largely achieved. The newly-incorporated and acculturated second-generation American Jews were believers in the "cult of gratitude," Melvin M. Tumin charged in 1969: the American Jew "instead of asking that America accept him as he is and treat him as an equal in his full self-proclaimed identity . . . is, in effect, asking that his separateness shall be forgotten and ignored."[8] The change in self-perceptions of their own identity, needs, and demands among American Jews since then has been attributed not only to their identification with Israel in the 1967 Six-Day War but also to their reaction to the Black Power movement in the U.S. It had the effect of also raising the self-consciousness of other ethnic and racial groups.

Contemporary Jews have asserted a new compact with the nation-state, Hertzberg declares, one which allows for the expression (rather than repression) of Jewish uniqueness, yet the basis of that uniqueness is changed.

> The conclusion is simple and inescapable: the very secular, "like all the nations" State of Israel has become the contemporary equivalent of the older Jewish religion; that is, the loyalties that it evokes throughout the Jewish world is the contemporary factor of Jewish

---

[4] Robert Weisbrot, *The Jews of Argentina from the Inquisition to Peron*, Philadelphia, Pa., 1979, pp. 210–215.

[5] Jacobo Timmerman, *Prisoner Without a Name, Cell Without a Number*, New York, 1981.

[6] The concept of over-representation is used here in a statistical rather than a normative sense; if the proportion of group members in a given occupation or category is greater than its proportion in the population, it is said to be over-represented.

[7] William David Rubinstein, *The Left, the Right and the Jews*, New York, 1982, pp. 60–64.

[8] "The Cult of Gratitude," in Peter I. Rose, *The Ghetto and Beyond*, New York, 1969.

uniqueness and Jewish distinctiveness. This is the contemporary embodiment of "their ways are different from those of all other people."[9]

Hertzberg rejects the assumption made by Sartre[10] and other universalists that distinctive Jewish characteristics would disappear when and if antisemitism waned since, Sartre reasoned, adherence to traditional Judaism had greatly diminished among Jews (which is probably less true in the 1980s than at the time Sartre wrote). This perception of Jewish distinctiveness and the interaction of the Arab-Israeli, US-USSR, and north-south conflicts has had different effects on Jews in different states. We shall first inquire into the origin and causes of Soviet antisemitism and ask what its status is in communist theory and what functions it might serve.

Theories linking antisemitism to the functions of a powerless scapegoat during crises are usually based on capitalist or precapitalist systems.[11] One may ask if we can explain the employment of antisemitism by communist states by similar mechanisms. While many have remarked how the Soviet-bloc states have used Jews as a scapegoat to deflect attention from leadership purges and arouse and displace hostility during internal crises,[12] the continuity and the changes in the policy of the Soviet Union toward the Jews of the USSR and world Jewry demand deeper analysis. For both the production and inhibition of expressions of antisemitism in the Soviet Union is (unlike the west) a state function as is the production and inhibition of other ideologies and opinions.

Goldhagen reviews the changing responses to antisemitism in socialist theories and in Soviet law and responses to Jews up to 1960, showing how the Soviet state has abandoned the principled rejection of antisemitism by Lenin and Trotsky. R. Nudelman[13] and Gitelman[14] both show there has been a quantitative escalation and intensification of antisemitic propaganda published in the USSR since 1968, reviving themes which predate the Soviet Revolution and exploiting classic Russian antisemitic canards. Rather than antisemitism being an outgrowth of anti-Zionism, these classic theses

---

[9] Arthur Hertzberg, "Anti-Semitism and Jewish Uniqueness," *Encyclopedia Judaica Yearbook,* Jerusalem, 1976, p. 216.

[10] See Part 1.

[11] See Part 3, introduction.

[12] Paul Lendvai, *Anti-Semitism Without Jews,* Garden City, N.Y., 1971.

[13] Herein.

[14] Zvi Gitelman, "Moscow and the Soviet Jews: A Parting of the Ways," *Problems of Communism* 29, 1, 1980, pp. 18–34.

(which infer that the evil character of Jews is grounded in their religion) are used to "explain" the alleged sins of Zionism.

One question which is sometimes obscured by the weight of documentation of Soviet antisemitism is: What is its goal or function? Goldhagen[15] and others have concluded it is the total assimilation or cultural extinction of Soviet Jewry. Yet the USSR's reiteration of hostile propaganda against Jews makes this unlikely. Nudelman[16] asserts that the mobilization of antisemitism serves several functions related to internal and external conflict involving the USSR; these include replacing the "former 'Russian-Jewish' intelligentsia by a new nationalist intelligentsia;" isolating and stigmatizing dissidents in the Soviet republics, in other eastern European communist states, and in foreign communist parties, to fortify Soviet control; and creating an international united camp against common enemies and appealing to non-democratic African and Asian regimes. We may label these functions as resolving competition, restoring solidarity and exorcising deviation, and international mobilization.

Many infer the function of Soviet antisemitism from Soviet discrimination against Jews seeking education and positions. Discrimination against Jews is functional for Russian elites competing for places. Korey has shown how Jews are systematically restricted from entering schools and universities that offer training prerequisite for higher-ranking careers.[17] Jews have been progressively excluded from influential sectors of Soviet life for several decades, restricted from access to military, diplomatic, administrative, or party posts, or consigned to a token number. However, restrictions against Jews in science has had the greatest impact on Soviet Jews since 1950. Soviet discrimination against Jews in science has also been related to the government's attempt to equalize the proportions of ethnic groups in science to correspond to the proportion of such groups in the population as advocated by the theory of equality of V. Mishin, a Soviet sociologist. Given this criterion, the Jews are the most over-represented of Soviet nationalities: "There are 315 research scientists per every 10,000 Jews in the USSR at present."[18] However, the decline in the number of Jewish workers in science (a drop of 60 percent between 1950 and 1973) has been far steeper than the decline among the Georgians and Armenians, other

---

[15] Herein.
[16] Herein.
[17] William Korey, "Aspects of Soviet Anti-Semitism," paper presented at the Aspen Institute Berlin Seminar, Sept. 25–28, 1983.
[18] I. Domal'ski, "New Developments in Anti-Semitism," in *Anti-Semitism in the Soviet Union: Its Roots and Consequences*, Vol. 1, Jerusalem, 1979, p. 249.

nationalities also over-represented in science. While some nations are encouraged, others are inhibited; both are accomplished by double-standards in admission and examination.[19] By the 1980s Jewish students in Moscow were under-represented in admission to Moscow universities, although their parents constituted 11 percent of the Moscow scientific community.[20]

Yet, the unfolding Soviet policy towards the Jews contained seeming contradictions in its objectives and impact that are puzzling. During the period after 1967, when Soviet anti-Zionist propaganda increased, the USSR allowed an increasing number of its Jews to emigrate to Israel; their numbers declined between 1974 and 1976, climbed to over 50,000 in 1979, and have sharply dropped since 1980. Gitelman asked:

> If the USSR is so hostile to Zionism, why does it permit the migration of its own citizens to the Zionist state, where, by all accounts, they make a significant contribution to Israel's economy and military capacity? It is not clear that Soviet policymakers intended to create this contradiction or are necessarily happy with it. Rather, the policies have gained a momentum of their own and have merged intentionally or unintentionally with deep strands of popular-antisemitism to create a perhaps irreversible alienation of Soviet Jews from their society.[21]

Gitelman theorized that, originally, the anti-Zionist campaign was intended to dissuade Jews from trying to leave the USSR, but that it became "a vehicle for those motivated purely by anti-semitism or by careerist ambitions and other considerations" and, rather than deterring Jews, convinced them (along with discrimination against them) that they had no future in the USSR. This led to a vicious cycle, enabling the authorities to justify denying higher education to this "unstable element," now seen as a "fifth column," which, in turn, moved more Jews to emigrate. Depending on their predispositions, other Russians viewed their departure either with jealousy, puzzlement, and defensive patriotism, or positive feelings about their rejection ("saying 'good riddance' to them").

Soviet Jews have responded with increased nonviolent and public struggle for their right to emigrate, practice as Jews, and learn Hebrew – at present, an estimated 300,000 to 500,000 Soviet Jews, or 17% to 28% of all Soviet Jews, have applied for permission to emigrate. Some Soviet Jews in elite positions apparently attempting to accomodate to and coexist with the

---

[19] *Ibid.*, pp. 247–267.
[20] Korey, *op. cit.*, pp. 2–3.
[21] Gitelman, *op. cit.*, p. 25.

regime, have publicly denied there is antisemitism in the Soviet Union. Simultaneously, Soviet repression and false charges of crimes against prominent dissidents and potential Jewish émigrés and Hebrew teachers have increased in the '80s. At the same time, the USSR has assigned more state resources to Yiddish culture (whose existence, Goldhagen herein and others noted, was denied for decades) in the 1980s. The significance of this policy is open to question, given the simultaneous repression of Hebrew culture.

What is singular about Soviet official responses to its Jews that may be labeled antisemitic is not simply its discrimination or denial of cultural freedom – Pentacostalists, Baptists, and Ukrainian nationalists are also denied cultural and personal freedom –, but the virulent hostility and demonization of the Jews which the state propagates.

Despite the fact that discrimination against Jews in the USSR opens up opportunities for other Soviet citizens, competition alone is an insufficient motive to account for the intensity of the Soviets' antisemitic propaganda campaign. Jews could be discriminated against on the same bases as Georgians or Armenians without any ideology singling them out. Nor can Soviet bonds with African and Asian states account for the extent and intensity of antisemitic propaganda within the Soviet Union, as described by Nudelman.

The most plausible theses are those linking Soviet antisemitism to restoring solidarity and exercising control against deviance in the USSR and eastern Europe. It is understandable that the ruling Soviet elite seeks to revive flagging Soviet solidarity by appealing to antisemitism, since it is the least common denominator among most East-European peoples antagonistic to Marxism. Thus, national socialism may replace internationalist socialism with the myths of *Mein Kampf* replacing the class struggle.

Further, antisemitism has also become a means to stigmatize dissidents in the Soviet Union and eastern Europe. This strategy is believable within the USSR itself, because of the extent of identification of Jews and dissidents, despite the denial of the Jewish movement of/for Soviet Jewry that reform of the USSR is its goal. Just as Jews are over-represented in the Soviet scientific elite, they are over-represented in the "Soviet democratic dissent movement – 60 to 70 percent of whose members are Jewish or married to Jews."[22] Also, many members of the independent peace move-

---

[22] William Orbach, *The American Movement to Aid Soviet Jewry*, Amherst, Mass., 1979, p. 43.

ment in the USSR "are Jewish refusniks who have been denied permission to emigrate for arbitrary reasons."[23]

This has both theoretical and practical implications. Theoretically, Soviet antisemitism can be distinguished from, but related to, the functions of myth and ideology specified in Part I.

> 15. When threats and crises arose whose source could not be understood or agreed upon, the anti-Judaic myth framed social cognitions . . .
> 27. Antisemitism provided a paradigm by which generalized threats of social chaos or revolution were made comprehensible by displacing blame for them onto the Jews . . .

It is because of the threats of rebellion against Soviet domination by the satellites (DDR 1953, Hungary 1956, Czechoslovakia 1968, Poland 1982) and the demand by the human rights movement in the USSR for individual freedoms can be understood that stigmatization of the leaders and displacing blame onto the Jews is needed.

Were there a real threat of internal breakdown in the Soviet Union along national lines or should rebellion spread, Soviet Jews could be in great jeopardy. For the latent implication of Soviet antisemitism is genocidal: the collective attack on Jews as Jews does not justify their assimilation but their elimination. Defining a group outside the universe of obligation of the dominant group is a prerequisite for annihilating them – a necessary, but not sufficient, condition.[24] In communist states, to become an enemy of the people is the first step to becoming a non-person. Further, the Soviet Union has the structural capacity to readily eliminate groups: the bureaucracy and facilities like prisons, camps, Gulags are in place and potential victims are defined and registered by the passport system. Nor would this be an unprecedented departure from past history. The USSR deported eight nationalities – suspected without charge, evidence, or trials – between 1941 and 1943 under conditions and to destinations leading to many deaths. Although the toll of these victims is a small percentage of the total of Soviet victims – "probably a little over half a million people died as a result"[25] – imposing conditions leading to the mass death of a national or ethnic group is an indictable offense under the Genocide Convention.

---

[23] Helsinki Watch Committee, *Violations of the Helsinki Accords: August 1983–September 1984.*

[24] Helen Fein, "Anticipating Deadly Endings: Models of Genocide and Critical Response," in Israel W. Charney (ed.), *The Book of the International Conference on Holocaust and Genocide: Towards Understanding, Intervention and Prevention of Genocide*, Vol. 2, Boulder, Colo., 1984.

[25] Robert Conquest, *The Nation Killers: The Soviet Deportation of Nationalities*, New York, 1970, Introduction.

Stalin also produced mass famine in the Ukraine in 1933 to squash nationalistic tendencies there by destroying the Ukrainian peasantry. It led to millions of deaths;[26] this also may be considered genocide. Thus, the USSR has much experience in eliminating suspect peoples as well as persons.

While Soviet antisemitism predated conflict between the USSR and Israel and the USSR and Soviet Jewry, it has intensified since the 1967 War. The conflict between Jewish and Arab nationalism in the mid-East also preceded 1967 but has become more exacerbated and mobilized since then.

How group conflict has led the Arabs as antagonists to exploit antisemitism is shown by Y. Harkabi in this selection from *Arab Attitudes to Israel*.[27] Harkabi firstly makes clear that Jews (like Christians) were always discriminated and subordinated under Islam, outside of the sacred Islamic universe of obligation.[28] A repertoire of negative images about Jews was available; there were also less well-known positive images. However, modern Arab antisemitism arises from the top, produced and controlled by the government, and is a response to the conflict with Israel, not to the Jews of Arab lands, although at times it has been displaced against them.

> The Arabs did not oppose Jewish settlement for anti-Semitic motives; their opposition aroused anti-Semitic emotions among them. . . . The fundamental characteristic of the Israelis is that they are Jews, and their Israeli identity is only a shallow surface layer – especially as the Diaspora Jews assist Israel and are connected with them by bonds of kinship and aid.

While intergroup conflict and prejudice may be distinguished,[29] Harkabi's analysis herein illustrates how intergroup conflict between contending racial, religious, or ethnic groups can often become embroiled by prejudice, reinforcing fear and hostility. Conflict between contenders divided on issues along ethnic/racial/religious lines without any common loyalty to an overarching association or overlapping bonds in other relationships is especially apt to be violent if not genocidal.[30] Prejudice is instrumental for unifying antagonistic groups in intergroup conflict against a common enemy. Antisemitism is also a significant resource because

---

[26] James E. Mace, "Famine and Nationalism in Soviet Ukraine," *Problems of Communism*, May–June 1984, pp. 37–50.

[27] Jerusalem, 1972.

[28] See Introduction, Part 3.

[29] As discussed by Fein, Langmuir and Weil in Part 2.

[30] Leo Kuper, *Genocide: Its Political Use in the Twentieth Century*, New Haven, Conn., 1981, p. 58.

of its rich resonance with western cultural traditions[31] and folk-beliefs, enabling the Arabs (themselves often an object of prejudice) to sell their case in a coin which is accepted currency in the Christian western world. (While antisemitic themes have been espoused by Arab spokesmen, at other times antisemitism has been repudiated by them and distinguished dogmatically from anti-Israel ideologies.) Harkabi's more recent writing and statements on the Arab-Israeli conflict focus on how unrealistic trends in Zionism, based on romanticization of heroic myth, ignore the limits of power and impede settlement of the conflict.[32]

Turning to the west, Eric Hobsbawm[33] relates the decline of antisemitism to the ideological and structural conditions of the quarter-century following World War II. Comparisons and judgments about Jews, as about all groups, depend upon how their status is related to one's own.

> Thus, the influx of Jews into the vast and growing American universities apparently created no significant resentment, while the influx of American academics into the much smaller Canadian academic job market, particularly during the Vietnam war, undoubtedly did.

Hobsbawm observes that the check on the inhibition of antisemitism has eroded in the north Atlantic states since 1970 for several reasons: first, due to population replacement, fewer citizens recall or experience guilt over the Holocaust; second, these states face depression, high unemployment, and little hope of expansion. However, unlike many theorists who look on Jews as a perpetual scapegoat, Hobsbawm expects that hostility aroused by structural crises will be displaced against other minorities. Yet, this is not an either-or choice for many social movements and parties in western states which are focused primarily on foreign workers and migrants are also antisemitic, as is the National Front in Britain.

Has antisemitism or the potential for it increased in the west during the last decade? Although attitude research does not corroborate this,[34] overt expressions of violence – some organized and others apparently not –, ideological attacks, and verbal threats against Jews in Europe and North

---

[31] See Ruether, Part 1.
[32] Yehoshafat Harkabi, *The Arab-Israel Conflict: a Future Perspective*, International Center for Peace in the Middle East, Tel Aviv, 1985; *The Bar Kokhba Syndrome: Risk and Realism in International Politics*, trans. Max D. Ticktin, ed. David Altshuler, Chappaqua, New York, 1983, pp. 129–186; "Dissent on the West Bank from Israeli Insider," *New York Times*, May 25, 1980, Pt. IV, p. 5; "Policy, Not Illusions," *New Outlook* Vol. 21: No. 3 (May/June 1978), pp. 29–33.
[33] Herein.
[34] See Part 2.

America since 1980 has caused many observers to perceive and fear a new rise in antisemitism. This preceded the worldwide predominantly hostile response to the Israeli invasion of Lebanon in 1982. There had been a rising number of terrorist incidents against Jews in Europe during the preceding two years (which claimed 25 lives and wounded 373 persons from 1980 to October 1982). The greatest number of European incidents was in France, and almost two out of three incidents were directed against Jewish (rather than Israeli) targets; bombs were thrown or shots were fired at schools, synagogues, and a Jewish restaurant. This aroused vocal protests by French leaders and sympathy marches in identification with the Jews. The incidents themselves raised questions about the extent and organization of antisemitism (especially in France) and about Arab terrorism since such violence has been linked to extremist left- and right-wing groups who have been instigated, trained, or supplied with arms by Soviet sources.[35]

Patterns of Prejudice conducted a symposium in 1982, asking participants about their sense of the meaning of these events, the sources of terrorism and antisemitism, and the anti-Zionism – antisemitism linkage. Replies were received from 21 people, mainly Jewish academics, leaders and staff of Jewish defense organization and rabbis in the north Atlantic states and Israel. Most participants recognized an increase in the expression of antisemitic attacks and ideology, but they were divided as to whether this simply reflected a disinhibition of the post-Holocaust taboo against expressing hostility towards the Jews, or a real increase, and most were reserved about the extent of that increase. Virtually all agreed that the target was no longer the civil rights or status achieved by individual Jews in western states but the legitimacy of Jewish claims as a collectivity identified with a nation-state under attack (Israel). There was general agreement that the latter had been undermined by the politically-inspired labeling of Zionism as racism (affirmed by the U.N. General Assembly in 1975). The Soviet Union and the Arab bloc were generally recognized as organizational bases diffusing anti-Zionist and antisemitic activity, i.e., ideological attacks on Jews' claims as a collectivity. Many belived these were related to physical attacks on Jews in Europe and North America, although there are indigenous organizational bases of terrorism on the extremist left and right in many states.

The most interesting question which divided respondents was the relationship between antisemitism and anti-Zionism and the implications of their conceptions. While most agreed that criticism of policies of the state

---

[35] Claire Sterling, *The Terror Network*, New York, 1981.

of Israel can not automatically be construed as anti-Zionist, there were no parameters or examples given of which criticisms are not anti-Zionist. Thus we can not really appraise how much consensus there was on the limits of legitimate dissent. Three major theses can be discerned regarding the links between anti-Zionism and antisemitism, with their pragmatic corollaries (in parentheses):

(1) Anti-Zionism is functionally the equivalent of antisemitism. (To oppose antisemitism is to oppose anti-Zionism.)

(2) Ideologically, anti-Zionism and antisemitism are discrete ideologies, but one may instigate, exploit, or draw upon the other, so that hostility towards the state of Israel leads towards hostility towards Jews, and vice versa. (This has mixed implications.)

(3) Labeling anti-Zionism as antisemitism is an act of semantic fiat which, by attribution, creates antisemitism and thus simulates a self-fulfilling prophecy. (These critics propose to Jews to discriminate rather than to conflate causes and/or consider resolving underlying causes for conflict, i.e., the Arab-Israeli question.)

Although we are talking about too few participants to infer national differences reliably, it is striking that the first position was more likely to be taken by the Israeli respondents, the second or third by the British respondents.

The first position was expressed by Shlomo Avineri, Yehuda Bauer, and Leon Wieseltier. Avineri asserted that

> Israel – the historical product of Zionism – is today the broadest possible common denominator for Jewish self-consciousness all over the world. . . . To strike at the legitimacy of Israel today through anti-Zionism as an ideology of delegitimizing Israel means striking at the centre of the normative self-determination of the Jewish people as Jews understand it. Should Israel disappear, or a major catastrophe befall it, practically all Jewish people would conceive it as a major tragedy for their own existence as Jews. Therefore, a delegitimization of Israel is tantamount to the delegitimization of Jewish existence as understood today by most Jews. . . . It is in this deeper sense – not in the facile semantic equation of anti-Zionism with antisemitism – that anti-Zionism is identical in its fundamental attitudes to former modes of traditional antisemitism. Just like Christian theology in the Middle Ages and modern racist antisemitism, current anti-Zionism aims at extirpating the basic legitimacy of Jewish existence.

Thus, denying Jews' claims to collective rights is, in effect, to deny Jews' claim to existence qua Jews.

Wieseltier asserted that critics of Israel must prove they are not enemies of the Jewish state (unlike Bauer and Avineri), concluding:

Anti-Zionism is antisemitism in theory and in practice. . . . It is the delegitimization of the Jews – their exclusion from the ranks of the collectively respectable – that prepares the ground for the new antisemitic violence. The air abounds with ideas that issue in the attack upon Goldenberg's [restaurant in Paris bombed in 1981]. . . . The attack upon Goldenberg's was an attack upon Jews that was justified in the minds of the attackers as an attack upon Zionists. But there is no such thing as a Zionist restaurant.

The second and third position are alike in that both oppose any sterotyped linkage between anti-Zionism and antisemitism, Rabbi Immanuel Jakobovits, Chief Rabbi of Great Britain and the Commonwealth, opposed linkage, citing his "Message to Anglo-Jewry" early during the war in Lebanon:

> By charging people [who criticize Israel] with antisemitism, you help to breed antisemitism. You give aid and comfort to the real antisemites and their movements, and you alienate true friends. . . . I believe that, generally, the unqualified equation of anti-Zionism with antisemitism holds true only in the Communist and Third Worlds. The causes of the antagonism towards Israel are many and complex. . . . But we must distinguish between cause and effect. That intense hostility to Israel spills over into antipathy against Jews is manifestly obvious. Anti-Zionism is certainly a cause of antisemitism. But the reverse is much more questionable, and often plainly untenable as a fact.

Metaphors and analogies used by some Israeli spokesmen which relate their isolation to that of the Jews of the Holocaust do not explain, as Gould and Beloff noted, but distort the causes of current conflict. Similarly, the antagonists of Israel and their sympathizers have appropriated the imagery and themes of the Holocaust to legitimate their cause, reversing roles to depict the Israelis as victimizers, perpetrators of genocide,[36] just as Israeli spokesmen and supporters have cast the Palestinians as Nazis and demonized them[37]. In both cases, the casting of villains, victims, motives, and plot by imposing the Holocaust as the paradigm serves both to obscure and intensify the conflict and diminish understanding of, and respect for, the meaning of the Holocaust.[38]

It is the conflict itself (or how it has been fought) which has produced the hostility, Wasserman observed:

> . . . it is not antisemitism which in general now lies behind anti-Zionism but, if anything, the reverse: anti-Zionism gives renewed impetus to antisemitism. That is to say, it is the

---

[36] Edward Alexander, "Stealing the Holocaust," *Midstream,* November 1980.
[37] Joseph Alpher, "From Wagner to Arafat: Demonology and Survival," *The Jerusalem Quarterly* 33, 1984, pp. 3–13.
[38] Helen Fein, "Unveiling the Second Text: Implications of the Holocaust," paper presented at the Eisner Institute for Holocaust Studies, Graduate Center, City University of New York, February 23, 1983.

deepening hostility to Israel almost everywhere (a hostility in large part evoked by the current Israeli government's actions) which is strengthening antisemitic currents . . .

Some conclude as has Yehoshua, that the latent effects of the strategy "of calling every anti-Zionist an anti-Semite will not diminish the number of anti-Zionists; it will only enlarge the ranks of the anti-Semites."[39]

Advocates of avoiding linkage often point to the need to resolve underlying sources of conflict, such as the late Nahum Goldmann, former president of the World Jewish Congress, who observed that only a solution of the Near East problem, including the Palestinian question, will do away with anti-Zionism and its consequences.

Few social scientists have researched or aimed to clarify the linkage question. Survey evidence as to the relationship between anti-Zionism and antisemitism is obscure firstly, because the constellation of ideas labeled anti-Zionism is not tapped by surveys. Looking at the American evidence based on surveys, we find little evidence of a carry-over of attitudes towards Jews and towards Israel.[40] Movements based on groups with a history of Christian theological particularism associated with antisemitism, whose spokesmen sometimes voice overt antisemitic stereotypes (such as the Moral Majority in the U.S.), are now uncritically pro-Israel (i.e., in favor not only of the existence but of the present policies of Israel).[41] Liberal university faculty who tend to be ideologically opposed to discrimination and antisemitism are more critical of Israel.[42]

As conflicts between Israel and the Arab states were related to class interests of the elites in the north Atlantic states, these political elites began to distinguish Jewish claims for civil rights from claims for Israel based on group interest, ranking group-interest claims against the claims of other classes and groups. The threat of antisemitism was revived by direct

---

[39] Abraham B. Yehoshua, *Between Right and Right*, Garden City, N.Y., 1981, p. 127.

[40] Gregory Matire and Ruth Clark, *Anti-Semitism in the United States: A Study of Prejudice in the 1980s*, New York, 1982, pp. 90–94; Seymour Martin Lipset and William Schneider, "Israel and the Jews in American Public Opinion," unpublished manuscript, n.d., pp. 68–69.

[41] The Rev. Dan Fore, Chairman of the Moral Majority in New York State, said, "Jews have a God-given ability to make money, almost supernatural ability to make money. . . . They control the media, they control this city" (*New York Times*, Feb. 5, 1981); he subsequently resigned in response to public criticism. Rev. Bailey Smith, President of the Southern Baptist Convention, said in August 1980: "God Almighty does not hear the prayer of the Jew, for how in the world can God hear the prayer of a man who says Jesus Christ is not the true Messiah?" (Jack Newfield, "Anti-Semitism and the Crime of Silence," *The Village Voice*, June 17–23, 1981, p. 13).

[42] Lipset and Schneider, *op. cit.*, p. 54.

attempts by political leaders to delegitimate Jewish claims related to Israel. Leonard Fein recalls[43] the successful campaign by President Reagan to press the U.S. Senate to approve the sale of AWACS planes to Saudi-Arabia in 1981 against opposition by American Jewish organizations and Israel:

> Specifically, the readiness of an incumbent President and two of his predecessors in office (Nixon and Ford) to engage in blatantly anti-semitic behaviour in their effort to prevail in the debate, together with similar manifestations within the American corporate elite was – and remains – a deeply disturbing phenomenon. I had imagined – mistakenly, as it turns out – that antisemitism was the preserve of the yahoos, of the know-nothings, of the bar-room brawlers. And now it develops that in addition to the anti-semitism of the bar-room, we must contend with the antisemitism of the board-room. . . . if ever there should be a move to build a coalition between the know-nothings and the care-nothings, between the beer-guzzlers and the martini-sippers, we are in very serious trouble.

What may be seen in the U.S. is the expression of existing prejudices and distrust of Jews which was previously publicly inhibited rather than any increase of antisemitism; this is both drawn on and fomented by elites in conflict with organized Jewry.[44] What the Arab-Israeli conflict has done in current American politics is to activate both Jewish organization and claims and the opponents of such claims who draw upon stereotypes of Jewish power and manipulation. The threat of invoking antisemitism or blaming Jews for provoking antisemitism is a resource for their antagonists which can put Jews in a double-bind as political actors: to challenge their opponent's charges directly and successfully may reinforce belief in the charges while not to respond may give credence to the charges and/or demonstrate their vulnerability.

To sum up, we may restate the question in 1985: Was there a significant increase in antisemitism in the early 1980s? The answer given by the participants in the *Patterns of Prejudice* symposium depended first on their conception and definition of antisemitism. Bauer (Israel), Ettinger (Israel) and DiNola (Italy) asserted there was a significant increase of antisemitism in the west; Brand (Federal Republic of Germany), Kriegel (France), and Wasserstein (Great Britain) asserted there was not. Other participants were more equivocal. Secondly, it reflected critical methodological problems of linkage between the levels of antisemitism and broader questions of political prognosis.[45]

---

[43] *Patterns of Prejudice*, 1982.
[44] See also Stephen S. Rosenfeld, "Dateline Washington: Anti-Semitism and U.S. Foreign Policy," *Foreign Policy* 47, 1982, pp. 172–183.
[45] See Part 2.

There was general agreement on the upsurge in antisemitism within the USSR and antisemitism generated internationally by the USSR since 1968. While there was much testimony on the impact of government-sponsored antisemitism from the top within the Soviet Union (and antisemitic currents from underneath which motivate it), there has been relatively little consideration of the impact of its propaganda on people without an antisemitic tradition outside the Soviet orbit.

Among the "third-world" states, many non-Arab and non-Islamic states have no tradition of antisemitism and have had little interaction with Jews; further, some African states have enjoyed cooperative relationships with Israel. Were anti-Zionism just a shibboleth, rallying-cry, flag, or standard, antisemitism would be superfluous. Anti-Zionism could not become a code-word for antisemitism were there not hostility toward Israelis and Jews among those who embrace it.

The fluctuation of policy toward the Jews before and during World War II in Italy and Japan,[46] states which had adopted antisemitic legislation and ideology without a popularly grounded antisemitic tradition, suggests that antisemitism not supported by fear and hostility toward Jews may have a shallow impact. Nor was there consideration of the impact of Soviet propaganda in Soviet satellites; one might conjecture that consciousness of the way it has been repeatedly used to discredit dissidents might lead opponents to repudiate antisemitism, as it did the leadership of Solidarity in Poland in 1982.[47]

Focusing on western Europe and North America, all participants acknowledged the rise of incidents of violence against Jews up to 1982 but disagreed as to their significance as an indicator. The B'nai B'rith U.S. Antidefamation League's annual audit of antisemitic incidents was over five times higher in 1984 than in 1979, and the number of the relatively few violent attacks was also significantly higher; however, in Europe, terrorist attacks against Jews almost ceased after 1982. This makes it appear more likely that the earlier European attacks were of terrorist and external origin rather than of indigenous social movements. It is difficult to draw reliable inferences from the U.S. audit (except as an index of diffuse hostility against Jews) because of the way it is compiled.[48]

---

[46] See Introduction, Part 3.

[47] Abraham Brumberg, "The Ghost in Poland," *New York Review of Books,* June 2, 1983, pp. 41–42.

[48] The ADL U.S. audit aggregates very different events on a scale of violence, such as painting swastikas on synagogue walls and throwing bombs without discriminating as to intensity or organization. Participants in vandalism which creates, at most, temporary property

Mass public opinion and public opinion surveys did not appear to be considered relevant by most of the participants in the symposium, except for Lipset who commented on the long-term decline in survey indicators of antisemitism in the west.[49] Ideologies and social movements' orientation toward antisemitism did seem relevant to many participants. However, there was dissensus whether specific movements were antisemitic, tolerated antisemitic expressions, or might lead to conditions threatening Jews as Jews. Bauer (in Israel) saw American Protestant fundamentalism as a threat to American democracy (and thus to the Jews) while Lipset (in the U.S.) saw it as a force upholding traditional values. This highlights the problem of confusing questions of long-term Jewish interest with observations on antisemitism; there are (and will probably continue to be) long-standing divisions of opinion among Jewish leaders and ordinary Jews in the U.S. as to what are Jewish interests, and which social policies, parties, and trends serve and threaten them.

Participants were also concerned with the symbolic responses of movements, traditionally opposed to racism, to antisemitism, or their lack of response. Kriegel (in France) saw the international left (especially the Communists) exploiting the threat of "an antisemitism which is largely mythical" to unite the left, while DiNola (in Italy) remarked on the "emergence of clearly antisemitic trends within the democratic left." Participants in similar discussions have distinguished the spectre of antisemitism amid the non-democratic left from resistance to it among the democratic left.[50] Some feminists have denounced the use and toleration of antisemitism among some in the women's movement, particularly on the international scene.[51] These illustrate the difficulty of generalizing about movements which are broadly-based, non-centralized, with numerous groups, organizations, shifting members and sympathizers, with many expressions.

In the end, most observers agree that insofar as Jewish identity or uniqueness is now based on the common identification of Jews with Israel,

---

damage and symbolic desecration, have often been youth with no antisemitic motive (Herman D. Stein and John M. Martin, "Swastika Offenders: Variation in Etiology, Behavior and Psycho-Social Characteristics," *Social Problems* 10, 1962, pp. 56–70). In one well-publicized spate of incidents in West Hartford, Connecticut in 1983, several acts of arson against Jewish targets were the work of a Jewish teenager. Nevertheless, such a count may be as valid an indicator of a communal climate of hostility as is possible if compiled by the same methods each year, but it can not be reagrded as more than a crude indicator.

[49] See Introduction, Part 2.
[50] Strauss in CCS 1984.
[51] Noonan in CCS 1984; Letty Cottin Pogrebin, "Anti-Semitism in the Women's Movement," *Ms.,* June 1982, pp. 45–72.

negative perceptions of Israel will have a negative impact on Jewish communities in the diaspora regardless of whether one believes anti-Zionism revives or is reinforced by antisemitism or whether anti-Zionism is inherently antisemitism. Collective claims of Jews are also more likely to be viewed by elites and governing circles as against state interests if they imply conflict with allies with whom such elites have common interests. Since groups must draw on power to make claims credible, Jewish claims must invoke some backing – votes, contributions, political exchanges. Such assertions may, in turn, make the stereotypes more salient.

One may also inquire what is the effect of the perception or labeling of action or allegations as antisemitic in social interaction. To this date, it is a label generally rejected by critics of Jews as derogatory.

Just as antisemitism can be a resource enabling antagonists to attract supporters and mobilize against the Jews, labeling critics as antisemitic may sometimes be a resource for Jewish and other leaders. Yet, it is a resource that may create its own backlash, commentators observed, for several reasons: it may tend to legitimate antisemitism as a form of dissent; it may incense critics who feel defamed and increase their hostile affect to Jews, creating a self-fulfilling prophecy; and finally, it may obscure the causes of intergroup conflict, leading both parties to be more intransigent.

This suggests that scholars – also participants in social action and interpretation – have a special responsibility to analyze and label social acts dispassionately, to discriminate the motives, ideology, and organization of antisemitic persons, parties, and movements rather than reifying antisemitism as a monolithic entity.

ERIC J. HOBSBAWM

Are We Entering a New Era of Anti-Semitism?*

In the long history of the Jews, the twelve years of Hitler form a brief and uniquely terrible episode. The scale of this catastrophe, which has probably spared no Jewish family in Europe and the Americas, is impossible to grasp, because the human mind is not so constructed as to form images of numbers above a certain magnitude, though greater ones may be manipulated intellectually. At all events, something like one third of all Jews were quite deliberately and systematically massacred.

This catastrophe has been followed by 35 years of equally unique prosperity and success for this extraordinary people. It was accompanied by, and to some extent made possible by, a striking though not universal recession of anti-semitism.

Is this period now coming to an end?

The remarkable achievements of Jews collectively and individually since 1945 are not confined to the establishment of the state of Israel. Paradoxically, as zionism triumphed, based on the assumption that there could be no satisfactory place for a scattered, persecuted minority in a gentile world, a large part of that world welcomed them on their merits, refusing to discriminate between Jews and non-Jews.

It is difficult to decide which is more significant: the fact that a consciously Jewish presence was welcomed and praised, as in America literature (Bellow, Malamud, Roth, Singer), or the fact that Jewish prominence in various fields of national life was hardly even noticed – except by Jews themselves. By prewar standards, the career of Henry Kissinger in an American Republican administration is as astonishing as the presence of four Jews in the current British Conservative government. The absence of anti-semitic comment about them (except presumably on the usual fascist fringe) is amazing.

---

* From: *New Society*, 11 December 1980, pp. 503–504.

No doubt it is less surprising that Jews florished in branches of activity with which they had long been associated, such as business, entertainment, and the world of the intellect; but the degree to which Jews came to be accepted without trying to assimilate their names or appearance – for instance, as film stars – is new. In short, for more than a generation in most countries containing large numbers of Jews, anti-semitism has ceased to be a serious problem.

Several reasons for this remarkable transformation may be suggested. The first is the recoil effect of the holocaust itself. When anti-semitism became identified with Hitler and massacre, nobody except unregenerated fascists cared to be anti-semitic in public, at least among the generation which had lived through the war. It was simply no longer possible to express a dislike and distrust of, or a contempt for, Jews as freely as English upper middle class people even of relatively liberal views (Virginia Woolf, Harold Nicolson) had habitually done among themselves before the war.

If they were not now ashamed of the feeling, as most of them may well have been, they were ashamed of giving expression to it. The shadow of the gas ovens hung over any criticism by non-Jews of Jews as a people, even of individual Jews, and inhibited it.

The second is, paradoxically, the existence of Israel itself. The very fact that Israel concentrated on demonstrating that Jews were good at the sort of activities previously and typically associated with gentiles – notably soldiering – transformed the gentile attitude towards them, particularly on the political right. (On the left, especially the revolutionary left, it was not news that Jews could demonstrate proficiency in arms and physical heroism.)

It is one of the ironies of history that the Jews won more respect as a small military people than they had as the people of Einstein. History had cast the minorities of the diaspora for the role of potential victims, and they themselves had adapted to it, mostly preferring the low profile, the tactics of evasion, propitiation, and payment for protection, to self-assertion. There could be no more conclusive and brutal self-assertion than for Jewish armies to win several wars rapidly and decisively in a few years. It reflected back on the standing of the diaspora.

Thirdly, new immigrant minorities now became the main targets for racism in a number of countries and thus provided a protective screen for the Jews. There is little doubt that the admirers of Hitler who inspire such movements as the National Front would give anti-semitism as high a priority as ever. But their potential followers in Britain today are primarily mobilisable against blacks, Indians and Pakistanis. Jews moved out of the firing line, if only because prosperity and changes in occupation dispersed the old ghetto quarters of the poor. More exactly, the firing line moved away from them.

Last, but by no means least, a generation of prosperity and economic expansion blunted a good deal of the social and economic resentment which gave anti-semitism its cutting edge. It is fashionable to stress the permanence and the non-economic roots of xenophobia and racism, but economic and social discontent undeniably sharpens the hatred of out-groups, native or foreign, whether considered as competitors, supposed exploiters, parasites or some other form of menace. Conversely, growing comfort makes other people's wealth appear more tolerable, and rivalry is less acute when opportunities for all seem available.

Thus, the influx of Jews into the vast and growing American universities apparently created no significant resentment, while the influx of American academics into the much smaller Canadian academic job market, particularly during the Vietnam war, undoubtedly did. Financial scandals which would have led to political uproar between the wars (with or without the prominence of Jews) hardly caused more than minor ripples in the confident years of the great global boom.

Belloc, Chesterton, Private Eye

Whereas before 1914 in Britain a handful of new Jewish millionaires provided endless material for anti-semitic campaigning by the Bellocs and the Chestertons, the Jews who had risen to wealth in the 1950 and 1960s – some very rapidly indeed – attracted very little attention as such. Only in the middle 1970s can one detect a certain, though generally muted, note of anti-semitism in the press reaction to Harold Wilson's ill-fated final honours list, and in some sniping by *Private Eye.*

In all these unusually tolerant years, significant anti-semitism survived (other than as a carry-over from earlier profascist sentiment, as perhaps in Argentina) mainly in two major regions: under Islam and – unfortunately – in some countries officially committed to an ideology which rejected racism, notably the Soviet Union.

In the Arab world, it is plainly a response to the creation and expansion of Israel. In eastern Europe, the situation is more complex. Several countries in this region had long native traditions of bitter popular anti-semitism, given full scope under the German occupation. And Jews were unusually prominent in the early phases of their communist regimes, thus concentrating against themselves both nationalist and anti-communist sentiment.

As nationalism tended to become the major bond between regimes and their citizens (whether Great Russian or anti-Russian), antisemitism, which was historically linked with it, was also tolerated and sometimes encouraged. Some laudable exceptions should be singled out: Hungary, German Democratic Republic, Yugoslavia, probably Bulgaria.

The existence of Israel complicated the problem further, because it tempted local Jews into a dual loyalty which (given the identification of Israel with the west) might be regarded as dangerous in eastern Europe: and because Israel itself was deeply committed to the mass immigration of Jews into their national state.

Israel failed almost totally to attract western Jews who, content enough where they were, preferred long-distance zionism. After the bulk influx of oriental Jews, east European (mainly Soviet) Jewry remained the only major reservoir for potential immigrants. It was essential for Israel to attract its members.

To this extent, Soviet anti-semitism was both a justification for Israel and a means for increasing its population, while the obvious desire of a lot of Soviet Jews to emigrate (not, as it happens, particularly to Israel) confirmed the authorities in their suspicion and provided an excuse for anti-semitism: let them go to "their own country." Probably east European anti-semitism diminished after the death of Stalin: but there are signs of some not unchallenged revival in the 1970s.

This is all mainly an issue for the Soviet Union which includes two-and-a-half millions Jews. Of the remaining twelve million or so Jews in the world, only some 300,000 live in Islamic or other communist countries. But, still, it is argued by some that anti-semitism is today spreading much more widely in the west – in France, in West Germany, even in America. Is it?

There is no reason to believe that the roots of xenophobia, racism in general, or anti-semitism in particular, have permanently atrophied anywhere. Three of the four reasons for the recession of anti-semitism since 1945 are plainly losing force. For most of the 60 or 70 per cent of Europeans and North Americans who are less than 45 year old, the twelve years of Hitler are ancient history. For Israel, the returns of reminding the world of the Holocaust have diminished sharply. For diaspora Jews, gentile admiration for Israel is also a wasting asset. Their own (often privately reluctant) solidarity with a state led by Menachem Begin hardly wins friends, and the fact that it sometimes influences people is resented.

After the Golden Years

A long period of world depression and social unrest has followed the golden 1950s and 1960s. Economic decline, relative or absolute, haunts states containing vast Jewish communities – the United States and Britain. Social meteorologists might well forecast a climatic deterioration.

Yet we must specify what we are forecasting and what we are afraid of. It will not do to think of anti-semitism in terms of Hitler and a new holocaust. In spite of some incidents of anti-Jewish terrorism and Hitlerite slogans, there is fortunately little sign of a mass revival of neo-fascism. The transformations in social structure have almost certainly deprived antisemitic fascist movements of their traditional mass basis. It is not massacre, or even mass expulsion, which can be reasonably expected.

What is to be expected depends on our assessment of developments in the halfdozen or so countries which (together with Israel and the Soviet Union) now contain the great bulk of the world's Jews: the United States, France, Britain, Argentina, Canada, Brazil and South Africa.

In none of these (except possibly Argentina) is the position of Jews, even after some deterioration, likely to be as unsatisfactory, within the foreseeable future, as that of some other racial and national groups. In the largest of them, the electoral leverage of the Jews provides a powerful counterweight. This does not make the growth of anti-semitism any more tolerable, but it must be said.

What can reasonably be expected is a revival of the public and private suspicion and dislike of Jews, though not so much of contempt for them; and a much greater identification of Jews in the public domain as Jews. Many of the gates so widely opened to them since 1945 may half-close. There may again be some gentlemanly or ungentlemanly discrimination at other than the golf-club level. In the few grey areas, where embittered and resentful people without jobs, prospects or hope – whether white or black – come face to face with Jews, there may be some physical aggression: probably more in North America than in Europe.

We may once again live in conditions familiar to those old enough to have known Europe before 1933, though they will almost cetainly be milder. In the atmosphere of international crisis and fear of nuclear war, the policies of Israel as at present conducted, will not make the lives of Jews in the diaspora easier. Conversely, the association of some non-zionist Jews with the revolutionary left will not endear their people to the forces of law, order and conservatism.

We live in times of insecurity and nerves. We also live in times when civility is on the retreat before barbarism. It is a serious matter for all of us when civilisation, after a generation of partial recovery, looks as though it may again go into reverse in the matter of anti-semitism. It is not surprising that a people with the Jews' historical experience looks at the future with foreboding.

However, anti-semitism must be resisted wherever it occurs. One should not forget that in the coming years Jews will not be the only people to suffer nor, short of a major war, will they probably be the worst sufferers. One should not forget, either, that their numbers even today are smaller than they were 50 years ago.

ERICH GOLDHAGEN

Communism and Anti-Semitism*

"Judaism kills the love for the Soviet Motherland."
Sovetskaia Moldavia, July 23, 1959.

"They do not like collective work, group discipline . . .
They are individualists . . . Jews are interested in everything,
they want to probe into everything, they discuss everything, and end up by having profoundly different opinions."

Khrushchev in an interview with Serge
Goussard, correspondent of *Le Figaro* (Paris),
April 9, 1958.

The existence of anti-Semitism in the USSR, its employment as a tool by
the Communist leadership, and its absorption into the *Weltanschauung* of
the "New Class" should no longer come as a surprise to anyone familiar
with the realities of Soviet life. Yet few are aware of the genealogy of this
unique phenomenon – of its historical roots and ideological evolution. For
it is a fact that anti-Semitism is not alien to the radical tradition – in Western
Europe, and more particularly in Russia. Indeed, the ancestry of Communist anti-Semitism may be traced to the precursors of Leninism and
Stalinism – the revolutionary terrorists, the so-called "Populists," who
dominated the revolutionary scene in Russia in the second half of the 19th
century.

"Lubricant on the Wheel of Revolution"

When socialism as a current of political thought made its appearance in
Western Europe, it tended to look upon the Jews with unfriendly eyes,
regarding them as the embodiment of those qualities of social life which

---

* From: *Problems of Communism* 9/3, 1960, pp. 34–43.

socialists denounced as evil and which they were sworn to undo. Barred from the ownership of land and excluded from the Guilds, the Jews had long ago been driven to devote themselves primarily to the pursuit of commerce; and throughout Western Europe the name Jew came to be almost synonymous with that of trader. The belief was thus born that the pursuit of money was a national vocation of the Jews, enjoined by their religion and practiced with unrivaled skill and zeal. It seemed that the spirit of commerce had found its purest embodiment and its consummate practitioners in the Jews.[1]

The Jews thus incurred the contempt and hatred that socialists harbored against the world of finance. The comprehensive condemnation of commerce and finance as useless and parasitic occupations, as unproductive activities whereby those who shun honest labor could derive undeserved riches from the toil of others was bound to embrace the Jews. This attitude was reinforced by the sinister tales which popular lore came to weave around the name of Rothschild, whose enormous wealth was believed to be a source of evil power – swaying monarchs, making and unmaking governments, and determining the destinies of nations. The vagaries of history, its irrationalities, the injustices and sufferings which it inflicted were traced not to the impersonal forces of economic and social processes but to villains of flesh and blood to whom one could assign guilt and upon whom one could discharge that hatred in which suffering and discontent often seek relief.

It was this outlook which Marx in part echoed in his famous essay *Zur Judenfrage:*

> What is the object of the Jew's worship in this world? Usury. What is his worldly god? Money . . .
>
> Money is the zealous one God of Israel, beside which no other God may stand. Money degrades all the gods of mankind and turns them into commodities. Money is the universal and self-constituted value set upon all things. It has therefore robbed the whole world, of

---

[1] It is interesting to note, in this connection, that all utopian reformers viewed money as a pernicious force serving no purpose save that of breeding injustice and perverting authentic human values, and foresaw its disappearance in the desired society of the future. The citizens of Thomas More's *Utopia*, for instance, "hold gold and silver up to scorn in every way . . . They hang gold rings from the ears of criminals, place gold rings on their fingers, gold collars around their necks, and gold crowns on their heads." T. More, *Utopia*, New York, 1949, p. 44. And Karl Marx, in his *Nationale Ökonomie und Philosophie*, had the following to say about the evil influence of money: "It turns loyalty into disloyalty, love into hate, virtue into vice, vice into virtue, slave into master, master into slave, stupidity into intelligence, intelligence into stupidity." Quoted in Kenneth Muir's "Marx's Conversion to Communism," *The New Reasoner*, London, No. 3, 1957–58, p. 63.

both nature and man, of its original value. Money is the essence of man's life and work, which have become alienated from him. This alien monster rules him and he worships it.[2]

In Russia, too, disdain towards the Jews was the prevalent attitude of the early revolutionaries. The abysmal conditions of the Jews – constrained in their movement, compelled to live only in assigned regions known as the Pale of Settlement, and reduced (save for a tiny minority) to a state of poverty verging on starvation – evoked little sympathy in the breasts of the radical intellectuals of the 1870's and 1880's, however virulent their hatred of the Tsarist autocracy. To be sure, the Jews were wretched and poor, but their wretchedness and poverty was not graced by those lofty virtues which the fertile imagination of the revolutionaries ascribed to the Russian peasantry. Unlike the peasants, who earned their meager subsistence by toil and who were regarded by the intellectuals as noble beings endowed with the qualities of selflessness and instincitve communalism, the Jews were a work-shirking lot, engaging in the "parasitic" and "exploitative" occupations. Even poverty, their only reward, could not redeem them.

But some revolutionaries did not content themselves with passive disdain; they acclaimed and encouraged active violence against the Jews.

In the spring and summer of 1881 a wave of violence swept through the southern part of the Pale of Settlement. Over one hundered Jewish communities were visited by orgies of destruction, claiming, apart from enormous material damage, scores of dead and hundreds of wounded. This outbreak of unprovoked brute force visited upon a defenseless community moved the Executive Committee of the Narodnaya Volya (People's Will) – the largest revolutionary-terroristic organization at that time – to issue a proclamation in Ukrainian on August 30, 1881, blessing the riots and exhorting the peasants to further violence against "the parasitic Jews" and

---

[2] Karl Marx, *A World Without Jews,* New York 1959, p. 41. This is not to say that Marx was anti-Semitic in the accepted sense of the term. Indeed, the main theme and purport of his essay was to expose the hollowness of the civic equality granted by the bourgeois order. As for Marx's linking of Jews and capitalism, the most original and freshest explanation of it, in this author's opinion, was offered by the East German scholar Leo Kofler, in his *Zur Geschichte der Bürgerlichen Gesellschaft* (On the history of the Bourgeois Society) *n. d.,* Halle/Saale, pp. 478–496 – a unique exception to the otherwise dreary gibberish that passes off as "social science" in the Communist bloc. According to Kofler, capitalism found its purest manifestation in the Jewish ethos because unlike Gentile capitalists who, being linked to the native proletariat by ties of common nationhood, have endeavored to disguise and temper their avarice and exploitative ambitions, the Jews knew no such restraint. Strangers to the society in which they have lived, they pursued their vocation with uninhibited ruthlessness and without an embellishing guise. They thus have mirrored capitalism in its stark nakedness.

the "Tsar of the Jews." "The people of the Ukraine," the proclamation stated, "suffer more than anyone else from the Jews ... you have already begun to rise against the Jews ... you have done well."[3]

This proclamation cannot be simply explained, of course, by the anti-Semitic spirit of the radical intelligentsia. No doubt its authors were imbued with anti-Semitic prejudices; yet it would be naive to assume, for instance, that they were in earnest in affixing the label "Tsar of the Jews" on Alexander III: his disdain for the Jews and his oppressive and discriminatory policies against them were certainly known to the leaders of the Narodnaya Volya. Thus there is little doubt that the proclamation was first and foremost a *calculated device*. Underlying it, apart from the Bakuninist conviction that the "passion for destruction is a constructive passion," lay Machiavellian calculation, the wish and the hope that the violence against the Jews would be extended to the autocracy. By linking the Jews with the Tsar, the leaders of the Narodnaya Volya sought to telescope the pogroms into the social revolution, to fan its fire into a conflagration engulfing the authorities. They were consciously lying, but to their minds this was a "noble lie," graced by the lofty purpose it served. The blood of the Jews might have been wholly innocent, but it was nonetheless the "lubricant on the wheels of revolution."

In the society of radical émigrés in Geneva, one by the name of Zhukov-sky defended the pogroms in the following terms:

> Sixty percent of the Jewish population are engaged in commerce. This is the background against which the peasant hunts down the Jew ... To be sure, from a humanitarian standpoint, it is a piece of barbarism when peasants fall like savages upon a frightened Jew and beat him until he bleeds. However, take this event in the context of social dynamics. Why does he beat? Because [beating] is his political ballot. He has no other way of venting his wrath against his exploitation by the government. It is indeed a pity that the peasant beats the Jew – the most innocent of his exploiters. But he beats, and this is the beginning of his struggle for liberation. When ... his fists will have grown strong and hard he will strike those who are above the Jews.[4]

But even those radicals who did not view the pogroms with approval could not bring themselves to call for an end to the bloodshed. Anti-Semitism was endemic to the Russian peasantry. It was its daily psychic bread

---

[3] Quoted in E. Tcherikover, *geshikhte fun der yidisher arbeter bavegung in di fareynikte shtatn* (History of the Jewish Labor Movement in the USA – in Yiddish) New York, 1945, Vol. II, p. 174.

[4] F. Kurski, "di zhenever grupe sotsialistn yidn un ir oyfruf" (The Geneva Group of Jewish Socialists and its proclamation – Yiddish), *Historishe Shriftn*, Vilna/Paris, 1939, Vol. III, p. 561.

designed to still the grievances and frustrations born of hunger – hunger for land and hunger for food. The Russian intelligentsia which had for two decades tried with only limited success to strike roots in the Russian peasantry, to secure its confidence and to persuade it to follow the intellectuals as the champions of its aspirations, feared that by showing concern for the Jews they would unwittingly alienate the peasants. To come out in defense of the Jews would have branded them as "Jewish stooges." Was it worth endangering, for the sake of a small national minority, the cause of socialism? These were the arguments with which radicals who had dissociated themselves from violence justified their refusal to come out publicly against the pogroms. The radical philosopher P. L. Lavrov, who was to describe anti-Semitism as the "most tragic epidemic of our era," declined to print a pamphlet against the pogroms submitted to him by the Social Democratic leader Akselrod:

> I must confess that I regard this question as a very complicated one, indeed an exceedingly difficult one for a party which seeks to come closer to the people. Theoretically, on paper, the question can be easily answered. But in view of the prevailing popular passions and the need of the Russian socialists to have the people on their side whenever possible the question is quite different.[5]

The New Spirit

The succeeding generation of Russian revolutionaries did not share the Populist view that anti-Semitic outrages have a redemptive quality. Manifestations of anti-Semitism were not tolerated in the Marxist-Socialist movement which dominated the Russian revolutionary scene during the next two decades. In his pamphlet *Our Differences* (1884), which set forth the program of the Social Democrats and the reasons for their opposition to the Narodnaya Volya, Plekhanov, the "father of Russian Marxism," condemned the proclamation of 1881 as "a base flattery of the national prejudices of the Russian people."[6] Similarly Lenin, after the notorious Kishinev pogrom in 1903, recalled with shame the "infamous proclamation" and called on all socialists to defend the Jews against the mob as a matter of honor.

Indeed, by the turn of the century both Russian and West European socialists tended to view anti-Semitism in a new light. Hitherto, socialists

---

[5] *Iz Arkhiva* P. G. *Akselroda* (From the P. G. Akselrod archive – in Russian) Berlin, 1924, Vol. II, p. 30.

[6] G. V. Plekhanov, *Izbrannye filosofskie proizvedeniia* (Collected Philosophical Works), Moscow, 1956, Vol. I, p. 217.

had regarded it as a misguided protest against existing social conditions by petty bourgeois and proletarians – "the socialism of fools," in the words of August Bebel. They had hoped that sooner or later those ensnared by it would recognize that not only capitalist Jews were the cause of their misery but Gentile and Jewish capitalists alike; and that this recognition would bring them into the fold of socialism. But when it seemed that instead of being a vestibule of socialism, anti-Semitism had become a useful tool in the hands of the ruling class, the socialist attitude changed. Anti-Semitism came to be treated unequivocally as a hostile ideology. During the two decades before 1917, there were few recorded overt expressions of anti-Jewish bias in the Russian socialist movement. In fact, there is no doubt that by and large the leaders of the Russian socialist parties did not harbor anti-Semitic sentiments. Such sentiments were certainly absent from Lenin, who was a genuine "internationalist," singularly free from national intolerance, and determinedly hostile to any manifestations of xenophobia or "Great Russian chauvinism" on the part of his comrades-in-arms.

Nevertheless, the Russian Social Democrats still shunned prominent association with specifically Jewish causes. To be sure, the central organs of their press denounced anti-Semitism in forceful terms; but they did not carry these denunciations in popular leaflets and pamphlets. For a socialist agitator, working among the grass-roots of the working-class, it was still unwise to appear in the role of an advocate of the Jews.

After the October Revolution the Bolsheviks adopted an uncompromising attitude against anti-Semitism. As the White armies converged to extinguish the infant regime with the battlecry "Beat the Jews and Save Russia," the denunciation of anti-Semitism as counter-revolutionary became not only a duty enjoined by faith but a course dictated by the imperatives of the struggle in which the Bolsheviks were engaged. The weapon had to be wrested from the hands of those seeking to restore the *ancien regime.* Anti-Semitism was outlawed and suppressed; and the Red Army was hailed by the Jews as a protector and liberator from the White troops which were bringing upon them nothing but death and destruction. There was exaggeration but no falsification in the picture of Eastern Europe drawn by the American-Yiddish poet, A. Liesin, who was not a Communist: "While in all the countries surrounding Bolshevik Russia anti-Semitism is fanned with increasingly infernal power ... Bolshevik Russia presents an example of humaneness and justice, the like of which the history of the Jewish Diaspora has never seen before."[7] Anti-Semitism

---

[7] A. Liesin, in *di tsukunft* (Yiddish), January 1920, p. 1.

could not figure in any indictment drawn up against the Soviet dictatorship during the 1920's. But with the advent of the 1930's a new picture began to unfold itself.

Stalinist Nationalism

The revival of Great Russian nationalism under Stalin's dispensation in the early 1930's created a climate less congenial to the Jews than that which had prevailed throughout the preceding decade. With the building of "socialism in one country" proceeding apace, Bolshevik Russia began to shed many of the features which revolutionary enthusiasm and devotion had bestowed upon her. A new spirit pervaded the party, disillusioned by the dearth of revolutionary outbreaks in West Europe to which it had looked forward in the days of Lenin and Trotsky, and deeply immersed in its own "revolution from above." Under these circumstances, the Russian nationalist tradition, renounced and abused by the sweeping wave of revolutionary triumph, gradually reasserted its claims, casting the revolutionary *élan* into more traditional mold. Within these confining walls the cosmopolitan radiance of the revolution grew dimmer and dimmer. The old revolutionary leadership reared in the tradition of Marxist internationalism was replaced by a new generation of bureaucrats imbued with that peculiar mixture of Marxist militancy and Russian chauvinism which henceforth was to mark the ethos of Soviet society.

A chilly wind began to envelop the Jews, especially the Jewish intelligentsia which had been everywhere in the modern world the bearer of cosmopolitanism. In this new climate the dictatorship was less disposed to resist the envious and subdued demands that the high proportion of the Jews in administrative positions and universities be reduced and that the vacancies thus created be filled by native sons. Indeed, the dictatorship viewed such restrictive measures as salutary: they would earn the regime fresh popularity at home, and at the same time blunt the edge of anti-Communist propaganda throughout the world (emanating from the extreme right) that Mother Russia had fallen under the domination of the Judeo-Communist conspiracy. Accordingly, the Soviet government proceeded to reduce sharply the number of Jews in the leading bodies of the party and government, to introduce a *numerus clausus* into some institutions of higher learning, and virtually to exclude Jews from the diplomatic service.[8] To be a Jew again became a source of discomfort and a handicap.

---

[8] Hitler revealed in the course of one of his celebrated table talks that "Stalin made no secret before Ribbentrop that he was waiting only for the moment of maturation of a sufficiently

These measures did not spring from anti-Semitic sentiment in the strict traditional sense of the term, but were motivated by coldly calculated *raison d'état*. They were sometimes accompanied by regrets (privately voiced) about the necessity of sacrificing principles to this greater consideration. *Lex revolutiae suprema est*, Plekhanov had proclaimed in faulty Latin at the Second Congress of the Russian Social Democratic Party (1903), scarcely aware of the horrifying deeds with which that tenet was pregnant. Would a movement which could massacre proletarians in the name of the dictatorship of the proletariat, practice terror in order to achieve social harmony, glory in autocracy in order to establish universal self-government – would such a movement shrink from the appeasement of anti-Semitism if it thought such appeasement would further the "lofty" cause of communism? The head of the Central Committee's department on national minorities met the complaints of a Yiddish writer, Katcherginski, concerning the discrimination against Jews practiced by Soviet authorities in Lithuania, with the explanation that "the Jews of Lithuania may have to be sacrificed to the general cause."[9] The rich and indiscriminate armory of means wherewith bolshevism professed to pursue Utopia acquired a fresh instrument, time-honored and of proven efficacy; and the anti-Semitic spirits, which had been outlawed by bolshevism and driven to lead a repressed existence in the subterranean dwellings of Soviet society, were now emboldened to emerge and engage in their practice in the guise of a Communist *raison d' état*.[10]

---

large indigenous intelligentsia to make short shrift (Schluß zu machen) of Jews as a leadership stratum which he still needs today." *Henry Picker (ed.), Hitlers Tischgespräche im Führerhauptquartier*, Bonn, 1951, p. 119.

[9] Sh. Katcherginsky, *tsvishn hamer un serp* (Between hammer and sickle – Yiddish), Buenos Aires, 1950, p. 96.

[10] Trotsky diagnosed the first stealthy manifestations of official anti-Semitism in Soviet Russia as symptoms of the bureaucratic degeneration afflicting Soviet society. According to him, having usurped the dictatorship of the proletariat and betrayed the spirit of the Marxist-Leninist legacy, the Stalinist bureaucacy was seeking to use the Jews as a scapegoat for its misrule and betrayal. L. Trotsky, "Thermidor and Anti-Semitism," *The New International*, May 1941, pp. 91–94. The article bears the date February 22, 1937. This diagnosis, however, was less applicable for the 1930's than to the period after World War II. Thus in 1956 during the ferment in the Polish Communist Party which brought Gomulka to power, the Stalinist elements, known as the Natolin faction, proposed that the popular hatred besieging the Communist rulers be placated by offering the Jewish party members as a sacrificial lamb. They advocated, in the words of a contemporary revisionist account, that the governmental and party apparatus be reconstructed by applying "the criterion of pure Aryan blood." Ryszard Turski, *Po Prostu*, October 28, 1956. See also Czeslaw Milosz, "Anti-Semitism in Poland," *Problems of Communism*, May-June 1957.

From Intolerance to Repression

In 1948 Soviet policy towards the Jews acquired a fresh and disturbing dimension. If hitherto anti-Semitism had been a tool wielded with dispassion and calculated moderation without deeply engaging the spirit of the Communist leaders, and affecting only those Jews aspiring to careers in certain fields, now it was fed by passion and conviction, and was directed against the entire Jewish community. It was not only anti-Semitism *de logique*, to paraphrase Camus' famous phrase; it was at once logical and passionate.

The affection and enthusiasm displayed by the Jews of Russia for the newly created state of Israel, to whose birth the Soviet Union itself had made a modest contribution, provoked Stalin's suspicion that the Jews were an untrustworthy element whose ties with their numerous brethren abroad made them potential traitors. He proceeded to treat them accordingly. He decided not only to render them harmless by encouraging their removal from jobs as security risks, but also to extinguish their ethnic consciousness. With characteristic totalitarian swiftness all Jewish cultural institutions were abolished and several hundred Yiddish writers were arrested: the more prominent among them were executed after a secret trial (in 1952), while others expired in the penal camps of the arctic wasteland. The entry "Jews" in Soviet Encyclopedia appearing during that period described the Jews as if they were an extinct tribe.[11] Before World War II an elaborate network of cultural institutions had served the Jews of Russia: schools attended by over 100,000 children, a Yiddish press, a large and prolific Yiddish literary community, and a theatre rated among the best in the Soviet Union. By the autumn of 1948 almost nothing was left in existence. By a stroke of the dictator's pen all organized Jewish endeavor came to an abrupt end. Only a score or so of defunct synagogues survived. These and the withered label of Birobidzhan still incongruously attached to that region on the Amur, which had never acquired a Jewish character and in which the Jews formed a hopeless minority, were the only visible signs of a community of two and a half million.[12]

From 1948 until the death of Stalin Soviet Jews lived under a reign of terror amid rumors of their imminent mass deportation.[13]

---

[11] *Bolshaia Sovetskaia Entsiklopedia*, 2nd ed., Vol. 15, Moscow, 1952, pp. 377–79.

[12] Birobidzhan, an area in eastern Siberia, was set up in the late 1920's as a "Jewish autonomous region," but due to its geographic location and severe climatic conditions it never attracted many Jews, whose roots were in the Ukraine and Belorussia primarily.

[13] See Communist weekly *World News*, Jan. 12, 1957.

Rehabilitation with a Difference

The death of Stalin and the acquittal of the doctors involved in the "Doctors' Plot," as well as *Pravda's* (April 6, 1953) admission that the affair of the doctors was a "fabrication" intended to "inflame nationalist hostilities among the Soviet peoples," removed the nightmare which had hovered over the Jewish community. The terror relented. But the fundamentals of Stalin's policies towards the Jews were retained. As in many other spheres of Communist endeavor the Stalinist aims were preserved, only the methods were changed. The carrot gained ascendancy over the stick, the peaceful incentive over terror, the indirect approach over the direct brutal assault.

Stalin's heirs, in the process of their cautious detachment from the most severe features of Stalin's legacy, set out to right the wrongs inflicted on some nationalities. It will be recalled that seven other ethnic groups had fallen victim to Stalin's suspicion and vindictiveness: the Ingush, the Chechens, the Volga Germans, the Crimea Tatars, the Kalmyks, the Karachai and the Balkars. All of them were uprooted at various times during World War II and banished in their entirety, including members of the party and the Komsomol, to remote places. While the expulsion of the Volga Germans was justified by the authorities as a security measure – and it was perhaps a more rational measure than the removal of the Japanese-Americans from the Pacific coast during World War II – the deportation of the other national groups was undertaken on the principle of collective guilt. The sins of the few were visited upon the entire community. The preamble to the official decree published in *Izvestia,* June 26, 1946, announcing, two years after the expulsion, the dissolution of the Chechen-Ingush and the Crimean Tatar autonomous republics, stated that collective punishment had been meted out for the failure of the peoples to combat those in their midst who were collaborating with the German enemy. It was this tribal notion of justice which Khrushchev included in his indictment of Stalin at the 20th Party Congress:

> Not only a Marxist-Leninist but also no man of common sense can grasp how it is possible to make whole nations responsible for inimical activity, including women, children, old people, Communists and Komsomols, to use mass repression against them, and to expose them to misery and suffering for the hostile acts of individual persons or groups of persons.[14]

---

[14] See Khrushchev's "secret speech" in *The Anti-Stalin Campaign and International Communism*, New York, 1956, pp. 57–58.

The repressed nationalities have since been restored to their public identity and some have even been permitted to return to their native lands. They ceased to be Orwellian "un-peoples." Their names reappeared on maps and in reference works. Even the Volga Germans have been provided with schools and newspapers.[15]

This wholesale rehabilitation has not embraced the Jews. To be sure the Jews had not been deported – although Soviet Jews are convinced that only Stalin's death saved them from that fate.[16] But condemned to the status of an "un-people," they had been marked out for cultural extinction and their institutions had been destroyed. However, it would seem that in Khrushchev's view this particular action of Stalin did not fall into the category of "monstrous acts" and "rude violations of the basic Leninist principles of the nationality policy of the Soviet state;"[17] it was a deed of prudent statesmanship. In the course of an interview with a Canadian Communist delegation, Khrushchev, in one of the unguarded moments of candor to which he is so often given, showed himself to share Stalin's view of the Jews as inherent security risks. "Khrushchev," relates the Canadian Communist, Salsberg, "agreed with Stalin that the Crimea, which had been depopulated at the war's end, should not be turned into a Jewish colonization center, because in case of war it would be turned into a base for attacking the USSR . . ."[18]

Surely, a people harboring such a ready propensity to treason could not be allowed to possess cultural institutions fostering and perpetuating that tendency.

The treatment of the Jews by the Soviet dictatorship is without a full parallel among its policies toward the other national minorities. A unique people, the Jews have drawn themselves singular treatment. As Stalinism departed from the ideals of internationalism and cosmopolitanism which had inspired the Bolshevik Revolution, it cynically resorted to anti-Semitism as a tool of its designs, harkening back to the tradition of the Narodnaya Volya, in many ways its spiritual ancestor. The xenophobia born of its totalitarian isolation – a xenophobia incongruously linked to its international aspirations and professions – exposed the Jews to grave suspicion. They were members of a worldwide fraternity, the greater part

---

[15] For an account of the rehabilitation, see Walter Kolarz, "Die Rehabilitierung der liquidierten Sowjetvölker," (The rehabilitation of Soviet nationalities), *Ost Europa*, June 1957, pp. 414–20.
[16] See *World News, op. cit.*
[17] Khrushchev, *op. cit.*, p. 57.
[18] Quoted in *The New Leader*, Sept. 14, 1959, p. 9.

of which lived in the camp of "imperialism," and the creation of the state of Israel intensified that suspicion. Alone among all the national minorities the Jews have been condemned to total assimilation. The Jews are indeed a "chosen people" in Russia – chosen for cultural extinction.

R. NUDELMAN

Contemporary Soviet Anti-Semitism: Forms and Content[*]

In recent years Soviet anti-Semitism has increased dramatically. Its most important feature at the present is that it has turned into a phenomenon of international dimensions, and has become a threat to the *existence of the Jewish people.* The other special feature is that internationally, *Soviet imperialism, Arab and Afro-Asian nationalism, and left-wing anti-Zionism,* combine with Soviet anti-Semitism to provide the *ideological base* for an all-out attack against Zionism, the State of Israel, and Jews in general.

In the first decades after the establishment of the Soviet rule, official anti-Semitism was unknown in the USSR and manifestations of popular anti-Semitism were severely suppressed. This situation had two causes. First, since communist ideology was internationalist at the time, it did not include any specific anti-Jewish elements. The official policy line of the regime in relation to Jews was that of *voluntary assimilation,* proclaimed in Lenin's works. Second, these decades saw the formation of a close alliance between the Soviet regime and the Jewish working masses freed from the Pale of Settlement. A disproportionately high number of Jews took part in the revolution, occupied appropriate positions in the Soviet state and party machine and, more importantly replaced the old intelligentsia which was recruited from the gentry and non-gentry *(raznochintsy)* of Russian society, which was thrown out of the country by the revolution. One may speak of a new "Russian-Jewish" intelligentsia which was formed during these decades and until recently played a leading role in Soviet life.

The revival of anti-Semitism took place during World War II. It proceeded simultaneously from the top and from the bottom. The Communist Party which, during the war years, had no choice but to rely on patriotic-national feelings for support, aimed at transforming the country into a nationalist-imperialist state. This necessitated displacing Jewish ele-

* Edited and abridged from: *Anti-Semitism in the Soviet Union: Its Roots and Consequences,* Vol. I (Jerusalem: The Hebrew University Centre for Research and Documentation of East European Jewry 1979).

ments from the leadership of industry, technology, science and, above all, of ideological and cultural areas. The new course found support in popular anti-Semitism which was revived during the war under the influence of German propaganda. The 1948–53 period was marked by an all-out offensive against Soviet Jews under the guise of the anti-cosmopolitan campaign culminating in the *Doctors' Plot.*

During these years Soviet anti-Semitism still had a purely internal character, and was directed against Soviet Jews. Attempts to link the *cosmopolitan* and *murderer doctors* with *world Zionism* had a strictly propaganda purpose and were intended primarily for internal consumption. Internationally the Soviet Union supported the State of Israel because of foreign policy considerations. Even the typical communist hostility to Zionism as a non-class-conscious bourgeois movement, was toned down.

Without attempting to delve into the reasons for subsequent changes in Soviet external and internal policies, it will be sufficient to name them:

– Changing international situation, the consolidation of the Soviet bloc, the break with China, the search for new partners in an anti-American and anti-Chinese coalition, an alliance with new African, Asian, and Arab political forces.
– Changed political situation in the Soviet bloc including disturbances in Hungary, East Germany, Poland, and Czechoslovakia, the growth of nationalist movements in Soviet borderland regions, the emergence of the dissident movement, the growth of Israel's prestige after the Six Day War, and the birth of the mass movement for aliya.

All of these factors contributed to the development of those internal processes which could already be detected in the USSR in the postwar years. At present the Soviet regime is quickly divesting itself of the remnants of Marxist and internationalist ideology. It is turning increasingly into a genuine nationalist-imperialist, Russian great-power regime whose totalitarian character is consistent with Russian historical tradition. This is suitable for accomplishing internal social and cultural tasks set by ideology and for rallying around Russia similar genuinely nationalist-totalitarian regimes. The process is twofold: the USSR is the world's largest supplier of armaments and of a new model of society for developing nations. These countries, in turn, tend to accelerate internal changes in the USSR.

Viewed against this historical background, the escalation of Soviet anti-Semitism should be interpreted as anything but accidental or temporary. It could easily be demonstrated that each stage in the expansion of this process war accompanied by respective changes in the character of Soviet

anti-Semitic propaganda and practice. Moreover, by observing the escalation of anti-Semitism, one could follow the various changes in the nature
and policies of the Soviet regime. Anti-Semitism thus appears as a vital
constituent of the historical process, an important organic part of Soviet
ideology which is constantly evolving in accordance with the requirements
of the internal and external political development of the USSR and of the
communist regime. Several such requirements are:

– To replace the former "Russian-Jewish" intelligentsia by a new national
intelligentsia which will become a mainstay of the nationalist-imperialist
regime in its fight with dissidents and national movements in the Soviet
empire's outlying regions.
– To fortify the position of the Soviet regime in the Eastern European bloc
in order to suppress national-dissident movements in socialist countries,
and to consolidate them into an effective military force.
– To undermine the positions of independents, such as dissidents, intellectuals, and nationally-oriented elements in other communist parties in
order to turn them into a reliable force in the struggle for hegemony in
Europe.
– To win over anti-Western national-totalitarian Afro-Asian regimes in
order to create a unified camp in the struggle against the United States and
China.

The first of the above requirements dictates a massive and final onslaught
on Jewry inside the USSR. The second adds to it the task of weeding out
Jewish-dissident elements within satellite countries. The third demands
that the anti-Jewish crusade be combined with anti-Bourgeois propaganda,
so attractive to the rank and file in Western parties, to Western youth and to
leftist intellectuals. This might be stated in reverse: To give anti-bourgeois
propaganda a clearly anti-Jewish, concrete character. The fourth require-
ment adds Zionism to this ideological complex as the banner under which
it is particularly easy to rally Afro-Asian anti-colonial regimes.

Consequently, Soviet anti-Semitism inevitably assumes a total ideological, political, and practical character within the USSR and of necessity
extends beyond its border, thus becoming an important part of Soviet
international politics.

As pointed out by M. Domalskii,[1] one of the investigators of Soviet
neo-anti-Semitism, contemporary anti-Semitism is still secret, that is, it

---

[1] M. Domalskii "Psikhologiia nenavisti" ("The Psychology of Hatred"), *Vremia i my* journal,
No. 25–26, 1978.

resorts to various kinds of camouflage, of which anti-Zionism is the most common. This is both true and untrue. It is true that Soviet propaganda goes out of its way to refrain from any wholesale accusations against all Jews in official statements. But on the level which escapes the notice of the Western public such as lectures on current events, administrative activity, and belles lettres, this limitation is increasingly removed. The contention that anti-Zionism is no more than a camouflage for Soviet anti-Semitism is not true. As has been indicated, it plays an integral role mainly in international policy. It is in tune with general communist ideology and finds a response and support in different circles of Western leftists and Eastern nationalists. The mainstay of internal anti-Semitism is formed by the nationalist new intelligentsia and the mass worker and administrative plebes in the USSR, and in satellite countries. Generally, one may note the formation of a broad alignment of various forces offering suitable ground for Soviet anti-Semitic propaganda. With every year of its escalation, the effect of this propaganda becomes more and more irreversible, resulting in *irreversible changes* both within and outside the Soviet bloc.

The main danger of modern Soviet anti-Semitism lies in the fact that, in contradistinction to the anticosmopolitan campaign of 1948–53, for example, it is now directed not so much against individual Jewish groups, but against *the Jewish people as a whole.* Secondly, the brunt of the attack is not directed against some specific aspect of Jewish existence, but rather against *the Jewish people.* Third, this attack is ideologically substantiated by introducing an outline, mendacious in essence and fascist and racist in character, of Jewish history and religion which repeats the most atrocious fabrications ever concocted by anti-Semites of all time – from Roman historians and early Christian apologists to the authors of the *Protocols of the Elders of Zion, Der Stürmer,* and the agitators of the Russian *Alliance of Michael the Archangel.* Soviet anti-Semitism is meticulously collecting in its arsenal all so-called doctrines and theories produced by anti-Semitism during the whole of its history: religious, historical, social, cultural, psychological, mystical, and irrational. It consolidates these elements into some new all-embracing ideology to suit modern conditions, and in this way becomes the chief originator of a new global model of anti-Semitism and subsequently its main supplier as well as organizer and initiator of a world anti-Jewish front.

Soviet anti-Semitism began to acquire its present character immediately after the Six Day War, the period marked by the growth of dissident and national movements in the Soviet bloc. In 1968 Soviet bloc propaganda for the first time openly declared that Jews were the main source of every dissidence as such. It was crystallized by the Polish party theoretician Andrzej Werblan in one of his articles which said that all Jews without exception were "particularly inclined to revisionism, Jewish nationalism and Zionism," and that for this reason wherever "there is a large concentration of Jews . . ." a bad political atmosphere is created.[2] In 1971 a Soviet author, V. Bolishukhin, wrote in *Pravda* that every person who becomes a Zionist automatically becomes an enemy of the Soviet people. *Enemy of the people* is the same official term that was the watchword during all of Stalin's mass reprisals of the 1930s. Finally, soon afterwards, G. Artatov, an adviser of the Kremlin politburo, said that 90 percent of Soviet Jews who remain in the USSR "appear in an unfavorable light," meaning they are suspicious elements.

The logic behind these statements is obvious. All Jews by their nature are inclined to become Zionists. All Zionists automatically become "enemies of the people." It could be added that internal Soviet propaganda in the form of public lectures concealed from outsiders claims that Jews may become Zionists "without being conscious of it." Soviet Jews leaving for Israel are thus open Zionists while those remaining – at least 90% according to Arbatov – are hidden Zionists, and therefore enemies of the people.

This new global doctrine of indiscriminate distrust toward Jews has become a theoretical basis for the systematic displacement of Soviet Jews from all spheres of social, industrial, and cultural life in the USSR – a process which has intensified and reached global proportions in recent years. The facts about this discrimination are widely known: *numerus clausus* for Jews who wish to enter institutions of higher learning or who seek employment, limitations in social activities, in the sciences, in international contacts, and simply in trips abroad. Other examples include the ruthless persecution of the Jewish religion and culture as well as suppression of every attempt at Jewish self-expression, such as the trials of Hebrew teachers I. Begun and P. Abramovich, the closing of the Moscow symposium on Jewish culture, and extra legal persecution of the Jewish Samizdat journal *The Jews in the USSR*. It should be noted that although national discrimination in the USSR is also being intensified toward other nations and ethnic groups – dictated by the Soviet leadership's fear of the growing nationalism in outlying regions – only the discrimination against Jews has such a total character and only this discrimination tends to turn into undisguised spiritual and cultural genocide, since the special position of Soviet Jewry, including the lack of territory, national institutions, and

---

[2] According to Polish dissidents, Werblan's article was Moscow-inspired.

national representation, makes it defenseless in the face of total displacement from Soviet life. The situation of Soviet Jewish youth appears particularly dangerous in this regard.

This discrimination has received further theoretical validation in the writings of the Soviet sociologist Mishin[3], who has proclaimed that at the present stage of development of Soviet society, it has become possible to realize the Marxist principle of "equal conditions for all nations," and this, he argues, must be preceded by a preliminary "equalization of the level of development of all peoples in the USSR." This artificial equalization in the case of the Jews is, of course, tantamount to artificial inhibition and limitation of their social and cultural development.

Meanwhile, Soviet authorities prevent the Jews of the USSR from finding a way out of the present situation either through assimilation or emigration.

Assimilation of the Jews in the USSR, which seemed, at least formally, possible during the first decades of Soviet rule, is absolutely impossible at present, since both the population and administration have, for many decades to come, been deeply infected with morbid anti-Semitic alertness, suspiciousness, and readiness to expose Jews. It would be naive to think that the results of such education, which has already been inculcated in the second generation, could be eliminated by decree. Further, anti-Semitic social attitudes, while forcing Jews to disguise themselves and their children still more thoroughly, are meanwhile continually intensifying their own national awareness. Whereas during the first decades of Soviet rule the dominant desire was for total assimilation, today the desire for "outward mimicry" prevails among assimilationists.

Those Jews who decide upon the other alternative – aliya – find themselves confronted with a system of obstacles consisting of direct refusals calculated to intimidate them. They also face an intensive propaganda campaign aimed at discrediting Israel and exaggerating out of all proportion those real and imaginary problems encountered by new olim in Israel. The scope of this campaign defies all description. According to Domalskii's[4] estimates, during certain days or weeks, the total volume of this kind of misinformation about Israel in Soviet media exceeds the aggregate of all other items of world news. The Soviet propaganda apparatus daily fabricates lies about the Jewish state and the Jewish nation, including

---

[3] V. Mishin. "Sotsial 'nyi progress" (Social progress), Moscow, 1970.

[4] M. Domal'skii. *Novoe v antisemitisme* (New trends in anti-Semitism). (Jewish Samizdat materials in publications of the Centre for the Documentation of East-European Jewry).

descriptions of torture in Israeli jails and reports about whole families in Israel using a single towel and obtaining water upon presenting a ration card. Regrettably, the absurdity of such falsehoods often prevents us from realizing the full extent of their influence on the Jewish population of the USSR, which is assaulted this way daily. Recent repatriates testify that such fabrications are widely believed in the Soviet Union. The systematic campaign of lies has succeeded in sowing seeds of doubt in the minds of many Soviet Jews with regard to foreign and Israeli press reports about Israel and Israeli life. Soviet Jews sometimes form unbelievably distorted and absurd ideas about the Israeli way of life. Finally, one should not disregard another result of this systematic brainwashing: the breeding of anti-Semitism among Jews themselves. The absence of national traditions and culture, a distorted image of Israel as a militarized, clerical- and poverty-ridden country, and unconscious Jewish anti-Semitism, are the elements of this mentality which to a large extent determine the growth of *neshira*.[5]

On the whole, Soviet propaganda continually depicts a Jew, who above all wants to flee once and for all from his Jewishness, a Jew who does not believe in the possibility of a normal Jewish existence. The condition of Soviet Jewry, living under an enormous and increasing double pressure, is becoming objectively tragic and historically dangerous.

The main thrust of Soviet propaganda, however, is directed not so much at Soviet Jews as at the indigenous population of the USSR, the satellite countries, the leftist Western public and the semiliterate Afro-Asian masses. Naturally, the scope and character of this propaganda should be evaluated, first and foremost, on the basis of that portion which is intended for internal consumption, since it is here that the government gives the finishing touches to the principal new elements of Soviet anti-Semitism before including it in the international version. There are, in fact, several international versions, varieties of Soviet international anti-Semitism which are meant for, let us say, leftist intellectuals, or for Afro-Asian states, or as ideological weapons for terrorist and extremist groups in different countries.

Modern Soviet anti-Semitism uses all means of mass brainwashing and is directed at all strata of the Soviet population. In each sector and in each direction it displays the aforementioned traits, including attempts to discredit the Jewish people by spreading lies about Jewish history, religion,

---

[5] Neshira (Hebrew for *dropout*). Emigrants from the Soviet Union, who, despite possibilities of going to Israel, opt to go to other countries.

culture, the national movement, the character and specific features of the Jewish people, and their role in world history, and modern times.

Cinema and television. Mass circulation in the USSR of anti-Semitic books, articles, and brochures (by Kichko, Evseev, Ivanov and others) is now widely acknowledged. The use of mass media such as cinema and television for the same purposes is relatively new. On January 22, 1977 Soviet television showed a one-hour documentary, "Traders in Souls." The program featured caricatures of Jews and Israelis portrayed in the spirit of Nazi newspapers and journals. A disgusting man with the traditional anti-Semitic Jewish look is shown giving five pound notes to English people protesting the persecution of Soviet Jews. An American tourist interrogated by the KGB confesses to having tried to smuggle forbidden literature into the Soviet Union "on the instructions of Zionist organizations which might be connected with the CIA." Scenes showing aliya activists embracing Israeli athletes beg the question: "How has it become possible that Zionist agents have appeared in our country?" Shown on the screen were photos of activists supplemented by their addresses and the following comment: "These people are Zionism's agents within our country and conduct their subversive activities here."

This film has been shown twice. Another film, "The Overt and the Covert," with a still more openly pogromist character, was not shown to mass audiences[6] but according to available information, was screened in a narrow circle which included groups of Soviet officers. This film begins with a revolver shot and the voice of the announcer saying: "That was how the Jewess Kaplan attempted to murder Vladimir Il'ich Lenin." This is followed by appropriately selected episodes from Soviet History. When German tanks are shown entering a Soviet city, the announcer says, "Hitler was brought to power by Jewish capital."

Anti-Semitic indoctrination in the army. A new, alarming feature of modern Soviet anti-Semitism is intensified ideological indoctrination in the army. The previously mentioned film shown in officers' clubs may be included among the evidence of such activities. The same contingent – officers and propagandists on the army staff – is catered to by anti-Semitic articles by a certain Lev Korneyev, a "specialist on the Jewish question." His articles appear regularly in the principal military newspaper *Krasnaia Zvezda* and the main political organ of the Soviet armed forces *Kommunist vooruzhennykh sil.* Both publications are obligatory for all army libraries,

---

[6] According to other data the film was screened in large movie theatres of a number of cities, e.g. in Odessa.

and compulsory reading for all officers and propagandists. During last year alone Korneyev published more than 10 articles under such characteristic titles as "Nazism from Tel Aviv," "Zionism's Mercenaries," "Israel's Army – An Instrument of Aggression," "Raiders and Bandits," "Terror – the Weapon of Zionism," "The Espionage, Tentacles of Zionism,"[7] "Zionism's Secret War," and "The Poisonous Weapon of Zionism."[8] Korneyev claims that Zionists are at the head of the American Mafia and that the Mafia chief Meyer Lansky received Golda Meir's personal invitation to settle in Israel. Quoting the Arab press, Korneyev further claims that the Israeli army recruits disguised criminals after they have changed their appearance, and that strikes in Israel are suppressed by some "Civil Guard Corps" numbering 50,000 men. He also reports that Zionists are in control of 158 out of 163 of the world's largest arms factories.[9]

Lecture propaganda. One of the distinctive features of the Soviet propaganda system is the daily delivery of lectures and reports in thousands of schools, institutes, offices, and industrial plants. These lectures are usually the main source of additional information for the listeners, and a main source of information on new party directives and trends. The scope of this branch of Soviet propaganda is not secondary to that of newspapers, radio and television. But it differs from the mass media in that it is concealed from outsiders, and the lecturers, therefore, feel at liberty to go further in expounding anti-Zionist views and "theories."

One such lecture delivered by Moscow party committee representative V. Eemel'ianov, which arrived through Samizdat channels, may serve as an example of this propaganda. The lecture is entitled "Judaism and Zionism:"[10] "Of all Semitic peoples the Jews are the youngest. The Bedouins, i.e., Arabs are the most ancient. The principle of Judaism has been formulated in the Torah. The Torah is the blackest book in mankind's entire history. Its main theses are that the Jews are a chosen people and should seize the territories of others. Joshua is like Genghis Khan. Jerusalem is translated as "the city of peace," but in reality it is a den of thieves and criminals. The Jews have contributed nothing original, they have proclaimed the racist principle: Jews must not work, work is for the Goyim. That was the origin of the division of humankind into humans

---

[7] *Krasnaia Zvezda* of 1977; *Kommunist vooruzhennykh sil* No. 24, Dec. 1977.

[8] L. Korneyev, "Tainaia voina sionizma."

[9] *Nedelia* November 21-27, 1977 "Vozhdi-gangstery" (Gangster Leaders); *Moskovskaia pravda* of 16, February 1977.

[10] *Evreiskii Samizdat*. Vol. 10, 1976 (reprint of *Evrei v SSSR* No. 8, 1974), published by the Centre for the Documentation of East-European Jewry at the Hebrew University.

proper – the Jews, and two-legged cattle – the Goyim. All nations must become the Jews' slaves. The Zionists have planned to achieve world domination by the year 2000. But they lack cadres. And then appears freemasonry, Judaism's fifth column. The aim of freemasonry is to shatter the Goyim's regimes. The converted Jew Loyola, under the pretext of fighting freemasonry, organized the Jesuit Order which created the Inquisition. The best Goyish minds were burnt at the stake by the Inquisition. The zionists are supported by the Judeo-Masonic pyramid, by the economies of 80 percent of the capitalist countries, and by 90–96 percent of the information media, which dupe the people. There will be a struggle, but we shall be victorious. But victory requires sacrifices. This does not mean that we must distrust all Jews, but we must take into account the fact that 40,000 leave annually for a state which is not just capitalist, but fascist."

Scholarly guidance for lecture propaganda of this kind in the USSR is provided by a special Commission for the Struggle Against Zionism attached to the Presidium of the Academy of Sciences of the USSR.

In February 1976 this commission held its regular session at which urgent problems of the ideological struggle against Zionism were discussed. The materials of this discussion became available to one of the Jewish activists and were published under the pseudonym of Sol'mar in Moscow in the Samizdat journal *Evrei v SSSR* and in Israel in the *Sion* journal. They show that timid attempts on the part of moderate scholars to give Soviet anti-Semitic propaganda at least a semblance of scientific character met with a fierce counterattack by the commission's leadership. The session vindicated the writings of the rabid anti-Semite V. Begun. It was declared that Begun's activities had the full approval of the Kiev city committee of the CPSU, that the "Znanie" (Knowledge) society had awarded him an honorary diploma for his book *Creeping Counter-revolution*, and that books and speeches of V. Evseev were fully approved of by the administration of the Institute of Philosophy of the Soviet Academy of Sciences.[11]

Fiction. Works of fiction are used to teach the masses the false image of the Jew constructed by Soviet propaganda: the image of a Zionist, a spy, a money-grubber, and the enemy of the people and humanity. In a novel by Ukrainian writer I. Vil'de, *The Sisters Richinskii,* a Jew is represented as a lascivious sadist and a greedy usurer. In the novels of the well-known writer Tevekelian *Granite Does Not Melt* and *Beyond the Moskva River,* Jews are depicted as avaricious underground financiers, money-changers, and crooks. But in the novels of the vicious anti-Semite I. Shevtsov *In the*

---

[11] *Sion* 21, 1977.

Name of the Father and the Son and *Love and Hatred,* Jews are painted in the most apocalyptic colors of all. The main character of the second book, a Jewish journalist named Naum Holtser, murders his mother, rips open her belly, wraps the corpse in the intestines and covers it with bank books. He seduces Russian girls and, for fear of being exposed, kills them, and rapes their dead bodies. In Shevtsov's novels, Jewish writers own luxury dachas and cars, possess untold wealth, and innumerable mistresses. They are connected with foreign intelligence services and spread Zionist literature in the USSR. Jewish scientists are spies who sell Soviet atomic secrets to American intelligence agents and kill a young Russian scientist for having "exposed" the relativity theory of the Jew Einstein.

This kind of literature is supplied to the wide reading public in a systematic manner, in amounts typical of a state-sponsored activity. Vil'de's novel was quickly translated into Russian, while the novels by Shevtsov, which were sharply criticized by some readers, were nevertheless reprinted – the second and the third printings amounting to 200,000 copies each – by the central publishing houses "Moskovskii rabochii" and "Voenizdat."

Quite recently, Soviet anti-Semitic literature has been reinforced by the publication of Ts. Solodar's *Wild Wormwood* in such journals as *Ogonek* and *Krokodil,* with circulations of five and eight million respectively. Solodar's book is sufficiently well characterized by the author's statement, "The similarity between Zionism and Nazism has finally been proven by the inhuman practices of the State of Israel . . . These facts make one reflect more and more on the deep spritual affinity between the followers of Adolf Hitler and those of Theodore Herzl."[12]

Scientific criticism of Zionism and Judaism. Anti-religious propaganda is a permanent element of Soviet life. Recently, however, that portion of this propaganda which is devoted to the "criticism of the Judaic religion," has assumed a plainly anti-Semitic character. Articles and brochures of such authors as Belen'kii, Skurlatov, Epshtein, and others systematically distort the true character and meaning of the Jewish religion and its basic texts. An article by Epshtein, a lecturer at the Kharkov Aviation Institute with a Master's degree in history, appears in Our Reply to Slanderers,[13] a collection published in Kharkov in 1976, and serves as an example. In this article, "When Zionists Are in Power," each page is divided into two parts, one of which contains quotations dredged up from Jewish and Zionist

---

[12] "Sionizm bez maski" (review of Ts. Solodar's book in the journal *Ogonek* of March 12, 1977 Moscow).
[13] *Nash otvet Klevetnikam,* Prapor, Kharkov, 1976.

literature, intending to prove the Jew's alleged claim to superiority and their racial conceit. These sayings are juxtaposed with quotes from Hitler.

Soviet propaganda widely uses scholars not only in the struggle against Judaism but also in their anti-Zionist attacks. The collection *Zionism: Its Theory and Practice,* produced by the Academy of Sciences[14] is a fundamental "theoretical" work aimed at providing a basis for the mendacious fabrications of Soviet anti-Semitic propaganda.

Although papers on "the criticism of Zionism" were not previously accepted at Soviet institutes as suitable thesis topics for degree candidates, characteristic changes recently occurred in this sphere also. On December 28, 1977 the Academy of Social Sciences attached to the Central Committee of the CPSU confirmed Nikitina's doctoral thesis written as a book, *The State of Israel.* Some speakers who spoke during the defense proceedings openly called Nikitina's book "a specimen of anti-Semitism," but were denounced by the majority of others as "dyed-in-the-wool Zionists" and "anti-Soviets," and the dissertation was confirmed by a majority of votes.[15]

It should be added in conclusion that the latest inventions of Soviet anti-Semitic propaganda are regularly transmitted abroad in a great number of broadcasts by the Soviet, German, and Arabic radio, or through publications for the foreign listener and reader and by other means.[16] Meanwhile, the Soviet press makes wide use of fabrications produced by Arab propaganda. This coordinated effort is exemplified by a book written by someone named Jahiya and published in Beirut and Damascus under the title *Zionism's Ties with Nazism.* Reports about this book have already appeared in many Soviet newspapers. The work is a rehash of Soviet anti-Semitic propaganda's fabrications, but at this point the Soviets are using it as "independent evidence of authenticity" of their own concoctions.

As is known, the Soviet Union has succeeded, by using its voting strength in the UN, in having the organization adopt the scandalous resolution equating Zionism with racism. Since then, this formula has

---

[14] *Sionism – teoriia i praktika,* Academy of Sciences of the USSR, Moscow, 1973.

[15] S. Lukin, "Novyi povorot staroi temy" (A new twist of an old theme) (Materials of the Jewish Samizdat at the disposal of the Centre for the Documentation of East-European Jewry).

[16] A T report for foreign countries in English of February 1, 1978. See also in *Ogonek,* No. 2 of January 1, 1978, a report on the translation into Arabic of Ts. Solodar's book *Byvshie (Anachronistic People),* which has been published by the PLO's United Information Centre.

become a conventional cliche of all Soviet anti-Semitic propaganda. At present this propaganda is intensively developing a new thesis, which is gradually coming into use as its regular tool: *Zionism is the fascism of today.*

Here are a few recent examples. *Korneyev:* The Jewish population of Palestine was, as far back as the 1930s, infected with the fascist virus; the similarity between Zionist and fascist doctrines led to their lengthy, cooperation from 1933 to 1945; "Zionism borrowed Hitler's methods of mass extermination of civilian population;" Weizman was making arrangements with Mussolini for the use of Jewish troops in the conquest of Africa in exchange for a promise that Hitler would help the Zionists to "rob the German Jews and bring them to Palestine by force;" the pogroms during Kristallnacht had been "agreed upon with Tsvi Grinberg, an agent of the Zionist secret service;" the World Zionist Organization and the Jewish Agency intentionally kept silent about the German's extermination of European Jewry, "because the Zionists helped the Nazis to murder Jews – women, children and old people."[17] Weizman was the chief Zionist murderer, having said, according to Korneyev "let the Germans burn and kill unnecessary Jews, we shall bring only the rich and young ones" to Palestine. *V. Begun:* "Collusion between the Nazis and the Hungarian Zionist leader Kastner, who helped the Nazis to send thousands of Jews to gas chambers, is not common knowledge. In Czechoslovakia, Kastner's role was played by Mandler. This highly placed official of the Zionist Centre for Jewish Resettlement helped the fascists to fill German camps with Jews."[18] *Brodskii and Shulmaister,* the authors of the Book *Zionism: a Tool of Reaction:* In Lvov's archives new documents have been found corroborating the fact of fascist-Zionist cooperation in mass executions of Jews in the Ukraine in 1941; "In the Warsaw ghetto cooperation between the fascists and Jews had reached such proportions, and the number of Jews who were secret agents of the Gestapo was so great that the Poles had to execute a few Jewish Gestapo men;" "the insurgents of the Warsaw ghetto were fighters against the fascist occupiers and the Zionist lackeys".[19] *Epshtein* in the *Our Reply to Slanderers* collection: "Numerous facts have clearly and convincingly corroborated the fascist character of the ideology

---

[17] L. Korneev. "Mrachnye tainy sionisma" (The Dismal Secrets of Zionism), in: *Ogonek,* Aug. 1977.

[18] V. Begun. *Vtorzhenie bez oruzhiia* Moscow, 1976; *Polzuchaia kontrarevoliutsiia* (Creeping Counterrevolution), Minsk, 1974.

[19] *Sionism - oruzhie reaktsii,* Lvov, 1976.

and policies of Zionism. Fascism is disgusting in any of its manifestations. Its Zionist version is no better than the Hitlerite one."[20] *Solodar'* in the book *Wild Wormwood:* "The Eichmann trial was designed to conceal the cooperation with the Nazis of such Jewish leaders as Weizman, Ben-Gurion, Moshe Sharett, Levi Eshkol. It is immaterial just how many Jews were killed with the aid of Zionist leaders; it is, in any case, an incontestable fact that the founders of the State of Israel are covered with Jewish blood."[21] The *Sovetskaia Rossiia* newspaper of February 2, 1978 in its review of the abovementioned book by Faris Jahiya: "Collaboration between the Zionists and the Nazis led to a catastrophe which cost the lives of almost six million Jews."

The most important new element of Soviet anti-Semitism, however, in our view, is the comparatively recent and increasingly frequent attempts to demonstrate that *Zionism itself and its "fascist content" are a natural and necessary outcome of the whole of Jewish history which, in its turn, has been predetermined by the nature of the Jewish religion and the national character of the Jewish people as such.* This new trend in Soviet anti-Semitism appears to be of paramount importance because it provides all the other aspects with that formerly missing link transforming isolated anti-Semitic inventions into a kind of *unified and global historical-religious doctrine* whose edge is directed not so much against Zionism or the State of Israel as against the Jewish people as a whole.

The first outlines of this new doctrine began to appear in the Soviet press following the Six-Day War when, at the authorities' bidding, on the same day hundreds of provincial newspapers published the same article entitled "What is Zionism?"[22] The article claimed – in the spirit of the "Protocols of the Elders of Zion" – that there existed a secret world Zionist conspiracy aimed at gaining world domination. This idea was developed in the lecture of Emel'ianov (1972). It has been further explored by a certain Skurlatov, a former important Komsomol official, expelled from the party in 1965 for fascist agitation, but since promoted to a position in the History Department of the Social Information Institute of the Academy of Sciences of the USSR.

In his book *Zionism and Apartheid*[23] Skurlatov sketches the following pattern of Jewish history from ancient times to modern Zionism: even in

[20] *Nash otvet klevetnikam*, Prapor, Kharkov, 1976.
[21] See Ts. Solodar's book, *Dikaia polyn'*.
[22] See, for example, the *Leningradskaia pravda* of July 3, 1967.
[23] V. Skurlatov, *Sionizm i aparteid*, Kiev, 1975.

ancient times the world needed middlemen for trade and in the course of centuries a trade clan or order formed whose most successful embodiment was the upper crust of ancient Jewish society. In ancient times this upper class had already turned into a "transnational Jewish corporation." From then on this "transnational Jewish corporation" has appeared under different guises in world history but always with a single purpose: to win supremacy over the world. With this aim in view, the corporation first created "the religion of the God-chosen," Judaism, a religion created by stealing, in its usual manner, "not only material but also cultural values, from other peoples." Judaism proved to be a very useful religion for gaining world domination, for it "very consistently generates a solid ideology of race superiority and apartheid." Later on, "Judaism's racial concept served as a prototype for European racism," first of all Catholic (because Catholicism posed as "New Israel"), then Protestant ("Protestantism is a version of Christianity pregnant with racism"), and finally Masonic ("Masonry is secular Judaism"). In modern times "the racist God-chosen prescripts of the Jewish corporation proved even more compatible with the bourgeoisie." This was particularly evident in the USA: "The Judeo-Protestant influence made itself distinctly felt in the formation of American imperialist ideology." And now, having inculcated Judaic formulas of conduct throughout the world, "the international Jewish elite already knows no bounds to its worldpower ambitions." But bourgeois ideologists, "although imbued with Judaic components," proved insufficiently useful for this purpose, writes Skurlatov, and so "the financial-monopolistic corporation of the Jewish bourgeoisie concluded that it was necessary to equip itself with a caste-exclusive doctrine, Zionism." Today, concludes the author, "because it considers itself God-chosen," this corporation "openly lays claim to world domination."

Soviet propaganda adds two aspects necessary to "complete" this scheme. On the one hand, this veritably Manichean irrational "theory" of a mysterious, eternal and omnipresent "Jewish transnational corporation" in the role of world evil, with Zionism as its latest embodiment is supplemented by an "exposure" of Judaism, i. e., the Jewish national religion as the ideological inspiration for all Jewish rapacious ambitions. On the one hand, it is supplemented by an "analysis" of the essence of Zionism as an insidious and well-calculated plan for speedy attainment of world domination by the Jews.

An example of the first kind of supplement is V. Begun's new book *Invasion without Arms*, of which 150,000 copies have appeared, and is sold at the cheapest, i.e., popular, price. In this book (which has recently arrived in Israel) Begun writes: "The apologists of Judaism extol this religion in every possible way ... It should, however, be noted that Judaism was basically borrowed from other peoples. As Engels points out, so-called holy scripture is a record of ancient Arabic religious traditions." Begun then characterizes Judaism itself: "The Judaic religion divides humanity into "God-chosen" Jews and "God-disdained" non-Jews. Judaic chauvinism and racism are already rooted in this division and date back to the most ancient times." Further, "holy scripture elaborates a double standard of morals," which, in relation to the gentile, is "shameless and inhuman." "It is quite understandable," Begun claims, "that the Judaic religion provoked other peoples' suspiciousness and enmity" toward Jews. Thus, the Jews themselves are to blame for the pogroms.

The history of ancient, medieval, and Russian anti-Semitism is related by Begun in a chapter bearing the eloquent title "Tears that should not be believed." In it he writes, among other things, that before condemning the pogromists one must investigate what kind of Jews they were killing – poor or rich. The trouble with the Jews, according to Begun, is that they always follow the chauvinistic idea of world domination formulated in holy scripture. Later, while discussing the modernization of Judaism in recent times Begun, in passing characterizes Ahad Ha'am ("he reeks of dyed-in-the-wool fascism a mile off"), Bialik and Jabotinsky (they demonstrate "unsurpassed examples of racism and national egoism") and other Zionist leaders.

Begun's task is to prove that Zionism is no more than a secular variation of Judaism, permeated with the same morality, ideology, and practical prescripts. What then are these morals and prescripts? Begun answers: "If one views the Torah in the light of modern civilization, it will appear as an unsurpassed manual of bloodthirstiness, hypocrisy, treachery, perfidy, moral dissoluteness – all base human qualities." Begun admits that other peoples have long ago given up their ancient religions, and only the Jews remain faithful to the Torah as a manual of modern conduct. He concludes: "Thus one can trace the links of a single chain: The Torah – ideological prescripts of Zionist theoreticians – aggression in the Middle East – corruption of minds both in Israel, openly, and in other countries, secretly – world domination, this is the dream of Zionist fanatics."[24]

That part of Soviet propagandist doctrine in which Zionism is represented as the logical result and the latest variant of the Jewish people's perpetual desire for world domination, may be illustrated by an article

---

[24] See above in V. Begun's book *Invasion without Arms*.

published in the book *Our Reply to Slanderers* and entitled "Zionism, a Variety of Racism." The author, Prof. A. Zuban', Doctor of History, writes: "Zionism is the most blatant form of modern racism. Its ideological sources are the reactionary ideas of the Jewish religion, which substantiates the Jews' superiority over all other peoples (in this Zuban' joins Skurlatov and Begun). It was not accidental that Zionist ideologists at first disagreed on the question in which country and in which part of the world to found the so-called "Jewish state." At last they decided on Palestine, the country situated near the Suez Canal, an important military and economic artery. Palestine lay at the international crossroads between the West and the colonial East and promised great advantages. Therefore the Jewish imperialist bourgeoisie and all the Zionist ideologists dragged out into the light of day the Judaic dogma of the "Promised Land," supposedly promised by God to the Jews. While preparing for the seizure of Palestine, Zionists started, even before the establishment of a state there, to develop theories about Palestine as some sort of a world centre of Jewish culture. Today, the Israeli press writes that the Arabs must return to Israel the Sinai, Palestine, Jordan, Syria, the Lebanon, Iraq, and part of Saudi Arabia, because all these lands were promised by God to Abraham's descendants."

These statements about Jewry, Judaism, and Zionism pass from article to article, from book to book, from lecture to lecture.[25] The repetition shows that somewhere in the depths of the Soviet propaganda machine, work is in progress on collecting, testing and polishing the elements of an all-embracing ideological doctrine which must convince the world that the Jewish religion preaches the slogan of world domination; that the Jewish people, therefore, has been consciously and methodically striving for such domination throughout its history; that to achieve its aims it has formed a worldwide secret conspiracy in the shape of a "transnational Jewish trade corporation;" that at present the chief instrument of this corporation is Zionism, whose methods and ideology are racism and fascism; that in their struggle for attaining world domination Zionists helped Hitler to exterminate six millions of their own fellow Jews; and that Zionism had purposely captured Palestine as the main springboard for the occupation first of all Arab lands and then of the rest of the world.

---

[25] See, for example, the journal *Aziia i Afrika segodnia* (Asia and Africa Today) 12, 1978 for G. Nikitina's review of such books as *Sionism - orudie antikomunizma (Zionism: A Tool of Anticommunism)* by D. Soifer (*Promin'*, Dnepropetrovsk, 1976), G. Fain, *Moral' iudaizma* (The Morality of Judaism) (*Maiak*, Odessa, 1976). These books reiterate or are variations of V. Begun, V. Skurlatov, V. Emeli'anov and A. Zuban'.

It would seem superfluous to prove that this anti-Semitic doctrine, which includes all the former "achievements" of Soviet propaganda, is directed against the Jewish people as a whole and threatens the very foundations of Jewish existence. That is why we have to state that to date Soviet anti-Semitism is the initiator and organizer of a worldwide crusade against Jewry, Judaism, and Zionism.

Occasionally one hears it claimed that individual glaring manifestations of Soviet anti-Semitism do not represent government policy, that propaganda can be separated from the state which, allegedly, is not responsible for the excesses of Beguns and Emel'ianovs. If the above facts in their entirety are not sufficiently convincing to disprove so naive a conception, then another striking fact may be cited. We have at our disposal a memorandum that Emel'ianov sent to the Central Committee of the CPSU. In this memorandum which arrived through Samizdat channels,[26] he sets forth his wild "theory" the worldwide "Jewish-Masonic conspiracy" and concludes by proposing a program of concrete measures to fight the "Jewish danger."

Here is this program (in excerpts):

1. Widest publicity to the ultimate world-power aims of Zionism and Masonry and their common source, Judaism.

2. Wide-scale publication of works on the history of Zionism, its strategy and tactics (by Ivanov, Evseev, Zhukov and others).

3. The creation of an Institute for the Study of Zionism and Masonry attached to the Central Committee of the CPSU.

4. A policy of cadre selection which would bar potential carriers of Zionist ideas from work.

5. Introduction of a compulsory course on "scientific anti-Zionism and anti-Masonry" in all high schools and institutions of higher learning in the country.

6. Introduction of a "scientific anti-Zionism and anti-Masonry" section into educational television programs.

7. Inclusion of this subject into the compulsory training program of the Armed Forces of the USSR.

8. Retraining programs on this subject in all agencies which are responsible for mass information programs and cultural and artistic phenomena.

---

[26] From the Jewish Samizdat materials now at the disposal of the Documentation Centre.

9. Inclusion into the criminal code of articles providing stiff penalties for membership in Zionist or Masonic oranizations; concealment of such membership must be viewed as infiltration of an enemy agent into our society.

10. Outlawing Zionism and Masonry.

11. Ruthless struggle against all kinds of organized Masonic-Zionist activities (the Sakharov Committee, Helsinki groups, the Solzhenitsyn fund, Amnesty International, Symposia on Jewish culture, etc.).

12. Since Masonry and Zionism are organizations of the radical bourgeoisie, the struggle against them must be conducted in a no less radical way, especially considering that the dissidents led by Zionists have switched over to acts of murderous terror against the civilian population in the Metro. They planned these acts as far back as 80 years ago in the Metro's early days.

This memorandum is dated January 10, 1978. The author's obvious paranoia could provoke only a smile but for the amazing fact that even the cursory analysis of Soviet reality offered above shows that all the items of the Emel'ianov program from the first to the eighth have in fact been realized or are in the process of being carried out in the USSR under state auspices. This means that the pogromist writings and speeches of Emel'ianov, Begun and their ilk, rather than expressing their "personal" point of view, reflect a certain objective tendency which is gradually making headway in Soviet society.

What is this tendency? ...

As has already been pointed out, the Soviet regime is now undergoing a nationalistic evolution in the course of which it becomes more and more "popular" or, in other words, takes on a more nationalistic, great-power character. The ideology of this process is provided by nationalistically-minded intelligentsia who are gradually gaining influence in Soviet official and unofficial circles, and closing ranks with the ever more entrenched official anti-Semitism exemplified by the likes of Evseev and Ivanov. (A vivid symbol of this link is the united stand taken by "intellectuals" and "official figures" at Nikitina's defense, or the public debate on "The Classics and Modernity," which took place a little earlier, on December 21, 1977 in the Central Writers' Club where nationalistic intelligentsia openly attacked "ethnically foreign elements" in Soviet culture). In this historic situation the role of Soviet Jewish – or, in a broader sense, "Russian-Jewish," intelligentsia has come to an end. The time has come when the

Jewish element in the USSR has become "superfluous" and "alien," and this is already irreversible. Soviet anti-Semitism of today, which goes hand-in-hand with the general anti-intellectual and anti-democratic campaign in the USSR, is an objective expression of this fact.

Undoubtedly, one must distinguish between anti-Jewish and anti-Semitic tendencies. Not every anti-Jewish statement is anti-Semitism. The desire of certain groups among the Soviet bureaucracy and intelligentsia to oust Jews and to occupy their positions is dictated by an entirely rational factor, competition. Anti-Semitism, on the other hand, is characterized by an irrational hatred for Jewry as such, the conception of Jewry as the "universal evil," the various sketches of a "world-wide Jewish conspiracy" dating from ancient times and stemming from the national peculiarities of the Jewish people, etc. These special features of anti-Semitism were most completely expressed in Nilus' "Protocols of the Elders of Zion" and in the anti-Semitic propaganda based on this book spread by the members of the Russian Black Hundred organization of the 19th–20th centuries. In tsarist Russia *this* anti-Semitism did not constitute an integral part of state ideology; the "world-wide Jewish conspiracy" scheme was not an officially proclaimed doctrine, but this is occurring in the USSR now: the schemes of V. Begun, V. Skurlatov, V. Emel'ianov and others are proclaimed in the official press, sanctioned by *official* organs and gradually are becoming part of the *state* ideology. These schemes are integrated into the official reigning Marxist ideology by using the thesis that Zionism is the contemporary expression of the "Jewish conspiracy." The struggle against Zionism is the point where the Begun-Emel'ianov "home-made" anti-Semitism emanating from "below" meets with Marxist anti-Zionism directed from "above."

This compels us to define the present tendency of official Soviet propaganda with respect to Jews as specifically *anti-Semitic* with all specific features and aims inherent in any form of anti-Semitism. . . .

This tendency is being reinforced – irreversibly – by external circumstances . . . In the collectivist East's offensive against the individualist West, Soviet anti-Semitic theories of a "world-wide Zionist conspiracy" as an expression of Western imperialist plans play the same role on the international arena that the theories of "Jewish contagion" play in the nationalist offensive against the intelligentsia and intellectuals inside the USSR. Anti-Semitism has proven an effective instrument in consolidating all both internal and external nationalistic forces in their fight against the forces of democracy, liberalism, and humanism.

YEHOSHAFAT HARKABI

Contemporary Arab Anti-Semitism: its Causes and Roots*

1. Islam and the Jews

The Arabs frequently emphasize that the Muslim countries, unlike the Christian ones, have never persecuted the Jews, that Arabs and Jews have lived together in peace and mutual respect, and that whenever the Jews were compelled to leave Europe they found refuge in the Arab world. Anti-Semitism was born in the West; Zionism, which was a reaction to it, also originated in Europe.[1]

It is true that the position of the Jews was much better in the Arab countries. Although there were outbreaks and restrictions there, too, they were not so severe, or on the same scale, as in Europe.[2] The Muslims did not impose their creed on the Jews by force, or expel them, as the Christians did.

The modern emphasis on equality of civil rights may lead us to equate toleration with lack of discrimination and civil equality. This is the impression that Arab spokesmen like Shukairy try to create. Aḥmad writes, for example:

> "Since God decreed their dispersion in the countries of the world, we have never heard that they were saved from harm and found a good life and security for themselves and their property anywhere except in the Islamic countries ... In every Muslim country, they

---

* From: Yehoshafat Harkabi, *Arab Attitudes to Israel*, trans. by Misha Louvish (Jerusalem: Israel Universities Press, 1972), Ch. 5, abridged.

[1] Ahmad Bahā' al-Dīn, *Isrā'īliyyāt* ("Judaica"), Kitāb al-Hilāl, No. 158, Cairo, March 1965, p. 196.

[2] The pogrom at Granada in 1066, in which a mob attacked and murdered three or four thousand Jews, was undoubtedly exceptional (see Samuel Rosenblatt, "The Jews in Islam," in Koppel S. Pinson (ed.), *Essays on Antisemitism,* New York, 1946, pp. 111–120). On the literary incitement that preceded the pogrom, see Moshe Perlman's article "Eleventh Century Andalusian Authors on the Jews of Granada," *American Academy for Jewish Research* 8, 1948–1949, pp. 269–290.

enjoyed the protection of Islam and lived under its wing, safe, peaceful, free to trade, enjoying equality in all civil rights and not suffering from any oppression whatsoever."[3]

The atmosphere of the conflict leads to some expressions of compunction over the tolerance extended to the Jews, which Sharāra says they exploited in order to bring about the corruption and disintegration of Islam.[4] He sums up:

"The liberation of the Jews in the framework of Arab civilization paved the way to its destruction."[5]

Jews in the Arab countries, it is sometimes stated, were Arabs of the Mosaic faith until Zionism came along and spoiled it all. Dr. Sayegh writes, for example:

"There were in Palestine at the end of World War I not more than 57,000 Jews. Many of these Jews were *Arabs of Jewish faith*, who, throughout Arab history, had lived in friendship and harmony with *Arabs of Christian or Muslim faith*."[6]

The truth is that this tolerance of Islam toward the Jews was founded on discrimination: it was a tolerance towards inferiors. Morroe Berger, in *The Arab World*, sums up the position: "Tolerance was not equality."[7] According to the basic Islamic approach, there was no room for pagans, who must be destroyed, but the Jewish and Christian "People of the Scripture" were recognized as inferior groups. Professor von Grunebaum says:

"Their personal safety and their personal property are guaranteed them at the price of permanent inequality."

"The minority situation within the world of Islam is, however, most clearly portrayed by saying that the minorities bought their safety at the price of *Geschichtslosigkeit*, at the price of having more or less the status of crown colonies in our day."[8]

He adds that non-Muslims, indeed, sometimes rose to high positions in the State, but this was illegal; and was opposed by religious circles.

Professor Bernard Lewis describes their position as follows:

"The Dhimmis were second-class citizens, paying a high rate of taxation, suffering from certain social disabilities, and on a few rare occasions subjected to open persecution. But by

[3] Ahmad Yūsuf Ahmad, *al-Sh'b al-Dalīl, Isrā'īl* ("Israel – the Misled People"), Kutub Qawmiyya, No. 176, Cairo, 1962, p. 75.
[4] 'Abd al-Latīf Sharāra, *al-Sahyūniyya, Jarimat al-'Asr al-Kubrā* ("Zionism, the Greatest Crime of the Age"), Dār al-Makshūf, Beirut, 1964, p. 23.
[5] *Ibid.*, p. 24.
[6] Fayez E. Sayegh, *The Arab-Israel Conflict*, 1956, pp. 5–6.
[7] London, 1962, p. 259.
[8] *Medieval Islam*, University of Chicago, 1961, pp. 178–81.

and large their position was infinitely superior to that of those communites who differed from the established church in Europe."[9]

The position of the Jews in the Arab countries was not so idyllic as it is portrayed today by Arab spokesmen. They were liable to degrading restrictions – though these were not always enforced. It is typical, perhaps, that they suffered particularly from discrimination, pressure and insult in the Yemen, which Professor Goitein has called "the most Arab of all the Arab countries;"[10] Jewish orphans were regarded as State property and forcibly converted to Islam;[11] Jews were set apart by their dress, and frequently stoned.[12]

It may be assumed that the attitude of the Quran, which contains numerous anti-Jewish expressions, especially from the Medina period, had a major influence of the image of the Jews in the eyes of the Arab populace. Special importance may be attributed to sayings that are repeated twice with slight differences in wording: for instance, that

> ". . . humiliation and wretchedness were stamped upon them and they were visited with wrath from Allah."[13]

These passages were understood, not as referring to the punishment of the Jews in the time of Moses, but as of wide historical significance: a divine decree, which, as the Arabs understood it, was fulfilled under historical, political and cultural conditions by lack of political independence and a position of inferiority. Bayḍāwī, one of the greatest commentators on the Quran, who lived in the 13th century, gives this interpretation of the verse in the first place where it appears:

> "The Jews are, in most cases, inferior and wretched, whether in truth or as a pretence in order to reduce the *jizya*" (the "part" or tax which was imposed on the tolerated infidels).

On the second passage he comments:

---

[9] *The Arabs in History,* London, 1964, p. 94, cited by Berger, *op. cit.,* p. 259. Professor Ben-Sasson writes in a similar vein: "In Islam – Ishmael – bodily injuries and mob violence were not the main phenomena of exile. Religious coercion was limited to a few fanatics, like the al-Muwaḥḥidūn (Almohades) in 12th-century Spain and North Africa, but degradation and social oppression were part of the law of the Islamic state and society, and were particularly marked in those countries where they were not overshadowed by the threat of death" (*Encyclopaedia Hebraica,* Vol. 10, article *"Galut,"* p. 822).

[10] Soloman D. Goitein, *Jews and Arabs, their Contact through Ages,* New York, 1964, p. 73.

[11] *Ibid.,* p. 77.

[12] *Ibid.,* p. 76.

[13] Sura II, The Cow, v. 61; Sura III, The Family of 'Imrān, v. 112.

"The Jews were in most cases poor and wretched."[14]

The Quranic phrase *"al-dhilla wa-al-maskana"* ("humiliation and wretchedness") is very frequently used in Islamic reference to the Jews. It is also to be found in Judah Halevi's philosophical work *The Khazar:*

> "The Scholar said: I see that you denounce us for poverty and wretchedness."[15]

The "humiliation and wretchedness" of the Jews were presented by the Muslims as a proof of the falsity of the Jewish faith, while the righteousness of Islam was demonstrated by its worldy success.

The Opening to the Quran, which every Muslim repeats in every prayer, reads:

> "Show us the straight path, the path of those whom Thou has favoured; not (the path) of those who earn Thine anger nor of those who go astray."

According to a common interpretation, though almost certainly not the original intention, it is the Jews who are meant, for they are rebuked by God. Al-Jiyār, whose approach is a Muslim one, emphasizes that the dispersion of the Jews and their continued exile is the will of God, who never wants them to have a Government[16]; in another passage, he says that their dispersion is an expression of the doom of wretchedness and humiliation.[17]

The divine verdict is described as a punishment for the evil character of the Jews. Ahmad writes:

> "This group (*fi'a*) was the lowest (*dhalīla*), most despicable (*khasīsa*) and degraded (*mahīna*)."

He goes on to explain that this verdict was carried out in the history of the Jews, as described in the Holy Scriptures, as a long chain of tribulations and invasions by Shishak, Tiglath-Pileser, Sennacherib, Pharoah Necho, and so forth.[18]

---

[14] A similar explanation, quoting the same verse from the Quran, is given by Ibn Khaldūn, who explains that in the past the Jews were endowed with a collective consciousness (*'asabiyya*), but they lost it "and degradation was their lot for many generations" (p. 91 in Emanuel Koplewitz's Hebrew translation). The Arabic expression is *rusūkh al-dhall,* which indicates that degradation had become rooted in them.

[15] Part I: 113; in Hirschfeld's Arabic version, p. 62.

[16] 'Abd al'Ghaffār al-Jiyār, *Filastīn lil-'Arab* ("Palestine for the Arabs"), Dār al-Kitāb al-'Arabī, Cairo, 1947, p. 4.

[17] *Ibid.,* p. 33.

[18] Ahmad, *op. cit.,* pp. 51–52.

The *jizya* tax was not only a source of income but a mark of subordination and humiliation, and payment was often accompanied with humiliating gestures, in keeping with the interpretation of the words of the Quran:

> "Fight against such of those who have been given the Scripture as believe not in Allah nor the Last Day, . . . until they pay the tribute readily, being brought low."[19]

Muhammad hoped that the Jews would accept his mission, and was ready to make gestures of goodwill towards them, but when they refused, he was furious and denounced them vehemently. The existence of the Jews did not in itself constitute a provocation and an affront to Islam, as it did to Christendom, particularly as they were recognized as subordinate and degraded. Since the image of the Jews in Islam was connected with wretchedness and humiliation, however, the establishment of the State of Israel as the result of a military victory appeared to be incompatible with the traditional view. Thus the Quranic image became a matter of importance.

---

[19] Sura IX, Repentance, v. 29; Al-Baydāwī explains that this verse means that "the sparing of them in return for the *jizya* was a great mercy." (According to a tradition from Ibn 'Abbās, when the *jizya* was collected the vassal was struck on the nape of the neck. The *Encyclopaedia of Islam* (new edition, Vol II, p. 562a) explains that apart from Shāfi'ī, commentators and jurists demanded payment by a degrading process, and that it was on the basis of this verse that the degrading signs on the clothing of the unbelievers were instituted.)

The original meaning of the expression *'an yad*, here translated "readily," was, as Professor Kister shows, "according to their capacity" ("'An Yadin Quran IX/29," *Arabica*, Tome XI, 1964, pp. 272–278). But the accepted interpretation was that the payment must be made by hand, directly, and not through an intermediary.

The verses referring to the degradation of the Jews were translated into action by those who observed them. Maimonides suffered this degradation and, since he was unaware of the sufferings of the Jews in Europe from the persecutions that accompanied the Crusades, he could not make a balanced judgement and declared that the position of the Jews in the Muslim countries was worse than anywhere else. In *Iggeret Teiman* ("The Epistle of Yemen"), he writes: "The nation of Ishmael injures us greatly and legislates to do us harm and make us hate . . . For never has a nation risen up against Israel to injure us more than it, nor has anyone gone so far in degrading and scorning and hating her as they do" (pp. 54 and 85 in the Halkin edition). Similarly, Rabbi Bahya said, "The sons of Ishmael are worse for Israel than the sons of Esau" (quoted by Halkin, note on p. 94).

In later generations, the picture appeared to be more balanced. Iliyās al-Ayyūbi, in his pamphlet *The Voice of Liberty for the Defence of Jewish Nation* (Alexandria, 1913), wrote: "The Jews in the countries where Islam spread were in a position of degradation and wretchedness according to the formula of the verse which stipulates that they must pay the *jizya* and be brought low." But their position was better than in the Christian countries, as they suffered degradation but not confiscation of property and burning at the stake (pp. 50–51). It should also be noted that this rule of degradation was not always observed and the position of the Jews in general improved.

The inconsistency between the political reality of sovereign independence today and the divine decree of wretchedness seemed to call for some explanation. Tabbāra explains, on the basis of another part of Sura III, The Family of 'Imrān, v. 112

"Ignominy shall be their portion wheresoever they are found save (where they grasp) a rope from Allah and a rope from men,"

that "a rope from men" means that the assistance the Jews receive from the Western countries, as a result of which the divine verdict has not been realized, and that "a rope from Allah" means that God wished the Jews to win their victory so as to draw the attention of the Arab peoples to the corruption that had spread amongst them, so that they should rectify the situation.[20]

Another element in the image of the Jews is, no doubt, connected with the attribution to them of deceit, cunning and treachery (*ghadr*). This is associated with Muhammad's dispute with the Jewish tribes in Arabia, who, according to Muslim tradition, violated their agreements and tried to seduce the believers, as well as to deceive him. I will return to these points later.

Ancient Arabic literature, including the Quran, contains not only expressions of opprobrium and contempt for the Jews, but also laudatory passages.[21] Within the framework of the present work, it is impossible to make any scientific estimate of the relative influence of the various factors in creating the image of the Jew. Thorough and comprehensive literary and historical research would be required for the purpose.[22] Generally, how-

---

[20] 'Afīf 'Abd al-Fattāh Tabbāra, *al-Yahūd fī al-Qur'ān* ("The Jews in the Quran"), Dār al-'Ilm lil Malāyīn, Beirut, 1966, pp. 45–46.

[21] For example, according to a tradition quoted too by Rosenblatt from Balādhurī's *The Conquest of the Lands* (p. 162), Muhammad said: "He that does harm to a protected person [Christian or Jew], I shall be his prosecutor on the Day of Judgment." There are also other examples. As an example of an opprobrious statement, there is Jāhiz's saying (quoted by Rosenblatt – Bayān, I, p. 165): "A Jew cannot talk to an Arab without plotting to kill him."

[22] The subject is discussed in H. Z. Hirshberg's paper "The Jews in the Countries of Islam" in *Chapters in the History of the Arabs and Islam* (Hebrew), edited by Hava Lazarus-Yaffe, Tel Aviv, 1967, pp. 262–315; S. D. Goitein, "The Grim Creed," in *The Dinaburg Volume* (Hebrew); Leon Poliakov, *De Mahomet aux Marranes*, Paris, 1961.

It should be noted that there has been a lack of balance in the treatment of this subject. Research has concentrated mainly on the positive aspects of the relationships between Jews and Islam (Goitein, 1964, *op. cit.*, Rosenthal, *Judaism and Islam*, and others), or on the influence of Judaism on Islam, and has neglected manifestations of opposition and hostility. It may well be that in addition to the fact that it is more pleasant to deal with "positive" subjects, scholars were also influenced by psychological motives to deal with the encour-

ever, the impression is that the image is a negative one, emphasizing their disloyalty, treachery and cunning. This is the conclusion of the orientalist Vajda, who writes that in the Ḥadīth, the traditional lore about the life of the Prophet, which was of major importance in Islamic religious consciousness, the Jews are presented "in very dark colours."[23] Among the vices ascribed to them are treachery, religious particularism, forgery of the Holy Scriptures and incitement; they are accused of cursing the Prophet by saying *"samm 'alayka"* ("Poison upon you") instead of *"Salām 'alayka"* ("Peace be upon you").

Anti-Jewish motifs are to be found in medieval Islamic religious polemics. For example, there are criticisms of the "chosen people" idea, which became of topical significance in the circumstances of the conflict, supporting the denunciations of Zionism, of Jewish separatism and of preferential treatment for the Jews. It may be assumed that, even if the conflict exists mainly on the secular, political plane, it reinforces religious antagonisms, as we have already seen in the writings of Tall and 'Alūba. But it is no accident that a 12th-century anti-Jewish book, *Ifḥām al-Yahūd* ("Silencing the Jew") was reprinted in Egypt in 1961 in the Library of the Great Jihad.[24]

The Arab-Israel conflict and Arab hostility to Israel were not the result of Islam's attitude to Judaism and its unfavorable image of the Jews, but once the conflict arose the antagonism to Israel was liable to derive ideas and emotions from these attitudes. The Islamic factor is neither a primary nor a principal one in the Arab attitude, but it is one of those that affect its character.

Since it is the conflict that has brought to the fore the anti-Jewish elements in Islam, such anti-Jewish expressions are rare in those parts of the non-Arab Muslim world where it does not exist, and insofar as they do

---

aging aspects. Where Israel is concerned, the discussion of the kinship between Judaism and Islam may have been regarded as a contribution to better relations.

[23] "Juifs et Musulmans selon de Hadith," *Journal Asiatique* II, 1937, p. 124.

[24] This is an anti-Jewish work written by Samuel al-Maghribī, a Jew converted to Islam, in the 12th century. It was published recently by Professor M. Perlman in a scientific edition with English translation and notes – see Bibliography. (I am grateful to Professor Ben-Sasson for drawing my attention to this book.) According to Professor Perlman, the book was reissued in Egypt in 1939, but there may be particular significance in the fact that it was reissued there in 1961 in Maktabat al-Jihād al-Kubrā "Library of the Great Jihad" (consolidated list of publications of the Government of the UAR, No. 613). The same publisher also issued another book, which, according to its name, also deals with religious polemics: *Al-Risāla al-Sab'iyya bi-Ibṭal al-yahūdiyya* ("The Abrogation of Judaism"), by Israel Samuel Ha-Yerushalmi (No. 614 in the same list).

appear, they may be assumed to be due to Arab influence. There is little feeling of involvement in the conflict in the non-Arab Muslim world, for which the rise of Israel does not constitute a provocation. Muslim anti-Jewish feeling, therefore, is particularly prominent in Arab Islam.

2. The Study and Sources of Arab Anti-Semitism

It is somewhat inappropriate to use the term "anti-Semitism" for Arab hatred of the Jews. Arabs themselves find it difficult to translate, and often use such terms as *"muḍāddat al-yahūd"* ("opposition to the Jews") or *"al-haraka al-mu'adiyya lilyahūd"* ("the movement hostile to the Jews") instead. However, the word has been specifically applied to Jew-hatred, and the argument that Arab anti-Semitism is a contradiction in terms is only a play upon words. If the publication of *The Protocols of the Elders of Zion* is an anti-Semitic act in Sweden, why should the issue of an Arabic translation be regarded in any other light?

Books written in an anti-Semitic spirit by Christian (especially Catholic) Arabs appeared in the Middle East in the second half of the 19th century under French influence. Brief surveys of this phenomenon may be found in articles by Eliahu Sapir, Joshua Ben-Hanina and Sylvia Haim.[25] As is explained by Sylvia Haim and Professor Perlman, who added a brief footnote to her article, these publications were at first sporadic and did not indicate any social or national trend. The suspicion aroused by Jewish settlement in Palestine led to Arab denunciation and the resort to ideas drawn from the stock of anti-Semitic arguments. Thus a number of books displaying anti-Semitic tendencies appeared in the twenties, thirties and forties, and anti-Semitic ideas made their appearance in the Arabic press. As Sylvia Haim states, *The Protocols of the Elders of Zion* was translated as far back as the twenties. In the thirties the German factor joined in as collaborator and supplier of ideas. The sharpening of the conflict since 1948 has been accompanied by an increase in manifestations of anti-Semitism in literature and press.

Isolated Arabic works of this type need not have caused any particular concern. Anti-Semitic books, pamphlets, and manifestoes are published by

---

[25] Eliahu Sapir, "Hatred for the Jews in Arabic Literature," *Ha-Shiloah*, Vol. VI (1899), pp. 272–279; Joshua Ben Haninah (Jacob Joshua), "Arab Anti-Zionist Literature," *Ha-Shiloah*, Vol. XLIII, 1925/6, pp. 272–79; "An Anti-Jewish Book in Arabic," *Haaretz*, December 19, 1926; "A Book on Hitler in Arabic," *Davar* (evening edition), February 24, 1935; "The Jews in Arabic Literature," *Moznavim*, Vol. XVIII, 1934/5, pp. 34–38, 305–309, 394–397; Sylvia Haim, "Arabic anti-Semitic Literature," *Jewish Social Studies* 17, 1955, pp. 307–312.

individuals in many countries of the world and the Arab world cannot be expected to remain immune. It might even be argued that the Egyptian propaganda machine is so extensive and ramified that some subordinate may have interpreted the order to issue anti-Israel books as meaning that he should publish an anti-Semitic work as well. After all, we cannot assume such strict control that every word printed exactly represents the will of the authorities and is issued with their specific blessing.

The picture is changed, however, by the multiplicity of such publications in Arabic, as well as anti-Jewish statements in newspapers and broadcasts. Several of the anti-Semitic publications have the official stamp of approval, which makes them particularly important. Several official Egyptian series of books for national guidance and training include a number of anti-Semitic works. Others have been translated into Arabic from various European languages and published under official auspices. Well-known Arab leaders use anti-Semitic themes and give their patronage to anti-Semitic publications by signed introductions. For example, 'Alūba's anti-Semitic book *Palestine and the Conscience of Mankind*[26] is prefaced by a letter from Nasser describing it as "a historic treasure" and "a political document," which "reveals truths." All this can hardly be mere chance; it appears to be a matter of deliberate policy. Arab anti-Semitism, by all indications, is a part of the official ideology; it stems not from the fringes of Arab society but from its centre.

Arab anti-Semitism, as we shall review it here, is of a literary character and, especially in the UAR, it appears to be guided by the Government. It can therefore be controlled, directed, and halted if the authorities so desire, especially if it proves to lead to criticism abroad. The study of these manifestations and the publication of the results may perhaps have an influence on them; indeed, publicity and criticism in various foreign circles may already have had some moderating influence.

Arab anti-Semitism is the outcome of political circumstances. As has been emphasized in connection with the psychological and sociological factors involved, it is not a cause of the conflict but a product of it. The Arabs did not oppose Jewish settlement for anti-Semitic motives; their opposition aroused anti-Semitic emotions among them. However, once the conflict exists and anti-Semitism has been created, it becomes one of the factors that give the conflict its character, and it must therefore be included in a study of this nature.

---

[26] Muḥammad 'Alī 'Alūba, *Filastīn wa-al Dāmīr al-Insānī* ("Palestine and the Conscience of Mankind"), Dār al-Hilāl, Cairo, March 1964.

3. Summary

The theories commonly advanced to explain the rise of anti-Semitism in the West during the past two centuries, on the basis of social, economic, and psychological factors, are not applicable to the phenomenon in the Arab countries. Anti-Semitism in the West is connected with the rise of the Jews in European society after emancipation and their achievement of positions in the economic and cultural spheres. Ambition was the main feature of the Jewish stereotype. Among the Arabs, however, there was no emancipation to raise the status of the Jews to a level that aroused the envy of the population; they did not symbolize the development of capitalism or occupy such an important place in life as in the West; they were not prominent in political or party activities; they never became prime ministers. The Arab could always regard the Quran's decree on Jewish degradation and wretchedness as vindicated, generally, by the absence of a Jewish political centre, and, more literally, in respect of at least part of the Jewish community. Some authorities have ascribed the rise of anti-Semitism in the West to various upsets and crises, but Arab anti-Semitism has nothing to do with internal crises or the processes of modernization. For others, the Jews symbolize the discomforts of urbanization,[27] but this is not applicable to the Arab world. In Europe the Jews occupied an irritatingly central place in the self-image of the population, but again this did not apply to the Arabs, among whom they were not outstanding in literature, the theatre or the press, as in the West. In the United States, an elaborate theoretical structure has been erected on the basis of a tendency to anti-Semitism which was attributed to certain particular types, such as the "prejudiced personality." It cannot be denied that such types exist in the Arab countries; perhaps, as we have noted, they may even be common, but Arab anti-Semitism cannot be founded mainly on psychological reasons. In the West there was an element, noted by the pioneer Zionist thinker Pinsker, of fear of the Jews as an unnatural element, but no such fear existed in the Arab world; on the contrary, the Arabs were confident of their own superiority. For the Christians, the very existence of the Jews, who refused to accept the Gospel, was a provocation, while Islam accepted their presence in its midst, though under conditions of subordination.

While the Jews may be hated because they are regarded as different and alien, Islamic society was founded on the recognition of religious groups existing side by side, with power and superiority reserved for the Muslim

---

[27] Gordon W. Allport, *The Nature of Prejudice*, New York, 1958, p. 242.

faith. The Ottoman Empire did not resent the foreignness of the Jews, for it was based on the existence of distinct religious groups, which it accepted as a matter of course. It is true that the rise of Arab nationalism, which inevitably creates a consciousness of national uniqueness and an aspiration for inner homogeneity, intensifies sensitivity towards aliens, but even this cannot be regarded as a primary cause of anti-Semitism.

Western anti-Semitism contained a popular element, which started from the Jewish stereotype and the prejudices current among the people, and was nourished by the charge that the Jews killed God. Arab anti-Semitism, on the other hand, is not basically popular, nor is it founded on the stereotype of the Jew that has been current in the Arab world. On the contrary, it tries to contradict the stereotype, which is based on weakness, and replace it by the image of a powerful, dangerous, and threatening enemy. People are inclined to despise the weak, and to fear and hate the strong. Arab anti-Semitism is not based on stereotypes and prejudices, but tries to implant them in the popular imagination. If the Arab-Israel conflict was settled, anti-Semitic manifestations would die out, but the continuation of the conflict is liable to deepen the anti-Semitic elements in the popular consciousness.

The distinctive feature of Arab anti-Semitism is that from the beginning it was not directed against Jews as a minority, whether as individuals or as a group living in the Arab countries, but against Israel and the Jews living outside the Arab world. When the authorities fomented anti-Semitism in Europe, it was part of their internal policies and strategies, or, at most, a means of subversion abroad, as it was used by Hitler. Arab anti-Semitism, however, is a part of the Arab countries' struggle against Israel and their strategy in foreign policy; its main stress is on the Jews as a political organism. It is rooted in external political motives.

To sum up, it should be stated with the utmost emphasis that Arab anti-Semitism is not the cause of the conflict but one of its results; it is not the reason for the hostile Arab attitude towards Israel and the Jews, but a means of deepening, justifying, and institutionalizing that hostility. Its rise is connected with the tension created as a result of Zionist activity, and expecially of the traumatic experience of defeat, the establishment of independent Israel and the struggle against her. Anti-Semitism is a weapon in this struggle. It is functional and political, not social: it presents the Jews mainly as a political, not a social threat, and it is partially directed by the administration which conducts the political struggle, or at least gives it its blessing. Hence, it describes the Jews, not as passive, shrinking parasites, but as aggressors. Unlike Western Christian anti-Semitism, it is not the result of generations of incitement which have created an archetype in the popular consciousness, although there are elements in Islam on which anti-Semitism could build.

It does not follow, however, from the difference between Arab and Western anti-Semitism that the numerous anti-Jewish books do not deserve to be called "anti-Semitic," or that there is no "Arab anti-Semitism." Western anti-Semitism contains a Christian religious element, but it does not follow that there cannot be another type, in which such a factor is not present. The limitation of anti-Semitism to the type that involves a Christian element and a popular emotion is purely arbitrary.

The difference between the hatred of the Jews in the West and in the Islamic world was defined by Sapir in his article "Hatred of the Jews in Arab Literature" (1899), in these terms:

> "The Muhammadan Arabs' hatred of the Jews was only an external hatred, or an external war which was necessary at the time: when the Jews were powerful they regarded them as a barrier to their victory and glory, but when the Jews were submissive and did not interfere with their positions, the hatred disappeared. On the other hand, we can see in the hatred of the other nations towards the Jews an inner hatred, a profound and ineradicable natural emotion, which appeared also – or particularly – at a time when the Jews were trampled upon and anyone could strike at them with impunity."[28]

On the establishment of the State of Israel, the Jews again became "a barrier to their victory and glory," and Jew-hatred came to life, with the old and new elements inextricably intermingled.

Despite the superficiality of Arab anti-Semitism and its shallow roots in popular feeling, there are a number of factors that are liable to make it particularly fervent and powerful. In the West there was something artificial and abstract in the presentation of the Jews as a danger; it could be done only by weaving ingenious tales of plots and stratagems. The Arabs, on the other hand, regard Israel as a real danger; they have experienced several defeats and fear more. Neither the Russians nor the Germans burned their fingers in their relations with the Jews as the Arabs did. The Germans accused them of responsibility for the "stab in the back," but for the Arabs the blow was direct, they were defeated by the Jews in face-to-face confrontation. Western anti-Semitism denounced the Jews as a secret enemy; for the Arabs, Israel is an enemy without pretence or concealment.

Anti-Semitism among the Arabs is, therefore, vigorous and aggressive; it is so ardent that it overcomes even the restraints created by the memory of the Nazi holocaust. Their motivation is so strong that they are not inhibi-

---

[28] *Hashiloah*, Vol. VI, p. 223.

ted even by the example of the moral, human and national havoc that
anti-Semitism wrought in Germany. Their anti-Semitism is fervent and
vengeful; its very existence is cathartic and helps to restore their wounded
self-respect.

The starting point of Arab anti-Semitism is the culpability of the State of
Israel; next it goes on to attribute odium to the Jews, which is then passed
back to their State. In Europe the Jews were an evil in themselves; the
Arabs regard them as partners with imperialism, the major satanic power
in the world today. The kingdom of darkness, in the Arab version, is ruled
by a trinity: imperialism, Israel (and the Jews), and reaction. The fundamental Arab conception was that imperialism, as an embodiment of aggression against the peoples, was the root of the evil, which "created" Israel
and from which the evil of Israel emanated as a manifestation and a product
of aggression, but Arab anti-Semitism has been developing the idea that
Israel's Jewishness produces a further evil. Its bond with imperialism is not
accidental; it is a result of its Jewishness.

Arab anti-Semitism might have been expected to be free from the idea of
racial odium, since Jews and Arabs are both regarded by race theory as
Semites, but the odium is directed, not against the Semitic race, but against
the Jews as a historical group. The main idea is that the Jews, racially, are a
mongrel community, most of them being not Semites, but of Khazar and
European origin. Their despicable qualities are transmitted not by biological inheritance, but through cultural and religious channels. The Jewish
creed and spirit are emphasized as the root of the evil. However, since the
Jewish religion is described as the creation of the Jews, who distorted the
element of truth it contained, the origin of the evil goes back to the ancient
Jews – which means that it is racial after all.

The first anti-Semitic books in Arabic were written by Christian Arabs
under French influence, but Arab anti-Semitism today is of an Islamic
religious character. It is no accident that this is emphasized in such books at
those of 'Aqqād, 'Alūba Tall, al-Jiyār, Tabbāra and Rousan, or in articles in
the al-Azhar monthly. This religious character, however, prevents the
struggle against Jewry being conceived as a confrontation between the slave
mentality and morality and that of the master race, as it was presented by
the Nazis. Nor, of course, does Arab anti-Semitism involve a war against
religion, as in the Soviet Union, for example.

A question of principle arises: Was the adoption of anti-Semitic ideas the
inevitable outcome of the refusal to acquiesce in the existence of the State of
Israel? It seems natural that a prolonged and virulent quarrel with Israel
was liable to lead to a tendency to denigrate its people. Once an interna-

tional conflict breaks out, it is not restricted to the political level; it spills over into the rival peoples. The denial of Israel's right to exist leads to the attribution of odious characteristics to the Israelis, and the odium is extended to their Jewishness, expecially as most of the Israelis are recent settlers: the fact that they are in Israel and not in the Diaspora is often accidental; it does not reflect any inherent difference between them and their brethren living abroad, and an Israeli identity, distinct from the Jewish identity, has not yet taken shape. The fundamental characteristic of the Israelis is that they are Jews, and their Israeli identity is only a shallow surface layer – especially as the Diaspora Jews assist Israel and are connected with them by bonds of kinship and aid.

Furthermore, Israel as the Arabs see her is so vile that she deserves no lesser penalty than extinction. It is not only a question of antagonism to some policy she adopts or some action she has perpetrated, or a quarrel over some limited subject, but a denunciation of the very existence of her political personality. Since this is a State doomed to death, it must be evil, and since it is the incarnation of evil, its odiousness is not limited merely to its political superstructure, but pervades all the strata of its population. Good men could not establish and maintain such a monstrosity. The evil in the State reflects the character of its inhabitants – and is reflected in them. Besides, in order to prepare for the brutality of liquidating Israel by violence, the Arabs must harden their hearts against her inhabitants and dehumanize them.[29] Anti-Semitism becomes an educational necessity in furtherance of the politicial aim.

Thus, Professor Faris wrote:

> "If we have to kill, the task is made less painful to the extent that we can define the victim as nonhuman. The soldier has to think of the enemy as subhuman, if he is to bring himself willingly to use the dagger against him."[30]

---

[29] Editor's note: In this selection, Harkabi assumes a single united aim among Arabs to physically annihilate Israel. In later work, he discriminated among Arab attitudes, goals, and strategies, observing differences in the willingness of some to coexist with Israel on a pragmatic basis. See *Arab Strategies and Israel's Response,* New York, 1977; *The Bar Kokhba Syndrome: Risk and Realism in International Politics,* Max D. Tricktin, ed. David Altshuler, Chappaqua, New York, 1983, pp. 139–140, 176–177.

[30] Robert E.L. Faris, "Interaction Levels and Intergroup Relations," in Muzafer Sherif (ed.), *Intergroup Relations and Leadership,* New York 1962, p. 37. Similarly, Jessie Bernard, citing Buchan, states that the negative image of the enemy has the value of making it easier for people to ignore the accepted dictates of morality and kill without pangs of conscience (*The Nature of Conflict,* Paris, 1957, p. 54).

It may, therefore, be assumed that the advocacy of the liquidation of Israel creates an inclination to develop anti-Semitic concepts. This is not a matter of logical determinism. Anti-Semitism is not a necessary condition for the advocacy of liquidation, but it helps. It closes the circle and makes the attitude more complete and consistent.

Even Nājī Alūsh, who does not resort to anti-Semitism, is not entirely free from it; citing Marx's analysis, he denounces the Jews as the embodiment of capitalism and Israel as the outcome of colonialism.[31] The implication is that Israel cannot possibly be immune from some kind of odium, whether through capitalism, or colonialism, or both.

Although the abuse of Israel, Zionism, and the Jews is a secondary phenomenon, motivated by the existence of the conflict, it serves to support and justify the aim of liquidating Israel. The hostility against the State overflows onto the Israelis and the Jews. Not only the State, but the Jew who lives in it and his brethren, wherever they may be, are also odious. Moreover, if the State deserves to be liquidated, the same applies to the odious Israeli. The growth of anti-Semitic ideas reflects a highly significant development in the Arab attitude in the conflict. In the name of the idea of justice for the Palestinians, which may arouse understanding and sympathy, the Arabs are summoned to perpetrate an act of politicide – the destruction of a State – and the ideology which defames Israel and the Israelis impels them to complete the circle by fostering genocidal tendencies. The existence of Israel involves the concentration of the Jews in it, and its liquidation, therefore, inevitably depends on the ending of this concentration, either by bloodshed or by some miraculous kind of bloodless "evaporation."

Anti-Semitism widens the scope of this conception. If the Jews aim at world destruction, the world is faced with the alternative of either submitting to them and accepting their rule or, on the contrary, subduing them and destroying the threat by abolishing their existence. If Judaism is loathsome, and so are the Jews who profess it, there must be an end to Judaism and the Jews. "A final solution" – no matter in what style, whether by violence or by gentler means – is an integral part of anti-Semitism. Since anti-Semitism regards the Jews as a pathological phenomenon, a cancer in the flesh of humanity, it rejects their right to a future and cherishes the ideal of a world without Jews. 'Aqqād says that, against the Jews,

"... the nations have no expedient except, ultimately, to subdue them or surrender to them completely. But this is a sheer absurdity on any assumption. The malady which is

---

[31] *al-Masīra Ilā Filastīn* ("The Journey to Palestine") Dār al-Talī'a, Beirut, Sept. 1964.

innate in this group is that they constitute a socially degenerate entity, for they are a group which can neither become a nation nor return to the Bedouin [tribal] organization. This group has become entangled with the world; it is in a stage of stagnation, unfit for growth. Any cure will be useless, so long as the world does not make it overcome its own nature, and absorb it compulsorily among its nations; this is what will inevitably happen, for nothing else will come to pass."[32]

Ahmad sums up:

"The day will soon come when this gang will be wiped out of existence and disappear from off the face of the earth, and then, with its obliteration, an era of robbery, treachery and crime will come to an end."[33]

The redemption of the world, in other words, will come with the disappearance of the Jews.

The demand that the Jews must assimilate is also repeated in Arab works which lay the emphasis on anti-Zionism rather than anti-Semitism, and it is thus a general one. Since the Jews are denied any unique character which would entitle them to a national life of their own, their failure to assimilate is denounced as racialism. Thus, for example, Darwaza condemns Moses Hess' statement that the Jews have survived because of their racial instinct, the theories of Pinsker and Herzl, and Ahad Ha'am's call for the preservation of Jewish distinctiveness, which reveal a tendency to racial superiority on the part of the chosen people.[34] A similar point of view is expressed by Dr. Sayegh. Bahā' al-Dīn also regards the continued survival of the Jews as deplorable; as we have seen, he identifies assimilation with liberalism and Zionism with anti-liberalism. The difference between the anti-Zionist approach and the anti-Semitic one is that the former sees no place in the world for Jewish distinctiveness, while the latter can find no room for Jews at all.

---

[32] 'Abbās Maḥmūd al-'Aqqād, al-Ṣahyūniyya al-'Alamiyya ("world Zionism"), Ikhtarna Lak, No. 27, Cairo, 1956, pp. 16–17.

[33] Op. cit., pp. 77–78.

[34] Alhakam Darwazah, A Short Survey of the Palestine Problem, Facts & Figures Series, No. 7, Research Center, Palestine Liberation Organization, Beirut, November 1966, pp. 15–16.

Acknowledgements

Armstrong, John A., Mobilized and Proletarian Diasporas. From: *American Political Science Review* 70, 1976, pp. 393–408. Reprinted by permission of the author.

Goldhagen, Erich, Communism and Anti-Semitism. From: *Problems of Communism* 9/3, 1960, pp. 34–43. Reprinted by permission of the author.

Harkabi, Yehoshafat, Contemporary Arab Anti-Semitism: its Causes and Roots. From: Yehoshafat Harkabi, *Arab Attitudes to Israel,* trans. by Misha Louvish. Jerusalem: Israel Universities Press, 1972, Ch. 5, abridged. Reprinted by permission of Keter Publishing House Jerusalem Ltd.

Hobsbawm, Eric J., Are We Entering a New Era of Anti-Semitism? From: *New Society* 11 December 1980, pp. 503–504. Reprinted by permission of the author.

Katz, Jacob, Anti-Semitism Through the Ages. Edited from: Jacob Katz, *From Prejudice to Destruction: Anti-Semitism, 1700–1933.* Cambridge, Mass.: Harvard University Press, 1980. © 1980 by Jacob Katz. Reprinted by permission of Harvard University Press.

Kershaw, Ian, The Persecution of the Jews and German Popular Opinion in the Third Reich. From: *Leo Baeck Yearbook* Vol. XXVI (1981), pp. 261–289. Reprinted by permission of the author and the editor.

Merkl, Peter, Dimensions of Nazi Prejudice. From: Peter Merkl, *Political Violence under the Swastika: 581 Early Nazis.* Copyright © 1975 by Princeton University Press. Excerpt, pp. 338–367, reprinted with permission of Princeton University Press.

Nudelman, R., Contemporary Soviet Anti-Semitism: Forms and Content. Edited and abridged from: *Anti-Semitism in the Soviet Union: Its Roots and Consequences,* Vol. I. Jerusalem: The Hebrew University Centre for Research and Documentation of East European Jewry 1979. Reprinted by permission of Hebrew University.

Quinley, Harold E. and Charles Y. Glock, Christian Sources of Anti-Semitism. Reprinted with permission of The Free Press, a Division of Macmillan, Inc. from *Anti-Semitism in America* by Harold E. Quinley and Charles Y. Glock. Copyright © 1979 by The Free Press.

Ruether, Rosemary R., The Theological Roots of Anti-Semitism. Edited and abridged from: Rosemary Ruether, *Faith and Fratricide: The Theological Roots of Anti-Semitism.* New York: Seabury Press, 1974. Reprinted with permission of the author.

Sartre, Jean Paul, What is an Anti-Semite? Edited and abridged from: Jean Paul Sartre, *Anti-Semite and Jew,* trans. by George J. Becker. New York: Grove Press, 1948, pp. 7–151. Reprinted by permission of Grove Press, Inc.

Wuthnow, Robert, Anti-Semitism and Stereotyping. From: *In the Eye of the Beholder: Contemporary Issues in Stereotyping,* edited by Arthur G. Miller. Copyright © 1982 Praeger Publishers; pp. 137–187, reprinted by permission of Praeger Publishers.

Zenner, Walter P., Middleman Minority Theories: a Critical Review. From: R. S. Bryce-Laportes (ed.), *Sourcebook on the New Immigration.* New Brunswick: Transaction Books 1980, pp. 413–425. Reprinted by permission of the author.

STUDIA JUDAICA

Scholarly Research on Judaism
Edited by Ernst Ludwig Ehrlich

PAUL WINTER

On the Trial of Jesus

2nd edition revised and edited by T. A. Burkill and G. Vermes
Large-octavo. XXIV, 225 pages. 1974.
Cloth DM 62,— ISBN 3 11 002283 4 (volume 1)

JOSEPH HEINEMANN

Prayer in the Talmud

Forms and Patterns

Large-octavo. X, 320 pages. 1977.
Cloth DM 122,— ISBN 3 11 004289 4 (volume 9)

IRA CHERNUS

Mysticism in Rabbinic Judaism

Studies in the History of Midrash

Large-octavo. approx. VIII, 160 pages. 1982.
Cloth DM 62,— ISBN 3 11 008589 5 (volume 11)

HAIM SCHWARZBAUM

Studies in Jewish and world folklore

Large-octavo. X, 604 pages. 1968.
Cloth DM 195,— ISBN 3 11 000393 7

Hebrew and Aramaic Dictionary of the Old Testament

Edited by Georg Fohrer

Octavo. XVIII, 334 pages. 1973.
Cloth DM 32,— ISBN 3 11 004572 9

Prices are subject to change

Walter de Gruyter

W
DE
G

Berlin · New York

HAROLD W. TURNER

From Temple to Meeting House

The Phenomenology and Theology of Places of Worship

Large-octavo. XIV, 406 pages. 1979.
Cloth DM 103,— ISBN 90 279 7977 4
(Religion and Society 16)

Ni Juif ni grec
Entretien sur le racisme

Actes du colloque tenu 16 au 20 juin 1975
au Centre Culturel International de Cerisy-la Salle

Publié sous la direction et avec une préface de
Léon Poliakov

Large-octavo. 190 pages. 1978.
Boards DM 26,— ISBN 90 279 7574 4
(Le Savoir Historique 12)

JOSHUA A. FISHMAN (Editor)
Never Say Die!

A Thousand Years of Yiddish in Jewish Life and Letters

1981. 21 × 28 cm. XVI, 762 pages.
With numerous figures and tables.
DM 95,— ISBN 90 279 7978 2
(Contributions to the Sociology of Language 30)

WILLIAM E. MITCHELL
Mishpokhe

A Study of New York City Jewish Family Clubs

Foreword by M. Sklare

Large-octavo. 262 pages, 11 tab., 2 figs. 1978. Cloth DM 41,—
ISBN 90 279 7695 3
(New Babylon. Studies in the Social Sciences 30)

Prices are subject to change

Mouton de Gruyter

Berlin · New York · Amsterdam